The

HUMAN
RECORD

Volume I

The
HUMAN
RECORD

SOURCES OF GLOBAL HISTORY

FIFTH EDITION / Volume I: To 1700

Alfred J. Andrea

Emeritus Professor of History, University of Vermont

James H. Overfield

Professor of History, University of Vermont

HOUGHTON MIFFLIN COMPANY   BOSTON NEW YORK

Editor-in-Chief: Jean L. Woy
Senior Sponsoring Editor: Nancy Blaine
Senior Development Editor: Julie Dunn
Editorial Associate: Annette Fantasia
Senior Project Editor: Margaret Park Bridges
Manufacturing Coordinator: Carrie Wagner
Senior Marketing Manager: Sandra McGuire

Cover image: © Erich Lessing/Art Resource, NY

Source credits appear on pages 501–505, which constitute an extension of the copyright page.

Printed in the U.S.A.

Library of Congress Control Number: 2003110176

ISBN: 0-618-37040-4

456789-MV-08 07 06 05

As always, our love and thanks to
Juanita B. Andrea and Susan L. Overfield

Contents

Geographic Contents

Topical
Contents

Violence, War, and Warriors

Preface

The fifth edition of *The Human Record: Sources of Global History* follows the principles that guided the first four editions. Foremost is our commitment to the proposition that all students of history must meet the challenge of analyzing primary sources, thereby becoming active inquirers into the past. Working with primary-source evidence enables students to see that historical scholarship is an intellectual process that involves drawing inferences and discovering patterns from clues yielded by the past, not of memorizing someone else's judgments. Furthermore, such analysis motivates students to learn by stimulating curiosity and imagination, and it helps them develop into critical thinkers who are equipped to deal with the complex intellectual challenges of life.

Themes and Structure

We have compiled a source collection that traces the course of human history from the rise of the earliest civilizations to the present. Volume I follows the evolution of cultures that most significantly influenced the history of the world from around 3500 B.C.E. to 1700 C.E., with emphasis on the development of the major social, religious, intellectual, and political traditions of the societies that flourished in Africa and Eurasia. Although our focus in Volume I is on the Eastern Hemisphere, we do not neglect the Americas. Volume I concurrently develops the theme of the growing links and increasingly important exchanges among the world's cultures down to the early modern era. Volume II picks up this theme of growing human interconnectedness by tracing the gradual establishment of Western global hegemony; the simultaneous historical developments in other civilizations and societies around the world; the anti-Western, anticolonial movements of the twentieth century; and the emergence of the twenty-first century's integrated but still often bitterly divided world.

To address these themes in the depth and breadth they deserve, we have chosen primary sources that present an overview of global history in mosaic form. Each source serves two functions: It presents an intimate glimpse into some meaningful aspect of the human past and simultaneously contributes to the creation of a single large picture — an integrated history of the world. With this dual purpose in mind, we have tried to avoid isolated sources that provide a taste of some culture or age but, by their dissociation, shed no light on patterns of cultural creation, continuity, change, and interchange — the essential components of world history.

In selecting and arranging the various pieces of our mosaic, we have sought to create a balanced picture of human history that reflects many different perspectives and experiences. Believing that the study of history properly concerns every aspect of past human activity and thought, we have chosen sources that mirror the practices and concerns of as wide a variety of representative persons and groups as availability and space allow.

Our pursuit of historical balance has also led us into the arena of artifactual evidence. Although most historians center their research on documents, the discipline of history requires us to consider all of the clues surrendered by the past, and these include its artifacts. Moreover, we have discovered that students enjoy analyzing artifacts and seem to remember vividly the insights they draw from them. For these reasons, we have included works of art and other artifacts that users of this book can and should analyze as historical sources.

New to This Edition

We have been gratified with the positive response by colleagues and especially students to the first four editions of *The Human Record.* Many have taken the trouble to write or otherwise contact us to express their satisfaction. No textbook is perfect, however, and these correspondents have been equally generous in sharing their perceptions of how we might improve our book and meet more fully the needs of its readers. Such suggestions, when combined with continuing advances in historical scholarship and our own deeper reflections on a variety of issues, have mandated periodic revisions. In the current revision, as was true in the previous three, our intent has been to make the book as interesting and useful as possible to students and professors alike.

As difficult as it is to let go of sources that have proved valuable and important for us and our students (and our classroom has always been the laboratory in which we test and refine *The Human Record*), we are always searching for sources that enable us and our students to explore more fully and deeply the rich heritage of world history. For this reason, almost one-third of the sources that appear in the fifth edition are new.

In Volume I we added eight new sources relating to the Silk Road and the peoples of Central Asia, scattering them among three chapters. The United States' heightened interest and involvement in the lands and cultures of that region was one factor that led to this decision, but equally important were the voices of many users of the text who asked for more material on the pastoral peoples of Inner Asia and the manner in which they related to their neighbors. Now students can study *The Old Tang History*'s account of how an eighth-century Chinese emperor used an imperial marriage alliance to gain the help of the Uighurs in putting down a civil war. Among the other new Silk Road sources, there is the biography of the nun An Lingshou, which illustrates how Buddhism infiltrated into China from Central Asia during the fifth century; a seventh-century Chinese description of Nalanda, India's premier Buddhist monastery and a magnet for wandering saints and scholars from lands as distant as Persia and Sumatra; and the Spaniard Ruy Gonzalez de Clavijo's description of how Samarqand became the most prosperous city in Central Asia during the Age of Tamerlane.

In response to an avalanche of recent interest in the Sufi poetry of Jalaluddin al-Rumi, Chapter 8 of Volume I contains several of this thirteenth-century mystic's poems and a short excerpt from Ahmed al-Aflaki's biography of al-Rumi, *The Virtues of Those Who Know.* Several other sources also offer the spe-

cial insight that poetry provides. New selections from the poetry of Du Fu provide, better than ever before, a privileged view of China's turbulent history in
the mid eighth century. To illustrate the vivacity of Egypt's New Kingdom, we
have included several love songs probably composed by an upper-class
woman. Love is also a key element in the *Pillow Book* of Sei Shonagon, an
eleventh-century Japanese court lady, whose frank and, at times, scandalous
ruminations force us to rethink stereotypical images of East Asian women and
their place in society.

American Indian civilizations also get a new look, thanks to three Mayan
sculptures and Diego Durán's *Book of the Gods and Rites,* which reveals the
confluence of commercial vitality and religion in the Aztec marketplace. Religion and tragic drama existed side by side in the theaters of Classical Greece,
and nowhere is this better illustrated than in Euripides' *The Bacchae.* Comple-
menting this masterpiece are three new Hellenic works of art, including the
provocative *Meanad,* or female Bacchic devotee.

Among the many other new sources in Volume I, several have received new
translations by A. J. Andrea that are improvements on flawed or antiquated
available translations. These include works by two first-century Roman authors: Pliny the Elder's description of Roman trade with India and other lands
to its east and Tacitus's two accounts of the rebellion of Queen Boudica in first-
century Britain. They also include several Roman sources relating to the persecution of Christians and an early-fourteenth-century description of China by
the Italian missionary Odoric of Pordenone.

A number of sources carried over from the fourth edition have been recon-
figured and revised. In Volume I these include excerpts from China's *Book of
Songs,* the *Analects of Confucius,* the *Quran,* Charlemagne's *Capitularies,* excerpts from the writings of Maimonides, as well as the already-mentioned
poems of Du Fu.

Longtime users of Volume II of *The Human Record* will note that its organization in the fifth edition has been changed in subtle but significant ways.
First, the chapter order of Part One has been recast. Ever since the second edition, this part has begun with a chapter on Europe, with those on Africa and
the Americas, South and Southwest Asia, and East and Southeast Asia following. This arrangement sent the unintended message to some of our students
that Europe came first because it was more important, more advanced, and
more powerful than other regions of the world. Putting Europe first for such
reasons might be defensible for later periods in world history, but certainly not
for the years covered in these initial chapters, when in most fields of human
endeavor — art, literature, technology, government, military power, agriculture, commerce, and manufacturing — Europe lagged behind the older civilizations of the Middle East, India, and East Asia. Now European material is
covered in Chapter 3, which follows chapters on East and Southeast Asia and
the Islamic heartland and precedes the material on Africa and the Americas,
the two regions most affected by Europe's overseas expansion.

The other organizational change in Volume II is that material on the world
since 1945 has been broken down into two chapters, meaning that for the first

time in its publishing history Volume II of *The Human Record* will have fourteen, not thirteen, chapters. The reason for the change is simple: Time marches on and history expands. Ever since the first edition of *The Human Record* Chapter 13 has been entitled "The Global Community since 1945." In the first edition this meant it covered forty-five years of recent history, already a formidable task. For the fifth edition the number of years to be covered increased almost 33 percent to almost sixty years. In these additional years the Cold War ended, the Soviet Union collapsed, the Internet revolution took place, globalization became a hot topic, new pandemics swept the world, and world terrorism emerged as a major threat. In this edition Chapter 13 covers the period from 1945 to the mid 1980s, while Chapter 14 covers the last two decades.

Of the approximately forty new sources in Volume II, four are in Chapter 14. Two sources are devoted to the debate on the role of free trade and open markets in the new global economy, with Ralph Nader's 1993 anti-NAFTA essay representing free trade's critics and the excerpt from Brookings Institution scholars' 1998 book *Globaphobia* presenting the views of free trade's defenders. Chapter 14 also includes a section on terrorism, with focus on the events of September 11, 2001. The subsection consists of two sources: first, excerpts from Osama bin Laden's 1996 "Declaration of Jihad against Americans," and second, excerpts from "The Last Night," the list of instructions drawn up by the chief planner of the September 11 suicide missions, Mohammed Atta, that was to be read by the participants on the evening of September 10.

The other new sources for Volume II fall into two main categories. First, a number of sources that appeared in one or more of the first three editions of the book and disappeared in later editions reappear in the fifth edition. Every source we drop from one edition of the book to the next is someone's favorite, and we usually hear about it via e-mail, phone calls, letters, or conversations at professional meetings. It appears that quite a few people favored some of the sources dropped from the fourth edition, such as Darwin's writings on evolution, Voltaire's moving defense of religious toleration, Anna Bijn's spirited poem "Unyoked Is Best," the "Declaration of the Rights of Man and of the Citizen," and the encomienda records from Nestalpa, Mexico. All of these have been reinstated.

Totally new sources make up the second category. They have been introduced to the fifth edition because we believe they will be more effective and useful for classroom teaching than those they replaced. Several new sources on women have been introduced to strengthen what has been an emphasis in *The Human Record* since it first appeared. They include excerpts from Leon Battista Alberti's *On the Family,* a book that provides instructive insights into upper-class Florentine male attitudes toward wives and daughters. It has the further advantage of adding a source on the Italian Renaissance. Chapter 2 includes a new source consisting of legal opinions and judgments by the seventeenth-century Islamic jurist Khayr al-Din Ramli pertaining to marriage, divorce, and sexual abuse in the region of Syria-Palestine in the Ottoman Empire. It is a fascinating source, with much more potential for classroom use than the short section on divorce from Ogier de Busbecq's *Turkish Letters* that had to suffice in previous editions.

Other new sources in Volume II include three documents in Chapter 3 on the motives behind Europe's overseas expansion (excerpts from Azurara's *Chronicle of Guinea*; the 1492 agreement between Columbus and the Spanish monarchs; and Hakluyt's *A Discourse on Western Planting*). Chapter 5 now includes a series of political cartoons that illustrates the loss of privilege on the part of the clergy and nobility in the early years of the French Revolution. A soldier's memoir has been added to Chapter 11 to convey the horrors and futility of trench warfare in World War I. It replaces poems by Wilfred Owen and two artworks, which our students found moving but did not spark much in the way of class discussion. Excerpts from Theodor Herzl's *The Jews' State* have been added to the section on European nationalism in Chapter 8, and sources on sixteenth-century Chinese commerce, German reaction to the Treaty of Versailles, and pre–World War II Japanese nationalism also appear for the first time.

We also have an obligation to reflect in our work the most up-to-date scholarly discoveries and controversies. With that in mind, we have revised many of our introductions and commentaries. More than one-third of the pages dedicated to editorial commentary and notes have been rewritten.

Learning Aids

Source analysis can be a daunting challenge for any student. With this in mind, we have labored to make these sources as accessible as possible by providing the student-user with a variety of aids. First there is the *Prologue,* in which we explain, initially in a theoretical manner and then through concrete examples, how a historian interprets written and artifactual sources. Next we offer *part, chapter, sub-chapter,* and *individual source introductions* — all to help the reader place each selection into a meaningful context and understand each source's significance. Because we consider *The Human Record* to be an interpretive overview of global history and therefore a survey of the major patterns of global history that stands on its own as a text, our introductions are significantly fuller than what one normally encounters in a book of sources.

Suggested *Questions for Analysis* precede each source; their purpose is to help the student make sense of each piece of evidence and wrest from it as much insight as possible. The questions are presented in a three-tiered format designed to resemble the historian's approach to source analysis and to help students make historical comparisons on a global scale. The first several questions are usually quite specific and ask the reader to pick out important pieces of information. These initial questions require the student to address two issues: What does this document or artifact say, and what meaningful facts can I garner from it? Addressing concrete questions of this sort prepares the student researcher for the next, more significant, level of critical thinking and analysis: drawing inferences. Questions that demand inferential conclusions follow the fact-oriented questions. Finally, whenever possible, we offer a third tier of questions that challenge the student to compare the individual or society that produced a particular source with an individual, group, or culture encountered earlier in the volume. We believe such comparisons help students fix more firmly in their minds the distinguishing cultural characteristics of the various societies they encounter in their survey of world history. Beyond that, it underscores the fact that global history is, at least on one level, comparative history.

Another form of help we offer is to *gloss the sources,* explaining fully words and allusions that first-year college students cannot reasonably be expected to know. To facilitate reading and to encourage reference, the notes appear at the bottom of the page on which they are cited. A few documents also contain *interlinear notes* that serve as transitions or provide needed information.

Some instructors might use *The Human Record* as their sole textbook. Most will probably use it as a supplement to a standard narrative textbook, and many of these might decide not to require their students to analyze every entry. To assist instructors (and students) in selecting sources that best suit their interests and needs, we have prepared *two analytical tables of contents* for each volume. The first lists readings and artifacts by geographic and cultural area, the second by topic. The two tables suggest to professor and student alike the rich variety of material available within these pages, particularly for essays in comparative history.

In summary, our goal in crafting *The Human Record* has been to do our best to prepare the student-reader for success — *success* being defined as comfort with historical analysis, proficiency in critical thinking, learning to view history on a global scale, and a deepened awareness of the rich cultural varieties, as well as shared characteristics, of the human family.

Using The Human Record: *Suggestions from the Editors*

Specific suggestions for assignments and classroom activities appear in the manual *Using* The Human Record: *Suggestions from the Editors*. In it we explain why we have chosen the sources that appear in this book and what insights we believe students should be capable of drawing from them. We also describe classroom exercises for encouraging student thought and discussion on the various sources. The advice we present is the fruit of our own use of these sources in the classroom.

Feedback

As already suggested, we want to receive comments and suggestions from professors and students who are using this book. Comments on the Prologue and Volume I should be addressed to A. J. Andrea, whose e-mail address is <Alfred.Andrea@uvm.edu>; comments on Volume II should be addressed to J. H. Overfield at <James.Overfield@uvm.edu>.

Acknowledgments

We are in debt to the many professionals who offered their expert advice and assistance during the various incarnations of *The Human Record*. Scholars and friends at The University of Vermont who generously shared their expertise with us over the years as we crafted these five editions include Abbas Alnasrawi, Doris Bergen, Robert V. Daniels, Carolyn Elliott, Bogac Ergene, Shirley Gedeon, Erik Gilbert, William Haviland, Walter Hawthorn, Richard Horowitz, William Mierse, George Moyser, Kristin M. Peterson-Ishaq, Abubaker Saad, Wolfe W. Schmokel, Peter Seybolt, John W. Seyller, Sean Stilwell, Marshall True, Diane Villemaire, Janet Whatley, and Denise Youngblood. Additionally, Ms. Tara Coram of the Arthur M. Sackler Gallery and Freer Gallery of Art of the Smithsonian Institution deserves special thanks for the assistance she rendered A. J. Andrea in his exploration of the Asian art holdings of the two museums.

We wish also to acknowledge the following instructors whose comments on the fourth edition helped guide our revision: Timothy Connell, Laurel School; Moshe Gershovich, University of Nebraska at Omaha; Erik Gilbert, Arkansas State University; Randee Brenner Goodstadt, Asheville-Buncombe Technical Community College; Richard S. Horowitz, California State University, Northridge; Cynthia Kosso, Northern Arizona University; Scott C. Levi, University of Louisville; Yihong Pan, Miami University; James A. Polk, College of Charleston; Harold M. Tanner, University of North Texas; and Ronald Young, Georgia Southern University.

Finally, our debt to our spouses is beyond payment, but the dedication to them of each edition of this book reflects in some small way how deeply we appreciate their constant support and good-humored tolerance.

A. J. A.
J. H. O.

Prologue

▾▾▾

Primary Sources and How to Read Them

Imagine a course in chemistry in which students never set foot in a laboratory; or a literature course in which they read commentaries on Shakespeare's plays but none of the plays; or a course on the history of jazz in which they never listen to a note of music. Most students would consider such courses strange and deficient, and many would soon be beating a path to the door of their academic advisor or college dean with complaints about flawed teaching methods and wasted tuition payments. No one can understand chemistry without doing experiments. No one can understand literature without reading plays, poetry, and fiction. No one can understand music without listening to performances.

In much the same way, no one can understand history without reading and analyzing *primary sources*. Although we shall see an exception to the rule when we look at oral traditions, in most instances, *primary sources are historical records produced at the same time the event or period that is being studied took place or soon thereafter.* They are distinct from *secondary sources* — books, articles, television documentaries, and even historical films — produced well after the events they describe and interpret. Secondary sources — *histories* in the conventional sense of the term — organize the jumble of past events into understandable narratives. They also provide interpretations, make comparisons, and discuss motive and causation. When done well, they provide pleasure and insight to their readers and viewers. But such works, no matter how well done, are still secondary, in that they are written well after the fact and, more important, derive their evidence and information from primary sources.

History is an ambitious discipline that deals with all aspects of past human activity and belief. This means that the primary sources historians use to recreate the past are equally wide-ranging and diverse. Most of the primary sources they use are written sources — government records, law codes, private correspondence, literary works, religious texts, merchants' account books, memoirs, and the list goes on almost endlessly. So important are written records to the study of history that societies and cultures that had or have no system of writing are called *prehistoric* — not because they lack a history but because there is no way to construct a detailed narrative of their histories due to the lack of written records. Of course, even so-called prehistoric societies leave behind evidence of their experiences, creativity, and belief systems in their *oral traditions* and their *artifacts*.

Let us look first at oral traditions — the remembered past passed down by word of mouth. The difficulty of working with such evidence is significant. You are aware of how stories change as they are transmitted from person to person. Imagine how difficult it is to use such stories as historical evidence. Yet, despite the challenge they offer us, these sources cannot be overlooked. Although the oral traditions of ancient societies were often written down long after they were first articulated, they are often the only recorded evidence that we have of a far-distant society or event. So, the farther back in history we go, the more we see the inadequacy of the definition of primary sources that we offered above ("historical records produced at the same time the event or period that is being studied took place or soon thereafter"). The early chapters of Volume I contain quite a few primary sources based on oral traditions. We will inform you when this is the case and offer you sufficient information and suggestions as to which questions you can validly ask of them to enable you to use them effectively.

Artifacts can help us place oral traditions into a clearer context by producing tangible evidence that supports or calls into question legends. Artifacts can also tell us something about prehistoric societies whose oral traditions are lost to us. They even serve as primary sources for historians who study literate cultures. Written records, no matter how extensive and diverse, never allow us to draw a complete picture of the past, and we can fill at least some of those gaps by studying what human hands have fashioned. Everyday objects, such as fabrics, tools, kitchen implements, weapons, farm equipment, jewelry, pieces of furniture, and family photographs, provide windows into the ways that common people lived. Grander cultural products — paintings, sculpture, buildings, musical compositions, and, more recently, film — are equally important because they also reflect the values, attitudes, and styles of living of their creators and those for whom they were created.

To be a historian is to work with primary sources. But to do so effectively is not an easy task. Each source provides only one glimpse of reality, and no single source by itself gives us the whole picture of past events and developments. Many sources are difficult to understand, and can be interpreted only after the precise meaning of their words have been deciphered and their backgrounds thoroughly investigated. Many sources contain distortions and errors that can be discovered only by rigorous internal analysis and comparison with evidence from other sources. Only after all these source-related difficulties have been overcome can a historian hope to achieve a coherent and reasonably accurate understanding of the past.

To illustrate some of the challenges of working with primary sources, let us imagine a time in the mid twenty-first century when a historian decides to write a history of your college class in connection with its fiftieth reunion. Since no one has written a book or article about your class, our historian has no secondary sources to consult, and must rely entirely on primary sources. What primary sources might he or she use? The list would be a long one: the school catalogue, class lists, academic transcripts, yearbooks, college rules and regulations, and similar official documents; lecture notes, syllabi, examinations, term papers, and textbooks; diaries and private letters; articles from the campus newspaper and programs for sporting events, concerts, and plays; posters and handbills; recollections written down or otherwise recorded by some of your classmates long after they graduated. With a bit of thought you could add other items to the list, among them some artifacts, such as souvenirs sold in the campus store, and other unwritten sources, such as recordings of music popular at the time and photographs and videotapes of student life and activity.

Even with this imposing list of sources our future historian will only have an incomplete record of the events that made up your class's experiences. Many of those moments — telephone conversations, meetings with professors, and gossip exchanged at the student union — never made it into any written record. Also consider the fact that all the sources available to our future historian will be fortunate survivors. They will represent only a small percentage of the material generated by you, your classmates, professors, and administrators over a two- or four-year period. Wastebaskets and recycling bins will have claimed much written material; the "delete" key and inevitable changes in computer technology might make it impossible to retrieve basic sources, such as your college's website, e-mail, and a vast amount of other online materials. It is also probable that it will be difficult to find information about certain groups within your class, such as part-time students, nontraditional students, and commuters. The past always has its so-called silent or near-silent groups of people. Of course, they were never truly silent, but often nobody was listening to them. It is the historian's task to find whatever evidence exists that gives them a voice, but often that evidence is tantalizingly slim.

For these reasons, the evidence available to our future historian will be fragmentary at best. This is always the case when doing historical research. The records of the past cannot be retained in their totality, not even those that pertain to the recent past.

How will our future historian use the many individual pieces of surviving documentary evidence about your class? As he or she reviews the list, it will quickly become apparent that no single primary source provides a complete or unbiased picture. Each source has its own perspective, value, and limitations. Imagine that the personal essays submitted by applicants for admission were a historian's only sources of information about the student body. On reading them, our researcher might draw the false conclusion that the school attracted only the most gifted, talented, interesting, and intellectually committed students imaginable.

Despite their flaws, however, essays composed by applicants for admission can still be important pieces of historical evidence. They certainly reflect the would-be students' perceptions of the school's cultural values and the types of people it hopes to attract, and usually the applicants are right on the mark because they have read the school's catalogue and the brochures prepared for prospective students by the admissions office. Admissions materials and, to a degree, even the catalogue, are forms of creative advertising, and both present an idealized picture of campus life. But such publications have value for the careful researcher because they reflect the values of the faculty and administrators who composed them. The catalogue also provides useful information regarding rules and regulations, courses, instructors, school organizations, and similar items. Such factual information, however, is the raw material of history, not history itself, and certainly it does not reflect anything close to the full historical reality of your class's collective experience.

What is true of the catalogue is equally true of the student newspaper and every other piece of evidence pertinent to your class. Each primary source is a part of a larger whole, but as we have already seen, we do not have all the pieces. Think of historical evidence in terms of a jigsaw puzzle. Many of the pieces are missing, but it is possible to put most, though probably not all, of the remaining pieces together in a fashion to form a fairly accurate and coherent picture. The picture that emerges will not be complete, but it can still be useful and valid. The keys to fitting these pieces together are hard work and imagination. Each is absolutely necessary.

Examining Primary Sources

Hard work speaks for itself, but students are often unaware that historians also need imagination to reconstruct the past. After all, many students ask, doesn't history consist of strictly defined and irrefutable dates, names, and facts? Where does imagination enter into the process of learning these facts? Again, let us consider your class's history and its documentary sources. Many of those documents provide factual data — dates, names, grades, statistics. While these data are important, individually and collectively they have no historical meaning until they have been *interpreted.* Your college class is more than a collection of statistics and facts. It is a group of individuals who, despite their differences, shared and helped mold a collective experience. It was and is a community evolving within a particular time and place. Any valid or useful history must reach beyond dates, names, and facts and interpret the historical characteristics and role of your class. What were its values? How did it change and why? What impact did it have? These are some of the important questions a historian asks of the evidence.

To arrive at answers, the historian must examine each and every piece of relevant evidence in its full context and wring from that evidence as many *inferences* as possible. *An inference is a logical conclusion drawn from evidence, and it is the heart and soul of historical inquiry.* Facts are the raw materials of history, but inferences are its finished products.

Every American schoolchild learns at an early age that "in fourteen hundred and ninety-two, Columbus sailed the ocean blue." In subsequent history classes, he or she might learn other facts about the famous explorer: that he was born in Genoa in 1451; that he made three other transatlantic voyages in 1493, 1497, and 1503; that he died in Spain in 1506. Knowing these facts is of little value, however, unless it contributes to our understanding of the motives, causes, and significance of Columbus's voyages. Why did Columbus sail west? Why did Spain support such enterprises? Why were Europeans willing and able to exploit, as they did, the so-called New World? What were the short- and long-term consequences of the European presence in the Americas? Finding answers to questions such as these are the historian's ultimate goal, and these answers can only be found in primary sources.

One noted historian, Robin Winks, has written a book entitled *The Historian as Detective,* and the image is appropriate although inexact. Like a detective, the historian examines evidence to reconstruct events. Like a detective, the historian is interested in discovering "what happened, who did it, and why." Like a detective interrogating witnesses, *the historian also must carefully examine the testimony of sources.*

First and foremost, the historian must evaluate the *validity* of the source. Is it what it purports to be? Artful forgeries have misled many historians. Even authentic sources still can be misleading if the author lied or deliberately misrepresented reality. In addition, the historian can easily be led astray by not fully understanding the *perspective* reflected in the document. As is soon learned by any detective who has examined eyewitnesses to an event, witnesses' accounts often differ widely. The detective has the opportunity to re-examine witnesses and offer them the opportunity to change their testimony in the light of new evidence and deeper reflection. The historian is not so fortunate. Even when the historian compares a piece of documentary evidence with other evidence in order to uncover its flaws, there is no way to cross-examine its author. Given this fact, it is absolutely necessary for the historian to understand as fully as possible the source's perspective. Thus, the historian must ask several key questions — all of which share the letter W.

- *What* kind of document is it?
- *Who* wrote it?
- For *whom* and *why*?
- *Where* was it composed and *when*?

What is important because understanding the nature of a source gives the historian an idea of what kind of information he or she can expect to find in it. Many sources simply do not address the questions a historian would like to ask of them, and knowing this can save a great deal of frustration. Your class's historian would be foolish to try to learn much about the academic quality of your school's courses from a study of the registrar's class lists and grade sheets. Student and faculty class notes, copies of syllabi, examinations, student papers, and textbooks would be far more useful.

Who, for whom, and *why* are equally important questions. The school catalogue and publicity materials prepared by the admissions office undoubtedly address some issues pertaining to student social life. But should documents like these — designed to attract potential students and to place the school in the best possible light — be read and accepted uncritically? Obviously not. They must be tested against student testimony discovered in such sources as private letters, memoirs, posters, the student newspaper, and the yearbook.

Where and *when* are also important questions to ask of any primary source. As a rule, distance from an event in space and time colors perceptions and can diminish the reliability of a source. Recollections of a person celebrating a twenty-fifth class reunion could be an insightful and valuable source of information for your class's historian. Conceivably this graduate would have a perspective and information that he or she lacked a quarter of a century earlier. Just as conceivably, that person's memory of what college was like might have faded to the point where his recollections have little value.

You and the Sources

This book will actively involve you in the work of historical inquiry by asking you to draw inferences based on your analysis of primary source evidence. This might prove difficult at first, but it is well within your capability.

You will analyze two types of evidence: documents and artifacts. Each source will be authentic, so you do not have to worry about validating it. Editorial material in this book also supplies you with the information necessary to place each piece of evidence into its proper context and will suggest questions you legitimately can and should ask of each source.

It is important to keep in mind that historians approach each source they consider with questions, even though they might be vaguely formulated. Like detectives, historians want to discover some particular truth or shed light on a particular issue. This requires asking specific questions of the witnesses or, in the historian's case, of the evidence. These questions should not be prejudgments. One of the worst errors a historian can make is setting out to prove a point or to defend an ideological position. Questions are essential, but they are starting points, nothing else. Therefore, as you approach a source, have your question or questions fixed in your mind and constantly remind yourself as you work your way through a source what issue or issues you are investigating. Each source in this anthology is preceded by a number of suggested *Questions for Analysis.* You or your professor might want to ask other questions. Whatever the case, keep focused on your questions and issues, and take notes as you read a source. Never rely on unaided memory; it will almost inevitably lead you astray.

Above all else, you must be honest and thorough as you study a source. Read each explanatory footnote carefully to avoid misunderstanding a word or an allusion. Try to understand exactly what the source is saying and what its author's perspective is. Be careful not to wrench items, words, or ideas out of context, thereby distorting them. Be sure to read the entire source so that you understand as fully as possible what it says and does not say.

This is not as difficult as it sounds. But it does take concentration and work. And do not let the word "work" mislead you. True, primary source analysis demands attention to detail and some hard thought, but it is also rewarding. There is great satisfaction in developing a deeper and truer understanding of the past based on a careful exploration of the evidence.

Analyzing Two Sample Sources

To illustrate how you should go about this task and what is expected of you, we will now take you through a sample exercise, in which we analyze two sources:

a document from the pen of Christopher Columbus and an early-sixteenth-century woodcut. We present each source as it would appear in this book: first an introduction, then suggested Questions for Analysis, and finally the source itself, with explanatory notes. Because we want to give you a full introduction to the art of documentary source analysis, this excerpt is longer than any other document in the book. Also, in order to help you refer back to the letter as we analyze it, we have numbered each fifth line. No other source in this book will have numbered lines. Our notes that comment on the text are probably fuller than necessary, but we prefer to err on the side of providing too much information and help rather than too little. But do not let the length of the document or its many notes intimidate you. Once you get into the source, you should find it fairly easy going.

"With the Royal Standard Unfurled"
▼▼▼
▼ *Christopher Columbus,*
A LETTER CONCERNING
RECENTLY DISCOVERED ISLANDS

Sixteenth-century Spain's emergence as the dominant power in the Americas is forever associated with the name of a single mariner — Christopher Columbus (1451–1506). Sponsored by King Ferdinand II of Aragon and Queen Isabella I of Castile, this Genoese sea captain sailed west into the Atlantic seeking a new route to the empires of East Asia described by John Mandeville, Marco Polo, and other travel writers he had avidly read. On October 12, 1492, his fleet of three ships dropped anchor at a small Bahamian island, which Columbus claimed for Spain, naming it San Salvador. The fleet then sailed to two larger islands, which he named Juana and Española (today known as Cuba and Hispaniola).

After exploring these two islands and establishing on Española the fort of Navidad del Señor, Columbus departed for Spain in January 1493. On his way home, the admiral prepared a preliminary account of his expedition to the "Indies" for Luis de Santángel, a counselor to King Ferdinand and one of Columbus's enthusiastic supporters. In composing the letter, Columbus borrowed heavily from his official ship's log, often lifting passages verbatim. When he landed in Lisbon in early March, Columbus dispatched the letter overland, expecting it to precede him to the Spanish royal court in faraway Barcelona, where Santángel would communicate its contents to the two monarchs. The admiral was not disappointed. His triumphal reception at the court in April was proof that the letter had served its purpose.

QUESTIONS FOR ANALYSIS

1. What does Columbus's description of the physical attributes of the islands suggest about the motives for his voyage?
2. Often the eyes only see what the mind prepares them to see. Is there any evidence that Columbus saw what he wanted to see and discovered what he expected to discover?
3. Is there any evidence that Columbus's letter was a carefully crafted piece of self-promotion by a person determined to prove he had reached the Indies?
4. Is there any evidence that Columbus attempted to present an objective and fairly accurate account of what he had seen and experienced?
5. In light of your answers to questions 2–4, to what extent, if at all, can we trust Columbus's account?
6. What do the admiral's admitted actions regarding the natives and the ways in which he describes these people allow us to conclude about his attitudes toward these "Indians" and his plans for them?
7. What does this letter tell us about the culture of the Tainos on the eve of European expansion into their world? Is there anything that Columbus tells us about these people that does not seem to ring totally true?
8. How, if at all, does this letter illustrate that a single historical source read in isolation can mislead the researcher?

Sir, as I know that you will be pleased at the great victory with which Our Lord has crowned my voyage, I write this to you, from which you will learn how in thirty-three days, I passed from the Canary Islands to the Indies[1] with the fleet which the most illustrious king and queen, our sovereigns, gave to me. And there I found very many islands filled with people[2] innumerable, and of them all I have taken possession for their highnesses, by proclamation made and with the royal standard unfurled, and no opposition was offered to me. To the first island which I found, I gave the name *San Salvador*,[3] in remembrance of the Divine Majesty, Who has marvelously bestowed all this; the Indians call it "Guanahani." To the second, I gave the name *Isla de Santa Maria de Concepción;*[4] to the third, *Fernandina;* to the fourth, *Isabella;* to the fifth, *Isla Juana,*[5] and so to each one I gave a new name.

When I reached Juana, I followed its coast to the westward, and I found it to be so extensive that I thought that it must be the mainland, the province of Catayo.[6] And since there were neither towns nor villages on the seashore, but only small hamlets, with the people of which I could not have speech, because they all fled immediately, I went forward on the same course, thinking that I should not fail to find great cities and towns. And, at the end of many leagues,[7] seeing that there was no change and that the coast was bearing me northwards, which I wished to avoid, since winter was already beginning, . . . [I] retraced my path as far as a certain harbor known to me. And from that point, I sent two men inland

---

[1]A term that referred to the entire area of the Indian Ocean and East Asia.

[2]The Tainos, a tribal branch of the Arawak language family. Arawak speakers inhabited an area from the Amazon River to the Caribbean.

[3]"Holy Savior," Jesus Christ.

[4]"The Island of Holy Mary of the Immaculate Conception." Catholics believe that Mary, the mother of Jesus, was abso-

lutely sinless, to the point that she was conceived without the stain of Original Sin (the sin of Adam and Eve) on her soul.

[5]Named for Prince Juan, heir apparent of Castile.

[6]The Spanish term for *Cathay* — technically northern China. Columbus, however, meant by it the entire Chinese Empire of the Great Khan (see note 23).

[7]A league is about three miles.

to learn if there were a king or great cities. They traveled three days' journey and found an infinity of small hamlets and people without number, but nothing of importance. For this reason, they returned.

I understood sufficiently from other Indians, whom I had already taken,[8] that this land was nothing but an island. And therefore I followed its coast eastwards for one hundred and seven leagues to the point where it ended. And from that cape, I saw another island . . . to which I at once gave the name "Española." And I went there and followed its northern coast. . . . This island and all the others are very fertile to a limitless degree, and this island is extremely so. In it there are many harbors on the coast of the sea, beyond comparison with others which I know in Christendom, and many rivers, good and large, which is marvelous. Its lands are high, and there are in it very many sierras and very lofty mountains, beyond comparison with the island of Teneriffe.[9] All are most beautiful, of a thousand shapes, and all are accessible and filled with trees of a thousand kinds and tall, and they seem to touch the sky. And I am told that they never lose their foliage, as I can understand, for I saw them as green and as lovely as they are in Spain in May, and some of them were flowering, some bearing fruit, and some in another stage, according to their nature. And the nightingale was singing and other birds of a thousand kinds in the month of November there where I went. There are six or eight kinds of palm, which are a wonder to behold on account of their beautiful variety, but so are the other trees and fruits and plants. In it are marvelous pine groves, and there are very large tracts of cultivable lands, and there is honey, and there are birds of many kinds and fruits in great diversity. In the interior are mines of metals, and the population is without number. Española is a marvel.

The sierras and mountains, the plains and arable lands and pastures, are so lovely and rich for planting and sowing, for breeding cattle of every kind, for building towns and villages. The harbors of the sea here are such as cannot be believed to exist unless they have been seen, and so with the rivers, many and great, and good waters, the majority of which contain gold.[10] In the trees and fruits and plants, there is a great difference from those of Juana. In this island, there are many spices and great mines of gold and of other metals.

The people of this island, and of all the other islands which I have found and of which I have information, all go naked, men and women, as their mothers bore them,[11] although some women cover a single place with the leaf of a plant or with a net of cotton which they make for the purpose. They have no iron or steel or weapons, nor are they fitted to use them, not because they are not well built men and of handsome stature, but because they are very marvelously timorous. They have no other arms than weapons made of canes, cut in seeding time, to the ends of which they fix a small sharpened stick. And they do not dare to make use of these, for many times it has happened that I have sent ashore two or three men to some town to have speech, and countless people have come out to them, and as soon as they have seen my men approaching they have fled, even a father not waiting for his son. And this, not because ill has been done to anyone; on the contrary, at every point where I have been and have been able to have speech, I have given to them of all that I had, such as cloth and many other things, without receiving anything for it; but so they are, incurably timid. It is true that, after they have been reassured and have lost their fear, they are so guileless and so generous with all they possess, that no one

---

[8]Columbus took seven Tainos on board at San Salvador to instruct them in Spanish and use them as guides and interpreters.

[9]One of the Canary Islands.

[10]Although Columbus obtained items of gold and received plenty of reports of nearby gold mines, the metal was rare in the islands.

[11]Marco Polo described a number of islanders in South Asia who went naked. Compare also Columbus's description of this nudity with John Mandeville's account of the people of Sumatra in Volume I, Chapter 12, source 98.

120 would believe it who has not seen it. They never refuse anything which they possess, if it be asked of them; on the contrary, they invite anyone to share it, and display as much love as if they would give their hearts, and whether the thing be of
125 value or whether it be of small price, at once with whatever trifle of whatever kind it may be that is given to them, with that they are content.[12] I forbade that they should be given things so worthless as fragments of broken crockery and scraps of
130 broken glass, and ends of straps, although when they were able to get them, they fancied that they possessed the best jewel in the world. So it was found that a sailor for a strap received gold to the weight of two and a half *castellanos,*[13] and others
135 much more for other things which were worth much less. As for new *blancas,*[14] for them they would give everything which they had, although it might be two or three *castellanos'* weight of gold or an *arroba*[15] or two of spun cotton. . . .
140 They took even the pieces of the broken hoops of the wine barrels and, like savages, gave what they had, so that it seemed to me to be wrong and I forbade it. And I gave a thousand handsome good things, which I had brought, in order that they
145 might conceive affection, and more than that, might become Christians and be inclined to the love and service of their highnesses and of the whole Castilian nation, and strive to aid us and to give us of the things which they have in abun-
150 dance and which are necessary to us. And they do not know any creed and are not idolaters;[16] only they all believe that power and good are in the heavens, and they are very firmly convinced that I, with these ships and men, came from the heav-
155 ens, and in this belief they everywhere received

me, after they had overcome their fear. And this does not come because they are ignorant; on the contrary, they are of a very acute intelligence and are men who navigate all those seas, so that it is amazing how good an account they give of every- 160 thing, but it is because they have never seen people clothed or ships of such a kind.

And as soon as I arrived in the Indies, in the first island which I found, I took by force some of them, in order that they might learn and give me 165 information of that which there is in those parts, and so it was that they soon understood us, and we them, either by speech or signs, and they have been very serviceable. I still take them with me, and they are always assured that I come from 170 Heaven, for all the intercourse which they have had with me; and they were the first to announce this wherever I went, and the others went running from house to house and to the neighboring towns, with loud cries of, "Come! Come to see 175 the people from Heaven!" So all, men and women alike, when their minds were set at rest concerning us, came, so that not one, great or small, remained behind, and all brought something to eat and drink, which they gave with ex- 180 traordinary affection. In all the island, they have very many canoes, like rowing *fustas,*[17] some larger, some smaller, and some are larger than a *fusta* of eighteen benches. They are not so broad, because they are made of a single log of wood, but a 185 *fusta* would not keep up with them in rowing, since their speed is a thing incredible. And in these they navigate among all those islands, which are innumerable, and carry their goods. One of these canoes I have seen with seventy and 190 eighty men in her, and each one with his oar.

---

[12]Compare this with Mandeville's description of the people of Sumatra's attitude toward possessions (see note 11).

[13]A gold coin of considerable value that bore the seal of Castile.

[14]The smallest and least valuable Spanish coin, it was worth about one-sixtieth of a castellano. It had a whitish hue, hence the name *blanca,* or white.

[15]The equivalent of about sixteen skeins, or balls, of spun textile.

[16]Normally *idolater* means someone who worships idols, or sacred statues, but it is unclear exactly what Columbus

means here. The Tainos worshiped a variety of deities and spirits known as *cemis,* whom they represented in stone statues and other images, also known as cemis. It is hard to imagine Columbus's not having seen carved cemis, which filled the Tainos' villages. To compound the problem of what Columbus meant by their not being idolaters, consider lines 289–291 of this letter, where he refers to idolaters who will be enslaved.

[17]A small oared boat, often having one or two masts.

In all these islands, I saw no great diversity in the appearance of the people or in their manners and language. On the contrary, they all under-
195 stand one another,[18] which is a very curious thing, on account of which I hope that their highnesses will determine upon their conversion to our holy faith, towards which they are very inclined. . . .

200 I can say that [Juana] is larger than England and Scotland together,[19] for . . . there remain to the westward two provinces to which I have not gone. One of these provinces they call "Avan,"[20] and there the people are born with tails;[21] . . . as I
205 could understand from those Indians whom I have and who know all the islands.

The other, Española, has a circumference greater than all Spain.[22] . . . It is a land to be desired and, seen, it is never to be left. And . . . I
210 have taken possession for their highnesses . . . this Española, in [a] situation most convenient and in the best position for the mines of gold and for all intercourse as well with the mainland . . . belonging to the Grand Khan,[23] where will be
215 great trade and gain. I have taken possession of a large town, to which I gave the name *Villa de Navidad*,[24] and in it I have made fortifications and a fort, which now will by this time be entire-

ly finished, and I have left in it sufficient men for such a purpose with arms and artillery and provi-220 sions for more than a year, and a *fusta,* and one, a master of all seacraft, to build others, and great friendship with the king of that land, so much so, that he was proud to call me, and to treat me as a brother. And even if he were to change his atti-225 tude to one of hostility towards these men, he and his do not know what arms are and they go naked, as I have already said, and are the most timorous people that there are in the world, so that the men whom I have left there alone would 230 suffice to destroy all that land, and the island is without danger for their persons, if they know how to govern themselves.[25]

In all these islands, it seems to me that all men are content with one woman, and to their chief or 235 king they give as many as twenty.[26] It appears to me that the women work more than the men. And I have not been able to learn if they hold private property; what seemed to me to appear was that, in that which one had, all took a share, es-240 pecially of eatable things.[27]

In these islands I have so far found no human monstrosities, as many expected,[28] but on the contrary the whole population is very well-formed, nor are they negroes as in Guinea,[29] but 245

---

[18]This is not totally accurate. Columbus's Taino interpreters knew only a little of the language of the Ciguayos whom the admiral encountered on Española in January 1493 (note 30).
[19]Not so.
[20]Which the Spaniards transformed into La Habana, or Havana.
[21]Marco Polo reported the existence of tailed humans in the islands of Southeast Asia. In his description of the various fantastic people who supposedly inhabited the islands of Southeast Asia, John Mandeville listed hairy persons who walked on all fours and climbed trees.
[22]Not so.
[23]The Mongol emperor of Cathay (Volume I, Chapter 12, source 103). Columbus did not know that the Mongol khans had been expelled from power in China in 1368.
[24]"Village of the Nativity" (of the Lord). The destruction of the *Santa Maria* off the coast of Española on Christmas Day (Navidad del Señor) forced Columbus to leave behind thirty-nine sailors at the village garrison, which he named after the day of the incident.
[25]When Columbus returned in November 1493, he discovered the fortification burned to the ground and all thirty-

nine men dead. Almost as soon as Columbus had sailed away, the Spaniards began fighting among themselves and split into factions, with only eleven remaining to garrison the fort. The widely scattered groups of Spaniards were wiped out by Tainos led by a chief named Caonabó. Guacanagarí, the king to whom Columbus refers, apparently was wounded trying to defend the Spaniards.
[26]Generally only chiefs could afford large numbers of wives because of the substantial bride prices that were paid, in goods or services, to the families of the women. Notwithstanding, many commoners could and did have two or three wives.
[27]See note 12.
[28]Based on the Greek, Roman, and Arab geographies available to them, Europeans were prepared to find various races of monstrous humans and semihumans in the Indies. Accepted accounts of the wonders of the East, such as the travelogue of John Mandeville, told of dog-headed people and a species of individuals who, lacking heads, had an eye on each shoulder.
[29]Sub-Saharan West Africa (see Volume I, Chapter 12, source 108).

their hair is flowing, and they are not born where there is intense force in the rays of the sun; it is true that the sun has there great power. . . .

As I have found no monsters, so I have had no report of any, except in an island "Quaris," the second at the coming into the Indies, which is inhabited by a people who are regarded in all the islands as very fierce and who eat human flesh. They have many canoes with which they range through all the islands of India and pillage and take as much as they can.[30] They are no more malformed than the others, except that they have the custom of wearing their hair long like women, and they use bows and arrows of the same cane stems, with a small piece of wood at the end, owing to lack of iron which they do not possess. They are ferocious among these other people who are cowardly to an excessive degree, but I make no more account of them than of the rest. These are those who have intercourse with the women of "Matinino," which is the first island met on the way from Spain to the Indies, in which there is not a man. The women engage in no feminine occupation, but use bows and arrows of cane, like those already mentioned, and they

arm and protect themselves with plates of copper, of which they have much.[31]

In another island, which they assure me is larger than Española, the people have no hair.[32] In it, there is gold incalculable, and from it and from the other islands, I bring with me Indians as evidence.[33]

In conclusion, to speak only of that which has been accomplished on this voyage, which was so hasty, their highnesses can see that I will give them as much gold as they may need, if their highnesses will render me very slight assistance; moreover, spice and cotton,[34] as much as their highnesses shall command; and mastic,[35] as much as they shall order to be shipped and which, up to now, has been found only in Greece, in the island of Chios,[36] and the Seignory[37] sells it for what it pleases; and aloe wood, as much as they shall order to be shipped, and slaves, as many as they shall order to be shipped and who will be from the idolaters.[38] And I believe that I have found rhubarb and cinnamon,[39] and I shall find a thousand other things of value, which the people whom I have left there will have discovered, for I have not delayed at any point, so far as

---

[30]These were the Caribs, who shortly before the arrival of Columbus began to displace the Arawak peoples of the Lesser Antilles, the archipelago to the east and south of Hispaniola. Sixteenth-century Spanish writers unanimously agreed that the Caribs were fierce warriors and cannibalistic. On January 13, 1493, Columbus and his men had a short skirmish on Española (Hispaniola) with some previously unknown natives, whom the admiral incorrectly assumed were Caribs. They were actually Ciguayos, who were less peaceful than the Tainos.

[31]The same account appears in Columbus's log. Father Ramón Pane, who composed an ethnographic study of Taino culture during Columbus's second voyage of 1493–1494, also related in great detail the legend of the island of Matinino, where only women resided. The story, as reported by Pane, however, contains no hint that they were war-like women. Apparently Columbus took this Taino legend and combined it with the Greco-Roman myth of the warrior Amazons. Mandeville wrote of the land of Amazonia, populated totally by warrior women, and Marco Polo described two Asian islands, one inhabited solely by women and another exclusively by men. There is no evidence that this female society reported by Columbus and Pane ever existed in the Caribbean. The Tainos, however, who were essentially a stone-age people, did import from South America an alloy of copper and gold, which they used for ornaments.

[32]John Mandeville described people with little body hair, and Marco Polo told of Buddhist monks whose heads and faces were shaved.

[33]Columbus brought seven Tainos back to Spain, where they were baptized, with King Ferdinand and Prince Juan acting as godparents. One remained at the Spanish court, where he died, and the others returned with Columbus on his second voyage of 1493.

[34]The only indigenous spice was the chili pepper; the wild cotton was excellent but not plentiful.

[35]Columbus and his men wrongly identified a native gumbo-limbo tree, which contains an aromatic resin, with the rare mastic tree, whose costly resin was a profitable trade item for Genoa (note 37).

[36]An island in the eastern Mediterranean.

[37]The ruling body of Genoa, Columbus's native Italian city-state. Chios was a possession of Genoa, whose merchants controlled the mastic trade.

[38]Church law forbade the enslavement of Christians, except in the most exceptional circumstances.

[39]Actually, when members of the crew showed Columbus what they thought were aloe, mastic, and cinnamon, the admiral accepted the aloe and mastic as genuine but rejected the supposed cinnamon. One of his lieutenants reported seeing rhubarb while on a scouting expedition.

the wind allowed me to sail, except in the town of Navidad, in order to leave it secured and well established, and in truth, I should have done much more, if the ships had served me, as reason
300 demanded.

This is enough . . . and the eternal God, our Lord, Who gives to all those who walk in His way triumph over things which appear to be impossible, and this was notably one; for, although
305 men have talked or have written of these lands, all was conjectural, without suggestion of ocular evidence, but amounted only to this, that those who heard for the most part listened and judged it to be rather a fable than as having any vestige
310 of truth. So that, since Our Redeemer[40] has given this victory to our most illustrious king and

queen, and to their renowned kingdoms, in so great a matter, for this all Christendom ought to feel delight and make great feasts and give solemn thanks to the Holy Trinity[41] with many 315 solemn prayers for the great exaltation which they shall have, in the turning of so many people to our holy faith, and afterwards for temporal benefits,[42] for not only Spain but all Christians will have hence refreshment and gain. 320

This in accordance with that which has been accomplished, thus briefly.

Done in the caravel,[43] off the Canary Islands, on the fifteenth of February, in the year one thousand four hundred and ninety-three. 325

At your orders.   El Almirante.[44]

---

[40]Jesus Christ.
[41]The Christian belief of three divine persons — Father, Son, and Holy Spirit — contained in a single divine essence.
[42]Benefits that are of this world and last only for a time, as opposed to eternal, or heavenly, rewards.

[43]A Spanish ocean-going ship.
[44]The Admiral.

Interpreting Columbus's Letter

As already noted, a historian always has to evaluate the worth of each source, which means understanding its point of view and reliability. So let us concentrate on those two issues. By so doing, we will address questions 1–5 and 8.

In this letter several things are obvious. Columbus believed he had reached Asian islands (lines 5–23). Marco Polo, John Mandeville, and other writers had provided a number of reference points by which to recognize the Orient (notes 11, 12, 21, 28, 31, and 32), and Columbus believed he had found many of them. It is equally obvious that Columbus tried to present his discoveries in the best light possible. He sent this letter ahead to the court of Ferdinand and Isabella to ensure that when he arrived he would be received with due honor.

There is plenty of exaggeration, self-puffery, error, coverup, and even some deliberate distortion in this account. He overestimated the size of several islands (lines 200–201 and 207–208) and, except for chilies, the spices he claimed to have discovered (lines 85, 283, and 292) were not there. The admiral also failed to mention that the *Santa Maria* had been lost (note 24). Columbus could not escape informing his royal patrons of this unhappy incident, but presumably he wanted to wait until he was at the court, where he could put his own spin on the facts surrounding the incident. Also not mentioned is a skirmish that he and his men had on January 13, 1493, with some hostile strangers, whom he incorrectly assumed were Caribs (note 30). That incident, if reported without explanation, probably would have weakened the admiral's implied claim that Spain could easily subjugate these timid Indians (lines 93–113 and 225–233). Indeed, his statement that the crew members he left behind at Navidad del Señor were in no danger "if they know how to govern themselves" (lines 232–233) suggests that he chose not to mention that some ugly incidents had already taken place, possibly rape of island women, and he feared the Tainos would not tolerate further outrages. And this proved to be the case as note 25 informs us.

Generally, however, despite Columbus's enthusiasm and understandable tendency to exaggerate, to neglect mentioning anything negative, and to see what he wanted to see, the admiral *seems* to have wanted to present an essentially factual account. Well, that certainly sounds like a strange conclusion, given all of the flaws that we just pointed out or alluded to.

One feature of the letter that leads us to this position is how Columbus described the people of the islands. His reading of popular travel accounts had prepared him to encounter every sort of human monstrosity (note 28), and undoubtedly he would have enjoyed reporting such contacts. But he honestly reported that all the natives he encountered were quite unmonstrous in appearance and temperament (lines 242–245). Of course, he reported stories of people with tails, cannibals, and warlike women who lived apart from men (lines 204–206 and 249–272), but it is unlikely that the admiral was deliberately misleading anyone on this issue. The Carib cannibals were real enough. Rumors of tailed people and latter-day Amazons conceivably were nothing more than the natives' effort to please Columbus or simply the result of poor communication. It is not difficult to imagine that when the admiral inquired after the locations of the various human curiosities whom Mandeville, Polo, and others had placed in the islands of the Indian Ocean, the Tainos, not knowing what he was asking, agreeably pointed across the waters to other islands.

This raises one issue that has long vexed historians and goes straight to the heart of the question of this source's overall reliability. *How well was Columbus able to communicate with these people?* Columbus insisted that through gestures and learned words the Spaniards and Tainos were able to communicate with one another (lines 163–169), and he certainly learned enough of the Tainos' language to report that they called the island on which he initially landed *Guanahani* (line 15). Nevertheless, we suspect that, despite Columbus's use of captive interpreters, only the most primitive forms of communication were possible between the Europeans and the Tainos in 1492–1493. We should, therefore, have a healthy skepticism about anything that Columbus reports about the Tainos' beliefs and cosmological perspectives (for example, lines 150–156 and 170–176).

All things considered, it seems reasonable to conclude that Columbus's letter can be accepted as a somewhat honest but far from accurate account of his discoveries and experiences. Put another way, Columbus was a "spin doctor," very much like some modern politicians who think they are speaking the truth, but their version of the truth is colored by their hopes, dreams, ambitions, and promises made. Columbus's honesty, compromised by an understandable enthusiasm to present his accomplishments positively, comes through in his attempt to describe the islands' physical qualities and the people he encountered. The picture that emerges tells us a lot about the complex motives that underlay his great adventure.

We notice that Columbus had taken possession of the lands in the names of the Spanish monarchs and even renamed the islands, without once giving thought to the claims of anyone else (lines 7–19). He also thought nothing of seizing some natives as soon as he arrived (lines 40–41 and 164–169) and of carrying several Indians back to Spain (lines 276–277). Moreover, he noted toward the end of his letter that the monarchs of Spain could obtain as many *slaves* as they desired from among the islands' *idolaters* (lines 289–291). At the same time (and this might strike the modern student as curious), Columbus claimed that he had acted generously and protectively toward the native people (lines 107–112 and 140–145), and he conveys in his letter a tone of admiration and even affection for the people whom he had encountered. Indeed, the admiral expressed a deep interest in winning over the native people in an avowed hope that they might become Catholic Christians and loyal subjects of Ferdinand and Isabella (lines 143–150), and he even claimed that they were strongly inclined toward religious conversion (lines 197–199). Yet the very qualities that Columbus implied made the Tainos prime candidates for conversion — intelligence, timidity, naiveté, generosity, ignorance, technological backwardness, lack of an articulated religious creed, an ability to communicate freely among themselves, and a sense of wonder at the Europeans — also made them ripe for subjugation.

The tone of this letter suggests that Columbus was concerned with these people as humans and was genuinely interested in helping them achieve salvation through conversion. It is equally clear, however, Columbus believed that he and Catholic Spain had a right and duty to subjugate and exploit these same people. Such tension continued throughout the Spanish colonial experience in the Americas.

Subjugation of the Indians and their lands involved more than just a sense of divine mission and Christian altruism — as real as those motives were. Columbus, his royal patrons, and most others who joined overseas adventures expected to gain in earthly wealth as well (see especially lines 278–295). Even a superficial reading of his letter reveals the admiral's preoccupation with the riches of the islands — riches that he appears to have exaggerated and even misrepresented (note 39). Gold, spices, cotton, aromatic mastic, and, of course, slaves were the material rewards that awaited Christian Europeans, and Columbus was fully interested in them and wanted Ferdinand and Isabella to underwrite future trips so that he could discover them in abundance. So exaggeration can be found in this account, but it seems to be largely exaggeration based on conviction.

Was Columbus being cynical, hypocritical, or deliberately ironic when in his closing words he claimed that Jesus Christ had provided this great victory to the Spanish monarchs (and indeed to all Christendom) and from that victory would flow the dual benefits of the conversion of so many people and worldly riches (lines 310–320)? Cynicism, hypocrisy, and conscious irony are not likely explanations. It seems more likely that these closing remarks reveal the mind of a man who saw no contradiction between spreading the faith and benefiting materially from that action, even if doing so meant exploiting the converts.

Perhaps you disagree with our conclusion that Columbus's letter is basically an honest and valuable source, despite its shortcomings. Well, if you do, you are in excellent company. Two eminent historians — William D. Phillips Jr. and Carla Rahn Phillips, in their book *The Worlds of Christopher Columbus* — characterize this letter as "a tissue of exaggerations, misconceptions, and outright lies." Although we acknowledge the letter's exaggerations, misconceptions, and prevarications (a somewhat less damning form of falsehood), we disagree as to the degree, nature, and extent of the letter's misstatements. Well, no historian is infallible, and certainly we do not claim that distinction. Moreover, no source is so clear in all respects that it lacks areas of potential disagreement for historians. That, in fact, is one of the exciting aspects of historical research. Despite all the facts and conclusions that historians generally agree on, there are numerous areas in which they carry on spirited debate. *The very nature of history's fragmentary, flawed evidence makes debate inevitable.*

What is more, no historian can possibly see everything there is to be seen in every source. What this means, so far as you are concerned, is that *there is plenty of latitude in the sources that appear in this book for you to arrive at valid insights that are unique to you.* In so doing, however, you must at all times attempt to divorce yourself of present-mindedness and to enter imaginatively into the world of the author whose work you are analyzing.

We can ask many other questions of Columbus's letter and garner other insights from it. Certainly it tells us a lot about Taino culture. Despite his cultural blinders, his naiveté, his tendency to see what he wanted to see, and his probably exaggerated belief in his ability to communicate with these people, Columbus seems to be a reasonably accurate and perceptive observer. Thus anyone interested in Caribbean cultures before the Europeans had much of a chance to influence them must necessarily look to this and similar accounts of first contacts. In fact, it would be good practice for you, right now, to try to answer question 7, which we have deliberately left unanswered. You will be surprised at how much you can learn about the Tainos from this brief description. As you do this exercise, however, do not forget to ask yourself constantly: How reliable does Columbus appear to be on this specific point, and what is the basis for my conclusion?

After you have tested your own powers of historical analysis in this exercise, it would be wise to put the letter aside for the present. We trust that by now you have a good idea of how to examine and mine a documentary source. Now let us consider an artifact and proceed to interpret it.

The Family Dinner

▼▼▼

▼ *AN ANONYMOUS WOODCUT OF 1511*

Columbus arrived in Barcelona in April 1493 to learn not only had his letter arrived, but it had already been published and publicly circulated. Within months the letter was translated into several languages; the Latin translation alone went through nine editions, several of which were lavishly illustrated, before the end of 1494. Printers discovered that educated Europeans had an almost insatiable desire to learn about the peoples and lands Columbus and other explorers were discovering, and they catered to that interest. Their clientele wanted not only to read about the fascinating peoples, plants, and animals of these lands — they wanted also to see them. Consequently, as books on the new explorations proliferated, so did the number of printed illustrations. Many are fanciful and tell us more about the Europeans who created them than the peoples and regions they supposedly portrayed. The woodcut print we have chosen appeared in a popular English pamphlet of 1511.

QUESTIONS FOR ANALYSIS

1. What scene has the artist set? What has the artist placed to the immediate right of the standing man, and what function does it have in this scene?
2. What do each person's actions, dress, and demeanor tell us about her or him?
3. What does this illustration tell us about popular European notions concerning the natives of the New World?

Interpreting the Woodcut

What a charming, even idyllic domestic scene! An attractive mother nurses an infant at her breast while amusing an older child with a feather. A well-muscled, equally attractive, and proud father stands nearby, holding the tools of his trade while next to him the family's dinner is slowly cooking. Dinner, of course, may strike us as macabre, as these are cannibals, and it looks like roast human is on the menu. The tools of the father's trade are weapons. Both children are naked, and the parents are virtually nude, save for what appear to be leaves that cover their loins, decorative necklaces, armbands and anklets of some indeterminate material, and feathers in their long and unkempt hair.

What is the message? What we have is a reprise of the image provided by Columbus in his letter of 1493: the *noble savage.* These are fully human beings with human bonds and affections. Yet they are still savages, as their clothing (or lack of it), decorations, hair styles, weapons, and choice of food would have suggested to most sixteenth-century Europeans. Here, as Columbus and many of those who followed agreed, were a people who could become Christians but who also, by virtue of their backwardness, were to be subjugated. There is something appealing about their innocent savagery, but what of that poor fellow whose severed leg and head are slowly roasting?

Have we read too much into the woodcut? It is arguable that we may have. The historian always faces this problem when trying to analyze an isolated piece of evidence, particularly an artifactual source. Yet this artifact is not completely isolated, for we brought to its analysis insight gained from documentary evidence — Columbus's letter. That is how we generally read the artifacts of historical cultures. We attempt to place them in the context of what we have already learned or inferred from documentary sources. Documents illuminate artifacts, and artifacts make more vivid and tangible the often shadowy world of words.

As you attempt to interpret the unwritten sources in this book, keep in mind what you have learned from the documents you have already read, your textbook, and class lectures. Remember that we have chosen these artifacts to illustrate broad themes and general trends. You should not find their messages overly subtle. As with the documents, always try to place each piece of artifactual evidence into its proper context, and in that regard, read the introductions and Questions for Analysis very carefully. We will do our best to provide you with all the information and clues you need.

Good luck and have fun!

Part One

▼▼▼

The Ancient World

The term *Ancient World* presents a problem to the student of world history because it is a creation of Western historical thought. Historians in the West originally used the term to refer only to the early history of one small region of the world — the area that stretches from the northwest corner of the Indian subcontinent to Western Europe. Understood within this narrow context, ancient history involves the period from the rise of civilizations in Southwest Asia and Egypt (collectively known today as the *Middle East*) to the collapse of Roman civilization: from approximately 3500 *Before the Common Era* (B.C.E.) to about 500 in the *Common Era* (C.E.). Within this Western scheme of history, antiquity passed away about 1,500 years ago but not before it had laid the roots of Western civilization. Having spent itself, the ancient world was followed by the so-called *Middle Ages* (500–1500), and this era, in turn, was followed by the early modern (1500–1789), modern (1789–1914), and contemporary eras.

Such neat divisions of the past, which might reflect the Western historical experience (and there is debate over their accuracy even in regard to the history of the West), make little sense when history is studied globally. Nevertheless, the category *Ancient World* is useful for the global historian if we redefine it in two ways: (1) by expanding the term to include all of the world's *primary,* or earliest, *civilizations,* and (2) by distinguishing between the *Afro-Eurasian* and *American* worlds of antiquity.

Ancient civilizations arose independently on two grand *world islands:* the Afro-Eurasian landmass and the Americas. The first to witness the phenomenon was the Afro-Eurasian supercontinent, where primary civilizations appeared in the river valleys of Mesopotamia, Egypt, northwest India, and China, between approximately 3750 and 2200 B.C.E. Although distinct and largely indigenous, these four early centers of civilization influenced one another in varying degrees.

Across the Atlantic and Pacific oceans, unknown to and uninfluenced by the civilizations of Eurasia and Africa, civilizations appeared in two widely separated centers: the Pacific coast and Andean highlands of Peru around 1900 B.C.E. and the Gulf coast of Mexico around 1500 B.C.E. From these two points of origin, civilization slowly spread outward. As was the case in the Afro-Eurasian world island, the civilizations of the Americas cross-fertilized one another through their extensive trade networks but were essentially isolated from the rest of the world. As was also the case in the Afro-Eurasian hemisphere of the globe, the original centers of civilization in the Americas — Peru and Mexico — served as the American hemisphere's dominant matrices of civilized culture for thousands of years and well beyond the period Europeans characterize as *antiquity*.

The four original centers of civilization within the Afro-Eurasian World — Mesopotamia, Egypt, the Indus Valley, and China — were fairly self-contained, compact, and separate, but never isolated. Plenty of evidence (such as source 8) indicates that the river-valley civilizations of Mesopotamia, Egypt, and the Indus enjoyed a measure of commercial and cultural exchange from early days. The vast steppes, deserts, and mountain ranges of Central Asia meant that China at the eastern end of the Eurasian landmass was more isolated than the three other primary centers of civilization, but its isolation was never absolute. By the middle of the second millennium (the 1000s) B.C.E., wheat and barley had made their way from Southwest Asia to China. The techniques of painted pottery and bronze casting might also have made the same journey, but the process of transmission is obscure and in dispute. Less controversial is the horse chariot, an invention of northern Iran, which appeared in China before the twelfth century B.C.E. On the other end of the scale of exchange, scraps of Chinese silk have been found in Egyptian tombs dating from around 1000 B.C.E.

As these separate but connected civilizations evolved over the course of several thousand years, each spread outward, encompassing a large region on which it imprinted a distinctive culture. By 300 B.C.E. the four major Afro-Eurasian cultural regions, or pools, were Southwest Asia, India, China, and the Mediterranean. Of these, China's relative isolation dictated that its culture would be the most singular and least stimulated by foreign influences. Conversely, the culture of Southwest Asia — the crossroads of the Afro-Eurasian world — was the most variegated and eclectic. A close second in the realm of diversity was the Mediterranean, which drew deeply from the cultural traditions of Mesopotamia, Egypt, and all of the various peoples of the Mediterranean Basin, especially the Greeks.

During the last few centuries B.C.E. and the first several centuries C.E., the cultures at both ends of the great Eurasian expanse of land, China and the Greco-Roman world, achieved political unity and consequently expanded at the expense of their less organized neighbors, such as Koreans and Southeast Asians in the East and various Celtic peoples in the West. The result was two massive empires linked by Central Asian, Indian, Southwest Asian, and East African intermediaries. Consequently, goods, ideas, and diseases were exchanged throughout Eurasia and portions of Africa more freely and quickly than ever before, especially along the so-called *Silk Road,* a complex network of caravan routes that opened up around 100 B.C.E. and connected China with India and the Mediterranean Sea.

Between approximately 200 and 550 C.E. internal and external pressures, including diseases that traveled along the trade routes, precipitated the collapse of empires in China, India, Southwest Asia, and the Roman Mediterranean. With those disasters, which were neither totally contemporaneous nor equally severe, the first grand epoch of Afro-Eurasian history — the Ancient World — was at an end. The era that followed rested on the foundations of antiquity but also differed substantially from the Ancient World, in part because of three world religions — Mahayana Buddhism, Christianity, and Islam — which played transforming roles throughout Eurasia and Africa between roughly 600 and 1500 C.E.

Across the oceans, the civilizations of Mexico and Central and South America continued their development in isolation from the cares and trends of the Eastern Hemisphere. Cities and empires rose and fell, and societies continued to develop along cultural lines set down by the Americas' first civilizations. To be sure, changes took place. One important new trend between roughly 600 and 1200 C.E. was the rise of North American civilizations in what are today the deserts of the southwestern United States and the lands washed by the Mississippi and Ohio rivers. Despite these new centers of civilization, the American Indian World was only wrenched out of its ancient patterns when European invaders and colonists began arriving in significant numbers in the early sixteenth century.

Because of a relative lack of documentary evidence relating to preconquest American Indian cultures and civilizations, the sources in Part One deal exclusively with ancient Afro-Eurasian history. We will consider the story of antiquity in the Western Hemisphere in Part Three, Chapter 11.

Chapter 1

▼▼▼

The First Civilizations

The word *civilization* derives from the Latin adjective *civilis,* which means "political" or "civic." No matter how else we define civilization, an organized civic entity, known as a *state,* serves as the core of every society we call civilized. A state is a sovereign public power that binds large numbers of people together at a level that transcends the ties of family, clan, tribe, and local community and organizes them for projects far beyond the capabilities of single families or even villages and towns.

Modern states tend to be *secular,* or oriented toward this world, and most rulers today claim no particular spiritual or religious authority. In fact, many modern states are based on the principle that legitimate power derives solely from the people. In contrast, the world's first states were all *sacred states,* in which rulers claimed to govern by divine mandate. Such rulers either governed in the name of some divine or heavenly authority or were themselves perceived as gods. Religious beliefs, as well as political and social institutions, varied greatly among the world's ancient civilizations, but ancient civilized peoples shared a common perception that authority is indivisible because it is divine. In other words, they saw no distinction between the state's sacred and secular functions.

Rulers and those who carried out their wills — priests, bureaucrats, and soldiers — were a small minority and maintained power by exploiting the many. This was a fact of early civilized life largely because, until recent times, states could produce only severely limited surpluses of resources, due to the narrow agrarian base of their economies. That surplus of goods, which is so necessary for the creation of a state, could be channeled into state-building activities only if rulers kept the majority of their subjects at a fairly low level of subsistence by exacting from them a major portion of the surplus through taxes, labor services, and military conscription. Consequently, the more agreeable benefits of civilization, such as literature and the other arts, were largely the exclusive property and tools of the few.

Most of the world's first civilizations evolved systems of writing, and in each case the art of writing served, at least initially, to strengthen the authority of rulers. Whether writing was used to record temple possessions or tax obligations, to give permanence to laws, or to provide priests with a coherent body of sacred texts, writing set apart the powerful from the powerless.

Not all of the records left behind by the first civilizations are open to us. Some ancient systems of writing still defy decipherment. Happily, this is not the case with the written languages of Mesopotamia, Egypt, and China. The documentary sources left behind by these three civilizations reveal societies that were strikingly different in perspective and structure, even as they shared characteristics common to all early civilizations.

▼▼▼

Mesopotamia: The Land of Two Rivers

According to the eminent historian Samuel N. Kramer, "History begins at Sumer," and there is a good deal of truth to that judgment. It is in *Sumer,* which lay just to the north of the Persian Gulf in an area encompassed by the southern regions of modern Iraq, that we discover the first evidence of human civilization. Around 3750 B.C.E. Uruk emerged as a city — apparently Sumer's first city — and other Sumerian city-states followed in succeeding centuries.

The origin of the Sumerians is a mystery. Their language is unique, with no connection to any other known language or language family. Evidence of a number of non-Sumerian words in their language, especially for terms associated with such basic skills as farming and metalworking, suggests that the Sumerians were migrants who learned the techniques essential for a settled life from an indigenous population that they absorbed or, at least, controlled.

Generally we call the Sumerians, and the other peoples who inhabited this region of Southwest Asia, *Mesopotamians*. The term is Greek, and it means "those who dwell between the rivers." The rivers are the Tigris in the east and the Euphrates to its west. The former is about 1,180 miles long, and the latter flows for about 1,740 miles. Rising in the mountains, they descend southeast, providing water to the inhabitants of the steppes, plains, and marshes through which they pass. Without the fertile soil produced by these two rivers and the challenge of harnessing this life-giving water through irrigation systems, Sumerian civilization is inconceivable.

By approximately 1800 B.C.E., the Sumerians had been absorbed by waves of infiltrators and invaders and ceased to exist as an identifiable people. Moreover, the cultural center of gravity within Mesopotamia had shifted northward to the region of middle Mesopotamia, centering on the city of *Babylon* on the Euphrates.

Despite their disappearance as a people, the Sumerians had set the framework for a dynamic Mesopotamian civilization that exercised profound cultural influence throughout West Asia and beyond for about 3,000 years. Between roughly 3750 and 500 B.C.E. Mesopotamia was where much of the action was, so far as the history of West Asian civilization was concerned.

That action was both constructive and destructive. The Mesopotamians are credited with having created the world's first system of writing, as well as its first governments, schools, codes of law, ethical systems, and epic literature. Just as prominent in Mesopotamian life were disasters, both natural and human generated.

As noted, the geography of Mesopotamia provided its people with the challenge of harnessing the waters of its two great rivers, and from that necessary cooperative effort civilization arose. Yet those rivers also threatened to destroy the fragile fabric of civilized society because they were unpredictable and could easily turn into uncontrollable torrents, especially in the south. Moreover, most of southern Mesopotamia was covered by either arid plains or marsh. Consequently, Sumerian civilization was built upon heroic labor in the midst of a hostile environment.

Another significant geographical aspect of Mesopotamian life, which also proved to be an important factor throughout its history, is the land's openness to incursions. To the north and east lie the hills and mountains of Iran and Armenia, from which wave after wave of invaders descended into the inviting valley of cities. To the south and west lies the desert of Arabia, out of which came countless nomads century after century. In many instances these invaders toppled a preexisting state and then settled down to become, in turn, Mesopotamians.

Some came from the desert fringes, such as the *Amorites,* speakers of a *Semitic* language who established the first Babylonian Empire in the eighteenth century (1700s) B.C.E. Others were mountain folk, such as the chariot-driving *Kassites,* speakers of an Indo-Iranian language who toppled Babylon late in the seventeenth century B.C.E. Regardless of their origin, language, or native culture, all eventually became part of a Mesopotamian cultural complex, with modes of life and thought the Sumerians had set in place at the dawn of human civilization.

The Search for Eternal Life in Mesopotamia

▼▼▼

1 ▼ *THE EPIC OF GILGAMESH*

Humans share many basic concerns, and among them two are of primary importance: finding meaning in life and confronting the reality of death. In Mesopotamia, where life and human fortune were so precarious, people deeply probed these issues and made them the subjects of numerous myths. The word *myth* derives from the ancient Greek word for "a poetic story." As understood by modern scholars, however, a myth is not just any poetic story, and it certainly is not a deliberate piece of fiction or a story told primarily to entertain, even though myths do have entertainment value. First and foremost, a myth is a vehicle through which prescientific societies explain the workings of the universe and humanity's place within it. Whereas the scientist objectifies nature, seeing the world as an *it,* the myth-maker lives in a world where everything has a soul, a personality, and its own story. A raging river is not a body of water responding to physical laws but an angry or capricious god. In the same manner, the fortunes of human society are not the consequences of chance, history, or any patterns discoverable by social scientists. Rather, the gods and other supernatural spirits intervene directly into human affairs, punishing and rewarding as they wish, and divine interventions become the subjects of mythic stories. The stories, in turn, provide insight into the ways of the gods, thereby largely satisfying the emotional and intellectual needs of the myth-maker's audience.

So far as the issues of the meaning of life and death were concerned, ancient Mesopotamia created its classic mythic answer in the form of its greatest work of literature, *The Epic of Gilgamesh.* An *epic* is a long narrative poem that celebrates the feats of some legendary hero who is involved in a journey or similar severe test. In the process of his trials, the hero gains wisdom and, because of that wisdom, greater heroic stature.

The most complete extant version of *The Epic of Gilgamesh* exists in Akkadian, a Semitic language that gradually supplanted Sumerian as the dominant language of Mesopotamia after about 2300 B.C.E. and became *the* language of diplomacy and commerce throughout Southwest Asia after about 1450 B.C.E. The text was discovered on fragments of about seventy clay tablets in the ruins of an Assyrian library that dated to the late seventh century B.C.E. Other, earlier versions of the epic show, however, that the story, at least in its basic outline, is Sumerian in origin and goes back to the third millennium B.C.E. (2000s). The Akkadian version of the epic that survives is about 80 percent complete. About 575 lines are missing out of an original 3,000 or so. Despite these holes, some of which might have been filled from yet-to-be-translated cuneiform tablets looted or destroyed in 2003 in the wake of the Second Gulf War, the story that survives is coherent and its characters emerge as multidimensional.

The hero, Gilgamesh, was a historical figure. Originally known by his Sumerian name, Bilgames, he ruled the city-state of Uruk sometime around 2800–2700 B.C.E. and was remembered as a great warrior, as well as the builder of Uruk's massive walls. His exploits were so impressive that he became the focal point of a series of sagas that recounted his legendary heroic deeds. Around 1700 B.C.E. an unknown Babylonian poet reworked some of these Sumerian tales, along with other stories — such as the adventure of Utnapishtim that appears in our selection — into an epic masterpiece that became widely popular and influential throughout Southwest Asia and beyond.

The epic contains a profound theme, the conflict between humanity's talents and aspirations and its mortal limitations. Gilgamesh, "two-thirds a god and one-third human," as the poem describes him, is a man of heroic proportions and appetites who still must face the inevitability of death.

As the epic opens, an arrogant Gilgamesh, not yet aware of his human limitations and his duties as king, is exhausting the people of Uruk with his manic energy. The people cry to Heaven for relief from his abuse of power, and the gods respond by creating Enkidu, a wild man who lives among the animals. Enkidu enters Uruk, where he challenges Gilgamesh to a contest of strength and fighting skill. When Gilgamesh triumphs, Enkidu embraces him as a brother, and the two heroes set out on a series of spectacular exploits.

In the course of their heroic adventures, they insult Ishtar (Inanna in Sumerian), goddess of sexual love and fertility, and for this a life is owed. The one chosen by the gods to die is Enkidu. As our selection opens, Enkidu, after having cursed his heroic past which has brought him to this fate, tells Gilgamesh of a vision he has had of the place Mesopotamians knew as "the land of no return."

QUESTIONS FOR ANALYSIS

1. What was the Mesopotamian view of the afterlife?
2. What is the message of Siduri's advice to Gilgamesh?
3. Consider Utnapishtim's initial response to Gilgamesh's request for the secret of eternal life. How does his message complement what Siduri has said?
4. Consider the story of Utnapishtim. What do the various actions of the gods and goddesses allow us to infer about how the Mesopotamians viewed their deities?
5. According to the epic, what are the respective roles of the gods and humans? What do the Mesopotamian deities require of humanity? What do humans expect of their gods?
6. What wisdom has Gilgamesh gained from his epic struggles? How has he changed as a result of his quest?
7. Despite the failure of his quest for eternal life, has Gilgamesh earned anything? If so, what is it?
8. Review your answers to questions 2 and 3 in light of the epilogue, where the poet lays out for us the moral of the story. Basing your answer on the entire story, and especially the epilogue, what would you say was the Mesopotamian view of the meaning of life?

As Enkidu slept alone in his sickness, in bitterness of spirit he poured out his heart to his friend. "It was I who cut down the cedar, I who leveled the forest, I who slew Humbaba[1] and now see what has become of me. Listen, my friend, this is the dream I dreamed last night. The heavens roared, and earth rumbled back an answer; between them stood I before an awful being, the sombre-faced manbird; he had directed on me his purpose. His was a vampire face, his foot was a lion's foot, his hand was an eagle's talon. He fell on me and his claws were in my hair, he held me fast and I smothered; then he transformed me so that my arms became wings covered with feathers. He turned his stare towards me, and he led me away to the palace of Irkalla, the Queen of

---

[1] A monstrous giant who guarded the sacred cedar forest in the mountains of Lebanon and was slain by Gilgamesh.

Darkness,[2] to the house from which none who enters ever returns, down the road from which there is no coming back.

"There is the house whose people sit in darkness; dust is their food and clay their meat. They are clothed like birds with wings for covering, they see no light, they sit in darkness. I entered the house of dust and I saw the kings of the earth, their crowns put away forever; rulers and princes, all those who once wore kingly crowns and ruled the world in the days of old. They who had stood in the place of the gods like Anu and Enlil,[3] stood now like servants to fetch baked meats in the house of dust, to carry cooked meat and cold water from the waterskin. In the house of dust which I entered were high priests and acolytes, priests of the incantation and of ecstasy; there were servers of the temple, and there was Etana, that king of Kish whom the eagle carried to Heaven in the days of old.[4] There was Ereshkigal[5] the Queen of the Underworld; and Belit-Sheri squatted in front of her, she who is recorder of the gods and keeps the book of death. She held a tablet from which she read. She raised her head, she saw me and spoke: 'Who has brought this one here?' Then I awoke like a man drained of blood who wanders alone in a waste of rushes; like one whom the bailiff has seized and his heart pounds with terror."

▷ Enkidu dies, and Gilgamesh now realizes that heroic fame is no substitute for life. Facing the reality of his own death, he begins a desperate search for immortality. He travels to the end of the Earth, where he encounters Siduri, a female tavern keeper, who advises him:

"Gilgamesh, where are you hurrying to? You will never find that life for which you are looking. When the gods created man they allotted to him death, but life they retained in their own keeping. As for you, Gilgamesh, fill your belly with good things; day and night, night and day, dance and be merry, feast and rejoice. Let your clothes be fresh, bathe yourself in water, cherish the little child that holds your hand, and make your wife happy in your embrace; for this too is the lot of man."

▷ Gilgamesh, however, refuses to be deflected from his quest. After a series of harrowing experiences, he finally reaches Utnapishtim, a former mortal whom the gods had placed in an eternal paradise, and addresses him.

"Oh, father Utnapishtim, you who have entered the assembly of the gods, I wish to question you concerning the living and the dead, how shall I find the life for which I am searching?"

Utnapishtim said, "There is no permanence. Do we build a house to stand forever, do we seal a contract to hold for all time? Do brothers divide an inheritance to keep forever, does the flood-time of rivers endure? It is only the nymph of the dragon-fly who sheds her larva and sees the sun in his glory. From the days of old there is no permanence. The sleeping and the dead, how alike they are, they are like a painted death. What is there between the master and the servant when both have fulfilled their doom? When the Anunnaki,[6] the judges, come together, and Mammetun[7] the mother of destinies, together they decree the fates of men. Life and death they allot but the day of death they do not disclose."

Then Gilgamesh said to Utnapishtim the Faraway, "I look at you now, Utnapishtim, and your appearance is no different from mine; there is nothing strange in your features. I thought I

---

[2]Goddess of the Underworld and sister of Ishtar/Inanna.
[3]Dead earthly kings. Anu, whose name meant "heaven," was the supreme but remote king of the gods and the ultimate source of all order and government. Enlil, second only to Anu in power and importance, was more involved in earthly affairs. He directed the forces of nature and bestowed royal authority on earthly leaders.
[4]A legendary king of the Sumerian city of Kish who flew to Heaven on the back of an eagle in order to obtain a magical plant that would give him the potency to father an heir.
[5]The more common name of the goddess of the Underworld (see note 2).
[6]An assemblage of lesser deities (numbering either 60 or 600) who had multiple functions.
[7]A mother goddess of fate.

should find you like a hero prepared for battle, but you lie here taking your ease on your back. Tell me truly, how was it that you came to enter the company of the gods and to possess everlasting life?" Utnapishtim said to Gilgamesh, "I will reveal to you a mystery, I will tell you a secret of the gods."

"You know the city Shurrupak,[8] it stands on the banks of Euphrates? That city grew old and the gods that were in it were old. There was Anu, lord of the firmament, their father, and warrior Enlil their counselor, Ninurta[9] the helper, and Ennugi[10] watcher over canals; and with them also was Ea.[11] In those days the world teemed, the people multiplied, the world bellowed like a wild bull, and the great god was aroused by the clamor. Enlil heard the clamor and he said to the gods in council, 'The uproar of mankind is intolerable and sleep is no longer possible by reason of the babel.' So the gods agreed to exterminate mankind. Enlil did this, but Ea because of his oath[12] warned me in a dream. He whispered their words to my house of reeds, 'Reed-house, reed-house! Wall, O wall, hearken reed-house,[13] wall reflect; O man of Shurrupak, son of Ubara-Tutu; tear down your house and build a boat, abandon possessions and look for life, despise worldly goods and save your soul alive. Tear down your house, I say, and build a boat. . . . Then take up into the boat the seed of all living creatures.'

"When I had understood I said to my lord, 'Behold, what you have commanded I will honor and perform, but how shall I answer the people, the city, the elders?' Then Ea opened his mouth and said to me, his servant, 'Tell them this: I have learnt that Enlil is wrathful against me, I dare no

longer walk in his land nor live in his city; I will go down to the Gulf to dwell with Ea my lord. But on you he will rain down abundance, rare fish and shy wildfowl, a rich harvest-tide. In the evening the rider of the storm will bring you wheat in torrents.' . . .

"On the seventh day the boat was complete. . . .

"I loaded into her all that I had of gold and of living things, my family, my kin, the beast of the field both wild and tame, and all the craftsmen. I sent them on board. . . . The time was fulfilled, the evening came, the rider of the storm sent down the rain. I looked out at the weather and it was terrible, so I too boarded the boat and battened her down. . . .

"For six days and six nights the winds blew, torrent and tempest and flood overwhelmed the world, tempest and flood raged together like warring hosts. When the seventh day dawned the storm from the south subsided, the sea grew calm, the flood was stilled; I looked at the face of the world and there was silence, all mankind was turned to clay. The surface of the sea stretched as flat as a roof-top; I opened a hatch and the light fell on my face. Then I bowed low, I sat down and I wept, the tears streamed down my face, for on every side was the waste of water. I looked for land in vain, but fourteen leagues distant there appeared a mountain, and there the boat grounded; on the mountain of Nisir the boat held fast, she held fast and did not budge. . . . When the seventh day dawned I loosed a dove and let her go. She flew away, but finding no resting-place she returned. Then I loosed a swallow, and she flew away but finding no resting-place she re-

---

[8]Located at modern Fara, about equidistant between Baghdad in the north and Basra in the south, the ruins of Shuruppak contain a two-foot-thick layer of mud, evidence of a local flood that took place around 2750 B.C.E. The flood did not cover all of Sumer, much less all of Mesopotamia, but it might have served as the basis for a flood epic. Evidence also shows that the city survived the flood and life went on.

[9]Originally a god of irrigation and agriculture, Ninurta became a god of war with the rise of Mesopotamian imperialism.

[10]God of irrigation and of the dead.

[11]Also known as Enki, Ea was the god of water and the secret wisdom of sorcery and crafts. He was also the god of providence who protected those in crisis.

[12]Apparently an oath to protect humanity, because he was the god of life-giving water and good fortune.

[13]Reed houses probably go back to neolithic times. Because of their fragility, they served Mesopotamians as a metaphor for impermanence. The so-called Marsh Arabs of southern Iraq built reed houses well into the late twentieth century, until Saddam Hussein destroyed the marshes in order to root out their opposition to his rule.

turned. I loosed a raven, she saw that the waters had retreated, she ate, she flew around, she cawed, and she did not come back. Then I threw everything open to the four winds, I made a sacrifice and poured out a libation[14] on the mountain top. Seven and again seven cauldrons I set up on their stands, I heaped up wood and cane and cedar and myrtle. When the gods smelled the sweet savor, they gathered like flies over the sacrifice.[15] Then, at last, Ishtar also came, she lifted her necklace with the jewels of Heaven that once Anu had made to please her. 'O you gods here present, by the lapis lazuli round my neck I shall remember these days as I remember the jewels of my throat; these last days I shall not forget.[16] Let all the gods gather round the sacrifice, except Enlil. He shall not approach this offering, for without reflection he brought the flood; he consigned my people to destruction.'

"When Enlil had come, when he saw the boat, he was wrath and swelled with anger at the gods, the host of Heaven, 'Has any of these mortals escaped? Not one was to have survived the destruction.' Then the god of the wells and canals Ninurta opened his mouth and said to the warrior Enlil, 'Who is there of the gods that can devise without Ea? It is Ea alone who knows all things.' Then Ea opened his mouth and spoke to warrior Enlil, 'Wisest of gods, hero Enlil, how could you so senselessly bring down the flood? . . . It was not that I revealed the secret of the gods; the wise man learned it in a dream. Now take your counsel what shall be done with him.'

"Then Enlil went up into the boat, he took me by the hand and my wife and made us enter the boat and kneel down on either side, he standing between us. He touched our foreheads to bless us saying, 'In time past Utnapishtim was a mortal man; henceforth he and his wife shall live in the distance at the mouth of the rivers.' Thus it was that the gods took me and placed me here to live in the distance, at the mouth of the rivers."

Utnapishtim said, "As for you, Gilgamesh, who will assemble the gods for your sake, so that you may find that life for which you are searching?"

▷   After telling his story, Utnapishtim challenges Gilgamesh to resist sleep for six days and seven nights. When Gilgamesh fails the test, Utnapishtim points out how preposterous it is to search for immortality when one cannot even resist sleep. Out of kindness, Utnapishtim does tell Gilgamesh where he can find a submarine plant that will at least rejuvenate him. Consequently, the hero dives to the bottom of the sea and plucks it. However, humanity is to be denied even the blessing of forestalling old age and decrepitude, because the plant is stolen from Gilgamesh by a serpent. His mission a failure, Gilgamesh returns to Uruk.

The destiny was fulfilled which the father of the gods, Enlil of the mountain, had decreed for Gilgamesh: "In nether-earth the darkness will show him a light: of mankind, all that are known, none will leave a monument for generations to come to compare with his. The heroes, the wise men, like the new moon have their waxing and waning. Men will say, 'Who has ever ruled with might and with power like him?' As in the dark month, the month of shadows, so without him there is no light. O Gilgamesh, this was the meaning of your dream. You were given the kingship, such was your destiny, everlasting life was not your destiny. Because of this do not be sad at heart, do not be grieved or oppressed; he has given you power to bind and to loose, to be the darkness and the light of mankind. He has given unexampled supremacy over the people, victory in battle from which no fugitive returns, in forays and assaults from which there is no going back. But do not abuse this power, deal justly with your servants in the palace, deal justly before the face of the Sun." . . .

Gilgamesh, the son of Ninsun, lies in the tomb. At the place of offerings he weighed the

---

[14]Poured out wine or some other beverage as an offering to the gods.
[15]Many myth-making people believe that the gods gain nourishment from the greasy smoke of burnt sacrifices.

[16]The necklace is a rainbow. Lapis lazuli is not indigenous to Mesopotamia and was imported from Afghanistan.

bread-offering, at the place of libation he poured out the wine. In those days the lord Gilgamesh departed, the son of Ninsun, the king, peerless, without an equal among men, who did not neglect Enlil his master. O Gilgamesh, lord of Kullab,[17] great is thy praise.

---

[17]Part of Uruk.

Bringing Order to an Uncertain World
▼▼▼

2 ▼ *THE JUDGMENTS OF HAMMURABI*

Mesopotamia's characteristic sense of insecurity resulted in its producing not only great philosophical literature but also detailed legal codes. The so-called *Code of Hammurabi* is the most famous but certainly not the earliest of the many collections of law produced throughout the first 3,000 years of Mesopotamian civilization. Discovered in 1901, this Babylonian text from the eighteenth century B.C.E. is inscribed on a stone pillar (technically known as a *stele*) that measures over seven feet in height and more than six feet in circumference. Apparently Hammurabi wanted it to last forever.

Whether Mesopotamia's numerous compilations of law were Sumerian, Babylonian, Assyrian, or Chaldean, a number of common elements united them. Chief among them was the expressed purpose, as the prologue to Hammurabi's collection declares, "to promote the welfare of the people . . . to cause justice to prevail in the land, to destroy the wicked and the evil, that the strong might not oppress the weak." There is good reason to believe that even conquerors such as Hammurabi (reigned ca. 1792–1750 B.C.E.), who briefly united Mesopotamia and transformed Babylon into the capital of an empire, sought to promote justice through law.

Hammurabi's code is actually not a coherent and systematic code of laws but rather a compilation of decisions, or *misharum* (equity rulings), that the king made in response to specific cases and perceived injustices. Nevertheless, this collection of judgments covers a wide variety of crimes and circumstances, thereby allowing extensive insight into the structure and values of eighteenth-century Babylonian society.

QUESTIONS FOR ANALYSIS

1. What specific actions did Hammurabi take in his attempt to provide for the good order of society and the basic welfare of his subjects?
2. What evidence is there of class distinctions in Babylon?
3. What was the status of women in this society? Did they enjoy any protection or liberties?
4. What about children? What was their status? Did they enjoy any protection or liberties?
5. Mesopotamian society has been characterized as a *patriarchal* (dominated by male heads of households) society. Does the evidence in this collection of decisions tend to support or refute that judgment?

6. What principles and assumptions underlay these judgments? In other words, what does this collection reveal about the worldview, basic values, and ideals of Hammurabi's Babylon?

PROLOGUE

When Marduk[1] had instituted me governor of men, to conduct and to direct, Right and Justice I established in the land, for the good of the people.

THE ADMINISTRATION OF JUSTICE

3. If in a lawsuit a man gives damning evidence, and his word that he has spoken is not justified, then, if the suit be a capital one,[2] that man shall be slain. . . .

5. If a judge has heard a case, and given a decision, and delivered a written verdict, and if afterward his case is disproved, and that judge is convicted as the cause of the misjudgment, then he shall pay twelve times the penalty awarded in that case. In public assembly he shall be thrown from the seat of judgment; he shall not return; and he shall not sit with the judges upon a case. . . .

FELONS AND VICTIMS

22. If a man has perpetrated brigandage, and has been caught, that man shall be slain.

23. If the brigand has not been taken, the man plundered shall claim before god[3] what he has lost; and the city and governor in whose land and boundary the theft has taken place shall restore to him all that he has lost.

24. If a life, the city and governor shall pay one mina[4] of silver to his people.[5] . . .

PROPERTY

29. If his son is under age, and unable to administer his [deceased] father's affairs, then a third part of the field and garden shall be given to his mother, and his mother shall bring him up. . . .

38. A captain, soldier, or official may not give his field, or garden, or house to his wife or his daughter; neither can they be given as payment for debt.[6]

39. He may bequeath in writing to his wife or daughter a field, a garden, or a house that he may have bought, and may give it as payment for debt. . . .

WINESELLERS AND TAVERNS

109. If rebels meet in the house of a wineseller and she[7] does not seize them and take them to the palace, that wineseller shall be slain.

110. If a priestess who has not remained in the temple,[8] shall open a wine-shop, or enter a wine-shop for drink, that woman shall be burned. . . .

DEBT SLAVERY

117. If a man has contracted a debt, and has given his wife, his son, his daughter for

---

[1]The chief god of Babylon.
[2]A case in which death is the penalty.
[3]The god or goddess of the city. Each city had its special protector deity.
[4]A unit of measure that equaled eighteen ounces of silver. Coins were invented around 700 B.C.E. in the Anatolian kingdom of Lydia.
[5]The family of the slain person.

[6]The monarch retained ultimate ownership of the property handed out to soldiers and bureaucrats who received land as payment for their services.
[7]Women traditionally filled this role in ancient Mesopotamia. See Siduri in source 1.
[8]Thereby breaking her vow to devote her life to serving the temple deity.

silver or for labor, three years they shall serve in the house of their purchaser or bondsmaster; in the fourth year they shall regain their original condition. . . .

MARRIAGE AND THE FAMILY

129. If the wife of a man is found lying with another male, they shall be bound and thrown into the water. If the husband lets his wife live, then the king shall let his servant[9] live. . . .

134. If a man has been taken prisoner, and there is no food in his house, and his wife enters the house of another, then that woman bears no blame.

135. If a man has been taken prisoner, and there is no food before her, and his wife has entered the house of another, and bears children, and afterward her husband returns and regains his city, then that woman shall return to her spouse. The children shall follow their father.

136. If a man has abandoned his city, and absconded, and after that his wife has entered the house of another, if that man comes back and claims his wife, because he had fled and deserted his city, the wife of the deserter shall not return to her husband.

137. If a man has decided to divorce . . . a wife who has presented him with children, then he shall give back to that woman her dowry,[10] and he shall give her the use of field, garden, and property, and she shall bring up her children. After she has brought up her children, she shall take a son's portion of all that is given to her children, and she may marry the husband of her heart.

138. If a man divorces his spouse who has not borne him children, he shall give to her all the silver of the bride-price,[11] and restore to her the dowry which she brought from the house of her father; and so he shall divorce her.

139. If there was no bride-price, he shall give her one mina of silver for the divorce.

140. If he is a peasant, he shall give her one-third of a mina of silver.

141. If a man's wife, dwelling in his house, has decided to leave, has been guilty of dissipation, has wasted her house, and has neglected her husband, then she shall be prosecuted. If her husband says she is divorced, he shall let her go her way; he shall give her nothing for divorce. If her husband says she is not divorced, her husband may marry another woman, and that [first] woman shall remain a slave in the house of her husband.

142. If a woman hates her husband, and says "You shall not possess me," the reason for her dislike shall be inquired into. If she is careful, and has no fault, but her husband takes himself away and neglects her, then that woman is not to blame. She shall take her dowry and go back to her father's house. . . .

148. If a man has married a wife, and sickness has seized her, and he has decided to marry another, he may marry; but his wife whom the sickness has seized he shall not divorce. She shall dwell in the house he has built, and he shall support her while she lives. . . .

168. If a man has decided to disinherit his son, and has said to the judge, "I disown my son," then the judge shall look into his reasons. If the son has not been guilty of a serious offense which would justify his being disinherited, then the father shall not disown him.

169. If the son has committed a serious offense against his father which justifies his being disinherited, still the judge shall overlook

---

[9] The wife's lover.
[10] The required money or goods she brought to the marriage.

[11] The price he paid her family in order to marry her.

this first offense. If the son commits a grave offense a second time, his father may disown him. . . .

PERSONAL INJURY

195. If a son has struck his father, his hands shall be cut off.
196. If a man has destroyed the eye of another free man, his own eye shall be destroyed.
197. If he has broken the bone of a free man, his bone shall be broken.
198. If he has destroyed the eye of a peasant, or broken a bone of a peasant, he shall pay one mina of silver.
199. If he has destroyed the eye of a man's slave, or broken a bone of a man's slave, he shall pay half his value.
200. If a man has knocked out the teeth of a man of the same rank, his own teeth shall be knocked out.
201. If he has knocked out the teeth of a peasant, he shall pay one-third of a mina of silver.
202. If a man strikes the body of a man who is superior in status, he shall publicly receive sixty lashes with a cowhide whip. . . .
206. If a man has struck another man in a dispute and wounded him, that man shall swear, "I did not strike him knowingly"; and he shall pay for the physician.
207. If he dies of his blows, he shall swear likewise; and if it is the son of a free man, he shall pay half a mina of silver.
208. If he is the son of a peasant, he shall pay a third of a mina of silver.
209. If a man strikes the daughter of a free man, and causes her fetus to abort, he shall pay ten shekels[12] of silver for her fetus.
210. If that woman dies, his daughter shall be slain.

211. If he has caused the daughter of a peasant to let her fetus abort through blows, he shall pay five shekels of silver.
212. If that woman dies, he shall pay half a mina of silver. . . .

CONSUMER PROTECTION

215. If a physician has treated a man with a metal knife for a severe wound, and has cured the man, or has opened a man's tumor with a metal knife, and cured a man's eye, then he shall receive ten shekels of silver.
216. If the son of a peasant, he shall receive five shekels of silver. . . .
218. If a physician has treated a man with a metal knife for a severe wound, and has caused the man to die, or has opened a man's tumor with a metal knife, and destroyed the man's eye, his hands shall be cut off. . . .
229. If a builder has built a house for a man, and his work is not strong, and if the house he has built falls in and kills the householder, that builder shall be slain.
230. If the child of the householder is killed, the child of that builder shall be slain.
231. If the slave of the householder is killed, he shall give slave for slave to the house holder.
232. If goods have been destroyed, he shall replace all that has been destroyed; and because the house that he built was not made strong, and it has fallen in, he shall restore the fallen house out of his own personal property.
233. If a builder has built a house for a man, and his work is not done properly, and a wall shifts, then that builder shall make that wall good with his own silver. . . .

---

[12]Three ounces of silver. A mina (note 4) was divided into sixty shekels, each of which was three-tenths of an ounce of silver.

EPILOGUE

The oppressed, who has a lawsuit, shall come before my image as king of justice. He shall read the writing on my pillar, he shall perceive my precious words. The word of my pillar shall explain to him his cause, and he shall find his right. His heart shall be glad [and he shall say,] "The Lord Hammurabi has risen up as a true father to his people; the will of Marduk, his god, he has made to be feared; he has achieved victory for Marduk above and below. He has rejoiced the heart of Marduk, his lord, and gladdened the flesh of his people for ever. And the land he has placed in order." . . .

In after days and for all time, the king who is in the land shall observe the words of justice which are written upon my pillar. He shall not alter the law of the land which I have formulated,

or the statutes of the country that I have enacted. . . . If that man has wisdom, and desires to keep his land in order, he will heed the words which are written upon my pillar. . . . The . . . people he shall govern; their laws he shall pronounce, their statutes he shall decide. He shall root out of the land the perverse and the wicked; and the flesh of his people he shall delight.

Hammurabi, the king of justice, am I, to whom Shamash[13] has granted rectitude. My words are well weighed: my deeds have no equal, leveling the exalted, humbling the proud, expelling the haughty. If that man heeds my words that I have engraved upon my pillar, departs not from the laws, alters not my words, changes not my sculptures, then may Shamash make the scepter of that man to endure as long as I, the king of justice, and to lead his people with justice.

[13]The sun-god: god of justice and vindicator of the oppressed. During the eighteenth century B.C.E. he rose in prominence among the deities of Babylon. The sculpture that is carved at the top of the stele on which Hammurabi's judgments are inscribed shows the king humbly receiving from Shamash a measuring-line and a rod, the symbols of equity and justice.

▼▼▼

Egypt: The River of Two Lands

Civilization seems to have arisen in Egypt shortly after it first appeared in Sumer. Although there is evidence of early Sumerian contact with the Egyptians, Egypt's civilization was largely self-generated, and its history and cultural patterns differed substantially from those of Mesopotamia. Egyptians, however, shared the same myth-making way of perceiving reality.

An integral element of Egyptian myth was the belief that Egypt was the land of divine harmony ruled by a living god-king, or *pharaoh,* who balanced all conflicting cosmic forces. Around 3100 B.C.E. the land of the Nile was unified into a single state, although culturally it remained two distinctive lands: the rich delta region of the north, known as *Lower Egypt* (because the Nile flows north), and the long but narrow strip of green land that borders the Nile to the south, known as *Upper Egypt.* Before their unification, Lower and Upper Egypt had been separate kingdoms. As far as Egyptians were concerned, they forever remained two antithetical yet complementary lands brought into harmony by a unifying king who was a god on Earth. As the embodiment of the union of Upper and Lower Egypt, the king was likewise the personification on Earth of the goddess *Ma'at,* whose name meant "what is right." In other words, the god-king of Egypt *was* truth, law, and justice.

The state that resulted from the union of Egypt's two lands enjoyed about 3,000 years of unparalleled prosperity and stability. Between approximately 3100 and 343 B.C.E. Egypt experienced only a handful of relatively short-lived periods of either major internal turmoil and the consequent breakdown of central authority or domination by foreign powers. This long history of centralized monarchy and native rule was due in large part to the blessings of geography. Egypt was fairly secure behind its barriers of sea and desert, and the Nile's annual flooding was normally predictable and usually beneficial.

The sense of security that followed from these geographical and historical circumstances was reflected in much of ancient Egypt's religion, philosophy, and arts. At the same time, codes of law, which figure so prominently in the historical records of Mesopotamia, are not to be found in the literature of ancient Egypt. Though the Egyptians were equally concerned with maintaining a well-ordered society, their avenue to this goal differed greatly from that of the Mesopotamians.

The Search for Eternal Life in Egypt
▼▼▼
3 ▾ *THREE MORTUARY TEXTS*

Historians have traditionally divided the first 2,000 years of Egyptian civilization into six ages: the Early Dynastic Period (ca. 3100–2600 B.C.E.); the Old Kingdom (ca. 2600–2125); the First Intermediate Period (ca. 2125–2025); the Middle Kingdom (ca. 2060–1700); the Second Intermediate Period, or Age of the Hyksos (ca. 1700–1550); and the New Kingdom, or Empire (ca. 1550–1069).

The *Early Dynastic Period* was Egypt's era of initial unification and state-building under the guidance of its first three royal dynasties. The *Old Kingdom* that followed centered on Egypt's god-kings, whose mummified remains were reverently entombed in pyramids in preparation for the journey to eternal life in the *Land of the West.* During this age, Egyptians believed (or at least the priests taught) that immortality was the exclusive preserve of the divine pharaoh, members of the royal family, the priests, and a handful of favored royal servants. They further believed that in order to insure the king's safe journey to the afterlife, all that was needed was proper attention to the many details of the royal funeral ceremony. Beginning with the entombment of King Unas, who died around 2345 B.C.E., Egyptians carved magical incantations on the walls of royal burial chambers as a means of assuring the king's safe journey into eternal life. Modern scholars have discovered and catalogued over 750 distinct incantations, which they term collectively the *Pyramid Texts.* We do not know what the Egyptians called them, but regardless, they provide a privileged view of funeral practices and beliefs regarding immortality during the Old Kingdom. Our first selection comes from the tomb of King Teti, who followed Unas to the throne.

Ancient Egyptians continued to bury their dead with great ceremony for thousands of years and intermittently constructed pyramids throughout their long history. None, however, reached the monumentality and engineering excellence of the massive pyramids at Giza, near Cairo, which entombed several kings of the Fourth Dynasty (about 2600–2500 B.C.E.). For over 4,500 years they have served as tokens of the power wielded by early Egypt's god-kings. The reign of Pepi II (ca. 2275–2185 B.C.E.) marked the end of the Old Kingdom. Shortly after Pepi's death, pharaonic power collapsed, plunging Egypt into an era of internal turmoil known as the *First Intermediate Period.* A century later this age of local rule and social upheaval gave way to the *Middle Kingdom,* an era of revived central authority and of a deepening awareness of social justice and personal moral responsibility. Befitting the new spirit, many Egyptians came to view eternal life as available to all Egyptians who met certain criteria.

A new body of funerary inscriptions appeared, which scholars today refer to as the *Coffin Texts.* The texts, usually inscribed within the wooden coffins of people who could afford elaborate funerals, were ritual resurrection spells. Some were modeled upon the earlier *Pyramid Texts,* but most were new and displayed an obsession with the dangers of Earth and the terrors of death that was lacking in the pyramid inscriptions. Despite their hope in a blissful afterlife, Egyptians were not immune to the miseries and fears, especially fear of disaster and death, that beset all humans.

Our second selection is a much-used coffin spell that takes the form of a two-part speech. In the first part the sun-god Re speaks, reminding humanity of his four good deeds at the time of creation. In the second part the deceased speaks, laying his claim on eternal life.

The process of widening access to the afterlife evolved to another level with the creation of *The Book of the Dead.* This is the modern name for a collection of papyrus texts that the Egyptians knew as *The Chapters for Coming Forth by Day.* Although it did not reach its final form until around the sixth century B.C.E., this collection of chapters was largely a creation of the New Kingdom. Like the pyramid and coffin inscriptions from which it evolved, it was a body of magical incantations for use in burial ceremonies, but unlike the pyramid and coffin inscriptions, it had a fairly standardized text. It was also available to a larger but still necessarily prosperous clientele. Divided into more than 150 chapters, which were gathered together into papyrus scrolls, the book had a certain mass-produced quality. One could purchase a scroll, fill in the name of the deceased, and bury it with the person's body. Resurrection had become a cut-rate enterprise.

Of all the chapters, the most famous is Chapter 125, the lengthy "Judgment of the Dead," from which we have extracted the *The Negative Confession.* The scene is the Hall of the Two Truths, or the Double Ma'at, where *Osiris,* king of the Underworld, presides over an assembly of forty-two minor deities. It is these forty-two who judge the deceased's suitability to become an eternally blessed spirit. Upon entering the hall, the deceased (N, or fill in the name) proclaims her or his purity.

QUESTIONS FOR ANALYSIS

1. What are the underlying assumptions of King Teti's pyramid text?
2. According to the coffin text, how does a person guarantee eternal life?
3. Consider the speech of Re. Does it contain a moral element? If so, how is that message connected, if at all, with the dead person's spell?
4. One scholar has written of the *Coffin Texts:* "Because the individuals who were seeking an afterlife as divine beings stood outside of the royal circle, their coffin inscriptions reflected both paranoid fear and delusions of grandeur." Do you agree or disagree?
5. What does *The Negative Confession* allow us to infer about Egyptian values in the New Kingdom?
6. Each of the three texts provides a path to eternal life. What do their similarities and differences suggest about continuities and changes within Egyptian society over this millennium?
7. Compare these three texts with *The Epic of Gilgamesh*. What are their different messages? What do those messages suggest about the differences between the two civilizations?

A PYRAMID TEXT

Oho! Oho! Rise up, O Teti!
Take your head,
Collect your bones,
Gather your limbs,
Shake the earth from your flesh!
Take your bread that rots not,
Your beer that sours not,
Stand at the gates that bar the common people!
The gatekeeper comes out to you,
He grasps your hand,
Takes you into heaven, to your father Geb.[1]
He rejoices at your coming,
Gives you his hands,
Kisses you, caresses you,
Sets you before the spirits, the imperishable
    stars.
The hidden ones worship you,
The great ones surround you,
The watchers wait on you.
Barley is threshed for you,
Emmen is reaped for you,

Your monthly feasts are made with it,
Your half-month feasts are made with it,
As ordered done for you by Geb, your father,
Rise up, O Teti, you shall not die!

A COFFIN TEXT

Words spoken by Him-whose-names-are-hidden, the All-Lord, as he speaks before those who silence the storm, in the sailing of the court:[2]

Hail in peace! I repeat to you the good deeds which my own heart did for me from within the serpent-coil,[3] in order to silence strife. I did four good deeds within the portal of lightland:

I made the four winds, that every man might breathe in his time. This is one of the deeds.

I made the great inundation,[4] that the humble might benefit by it like the great. This is one of the deeds.

I made every man like his fellow; and I did not command that they do wrong. It is their hearts that disobey what I have said. This is one of the deeds.

---

[1]The god of Earth and father of Osiris, the god of resurrection and king of the dead.
[2]The deities who accompany Re as he sails daily across the sky (note 9).

[3]The serpent-dragon Apophis, a mythic symbol of the lurking dangers in the world.
[4]The annual flooding of the Nile.

I made that their hearts are not disposed to forget the West,[5] in order that sacred offerings be made to the gods of the nomes.[6] This is one of the deeds.

I have created the gods from my sweat, and the people from the tears of my eye.

The Dead Speaks

I[7] shall shine and be seen every day as a dignitary of the All-Lord, having given satisfaction to the Weary-hearted.[8]

I shall sail rightly in my bark,[9] I am lord of eternity in the crossing of the sky.

I am not afraid in my limbs, for Hu and Hike[10] overthrow for me that evil being.

I shall see lightland, I shall dwell in it. I shall judge the poor and the wealthy.

I shall do the same for the evil-doers; for mine is life, I am its lord, and the scepter will not be taken from me.

I have spent a million years with the Weary-hearted, the son of Geb, dwelling with him in one place; while hills became towns and towns hills, for dwelling destroys dwelling.

I am lord of the flame who lives on truth; lord of eternity, maker of joy, against whom that worm shall not rebel.

I am he who is in his shrine, master of action who destroys the storm; who drives off the serpents of many names when he goes from his shrine.

Lord of the winds who announces the northwind, rich in names in the mouth of the Ennead.[11]

Lord of lightland, maker of light, who lights the sky with his beauty.

I am he in his name! Make way for me, that I may see Nun[12] and Amun![13] For I am that equipped spirit who passes by the guards.[14] They do not speak for fear of Him-whose-name-is-hidden, who is in my body. I know him, I do not ignore him! I am equipped and effective in opening his portal!

As for any person who knows this spell, he will be like Re in the eastern sky, like Osiris in the netherworld. He will go down to the circle of fire, without the flame touching him ever!

THE NEGATIVE CONFESSION

(1) To be said on reaching the Hall of the Two Truths[15] so as to purge N of any sins committed and to see the face of every god:

> Hail to you, Great God, Lord of the Two
>   Truths!
> I have come to you, my Lord,
> I was brought to see your beauty.
> I know you, I know the names of the forty-
>   two gods,
> Who are with you in the Hall of the Two
>   Truths.
> Who live by warding off evildoers,
> Who drink of their blood,
> On that day of judging characters before
>   Wennofer.[16]
> Lo, your name is "He-of-Two-Daughters,"

---

[5]The Land of the Resurrected Dead.

[6]The forty-two religious and administrative districts into which Egypt was divided. Note that the dead person is being judged by forty-two deities.

[7]The dead person now becomes the speaker, assuming the identity of Re.

[8]One of Osiris's titles. One must first satisfy Osiris before joining Re.

[9]Re sails across the sky in a bark, or boat.

[10]Personifications of effective speech and magic, they are probably a reference to this magical spell, which has been uttered at entombment and carved in the coffin.

[11]The company of Egypt's nine chief deities.

[12]The watery void outside of the temporal and spatial boundaries of creation from which the creator emerged, Nun was personified as the god of the Abyss.

[13]A primeval god who existed as a force before creation, he became the chief god of Thebes. He rose to preeminence in Egypt when the princes of Thebes reunited Egypt after the Second Intermediate Period.

[14]The guards to the Land of the West.

[15]Ma'at takes a dual form here in Isis, goddess of Right, and Nephthys, goddess of Truth. Isis was the sister and wife of Osiris. It was she who brought the dead and dismembered Osiris back to life, thereby assuring his status as god of resurrection and king of the Underworld. Nephthys, also Osiris's sister, had assisted in his resurrection.

[16]One of Osiris's names.

(And) "He-of-Ma'at's-Two-Eyes."
Lo, I come before you,
Bringing Ma'at to you,
Having repelled evil for you.

I have not done crimes against people,
I have not mistreated cattle,
I have not sinned in the Place of Truth.[17]
I have not known what should not be
    known,[18]
I have not done any harm.
I did not begin a day by exacting more than
    my due,
My name did not reach the bark of the
    mighty ruler.[19]
I have not blasphemed a god,
I have not robbed the poor.
I have not done what the god abhors,
I have not maligned a servant to his master.
I have not caused pain,
I have not caused tears.
I have not killed,
I have not ordered to kill,
I have not made anyone suffer.
I have not damaged the offerings in the
    temples,
I have not depleted the loaves of the gods,
I have not stolen the cakes of the dead.[20]

I have not copulated nor defiled myself.[21]
I have not increased nor reduced the
    measure, . . .

I have not cheated in the fields.
I have not added to the weight of the balance,
I have not falsified the plummet of the scales.
I have not taken milk from the mouth of
    children,
I have not deprived cattle of their pasture.
I have not snared birds in the reeds of the
    gods,
I have not caught fish in their ponds.
I have not held back water in its season,
I have not dammed a flowing stream,
I have not quenched a needed fire.
I have not neglected the days of meat
    offerings,
I have not detained cattle belonging to the
    god,
I have not stopped a god in his procession.

I am pure, I am pure,
I am pure, I am pure! . . .
No evil shall befall me in this land,
In this Hall of the Two Truths;
For I know the names of the gods in it,
The followers of the great God!

---

[17]He has not sinned in any holy place.
[18]Secrets of the gods.
[19]As he sails across the sky in his bark, Re has not heard of any misdeeds by the deceased.

[20]Food to accompany the dead on their journey.
[21]Presumably, in a holy place.

Another Side of Egyptian Life
▼▼▼

4 ▼ *A CRIB INCANTATION and TWO LOVE SONGS*

A cursory examination of the Egyptian funerary monuments, sarcophaguses, and mummified bodies that fill museums might lead a person to conclude that ancient Egyptians spent their lives obsessing about death. Certainly the previous source might also seem to support that judgment. The brief pieces that appear here allow us to put that supposed Egyptian preoccupation with death into a fuller perspective.

Our first document is a magical incantation to be spoken by a mother over her sleeping child. The papyrus on which this magical charm was written dates from around the sixteenth century B.C.E., although the incantation itself and the beliefs that underlay it had their roots in prehistory.

The second document contains two excerpts from a collection of love songs from the later years of the New Kingdom — ca. 1300–1100 B.C.E. The New Kingdom, or Empire, was a time of exciting new directions in the arts. Its literature and representational art gloried in the beauty of nature and the joys of sensual love, as these songs make clear. As you read the poems, be aware that the terms *brother* and *sister* do not refer to blood siblings; it was the fashion to speak of one's beloved as brother or sister.

QUESTIONS FOR ANALYSIS

1. How did the Egyptians explain infant crib death?
2. How did they attempt to prevent it?
3. Consider the vision of death in this incantation and compare it with that of the roughly contemporaneous *Coffin Text*. What similarities do they share? How are they different? What do those similarities and differences suggest to you?
4. What might we infer from the love songs about the status and freedom enjoyed by this female lover?
5. "Egypt's love songs and funerary texts were equally the products of a culture that emphasized the sweetness of life over the sting of death." What does this anonymous commentator mean? Do you agree? Be specific in your evaluation of this statement.

A MOTHER'S INCANTATION FOR HER SLEEPING CHILD

Another (charm). Mayest thou flow away, he who comes in the darkness and enters in furtively, with his nose behind him, and his face reversed, failing in that for which he came![1]

Mayest thou flow away, she who comes in the darkness and enters in furtively, with her nose behind her, and her face turned backwards, failing in that for which she came!

Hast thou come to kiss this child? I will not let thee kiss him! Hast thou come to silence (him)? I will not let thee set silence over him! Hast thou come to injure him? I will not let thee injure him! Hast thou come to take him away? I will not let thee take him away from me!

I have made his magical protection against thee out of *clover* — that is what *sets an obstacle* — of onions — what injures thee[2] — out of honey — sweet for men, (but) bitter for those who are yonder[3] — out of the *roe* of the *abdju*-fish, out of the jawbone of the *meret*-fish, and out of the backbone of the perch.

---

[1] A ghost of the dead. Having no future, it looks backward.
[2] A pun: *hedjw* means "onions" and *hedjet* means "what injures."

[3] The ghosts of the dead.

TWO LOVE SONGS FROM THE NINETEENTH DYNASTY

The beginning of the beautiful songs of entertainment of thy sister, the beloved of thy heart, as
she comes from the meadow.

My brother, my beloved,
My heart pursues the love of thee,
All that thou hast brought into being.
I say to thee: "See what I am doing!"
I have come from setting my trap with my
     (own) hand;
In my hand are my bait and my snare.[4]
All the birds of Punt, they alight in Egypt,
Anointed with myrrh.[5]
The first one comes and takes my worm.
Its fragrance is brought from Punt,
And its talons are full of resin.
My wish for thee is that we loose them
     together,
When I am alone with thee,
That I might let thee hear the cry
Of the one anointed with myrrh.[6]

How good it would be
If thou wert there with me
When I set the trap!
The best is to go to the fields,
To the one who is beloved!
The End.

▼▼▼

The voice of the swallow speaks and says:
"The land has brightened — What is thy
     road?"[7]
Thou shalt not, O bird, *disturb* me!
I have found my brother in his bed,
And my heart is still more glad,
(When he) said to me:
"I shall not go afar off.
My hand is in thy hand,
I shall stroll about,
And I shall be with thee in every pleasant
     place."
He makes me the foremost of maidens.
He injures not my heart.
The End.

---

[4]She is hunting these exotic birds, who later in the poem become a metaphor for her.
[5]Punt, the southwestern tip of the Arabian Peninsula —
modern Yemen — was famous for its perfumes and aromatic
resins, such as myrrh. Perfume was highly valued in Egyptian society and widely used by its elites.

[6]A double image: The "one anointed with myrrh" is the bird
and the woman.
[7]"Where are you going?"

▼▼▼

China: The Land of the Yellow and Yangzi Rivers

The study of history has been one of China's most revered and continuous traditions for over 2,000 years. By the second century B.C.E. the Chinese claimed a detailed history that reached back into the early third millennium. According to their
vision of the past, Chinese civilization was sparked not by the actions of gods but
by extraordinary men, beginning with the *Three Sovereigns,* who laid the basis of
Chinese culture by bestowing such gifts as agriculture and fire. The last of the
three was the *Yellow Emperor,* who established an organized state around 2700

B.C.E. Four other emperors succeeded in turn, each ascending the throne through merit and genius rather than by birth. Known as the *Five Sage Emperors,* they crafted all of the basic elements of Chinese civilization, such as hydroengineering (harnessing the waters of the violent Yellow River) and silk production. The last of the five was succeeded onto the throne by his son, thereby establishing China's first royal dynasty — the *Xia* family, which ruled from 2205 to 1766 B.C.E. After Xia's collapse, the *Shang* Dynasty succeeded and held power, until it gave way to the *Zhou* Dynasty.

Until the late 1920s scholars lacked hard evidence that either the Xia or Shang dynasties ever existed, and Western historians generally dismissed them as romantic legends. The work of archaeologists over the past sixty years, however, proved the Shang Era was a historical reality, and recent evidence suggests its period of efflorescence stretched from about 1600 to around 1050 B.C.E. Xia remains an enigma due to a lack of conclusive evidence. Recent excavations, however, show that China enjoyed a period of civilization before Shang, possibly as early as 2200 or 2100 B.C.E., and certainly by 2000 B.C.E. Whether or not there was a full-fledged Xia Dynasty of kings during those pre-Shang centuries is an open question. One theory that has some evidentiary support holds that Xia, Shang, and Zhou were three co-existing centers of civilization in northern China in the area of the Yellow River, and the Xia, Shang, and Zhou Eras were largely the shifting of dominance through warfare from one state and family of royal warlords to another. It appears that from as early as the late third millennium B.C.E., northern China was home to many competing small states, each centered on a clan and its walled town. Warfare and alliances allowed some states to grow at their neighbors' expense and others to lose their independence. Apparently none of the families or their states ever totally dominated northern China until the victory of the Qin state in 221 B.C.E. (see Chapter 4), but certain families, certainly Shang and Zhou and possibly Xia, successively and successfully claimed wide-sweeping royal hegemony.

Although the details of early Chinese history still largely elude us, archaeology is providing tantalizing clues that are forcing us to question and even abandon once-dominant notions regarding early Chinese civilization. In the 1980s discoveries south of the Yangzi River and also in the southwestern province of Sichuan forced scholars to reevaluate the prevailing diffusionist theory of the origins of Chinese civilization. According to that model, civilization began in the north, around the Yellow River, in the late third millennium B.C.E. and slowly spread out from there, not fully penetrating the southern region of the Yangzi River Valley until the early centuries C.E. Earlier editions of *The Human Record* reflected that picture. However, the discovery of bronzes and other artifacts far to the south and the southwest of the Yellow River have forced a rethinking of that model. Many of the artifacts in the Yangzi River area, which date to the late Shang Era, show clear Shang characteristics, indicating that Shang cultural influences had spread far beyond its political borders. More significant, the artifacts discovered in the southwestern region of Sichuan, as well as some items from the Yangzi River area, exhibit styles and forms that differ greatly from those of Shang. This has led many scholars to posit the theory that Chinese civilization emerged out of the confluence of several independent cultures, all of which were flourishing around 1200 B.C.E. It certainly seems as though the Yangzi River Valley, which previous generations of historians thought was a latecomer to Chinese culture, played a role in the evolution of early Chinese civilization. It might not have been as dominating as that of the Yellow River, but it was significant.

The history of early southern Chinese civilization has yet to be written, so we must turn to the north, to the states of the Yellow River, for the story of early Chinese political development.

Our knowledge of the Xia state, if there was one, and its presumed age of predominance is less than sketchy. We know much more about the Shang, thanks to the work of archaeologists, who have unearthed two huge capital cities, royal tombs, magnificent bronze ceremonial vessels, and an early form of Chinese ideographic writing on what are known as *oracle bones*. Because they served the purpose of magical divination of the future, the inscriptions on oracle bones are brief and often cryptic. Nevertheless, in the hands of experts, they provide useful insights into Shang society and culture.

The Shang kings reigned over a loose confederation of family-centered states that collectively encompassed most but not all of northern China. Their world was precarious because military alliances and loyalties were constantly shifting. Today's subordinate ally might be tomorrow's enemy. Despite these limitations on the Shang kings' political powers, they enjoyed substantial authority as chief priests in the worship of Di, the high god of the Shang. It was believed that the ancestral spirits of the Shang family provided the king a privileged avenue of communication to Di. Moreover, excavated Shang royal tombs indicate that the Shang kings were able to mobilize large numbers of workers and extensive resources in a world where slavery and ritual sacrifice of human victims were accepted practices.

If, however, we desire a fuller story based upon narrative documents, we must wait until the Zhou Dynasty (ca. 1050–256). Because China's earliest extant literary and political documents date from the age of Zhou rule, we know much more about the Zhou Dynasty than about the Xia and Shang combined. The era of Zhou rule began around 1050 when the Zhou conquered the Shang and established a royal dynasty that lasted eight centuries. The Zhou Era is divided into two periods: Western and Eastern. The age of Western Zhou witnessed a fairly strong but decentralized monarchy that presided over fifty or more subordinate states. What this means is that the Zhou kings delegated authority to the rulers of these states in elaborate ceremonies that emphasized the king's primacy. As time went on, however, power tended to slip away from the Western Zhou kings into the hands of local lords. In 771 B.C.E. a group of rebellious northern nobles killed King Yu and overran the capital city, Chang'an (modern Xi'an), and the royal heir fled eastward to Luoyang. Here the Zhou continued to reside as kings until 256 B.C.E., but the kings of Eastern Zhou never enjoyed the power of their western forbearers. For 500 years they reigned over but did not rule a kingdom where military and political power resided in the smaller regional states and the families that controlled them. As the *Son of Heaven,* however, the king continued to enjoy the exclusive right to offer sacrifices to Heaven and to preside over ceremonies dedicated to the royal ancestors.

The Mandate of Heaven
▼▼▼

5 ▼ *THE BOOK OF DOCUMENTS*

The *Shujing,* or *Book of Documents,* is the oldest of the *Five Confucian Classics.* These five works, which also include the *Book of Songs* (source 6), the *Book of Changes,* the *Book of Rites,* and the *Spring and Autumn Annals,* are incorrectly ascribed to the editorship of *Confucius* (Chapter 4, source 21). Known collectively as the *Wujing (The Five Scriptures),* the books became the basic elements of the Confucian educational system during the second century B.C.E., when they were reconstructed by order of several emperors of the Han Dynasty (202 B.C.E.–220 C.E.), who reversed the policy of the earlier *Qin Dynasty* to destroy all traces of Confucian ideology. Regardless of this reconstruction and later editing, the *Shujing* that has come down to us is probably pretty much the same already-ancient text that Confucius admired, studied, and accepted as an authentic record of Chinese civilization.

Also known in English translation as the *Classic of History,* the *Shujing* is not a work of historical interpretation or narration. Rather, it is a collection of documents spanning about 1,700 years of Chinese history and legend, from 2357 to 631 B.C.E. Despite their ascriptions, many of the documents are the spurious creations of much later periods and therefore reflect the attitudes of those subsequent eras.

The document that appears here was composed in the age of Zhou but purports to be the advice given by the faithful Yi Yin to King Tai Jia, second of the Shang kings. According to the story behind the document, when the first Shang king, Zheng Tang, died around 1753, his chief minister, Yi Yin, took it upon himself to instruct the new, young king in the ways and duties of kingship and the workings of the Mandate of Heaven.

The *Mandate of Heaven (Tianming)* was a political-social-cosmological philosophy that served as the basic Chinese explanation for the success and failure of monarchs and states down to the end of the empire in 1912 C.E. Whenever a dynasty fell, the reason invariably offered by China's sages was that it had lost the mandate, or authorized right, to rule, which is given by Heaven alone. In this context, Heaven did not mean a personal god but a cosmic, all-pervading power. The theory of the Mandate of Heaven and the very concept of Heaven were probably joint creations of the Zhou, who used them to justify their overthrow of the Shang around 1050 B.C.E. The king, after all, was the father of his people, and paternal authority was the basic cement of Chinese society from earliest times. Rebellion against a father needed extraordinary justification.

QUESTIONS FOR ANALYSIS

1. What virtues and values does this document extol?
2. Define the Mandate of Heaven. How does a ruler earn it? How and why is it lost?

3. What are the consequences of losing the Mandate of Heaven?
4. Is there any evidence in this passage to support the conclusion that Chinese political philosophers perceived the state as an extended family?
5. Would Yi Yin accept the notion that one must distinguish between a ruler's private morality and public policies?
6. What does the theory of the Mandate of Heaven suggest about the nature of Chinese society?
7. Modern politicians often promise "innovative answers to the challenges of tomorrow." What would Yi Yin think about such an approach to statecraft? What would Yi Yin think about modern politicians who attempt to appear youthful? What would he think of popular opinion polls?
8. Compare the Chinese vision of its ideal monarch with Egyptian and Mesopotamian views of kingship. Despite their obvious cultural differences, did each society expect its king to perform essentially the same task? If so, what was that task?

In the twelfth month of the first year . . . Yi Yin sacrificed to the former king, and presented the heir-king reverently before the shrine of his grandfather. All the princes from the domain of the nobles and the royal domain were present; all the officers also, each continuing to discharge his particular duties, were there to receive the orders of the chief minister. Yi Yin then clearly described the complete virtue of the Meritorious Ancestor[1] for the instruction of the young king.

He said, "Oh! of old the former kings of Xia cultivated earnestly their virtue, and then there were no calamities from Heaven. The spirits of the hills and rivers likewise were all in tranquility; and the birds and beasts, the fishes and tortoises, all enjoyed their existence according to their nature. But their descendant did not follow their example, and great Heaven sent down calamities, employing the agency of our ruler[2] who was in possession of its favoring appointment. The attack on Xia may be traced to the orgies in Ming Tiao.[3] . . . Our king of Shang brilliantly displayed his sagely prowess; for oppression he substituted his generous gentleness; and the millions of the people gave him their hearts. Now your Majesty is entering on the inheritance of his virtue; — all depends on how you commence your reign. To set up love, it is for you to love your relations; to set up respect, it is for you to respect your elders. The commencement is in the family and the state. . . .

"Oh! the former king began with careful attention to the bonds that hold men together. He listened to expostulation, and did not seek to resist it; he conformed to the wisdom of the ancients; occupying the highest position, he displayed intelligence; occupying an inferior position, he displayed his loyalty; he allowed the good qualities of the men whom he employed and did not seek that they should have every talent. . . .

"He extensively sought out wise men, who should be helpful to you, his descendant and heir. He laid down the punishments for officers, and warned those who were in authority, saying, 'If you dare to have constant dancing in your palaces, and drunken singing in your chambers, — that is called the fashion of sorcerers; if you dare to set your hearts on wealth and women, and abandon yourselves to wandering about or to the chase, — that is called the fashion of extravagance; if you dare to despise sage words, to resist the loyal and upright, to put far from you the aged and virtu-

---

[1]Zheng Tang, founder of the Shang Dynasty, who was supposedly enthroned in 1766 B.C.E.
[2]Zheng Tang (see note 1).

[3]According to legend, Jie, the last Xia king, held notorious orgies at Ming Tiao.

ous, and to seek the company of . . . youths, — that is called the fashion of disorder. Now if a high noble or officer be addicted to one of these three fashions with their ten evil ways, his family will surely come to ruin; if the prince of a country be so addicted, his state will surely come to ruin. The minister who does not try to correct such vices in the sovereign shall be punished with branding.' . . .

"Oh! do you, who now succeed to the throne, revere these warnings in your person. Think of them! — sacred counsels of vast importance, admirable words forcibly set forth! The ways of Heaven are not invariable: — on the good-doer it sends down all blessings, and on the evil-doer it sends down all miseries. Do you but be virtuous, be it in small things or in large, and the myriad regions will have cause for rejoicing. If you not be virtuous, be it in large things or in small, it will bring the ruin of your ancestral temple."

Zhou Viewed from Above and Below
▼▼▼

6 ▼ THE BOOK OF SONGS

The *Shihjing,* or *Book of Songs,* another of the Five Confucian Classics that served as basic texts of an educational system that molded China's leaders for more than 2,000 years, consists of 305 poetic songs, composed largely between about 900 and 600 B.C.E. Some of them were sung at the Zhou court on ceremonial occasions, but others, such as ballads that complain about Zhou rule, celebrate love, or depict or dinary people at work, probably began as folk songs. We know nothing about the process by which songs were selected for inclusion, especially certain love songs that scandalized some later commentators. Regardless of the high percentage of light-hearted, homey, and even frankly sexual songs in the collection, the *Book of Songs* ultimately became Confucian because Confucius and his many generations of disciples interpreted these troublesome songs as metaphors and allegories, transforming them into texts of moral instruction.

The following songs illustrate several important aspects of early Chinese civilization and thought: marriage customs; relations between men and women, the perceived role of Heaven (and women) in human affairs, and the cult of ancestor veneration. The first song is that of a woman who is being pressured to marry against her will. The second is of a young woman who loves someone her family does not favor. The third tells of a moment shared between a woman and a man. The fourth reflects on troubles and the reasons for them. The fifth is a hymn meant to be sung in a ceremony in which the spirits of the ancestors are offered wine and food.

QUESTIONS FOR ANALYSIS

1. Consider the first three songs as a group. What do they suggest about marriage customs and the status and role of women in Zhou China? Is the picture that emerges simple or complex?
2. What are the author's specific complaints in the fourth song? Whom does he blame for China's woes?

3. Compare the philosophy that undergirds this song with that of the selection from the *Book of Documents* (source 5). What conclusions do you reach?
4. Compose a reply by the author of any of the first three songs to the fourth song. A prose answer is sufficient.
5. Compare the love songs from the Egyptian New Kingdom (source 4) with the first three songs here. What are more striking, the similarities or the differences? Be specific. What do you conclude from your answer?
6. According to the fourth and fifth songs, how and why were the ancestors honored?

CYPRESS BOAT

Tossed is that cypress boat,
Wave-tossed it floats.
My heart is in turmoil, I cannot sleep.
But secret is my grief.
Wine I have, all things needful
For play, for sport.

My heart is not a mirror,
To reflect what others will.
Brothers too I have;
I cannot be snatched away.
But lo, when I told them of my plight
I found that they were angry with me.

My heart is not a stone;
It cannot be rolled.
My heart is not a mat;
It cannot be folded away.
I have borne myself correctly
In rites more than can be numbered.[1]

My sad heart is consumed, I am harassed
By a host of small men.
I have borne vexations very many,
Received insults not few.
In the still of night I brood upon it;
In the waking hours I rend my breast.

O sun, ah, moon,
Why are you changed and dim?
Sorrow clings to me
Like an unwashed dress.
In the still of night I brood upon it,
Long to take wing and fly away.

I BEG YOU, ZHONG ZI

I beg of you, Zhong Zi,
Do not climb into our homestead,
Do not break the willows we have planted.
Not that I mind about the willows,
But I am afraid of my father and mother.
Zhong Zi I dearly love;
But of what my father and mother say
Indeed I am afraid.
I beg of you, Zhong Zi,
Do not climb over our wall,
Do not break the mulberry-trees we have
    planted.
Not that I mind about the mulberry-trees,
But I am afraid of my brothers.
Zhong Zi I dearly love;
But of what my brothers say
Indeed I am afraid.

I beg of you, Zhong Zi,
Do not climb into our garden,
Do not break the hard-wood we have planted.
Not that I mind about the hard-wood,
But I am afraid of what people will say.
Zhong Zi I dearly love;
But of all that people will say
Indeed I am afraid.

---

[1]Family rites, or ceremonies, honoring the ancestors. See the fifth song.

SPLENDID

How splendid he was!
Yes, he met me between the hills of Nao.[2]
Our chariots side by side we chased two boars.
He bowed to me and said I was very nimble.

How strong he was!
Yes, he met me on the road at Nao.
Side by side we chased two stags.
He bowed to me and said "well done."

How magnificent he was!
Yes, he met me on the south slopes of Nao.
Side by side we chased two wolves.
He bowed to me and said "that was good."

HIGH REGARD

In high regard we hold mighty Heaven,
But even it is unkind to us.
We are forever without peace;
It brings down this scourge upon us.
All the states are filled with unrest,
Low and noble both suffer this disease.
As with parasites and pests,
There is no controlling it.
The guilty are not apprehended,
There is no respite, no cure.
The people have farm and field,
But these you seize without warning.
The people have working folk,
But these you commandeer.
There are some people quite innocent,
But still you have them jailed.
Then there are those with offenses
Whom you let go free.

A clever man builds a city;
A clever woman tears it down.
Oh, that clever woman,
She is an owl, she is a shrike.

The wagging tongues of women
Are the instruments of our decline.
No, disorder does not come down from Heaven,
Rather it is the spawn of these women.
You can neither teach, nor instruct
Women and their eunuchs.[3]

They attack others in anger and spite,
Slander arises, backs are turned.
You ask if they are not right,
You ask what harm can they do.
They are like merchants with a three-fold
    profit;[4]
Noble lords understand this well.
Thus no woman serves the public,
They stay with their weaving and their loom.

Why does Heaven so reprove you?
Why do spirits not give their blessings?
Because you pay the enemy no attention,
And yet view us with resentment.
This is neither good nor auspicious;
Your demeanor is not fitting.
People flee for their lives,
The state is injured and exhausted.

Heaven casts down its net,
Indeed it is very wide.
People flee for their lives,
Their hearts filled with grief.
Heaven casts down its net,
It is very close-knit indeed.
People flee for their lives.
Their hearts filled with melancholy.

The geyser spews high in the sky;
It must be very deep indeed.
Our hearts are filled with grief
Why has this come to us now?
And not before?
Or not after?
Expansive is mighty Heaven;

---

[2]In northeastern China.
[3]Castrated court officials who wielded great influence. They were castrated so that they would have no family ties and would owe their loyalty totally to the king. Often they and

the women of the court were accused, rightly or wrongly, of intrigues aimed at grabbing power.
[4]Exorbitant profit.

There is nothing it cannot assure.
Insult not the august ancestors,
And your descendants will be secure.

GLORIOUS ANCESTORS

Ah, the glorious ancestors —
Endless their blessings,
Boundless their gifts are extended;
To you, too, they needs must reach.
We have brought them clear wine;
They will give victory.
Here, too, is soup well seasoned,
Well prepared, well mixed.
Because we come in silence,

Setting all quarrels aside,
They make safe for us a ripe old age,
We shall reach the withered cheek, we shall go
    on and on.
With our leather-bound naves,[5] our bronze-clad
    yokes,
With eight bells a-jangle
We come to make offering.
The charge put upon us is vast and mighty,
From Heaven dropped our prosperity,
Good harvests, great abundance.
They come,[6] they accept,
They send down blessings numberless.
They regard the paddy-offerings,[7] the offerings
    of first-fruits
That Tang's descendant brings.[8]

---

[5]The hub of a wheel. The image here is of their driving a chariot.
[6]The spirits of the ancestors.
[7]An offering of rice.

[8]Zheng Tang, founder of the Shang Dynasty (see source 5). This hymn comes from the state of Song, whose people claimed descent from the Shang.

▼▼▼

Mute Testimony

Some of the world's earliest civilizations have left written records that we cannot yet decipher and might never be able to read. These include India's *Harappan* civilization, which was centered in the Indus valley from around 2600 to about 1700 B.C.E.; the *Minoan* civilization of the Aegean island of Crete, which flourished from roughly 2500 to about 1400 B.C.E.; and the African civilization of *Kush*, located directly south of Egypt, which reached its age of greatness after 800 B.C.E. but with much earlier origins as a state. For many other early civilizations and cultures we have as yet uncovered no written records. This is the case of the mysterious peoples who, between approximately 6000 B.C.E. and the first century C.E., painted and carved thousands of pieces of art on the rocks of *Tassili n' Ajjer* in what is today the central Sahara Desert.

The following pieces of artifactual evidence provide glimpses into these often forgotten cultures. As is always the case when dealing with unwritten sources, the historian discovers that such clues from the past raise more questions than they answer.

Bringing in the Sheaves
▼▼▼

7 ▼ *A TASSILI ROCK PAINTING*

Tassili n' Ajjer is today a desiccated, largely uninhabited plateau deep in the heart of southern Algeria's Sahara Desert. Its name, however, which translates as "plateau of the rivers," suggests a past quite different from its current condition. Before the Sahara crept into the region about 2,000 years ago, Tassili n' Ajjer was a lush area that supported a wide variety of animal species and human cultures. The latter left behind a rich artistic record of over 6,000 years of human habitation on the plateau.

In 1956 an expedition of French scholars studied and copied more than 4,000 rock paintings at Tassili and an equally impressive number of rock carvings. This art reflects four major cultural stages of the peoples who lived there. The earliest examples of rock paintings reach back to before 6000 B.C.E. and were the products of a preagricultural, gatherer-hunter society. The rock art produced between about 5000 and 1200 B.C.E. was the work of a pastoral people whose cattle figure prominently in their paintings. Around 1200 B.C.E. the horse and chariot appear in

Tassili Rock Painting: Grain Harvesters

Tassili's rock art, evidence of a significant new equine technology due to influences from the Mediterranean. Finally, as the desert was expanding, the domesticated single-humped Arabian camel appears on the faces of these rocks, signifying yet another and now final stage of cultural development for the terminally endangered people of this area.

The painting that appears here is generally interpreted as portraying a group of people harvesting wild grains. It might date anywhere from 4000 to 1500 B.C.E.

QUESTIONS FOR ANALYSIS

1. What appears to be the sex of the seven harvesters and the person in the lower right who seems to be going to the field?
2. Consider the person at the upper left of the painting. What does he/she seem to be doing? What appears to be the person's sex?
3. What do your answers suggest about gender roles in this society?

Cultural Impressions
▼▼▼

8 ▼ *INDUS, MESOPOTAMIAN, AND CRETAN SEALS*

The stamps and seals that grace the many documents certifying who we are and what we have attained have their origins in the carved magic amulets of prehistory. As official signatures and tokens of authority, seals and stamps have been used by individuals and states since the dawn of civilization. In Mesopotamia carved stone cylinder seals that were rolled into soft clay were used at Uruk and other Sumerian cities as early as 3500 B.C.E. and continued to be produced in large numbers throughout Southwest Asia for the next 3,000 years. When papyrus and parchment replaced clay as preferred writing surfaces, stamps and stamp seals replaced cylinder seals in popularity.

Ancient Southwest Asians did not have a monopoly on the use of such marks of ownership, authenticity, and official approval. More than 2,000 stamp seals and seal impressions have been discovered at Harappan sites in the Indus Valley of what is today the nation of Pakistan. Collectively, the seals contain some 400 different characters of what appears to be a pictographic form of writing. However, scholars have, as yet, been unable to crack the code represented by these signs. Happily, the seals contain more than undecipherable words; they contain carved images that allow us to infer something about this largely mysterious civilization.

Our first grouping contains six modern drawings (done in negative for clarity) of Indus seal impressions from the period 2100–1750 B.C.E., the age of Harappan cultural maturity. Seal 1 depicts a hairy person holding two tigers by the throat. Seal 2 portrays a horned, tailed, and cloven-footed individual grappling with a horned tiger under a tree. Seal 3 depicts two unicorn (single-horned) heads twisted around what appears to be a stylized *pipal,* or fig, tree, the sacred tree of India. Seal 4 shows four human figures somersaulting forward and backward over the raised horns of a bull. Seal 5 shows a humped bull, often called a Brahman bull. Seal 6 presents a male individual with a deeply furrowed or painted face who is wearing a water-buffalo-horn headdress, numerous bangles, bracelets, and a V-shaped collar or necklace. The individual is sitting with his knees angled to either side and the soles of his feet pressed together in front of him. His arms extend away from his body and his hands rest on his knees, with fingers pointed downward. Surrounding him are wild animals: a rhinoceros and water buffalo to his left; an elephant and tiger to his right; underneath him are two antelope-like creatures (one is largely broken off; only its horns remain). A stick-figure human also stands or walks to his right. Some viewers see two side faces in this seated figure.

1

4

2

5

3

6

Indus Seals

7

8

Mesopotamian Seals

9

Cretan Seal

For reasons of comparison, consider the second group of three seal impressions. Items 7 and 8 are rolled-out impressions from Mesopotamian cylinder seals. Number 7, which is from Sumer and dates to somewhere between 2600 and 2350 B.C.E., depicts two heroes struggling with animals. On our left is a nude, muscular, hairy man fighting two bulls. This is probably Gilgamesh (source 1). On the right is a creature who is half bull and half human grasping two lions. This is probably Gilgamesh's companion Enkidu. Number 8 was crafted in Akkad in central Mesopotamia in the period 2340–2180 B.C.E. and shows a bull-man on the left and a hairy hero on the right (probably Enkidu and Gilgamesh). Each holds a rampant bull by the mane and tail. The forelegs of each bull touch the top of a stylized mountain and what seems to be a sacred tree on the mountain. The final impression (9) is of a seal from the island civilization of Crete. The seal dates to ca. 1550–1500 B.C.E. and depicts two bulls and two acrobats. One athlete has just vaulted over a bull, while the second bull-leaper stands ready to vault.

QUESTIONS FOR ANALYSIS

1. Seals 2–9 contain horned figures. What do you suppose the horn symbolized to these societies? Why, of all horned creatures, do you think the bull figures so prominently in these seals? Based on your answers, what can you infer about the religious and social values of these societies?

2. Consider the hairy males in seals 1, 7, and 8. What does hairiness seem to symbolize in each instance? Again, what do you infer about their societies' religious and social values from this evidence?

3. Consider the central figure in seal 6. How do you interpret his posture, and what does your answer suggest about the individual and his function? Consider his dress and the figures that surround him. Do these suggest humanity or divinity? If a human, what is his class? If a god, what sort of god?

4. What can you infer from these seals about possible lines of cultural contact and influence? Who *seems* to have influenced whom, and how? On a map, trace the possible routes of cultural exchange.

Sacred Kingship along the Nile
▼▼▼

9 ▼ TWO TEMPLE RELIEFS

It is unclear whether several of the Indus seals that we have studied portray humans or deities, but the two temple *reliefs* (raised carvings on flat backgrounds) that follow clearly depict gods and kings. The piece on the top is Egyptian and dates from the thirteenth century B.C.E. Located at the temple of King Seti I at Abydos in Upper Egypt, it portrays, from right to left, Horus the falcon-god, King Seti, and the goddess Isis (see source 3). We will use it solely for comparison with the relief below it. This piece of art is Kushitic and dates from after 300 B.C.E. It is a small fragment of a temple tablet from Meroë, a *Nubian* city considerably distant from Abydos. It portrays a Nubian king of *Kush* and Apedemak, the lion-god of war.

The Nubians, who inhabited the region directly south of Egypt, were drawn into the orbit of their powerful neighbor to the north at an early date. Yet while they borrowed quite a bit from the Egyptians, the Nubians managed to retain their indigenous culture. Around 800 B.C.E. the Nubians created the independent kingdom of Kush and around 730 B.C.E. were strong enough to conquer Egypt, which Kushite pharaohs ruled for close to a century. After being driven out of Egypt by the Assyrians, the Kushites eventually established a new capital for their kingdom at Meroë on the Middle Nile. Between about 350 B.C.E. and the early fourth century C.E., Kush was a major economic power in Northeast Africa, largely because of Meroë's rich iron deposits.

In the bottom relief, one of those mighty monarchs of Kush stands face to face with the Nubians' most powerful deity. Unfortunately we cannot decipher the writing above each figure, so we can only guess at the meaning of this scene. Perhaps the relief of Seti I provides a vital clue. There Horus, the divine son of Isis, is handing the scepter of power to Seti, who, as long as he lives on Earth, will be identified with Horus, upon whose throne he sits. Note that the Meroitic tablet also portrays both god and king with what appear to be scepters.

QUESTIONS FOR ANALYSIS

1. What do these two sculptures allow us to infer about the nature of royal power in Kush?
2. What do they tell us about the balance that the Kushites struck between accepting Egyptian influences and retaining traditional Nubian ways?

Temple Relief: Isis, Seti I, and Horus

Temple Relief: Kushite King and Apedemak

Chapter 2

Newcomers
From Nomads to Settlers

The oldest town excavated to date by archaeologists is Jericho, which has been inhabited fairly continuously, but with some significant breaks, for the past 10,000 years. Around 8000 B.C.E. this site, which lies west of the Jordan River, covered more than eight acres and supported a population of 2,000 to 3,000 people. Most impressive of all are the town's massive watchtower, walls, and encircling ditch, which serve as silent witnesses of the residents' fear of outsiders.

That fear was well based. Archaeological evidence shows that Jericho suffered destruction on several occasions, and it is easy to imagine that some of those catastrophes were the handiwork of invaders, attracted by the town's wealth. Not all of Jericho's assailants were *nomads,* or groups of related individuals who migrated along well-established seasonal routes, tending herds of domesticated animals as they moved. But some were.

The tension between nomadic peoples and settled farmers is as old as agriculture itself, and it continued to be a major factor in global history well into modern times. To be sure, settled communities and the peoples who wandered their borders enjoyed many mutually beneficial relationships. Nomads served as mercenary soldiers, traders, and carriers of new ideas. But they could also be formidable foes, threatening the very existence of some civilizations. Threats and incursions cut both ways, however, and often nomads found their ways of life disrupted and imperiled by the outward expansion of neighboring civilizations.

In this chapter we shall consider the impact, settlements, and evolving cultures of three newcomers: the *Aryans* (the noble people), the *Greeks,* and the *Israelites,* all of whom appeared on the historical scene during the second millennium B.C.E. The state of current scholarship suggests that all three — Aryans, Greeks, and Israelites — engaged in some limited agriculture prior to their moving into their new homelands. Many of the Israelites, however, seem to have been more purely pastoralists when they marched into the light of history, very much like modern Bedouins who still wander the arid regions of Southwest Asia with their flocks.

▼▼▼

The Indo-Europeans

By the late first millennium B.C.E., many of Eurasia's settled peoples, from the *Celts* of the British Isles in the west to the *Tocharians* of Central Asia in the east, spoke a variety of related languages that linguists classify as *Indo-European*. As far as we can tell, a core group of people who spoke a language known as *Proto-Indo-European* lived in western Asia about 6,500 or more years ago. Some scholars push that date back as far as 6500 B.C.E.; a majority are more comfortable with the vague date ca. 4500–4000 B.C.E. Some linguists place the ancestral homeland of this language family in *Anatolia* (modern Asiatic Turkey); a majority find the steppe region of southern Ukraine and Russia, just north of the Black and Caspian seas, a more likely location. Whatever the time and place of Proto-Indo-European's origins, beginning possibly as early as 4500 B.C.E., and continuing for several thousand years, groups who spoke various forms of this language moved out of their ancestral homeland in waves and migrated east, west, north, and southeast. Once underway, the migration waves seem to have moved at a slow pace, but their historical impact was profound. The fact that *Aryan, Eire* (the Gaelic name for the Republic of Ireland), and *Iran* derive from the common archaic root-word *aryo,* which means "nobleman," eloquently attests to the extent of the ancient Indo-European wanderings and settlements. Today almost all of the languages of Europe (Basque, Finnish, Georgian, and Hungarian are the exceptions) belong to subgroups of the Indo-European family, as also do such disparate tongues as Armenian, Farsi (Persian), Hindi, Kurdish, and Romany (the language of the Gypsies).

In the course of these Indo-European migrations, the Aryans moved across the Hindu Kush mountain range and into the fertile Indus Valley, where they encountered the vestiges of Harappan civilization (source 8), and the Greeks moved into the Balkans, where they absorbed or displaced the native people they encountered. The dates of their respective arrivals are uncertain, but both were securely settled in their new homelands by the mid second millennium B.C.E.

Life, Death, and the Gods in Aryan India
▼▼▼

10 ▼ *THE RIG VEDA*

Until fairly recently, historians generally credited the Aryans with conquering and destroying a vigorous Harappan civilization. The evidence now suggests that these Indo-European immigrants moved into a region whose civilization was already in shambles, due probably to a series of natural disasters that occurred around 1700 B.C.E. What is clear is that by 1500 the Aryans were ruling northwestern India as an illiterate warrior aristocracy, and the arts of writing and statecraft had disappeared. India would not reemerge into the light of recorded history until around 600 B.C.E.

Because the early Aryans were a preliterate people, what little we know about them we derive from their *oral tradition,* which survives in four great collections of priestly hymns, chants, incantations, and ritual formulas known as the *Vedas,* all of which were composed in the Aryans' sacred language, *Sanskrit.* Veda means "wisdom" or "knowledge," and the Aryans accepted these collections of sacred poetry as the eternal word of the gods. For modern historians, however, the Vedas provide tantalizing glimpses into the historical dynamics of the era from roughly 1500 to about 600 B.C.E., a near millennium that is often referred to as India's *Vedic Age.*

As is common in preliterate societies, Aryan priests, known as *Brahmins,* were trained to perform prodigious feats of memory. Generation after generation they sang these songs and passed them on to those who followed. As a result, although the Vedas would not be written down until around 600 B.C.E., many of their songs reflect the religious, social, and political realities of Aryan life around 1500 or earlier. Conversely, other Vedic hymns were the products of much later centuries and mirror the more sophisticated culture of an emerging Indo-Aryan civilization. It is the historian's task to identify and make sense out of these different elements.

The most celebrated and earliest of the four Vedic collections is the *Rig Veda* (Verses of Knowledge), a compilation of 1,017 songs, which probably was largely put together in the form we know it between 1200 and 900 B.C.E., although it contains many elements that stretch back to long before the Aryans arrived in India. This Sanskrit masterpiece remains, even today, one of the sacred books of Hinduism. It is also, as far as we can determine, the earliest extant major work of literature in an Indo-European tongue, predating by several centuries the Homeric Greek epics.

The following three poems from the *Rig Veda* illustrate the evolution of Indo-Aryan religious thought. The first celebrates the victory over *Vritra,* the dragon of drought, by *Indra,* the early Aryans' chief deity. A lusty god of war, Indra was noted for imbibing every morning large amounts of *Soma,* a sacred hallucinogenic drink reserved for the gods and their priests, and for his military victories over the *Dasas* (slaves), the indigenous people of northern India whom the Aryans were subduing. In this particular hymn, however, Indra conquers another foe, Vritra, known as the *Encompasser,* and liberates the universe, which Vritra has swallowed. In his conquest, Indra releases life-giving monsoon rains, irrigating waters that were vital to the Aryans, who were now settling down and farming the land. As the Aryans were absorbed into the rich cultural fabric of India, their forms of religious expression also changed. Indra, whose worship was the central reality of early Vedic religious life, largely fell out of favor as a major deity in post-Vedic India, becoming simply the god of weather. Our second hymn hints at the change in religious perception that was taking place in later Indo-Aryan society as some Aryans even dared to doubt the very existence of this ancient god of battle. As this second hymn also indicates, the Aryans had originally envisioned Indra as the creator-god. Our third hymn, which is clearly one of the last Vedic songs to be crafted, presents another vision of creation. In this poem the gods create the universe (and themselves) by sacrificing *Purusha,* the Cosmic Man, to himself. The paradoxical view of reality presented in this hymn would become a hallmark of classic Hindu thought, as we shall see in Chapter 3 and elsewhere.

QUESTIONS FOR ANALYSIS

1. The hymn regarding the victory over Vritra is the earliest of the three poems. What sort of god is Indra? What does your answer suggest about the society that worshiped him as its chief deity?
2. Compare the first hymn with the second hymn. Do you perceive any differences in tone or substance? What are they, and what do they suggest to you about changes in Indo-Aryan society?
3. What are the clues in the hymn to Purusha that point to its late composition?
4. What evidence is there in the third hymn for the emergence of what would become the Hindu *caste* system (Chapter 3, source 15), and how is that system explained and justified?
5. Can you find in the hymn to Purusha evidence of the basic Hindu concept of the unity of all life?
6. Compare Indra and Purusha as deities. In what ways do they represent significant historical changes that took place within Indo-Aryan society?

VICTORY OVER VRITRA

I will declare the manly deeds of Indra, the first that he achieved, the thunder-wielder.

He slew the dragon, then disclosed the waters, and cleft the channels of the mountain torrents.

He slew the dragon lying on the mountain: his heavenly bolt of thunder Twashtar[1] fashioned.

Like lowing cows in rapid flow descending, the waters glided downward to the ocean.

Impetuous as a bull, he chose the Soma, and quaffed in threefold sacrifice the juices.

Maghavan[2] grasped the thunder for his weapon, and smote to death this firstborn of the dragons.

When, Indra, you had slain the dragon's firstborn, and overcome the charms of the enchanters.

Then, giving life to sun and dawn and heaven, you found not one foe to stand against you.

Indra with his own great and deadly thunder smote into pieces Vritra worst of Vritras.[3]

As trunks of trees, what time the axe has felled them, low on the earth so lies the prostrate dragon.

---

[1]The divine artisan.
[2]Lord Bountiful — another name for Indra.

[3]"Dragon, worst of dragons."

He, like a mad weak warrior, challenged Indra, the great impetuous many-slaying hero.

He, brooking not the clashing of the weapons, crushed — Indra's foe — the shattered forts in falling.[4]

Footless and handless still[5] he challenged Indra, who smote him with his bolt between the shoulders.

Emasculated yet claiming manly vigor, thus Vritra lay with scattered limbs dissevered. . . .

Nothing availed him. Lightning, nothing, nor thunder, hailstorm or mist which he had spread around him.[6]

When Indra and the dragon strove in battle, Maghavan gained the victory for ever. . . .

Indra is king of all that moves and moves not, of creatures tame and horned, the thunder-wielder.

Over all living men he rules as sovereign, containing all as spokes within a rim.

WHO IS INDRA?

The god who had insight the moment he was born, the first who protected the gods with his power of thought, before whose hot breath the two world-halves[7] tremble at the greatness of his manly powers — he, my people, is Indra.

He who made fast the tottering earth, who made still the quaking mountains, who measured out and extended the expanse of the air, who propped up the sky — he, my people, is Indra.

He who killed the serpent and loosed the seven rivers, who drove out the cows that had been pent up by Vala,[8] who gave birth to fire between

two stones,[9] the winner of booty in combats — he, my people, is Indra.

He by whom all these changes were rung, who drove the race of Dasas down into obscurity, who took away the flourishing wealth of the enemy as a winning gambler takes the stake — he, my people, is Indra.

He about whom they ask, 'Where is he?,' or they say of him, the terrible one, 'He does not exist,' he who diminishes the flourishing wealth of the enemy as a gambler does — believe in him! He, my people, is Indra.

He who encourages the weary and the sick, and the poor priest who is in need, who helps the man who harnesses the stones to press Soma, he who has lips fine for drinking — he, my people, is Indra.

He under whose command are horses and cows and villages and all chariots, who gave birth to the sun and the dawn and led out the waters, he, my people, is Indra.

He who is invoked by both of two armies, enemies locked in combat, on this side and that side, he who is even invoked separately by each of two men standing on the very same chariot,[10] he, my people, is Indra.

He without whom people do not conquer, he whom they call on for help when they are fighting, who became the image of everything, who shakes the unshakeable — he, my people, is Indra.

He who killed with his weapon all those who had committed a great sin, even when they did not know it, he who does not pardon the arrogant

---

[4]The clouds are pictured as forts imprisoning moisture.
[5]Vritra is serpentlike, lacking feet and hands.
[6]Vritra used magic to surround himself with storms and mist, but they failed him.
[7]Heaven and Earth.
[8]A demon who penned up Indra's cows, cows being tokens of wealth among the early Aryans.
[9]Indra is the bringer of fire, which is kindled by striking two

flints. He is also the creator of lightning (the fire between [the stones of] Heaven and Earth) and Soma, which is crushed between stones. He also created the sun, another fire between Heaven and Earth.
[10]Two persons rode in a war chariot, the priest/charioteer and the warrior-noble (see Chapter 3, source 15).

man for his arrogance, who is the slayer of the Dasyus,[11] he, my people, is Indra.

He who in the fortieth autumn discovered Sambara living in the mountains,[12] who killed the violent serpent, the Danu,[13] as he lay there, he, my people, is Indra.

He, the mighty bull who with his seven reins let loose the seven rivers to flow, who with his thunderbolt in his hand hurled down Rauhina[14] as he was climbing up to the sky, he, my people, is Indra.

Even the sky and the earth bow low before him, and the mountains are terrified of his hot breath; he who is known as the Soma-drinker, with his thunderbolt in his hand, with the thunderbolt in his palm, he, my people, is Indra.

He who helps with his favor the one who presses and the one who cooks,[15] the praiser and the preparer, he for whom prayer is nourishment, for whom Soma is the special gift, he, my people, is Indra.

You[16] who furiously grasp the prize for the one who presses and the one who cooks, you are truly real. Let us be dear to you, Indra, all our days, and let us speak as men of power in the sacrificial gathering.

TO PURUSHA

A thousand heads had Purusha,[17] a thousand eyes, a thousand feet.

He covered earth on every side, and spread ten fingers' breadth beyond.

This Purusha is all that yet has been and all that is to be;

The lord of immortality which waxes greater still by food.

So mighty is his greatness; yea, greater than this is Purusha.

All creatures are one-fourth of him, three-fourths eternal life in heaven.[18]

With three-fourths Purusha went up: one-fourth of him again was here.

Thence he strode out to every side over what eats not and what eats.

From him Viraj[19] was born; again Purusha from Viraj was born.

As soon as he was born he spread eastward and westward o'er the earth.

When gods prepared the sacrifice with Purusha as their offering,

Its oil was spring, the holy gift was autumn; summer was the wood.

They balmed as victim on the grass[20] Purusha born in earliest time.

With him the deities and all Sadhyas[21] and Rishis[22] sacrificed.

From that great general sacrifice the dripping fat was gathered up.

He formed the creatures of the air, and animals both wild and tame.

From that great general sacrifice Richas and Samahymns[23] were born:

---

[11]The Dasas, or slaves.
[12]A demon who kept Soma from Indra in mountain fortresses.
[13]Vritra.
[14]An obscure enemy about whom nothing else is known.
[15]Those who press and those who cook Soma.
[16]Indra.
[17]Purusha, the all-pervading universal spirit and source of all life, is conceived as a god with countless eyes, hands, and feet. Purusha is both limitless and able to be enclosed in the

smallest of spaces. In an act celebrated by this poem, Purusha is simultaneously the sacrifice and the sacrificer.
[18]One-quarter of Purusha is found in all mortal creation; three-fourths of Purusha is divine and eternal.
[19]The female creative germ.
[20]Special grasses laid out during Vedic sacrifices for the gods to sit upon.
[21]A class of demigods.
[22]Sages.
[23]The constituent elements of the *Rig Veda*.

Therefrom the meters were produced,[24] the Yajus[25] had its birth from it.

From it were horses born, from it all creatures with two rows of teeth:

From it were generated cows, from it the goats and sheep were born.

When they divided Purusha how many portions did they make?

What do they call his mouth, his arms? What do they call his thighs and feet?

The Brahmin[26] was his mouth, of both his arms was the Rajanya[27] made.

His thighs became the Vaisya,[28] from his feet the Sudra[29] was produced.

The Moon was gendered from his mind, and from his eye the Sun had birth;

Indra and Agni[30] from his mouth were born, and Vayu[31] from his breath.

Forth from his navel came mid-air; the sky was fashioned from his head;

Earth from his feet, and from his ear the regions. Thus they formed the worlds.

Seven fencing-logs had he, thrice seven layers of fuel were prepared,[32]

When the gods, offering sacrifice, bound, as their victim, Purusha.

Gods, sacrificing, sacrificed the victim: these were the earliest holy ordinances.

The mighty ones attained the height of heaven, there where the Sadhyas, gods of old, are dwelling.

---

[24]The verses of the *Sama Veda*. It is largely a collection of parts of the *Rig Veda* arranged for religious ceremonial use.
[25]The ritual formulas of the *Yajur Veda*. It was compiled a century or two after the *Rig Veda* and served as a collection of sacrificial chants.
[26]An Aryan priest.
[27]The *Rajanyas,* or *Kshatriyas,* comprised the ruling or warrior class, which later became a caste.
[28]This class initially encompassed free herders and farmers; later, when it was a caste, it included traders and artisans.

[29]The slave and servant class, which later became the fourth and lowest caste. The term was originally applied to the Dasas, the native people whom the Aryans conquered and subjugated when they entered India.
[30]The god of fire and sacrifice. This Sanskrit word is cognate with *ignis,* the Latin word for "fire" (hence, *ignite* in English).
[31]The wind.
[32]For a sacrificial fire.

A Journey to the Underworld
▼▼▼

11 ▼ *Homer, THE ODYSSEY*

By 1600 B.C.E. history's first identifiable Greeks, a people who called themselves the *Achaeans,* had created in the Balkan Peninsula a decentralized warrior civilization, which we term *Mycenaean.* The name derives from *Mycenae,* a city that exercised a loose leadership over the petty principalities of southern and central Greece. Around 1450 B.C.E. the Achaeans were masters of the island civilization of Crete (source 8) and, as accomplished pirates and maritime merchants, a major force in the eastern Mediterranean. It is against this background that we must place the Achaean expedition against *Troy,* a city in Anatolia, which took place around 1200.

The sack of rival Troy was the high-water mark for the Achaeans. Within a century Mycenaean civilization was collapsing, in part, at least, because of internecine wars among the various Achaean principalities. What other factors were involved remains a mystery. By 1100 B.C.E. the highly specialized arts and crafts, including literacy, that had characterized Bronze Age Greece at its height had disappeared or were severely reduced in quality and quantity. Greece had entered a period we call the *Greek Dark Age* (ca. 1100–ca. 800), a term that, more than anything else, implies our overall ignorance of what was happening in the Greek World during these centuries. About all we can say with any degree of certainty is that the Greeks lost the art of writing, their political and economic structures seem to have been drastically reduced in size, and a relatively weak and impoverished Greek World ceased to be a major power in the eastern Mediterranean. At the same time, however, recent archaeological finds have tended to underscore the continuities between late Mycenaean society and the classical *Hellenic World* that arose after 800 B.C.E., despite the losses and retrenchments. What is more, during this so-called Dark Age the Greek *polis,* or city-state, emerged as a major (many would say *the* major) component of Greek civilization. By 800 B.C.E., *poleis* (the plural of *polis*) were scattered all over the Greek World.

When Greek civilization (with its accompanying literacy) reemerged around the middle of the eighth century B.C.E., it was centered along the western shores of Anatolia, where Greek colonists had begun settling around the mid eleventh century B.C.E. Because so many of these Greek refugees spoke a Greek dialect known as *Ionian,* the region became known as *Ionia.* Here across the Aegean Sea, Greek settlers, benefiting from their contact with the far-older civilizations of Southwest Asia (and, to a lesser extent, Egypt), produced the first Greek literature known to us (as opposed to the bureaucratic lists left behind by Mycenaean civilization). Of all of this early literature, the most significant are two epic poems, the *Iliad* and the *Odyssey,* both ascribed to a bard called *Homer.*

The ancients had no doubt there was a historical Homer, a blind poet who created both works. Modern scholars are less certain, and most agree that we will never know the truth about Homer's identity or the exact process by which his epics were fashioned. Yet there are some points on which scholars are generally agreed. Internal evidence (the words, phrases, and allusions within each poem) has led most researchers to conclude that, regardless of whether Homer was one, two, or many poets, these two poems largely reached their final form in Anatolia during the late eighth century. Whether they were written down that early or still transmitted orally is impossible to say. What is clear, however, is that both epics exhibit all of the hallmarks of oral poetry, suggesting strongly that in the act of creation the poet or poets whom we call Homer drew heavily from a long tradition of oral poetic stories, which had been preserved for centuries in the memories of wandering professional bards.

Very much like the *Rig Veda,* therefore, the Homeric epics preserve vestiges of a much earlier age — in this case the Late Mycenaean Age — but are also overlaid with the values, social practices, and modes of perception of later Greek society. When used judiciously, the two epics tell us a good deal about life in the thirteenth century B.C.E. — the age of the Trojan War. At the same time, they often reflect the culture of Late Dark Age society, especially that of the ninth and eighth centuries. The problem facing the historian is to separate one from the other.

On one level both poems celebrate such warrior virtues as personal honor, bravery, and loyalty to one's comrades, and on a deeper level they probe the hidden recesses of human motivation and emotion. On a third level the poems address the issue of the meaning of human suffering. Why do humans experience pain and sorrow? Are they captive to the whims of the gods? Are they and the gods subject to an overarching destiny that neither can avoid?

More to human scale than the *Iliad,* the *Odyssey* tells two intertwined stories. One traces the ten-year-long homeward voyage of the Achaean hero *Odysseus.* This clever adventurer has to battle, with cunning and skill, the enmity of Poseidon, god of the sea, and a variety of superhuman opponents before finally arriving home to his island kingdom of Ithaca. The second story details the efforts of Odysseus's wife and son, Penelope and Telemachus, who, with equal cunning and skill, attempt to stall indefinitely the advances of a group of suitors who seek to marry the presumed widow. As the suitors impatiently wait to see whom she will marry, they despoil Odysseus and Penelope's home and waste Telemachus's patrimony. The two story lines merge when Odysseus returns and, with the aid of his son and several loyal servants, wreaks vengeance on the suitors by killing them all. Unlike most epics, the story ends happily with Penelope and Odysseus reunited and Telemachus assured of his inheritance.

The following selection describes one of Odysseus's most daring adventures on his troubled homeward journey — a visit to the House of Hades, or the Land of the Dead. Here he consults Teiresias, the blind Theban seer, who even in death retains his prophetic powers. Odysseus also meets the shades of many famous women and men, including his old comrade-in-arms Achilles, the Achaeans' greatest warrior and the central character of the *Iliad,* who was killed prior to the fall of Troy.

QUESTIONS FOR ANALYSIS

1. What values did Odysseus's society hold in highest esteem?
2. How does Homer address the issue of human responsibility for ill fortune?
3. Is there a destiny that humans cannot escape? If so, what role do the gods play in this destiny?
4. It is often stated that the Greeks focused on human beings and human concerns. Indeed, it is said that for the Greeks the human was the standard of measurement for all things. Does this selection seem to support or contradict that judgment?
5. Compare Achilles' sentiment toward the land of the dead with Enkidu's vision in *The Epic of Gilgamesh* (source 1). What do you conclude from your analysis?
6. Compare Achaean society with that of the Aryans. What strikes you as more significant, the similarities or the differences? What do you conclude from your answer?

Now the spirit of Teiresias of Thebes came forward, bearing a golden staff in his hand. Knowing who I am, he addressed me: "Son of Laertes, sprung from Zeus,[1] Odysseus, known for your many wiles, why, unhappy man, have you left the sunlight to behold the dead in this cheerless region? Step back from the trench and put aside your sharp sword so that I might drink the blood[2] and thereby prophesy the truth to you." Thus he spoke. I, stepping backward, drove my silver-studded sword into its scabbard. When he had drunk the black blood, this noble prophet addressed me with these words.

"Lord Odysseus, you seek a honey-sweet homeward journey, but a god will make your travels difficult. I do not think you can escape the notice of the Earth-shaker,[3] who has set his mind in enmity against you, enraged because you blinded his beloved son.[4] Even so, you still might be able to reach home, although in sorry circumstances, if you are willing to restrain your desires, and those of your comrades, beginning when your seaworthy ship leaves the deep blue waters and approaches the island of Thrinacie,[5] where you will see the grazing cattle and fat sheep of Helios,[6] who sees and hears everything. If you leave the animals untouched and concentrate solely on getting home, it is possible that all of you might reach Ithaca, although in sorry circumstances. If you injure these animals, however, I foresee destruction for your ship and its crew, and even if you yourself manage to escape, you will return home late, in a sorry state, in an alien ship, having lost all your companions.[7] And even there at

home you will find troubles. Overbearing men will be consuming your wealth, wooing your goddesslike wife, and offering her bridal gifts. Certainly, following your arrival, you will gain revenge on these suitors for their evil deeds. When you have slain the suitors in your halls, whether by stratagem or in an open fight with sharp bronze weapons, you must again set out on a journey. You must take a well-fashioned oar and travel until you reach a people who are ignorant of the sea and never eat food mixed with salt, and who know nothing about our purple-ribbed ships and the well-fashioned oars that serve as ships wings. And I say you will receive a sign, a very clear one that you cannot miss. When another traveler upon meeting you remarks that you are carrying a winnowing-fan across your broad back,[8] plant your well-fashioned oar in the earth and offer Lord Poseidon the sacrifice of a ram, a bull,[9] and a boar, the mate of the wild she-swine. Then return home and there make sacred offerings to all the immortal gods who inhabit wide Heaven, and do so to each in order of rank. As for death, it will come to you at last gently out of the sea in a comfortable old age when you are surrounded by a prosperous people. This I tell you truly." . . .

Next came the spirits of Achilles, son of Peleus, of Patroclus,[10] of noble Antilochus,[11] and of Aias,[12] who surpassed all the Danaans[13] in beauty of physique and manly bearing, except for the flawless son of Peleus.[14] The spirit of swift-footed Achilles of the house of Aeacus[15] recognized me, and mournfully spoke in winged words: "Son of

---

[1]The greatest of the Greek gods. The title implies Odysseus's godlike heroic qualities.
[2]The spirits of the dead can communicate with Odysseus only after they drink blood from animals he has sacrificed.
[3]Poseidon, god of the sea and of earthquakes.
[4]The Cyclops, a son of Poseidon, was a one-eyed, cannibal giant whom Odysseus had blinded in self-defense.
[5]The mythical island of the sun-god Helios, where he pastured his sacred cattle; ancient Greek commentators on Homer identified it as the island of Sicily.
[6]The sun-god.
[7]The crew will kill and eat the sun-god's flocks, and all, except Odysseus, will die as a result.
[8]Odysseus will be in a region where no one knows what an oar's function is. Rather, they will mistake it for the long-

handled shallow basket in which grain is tossed to separate cereal from the chaff.
[9]The bull was sacred to Poseidon. (See Chapter 1, source 8 for examples of the popularity of the bull as a sacred animal.)
[10]Achilles' best friend, who also died at Troy.
[11]An Achaean hero who fell at Troy while defending his father, King Nestor of Pylos (note 21).
[12]The Achaeans' second-greatest warrior; he committed suicide at Troy after Odysseus bested him in a contest for the armor of the dead Achilles.
[13]Another name for the Achaeans.
[14]Achilles.
[15]The ancestor from whom Peleus and his son Achilles were descended. Homer's heroes always identified themselves by reference to their fathers and other notable ancestors.

Laertes, sprung from Zeus, Odysseus, known for your many wiles! Rash man, what greater deed than this remains for you to devise in your heart? How did you dare to descend to Hades'[16] realm, where the dead dwell as witless images of worn-out mortals?"

Thus he spoke, and I answered in return. "Achilles, son of Peleus, by far the mightiest of the Achaeans, I came to consult with Teiresias in the hope of his giving me a plan whereby I might reach rocky Ithaca. For I have not yet come near the land of Achaea,[17] nor yet set foot on my own island, but have been constantly beset by misfortunes. How different from your situation, Achilles, you who are more fortunate than any man whoever was or will be. For in the old days, when you were alive, we Argives[18] honored you as though you were a god, and now that you are here, you rule nobly among the dead. Therefore, grieve not, Achilles, that you are dead."

So I spoke, and he immediately answered, saying: "Do not endeavor to speak soothingly to me of death, Lord Odysseus. I would rather live on Earth as the hired help of some landless man whose own livelihood was meager, than be lord over all the dead who have perished. Enough of that. Tell me about my son, that lordly young man. Did he follow me to war and play a leading role in it? And tell me about noble Peleus. . . . I am not there in the sunlight to aid Peleus with that great strength that was once mine on the broad plains of Troy, where I slew the best of the enemy's army in defense of the Argives. If, but for an hour, I could return to my father's house with such strength as I once had, I would give those who do him violence and dishonor him cause to rue my might and my invincible hands."

So he spoke, and I answered: "I have heard nothing about noble Peleus, but I will give you all the news you desire of your dear son, Neoptolemus.[19] It was I who brought him from Scyros[20] in my well-fashioned, hollow ship to join the ranks of the well-armed Achaeans. Whenever we held a council meeting during the siege of Troy, he was always the first to speak, and his words never missed the mark. Godlike Nestor[21] and I alone surpassed him. As often as we fought with bronze weapons on the Trojan plain, he never lagged behind in the ranks or crowd, but would always run far out in front, yielding first place to no one, and he slew many men in mortal combat. I could not name all whom he killed in defense of the Argives. . . . Again, when we, the best of the Argives, were about to enter into the horse that Epeus made,[22] and responsibility lay solely with me to either open or keep closed the door of our stout-built ambush, the other Danaan leaders and chieftains were wiping away tears from their eyes and each man's limbs shook beneath him. But never did my eyes see his fair face grow pale, nor did I see him wiping away tears from his cheeks. Rather, he earnestly begged me to allow him to sally forth from the horse, and he kept handling his sword-hilt and his heavy bronze spear in his eagerness to inflict harm on the Trojans. Following our sack of the lofty city of Priam,[23] he boarded his ship with a full share of the spoils and his special prize.[24] And he was unscathed, never cut by a sharp sword or wounded in close combat, as often happens in war, since Ares[25] rages in a confused fashion."

So I spoke, and the spirit of the son of Aeacus departed with long strides across the field of asphodel,[26] rejoicing that his son was preeminent among men.

---

[16]The god of the dead.
[17]The land of the Achaeans — mainland Greece.
[18]Another name for the Achaeans.
[19]Fittingly, his name means "New War."
[20]The Aegean island where Achilles' son had been raised.
[21]The aged king of Pylos noted for his wisdom and sage advice.
[22]The so-called Trojan horse, through which the Achaeans finally were able to capture Troy.

[23]The last king of Troy.
[24]At the division of the Trojan survivors, Neoptolemus was awarded Andromache, widow of Hector, Troy's greatest hero, whom Achilles had killed in single combat.
[25]The god of war.
[26]A flower that carpeted the Elysian Fields, where the spirits of dead heroes, such as Achilles, resided.

The Israelites and Their Neighbors

Excavations at the city of Ebla in northern Syria reveal that the land of Palestine-Syria (the region covered by the modern nations of Israel, Jordan, Lebanon, and Syria, and the emerging Palestinian state) has known urban civilization since about 3000 B.C.E., although its cities did not begin to reach significant size until around 2500. Inasmuch as this land is a bridge between Egypt and Mesopotamia, it has suffered the fate of all regions that serve as crossroads, being prey to numerous invaders. Its first known conqueror was Sargon the Great of Akkad in Mesopotamia, who sacked Ebla in the twenty-fourth century. Proximity to Egypt and Mesopotamia, especially the latter, also enriched the land and its people with trade and cultural imprints. The Eblaites mainly wrote in Sumerian on clay tablets, in imitation of their Mesopotamian neighbors, but they also adopted Sumerian *cuneiform* (wedge-shaped) script and words to write their own language — Eblaite. Ebla disappeared from history by 1600 B.C.E., but the region continued to be a focal point of exchange and invasion.

During the thirteenth century B.C.E., in the midst of a number of invasions and upheavals that tested all civilizations in Southwest Asia and the eastern Mediterranean, several groups of invaders penetrated the region of *Canaan* (roughly modern Israel, Palestine, and southern Lebanon) and established themselves there at the expense of an indigenous, ethnically diverse population. One of the invaders was a mixed group from the Aegean that settled in cities along the coast of what is today the state of Israel. These people, who included a large percentage of uprooted Mycenaean Greeks and Cretans, became known as the *Philistines*. A second wave was comprised of another hybrid mass of people, the *Israelites,* who spoke a Semitic language — *Hebrew*.

As is the case with the Indo-European language family, Semitic origins are lost in the mists of time. We do know, however, that the Akkadians, who spoke a Semitic language, inhabited the middle Tigris-Euphrates Valley as early as 2900 B.C.E., and the Eblaites also spoke a Semitic tongue. Evidence suggests that the early Semites migrated into Mesopotamia and northern Syria from the western and southern deserts, and consequently historians believe the original homeland of the Semitic language family was Arabia.

Whatever the distant origins of their language, the people whom history identifies as the Israelites seem to have been originally an ethnically mixed mass of Semitic peoples who infiltrated into Canaan out of the southern and eastern deserts and settled the inland high ground overlooking the Philistine cities. Egyptian sources suggest that the forerunners of the Israelites were viewed by their more settled neighbors as outlaws and raiders.

Prior to the waves of invaders, the Hittite and Egyptian empires had fought one another for mastery over Syria-Palestine. With the destruction of Hittite civilization and the concurrent severe weakening of the Egyptian empire around 1200, a momentary power vacuum occurred along the eastern rim of the Mediterranean. In the absence of any outside imperial power, the various cultural groups of Syria-

Palestine, including the Israelites, had several centuries of relative freedom in which to struggle with one another and to amalgamate.

For the Israelites, amalgamation was seductively easy and potentially disastrous. The vast majority of the peoples who already inhabited Canaan also spoke Semitic languages and shared other cultural characteristics with these ruder newcomers. Something, however, set the Israelites apart and enabled them to mold a distinctive culture. As they coalesced as an identifiable people, the Israelites evolved the idea that they enjoyed the special protection of a god whom they called *YHWH* (probably pronounced "Yahveh"). In return for that protection, this deity demanded their sole devotion. A corollary of that belief was the conviction that if the Israelites were to prosper in Canaan, a land that YHWH had promised them, they had to maintain religious purity and, therefore, cultural distance from all other peoples.

Establishing a Covenant with Humanity
▼▼▼
12 ▼ *THE BOOK OF GENESIS*

Other than a late-thirteenth-century B.C.E. Egyptian note that there was an entity called Israel inhabiting the land of Canaan, there is only silence in contemporary records regarding the settlement and even the very existence of the Israelites. Likewise, archaeological evidence regarding their activities in the first several centuries of their residence in Canaan is scanty and ambiguous. The major documentary source for both the process of cultural fusion and the fierce struggles that took place among the various groups of Iron Age settlers in Syria-Palestine is a collection of sacred Hebrew writings known as the Bible (from the Greek word *biblos,* which means "book").

The exclusively Hebrew portion of the Bible, known to Jews as the *Tanakh* but called by Christians the Old Testament, consists of a wide variety of different types of literature. These scriptures were mainly composed, edited, and re-edited between roughly 1000 B.C.E. to possibly as late as the second century B.C.E., although Jewish religious authorities did not fix the Tanakh's final *canon,* or official body of accepted texts, until after 100 C.E. This means that biblical accounts of early Israelite history are, in many cases, centuries removed from the events they narrate, although it appears that these later authors used early written and oral sources that are now lost to us. At the same time, we must keep in mind that these authors primarily wrote history from a theological perspective and consequently clothed their stories in myth. That is, history for them was not a narrative of verifiable human events. It was, rather, the story of Israel's special relationship with its god, and in telling that story the Bible's authors employed a variety of literary devices, many of which they adapted to their needs from the literary traditions of their neighbors.

The first book of the Bible is known as *Genesis* (the beginning) and recounts the story of humanity's relationship with YHWH from Creation through the settlement of the Children of Israel in Egypt. Tradition ascribes its authorship to *Moses,* one of the most enigmatic and elusive figures in the Bible. Modern scholars divide on the question of whether or not there was a historical Moses who led the Israelites out of Egypt and passed on to them a set of laws that made them uniquely YHWH's people (source 13). Later Israelites did not doubt Moses' historicity, but this did not necessarily mean they believed Moses actually wrote or dictated Genesis. Rather, within the context of their culture, calling this book "Mosaic" meant they understood Moses to be the one who provided the initial and pervading spirit behind the work. In all likelihood, a number of different authors composed and reworked Genesis over the period from before 900 to after 721 B.C.E., but they might well have drawn on traditions that stretched back to the time of the Israelites' infiltration into Canaan.

The following selection recounts a popular Southwest Asian theme that we saw in Chapter 1: the Flood. As you read it, be aware not only of the striking similarities between it and the story told by Utnapishtim but of the even more significant differences. Remember that the author is making a religious statement.

QUESTIONS FOR ANALYSIS

1. Why does YHWH destroy all humanity except Noah and his family? How does YHWH's reasoning compare with the Mesopotamian gods' reason for wanting to destroy humans and Ea's decision to warn Utnapishtim?
2. Compare YHWH's treatment of Noah and his descendants following the Flood with the Mesopotamian gods' treatment of Utnapishtim after the waters had receded.
3. What do the Mesopotamian gods demand of humans? What does Noah's god demand?
4. From these several comparisons, what picture emerges of the god of the Israelites? In what ways is their god similar to the gods of Mesopotamia? In what ways does their god differ?
5. Consider the story of Noah's curse on Canaan. What has Ham done to deserve such anger, and why is it that his son suffers as a consequence? Do your answers tell us anything about Israelite social values and practices at this time? (Hint: Review *The Judgments of Hammurabi,* source 2).
6. How does the story of the curse on Ham have relevance to the Israelites' settlement in the land of Canaan? What does this suggest about the story's date of composition? How does this illustrate the Israelites' use of myth to explain and justify historical events?

The Lord saw that the wickedness of man was great in the Earth, and that every imagination of the thoughts of his heart was only evil continually. And the Lord was sorry that he had made man on the Earth, and it grieved him to his heart. So the Lord said, "I will blot out man whom I have created from the face of the ground, man and beast and creeping things and birds of the air, for I am sorry that I have made them." But Noah found favor in the eyes of the Lord. . . .

Noah was a righteous man, blameless in his generation; Noah walked with God. And Noah had three sons, Shem,[1] Ham, and Japheth.

Now the Earth was corrupt in God's sight, and the Earth was filled with violence. And God saw the Earth, and behold, it was corrupt; for all flesh had corrupted their way upon the Earth. And God said to Noah, "I have determined to make an end of all flesh; for the Earth is filled with violence through them; behold, I will destroy them with the Earth. Make yourself an ark of gopher wood; make rooms in the ark, and cover it inside and out with pitch. . . . For behold, I will bring a flood of waters upon the Earth, to destroy all flesh in which is the breath of life from under Heaven; everything that is on the Earth shall die. But I will establish my covenant with you; and you shall come into the ark, you, your sons, your wife, and your sons' wives with you. And of every living thing of all flesh, you shall bring two of every sort into the ark, to keep them alive with you; they shall be male and female. Of the birds according to their kinds, and of the animals according to their kinds, of every creeping thing of the ground according to its kind, two of every sort shall come in to you, to keep them alive. Also take with you every sort of food that is eaten, and store it up; and it shall serve as food for you and for them." Noah did this; he did all that God commanded him.

Then the Lord said to Noah, "Go into the ark, you and all your household, for I have seen that you are righteous before me in this generation. Take with you seven pairs of all clean animals,[2] the male and his mate; and a pair of the animals that are not clean, the male and his mate; and seven pairs of the birds of the air also, male and female, to keep their kind alive upon the face of all the Earth. For in seven days I will send rain upon the Earth forty days and forty nights; and every living thing that I have made will blot out from the face of the ground." And Noah did all that the Lord had commanded him.

Noah was six hundred years old when the flood of waters came upon the Earth. And Noah and his sons and his wife and his sons' wives with him went into the ark, to escape the waters of the flood. Of clean animals, and of animals that are not clean, and of birds, and of everything that creeps on the ground, two and two, male and female, went into the ark with Noah, as God had commanded Noah. And after seven days the waters of the flood came upon the Earth.

In the six hundredth year of Noah's life, in the second month, on the seventeenth day of the month, on that day all the fountains of the great deep burst forth, and the windows of the heavens were opened.[3] And rain fell upon the Earth forty days and forty nights. . . .

And the waters prevailed so mightily upon the Earth that all the high mountains under the whole Heaven were covered. . . . He blotted out every living thing that was upon the face of the ground, man and animals and creeping things and birds of the air; they were blotted out from the Earth. Only Noah was left, and those that were with him in the ark. And the waters prevailed upon the Earth a hundred and fifty days.

But God remembered Noah and all the beasts and all the cattle that were with him in the ark.

---

[1]Shem was the eldest of Noah's sons and the one from whom the Israelites claimed direct descent. The term *Semite* is derived from the name.

[2]According to the Mosaic Law, a ritually clean animal, such as a sheep, was one worthy of sacrifice to YHWH. An unclean animal, such as a predator or a scavenger, would never be offered in sacrifice.

[3]The view of the world shared by the peoples of Southwest Asia at this time was that the world's firmament, or land, was totally surrounded, above and below, by water. The water above was normally kept in place by a translucent crystalline sphere. Rain was the seepage of water through that sphere.

And God made a wind blow over the Earth, and the waters subsided; the fountains of the deep and the windows of the heavens were closed, the rain from the heavens was restrained, and the waters receded from the Earth continually. At the end of a hundred and fifty days the waters had abated; and in the seventh month, on the seventeenth day of the month, the ark came to rest upon the mountains of Ararat. And the waters continued to abate until the tenth month; in the tenth month, on the first day of the month, the tops of the mountains were seen.

At the end of forty days Noah opened the window of the ark which he had made, and sent forth a raven; and it went to and fro until the waters were dried up from the Earth. Then he sent forth a dove from him, to see if the waters had subsided from the face of the ground; but the dove found no place to set her foot, and she returned to him to the ark, for the waters were still on the face of the whole Earth. So he put forth his hand and took her and brought her into the ark with him. He waited another seven days, and again he sent forth the dove out of the ark; and the dove came back to him in the evening, and lo, in her mouth a freshly plucked olive leaf; so Noah knew that the waters had subsided from the Earth. Then he waited another seven days, and sent forth the dove; and she did not return to him any more.

In the six hundred and first year,[4] in the first month, the first day of the month, the waters were dried from off the Earth; and Noah removed the covering of the ark, and looked, and behold, the face of the ground was dry. . . . Then God said to Noah, "Go forth from the ark, you and your wife, and your sons and your sons' wives with you. Bring forth with you every living thing that is with you of all flesh — birds and animals and every creeping thing that creeps on the earth — that they may breed abundantly on the Earth, and be fruitful and multiply upon the Earth." So Noah went forth, and his sons and his wife and his sons' wives with him. And every beast, every creeping thing, and every bird, everything that moves upon the Earth, went forth by families out of the ark.

Then Noah built an altar to the Lord, and took of every clean animal and of every clean bird, and offered burnt offerings on the altar. And when the Lord smelled the pleasing odor, the Lord said in his heart, "I will never again curse the ground because of man, for the imagination of man's heart is evil from his youth; neither will I ever again destroy every living creature as I have done. While the Earth remains, seedtime and harvest, cold and heat, summer and winter, day and night, shall not cease."

And God blessed Noah and his sons, and said to them, "Be fruitful and multiply, and fill the Earth. The fear of you and the dread of you shall be upon every beast of the Earth, and upon every bird of the air, upon everything that creeps on the ground and all the fish of the sea; into your hand they are delivered. Every moving thing that lives shall be food for you; and as I gave you the green plants, I give you everything. Only you shall not eat flesh with its life, that is, its blood.[5] For your lifeblood I will surely require a reckoning; of every beast I will require it and of man; of every man's brother I will require the life of man. Whoever sheds the blood of man, by man shall his blood be shed; for God made man in his own image. And you, be fruitful and multiply, bring forth abundantly on the Earth and multiply in it."

Then God said to Noah and to his sons with him, "Behold, I establish my covenant with you and your descendants after you, and with every living creature that is with you, the birds, the cattle, and every beast of the earth with you, as many as came out of the ark. I establish my covenant with you, that never again shall all flesh be cut off by the waters of a flood, and never again shall there be a flood to destroy the Earth." And God said, "This is the sign of the covenant

---

[4]Of Noah's life.
[5]Raw meat or meat dripping with blood could not be consumed.

which I make between me and you and every living creature that is with you, for all future generations: I set my bow[6] in the cloud, and it shall be
a sign of the covenant between me and the Earth.
When I brink clouds over the Earth and the bow
is seen in the clouds, I will remember my covenant which is between me and you and every living creature of all flesh; and the waters shall
never again become a flood to destroy all flesh.
When the bow is in the clouds, I will look upon
it and remember the everlasting covenant between God and every living creature of all flesh
that is upon the Earth." God said to Noah, "This
is the sign of the covenant which I have established between me and all flesh that is upon the
Earth."

The sons of Noah who went forth from the ark
were Shem, Ham, and Japheth. Ham was the
father of Canaan. These three were the sons of
Noah; and from these the whole Earth was peo-
pled.

Noah was the first tiller of the soil. He planted
a vineyard; and he drank of the wine, and became
drunk, and lay uncovered in his tent. And Ham,

the father of Canaan, saw the nakedness of his
father, and told his two brothers outside. Then
Shem and Japheth took a garment, laid it upon
both their shoulders, and walked backward and
covered the nakedness of their father; their faces
were turned away, and they did not see their father's nakedness. When Noah awoke from his
wine and knew what his youngest son had done
to him, he said

"Cursed be Canaan;
a slave of slaves shall he be to
his brothers."[7]

He also said,

"Blessed by the Lord my God be Shem;
and let Canaan be his slave.
God enlarge Japheth,
and let him dwell in the tents of Shem;[8]
and let Canaan be his slave."

After the flood Noah lived three hundred and
fifty years. All the days of Noah were nine hundred and fifty years; and he died.

---

[6]A rainbow. Compare this with Ishtar's rainbow (source 1).
[7]According to Hebrew legend, Ham and his son Canaan
were the direct ancestors of the Canaanites, a Semitic people
whom the Israelites were dispossessing of their lands.
[8]Japheth, according to Israelite tradition, was the ancestor of

the Indo-European peoples of northern Syria and beyond,
such as the Hittites and Hurrians. From the Israelite perspective, the Israelites and the northern Indo-Europeans
were dividing up the land of Syria-Palestine between them.

Establishing a Covenant with a Chosen People
▼▼▼
13 ▼ *THE BOOK OF DEUTERONOMY*

The story of Noah tells of YHWH's post-Deluge covenant with all living creatures;
the story of the Israelites' *Exodus* (going out) from Egypt tells of their special
Covenant, or pact, with this god and their becoming a *Chosen People* with a new
identity.

Forerunners of the Israelites had probably entered Egypt in the time of the conquest of Lower Egypt, or the Delta region, by the Hyksos (rulers from foreign
lands), who came in from the deserts of western Asia around 1700 B.C.E. With the
overthrow of the Hyksos and the re-establishment of native Egyptian rule around
1570, significant numbers of these people were probably enslaved, as happened to
many Asian prisoners of war in Egypt at that time. That at least seems to be a likely scenario if we seek to fit the story told in the Bible's Book of Exodus with the

sketchy picture we have of Egyptian history during the Second Intermediate Period and the New Kingdom that followed.

At this point reconstruction of the next stage of Israelite history becomes even more problematic, due to the many, sometimes contradictory, layers of legend and folktale motifs that we find in the biblical story of their flight from Egypt. Yet several aspects of the story have the ring of validity and lead many historians to accept the basic historicity of the Exodus, even though most question many of the details of the story as narrated in the Bible. The fact that the Israelites trace their origins as a people to an age of bondage and oppression, rather than claiming kings and heroes as their progenitors, suggests that this less-than-glorious beginning was rooted in historical reality. Equally telling is the origin of Moses' name, which most likely derives from the Egyptian verb *msy* (born). This hint of Egyptian heritage lends a certain credence to his presumed historicity, even though there is no known record of Moses outside of the Bible. Assuming that the Israelites' oral traditions retained a valid core memory of their flight from Egypt and subsequent wanderings, we can say with hesitant confidence that a charismatic leader, whom history remembers as Moses, arose to lead a band of Semitic peoples out of Egypt and to the borders of Canaan, probably sometime around the reign of Rameses the Great (r. 1279–1213 B.C.E.). Further, and most important of all, in the process of their migration, Moses molded these disparate peoples into a single people and wedded them to his god YHWH. No longer a loose band of nomads, they were now the Israelites — descendants of the patriarchs Abraham, Isaac, and Jacob (also called Israel).

The story of this transformation is told in several books of the Bible. This selection comes from *Deuteronomy,* which was initially shaped during the reign of King Josiah of Jerusalem (r. 640–609 B.C.E.) and subsequently revised in the following century. Deuteronomy was composed at a time of religious reformation, when Josiah and several successors were attempting to abolish all forms of pagan worship in the kingdom, especially the practices of the Assyrians, who had conquered the northern kingdom of the Israelites. Although Deuteronomy, as we know it, is essentially a creation of the seventh and sixth centuries, there is good reason to conclude it is based on sources that date from the time of Moses.

The setting of our excerpt is the frontier of Canaan, which the Israelites have reached after forty years of wandering in the desert. Moses, realizing he will die before his people cross the Jordan River into the *Promised Land,* delivers a final message to them.

QUESTIONS FOR ANALYSIS

1. What is the Covenant between YHWH and the people of Israel? What does God promise and demand in return? What does YHWH threaten for those who break the covenant?
2. Consider YHWH's promises again. What does YHWH have to say about rewards after death? What do you infer from your answer?
3. Which elements of Moses' message would the religious reformers of Jerusalem wish to emphasize?

4. Compare the Ten Commandments with either the *Judgments of Hammurabi* or the Egyptian Negative Confession (sources 2 and 3). Which strike you as more significant, the similarities or the differences? What do you conclude from your answer?

And Moses summoned all Israel,[1] and said to them, "Hear, O Israel, the statutes and the ordinances which I speak in your hearing this day, and you shall learn them and be careful to do them. The Lord our God made a covenant with us in Horeb.[2] Not with our fathers did the Lord make this covenant, but with us, who are all of us here alive this day. The Lord spoke with you face to face at the mountain, out of the midst of the fire, while I stood between the Lord and you at that time, to declare to you the word of the Lord; for you were afraid because of the fire, and you did not go up into the mountain. He said:

"'I am the Lord your God, who brought you out of the land of Egypt, out of the house of bondage.

"'You shall have no other gods before me.

"'You shall not make for yourself a graven image, or any likeness of anything that is in Heaven above, or that is on the Earth beneath, or that is in the water under the Earth; you shall not bow down to them or serve them; for I the Lord your God am a jealous God, visiting the iniquity of the fathers upon the children to the third and fourth generation of those who hate me, but showing steadfast love to thousands of those who love me and keep my commandments.

"'You shall not take the name of the Lord your God in vain: for the Lord will not hold him guiltless who takes his name in vain.

"'Observe the sabbath day, to keep it holy, as the Lord your God commanded you. Six days you shall labor, and do all your work; but the seventh day is a sabbath to the Lord your God; in it you shall not do any work, you, or your son, or your daughter, or your manservant, or your maidservant, or your ox, or your ass, or any of your cattle, or the sojourner who is within your gates, that your manservant and your maidservant may rest as well as you. You shall remember that you were a servant in the land of Egypt, and the Lord your God brought you out thence with a mighty hand and an outstretched arm; therefore the Lord your God commanded you to keep the sabbath day.

"'Honor your father and your mother, as the Lord your God commanded you; that your days may be prolonged, and that it may go well with you, in the land which the Lord your God gives you.

"'You shall not kill.

"'Neither shall you commit adultery.

"'Neither shall you steal.

"'Neither shall you bear false witness against your neighbor.

"'Neither shall you covet your neighbor's wife; and you shall not desire your neighbor's house, his field, or his manservant, or his maidservant, his ox, or his ass, or anything that is your neighbor's.'

"These words the Lord spoke to all your assembly at the mountain out of the midst of the fire, the cloud, and the thick darkness, with a loud voice; and he added no more. And he wrote them upon two tables of stone, and gave them to me. . . .

"Now this is the commandment, the statutes and the ordinances which the Lord your God commanded me to teach you, that you may do them in the land to which you are going over, to possess it; that you may fear the Lord your God,

---

[1]They referred to themselves as *Israel* and also as the *Children of Israel* and the *Israelites* because they traced their lineage to Jacob, whose name God had changed to Israel (God rules). Jacob, the grandson of Abraham and the son of Isaac, had twelve sons, each of whom became the patriarch of one of the twelve tribes of the Children of Israel.

[2]Also known as *Mount Sinai*. Here Moses had received the Law from YHWH during the period of desert wandering.

you and your son and your son's son, by keeping all his statutes and his commandments, which I command you, all the days of your life; and that your days may be prolonged. Hear therefore, O Israel, and be careful to do them; that it may go well with you, and that you may multiply greatly, as the Lord, the God of your fathers, has promised you, in a land flowing with milk and honey.

"Hear, O Israel: The Lord our God is one Lord; and you shall love the Lord your God with all your heart, and with all your soul, and with all your might. And these words which I command you this day shall be upon your heart; and you shall teach them diligently to your children, and shall talk of them when you sit in your house, and when you walk by the way, and when you lie down, and when you rise. And you shall bind them as a sign upon your hand, and they shall be as frontlets between your eyes. And you shall write them on the doorposts of your house and on your gates.

"And when the Lord your God brings you into the land which he swore to your fathers, to Abraham, to Isaac, and to Jacob, to give you, with great and goodly cities, which you did not build, and houses full of all good things, which you did not fill, and cisterns hewn out, which you did not hew, and vineyards and olive trees, which you did not plant, and when you eat and are full, then take heed lest you forget the Lord, who brought you out of the land of Egypt, out of the house of bondage. You shall fear the Lord your God; you shall serve him, and swear by his name. You shall not go after other gods, of the gods of the peoples who are round about you; for the Lord your God in the midst of you is a jealous God; lest the anger of the Lord your God be kindled against you, and he destroy you from off the face of the Earth. . . .

"When the Lord your God brings you into the land which you are entering to take possession of it, and clears away many nations before you . . . seven nations greater and mightier than yourselves, and when the Lord your God gives them over to you, and you defeat them; then you must utterly destroy them; you shall make no covenant with them, and show no mercy to them. You shall not make marriages with them, giving your daughters to their sons or taking their daughters for your sons. For they would turn away your sons from following me, to serve other gods; then the anger of the Lord would be kindled against you, and he would destroy you quickly. But thus shall you deal with them: you shall break down their altars, and dash in pieces their pillars, and hew down their Asherim,[3] and burn their graven images with fire.

"For you are a people holy to the Lord your God; the Lord your God has chosen you to be a people for his own possession, out of all the peoples that are on the face of the Earth. It was not because you were more in number than any other people that the Lord set his love upon you and chose you, for you were the fewest of all peoples; but it is because the Lord loves you, and is keeping the oath which he swore to your fathers, that the Lord has brought you out with a mighty hand, and redeemed you from the house of bondage, from the hand of Pharaoh king of Egypt. Know therefore that the Lord your God is God, the faithful God who keeps covenant and steadfast love with those who love him and keep his commandments, to a thousand generations, and repays those who hate him, by destroying them; he will not be slack with him who hates him. . . . You shall therefore be careful to do the commandments, and the statutes, and the ordinances, which I command you this day.

"And because you hearken to these ordinances, and keep and do them, the Lord your God will keep with you the covenant and the steadfast love which he swore to your fathers to keep; he will

---

[3]Sacred poles raised to Astarte (or Asherah), the Canaanite counterpart of Ishtar, the Mesopotamian goddess of fertility and love (source 1).

love you, bless you, and multiply you; he will also bless the fruit of your body and the fruit of your ground, your grain and your wine and your oil, the increase of your cattle and the young of your flock, in the land which he swore to your fathers to give you. You shall be blessed above all peoples; there shall not be male or female barren among you, or among your cattle. And the Lord will take away from you all sickness; and none of the evil diseases of Egypt, which you knew, will he inflict upon you, but he will lay them upon all who hate you. And you shall destroy all the peoples that the Lord your God will give over to you, your eye shall not pity them; neither shall you serve their gods, for that would be a snare to you."

Chapter 3

▼▼▼

Transcendental Reality

Developing the Spiritual Traditions
of India and Southwest Asia:
800–200 B.C.E.

Between about 800 and 200 B.C.E. profound changes in thought, belief, social organization, and government took place in China, India, Southwest Asia, and *Hellas* (the land of the Greeks). So pivotal were these changes, some historians favor calling this era the *Axial Age*. During these six centuries the Chinese, Indians, Southwest Asians, and *Hellenes* (the name by which the Greeks of classical antiquity identified themselves) formulated distinctive traditions and institutions that became essential features of their civilizations. In essence, their classical cultures took shape.

These developments became especially pronounced during the sixth century B.C.E. and following. It is no coincidence that Confucius, the Buddha, several authors of the Upanishads, Second Isaiah, and the earliest Greek scientists and philosophers all lived during or around the sixth century. Moreover, the Hindu caste system was taking early shape and the Persian Empire and the Hellenic city-states were thriving by the end of this century.

What accounts for these parallel developments? The *Age of Iron,* which began after about 1000 B.C.E., witnessed the development of considerably larger, more complex, and more competitive political and economic entities that challenged older social systems and values. This disruption of life was unsettling and led to the search for new answers to some fundamental questions: What is the meaning of life? How does one relate to the spiritual world? To the natural world? To other humans? What is the ideal government?

The historical frameworks of the various civilizations posing such questions often differed radically. Hence, their respective answers varied significantly. In one way, however, they displayed a striking similarity. Each emerging tradition challenged the myth-making notion that humankind is held hostage by a capricious, god-infested nature.

Indian thinkers did this by denying that the tangible world of observable nature is real in any meaningful sense and seeking, instead, reality in the transcendental world of the spirit. China witnessed several other approaches. One school of thought — *Daoism* — sought mystical union with nature; two other schools — *Confucianism* and *Legalism* — sought to control nature by imposing human discipline upon it. Whereas Confucians saw the solution in a moral order of virtuous behavior, Legalists found it in the order of strict and dispassionately applied human law. In Southwest Asia freedom from myth-laden nature was partially achieved through worship of and obedience to a totally spiritual yet personal God of the universe, who stood completely outside nature yet imposed moral order upon it. In Hellas the attempt to master nature took the form of rational philosophy and science. Here certain thinkers sought to control nature by studying it objectively, thereby discovering laws that would enable humans to define more surely their place in the universe. In this manner, four major world traditions emerged: Indian transcendental spirituality; China's distinctive blend of practical worldliness with a mystical appreciation of nature; Southwest Asia's preoccupation with ethical monotheism; and Greek rationalism, with its special focus on the human condition.

In this chapter we shall explore the spiritual and religious traditions that took shape in India and Southwest Asia. Religion has played a central role in human history, especially in the region of southern Asia that stretches from the eastern coast of the Mediterranean Sea to the Bay of Bengal. This vast area, which encompasses all of Southwest Asia and the whole Indian subcontinent, has been the birthplace of most of the world's major religions. Time and again we shall return to this region of the world to marvel at its spiritual fertility. For the present we focus on the emergence of two major spiritual traditions. The first was a world- and self-denying transcendentalism that took shape in India. Its most classic expressions were *Brahminical Hinduism* and *Buddhism*. Both sprang out of a common Indian notion that true peace and bliss do not lie in the momentary pleasures that come from satisfying the illusory desires of this world. Rather, lasting tranquility comes only with the discovery of Immutable Reality through a radical transformation of one's self. The second major religious tradition of southern Asia was the concept of a single, sole God of the universe. This God is transcendental, existing totally outside of time, space, and matter, all of which are this deity's creations. But this Universal God is also a personal, caring deity who directs human history and uses humans as historical agents. Moreover, this God demands a high degree of moral behavior from those called to divine service because by directing human history, God has sanctified it. This notion, which we term *ethical monotheism,* found its origins in Persia's *Zoroastrianism* and Israel's *Judaism.*

▼▼▼

The Emergence of Brahminical Hinduism

Religion for the early Aryans of India, as was also true for the early Greeks and Persians, centered on the sacrifice by fire of animals, especially horses and cattle. Chanting ritual hymns, which were later preserved in the four great Vedic collections, Aryan priests, known as *Brahmins,* offered these sacrifices in the hope of winning the favor of the gods, especially Indra (source 10). As important as the Brahmins were, however, early Aryan society appears to have been led by its warriors. Yet by the time of the composition of the *Rig Veda's* "Hymn to Purusha," the Brahmins, who composed and recited the hymn, claimed a position of primacy over the other three classes: *Rajanyas* or *Kshatriyas* (rulers and warriors); *Vaisyas* (workers); and *Sudras* (slaves and servants). This claim did not go uncontested by the Kshatriyas, and for many centuries both classes jockeyed for leadership. In the end the Brahmins won out, and their victory was manifested in a uniquely Indian religious-social system known as *caste.*

The Sanskrit term for caste is *varna,* which means "color," and might derive from the Aryans' early attempt to distinguish themselves from the darker-skinned natives of the subcontinent. It seems likely that initially the Aryans relegated these much-despised *Dasas* (slaves) to the fourth and lowest class — the Sudras — although over time many members of the native upper classes were incorporated into the higher strata of the Indo-Aryan World. Whatever its origins, sometime in the course of the so-called Axial Age, varna came to mean the four immutable groups of humanity that inhabited the *Hindu* (Indian) World, and at the top of this hierarchy stood the Brahmins. The four traditional Indo-Aryan classes were now castes, and strict rules codified each one. Castes became hereditary and permanent, with few exceptions, and they defined the most intimate aspects of each member's life. What was more important, caste defined one's place in the painful cycle of rebirth (*samsara*) as each soul journeyed from incarnation to incarnation in search of release (*moksha*) and return to the World Soul (*Brahman*). Needless to say, male Brahmins stood at the doorstep of release because of the merits of their previous lives that had brought them this far. With the evolution of caste, which in itself is based on the belief that the tangible world is a shadow of the true world of the spirit, *Brahminical Hinduism* had arrived, at least in its early stages of evolution.

On one level Hinduism can be defined as the entire body of Indian religious beliefs and ways of life that are centered on a caste system in which Brahmins hold the most exalted position. Yet on a more profound level Hinduism defies all attempts at simple definition. In fact, it is wrong to think of it, either today or several thousand years ago, as a single set of beliefs and practices. To the contrary, it is and always has been a fluid mass of religious and social expressions. It encompasses archaic folk rituals and the most abstract and speculative thought on the nature of Divine Reality. Although Brahmins constitute its priestly caste, historically its great *gurus,* or religious teachers, have come from all castes and walks of life. It is both polytheistic and monotheistic. It has thousands of gods and goddesses, but it also focuses on Brahman, the True One — limitless Divine Reality. One deity can have countless manifestations, but all the deities are manifestations of the One. Because Divine Reality is without bounds, Hindu religious expression is simultaneously earthy and metaphysical, and both erotic sexuality and extreme asceticism are equally valid religious traditions. More than a single religion, it is a family of connected religions that encompasses the living faiths of all the diverse peoples of India who call themselves Hindu, or Indian. Indeed, Hindus can choose from an apparently endless variety of beliefs and modes of worship because one of the key religious insights of Hinduism is that *there are an infinite number of paths to and manifestations of the limitless One.* Consequently, Hindus do not believe that the fullness of religious truth can be summed up in a neat package of doctrinal statements, nor do they believe that religion consists of a clear-cut struggle of truth versus error, good versus evil. The notion that a thing either is or is not, but cannot be both, has no place in a Hindu world where countless apparent contradictions exist comfortably alongside one another.

The Hindu Search for Divine Reality
▼▼▼

14 ▼ *THE UPANISHADS*

Despite the growing importance of the Brahmins, between roughly 700 and 500 B.C.E., a number of religious revolutionaries in the region of northeast India's Ganges Plain, the new demographic and cultural center of the subcontinent, created a form of spiritual literature known as the *Upanishads.*

Upanishad means "sitting down in front [of a teacher]," and these texts take the form of dialogues between teachers and pupils who seek to go beyond the Vedas in their search for ultimate wisdom. Many of the authors were probably Brahmins, but it seems clear that just as many, if not more, were Kshatriyas, which reflects not only a continuing struggle for supremacy between the two castes but also a discontentment by many Brahmins, as well as Kshatriyas, with what they perceived to be the empty formalism of Brahminical rituals.

Without rejecting the ancient Vedas and Brahminical sacrifices or the far-more-recent and still-evolving caste system, the Upanishadic teachers took certain concepts that were implied in the later Vedic hymns, such as the "Hymn to Purusha" (source 10), and articulated a vision of an all-inclusive Being, or Ultimate Reality, called *Brahman.* More than that, they articulated a way by which anyone, regardless of caste, could attain Brahman.

As we might expect, there is a good deal of contradiction among the 108 extant Upanishadic texts, yet a fundamental message binds them: Not only is there a Universal Soul, or Brahman, but the innermost essence of a person, the *atman,* or spiritual self, is one with Brahman, the True Self. Humans, therefore, are not outside Divine Reality; they are part of it. Those who wish to throw off the painful bonds of rebirth and earthly nonreality must reach that divinity within themselves.

Our first selection, which comes from the early and especially revered *Chandogya Upanishad,* presents two analogies to explain this theological message. Here we meet the conceited youth Svetaketu, who thinks that he has mastered all that he needs to know in order to win release from the shackles of life's cycle of suffering by virtue of his twelve-year apprenticeship with Brahmin priests, who have taught him all the sacred rituals. His father, however, teaches him an additional lesson: Reality transcends the world of tangible phenomena and yet is attainable. The second excerpt, taken from the later but equally important *Brihadaranyaka Upanishad,* deals with the issue of how that spark of Brahman, the Self, which is contained within each mortal body, migrates from one body to another until it finally achieves release and rejoins the One. Here we see an early enunciation of what are becoming two essential elements of Hindu religious thought: reincarnation and the law of *karma,* or the fruits of one's actions (see also source 15). The third selection, also from the *Brihadaranyaka,* describes the state of consciousness of a person who is on the verge of attaining release from the cycle of rebirth and union with Brahman.

QUESTIONS FOR ANALYSIS

1. What does the father mean when he states, "You, Svetaketu, are it"?
2. What is the law of karma?
3. Why are souls reincarnated, and how might one advance up the ladder of caste?
4. How does one end the cycle of rebirth?
5. How important or real is this world to the soul that is returning to Brahman?
6. Why do even good and evil cease to have meaning to the soul that has found Brahman?
7. Consider the closing lines of the *Brihadaranyaka Upanishad.* What hope does this text hold out to persons of the lowest castes and even to casteless *Untouchables?*
8. Is the Upanishadic vision of Brahman a logical development from the message of the "Hymn to Purusha"? If so, how?

THE CHANDOGYA UPANISHAD

There lived once Svetaketu. . . . To him his father Uddalaka . . . said: "Svetaketu, go to school; for no one belonging to our race, dear son, who, not having studied, is, as it were, a Brahmin[1] by birth only."

Having begun his apprenticeship when he was twelve years of age, Svetaketu returned to his father, when he was twenty-four, having then studied all the Vedas, — conceited, considering himself well-read, and stern.

His father said to him: "Svetaketu, as you are so conceited, considering yourself so well-read, and so stern, my dear, have you ever asked for that instruction by which we hear what cannot be heard, by which we perceive what cannot be perceived, by which we know what cannot be known?"

"What is that instruction, Sir?" he asked. . . .

"Fetch me . . . a fruit of the Nyagrodha tree."

"Here is one, Sir."

"Break it."

"It is broken, Sir."

"What do you see there?"

"These seeds, almost infinitesimal."

"Break one of them."

"It is broken, Sir."

"What do you see there?"

"Not anything, Sir."

The father said: "My son, that subtle essence which you do not perceive there, of that very essence this great Nyagrodha tree exists.

"Believe it, my son. That which is the subtle essence, in it all that exists has its self. It is the True. It is the Self, and you, . . . Svetaketu, are it."

"Please, Sir, inform me still more," said the son.

"Be it so, my child," the father replied.

"Place this salt in water, and then wait on me in the morning."

The son did as he was commanded.

The father said to him: "Bring me the salt, which you placed in the water last night."

The son having looked for it, found it not, for, of course, it was melted.

The father said: "Taste it from the surface of the water. How is it?"

The son replied: "It is salt."

"Taste it from the middle. How is it?"

The son replied: "It is salt."

"Taste it from the bottom. How is it?"

The son replied: "It is salt."

The father said: "Throw it away and then wait on me."

He did so; but the salt exists forever.[2]

Then the father said: "Here also, in this body,[3] . . . you do not perceive the True, my son; but there indeed it is.

"That which is the subtle essence,[4] in it all that exists has its self. It is the True. It is the Self, and you, Svetaketu, are it."

THE BRIHADARANYAKA UPANISHAD

"And when the body grows weak through old age, or becomes weak through illness, at that time that person, after separating himself from his members, as a mango, or fig, or pippala-fruit is separated from the stalk,[5] hastens back again as he came, to the place from which he started, to new life. . . .

"Then both his knowledge and his work take hold of him[6] and his acquaintance with former things.[7]

"And as a caterpillar, after having reached the end of a blade of grass, and after having made an-

---

[1]Note that *Brahmin* is the male gender variation of the neuter noun *Brahman*.
[2]The salt, although invisible, remains forever in the water.
[3]The human body.
[4]The soul, or atman.
[5]The image is of a fruit that carries the seed of new life, even as it decays.

[6]The law of karma, which is defined more fully later in this source.
[7]Acquaintance with things in a former life explains the peculiar talents and deficiencies evident in a child.

other approach to another blade, draws itself together towards it, thus does this Self, after having thrown off this body and dispelled all ignorance, and after making another approach to another body, draw himself together towards it.

"And as a goldsmith, taking a piece of gold, turns it into another, newer and more beautiful shape, so does this Self, after having thrown off this body and dispelled all ignorance, make unto himself another, newer and more beautiful shape. . . .

"Now as a man is like this or like that, according as he acts and according as he behaves, so will he be: — a man of good acts will become good, a man of bad acts, bad. He becomes pure by pure deeds, bad by bad deeds.

"And here they say that a person consists of desires. And as is his desire, so is his will; and as is his will, so is his deed; and whatever deed he does, that he will reap.

"And here there is this verse: 'To whatever object a man's own mind is attached, to that he goes strenuously together with his deed; and having obtained the consequences of whatever deed he does here on Earth, he returns again from that world . . . to this world of action.'[8]

"So much for the man who desires. But as to the man who does not desire, who, not desiring, freed from desires, is satisfied in his desires, or desires the Self only, his vital spirits do not depart elsewhere, — being Brahman, he goes to Brahman.[9]

"On this there is this verse: 'When all desires which once entered his heart are undone, then does the mortal become immortal, then he obtains Brahman.'"

▼▼▼

"Now as a man, when embraced by a beloved wife, knows nothing that is without, nothing that is within, thus this person, when embraced by the intelligent Self, knows nothing that is without, nothing that is within. This indeed is his true form, in which his wishes are fulfilled, in which the Self only is his wish, in which no wish is left, — free from any sorrow.

"Then a father is not a father, a mother not a mother, the worlds not worlds, the gods not gods, the Vedas not Vedas. Then a thief is not a thief, a murderer not a murderer, a Kandala not a Kandala,[10] a Sramana not a Sramana,[11] a Tapasa not a Tapasa.[12] He is not followed by good, not followed by evil, for he has then overcome all the sorrows of the heart."

---

[8]The law of karma, which means "action."

[9]By discovering and becoming one with the spark of Brahman within, the person ends the painful cycle of samsara.

[10]*Kandalas* were the lowest of all casteless persons. Beneath the lowly Sudra stood certain casteless persons whose inherited occupations, or subcastes *(jatis),* rendered them "un-

clean." Hence, they were Untouchables. (See Chapter 5, source 35 for additional material dealing with the Kandalas and other subcastes.)

[11]A holy beggar.

[12]A person performing penance

Dharma: The Imperative of Caste Law
▼▼▼
15 ▼ *THE BHAGAVAD GITA*

The Upanishadic texts offer one *yoga* (pathway of discipline) to total detachment from this world and, therefore, release: the *Yoga of Knowledge,* by which the atman acquires the sure knowledge of its own divinity. The *Bhagavad Gita (Song of the Blessed Lord),* Hinduism's most beloved sacred text, offers several others, of which we shall, at this time, consider only one: the *Yoga of Action,* by which one detaches oneself from this world through selfless devotion to caste duties (see Chapter 6, sources 41 and 42, for the *Yoga of Devotion*).

The *Gita* appears as an interjected episode in the *Mahabharata (The Great Deeds of the Bharata Clan),* the world's longest epic poem. Like the Homeric Greek epics, the *Mahabharata* is ascribed to a single legendary poet, Vyasa. In fact, however, it was the work of many authors over an extensive period of time, from perhaps 500 B.C.E. to possibly 400 C.E. Also like the Homeric epics, the *Mahabharata* deals on one level with the clash of armies and the combat of individual heroes, and simultaneously on a higher plane it expounds theological and philosophical insights. Among all of its spiritual passages, the *Bhagavad Gita* is the most profound.

Younger than most of the epic into which it was placed, the *Gita*'s date of final composition is uncertain; scholars fix it anywhere between 300 B.C.E. and 300 C.E. Whatever its date, Hindu commentators have consistently considered the song to be the last and greatest of the Upanishadic texts, for they see it as the crystallization of all that was expressed and implied in the Upanishadic tradition.

The core question addressed in the *Bhagavad Gita* is how a person can become one with Brahman while still functioning in this world. Answers to that primary quest of Hindu theology come from Lord *Krishna,* the incarnation of the god *Vishnu,* the Divine Preserver. In this particular corporeal form, or *avatara,* Krishna/Vishnu serves as charioteer to the warrior-hero *Arjuna.* Arjuna, son of a mortal mother and the god Indra, is a fearless warrior, but he shrinks from entering battle because his foes are his kinsmen. Overcome by a sense of the futility of this fratricidal war and overwhelmed by compassion, he wants no part in creating more suffering. The hero-god Krishna then proceeds to resolve Arjuna's quandary by explaining to him the moral imperative of caste-duty, or *dharma.*

QUESTIONS FOR ANALYSIS

1. Why should Arjuna not grieve for those whom he might kill?
2. Why should one perform one's caste-duty in a totally disinterested fashion?
3. According to Krishna, what constitutes sin? What is evil?
4. What hope, if any, does this theological message hold out to the lowest elements of Hindu society?
5. Is Krishna's message the same as that of the Upanishads? If so, how?

The deity said, you have grieved for those who deserve no grief. . . . Learned men grieve not for the living nor the dead. Never did I not exist, nor you, nor these rulers of men; nor will any one of us ever hereafter cease to be. As in this body, infancy and youth and old age come to the embodied self, so does the acquisition of another body; a sensible man is not deceived about that. The contacts of the senses, O son of Kunti![1] which pro-

duce cold and heat, pleasure and pain, are not permanent, they are ever coming and going. Bear them, O descendant of Bharata![2] For, O chief of men! that sensible man whom they (pain and pleasure being alike to him) afflict not, he merits immortality. There is no existence for that which is unreal; there is no non-existence for that which is real. And the correct conclusion about both is perceived by those who perceive the truth. Know

---

[1]The secondary name of Arjuna's mother (see note 4).
[2]King Bharata was the ancestor from whom Arjuna and his foes were descended.

that to be indestructible which pervades all this. . . . He who thinks it[3] to be the killer and he who thinks it to be killed, both know nothing. It kills not, is not killed. It is not born, nor does it ever die, nor, having existed, does it exist no more. Unborn, everlasting, unchangeable, and primeval, it is not killed when the body is killed. O son of Pritha![4] how can that man who knows it thus to be indestructible, everlasting, unborn, and inexhaustible, how and whom can he kill, whom can he cause to be killed? As a man, casting off old clothes, puts on others and new ones, so the embodied self casting off old bodies, goes to others and new ones. . . . It is everlasting, all-pervading, stable, firm, and eternal. It is said to be unperceived, to be unthinkable, to be unchangeable. Therefore knowing it to be such, you ought not to grieve. But even if you think that it is constantly born, and constantly dies, still, O you of mighty arms! you ought not to grieve thus. For to one that is born, death is certain; and to one that dies, birth is certain. , , , This embodied self, O descendant of Bharata! within every one's body is ever indestructible. Therefore you ought not to grieve for any being. Having regard to your own duty also, you ought not to falter, for there is nothing better for a Kshatriya than a righteous battle. Happy those Kshatriyas, O son of Pritha! who can find such a battle . . . an open door to Heaven! But if you will not fight this righteous battle, then you will have abandoned your own duty and your fame, and you will incur sin. . . . Your business is with action alone; not by any means with fruit. Let not the fruit of action be your motive to action. Let not your attachment be fixed on inaction. Having recourse to devotion . . . perform actions, casting off all attachment, and being equable in success or ill-success; such equability is called devotion. . . . The wise who

have obtained devotion cast off the fruit of action,[5] and released from the shackles of repeated births, repair to that seat where there is no unhappiness. . . . The man who, casting off all desires, lives free from attachments, who is free from egoism, and from the feeling that this or that is mine, obtains tranquility. This, O son of Pritha! is the Brahmic state; attaining to this, one is never deluded; and remaining in it in one's last moments, one attains the Brahmic bliss.[6] . . .

I have passed through many births, O Arjuna! and you also. I know them all, but you, O terror of your foes! do not know them. Even though I am unborn and inexhaustible in my essence, even though I am lord of all beings, still I am born by means of my delusive power. Whensoever, O descendant of Bharata! piety languishes, and impiety is in the ascendant, I create myself. I am born age after age, for the protection of the good, for the destruction of evil-doers, and the establishment of piety. . . . The fourfold division of castes was created by me according to the appointment of qualities and duties. . . . The duties of Brahmins, Kshatriyas, and Vaisyas, and of Sudras, too, O terror of your foes! are distinguished according to the qualities born of nature.[7] Tranquility, restraint of the senses, penance, purity, forgiveness, straightforwardness, also knowledge, experience, and belief in a future world, this is the natural duty of Brahmins. Valor, glory, courage, dexterity, not slinking away from battle, gifts, exercise of lordly power, this is the natural duty of Kshatriyas. Agriculture, tending cattle, trade, this is the natural duty of Vaisyas. And the natural duty of Sudras, too, consists in service. Every man intent on his own respective duties obtains perfection. Listen, now, how one intent on one's own duty obtains perfection. Worshiping, by the performance of his own duty, him from whom all

---

[3]The atman, or individual soul, and Brahman, which are one and the same (see source 14).

[4]The primary name of Arjuna's mother (see note 1).

[5]They do not concern themselves with the earthly consequences of their actions and develop no attachments to the rewards of this world (fame, wealth, family) that might result from those actions.

[6]*Brahma-nirvana,* or merging with Brahman and release

(moksha) from the cycle of rebirth. It is a state of simultaneous being and nonbeing.

[7]Each caste consists of persons born to that station by virtue of their nature. Each person's karma has made that person's nature suitable for a particular caste and only that caste. Brahmins teach and offer sacrifices; Kshatriyas rule and fight; Vaisyas work; and Sudras serve (see source 10, and Chapter 5, source 35).

things proceed, and by whom all this is permeated, a man obtains perfection. One's duty, though defective, is better than another's duty well performed. Performing the duty prescribed by nature, one does not incur sin. O son of Kunti! one should not abandon a natural duty though tainted with evil; for all actions are enveloped by evil, as fire by smoke. One who is self-restrained, whose understanding is unattached everywhere, from whom affections have departed, obtains the supreme perfection of freedom from action by renunciation. Learn from me, only in brief, O son of Kunti! how one who has obtained perfection attains the Brahman, which is the highest culmination of knowledge. A man possessed of a pure understanding, controlling his self by courage, discarding sound and other objects of sense, casting off affection and aversion; who frequents clean places, who eats little, whose speech, body, and mind are restrained, who is always intent on meditation and mental abstraction, and has recourse to unconcern, who abandoning egoism, stubbornness, arrogance, desire, anger, and all belongings, has no thought that this or that is mine, and who is tranquil, becomes fit for assimilation with the Brahman.

▼▼▼

A Challenge to Caste: The Teachings of the Buddha

By 600 B.C.E. the central spiritual question in Indian society was how to find liberation from karma and the painful cycle of rebirth. As we have seen, the Upanishadic teachers and the *Bhagavad Gita* offered different but complementary answers, and both sources of wisdom held out the possibility that anyone, regardless of caste, could find release in the present life by achieving a state of absolute selflessness. Regardless of these proffered avenues, the growing entrenchment of castes was not retarded, and about 300 B.C.E. the caste system was pretty well established throughout most of Indian society. Moreover, there was a widespread consensus — at least among the Brahminical teachers — that conformity to one's dharma, no matter how lacking in perfect selflessness it might be, and slow karmic progress up the chain of caste through a series of reincarnations were the dual keys to release from the bonds of matter. In opposition to this notion, however, some spiritual teachers offered their followers avenues to liberation that challenged the entire caste system.

Even as the Brahmin class was in the process of becoming the dominant Hindu caste and defining what would become mainstream Hinduism, several teachers emerged from the Kshatriya class to offer alternatives to the caste system. The most significant of these was *Siddhartha Gautama,* better known as the *Buddha* (the Enlightened One).

The Buddha and his doctrine are understandable only within the context of a Hindu cosmology. Although he formulated a spiritual philosophy that denied certain concepts basic to what was emerging as classical Brahminical Hinduism, the questions he asked and the answers he offered were predicated upon the world-denying assumptions that underlie all Indian spiritual thought.

Although grounded in Hindu spirituality, *Buddhism* eventually expanded well beyond the cultural boundaries of Hinduism and traveled far beyond the frontiers of India. By the first century C.E. the Buddha's teachings had already been transformed into a family of related religious sects, many of which worshiped the Buddha himself as a divine being (see Chapter 6). For well over 2,000 years, Buddhism in its various forms has profoundly shaped the lives of countless devotees throughout South and East Asia and remains a vital religious force today.

The Path to Enlightenment
▼▼▼

16 ▼ *The Buddha,*
SETTING IN MOTION THE
WHEEL OF THE LAW

Most details of the Buddha's life are uncertain. Unanimous tradition places Siddhartha Gautama's birth into a princely family residing in the Himalayan foothills of Nepal, but the written sources for his life and teachings, all of which were composed long after his time, differ as to his birth and death dates; the three strongest traditions are 624–544, 563–483, and 448–368 B.C.E. Significantly, all three agree that he lived to the age of eighty. Recent scholarship, based on archaeological evidence, has led to a growing consensus that the dates ca. 480–400 make the most sense.

Tradition holds that the prince led a sheltered court life up to age twenty-nine, when he viewed evidence of human aging, suffering, and death for the first time. Shrinking in horror at these manifestations of misery, he fled his comfortable life, his wife, and his newborn son and became an *ascetic* (someone who denies the pleasures of the body in order to liberate the soul), determined to find a remedy for suffering. *Mendicant* (begging) ascetics, known as *Shramanas,* who rejected the religious traditions of the Vedas and the primacy of the Brahmins, were already a major religious force in India. Siddhartha Gautama, however, found that the ascetic life offered him no liberating insight as to how one might escape the sorrows of mortal existence. In an act of desperation, he sat under a sacred *pipal tree* (see source 8, seal 3), vowing to meditate until he achieved his goal. Despite the attempts of the armies of *Mara,* "the Evil One," the divine Lord of the Realm of Desire, to deflect Siddhartha from his course, he persisted. Shortly after his victory over Mara's temptations, he achieved his goal. He was now the Buddha, the Enlightened One.

Legend tells us that seven weeks later he proceeded to share the path to Enlightenment, which he termed the *Middle Path,* by preaching a sermon in a deer park at Sarnath in northeastern India to five ascetics, former companions and students who had abandoned him as a false teacher when he had renounced asceticism as the path to Enlightenment. Through the aura of compassion that he now radiated, as well as by the words of his first sermon, the Buddha converted these five into his first disciples. Buddhists refer to that initial sermon as "Setting in Motion the Wheel of the Law," which means that the Buddha had embarked on a journey (turning the wheel) on behalf of the Law of Righteousness (Dharma). Now at age thirty-five, he had forty-five years ahead of him to preach his doctrine.

Our text is a reconstruction of that sermon as preserved in a body of Buddhist literature known as the *Pali Canon,* which contains the most authentic texts relating to the Buddha and his doctrine known to exist today. Assembled as an authoritative collection, or canon, of orally transmitted remembrances during the period between the Buddha's death and the late third century B.C.E., the texts were probably not written down in the form in which we have them until the late first century B.C.E. Composed in Pali, a language that is close to classical Sanskrit, they first appeared on the island of Ceylon (modern Sri Lanka) and traveled from there to Burma and Thailand, where they became the core canonical books of the branch of Buddhism known as *Theravada* (see Chapter 6). Each text is located in one of three groupings, or "baskets," a designation whose origin traces back to a time when the palm-leaf manuscripts of the texts were kept in three separate baskets. For this reason the entire collection is known as the *Tipitaka* (also spelled *Tripitaka*), or *Three Baskets*. Our source comes from *The Discipline Basket,* which consists of a number of books that concern the discipline, or regimented life, of Buddhist monks and nuns.

QUESTIONS FOR ANALYSIS

1. What is the Middle Path? Why is it, according to the Buddha, the proper path to Enlightenment?
2. What are the *Four Noble Truths,* and how does one's total comprehension and acceptance of them lead to *Nirvana,* or escape from the cycle of suffering?
3. Buddhists call the Law taught by the Buddha *Dharma*. How does Buddhist Dharma differ from that of Brahminical Hinduism?

And the Blessed One thus addressed the five Bhikkhus.[1] "There are two extremes, O Bhikkhus, which he who has given up the world ought to avoid. What are these two extremes? A life given to pleasures, devoted to pleasures and lusts: this is degrading, sensual, vulgar, ignoble, and profitless; and a life given to mortifications: this is painful, ignoble, and profitless. By avoiding these two extremes, O Bhikkhus, the Tathagata[2] has gained the knowledge of the Middle Path which leads to insight, which leads to wisdom, which conduces to calm, to knowledge, to the Sambodhi,[3] to Nirvana.[4]

"Which, O Bhikkhus, is this Middle Path the knowledge of which the Tathagata has gained, which leads to insight, which leads to wisdom, which conduces to calm, to knowledge, to the Sambodhi, to Nirvana? It is the Holy Eightfold Path, namely, Right Belief,[5] Right Aspiration,[6] Right Speech,[7] Right Conduct,[8] Right Means of

[1]Ascetics. The term later was used to refer to Buddhism's mendicant monks.
[2]One of the Buddha's titles. Literally it means "one who has gone thus," which is a way of saying "He who has arrived at the Truth."
[3]Total Enlightenment.
[4]The state of release from the limitations of existence and rebirth. The word means literally "extinction," in the sense that one has extinguished all worldly desires. In essence, it is Buddhahood. Like the Hindu Brahma-nirvana, Buddhist Nirvana is a state of absolute being and nonbeing.

[5]Understanding the truth about the universality of suffering, knowing the path leading to its extinction, and realizing it is attainable.
[6]Preparing for the journey to Enlightenment by freeing one's mind of ill will, sensuous desire, and cruelty.
[7]Abstaining from lying, harsh language, and gossip.
[8]Acting honestly by avoiding killing, stealing, and unlawful sexual intercourse.

Livelihood,[9] Right Endeavor,[10] Right Memory,[11] Right Meditation.[12] This, O Bhikkhus, is the Middle Path the knowledge of which the Tathagata has gained, which leads to insight, which leads to wisdom, which conduces to calm, to knowledge, to the Sambodhi, to Nirvana.

"This, O Bhikkhus, is the Noble Truth of Suffering: Birth is suffering; decay is suffering; illness is suffering; death is suffering. Presence of objects we hate, is suffering; Separation from objects we love, is suffering; not to obtain what we desire, is suffering. Briefly, . . . clinging to existence is suffering.

"This, O Bhikkhus, is the Noble Truth of the Cause of suffering: Thirst,[13] that leads to rebirth, accompanied by pleasure and lust, finding its delight here and there. This thirst is threefold, namely, thirst for pleasure, thirst for existence, thirst for prosperity.

"This, O Bhikkhus, is the Noble Truth of the Cessation of suffering: it ceases with the complete cessation of this thirst, — a cessation which consists in the absence of every passion — with the abandoning of this thirst, with the doing away with it, with the deliverance from it, with the destruction of desire.

"This, O Bhikkhus, is the Noble Truth of the Path which leads to the cessation of suffering: that Holy Eightfold Path, that is to say, Right Belief, Right Aspiration, Right Speech, Right Conduct, Right Means of Livelihood, Right Endeavor, Right Memory, Right Meditation. . . .

"As long, O Bhikkhus, as I did not possess with perfect purity this true knowledge and insight into these four Noble Truths . . . so long, O Bhikkhus, I knew that I had not yet obtained the highest, absolute Sambodhi in the world of men and gods. . . .

"But since I possessed, O Bhikkhus, with perfect purity this true knowledge and insight into these four Noble Truths . . . then I knew, O Bhikkhus, that I had obtained the highest, universal Sambodhi. . . .

"And this knowledge and insight arose in my mind: The emancipation of my mind cannot be lost, this is my last birth; hence I shall not be born again!"

---

[9]Avoiding any occupation that harms directly or indirectly any living being.
[10]Going beyond simply acting morally, a person now avoids all distractions and temptations of the flesh.
[11]Now that one has put aside distractions, one focuses the entire mind fully on important issues, such as life, suffering, and death.
[12]Total discipline of the mind, body, and spirit leading to a state of absolute awareness that transcends consciousness.
[13]Desire.

The Poison Arrow of Needless Speculation
▼▼▼

17 ▼ *The Buddha,*
QUESTIONS THAT TEND
NOT TO EDIFICATION

The *Pali Canon* contains thousands of sermons ascribed to the Buddha. Other than "Setting in Motion the Wheel of the Law," none is more famous or central to the Buddha's teaching than "Questions That Tend Not to Edification," also known as the "Poison Arrow." The sermon displays two characteristics common to most of the lessons ascribed to the Buddha in the *Tipitaka:* his use of earthy parables and analogies to convey his profound spiritual insights; and teaching by means of a dialogue between Enlightened Master and pupil.

QUESTIONS FOR ANALYSIS

1. Which issues or questions did the Buddha refuse to consider?
2. Did the Buddha consider such speculation simply a waste of time or was there a more profound reason for his antipathy to the search for answers to such questions?
3. What does his refusal to speculate on these issues suggest about his core doctrine?
4. Now that you have studied these four Indian sources, you are ready for the Big Questions: What assumptions and values do Brahminical Hinduism and Buddhism share? Where do they differ? Which are more significant, the similarities or the differences? What conclusions follow from your answers?

Thus I have heard.

On certain occasion the Blessed One[1] was dwelling at Savatthi in Jetavana monastery in Anathapindika's Park. Now it happened to the venerable Malunkyaputta,[2] being in seclusion and plunged in meditation, that a consideration presented itself to his mind as follows:

"These theories that the Blessed One has left unexplained, has set aside and rejected — that the world is eternal, that the world is not eternal, that the world is finite, that the world is infinite, that the soul and the body are identical, that the soul is one thing and the body another, that the saint[3] exists after death, that the saint does not exist after death, that the saint both exists and does not exist after death, that the saint neither exists nor does not exist after death — these the Blessed One does not explain to me. And the fact that the Blessed One does not explain them to me does not please me nor suit me. Therefore I will draw near to the Blessed One and inquire of him concerning this matter. If the Blessed One will explain them to me, . . . I will lead the religious life under the Blessed One. If the Blessed One will not explain them to me, . . . I will abandon religious training and return to the lower life of a layman."

Then the venerable Malunkyaputta arose in the evening from his seclusion, and drew near to where the Blessed One was; and having drawn near and greeted the Blessed One, he sat down respectfully at one side. And seated respectfully at one side, the venerable Malunkyaputta spoke to the Blessed One as follows:

"Reverend Sir, it happened to me, as I was just now in seclusion and plunged in meditation, that a consideration presented itself to my mind, as follows: 'These theories that the Blessed One has left unexplained, has set aside and rejected — that the world is eternal, that the world is not eternal . . . that the saint neither exists nor does not exist after death — these the Blessed One does not explain to me. And the fact that the Blessed One does not explain them to me does not please me nor suit me. I will draw near to the Blessed One and inquire of him concerning this matter. If the Blessed One will explain to me, either that the world is eternal, or that the world is not eternal . . . or that the saint neither exists nor does not exist after death, in that case I will lead the religious life under the Blessed One. If the Blessed One will not explain to me, either that the world is eternal, or that the world is not eternal . . . or that the saint neither exists nor does

---

[1] The Buddha.
[2] One of the Buddha's disciples.
[3] An *arahat,* or "one worthy of reverence," who has achieved the fourth and highest stage leading to Nirvana. The title is also spelled *arahant* and *arhat.*

not exist after death, in that case I will abandon religious training and return to the lower life of a layman.'

"If the Blessed One knows that the world is eternal, let the Blessed One explain to me that the world is eternal; if the Blessed One knows that the world is not eternal, let the Blessed One explain to me that the world is not eternal. If the Blessed One does not know either that the world is eternal or that the world is not eternal, the only upright thing for one who does not know, or who has not that insight, is to say, 'I do not know; I have not that insight.'"

"Pray Malunkyaputta, did I ever say to you, 'Come, Malunkyaputta, lead the religious life under me, and I will explain to you either that the world is eternal, or that the world is not eternal . . . or that the saint neither exists nor does not exist after death'?"

"No, indeed, Reverend Sir."

"Or did you ever say to me, 'Reverend Sir, I will lead the religious life under the Blessed One, on condition that the Blessed One explain to me either that the world is eternal, or that the world is not eternal . . . or that the saint neither exists nor does not exist after death'?"

"No, indeed, Reverend Sir." . . .

"That being the case, vain man, whom are you so angrily denouncing?

"Malunkyaputta, any one who should say, 'I will not lead the religious life under the Blessed One until the Blessed One shall explain to me either that the world is eternal. Or that the world is not eternal . . . or that the saint neither exists nor does not exist after death'; — that person would die, Malunkyaputta, before the Tathagata had ever explained this to him.

"It is as if, Malunkyaputta, a man had been wounded by an arrow thickly smeared with poison, and his friends and companions, his relatives and kinsfolk, were to procure for him a physician or surgeon; and the sick man were to say, 'I will not have this arrow taken out until I have learned whether the man who wounded me belonged to the warrior caste, or to the Brahmin caste, or to the agricultural caste, or to the menial caste.'

"Or again he were to say, 'I will not have this arrow taken out until I have learned the name of the man who wounded me, and to what clan he belongs.'

"Or again he were to say, 'I will not have this arrow taken out until I have learned whether the man who wounded me was tall, or short, or of the middle height.'

"Or again he were to say, 'I will not have this arrow taken out until I have learned whether the man who wounded me was black, or dusky, or of a yellow skin.'

"Or again he were to say, 'I will not have this arrow taken out until I have learned whether the man who wounded me was from this or that village, or town, or city.' . . .

▷   Many similar possibilities are mentioned.

"That man would die, Malunkyaputta, without ever having learned this.

"In exactly the same way, Malunkyaputta, any one who should say, 'I will not lead the religious life under the Blessed One until the Blessed One shall explain to me either that the world is eternal, or that the world is not eternal . . . or that the saint neither exists nor does not exist after death'; — that person would die, Malunkyaputta, before the Tathagata had ever explained this to him.

"The religious life, Malunkyaputta, does not depend on the dogma that the world is eternal; nor does the religious life, Malunkyaputta, depend on the dogma that the world is not eternal. Whether the dogma obtain, Malunkyaputta, that the world is eternal, or that the world is not eternal, there still remain birth, old age, death, sorrow, lamentation, misery, grief, and despair, for the extinction of which in the present life I am prescribing. . . .

"Accordingly, Malunkyaputta, bear always in mind what it is that I have not explained, and what it is that I have explained. And what, Malunkyaputta, have I not explained? I have not explained, Malunkyaputta, that the world is eternal; I have not explained that the world is not eternal; I have not explained that the world is finite; I have not explained that the world is infinite; I have not explained that the soul and the body are identical; I have not explained that the soul is one thing and the body another; I have not explained that the saint exists after death; I have not explained that the saint does not exist after death; I have not explained that the saint both exists and does not exist after death; I have not explained that the saint neither exists nor does not exist after death. And why, Malunkyaputta, have I not explained this? Because, Malunkyaputta, this profits not, nor has to do with the fundamentals of religion, nor tends to aversion, absence of passion, cessation, quiescence, the supernatural faculties, supreme wisdom, and Nirvana; therefore I have not explained it.

"And what, Malunkyaputta, have I explained? Misery, Malunkyaputta, have I explained; the origin of misery have I explained; the cessation of misery have I explained; and the path leading to the cessation of misery have I explained. And why, Malunkyaputta, have I explained this? Because, Malunkyaputta, this does profit, has to do with the fundamentals of religion, and tends to aversion, absence of passion, cessation, quiescence, knowledge, supreme wisdom, and Nirvana; therefore have I explained it. Accordingly, Malunkyaputta, bear always in mind what it is that I have not explained, and what it is that I have explained."

Thus the Blessed One spoke and, delighted, the venerable Malunkyaputta applauded the speech of the Blessed One.

Persians, Israelites, and Their Gods

Two peoples of Southwest Asia, the Persians and the Israelites, evolved visions of a single, uncreated God of the universe, who was the Creator of all goodness and who demanded wholehearted devotion and imposed an uncompromising code of moral behavior upon all believers. Both the Persian *Ahura Mazda* (Lord Wisdom) and the Israelite YHWH (I am Who am) were originally perceived as sky gods, existing among a multiplicity of other gods of nature; by the sixth century B.C.E., however, their respective devotees worshiped each as the sole source of all holiness. What is more, each of these two divinities was perceived as *the* sole God of history. That is, each God alone used humans as agents to serve the Divine Will and, thereby, to assist in the realization of the Divine Plan for humanity. For both the Persians and the Israelites, human history had a purpose and a goal. By serving as agents in the working out of God's holy plan for creation, humans assumed a spiritual dignity and importance that they could otherwise never have hoped to attain.

Although the Persian faith, known as *Zoroastrianism,* admitted the existence of a number of lesser divinities and, therefore, was not strictly monotheistic, it and the faith of the Israelites laid the basis for Southwest Asia's distinctive vision of ethical monotheism.

The Struggle between Good and Evil
▼▼▼

18 ▼ *Zarathustra, GATHAS*

During the second millennium B.C.E., about the same time that one branch of the Aryans wandered into the Indian subcontinent, another branch settled the highlands of *Iran* (the land of the Aryans). Initially, the religion and general culture of the people who settled Iran were almost identical to that of the Vedic Aryans of India. For example, the Iranians celebrated the slaying of Verethra, the drought, by their war-god Indara. The parallel with Indra's striking down Vritra, the dragon of drought, is obvious (see source 10). In time, however, these Iranians developed a civilization that differed radically from that of the Indo-Aryans. We call that ancient civilization *Persian.*

By the late sixth century B.C.E., the Persians possessed the largest empire the world had yet seen. For nearly two centuries they united Southwest Asia and portions of Central Asia, Northeast Africa, and the Balkan region of Europe into a politically centralized yet culturally diverse entity. During the reign of Darius the Great (r. 522–486 B.C.E.), who styled himself King of Kings, the royal house of Persia adopted as its religion the teachings of a native son, *Zarathustra* (or *Zoroaster,* as he was called by the Greeks). The highly ethical message of this Persian religious visionary appears to have been one of the major factors contributing to the empire's general policy of good government.

We know very little about the life of Zarathustra. According to a late Persian tradition, he lived 258 years before Alexander the Great, or around the first quarter of the sixth century B.C.E. As appealing as this putative date is for those who would place this religious revolutionary squarely into the so-called Axial Age, it seems likely that Zarathustra flourished many centuries earlier. The archaic language of his few extant hymns strongly suggests that he lived no later than 1000 B.C.E., probably closer to 1200, and possibly as early as the 1300s. Apparently he belonged to the priestly class that performed fire sacrifices, very much like the Indo-Aryan Brahmins. The religious world into which he had been born was filled with a multiplicity of lesser gods known as *daevas* (called *devas* by the Indo-Aryans) and three greater gods, each of whom bore the title *Ahura* (Lord), and all of these deities commanded worship. Zarathustra's great religious breakthrough seems to have been that he preached that one of these divine beings, *Ahura Mazda,* was the sole God of creation and the supreme deity of the universe. This uncreated God and source of all goodness alone was worthy of the highest worship. To be sure, Ahura Mazda had created lesser benign spirits, known as *yazatas,* to aid him, and they merited devotion, but all of the traditional Iranian daevas were evil demons, who deserved no worship. Indeed, these daevas were the creation of another uncreated entity, *Angra Mainyu* (Hostile Spirit), whose evil existence was the source of all sin and misery in the universe.

It is clear that Zarathustra claimed to be the *prophet* (a person speaking by divine inspiration and, thereby, revealing the will of God) of Ahura Mazda. Equally clear, Zarathustra taught his disciples that Ahura Mazda required all humans to join in the cosmic struggle against Angra Mainyu. Although coeternal with Lord Wisdom, Hostile Spirit was nowhere his equal. To be sure, Angra Mainyu (also known as the *Liar*) and his minions afflicted human souls with evil and led them away from the path of righteousness, but in the end Angra Mainyu and his daevas would be defeated. Strictly speaking, such a vision, which sees the universe engaged in a contest between two divine principles, one good and the other evil, is not monotheistic but rather *dualistic*. Nevertheless, Zarathustra's dualistic theology focused on a single God of goodness and should be seen as one of the major roots of Southwest Asian ethical monotheism.

Zarathustra's teachings took hold in Persia, especially with the rise of the first Persian Empire in the sixth century B.C.E. From 224 to 651 C.E. Zoroastrianism was the official state religion of a revived Persian Empire under the Sassanian house, and it was only in the Sassanian Era, possibly as late as the sixth century C.E., that the *Avesta,* the Zoroastrian collection of holy scripture, was written down in its final form. Although the *Avesta* encompasses many texts that date from well after Zarathustra's time, it contains a few short devotional hymns, known as *Gathas,* that date to the age of Zarathustra and probably owe their composition to him or an early disciple. Their archaic language and often unclear references make them hard, even impossible to interpret with full confidence. Yet, they are our only reliable sources for the original teachings of the Persian prophet. As such, they illustrate, but ambiguously so, his vision and message.

QUESTIONS FOR ANALYSIS

1. How are we able to infer that Zarathustra believed he had been called directly by Ahura Mazda to serve as a prophet?
2. What evidence indicates that Zarathustra saw Ahura Mazda as the sole creator of the universe?
3. Where and how does Zarathustra refer to Ahura Mazda's use of humanity and history to realize certain sacred purposes?
4. How does each person's life become a microcosm of the battle between Ahura Mazda and the Liar?
5. How do we know that Zarathustra believed Ahura Mazda would ultimately triumph over evil?
6. Does Zarathustra see his faith as only one of many paths to the truth or is it the Truth?
7. What is promised those who serve Ahura Mazda faithfully? What about those who do not accept and serve this God?

Then shall I recognize you as strong and holy, Mazda,[1] when by the hand in which you yourself hold the destinies that you will assign to the Liar and the Righteous . . . the might of Good Thought[2] shall come to me.

As the holy one I recognized you, Mazda

---

[1] *Mazda* means "wise" or "wisdom."
[2] Zarathustra conceived of Good Thought, Piety, and other such entities as spiritual beings whom Ahura Mazda had created to help in the battle against the forces of evil.

Ahura, when I saw you in the beginning at the birth of Life, when you made actions and words to have their reward — evil for the evil, a good Destiny for the good — through your wisdom when creation shall reach its goal.

At which goal you will come with your holy Spirit, O Mazda, with Dominion, at the same with Good Thought, by whose action the settlements[3] will prosper through Right. . . .

As the holy one I recognized you, Mazda Ahura, when Good Thought came to me and asked me, "Who are you? to whom do you belong? By what sign will you appoint the days for questioning about your possessions and yourself?"

Then I said to him: "To the first question, I am Zarathustra, a true foe to the Liar, to the utmost of my power, but a powerful support would I be to the Righteous, that I may attain the future things of the infinite Dominion, as I praise and proclaim you, Mazda." . . .

As the holy one I recognized you, Mazda Ahura, when Good Thought came to me, when the still mind taught me to declare what is best: "Let not a man seek again and again to please the Liars, for they make all the righteous enemies."

And thus Zarathustra himself, O Ahura, chooses that spirit of thine that is holiest, Mazda. May Right be embodied, full of life and strength! May Piety abide in the Dominion where the sun shines! May Good Thought give destiny to men according to their works!

▼ ▼ ▼

This I ask you, tell me truly, Ahura. Who is by generation the Father of Right, at the first? Who determined the path of sun and stars? Who is it by whom the moon waxes and wanes again? This, O Mazda, and yet more, I want to know.

This I ask you, tell me truly, Ahura. Who upheld the Earth beneath and the firmament from falling? Who the waters and the plants? Who yoked swiftness to winds and clouds? Who is, O Mazda, creator of Good Thought?

This I ask you, tell me truly, Ahura. What artist made light and darkness? What artist made sleep and waking? Who made morning, noon, and night, that call the understanding man to his duty? . . .

This I ask you, tell me truly, Ahura. Who created together with Dominion the precious Piety? Who made by wisdom the son obedient to his father? I strive to recognize by these things you, O Mazda, creator of all things through the holy spirit. . . .

This I ask you, tell me truly, Ahura. The Religion which is the best for all that are, which in union with Right should make prosperous all that is mine, will they duly observe it, the religion of my creed, with the words and action of Piety, in desire for your future good things, O Mazda?

This I ask you, tell me truly, Ahura — whether Piety will extend to those to whom your Religion shall be proclaimed? I was ordained at the first by you: all others I look upon with hatred of spirit.

This I ask you, tell me truly, Ahura. Who among those with whom I would speak is a righteous man, and who a liar? On which side is the enemy? . . .

This I ask you, tell me truly, Ahura — whether we shall drive the Lie away from us to those who being full of disobedience will not strive after fellowship with Right, nor trouble themselves with counsel of Good Thought. . . .

This I ask you, tell me truly, Ahura — whether through you I shall attain my goal . . . and that my voice may be effectual, that Welfare and Immortality may be ready to unite according to that promise with him who joins himself with Right.

This I ask you, tell me truly, Ahura — whether I shall indeed, O Right, earn that reward, even ten mares with a stallion and a camel,[4] which was promised to me, O Mazda, as well as through you the future gift of Welfare and Immortality.

▼ ▼ ▼

---

[3]People who are settled or civilized.

[4]Symbols of good fortune and earthly prosperity.

I will speak of that which Mazda Ahura, the all-knowing, revealed to me first in this earthly life. Those of you that put not in practice this word as I think and utter it, to them shall be woe at the end of life. . . .

I will speak of that which the Holiest declared to me as the word that is best for mortals to obey: he, Mazda Ahura said, "They who at my bidding render him[5] obedience, shall all attain Welfare and Immortality by the actions of the Good Spirit." . . .

In immortality shall the soul of the righteous be joyful, in perpetuity shall be the torments of the Liars. All this does Mazda Ahura appoint by his Dominion.

---

[5]Zarathustra.

A New Covenant for All Peoples
▼▼▼

19 ▼ THE BOOK OF ISAIAH

As we saw in Chapter 2, probably during the thirteenth century B.C.E. the Israelites moved into the land of Canaan. Once settled there, they waged a continuing battle to retain their independence, cultural identity, and exclusive devotion to YHWH. In the late eleventh century B.C.E., largely in response to Philistine pressure, the Israelites created a kingdom. Around 1020 B.C.E. their second king, David, captured Jerusalem and converted it into the religious and political capital of the Israelites.

The political stability of this kingdom was precarious at best. In 922 it was split into two independent entities: the larger kingdom of Israel in the north and the kingdom of Judah, centering on Jerusalem, in the south. In 722 the Assyrians obliterated Israel. The more compact and remote kingdom of Judah survived until 586 B.C.E., when finally a Semitic people from Mesopotamia known as the *Chaldeans* captured and destroyed Jerusalem and carried off most of Judah's upper classes into exile in Babylon, an episode known forever after as the *Babylonian Captivity.*

Cultural and religious stability was equally precarious. The cult of YHWH was in many ways more suitable to the life of the desert herder than to that of the settled farmer. As the Israelites settled down, they adopted many of the religious practices of their Canaanite neighbors. This action occasioned angry protests from a group of religious reformers known as the *prophets.* The prophets, who claimed inspiration from YHWH, now increasingly referred to simply as the *Lord,* protested vehemently against debasement of the Mosaic religion, but in the process of their protest they broadened considerably the moral and theological scope of the worship of the Lord.

One of the greatest and last of these prophets was a person we know only as *Second Isaiah.* He served as the voice of a new faith that was born out of the anguish of the Babylonian Captivity. We call that faith *Judaism.*

The original Prophet Isaiah had towered over the religious scene of Jerusalem from the middle to the late eighth century B.C.E. and left behind a rich legacy of teaching on the Lord's role as the God who controls the destinies of all people. Second Isaiah, who lived in the mid and late sixth century B.C.E., carried on this tradition. Consequently, the prophecies of this otherwise unknown person were appended to the writings of the earlier Isaiah and appear as chapters 40 through 55 in the Bible's Book of Isaiah.

The following passages were composed around 538 B.C.E., when Cyrus the Great, king of Persia and conqueror of the Chaldean (Neo-Babylonian) Empire, released the Israelites from captivity. Here Second Isaiah metaphorically describes the people of Israel as YHWH's *Suffering Servant* and delineates the historical role that the Lord has decreed for this servant.

This notion of a God of goodness who uses human agents to drive history forward certainly reminds us of Zarathustra's message, and clearly elements of Zoroastrian belief — such as angels, the Devil, Heaven, Hell, Limbo, the Resurrection of the dead, a Savior-to-Come, and a Day of Judgment — would later surface in some forms of Judaism, as well as in Christianity and Islam. Nevertheless, it is impossible to say with any certainty what influence, if any, Zoroastrian teachings might have had on Second Isaiah's prophetic vision. We can only speculate.

QUESTIONS FOR ANALYSIS

1. Consider the text's opening lines. In what manner has YHWH's special relationship with the people of Israel remained unchanged since the days of Moses?
2. What does Second Isaiah mean by the prophecy that the Lord will present Israel "as a light to the nations"? How will the Children of Israel's redemption from exile in Babylon serve a universal purpose?
3. What are the essential elements of Second Isaiah's vision of the Lord and this deity's Chosen People?
4. Consider YHWH's covenants with Noah (source 12) and with the wandering Israelites (source 13). To which of those covenants is this one closer? What do you conclude from your answer?
5. "For the Israelites and Persians religion became the means of transforming the world, not negating it." What does the author of this statement mean? Do you agree or disagree? Why?
6. How do Ahura Mazda and the Lord differ from Brahman?

"But now hear, O Jacob[1] my servant,
Israel whom I have chosen!
Thus says the Lord who made you, who formed
   you from the womb and will help you:
Fear not, O Jacob my servant,
Jeshurun[2] whom I have chosen.
For I will pour water on the thirsty land,
and streams on the dry ground;

I will pour my Spirit upon your descendants,
and my blessing on your offspring.
They shall spring up like grass amid waters,
like willows by flowing streams;
This one will say, 'I am the Lord's,'
another will call himself by the name of Jacob,
and another will write on his hand, 'The
   Lord's,'[3]

---

[1]Here *Jacob* means all of Jacob's descendants — the Children of Israel.
[2]"Upright one" — a term of endearment.

[3]Compare this with Moses' command that the Israelites tie the Law to their arms and wear it on their foreheads (source 13).

and surname himself by the name of Israel.
Thus says the Lord, the King of Israel[4]
and his Redeemer, the Lord of hosts:
"I am the first and I am the last;
besides me there is no God. . . .
Remember these things, O Jacob,
and Israel, for you are my servant;
I formed you, you are my servant;
O Israel, you will not be forgotten by me.
I have swept away your transgressions like a
    cloud,
and your sins like mist;
return to me, for I have redeemed you. . . .
I am the Lord, who made all things,
who stretched out the heavens alone,
who spread out the Earth —
    Who was with me? —
who frustrates the omens of liars,
and makes fools of diviners;
who turns wise men back,
and makes their knowledge foolish;
who confirms the word of his servant,
and performs the counsel of his messengers;
who says of Jerusalem, 'She shall be inhabited,'
and of the cities of Judah, 'They shall be built,
and I will raise up their ruins,' . . .
who says of Cyrus, 'He is my shepherd.
and he shall fulfill all my purpose';
saying of Jerusalem, 'She shall be built,'
and of the temple, 'Your foundation shall be
    laid.'"
Thus says the Lord to his anointed, to Cyrus,
whose right hand I have grasped,
to subdue nations before him
and ungird the loins of kings,
to open doors before him
that gates may not be closed:
"I will go before you
and level the mountains,
I will break in pieces the doors of bronze
and cut asunder the bars of iron,[5]

I will give you the treasures of darkness
and the hoards in secret places,
that you may know that it is I, the Lord,
the God of Israel, who call you by your name.
For the sake of my servant Jacob,
and Israel my chosen,
I call you by your name,
I surname you,[6] though you do not know me.
I am the Lord, and there is no other,
besides me there is no God;
I gird you, though you do not know me,
that men may know, from the rising of the sun
and from the west, that there is none besides
    me;
I am the Lord, and there is no other. . . .
I made the Earth,
and created man upon it;
it was my hands that stretched out the heavens,
and I commanded all their host.
I have aroused him[7] in righteousness,
and I will make straight all his ways;
he shall build my city[8]
and set my exiles free,
not for price or reward,"
says the Lord of hosts. . . .
"I the Lord speak the truth,
I declare what is right.
"Assemble yourselves and come,
draw near together,
you survivors of the nations![9]
They have no knowledge
who carry about their wooden idols,
and keep on praying to a god
that cannot save.
Declare and present your case;
let them take counsel together!
Who told this long ago?
Who declared it of old?
Was it not I, the Lord?
And there is no other god besides me,
    a righteous God and a Savior;

---

[4]This refers to all of the Israelites and should not be confused with the kingdom of Israel, which the Assyrians destroyed in 722 B.C.E.
[5]A reference to the great walls of Babylon.
[6]The Lord bestows on Cyrus the title *the Great*.

[7]Cyrus.
[8]Jerusalem will be rebuilt.
[9]All peoples who survive the collapse of the Chaldean, or Neo-Babylonian, Empire.

there is none besides me.
"Turn to me and be saved,[10]
all the ends of the Earth!
For I am God, and there is no other.
By myself I have sworn,
from my mouth has gone forth in righteousness
a word that shall not return:
'To me every knee shall bow,
every tongue shall swear.'
"Only in the Lord, it shall be said of me,
are righteousness and strength;
to him shall come and be ashamed,
all who were incensed against him.
In the Lord all the offspring of Israel
shall triumph and glory." . . .
Listen to me, O coastlands,
and hearken, you peoples from afar.
The Lord called me[11] from the womb,
from the body of my mother he named my
    name.
He made my mouth like a sharp sword,
in the shadow of his hand he hid me;
he made me a polished arrow,

in his quiver he hid me away.
And he said to me, "You are my servant,
Israel, in whom I will be glorified."
But I said, "I have labored in vain,
I have spent my strength for nothing and vanity;
yet surely my right is with the Lord,
and my recompense with my God."
And now the Lord says, . . .
"It is too light a thing that you should be my
    servant
to raise up the tribes of Jacob
and to restore the preserved of Israel;
I will give you as a light to the nations,
that my salvation may reach to the end of the
    Earth."
Thus says the Lord,
the Redeemer of Israel and his Holy One,
to one deeply despised, abhorred by the nations,
the servant of rulers:
"Kings shall see and arise;
princes, and they shall prostrate themselves;
because of the Lord, who is faithful,
the Holy One of Israel, who has chosen you."

---

[10]Most scholars conclude that the terms *save* and *salvation* used by Second Isaiah do not imply a promise of Paradise after death but only earthly peace and prosperity.

[11]The Children of Israel.

Chapter 4

▼▼▼

The Secular
Made Sacred

Developing the Humanistic Traditions
of China and Hellas: 600–200 B.C.E.

The Chinese and the Greeks, who inhabited the eastern and western extremes of civilized Eurasia in the sixth century B.C.E., had deities and spirits for every imaginable function and a wide range of religious taboos and rituals. But religion in its narrowest sense — reverence for a supernatural being — offered them little in the way of either intellectual stimulation or profound spiritual satisfaction. While contemporaries in India and Southwest Asia were raising religious speculation to high levels of abstract thought, religion for the Chinese and the Greeks remained, for the most part, a practical affair. One sacrificed to the gods and spirits in order to assure their benevolence. Religion was a form of magical insurance and not a relationship with Ultimate Reality.

At the same time, the social and psychic crises of the Age of Iron were just as real in China and Greece as elsewhere. In fashioning responses to the questions occasioned by the dislocation of traditional ways of life, both the Chinese and the Greeks looked more toward this world than the Beyond and created cultures that were essentially *humanistic* (human centered) and *secular* (of this world) in the sense that they focused on humanity's position within an observable universe of finite space and time. Social and political philosophy rather than theology engaged the intellectual energies of the Chinese and the Greeks as they endeavored to meet the challenges of the Iron Age.

In China various philosophers offered insights into how humans should behave in regard to their families, the state, and nature. These philosophers also struggled with the issue of personal excellence. They first inquired whether such a goal was achievable or even desirable, and many ultimately concluded that the cult of individuality that was inherent in such a quest for personal perfection threatened the harmony of the family, the state, and even the natural order. Therefore, it was to be avoided. For those who accepted, however tentatively and reluctantly, even a modified search for personal excellence, several questions remained: How is it achieved, and what purposes does it serve? Does cultivation of virtue have only personal value, or is it subordinate to a higher social purpose?

Many of the same concerns preoccupied Greek rationalists. Two issues particularly dominated Greek social thought: (1) How does the individual achieve excellence? This was a quality the Greeks assumed was the natural goal of all human striving and which they termed *arete*. (2) How does the individual function as an effective citizen within the city-state? Most Greek social philosophers, at least during the fifth and fourth centuries B.C.E., assumed that cultivation of personal talents and good citizenship were complementary and not antithetical pursuits. In other words, accomplished individuals were the best citizens.

Additionally, a small but highly influential group of Greek rationalists turned their attention to an objective study of the physical environment, thereby becoming the West's first natural scientists. Like its social philosophers, Greece's scientists attempted to explain the workings of the physical universe in response to human needs, the most basic of which was to provide knowledge that would allow people to control their lives and environment.

The Chinese and the Greeks did not look to divine forces for direction and meaning in life. Rather, they fashioned cultures in which humanity and the natural world were the measure of all that was important to them. However, concentration on the human-sized matters of this world did not mean that the Chinese and the Greeks lacked a sense of a sacred mystery. Nothing could be farther from the truth. In essence, they made the secular sacred.

China: Thought in Search of Harmony

Ages of political and social unrest often are times of intellectual ferment, as was true of the era of Eastern Zhou (770–256 B.C.E.). The collapse of the Western Zhou monarchy in 771 signaled the end of all effective royal power in China (limited though it had been) and ushered in a 500-year period when regional states held center stage. Zhou kings continued to perform their traditional religious roles and received tokens of nominal obedience from the great lords. True power, however, lay in the hands of the regional lords, who developed bureaucratic governments and strong standing armies. With each local prince essentially a sovereign, military and diplomatic maneuvering among their states became a constant fact of life. As disruptive as this was at times, it also proved to be a stimulus to intellectual activity. Both the demands of statecraft at the regional level and the occasional social dislocation that resulted from the conflicts among these states stimulated the development of political theory and social philosophy.

This was especially true from the fifth century B.C.E. onward, as wars became more frequent and bitter. Chinese historians traditionally catalogue the period from 403 to 221 B.C.E. as the *Age of Warring States.* Innovations such as cavalry, iron weapons, and the crossbow broke the battlefield superiority of the chariot-driving aristocracy. Armies of conscripted foot and horse soldiers became larger and more deadly. Concomitantly, intellectuals sought to keep pace with this changing world.

Between 260 and 221 B.C.E., *Qin,* the most aggressive and best organized of the warring states, conquered all rival powers in China and established a new ruling family, the short-lived but pivotal Qin Dynasty (221–206 B.C.E.). The triumph of the lord of Qin, the self-styled *Qin Shi Huangdi* (the First Emperor of Qin), who ruled from 221 to 210 B.C.E., not only inaugurated China's first age of empire, it brought with it the momentary victory of a political philosophy known as *Legalism.* In conforming to the principles of Legalism, the Qin regime was ruthless and brutal in its drive for complete centralization of authority. Undone by the harshness of its laws and policies, the Qin Dynasty collapsed in early 206 in the midst of rebellion and civil war. Within four years, however, a commoner general, Liu Bang, reformulated the empire by establishing the successful and long-lived *Han Dynasty* (202 B.C.E.–220 C.E.).

Although the extreme measures of the Qin regime discredited Legalism as a philosophy, Legalist-inspired organizational structures and administrative procedures served as the framework of the highly centralized Han Empire. By the late second century B.C.E., however, the Han Dynasty adopted as its official ideology the gentler and more humane philosophy of *Confucianism,* which had also taken shape in the disturbing period of Eastern Zhou.

Han imperial policies and institutions were, therefore, the products of a Confucian-Legalist synthesis, but these were not the only modes of thought to play a prominent role then and ever after in China. *Daoism,* an antirational, quite antipolitical, and somewhat antisocial philosophy, had also emerged from the confusion of Eastern Zhou and survived the hostility of Qin censors to become an integral part of Chinese thought and aesthetics.

Although they offered different answers to the ills of their day and presented some striking differences of perspective, all three schools of thought claimed to offer the correct *Way,* or path, to harmony. Daoism emphasized harmony with nature; Confucianism emphasized the harmony of human relationships; and Legalism emphasized the harmony of a well-regulated state. A fourth school of thought that emerged during this era of profound intellectual fertility also emphasized harmony but harmony on a grander scale. Philosophers who developed the dualistic theory of *Yin* and *Yang* encapsulated the entire universe in their explanation of the intrinsic harmony that infuses everything that exists. Integral to their philosophy was the belief that by understanding the natural harmony of the universe that results from the balance of Yin and Yang, one could set aright anything that had fallen into a state of disharmony — be it some element of nature, human relations, the social-political order, or even the human body.

Daoism: The Way That Is and Is Not
▼▼▼

20 ▼ *Laozi,*
THE CLASSIC OF THE WAY AND VIRTUE

Few if any philosophies are as enigmatic as *Daoism* — the teachings of the Way (Dao). The opening lines of this school's greatest masterpiece, *The Classic of the Way and Virtue (Dao Dejing),* which is ascribed to the legendary *Laozi,* immediately confront the reader with Daoism's essential paradox: "The Way that can be trodden is not the enduring and unchanging Way. The name that can be named is not the enduring and unchanging name." Here is a philosophy that purports to teach *the* Way of truth but simultaneously claims that the True Way transcends human understanding. Encapsulated within a little book of some 5,000 words is a philosophy that defies definition, spurns reason, and rejects words as inadequate.

The Dao is limitless and its origins are infinite. Somewhat like the Way that it purports to teach and not teach, Daoism has many manifestations and numerous origins. No one knows when or where it originated, but its roots probably lie in the animistic religions of prehistoric China. Daoism's earliest sages are equally shadowy. According to tradition, *Laozi* supposedly was born around 604 B.C.E. and died about 517, making him an older contemporary of Confucius (source 21). According to one popular story, when Confucius visited him, Laozi instructed the younger man to rid himself of his arrogant airs and then bade him farewell. As another story has it, the aged Laozi decided to leave the state in which he lived because he foresaw its imminent decay. At the frontier he was delayed by a border official, who implored him not to depart without first leaving behind his wisdom. In response, Laozi dashed off the *Dao Dejing* and left, never to be heard from again (although according to one story that sprang up in Daoist circles in the fourth century C.E., Laozi went to India where he became the Buddha). The fact that Laozi means "Old Master" suggests to many that this sage was more a composite figure of legend and imagination than a historic individual of flesh and blood. Indeed, many scholars conclude that the bulk of the language, ideas, and allusions contained within this classic indicate an intellectual environment closer to 300 than to 500 B.C.E.

Whatever its date and circumstances of its composition, the *Dao Dejing* is one of the most profound and beautiful works ever written in Chinese and one of the most popular. Daoism, especially as articulated in this little book, has exercised an incalculable influence on Chinese life, thought, and art over the centuries.

As you study the following selections, pay particular attention to the Daoist notion of *Actionless Activity.* Known in Chinese as *wuwei* and also translated as "Effortlessness," "Nonaction," and "Non-striving," this idea pervades all Daoist thought and comes closest to being Daoism's universal principle and driving force, if such is possible.

QUESTIONS FOR ANALYSIS

1. How does Laozi define the Way? How permanent is it? What are its limitations?
2. Does the Way acknowledge right and wrong?
3. What is *wuwei,* and how does it function?
4. How does the sage ruler who is in harmony with the Way govern?
5. What are the *Dao Dejing*'s major criticisms of Confucianism and Legalism?
6. Why would Daoism appeal to some individuals in the Age of Warring States?
7. When Buddhism initially entered China, many Chinese thought it to be a variation of Daoism. How and why was this perception possible? In what ways was this a misperception?

THE WAY

The Dao that can be trodden is not the enduring and unchanging Dao. The name that can be named is not the enduring and unchanging name.

Conceived of as having no name, it is the Originator of Heaven and Earth; conceived of as having a name, it is the Mother of all things.

▼ ▼ ▼

The Dao produces all things and nourishes them; it produces them and does not claim them as its own; it does all, and yet does not boast of it; it presides over all, and yet does not control them. This is what is called "The mysterious quality" of the Dao.

▼ ▼ ▼

When the Great Dao ceased to be observed, benevolence and righteousness came into vogue. Then appeared wisdom and shrewdness, and there ensued great hypocrisy.[1]

▼ ▼ ▼

Man takes his law from the Earth; the Earth takes its law from Heaven; Heaven takes its law from the Dao. The law of the Dao is its being what it is.

▼ ▼ ▼

All-pervading is the Great Dao! It may be found on the left hand and on the right.

All things depend on it for their production, which it gives to them, not one refusing obedience to it. When its work is accomplished, it does not claim the name of having done it. It clothes all things as with a garment, and makes no assumption of being their lord; — it may be named in the smallest things; . . . it may be named in the greatest things.

▼ ▼ ▼

He who has in himself abundantly the attributes of the Dao is like an infant.

---

[1]This is a criticism of the supposed hypocrisy of Confucians who claim to know and practice virtue (see source 21).

▼ ▼ ▼

The Dao in its regular course does nothing, for the sake of doing it, and so there is nothing which it does not do.

THE WISE PERSON

When we renounce learning we have no troubles.[2]

▼ ▼ ▼

If we could renounce our sageness and discard our wisdom, it would be better for the people a hundredfold. If we could renounce our benevolence and discard our righteousness, the people would again become filial and kindly.[3] If we could renounce our artful contrivances and discard our scheming for gain, there would be no thieves nor robbers.

▼ ▼ ▼

The sage manages affairs without doing anything, and conveys his instructions without the use of speech.

▼ ▼ ▼

Therefore the sage holds in his embrace the one thing of humility, and manifests it to all the world. He is free from self-display, and therefore he shines; from self-assertion, and therefore he is distinguished; from self-boasting, and therefore his merit is acknowledged; from selfcomplacency, and therefore he acquires superiority. It is because he is thus free from striving that therefore no one in the world is able to strive with him.

▼ ▼ ▼

When gold and jade fill the hall, their possessor cannot keep them safe. When wealth and honors lead to arrogance, this brings its evil on itself. When the work is done, and one's name is becoming distinguished, to withdraw into obscurity is the way of Heaven.

THE IDEAL GOVERNMENT

A state may be ruled by measures of correction;[4] weapons of war may be used with crafty dexterity; but the kingdom is made one's own only by freedom from action and purpose.

How do I know that it is so? By these facts: — In the kingdom the multiplication of prohibitive enactments increases the poverty of the people; the more implements to add to their profit that the people have, the greater disorder is there in the state and clan; the more acts of crafty dexterity that men possess, the more do strange contrivances appear; the more display there is of legislation, the more thieves and robbers there are.

Therefore a sage has said, "I will do nothing, and the people will be transformed of themselves; I will be fond of keeping still, and the people will of themselves become correct. I will take no trouble about it, and the people will of themselves become rich; I will manifest no ambition, and the people will of themselves attain to the primitive simplicity."

▼ ▼ ▼

Not to value and employ men of superior ability is the way to keep the people from rivalry among themselves;[5] not to prize articles which are difficult to procure[6] is the way to keep them from be-

---

[2]According to the Confucians, careful study and emulation of the virtues of the past is the primary avenue to harmony.

[3]These first two sentences reject the Confucian values of wisdom (saintliness), knowledge, human-heartedness, and righteousness, all of which, according to the Confucians, will result in *filial piety* (proper devotion and service to parents, ancestors, and superiors). See the introduction to source 21 for further discussion of the history of this Confucian principle.

[4]This aphorism rejects the principles and methods of Legalism (see source 22).

[5]Confucian political philosophy centered on the wise and learned superior man, also known as the gentleman (see source 21).

[6]Legalist policy favored trade.

coming thieves; not to show them what is likely to excite their desires is the way to keep their minds from disorder.

Therefore the sage, in the exercise of his government, empties their minds, fills their bellies, weakens their wills, and strengthens their bones.

He constantly tries to keep them without knowledge and without desire, and where there are those who have knowledge, to keep them from presuming to act on it. When there is this abstinence from action, good order is universal.

Confucianism: The Moral Way of the Past
▼▼▼

21 ▼ *Confucius, THE ANALECTS*

The Chinese refer to the period of Eastern Zhou as the *Age of a Hundred Schools*. Of the many schools of thought that flourished then, none has had a more substantial impact on Chinese culture than *Confucianism,* a philosophy ascribed to a teacher whom history identifies as *Confucius*.

Tradition records that this sage was born in 552 or 551 B.C.E. into the aristocratic but impoverished Kong family, which traced its lineage to the Shang Dynasty. Young Kong Qiu, as he was named, became an authority on court rituals and statecraft and rose to high office in his native state of Lu in northeastern China. In 497 he resigned his position when proper rituals were not performed during a state sacrifice to Heaven. Already an established teacher, he embarked on a fourteen-year period of wandering with his students. Traveling to the courts of various small states, he attempted without success to convince their princes to employ his philosophy of life and government — his *Moral Way* — which he believed would return Chinese society to a state of harmony and justice. Finally in 484, at age sixty-seven, Master Kong was recalled to Lu but not offered an office. He spent his remaining years teaching and died at age seventy-two in 479, convinced that he had failed to halt what he believed to be the moral corruption and political chaos of his day.

If Confucius died thinking himself a failure, he was wrong. His students achieved high positions of responsibility and became teachers themselves of the Moral Way. Through their students and the generations of students that followed, Confucius' ideas were widely disseminated. In the Age of Tang (618–907 C.E.) Confucianism became virtually synonymous with Chinese culture and played an almost equally important role in shaping Korean and Japanese thought. Because of Master Kong's profound impact on Chinese civilization, posterity accorded him the elegant title *Kongfuzi* (Reverend Master Kong), which seventeenth-century Western scholars Latinized into *Confucius*.

Recently some historians have challenged this story. Several claim that the historical Confucius was not a scholar-official but a conservative warrior-noble who held very few of the values that tradition later ascribed to him. Several others even question the historicity of Confucius, concluding that the man was a fictional construct of a much later age. Notwithstanding these challenges, most historians accept the overall outlines of the traditional story, even though they generally agree that later generations ascribed to Confucius some ideas and emphases that were never his.

Although later disciples of Confucian thought, such as *Mengzi,* or *Mencius* (ca. 370–300 B.C.E.), carried the ideas of the Master to points that he never imagined, it seems possible to identify the principles that served as bedrocks of Confucius' thinking. First, we must realize that Master Kong was a revolutionary conservative. He sought to transform Chinese society and government by returning it to the values and practices of the era of the duke of Zhou, a twelfth-century B.C.E. legislator and consolidator of the early Zhou Dynasty who, Kong was convinced, presided over a Golden Age of harmony and prosperity. In order to achieve this end, Kong Qiu emphasized several virtues. Chief among them were *xiao, li,* and *ren.* *Xiao* is best translated as "filial piety" (devotion and service to parents, ancestors, and superiors). *Li* is best understood as both "proper behavior" and "performance of the rituals." *Ren* is the richest of the terms and is variously translated as "human-heartedness," "benevolence toward humanity," "nobility of heart," and "humaneness."

As noted, Confucius revered the ways of the past. Consequently, he urged his students to master ancient traditions and texts, such as the *Book of Documents* and the *Book of Songs* (sources 5 and 6). But his philosophy went well beyond simple admiration and emulation. He took age-old Chinese values, such as filial piety and proper performance of ancient rituals, and turned them into moral principles. His genius was that he insisted human beings are moral creatures with social obligations and are, by that fact, obliged to comport themselves humanely and with integrity. He also taught that humans, or at least males, are capable of perfecting themselves as upright individuals. His ideal moral agent, so far as we can infer from the evidence, was the superior man (or gentleman), who cultivated virtue through study and imitation of the Moral Way of the past. This person by knowing the good would choose the good. What is more, he would act as an example to others, who would irresistibly follow the path he set along the Way of Goodness.

Although a traditionalist, Confucius was an innovator in that he was one of the first Chinese educators to offer instruction to any intelligent young man who sought the Moral Way, regardless of his social or economic status. Even so, Confucius' pupils were few. Tradition records that they numbered seventy-two, but we know the names of only about thirty-five.

As is true of so many great teachers whose words and example have placed a permanent stamp on a civilization, Confucius was not a productive writer. As far as we know, nothing he wrote or edited survives. Early Confucian disciples, however, managed to transmit to posterity a number of sayings ascribed to Master Kong and his immediate pupils. In time they were gathered into a book known as the *Lunyu (Ethical Dialogues),* which the modern West knows as the *Analects,* a term that means "Literary Gleanings." We do not know which of these maxims Confucius actually uttered, but collectively they provide us with the best available view of Master Kong's teachings as remembered by those who knew and followed him.

To assist your study, we have grouped our selections by general topic but have retained the traditional numbering of the maxims. Ancient editors arranged these

Confucian aphorisms into twenty chapters of unequal length. Thus 16.8 is saying 8 in Chapter 16. At the same time, be aware that there is a fair amount of thematic overlap. Several of the selections under the heading "The Well-Lived Life," for example, also deal with *ren*.

QUESTIONS FOR ANALYSIS

1. How and why does filial piety serve as a bedrock of Confucius' philosophical system?
2. Describe the superior man, or gentleman, as envisioned by Confucius? What are his qualities and how does he employ them?
3. What is Confucius' concept of good government and the ideal state?
4. Define what *ren* meant to Confucius. Was it absolute? Was it all-encompassing? In other words, did it have limitations? In what ways did it animate other virtues?
5. What role do the rituals play in the Confucian system?
6. "For Confucius propriety, or proper performance of rituals, meant much more than good manners or proper etiquette. Like *ren* and filial piety, it was an interior quality that set the superior man apart from all other humans." Comment on this anonymous statement. Do you agree or disagree with this analysis of Confucius' philosophy? Be specific in your answer.
7. Compare the Confucian Way and the Confucian vision of the well-lived life with those of Laozi. What do you conclude from your analysis?

FILIAL PIETY

1.2 Master You[1] said: "Those who are filial to their parents and obedient to their elder brothers but are apt to defy their superiors are rare indeed; those who are not apt to defy their superiors, but are apt to stir up a rebellion simply do not exist. The gentleman applies himself to the roots. Only when the roots are well planted will the Way grow. Filial piety and brotherly obedience[2] are perhaps the roots of humanity,[3] are they not?"

1.9 Master Zeng[4] said: "Show genuine grief at a parent's death,[5] keep offering sacri-

fices to them as time goes by, and the people's moral character shall be reinforced."

2.5 When Meng Yi-zi[6] asked about filial piety, the Master said: "Do not act contrary."[7]

When Fan Chi[8] was driving, the Master said to him: "When Meng-sun[9] asked me about filial piety, I replied: 'Do not act contrary.'"

Fan Chi said: "What do you mean?"

The Master said: "When your parents are alive, serve them in accordance with the rituals; when they die, bury them in accordance with the rituals; offer sacri-

---

[1]You Ruo, one of Confucius' chief disciples.
[2]The virtue of *ti,* whereby a younger brother obeys an older brother.
[3]*Ren.*
[4]Zeng Shen, one of Confucius' most important pupils. Mengzi (Mencius), the greatest Confucian after Kongfuzi himself, studied in the school begun by Zeng Shen.

[5]Here he addresses a ruler.
[6]A minister of Lu.
[7]Contrary to the ancient rituals.
[8]Also known as Fan Xu, he was a major disciple of the Master.
[9]Meng Yi-zi, who came from the aristocratic family of Meng-sun.

fices to them in accordance with the rituals."

4.18   The Master said: "In serving your parents, be gentle in remonstration. Seeing that they are not inclined to comply, remain reverent, and do not disobey them. Though weary, do not feel resentful."

13.18   The Duke of She[10] said to Master Kong: "In my native place, there is a man nicknamed Straight Body. When his father stole a sheep, he bore witness against him."

Master Kong said: "In my native place, straight people are different from this man: Father conceals for son and son conceals for father. Straightness lies therein."

THE GENTLEMAN

1.7   Zi-Xia[11] said: "He who loves worthy men instead of beautiful women; who, in serving his parents, can exert all his energy; who, in serving the sovereign, can exhaust his talent; and who, in associating with friends, is truthful to his word — although others may say he has not learned, I will surely say he has learned."

1.8   The Master said: "If a gentleman is not grave, he will not be awe-inspiring. If he learns, he will not be benighted.[12] He keeps whole-hearted sincerity and truthfulness as his major principles and does not befriend those beneath him. When he makes a mistake, he is not afraid to correct it."

4.10   The Master said: "The gentleman, in his attitude toward all under Heaven,[13] neither favors anyone nor disfavors anyone. He keeps close to whoever is righteous."

4.16   The Master said: "The gentleman is conversant with righteousness; the small man is conversant with profit."

7.36   The Master said: "The gentleman is broad-minded; the small man is always narrow-minded."

12.16   The Master said: "The gentleman helps others achieve their good ends; he does not help them achieve their evil ends. The small man does the opposite."

15.18   The Master said: "A gentleman considers righteousness his major principle: he practices it in accordance with the rituals, utters it in modest terms, and fulfils it with truthfulness. A gentleman indeed!"

15.34   The Master said: "The gentleman may not be recognized for small skills but can undertake great responsibilities; the small man cannot undertake great responsibilities but may be recognized in small skills."

16.8   Master Kong said: "The gentleman has three fears: he fears the decree of Heaven; he fears great men;[14] he fears the sage men's words. The small man, not knowing the decree of Heaven, does not fear it; he scorns great men and mocks the sage men's words."

GOOD GOVERNMENT

1.5   The Master said: "In governing a thousand-chariot state,[15] be reverent to your duties and truthful; economize expenditure and love men; employ the people at proper times."[16]

2.1   The Master said: "He who conducts government with virtue may be likened to the North Star, which, seated in its place, is surrounded by multitudes of other stars."

2.3   The Master said: "If you govern them with decrees and regulate them with

---

[10]A minister of Shu, a state south of the Yangzi River.
[11]Also known as Bu Shang, a member of Confucius' school. He figures prominently in the *Lunyu,* and became a major transmitter of the so-called *Confucian Classics* (see source 5).
[12]He will not be ignorant of the rituals.
[13]"All under Heaven" are all the Chinese.

[14]He is in awe of rulers.
[15]The military power of a state was computed by the number of chariots it could muster. A thousand-chariot state was fairly small.
[16]Employ their conscripted labor on public works during the slack times of the agricultural year.

punishments, the people will evade them but will have no sense of shame. If you govern them with virtue and regulate them with the rituals, they will have a sense of shame and flock to you."

2.19 Duke Ai[17] asked: "What must we do to make the people obedient?"

Master Kong replied: "Promote the upright, place them above the crooked, and the people shall be obedient. Promote the crooked, place them above the upright, and the people shall be disobedient."

2.20 Ji Kang-zi[18] asked: "How do you make the people reverent, loyal, and mutually encouraging?"

The Master said: "If you preside over them with dignity, they will be reverent; if you are filial and loving,[19] they will be loyal; if you promote the good and instruct the incapable, they will be mutually encouraging."

12.22 When Fan Chi asked about humanity, the Master said: "Loving men."

When asked about wisdom, the Master said: "Knowing men."

Fan Chi did not quite understand. The Master said: "Promote the upright, place them above the crooked, and you shall make the crooked upright."

Fan Chi retired and, on meeting Zi-xia, said: "A moment ago, I went to see the Master and asked him about wisdom. The Master said: 'Promote the upright, place them above the crooked, and you shall make the crooked upright.' What does it mean?"

Zi-xia said: "How rich is the statement! When Shun was in possession of the empire, he selected from the multitude and promoted Gao Yao.[20] Thus, inhumane men left him. When Tang was in possession of the empire, he selected from the multitude and promoted Yi Yin.[21] Thus, inhumane men left him."

13.1 When Zi-lu[22] asked about government, the Master said: "Guide them, and make them toil."

When asked to elaborate, the Master said: "Indefatigably."

REN

3.3 The Master said: "If a man is not humane, what can he do with the rituals? If a man is not humane, what can he do with music?"[23]

4.1 The Master said: "To live among humane men is beautiful. Not to reside among humane men — how can one be considered wise?"

4.3 The Master said: "Only a humane man is capable of loving men, and capable of loathing men."

4.4 The Master said: "If you bend your mind on humanity, you are free from evil."

4.5 The Master said: "Wealth and rank are what men desire: If you come by them undeservingly, you should not abide in them. Poverty and lowliness are what men loathe: If you come by them undeservingly, you should not abandon them. If a gentleman abandons humanity, how can he fulfill that name? A gentleman

[17]The prince of Lu (r. 494–466 B.C.E.), whom several of Confucius' disciples served.
[18]Prime minister to Duke Ai of Lu.
[19]Filial toward one's parents and loving to one's children.
[20]Yu Shun, last of the legendary Five Sage Emperors, chose the virtuous Gao Yao as his minister of justice.
[21]Tang, the founder of the Shang Dynasty and a figure highly revered by Master Kong. On Yi Yin, see source 5.
[22]Also known as Zhong Iou, he was one of the Master's best and most beloved students.
[23]The rituals were an elaborate, detailed code of proper etiquette governing all aspects of life, including sacrificial rites, state affairs, social relations, and day-to-day family matters. Specific rituals performed by an individual differed according to sex, age, social status, and context. Their purpose was to create harmony within a society where everyone knew his or her place and role and acted accordingly. Music, which represents the principle of harmony, accompanied court and family rituals. According to tradition, Confucius had a particular love of music and recommended that his followers become adept at it.

will not, for the space of a meal, depart from humanity. In haste and flurry, he always adheres to it; in fall and stumble, he always adheres to it."

13.19 When Fan Chi asked about humanity, the Master said: "Conduct yourself with respect; perform your duties with reverence; treat others with wholehearted sincerity. Even if you should journey to the Yis and Dis,[24] you cannot abandon these."

14.17 Zi-gong[25] said: "Guan Zhong was not a man of humanity, was he? When Duke Huan killed Prince Jiu, he not only was unable to die but became the duke's prime minister, instead."[26]

The Master said: "Guan Zhong helped Duke Huan become overlord of the various princes and set everything right in the empire. The people to this day benefit from his favors. But for Guan Zhong, we would be wearing our hair loose with our garments fastened on the left.[27] How could we expect him to be obstinately truthful like a common man or a common woman and hang himself in a gully without anyone knowing about it?"

15.24 Zi-gong asked: "Is there one single word that one can practice throughout one's life?"

The Master said: "It is perhaps 'like-hearted considerateness.' 'What you do not wish for yourself, do not impose on others.'"

17.23 Zi-gong said: "Does the gentleman also have people he loathes?"

The Master said: "Yes, I do. I loathe those who babble about other people's vices; I loathe those who, being in the lower stream, slander their superiors; I loathe those who are courageous but have no regard for the rituals; I loathe those who are resolute and daring but stubborn."

Then he said: "Ci,[28] are there also people you loathe?"

"I loathe those who plagiarize and consider themselves wise; I loathe those who are impertinent and consider themselves courageous; I loathe those who divulge other people's unseemly secrets and consider themselves straightforward."

THE RITUALS

6.27 The Master said: "A gentleman who is extensively learned in culture and restrains himself with the rituals is not likely to betray."[29]

12.1 When Yan Yuan[30] asked about humanity, the Master said: "'To restrain oneself and return to the rituals constitutes humanity.' One day one can restrain oneself and return to the rituals, all under Heaven will turn to humanity. The practice of humanity rests with oneself. Does it rest with anyone else?"

Yan Yuan said: "May I ask the details?"

The Master said: "That which does not conform to the rituals — do not look at it; that which does not conform to the rituals — do not listen to it; that which does not conform to the rituals — do not say it; that which does not conform to the rituals — do not do it."

---

[24]*Yi* is an ancient Chinese term for the non-Chinese, or barbarian, tribes to the east, especially Korea; *Di* is a similar term for the tribes to the north. "The Yis and Dis" meant, therefore, all the barbarian tribes on the borders of China.

[25]Also known as Duan-mu Ci, he was one of Master Kong's most faithful followers and later became prime minister of Lu and a famous diplomat.

[26]Guan Zhong (?–645 B.C.E.) was a brilliant statesman during the period described in the *Spring and Autumn Annals*, one of the *Five Confucian Classics* (see source 5). Rather than committing suicide when Duke Huan seized control of the state of Qi by murdering Guan Zhong's pupil, Prince Jiu, Guan Zhong became the duke's chief minister. As prime minister, he consolidated the state peacefully and protected its frontiers.

[27]Customs of non-Chinese tribes.

[28]Zi-Gong. See note 25.

[29]See note 23.

[30]Better known as Yan Hui (521?–481 B.C.E.), he had the reputation of being the most humane of Master Kong's students.

Yan Yuan said: "Slow-witted as I am, I beg to practice these remarks."

15.33 The Master said: "If a man's wisdom is equal to it,[31] but his humanity cannot keep it, even if he has acquired it, he will surely lose it. If his wisdom is equal to it and his humanity can keep it, but he does not preside over it with dignity, the people will not be reverent. If his wisdom is equal to it, his humanity can keep it, and he presides over it with dignity, but does not conduct it with the rituals, it is still not good."

17.10 The Master said: "'The rituals, the rituals,' they say. Do they merely refer to jade and silk? 'Music, music,' they say. Do they merely refer to bells and drums?"[32]

THE WELL-LIVED LIFE

6.22 When Fan Chi asked about wisdom, the Master said: "To apply oneself to the duties of man and, while revering the spirits and gods, to keep away from them[33] — this may be called wisdom."

When he asked about humanity, the Master said: "A man of humanity places hard work before reward. This may be called humanity."

7.3 The Master said: "Virtue uncultivated, learning undiscussed, the inability to move toward righteousness after hearing it, and the inability to correct my imperfections — these are my anxieties."

7.6 The Master said: "Aspire after the Way; adhere to virtue; rely on humanity; ramble among the arts."[34]

7.15 The Master said: "Eating coarse food, drinking plain water, and bending one arm for a pillow — happiness also lies therein. Wealth and rank acquired through unrighteous means are to me like drifting clouds."

7.33 The Master said: "As for sageness and humanity, how dare I claim them? But to learn it[35] insatiably and instruct others indefatigably — that much may be said of me, that is all."

Gong-xi Hua[36] said: "This is exactly what we disciples are unable to learn."

9.25 The Master said: "Keep wholehearted sincerity and truthfulness as your major principles. Do not befriend those beneath you. When you make a mistake, do not be afraid to correct it."

---

[31]The state.
[32]The external signs of the rituals and the instruments used to perform music are differentiated from the moral purposes behind them. See note 23.
[33]The spirits of the ancestors can influence a family's (or state's) fortunes for good or evil. The wise person employs rituals to keep the spirits happy and at a distance. In this aphorism Confucius also shows his all-consuming concern with human relations in the here-and-now.
[34]The Six Arts in the Era of Western Zhou were mastery of rituals, music, archery, charioteering, language, and arithmetic.
[35]The Way.
[36]This student of the Master became a respected diplomat.

Legalism: The Way of the State
▼▼▼

22 ▼ *Han Fei,*
THE WRITINGS OF MASTER HAN FEI

Daoism offered no active political program, whereas Confucius and his disciples preached a doctrine of benevolent reform based on virtuous imitation of the past. A third school of thought that emerged in the chaos of the late Zhou Era (and the several decades that followed) was *Legalism,* which rejected Daoism's Way of Nature and Confucianism's Moral Way. On their part, Legalist writers emphasized *law* as government's formulative force and advocated a radical restructuring of society in ways that were totally rational and up-to-date.

Legalism reached its apogee in the late third century B.C.E. in the writings of *Han Feizi* (Master Han Fei) and the policies of *Qin Shi Huangdi* (r. 221–210 B.C.E.). Han Fei was a prince of the state of Han who defected to its chief rival, the state of Qin, but eventually he ran afoul of Qin's chief minister and was forced to commit suicide in 233 B.C.E. Twelve years after Han Fei's death, the ruler of Qin, King Zheng (r. 247–221 B.C.E.), completed the conquest of "All under Heaven" and forged the First Chinese Empire — a unified entity upon which he imposed an empire-wide uniformity of law administered by a bureaucracy that was answerable to a central authority. Envisioning an empire that would last for centuries, he grandly styled himself Qin Shi Huangdi — the First Emperor of Qin (from which the term *China* is derived). The Qin Dynasty collapsed soon after Qin Shi Huangdi's death in 210 B.C.E., in large part because of rebellions against Qin's imperial structure and policies. In 202 B.C.E. a new dynasty arose, the Han, which adopted many of the policies of Legalist Qin but softened them by employing Confucian ideology, particularly the Confucian notion that there is a moral basis to the relationship between ruler and subjects. Thus, a Legalist-Confucian synthesis began to take shape — a synthesis that would serve Chinese emperors and their officials very well for more than 2,000 years.

Han Fei himself had been schooled in Confucian principles, but ultimately rejected the Moral Way for the Way of Law. He undoubtedly saw himself as a realist, as opposed to the idealists who had instructed him. To his mind, a strong dose of realism was needed to bring his present-day world out of the chaos that beset it. Before he died, Han Fei composed a number of essays on how to construct a stable and peaceful state. Our two selections present Han Fei's major principles of political philosophy.

QUESTIONS FOR ANALYSIS

1. In Han Fei's ideal state, which is the supreme governing authority: the will of the ruler or the law?
2. What are the "two handles," and how important are they to a Legalist state?
3. What roles do individuality and private initiative play in Han Fei's ideal state?
4. Imagine a conversation among a Legalist, a Daoist, and a Confucian regarding the ideal state and good government. Compose that conversation, giving each person the best possible arguments that reflect his particular school of thought.
5. Continue the conversation by having them debate the question: What makes something moral?

HAVING REGULATIONS

No country is permanently strong. Nor is any country permanently weak. If conformers to law are strong, the country is strong; if conformers to law are weak, the country is weak. . . .

Any ruler able to expel private crookedness and uphold public law, finds the people safe and the state in order; and any ruler able to expunge private action and act on public law, finds his army strong and his enemy weak. So, find out men following the discipline of laws and regulations, and place them above the body of officials. Then the sovereign cannot be deceived by anybody with fraud and falsehood. . . .

Therefore, the intelligent sovereign makes the law select men and makes no arbitrary promotion himself. He makes the law measure merits and makes no arbitrary regulation himself. In consequence, able men cannot be obscured, bad characters cannot be disguised; falsely praised fellows cannot be advanced, wrongly defamed people cannot be degraded. . . .

To govern the state by law is to praise the right and blame the wrong.

The law does not fawn on the noble. . . . Whatever the law applies to, the wise cannot reject nor can the brave defy. Punishment for fault never skips ministers, reward for good never misses commoners. Therefore, to correct the faults of the high, to rebuke the vices of the low, to suppress disorders, to decide against mistakes, to subdue the arrogant, to straighten the crooked, and to unify the folkways of the masses, nothing could match the law. To warn the officials and overawe the people, to rebuke obscenity and danger, and to forbid falsehood and deceit, nothing could match penalty. If penalty is severe, the noble cannot discriminate against the humble. If law is definite, the superiors are esteemed and not violated. If the superiors are not violated, the sovereign will become strong and able to maintain the proper course of government. Such was the reason why the early kings esteemed Legalism and handed it down to posterity. Should the lord of men discard law and practice selfishness, high and low would have no distinction.

THE TWO HANDLES

The means whereby the intelligent ruler controls his ministers are two handles only. The two handles are chastisement and commendation. What are meant by chastisement and commendation? To inflict death or torture upon culprits, is called chastisement; to bestow encouragements or rewards on men of merit, is called commendation.

Ministers are afraid of censure and punishment but fond of encouragement and reward. Therefore, if the lord of men uses the handles of chastisement and commendation, all ministers will dread his severity and turn to his liberality. The villainous ministers of the age are different. To men they hate they would by securing the handle of chastisement from the sovereign ascribe crimes; on men they love they would by securing the handle of commendation from the sovereign bestow rewards. Now supposing the lord of men placed the authority of punishment and the profit of reward not in his hands but let the ministers administer the affairs of reward and punishment instead, then everybody in the country would fear the ministers and slight the ruler, and turn to the ministers and away from the ruler. This is the calamity of the ruler's loss of the handles of chastisement and commendation.

Yin and Yang and the Dao of Good Health
▼▼▼

23 ▼ *THE YELLOW EMPEROR'S CLASSIC OF MEDICINE*

Of all the legendary Five Sage Emperors, none was more revered than the *Yellow Emperor (Huangdi).* The last of the mythic Three Sovereigns and the first of the Five Sage Emperors, the Yellow Emperor, who supposedly reigned in the twenty-seventh century B.C.E., was credited with fashioning China's first state and bestowing on its culture such gifts as wooden houses, ceramics, and writing, whereas his wife was credited with creating the first silk cloth. Daoists claimed the Yellow Emperor had articulated the basic principles of their philosophy, and Chinese physicians also claimed the Yellow Emperor as their own, believing he had laid down the foundations of their healing art.

The earliest known textbook of Chinese medicine is *The Yellow Emperor's Classic of Medicine,* which was written at some unknown time between maybe 1000 and 300 B.C.E. All we know for certain is that it was known and used during the Han Era (202 B.C.E.–220 C.E.), and scholars are certain that it could not have been composed anywhere near the supposed time of the Yellow Emperor. One indicator of this is the classic's focus on the cosmological theory of *Yin* and *Yang,* a way of explaining the natural world that developed during the Zhou Era.

The cosmology of Yin and Yang is based on the theory that the universe is composed of two basic principles: Yang is the male principle of light and life, the day and the sun, strength and activity; Yin is the female principle of darkness and death, the night and the moon, weakness and passivity. Heaven is the creation of Yang; Earth is the creation of Yin. Despite standing in opposition, the two principles are not at war with one another. To the contrary, they complement and complete one another. Every part of nature, including humans, contains its unique blend of Yin and Yang, and each element's mixture of Yin and Yang defines its essence and characteristics. From this it follows that maintaining the natural harmonious relationship of Yin and Yang that is special to each element of nature is essential for preserving its well-being and proper function.

In the following selection we see how the Chinese translated this cosmological theory into a philosophy of holistic, preventative medicine. Here we encounter an explanation of how the wise person must act in conformity with the four seasons, each of which is a manifestation of the cyclic interplay of Yin and Yang: Spring is when Yang is on the rise and Yin on the wane; summer is the season of Yang when Yin is dormant; fall is when Yin is on the rise and Yang on the wane; winter is the season of Yin when Yang is dormant.

QUESTIONS FOR ANALYSIS

1. How does this treatise offer a program for psychological and physical well-being?

2. Chinese philosophy was focused on the maintenance of harmony. Are the medical theories articulated in this treatise consistent with that focus? Please be specific in your answer.

3. This treatise speaks of conforming to the Dao. Review source 20. Are the principles contained in the Yellow Emperor's classic consistent with the principles articulated by Laozi?

4. Consider the following terms: secular; religious; naturalistic; scientific. Evaluate each in relation to the medical theories contained in this treatise. Which, if any, best characterizes this type of medicine? If you think none does, what term would you apply? Defend your choice.

Great Treatise on the Harmony of the Atmosphere of the Four Seasons with the Human Spirit

The three months of *Spring* are called the period of the beginning and development of life. The breaths of Heaven and Earth are prepared to give birth; thus everything is developing and flourishing.

After a night of sleep people should get up early in the morning; they should walk briskly around the yard; they should loosen their hair and slow down their movements; by these means they can fulfill their wish to live healthfully.

During this period one's body should be encouraged to live and not be killed; one should give to it freely and not take away from it; one should reward it and not punish it.

All this is in harmony with the breath of Spring and all this is the method for the protection of one's life.

Those who disobey the laws of Spring will be punished with an injury of the liver. For them the following Summer will bring chills and bad changes; thus they will have little to support their development in Summer.

The three months of *Summer* are called the period of luxurious growth. The breaths of Heaven and Earth intermingle and are beneficial. Everything is in bloom and begins to bear fruit.

After a night of sleep people should get up early in the morning. They should not weary during daytime and they should not allow their minds to become angry.

They should enable the best parts of their body and spirit to develop; they should enable their breath to communicate with the outside world; and they should act as though they loved everything outside.

All this is in harmony with the atmosphere of Summer and all this is the method for the protection of one's development.

Those who disobey the laws of Summer will be punished with an injury of the heart. For them Fall will bring intermittent fevers; thus they will have little to support them for harvest in Fall; and hence, at Winter solstice they will suffer from grave disease.

The three months of *Fall* are called the period of tranquillity of one's conduct. The atmosphere of Heaven is quick and the atmosphere of the Earth is clear.

People should retire early at night and rise early in the morning with the rooster. They should have their minds at peace in order to lessen the punishment of Fall. Soul and spirit should be gathered together in order to make the breath of Fall tranquil; and to keep their lungs pure they should not give vent to their desires.

All this is in harmony with the atmosphere of Fall and all this is the method for the protection of one's harvest.

Those who disobey the laws of Fall will be punished with an injury of the lungs. For them Winter will bring indigestion and diarrhoea; thus they will have little to support their storing of Winter.

The three months of *Winter* are called the period of closing and storing. Water freezes and the Earth cracks open. One should not disturb one's Yang.[1]

People should retire early at night and rise late in the morning and they should wait for the rising of the sun. They should suppress and conceal their wishes, as though they had no internal purpose, as though they had been fulfilled. People should try to escape the cold and they should seek warmth, they should not perspire upon the skin, they should let themselves be deprived of breath of the cold.

All this is in harmony with the atmosphere of Winter and all this is the method for the protection of one's storing.

Those who disobey the laws of Winter will suffer an injury of the kidneys; for them Spring will bring impotence,[2] and they will produce little. . . .

The sages followed the laws of nature and therefore their bodies were free from strange diseases; they did not lose anything which they had received by nature and their spirit of life was never exhausted.

Those who do not conform with the breath of Spring will not bring to life the region of the lesser Yang.[3] The atmosphere of their liver will change their constitution.

Those who do not conform with the atmosphere of Summer will not develop their greater Yang.[4] The atmosphere of their heart will become empty.

Those who do not conform with the atmosphere of Fall will not harvest their greater Yin.[5] The atmosphere of their lungs will be blocked from the lower burning space.[6]

Those who do not conform with the atmosphere of Winter will not store their lesser Yin.[7]

The atmosphere of their kidneys will be isolated and decreased.

Thus the interaction of the four seasons and the interaction of Yin and Yang is the foundation of everything in creation. Hence the sages conceived and developed their Yang in Spring and Summer, and conceived and developed their Yin in Fall and Winter in order to follow the rule of rules; and thus, together with everything in creation, maintained themselves at the gate of life and development.

Those who rebel against the basic rules of the universe sever their own roots and ruin their true selves. Yin and Yang, the two principles in nature, and the four seasons are the beginning and the end of everything and they are also the cause of life and death. Those who disobey the laws of the universe will give rise to calamities and visitations, while those who follow the laws of the universe remain free from dangerous illness, for they are the ones who have obtained Dao, the Right Way.

Dao was practiced by the sages and admired by the ignorant people. Obedience to the laws of Yin and Yang means life; disobedience means death. The obedient ones will rule while the rebels will be in disorder and confusion. Anything contrary to harmony with nature is disobedience and means rebellion to nature.

Hence the sages did not treat those who were already ill; they instructed those who were not yet ill. They did not want to rule those who were already rebellious; they guided those who were not yet rebellious. This is the meaning of the entire preceding discussion. To administer medicines to diseases which have already developed and to suppress revolts which have already developed is comparable to the behavior of those

---

[1]Yang is dormant and should be allowed to rest.
[2]The kidneys were believed to be the organ from which the sexual life force emanated.
[3]The human body has three regions, and each region has two divisions: a Yang and a Yin. Thus, every human has three Yin subregions and three Yang subregions. The subregion of the lesser Yang involves the gall bladder and the liver.
[4]The subregion of the greater Yang involves the small intestines and the heart.

[5]The greater Yin involves the lungs and the lower intestines.
[6]According to traditional Chinese anatomy, the body has three burning spaces — an upper, a middle, and a lower — that control their respective areas of the body. They also serve as a super cleansing system for the body. Apparently in this case the lungs will not be able to cleanse themselves properly.
[7]The lesser Yin involves the kidneys and the bladder.

persons who begin to dig a well after they have become thirsty, and of those who begin to cast weapons after they have already engaged in battle. Would these actions not be too late?

Hellenic Civilization:
A Rational Inquiry into Life

Early in the sixth century B.C.E., a small group of Greek intellectuals in Ionia began to challenge age-old mythic ways of explaining the workings of the universe by looking at the world as an objective phenomenon that could be studied in a rational, systematic manner. These thinkers, who sought to discover the physical underpinnings of the universe, are acknowledged as ancient Hellas's first philosophers and scientists and the people who established the Greek intellectual tradition of rational inquiry into all aspects of the physical and moral world.

As important as reason was in the formation of Greek thought, it never threatened to totally displace myth, mysticism, and religion. We would very much misunderstand Greek civilization by concluding that rational inquiry dominated every element of Greek life from the sixth century onward. Indeed, the nonrational permeated Greek society. This fact should not be surprising nor should it cause us to undervalue the achievements of Greek rationalists, whose modes of analysis became a hallmark of Greek civilization.

The period from about 750 B.C.E. down to the death of Alexander the Great in 323 B.C.E. is known as the *Hellenic Age* because, as we have seen, the people we call *Greeks* referred to themselves as *Hellenes* and their land as *Hellas.* (It was the Romans who began the tradition of calling all Hellenes *Greeks.*)

During the Hellenic Age the Greek World was very much a frontier society along the western periphery of the ancient civilized world. As a result, the Greeks were able to draw from the experiences of their more deeply rooted neighbors while simultaneously enjoying a certain amount of freedom to experiment culturally, especially in the areas of politics, thought, and art. This age was characterized by general Greek independence from foreign domination, political decentralization, intense rivalry among Hellas's many city-states, and a deep-seated ethnocentrism and even contempt for the non-Hellenic World. The Hellenes coined the term *barbarian* to refer to all non-Greek speakers, even the most civilized, because their alien languages sounded to Greek ears like so much babble, or *bar-bar.* The two dominating events of the Hellenic Age were the Persian Wars (499–450 B.C.E.) and the Peloponnesian War (431–404 B.C.E.). In the first, Greeks, under the leadership of Athens and Sparta, successfully withstood the threat of Persian domination. In the latter, again under Athenian and Spartan leadership, the whole Greek World was embroiled in a bitter family bloodletting. Despite the wars that dominated so much of the fifth century B.C.E., this hundred-year period is rightly regarded as the classical era of Hellenic civilization — an age when Hellas's intellectuals and artists soared to new heights as they explored the place of humans in a world that they confidently assumed was understandable and human-sized.

Hellenic Medicine
▼▼▼

24 ▼ *Hippocrates, ON THE SACRED DISEASE*

No matter how much they differed among themselves, early Greek scientists shared two basic assumptions: The world is a physical entity governed by regular, natural laws and not by mysterious supernatural forces or divine whims; and the human mind, unaided by magic or divine revelation, can understand how those laws function.

One area of Hellenic science that proved especially fruitful was medicine, especially as pioneered by the physicians of the island of Cos. Of the healers of Cos, the most famous in history and legend was *Hippocrates*. For all of his fame and reputed dominance in his field, we know very little about Hippocrates' life. Born on Cos around 460 B.C.E., he served as a member of that community's Guild of Aesculapius, a group of physicians who traced their origin back to the priesthood of the god of healing. Hippocrates' abilities as a practitioner and teacher of medicine eventually earned him a pan-Hellenic reputation, and he found himself traveling from city to city teaching his art and science — a science that stressed careful clinical observation of the nature and course of diseases. A late tradition holds that the Master Physician died in Thessaly in northern Greece around 377 B.C.E.

Succeeding generations of physicians looked to Hippocrates as the preeminent figure in their profession, and consequently his legend and stature grew beyond human proportions as the years passed. By 300 B.C.E. some seventy-two books were ascribed to him, but this Hippocratic body of medical knowledge clearly shows the hands of many different authors. It is impossible to say precisely which, if any, of these books Hippocrates composed, but it is reasonable to assume that they represent the medical tradition that he and generations of his students practiced and taught.

An integral part of that tradition was the theory of bodily *humors*. The physicians of Cos concluded from their observations of disease that the body contains four basic fluids, or humors: blood, phlegm, black bile, and yellow bile. Based on this, they further concluded that an excess of any humor — by reason of hereditary factors, environment, or accident — causes both psychic and physical imbalance. Depending on the humor that has thrown the body out of balance, the patient becomes sanguine, phlegmatic, melancholy, or bilious. Moreover, given human variability, no one's humors are ever in perfect balance; some humor always is dominant, which explains why people have different personalities and physical qualities. When, however, the imbalance becomes so great as to cause clinical illness, the physician must intervene. The Greek physician's art and science consisted of helping the body re-establish its natural harmony by administering or withholding foods and medicines that either reduced or increased one or more of the humors.

This theory underlies the document that appears here, an excerpt from *On the Sacred Disease,* one of the earliest treatises within the body of medical texts ascribed to Hippocrates. Here the author, putatively Hippocrates, deals with the issue of epilepsy.

QUESTIONS FOR ANALYSIS

1. Why does Hippocrates reject the notion that epilepsy comes from the gods?
2. How does he propose to cure this ailment?
3. Consider question 4 for source 23. Apply that same question to *On the Sacred Disease.*
4. Compare Chinese medicine as illustrated in source 23 with Hellenic medicine as illustrated in this source. Which strike you as more significant, the differences or the similarities? What conclusions follow from your answer?

In regard to the disease called "sacred," it seems to me to be no more divine or sacred than other diseases but has a natural cause from which it originates, like other afflictions. People regard its nature and cause as divine out of ignorance and credulity, because it is unlike other diseases. This notion of its divinity persists by virtue of people's inability to comprehend it and the simplicity of the means by which it is cured, for those afflicted are supposedly freed from it by purifications and incantations. If people reckon it divine because it incites awe, then instead of one sacred disease there would be many. As I will show, other diseases are no less awe-inspiring and strange, yet no one considers them sacred. . . . For example, one can see people grow mad and demented for no apparent reason and doing many strange things. I have known many persons to groan and cry out in their sleep . . . some jumping up and rushing out of doors, all deprived of their reason until they wake up. Afterward they are as healthy and rational as before, although pale and weak. And this will occur not once but frequently. There are many similar phenomena that it would be tedious to enumerate.

In my view, they who first associated this disease with the gods were people just like our present-day magicians, purifiers, charlatans, and quacks, who claim great piety and superior knowledge. Such persons, using superstition as camouflage for their own inability to offer any help, proclaimed the disease sacred . . . and instituted a method of treatment that protected them, namely purifications, incantations, and enforced abstinence from bathing and from many types of food. . . . Their course of treatment forbids the patient to have a black robe, because black is symbolic of death, or to sleep on a goatskin, or to wear one, or to put one foot on another, or one hand on another. All these things are reputed to be impediments to healing. . . . If the patient recovers they reap the honor and credit; if the patient dies, they have a perfect defense: The gods, not they, are to blame, seeing as they had administered nothing to eat or drink in the way of medicine, and they had not overheated the patient with baths. . . . To my way of thinking, if this course of treatment were correct, no Libyan living in the interior [of Africa] would be free of the disease, since they all sleep on goatskins and live on goat meat. . . . Then again, if such things, when administered as food, aggravate the disease, and if it is cured by abstinence from them, then the disease cannot be divine in origin, and the rites of purification provide no benefit. It is the food which is either beneficial or harmful. . . . Therefore, they who attempt to cure this disease in such a manner appear to me to be incapable of believing the disease is sacred or divine. . . .

Neither do I believe it to be a worthy opinion to maintain that a human body is polluted by the divine: the most impure substance being polluted by the most pure. . . . For it is the godhead that purifies, makes holy, and cleanses us from the greatest and most wicked of our offenses. . . . When we enter temples and the groves of gods we are sprinkled with holy water, not as a pollution but as a means of cleansing whatever pollution we had. And this principle seems to me to be the same in regard to purifications [offered by charlatan healers].

Consequently, this disease seems to me to be no more divine than others. It has the same nature and cause as other diseases. It is also no less curable than other diseases. . . . The key to its origin, as is the case with other diseases, lies in heredity. . . . There is nothing to prevent it from happening that where one or the other parent suffers from this malady, some of their children likewise suffer from it. . . . Another strong proof that this disease is no more divine in origin than any other is that it afflicts those who are by nature phlegmatic,[1] but it does not attack the bilious.[2] If this disease were more divine than other diseases, it should afflict all groups equally, making no distinction between the bilious and the phlegmatic. . . .

Since the brain, as the primary center of sensation and of the spirits, perceives whatever occurs in the body, if any unusual change takes place in the air, due to the seasons, the brain is changed by the state of the air. . . . And the disease called "sacred" arises from . . . those things that enter and leave the body, such as cold, the sun, and winds, which are constantly changing and never at rest. . . . Therefore the physician should understand and distinguish each individual situation, so that at one time he might add nourishment, at another time withhold it. In this disease, as in all others, he must endeavor not to feed the disease, but he must attempt to wear it out by administering whatever is most contrary to each disease and not that which favors and is allied to it. For it grows vigorous and increases through that which is allied to it, but it wears out and disappears under the administration of whatever is opposed to it.[3] Whoever is knowledgeable enough to render a person humid or dry, hot or cold by regimen can also cure this disease, if the physician recognizes the proper season for administering remedies. The physician can do so without attention to purifications, spells, and all other forms of hocus-pocus.

---

[1] A calm temperament that can reach sluggishness due to excessive phlegm.

[2] Those who, by reason of the dominance of bile in their systems, have peevish, sour-tempered dispositions.

[3] Specific foods and ministrations stimulate the production of specific humors; others reduce them.

The Athenian as Citizen
▼▼▼

25 ▾ Thucydides, *HISTORY OF THE PELOPONNESIAN WAR*

During the eighth century B.C.E., Homer, the putative author of the *Iliad* and the *Odyssey,* interpreted the past through the medium of poetic myth. By the mid fifth century certain Hellenic researchers were recapturing and interpreting the past through the more prosaic but accurate medium of history. The word *historia* is Greek and means "knowledge achieved through inquiry." As we have seen, the Israelites and the Persians had already evolved a sense of divinely directed history. However, it was the Greeks who became western Eurasia's first students of secular history. That means researchers who systematically studied worldly affairs divorced from any consideration of divine intervention or control. The particular genius of Greek *historiography* (the writing of history) was that certain thinkers, largely beginning with *Herodotus* (ca. 484–424 B.C.E.), believed that human events could be reconstructed and made comprehensible through careful research into the human record.

One such student of the human past was *Thucydides* (ca. 460–400 B.C.E.), widely reputed to have been classical Hellas's greatest historian. Thucydides was a citizen of Athens in an age when Hellenic civilization was dominated by rivalry among its many different city-states, or *poleis* (the plural of *polis*). During Thucydides' youth and young manhood, Athens was led by *Pericles,* who from 461 through 429 B.C.E. was a dominant force in shaping Athenian democracy.

Contrary to modern popular belief, democracy was not common in the Hellenic World. Hellas's competing poleis were organized along diverse political, social, military, and economic lines. Some were dictatorships, many were oligarchies (rule by small factions), and very few, like Athens, were democracies. Each of classical Hellas's poleis, including democratic Athens, were brotherhoods of warriors organized for the primary purpose of waging war — usually against other Hellenes — and organization for war played a major role in directing the course of a polis's political structures. The fact that Athens relied primarily on its navy raised significantly the importance of Athens's poorest citizens, who could not afford the time or the expense of training and serving as heavy-armed footsoldiers but could and did serve as rowers and marines in the city's fleet. With the new status of these poor citizens came political power, and under Pericles the city took its final steps toward full participatory democracy, although there was still plenty of opportunity for persuasive and gifted citizens such as Pericles to play leading roles in directing the city's fortunes.

In 431 B.C.E. Pericles led Athens into the *Peloponnesian War* against the oligarchic polis of *Sparta* and its allies. The war dragged on for a generation, ending in 404 with a Spartan victory. In the early stages of the conflict it had seemed as though there was no way Athens could lose the war, given its command of the sea lanes. In the winter of 431/430 Athens paused to honor those citizens who had fallen in battle during the first year of fighting and called upon Pericles, its unofficial First Citizen, to deliver the eulogy. Pericles used the occasion to praise the polis for which those citizens had lived and died and, by extension, to speak well of his own policies.

Thucydides undoubtedly attended that funeral and perhaps dreamed of his own glorious service to Athens. Six years later Thucydides commanded a small naval squadron that failed to relieve a besieged Athenian infantry force, and for that failure he was forced into exile. An avid student of human affairs, especially politics, Thucydides used his enforced retirement to study the war and write its history. As he noted in the opening lines of his *History,* he had begun writing about the war from its outbreak because he believed it would prove to be the most memorable conflict in all of Hellenic history, outstripping even the Trojan and Persian wars in magnitude. His purpose was simple: to provide all Hellenes with "an everlasting possession," whose careful study would enable them to avoid similar errors in the future.

In his attempt to create an aura of dramatic verisimilitude, thereby assuring his work's being read and preserved, Thucydides employed the convention of including numerous speeches into his *History*. As he admitted, the speeches were not verbatim accounts, but he claimed to preserve the sense of either what was said or what he judged should have been said on a particular occasion. Because Pericles' *Funeral Oration* was such a public and memorable speech, there is good reason to believe Thucydides has preserved the essence of Pericles' message. That message tells us a good deal about Hellenic secular culture in the fifth century B.C.E.

Just as telling is Thucydides' description of the plague that ravaged Athens in the summer of 430. Plato (source 27) implies that Hippocrates visited and taught medicine in Athens. Although it is not possible to verify this, it is clear that Hippocratic medical principles were part of Athens's intellectual atmosphere by the end of the fifth century B.C.E. It is equally clear that Thucydides had enjoyed all of the educational benefits available to a wealthy Athenian citizen, and that included at least an introduction to Hippocratic medicine.

QUESTIONS FOR ANALYSIS

1. How does Pericles define Athenian democracy? According to him, what sort of citizens does this democracy breed, and how does Athens help its citizens achieve their full potential?
2. In his idealized portrait of Athens, Pericles contrasts Athens's spirit with that of Sparta. According to him, how do the Spartans live? As Pericles sees it, what is wrong with the Spartan way of life?
3. Why is Athens, in Pericles' words, "the school of Hellas"?
4. How, if at all, does Pericles' speech provide evidence of Hellenic preoccupation with the human individual, the life of the polis, and rational analysis?
5. In what ways, if at all, does Thucydides' description of the plague conform to the principles of Hippocratic medicine?
6. How, if at all, does Thucydides' description of the consequences of the plague serve as a commentary on Pericles' speech? Please be specific.
7. Compose a commentary on this entire excerpt, the speech and the plague sequence, by Confucius.

During the . . . winter, . . . the funeral of those who first fell in this war was celebrated by the Athenians at the public charge. . . . Over those who were the first buried Pericles was chosen to speak. At the fitting moment he . . . spoke as follows: . . .

"I will speak first of our ancestors, for it is right and becoming that now, when we are lamenting the dead, a tribute should be paid to their memory. There has never been a time when they did not inhabit this land, which by their valor they have handed down from generation to generation, and we have received from them a free state. But if they were worthy of praise, still more were our fathers, who added to their inheritance, and after many a struggle transmitted to us their sons this great empire. And we ourselves assembled here today, who are still most of us in the vigor of life, have chiefly done the work of improvement, and have richly endowed our city with all things, so that she is sufficient for herself both in peace and war. . . . But before I praise the dead, I should like to point out by what principles of action we rose to power, and under what institutions and through what manner of life our empire became great. For I conceive that such thoughts are not unsuited to the occasion, and that this numerous assembly of citizens and strangers may profitably listen to them.

"Our form of government does not enter into rivalry with the institutions of others. We do not copy our neighbors, but are an example to them. It is true that we are called a democracy, for the administration is in the hands of the many and not of the few. But while the law secures equal justice to all alike in their private disputes, the claim of excellence is also recognized; and when a citizen is in any way distinguished, he is preferred to the public service, not as a matter of privilege, but as the reward of merit. Neither is poverty a bar, but a man may benefit his country whatever be the obscurity of his condition. There is no exclusiveness in our public life, and in our private intercourse we are not suspicious of one another, nor angry with our neighbor if he does what he likes; we do not put on sour looks at him which, though harmless, are not pleasant. While we are thus unconstrained in our private intercourse, a spirit of reverence pervades our public acts; we are prevented from doing wrong by respect for authority and for the laws. . . .

"And we have not forgotten to provide for our weary spirits many relaxations from toil; we have regular games and sacrifices throughout the year; at home the style of our life is refined; and the delight which we daily feel in all these things helps to banish melancholy. Because of the greatness of our city the fruits of the whole earth flow in upon us; so that we enjoy the goods of other countries as freely as of our own.

"Then, again, our military training is in many respects superior to that of our adversaries. Our city is thrown open to the world, and we never expel a foreigner or prevent him from seeing or learning anything of which the secret if revealed to an enemy might profit him. We rely not upon management or trickery, but upon our own hearts and hands. And in the matter of education, whereas they from early youth are always undergoing laborious exercises which are to make them brave,[1] we live at ease, and yet are equally ready to face the perils which they face. . . .

"If then we prefer to meet danger with a light heart but without laborious training, and with a courage which is gained by habit and not enforced by law, are we not greatly the gainers? Since we do not anticipate the pain, although, when the hour comes, we can be as brave as those who never allow themselves to rest; and thus too our city is equally admirable in peace and in war. For we are lovers of the beautiful, yet simple in our tastes, and we cultivate the mind without loss of manliness. Wealth we employ, not for talk and ostentation, but when there is a real use for it. To avow poverty with us is no disgrace; the true disgrace is in doing nothing to avoid it. An Athenian citizen does not neglect the state because he takes care of his own household; and even those of us who are engaged in business have a very fair idea of politics. We alone regard a man who takes no interest in public affairs, not as a harmless, but as a useless character; and if few of us are originators, we are all sound judges of a policy. The great impediment to action is, in our opinion, not discussion, but the want of that knowledge which is gained by discussion preparatory to action. For we have a peculiar power of thinking before we act and of acting too, whereas other men are courageous from ignorance but hesitate upon reflection. And they are surely to be esteemed the bravest spirits who, having the clearest sense both of the pains and pleasures of life, do not on that account shrink from danger. . . . To sum up: I say that Athens is the school of Hellas, and that the individual Athenian in his own person seems to have the power of adapting himself to the most varied

---

[1]Spartan training of their youth was noted for its rigor.

forms of action with the utmost versatility and grace. This is no passing and idle word, but truth and fact; and the assertion is verified by the position to which these qualities have raised the state. For in the hour of trial Athens alone among her contemporaries is superior to the report of her. No enemy who comes against her is indignant at the reverses which he sustains at the hands of such a city; no subject complains that his masters are unworthy of him. And we shall assuredly not be without witnesses; there are mighty monuments of our power which will make us the wonder of this and of succeeding ages; we shall not need the praises of Homer or of any other panegyrist whose poetry may please for the moment, although his representation of the facts will not bear the light of day. For we have compelled every land and every sea to open a path for our valor, and have everywhere planted eternal memorials of our friendship and of our enmity. Such is the city for whose sake these men nobly fought and died; they could not bear the thought that she might be taken from them; and every one of us who survives should gladly toil on her behalf.

"I have dwelt upon the greatness of Athens because I want to show you that we are contending for a higher prize than those who enjoy none of these privileges, and to establish by manifest proof the merit of these men whom I am now commemorating. Their loftiest praise has been already spoken. For in magnifying the city I have magnified them, and men like them whose virtues made her glorious. . . ."

Such was the order of the funeral celebrated in this winter, with the end of which ended the first year of the Peloponnesian War. As soon as summer returned, the Peloponnesian army[2] . . . invaded Attica,[3] where they established themselves and ravaged the country. They had not been there many days when the plague broke out at Athens

for the first time. A similar disorder is said to have previously smitten many places, particularly Lemnos,[4] but there is no record of such a pestilence occurring elsewhere, or of so great a destruction of human life. For a while physicians, in ignorance of the nature of the disease, sought to apply remedies; but it was in vain, and they themselves were among the first victims, because they most often came into contact with it. No human art was of any avail, and as to supplications in temples, inquiries of oracles,[5] and the like, they were utterly useless, and at last men were overpowered by the calamity and gave them all up.

The disease is said to have begun south of Egypt in Ethiopia; thence it descended[6] into Egypt and Libya,[7] and after spreading over the greater part of the Persian empire, suddenly fell upon Athens. It first attacked the inhabitants of the Piraeus,[8] and it was supposed that the Peloponnesians had poisoned the cisterns, no conduits having as yet been made there. It afterwards reached the upper city, and then the mortality became far greater. As to its probable origin or the causes which might or could have produced such a disturbance of nature, every man, whether a physician or not, will give his own opinion. But I shall describe its actual course, and the symptoms by which any one who knows them beforehand may recognize the disorder should it ever reappear. For I was myself attacked and witnessed the sufferings of others.

The season was admitted to have been remarkably free from ordinary sickness and if anybody was already ill of any other disease, it was absorbed in this. Many who were in perfect health, all in a moment, and without any apparent reason, were seized with violent heats in the head and with redness and inflammation of the eyes. Internally the throat and the tongue were quickly suffused with blood, and the breath became

---

[2]The Spartans and their allies. Sparta was located in the *Peloponnesus,* the southern peninsula of the Greek mainland.
[3]The peninsula on which Athens was located.
[4]An Aegean island.
[5]Priestesses of Apollo who looked into the future.

[6]The Nile flows northward; therefore, one descends the river while traveling from south to north.
[7]The region of North Africa immediately west of Egypt.
[8]Athens's port.

unnatural and fetid. There followed sneezing and hoarseness; in a short time the disorder, accompanied by a violent cough, reached the chest; then fastening lower down, it would move the stomach and bring on all the vomits of bile to which physicians have ever given names; and they were very distressing. An ineffectual retching producing violent convulsions attacked most of the sufferers; some as soon as the previous symptoms had abated, others not until long afterwards. The body externally was not so very hot to the touch, nor yet pale; it was of a livid color inclining to red, and breaking out in pustules and ulcers. But the internal fever was intense; the sufferers could not bear to have on them even the finest linen garment; they insisted on being naked, and there was nothing which they longed for more eagerly than to throw themselves into cold water. And many of those who had no one to look after them actually plunged into the cisterns, for they were tormented by unceasing thirst, which was not in the least assuaged whether they drank little or much. They could not sleep; a restlessness which was intolerable never left them. While the disease was at its height the body, instead of wasting away, held out amid these sufferings in a marvelous manner, and either they died on the seventh or ninth day, not of weakness, for their strength was not exhausted, but of internal fever, which was the end of most; or, if they survived, then the disease descended into the bowels and there produced violent ulceration; severe diarrhoea at the same time set in, and at a later stage caused exhaustion, which finally with few exceptions carried them off. For the disorder which had originally settled in the head passed gradually through the whole body, and, if a person got over the worst, would often seize the extremities and leave its mark, attacking the privy parts and the fingers and the toes, and some escaped with the loss of these, some with the loss of their eyes. Some again had no sooner recovered than they were seized with a forgetfulness of all things and knew neither themselves nor their friends.

The malady took a form not to be described, and the fury with which it fastened upon each sufferer was too much for human nature to endure. There was one circumstance in particular which distinguished it from ordinary diseases. The birds and animals which feed on human flesh, although so many bodies were lying unburied, either never came near them, or died if they touched them. This was proved by a remarkable disappearance of the birds of prey, who were not to be seen either about the bodies or anywhere else; while in the case of the dogs the fact was even more obvious, because they live with man.

Such was the general nature of the disease: I omit many strange peculiarities which characterized individual cases. None of the ordinary sicknesses attacked any one while it lasted, or, if they did, they ended in the plague. Some of the sufferers died from want of care, others equally who were receiving the greatest attention. No single remedy could be deemed a specific; for that which did good to one did harm to another. No constitution was of itself strong enough to resist or weak enough to escape the attacks; the disease carried off all alike and defied every mode of treatment. Most appalling was the despondency which seized upon any one who felt himself sickening, for he instantly abandoned his mind to despair and, instead of holding out, absolutely threw away his chance of life. Appalling too was the rapidity with which men caught the infection; dying like sheep if they attended on one another; and this was the principal cause of mortality. When they were afraid to visit one another, the sufferers died in their solitude, so that many houses were empty because there had been no one left to take care of the sick; or if they ventured they perished, especially those who aspired to heroism. For they went to see their friends without thought of themselves and were ashamed to leave them, even at a time when the very relations of the dying were at last growing weary and ceased to make lamentations, overwhelmed by the vastness of the calamity. But whatever instances there may have been of such devotion, more often the sick and the dying were tended by the pitying care of those who had recovered, because they knew the course of the disease and were themselves free from apprehension. For no one was ever attacked a second time, or not with a fatal result. All men congratulated them, and they themselves, in the excess of their joy at the moment, had an innocent fancy that they could not die of any other sickness.

The crowding of the people out of the country into the city aggravated the misery; and the newly-arrived suffered most. For, having no houses of their own, but inhabiting in the height of summer stifling huts, the mortality among them was dreadful, and they perished in wild disorder. The dead lay as they had died, one upon another, while others hardly alive wallowed in the streets and crawled about every fountain craving for water. The temples in which they lodged were full of the corpses of those who died in them; for the violence of the calamity was such that men, not knowing where to turn, grew reckless of all law, human and divine. The customs which had hitherto been observed at funerals were universally violated, and they buried their dead each one as best he could. Many, having no proper appliances, because the deaths in their household had been so frequent, made no scruple of using the burial-place of others. When one man had raised a funeral pile, others would come,

and throwing on their dead first, set fire to it; or when some other corpse was already burning, before they could be stopped would throw their own dead upon it and depart.

There were other and worse forms of lawlessness which the plague introduced at Athens. Men who had hitherto concealed their indulgence in pleasure now grew bolder. For, seeing the sudden change, — how the rich died in a moment, and those who had nothing immediately inherited their property, — they reflected that life and riches were alike transitory, and they resolved to enjoy themselves while they could, and to think only of pleasure. Who would be willing to sacrifice himself to the law of honor when he knew not whether he would ever live to be held in honor? The pleasure of the moment and any sort of thing which conduced to it took the place both of honor and of expediency. No fear of god or law of man deterred a criminal. Those who saw all perishing alike, thought that the worship or neglect of the gods made no difference. For offences against human law no punishment was to be feared; no one would live long enough to be called to account. Already a far heavier sentence had been passed and was hanging over a man's head; before that fell, why should he not take a little pleasure?

Bacchic Maenads: Feminine Religious Ecstasy
▼▼▼

26 ▾ *Euripides, THE BACCHAE*

Pericles concluded that Athens had become "the school of Hellas" because of the freedom its citizens enjoyed. As citizens with a vested interest in the polis, its people could develop independence and self-reliance easily and in many different directions. There is truth in Pericles' vision, and undoubtedly this freedom contributed substantially to Athens's vitality as Hellas's chief intellectual and artistic center during the fifth century B.C.E.

In the course of that century Athens created one of the Hellenic World's most enduring art forms — tragic drama. During the sixth century B.C.E. improvised songs and dance performed at festivals honoring Dionysus (also known as Bacchus), the god of wine, evolved into formal lyric narratives and dances, and from there became full-fledged dramas. The first known dramatic contest at which a prize was offered took place in Athens around 534 B.C.E. By the fifth century B.C.E., tragic dramas were annually offered in competition during Athens's six-day spring festival dedicated to Dionysus. The competition and production of the plays was supported by public funds, and money was even put aside to allow the poorest of Athens's citizens leisure time to attend the festivities and plays.

As Athenian tragic drama evolved, three playwrights emerged as the city's preeminent dramatists and dramatic innovators: *Aeschylus* (ca. 525–456 B.C.E.); *Sophocles* (ca. 496–406 B.C.E.); and *Euripides* (ca. 480–406 B.C.E.). Of the three, Euripides won the fewest first prizes, despite having composed about ninety plays, but more of his tragedies have survived (nineteen, but one is of doubtful authenticity) than those of Aeschylus and Sophocles combined. The reason for his later popularity, which assured the survival of so many of his plays, is that, more than any other Hellenic playwright, Euripides explored the dark side of the human psyche and the underside of Athenian life. Put simply, he was a master psychologist and an outspoken critic of the indignities suffered by those whom Athenian society exploited or overlooked: war victims, slaves, foreigners, and especially women.

Late in life he was forced to leave Athens, probably because of his outspoken opposition to Athenian atrocities in the Peloponnesian War, and he took up residence in the wilds of Macedon. Following Euripedes's death in 406 B.C.E., his son returned to Athens, bearing with him three plays that Euripides had written in exile. One of them, the *Bacchae,* was produced for the City Dionysia in 405, where it won first prize — only the fifth first prize that the Athenians accorded the great playwright.

The *Bacchae* is a troubling play. Some interpret it as the aged Euripides' recantation of the rationalism that pervaded his earlier work. Others see it as a final indictment of religion by an unregenerate skeptic. It is neither. The play unfolds as a rationalist's argument for a balanced acceptance of all religious expressions. Its underlying theme is that rejection of one religion in favor of another, no matter how irrational the rejected cult might appear to be, is intellectual arrogance that leads to dangerous imbalance and inevitable disaster. Composed of mind and body, humans need both lofty spirituality and earthy emotionalism.

The story revolves around the return of Dionysus to Thebes, where he was born from a union of Zeus, king of the gods, and a mortal, Semele, the daughter of Cadmus, who was then king of the city. The god has come out of western Asia (where his cult originated), followed by a group of ecstatic female devotees. His purpose is to redeem the reputation of his deceased mother, whose sisters said she lied when claiming Dionysus was the son of Zeus. Because they refused to recognize his divinity, Dionysus drove the sisters and every other woman in Thebes mad with frenzy, whereupon they took to the mountains to perform bacchanal rites in devotion to him. The young king of Thebes, Pentheus, grandson of Cadmus, refuses to accept this new religion. Determined to root out a pernicious rite that has led women to abandon their traditional roles, Pentheus disguises himself as a woman and goes to the mountains to spy on the bacchants. Dionysus blinds the women to Pentheus's identity and convinces them he is a mountain lion. Led by Pentheus's mother, Agave, and her two sisters (the three sisters who had rejected Semele's story of her divine pregnancy), the women tear Pentheus apart and carry his head back to Thebes in triumph. The still-living former king, Cadmus, informs Agave of her murderous error, which has extinguished the male line of his royal house.

Dionysus then appears and justifies Pentheus's death. He also announces that the three sisters will be banished from the city because of their blood guilt, and Cadmus and his wife will undergo great trials before eventual redemption. Full price has been paid for the blasphemy of not recognizing Dionysus's godhood.

Our selection comes from the play's midpoint, where a herdsman describes to Pentheus the activities of the bacchants, known as *Maenads* (literally, "mad women"), whom he observed on Mount Cithaeron.

QUESTIONS FOR ANALYSIS

1. Maenads were often accused of indulging in orgiastic rites of sexual license. Where did Euripides stand on the issue?
2. Maenads were also accused of uninhibited drunkenness. Where did Euripides stand on the issue?
3. Maenads were also accused of violence. Where did Euripides stand on the issue?
4. Why do you think Euripides has the herdsman report miracles performed by the Maenads?
5. It has been argued that bacchanal worship included "rituals of inversion," whereby women participated in acts that inverted, or turned on their head, normal female activities or modes of behavior. Can you find any in this passage?
6. Some scholars argue that the bacchanal rites were a safety valve that allowed women to break out momentarily from the confines of the roles assigned them by their society. Do you see any evidence to support that thesis in this source?
7. Some scholars argue that whatever other purposes the bacchanal rites served, rumors regarding what transpired during them reinforced men's stereotypes of women as out-of-control creatures when restraints were lifted, and helped justify male domination of them. Comment.

MESSENGER: Pentheus, king of Thebes, I come from Cithaeron[1] where the gleaming flakes of snow fall on and on forever —

PENTHEUS: Get to the point. What is your message, man?

MESSENGER: Sir, I have seen the holy Maenads, the women who ran barefoot and crazy from the city, and I wanted to report to you and Thebes what weird fantastic things, what miracles and more than miracles, these women do. But may I speak freely in my own way and words, or make it short? I fear the harsh impatience of your nature, sire, too kingly and too quick to anger.

PENTHEUS: Speak freely. You have my promise: I shall not punish you. Displeasure with a man who speaks the truth is wrong. However, the more terrible this tale of yours, that much more terrible will be the punishment I impose upon that man who taught our womenfolk this strange new magic.

---

[1]The mountain was sacred to Dionysus and the Muses.

MESSENGER: About that hour when the sun lets loose its light to warm the Earth, our grazing herds of cows had just begun to climb the path along the mountain ridge. Suddenly I saw three companies of dancing women, one led by Autonoë, the second captained by your mother Agave, while Ino led the third.[2] There they lay in the deep sleep of exhaustion, some resting on boughs of fir, others sleeping where they fell, here and there among the oak leaves — but all modestly and soberly, not, as you think, drunk with wine, nor wandering, led astray by the music of the flute, to hunt their Aphrodite[3] through the woods.

But your mother heard the lowing of our hornèd herds, and springing to her feet, gave a great cry to waken them from sleep. And they too, rubbing the bloom of soft sleep from their eyes, rose up lightly and straight — a lovely sight to see: all as one, the old women and the young and the unmarried girls. First they let their hair fall loose, down over their shoulders, and those whose straps had slipped fastened their skins of fawn[4] with writhing snakes[5] that licked their cheeks. Breasts swollen with milk, new mothers who had left their babies behind at home nestled gazelles and young wolves in their arms, suckling them. Then they crowned their hair with leaves, ivy and oak and flowering bryony. One woman struck her thyrsus[6] against a rock and a fountain of cool water came bubbling up. Another drove her fennel in the ground, and where it struck the Earth, at the touch of god, a spring of wine poured out. Those who wanted milk scratched at the soil with bare fingers and the white milk came welling up. Pure honey spurted, streaming, from their wands. If you had been there and seen these wonders for yourself, you would have gone down on your knees and prayed to the god you now deny.

We cowherds and shepherds gathered in small groups, wondering and arguing among ourselves at these fantastic things, the awful miracles those women did. But then a city fellow with the knack of words rose to his feet and said: "All you who live upon the pastures of the mountain, what do you say? Shall we earn a little favor with King Pentheus by hunting his mother Agave out of the revels?" Falling in with his suggestion, we withdrew and set ourselves in ambush, hidden by the leaves among the undergrowth. Then at a signal all the Bacchae whirled their wands for the revels to begin. With one voice they cried aloud: "O Iacchus![7] Son of Zeus!" "O Bromius!"[8] they cried until the beasts and all the mountain seemed wild with divinity. And when they ran, everything ran with them.

It happened, however, that Agave ran near the ambush where I lay concealed. Leaping up, I tried to seize her, but she gave a cry: "Hounds who run with me, men are hunting us down! Follow, follow me! Use your wands for weapons."

At this we fled and barely missed being torn to pieces by the women. Unarmed, they swooped down upon the herds of cattle grazing there on the green of the meadow. And then you could have seen a single woman with bare hands tear a fat calf, still bellowing with fright, in two, while others clawed the heifers to pieces. There were ribs and cloven hooves scattered everywhere, and scraps smeared with blood hung from the fir trees. And bulls, their raging fury gathered in their horns, lowered their heads to charge, then fell, stumbling to the earth, pulled down by hordes of women and stripped of flesh and skin more quickly, sire, than you could blink your

---

[2]The three were sisters.

[3]Goddess of erotic love.

[4]Maenads wore cloaks of animal skin, usually a fawn's skin because it was considered holy. See source 28.

[5]Some apparently also adorned their heads with snakes. See source 28.

[6]A shaft of fennel topped with ivy. It was carried in the right hand, with the ivy to the rear. See source 28.

[7]One of Dionysus's titles, it probably derives from a cry of joy in his honor.

[8]Another of his titles, it means "roarer," and refers to his manifestations as a bull-god and a lion-god.

royal eyes.[9] Then, carried up by their own speed, they flew like birds across the spreading fields along Asopus' stream[10] where most of all the ground is good for harvesting. Like invaders they swooped on Hysiae and on Erythrae[11] in the foothills of Cithaeron. Everything in sight they pillaged and destroyed. They snatched the children from their homes. And when they piled their plunder on their backs, it stayed in place, untied. Nothing, neither bronze nor iron, fell to the dark earth. Flames flickered in their curls and did not burn them. Then the villagers, furious at what the women did, took to arms. And *there,* sire, was something terrible to see. For the men's spears were pointed and sharp, and yet drew no blood, whereas the wands the women threw inflicted wounds. And then the men *ran,* routed by women! Some god, I say, was with them. The Bacchae then returned where they had started, by the springs the god had made, and washed their hands while the snakes licked away the drops of blood that dabbled their cheeks.

Whoever this god may be, sire, welcome him to Thebes. For he is great in many other ways as well. It was he, or so they say, who gave to mortal men the gift of lovely wine by which our suffering is stopped. And if there is no god of wine, there is no love, no Aphrodite either, nor other pleasure left to men.

(Exit messenger.)

---

[9]Maenads were accused of tearing living animals apart and eating their raw flesh during their ecstacies. We do not know what rites they performed, but it is imaginable that they ritually slaughtered and consumed animals, possibly raw, as a communion feast.

[10]The god of the river that also bore his name.
[11]Two nearby villages.

Socrates' Defense of Philosophy
▼▼▼

27 ▼ *Plato, APOLOGIA*

The *Dialogues* of Plato (427–348 B.C.E.) are the major source for the life and teachings of *Socrates* of Athens (ca. 469–399 B.C.E.), Hellas's first great ethical and social philosopher. Like Confucius, his near contemporary, Socrates left behind only a small number of students and no writings, but also like Confucius, he served *the* pivotal role in the development of his culture's approach to philosophy.

Socrates' main contribution to Greek thought was that he refused to accept easy answers as he searched after wisdom and virtue, which were to him the same. Like Confucius, Socrates had an implicit faith that action inevitably follows knowledge. The moral person, for Socrates, is one who knows the good and acts accordingly. Unlike Confucius, however, Socrates refused to accept the answers of tradition and the way of the past as infallible guides to wisdom and moral behavior.

Socrates' uncompromising search for truth and goodness of soul ultimately earned him a number of enemies, and he finally fell victim to the mood of bitter recrimination that followed Athens's defeat in the Peloponnesian War. In 399 a conservative politician charged Socrates with impiety against the gods and corruption of youth. On trial for his life, the seventy-year-old philosopher refused to defend himself against the charges, choosing instead to offer a justification of his life and methods of inquiry. He was found guilty and condemned to death by a jury that fully expected him to flee the city. Socrates, faithful to the end to his sense of morality, refused to avoid the sentence and went serenely to his death.

The best account of Socrates' defense, or *apologia,* at his trial comes to us from *Plato,* Socrates' brilliant pupil and, arguably, the most original of all of Hellas's great thinkers. It is impossible to say exactly where Socrates' ideas leave off and Plato's begin in the many philosophical dialogues Plato composed and in which his former master serves as hero. It is likely, however, that Plato's *Apologia* is faithful to the concepts, if not the actual words, that Socrates presented in his defense of philosophy.

Following the death of his teacher, Plato withdrew from his native Athens and did not return for twelve years. Upon return, he established his own school of philosophy, the *Academy,* which he presided over for nearly forty years, although later he again left Athens, this time for six years. When he returned, he again took up residence again in the Academy and for the rest of his life instructed there the men and women who attended in large numbers. The Academy continued to be a center of Greek philosophical inquiry until the Christian Emperor Justinian ordered its closing in 529 C.E. For more than 900 years the Academy served the cause of the unfettered pursuit of wisdom that Socrates so ably defended and died for.

QUESTIONS FOR ANALYSIS

1. What defense does Socrates offer against the charges of impiety and corruption of Athens's youth?
2. According to Socrates, what necessary social function does he serve?
3. What wisdom does Socrates claim to have?
4. What does he teach and what is his method of instruction? Can you discover in this text what the "Socratic method" of analysis, argumentation, and education is?
5. According to Socrates, what is a human being's highest function and greatest responsibility?
6. How was it possible for persons to perceive Socrates as guilty of all charges?
7. Hippocrates, Thucydides, Euripides, and Socrates: What basic cultural attitudes and assumptions did they share?
8. How does Socrates' definition of virtue parallel that of Confucius? How does it differ? Which are more significant, the similarities or the differences?

Men of Athens, do not interrupt me with noise, even if I seem to you to be boasting; for the word that I speak is not mine, but the speaker to whom I shall refer it is a person of weight. For of my wisdom — if it is wisdom at all — and of its nature, I will offer you the god of Delphi[1] as a witness. You know Chaerephon, I fancy. He was my comrade from a youth and the comrade of your democratic party.[2] . . . Well, once he went to Delphi and made so bold as to ask the oracle this question; and, gentlemen, don't make a disturbance at what I say; for he asked if there were

---

[1] The oracle, or prophetess, at Delphi spoke for the god Apollo.

[2] Socrates mistrusted the "unthinking masses" and was not a supporter of Athens's democratic faction.

anyone wiser than I. Now the Pythia[3] replied that there was no one wiser. And about these things his brother here will bear you witness, since Chaerephon is dead.

But see why I say these things; for I am going to tell you from where the prejudice against me has arisen. For when I heard this, I thought to myself: "What in the world does the god mean, and what riddle is he propounding?[4] For I am conscious that I am not wise to any degree. What then does he mean by declaring that I am the wisest? He certainly cannot be lying, for that is not possible for him." And for a long time I was at a loss as to what he meant; then with great reluctance I proceeded to investigate him somewhat as follows.

I went to one of those who had a reputation for wisdom, thinking that there, if anywhere, I should prove the utterance wrong and should show the oracle "This man is wiser than I, but you said I was wisest." So examining this man — for I need not call him by name, but it was one of the public men with regard to whom I had this kind of experience, men of Athens — and conversing with him, this man seemed to me to seem to be wise to many other people and especially to himself, but not to be so; and then I tried to show him that he thought he was wise, but was not. As a result, I became hateful to him and to many of those present; and so, as I went away, I thought to myself, I am wiser than this man; for neither of us really knows anything fine and good, but this man thinks he knows something when he does not, whereas I, as I do not know anything, do not think I do either. I seem, then, in just this little thing to be wiser than this man at any rate, that what I do not know I do not think I know either." From him I went to another of those who were reputed to be wiser than he, and these same things seemed to me to be true;

and there I became hateful both to him and to many others. . . .

Now from this investigation, men of Athens, many enmities have arisen against me, and such as are most harsh and grievous, so that many prejudices have resulted from them and I am called a wise man. For on each occasion those who are present think I am wise in the matters in which I confute someone else; but the fact is, gentlemen, it is likely that the god is really wise and by his oracle means this: "Human wisdom is of little or no value." And it appears that he does not really say this of Socrates, but merely uses my name, and makes me an example, as if he were to say: "This one of you, O human beings, is wisest, who, like Socrates, recognises that he is in truth of no account in respect to wisdom."

Therefore I am still even now going about and searching and investigating at the god's behest anyone, whether citizen or foreigner, who I think is wise; and when he does not seem so to me, I give aid to the god and show that he is not wise. And by reason of this occupation I have no leisure to attend to any of the affairs of the state worth mentioning, or of my own, but am in vast poverty on account of my service to the god.[5]

And in addition to these things, the young men who have the most leisure, the sons of the richest men, accompany me of their own accord, find pleasure in hearing people being examined, and often imitate me themselves, and then they undertake to examine others; and then, I fancy, they find a great plenty of people who think they know something, but know little or nothing. As a result, therefore, those who are examined by them are angry with me, instead of being angry with themselves, and say that "Socrates is a most abominable person and is corrupting the youth."[6]

And when anyone asks them "by doing or teaching what?" they have nothing to say, but

---

[3]The priestess who acted as the vehicle for the sacred serpent (the python), who was believed to be the actual soothsayer at Delphi.

[4]The pythia at Delphi answered all questions in riddles.

[5]Actually, Socrates had served Athens well as a soldier and as someone who did his civic duty when chosen by lot for office.

[6]In *The Clouds,* the comic playwright *Aristophanes* had lampooned Socrates' methods of investigation and argumentation. According to the picture he presented, Socrates' "thought factory" taught young men how to tie their elders into verbal and logical knots and catered to those who wanted to swindle people. Plato reports that Socrates thought this popular comedy damaged his reputation. See note 10.

they do not know, and that they may not seem to be at a loss, they say these things that are handy to say against all the philosophers, "the things in the air and the things beneath the Earth" and "not to believe in the gods" and "to make the weaker argument the stronger." For they would not, I fancy, care to say the truth, that it is being made very clear that they pretend to know, but know nothing. . . . If you should say to me . . . : "Socrates, this time we will not do as Anytus[7] says, but we will let you go, on this condition, however, that you no longer spend our time in this investigation or in philosophy,[8] and if you are caught doing so again you shall die"; if you should let me go on this condition which I have mentioned, I should say to you, "Men of Athens, I respect and love you, but I shall obey the god[9] rather than you, and while I live and am able to continue, I shall never give up philosophy or stop exhorting you and pointing out the truth to any one of you whom I may meet, saying in my accustomed way: "Most excellent man, are you who are a citizen of Athens, the greatest of cities and the most famous for wisdom and power, not ashamed to care for the acquisition of wealth and for reputation and honor, when you neither care nor take thought for wisdom and truth and the perfection of your soul?" And if any of you argues the point, and says he does care, I shall not let him go at once, nor shall I go away, but I shall question and examine and cross-examine him, and if I find that he does not possess virtue, but says he does, I shall rebuke him for scorning the things that are of most importance and caring more for what is of less worth. This I shall do to whomever I meet, young and old, foreigner and citizen, but most to the citizens, inasmuch as you are more nearly related to me. For know that the god commands me to do this, and I believe that no greater good ever came to pass in the city than my service to the god. For I go about doing nothing else than urging you, young and old, not to care for your persons or your property more than for the perfection of your souls, or even so much;

and I tell you that virtue does not come from money, but from virtue comes money and all other good things to man, both to the individual and to the state. If by saying these things I corrupt the youth, these things must be injurious, but if anyone asserts that I say other things than these, he says what is untrue. Therefore I say to you, men of Athens, either do as Anytus tells you, or not, and either acquit me, or not, knowing that I shall not change my conduct even if I am to die many times over. . . .

For know that if you kill me, I being such a man as I say I am, you will not injure me so much as yourselves. . . . And so, men of Athens, I am now making my defense not for my own sake, as one might imagine, but far more for yours, that you may not by condemning me err in your treatment of the gift the god gave you. For if you put me to death, you will not easily find another, who, to use a rather absurd figure, attaches himself to the city as a gadfly to a horse, which, though large and well bred, is sluggish on account of his size and needs to be aroused by stinging. I think the god fastened me upon the city in some such capacity, and I go about arousing, and urging and reproaching each one of you, constantly alighting upon you everywhere the whole day long. Such another is not likely to come to you, gentlemen; but if you take my advice, you will spare me. But you, perhaps, might be angry, like people awakened from a nap, and might slap me, as Anytus advises, and easily kill me; then you would pass the rest of your lives in slumber, unless the god, in his care for you, should send someone else to sting you. And that I am, as I say, a kind of gift from the god, you might understand from this; for I have neglected all my own affairs and have been enduring the neglect of my concerns all these years, but I am always busy in your interest, coming to each one of you individually like a father or an elder brother and urging you to care for virtue; now that is not like human conduct. If I derived any profit from this and received pay for these exhortations,

---

[7]The person who introduced charges against Socrates.
[8]A word coined by the Greeks that means "love of wisdom."

[9]Apollo.

there would be some sense in it; but now you yourselves see that my accusers, though they accuse me of everything else in such a shameless way, have not been able to work themselves up to such a pitch of shamelessness as to produce a witness to testify that I ever exacted or asked pay of anyone. For I think I have a sufficient witness that I speak the truth, namely, my poverty. . . .

I was never any one's teacher. If any one, whether young or old, wishes to hear me speaking and pursuing my mission, I have never objected, nor do I converse only when I am paid and not otherwise, but I offer myself alike to rich and poor; I ask questions, and whoever wishes may answer and hear what I say. And whether any of them turns out well or ill, I should not justly be held responsible, since I never promised or gave any instruction to any of them;[10] but if any man says that he ever learned or heard anything privately from me, which all the others did not, be assured that he is lying.

But why then do some people love to spend much of their time with me? You have heard the reason, men of Athens; for I told you the whole truth; it is because they like to listen when those are examined who think they are wise and are not so; for it is amusing.

---

[10]Socrates contrasts himself with the *Sophists* (those who are wise), professional teachers who offered, for pay, instruction in argumentation and the other skills that young men needed in order to distinguish themselves in public affairs. The charge against the Sophists was that they taught their pupils how to win debates at any cost, with no regard to the truth. Our term "sophistry" reflects the poor reputation of the Sophists. Aristophanes (note 6) portrayed Socrates as the worst of the Sophists.

Art and the Human Form
▼▼▼

28 ▼ *THREE HELLENIC WORKS OF ART*

It is often said that the ancient Hellenes used the human as the measure of all things. Their gods were humanlike in appearance and in their passions, and human concerns, especially morality and politics, consumed Greek thinkers and writers. Humanity, particularly the human form, was also the consuming interest of fifth-century B.C.E. Hellenic sculptural and graphic artists, as the following three pieces of art illustrate.

Our first masterpiece is a black-on-white painting found on the interior of a wine cup. The work, crafted around 490 B.C.E. by an artist known simply as the Brygos Painter, depicts a Maenad. Note the animal pelt around her neck, the panther she holds in her left hand, and the other accoutrements of bacchic worship that Euripides described in the *Bacchae* (source 26).

Our second work of art is the *Bronze Charioteer of Delphi,* which dates from around 470 B.C.E. This life-sized (5'11") charioteer was originally part of a four-horse chariot ensemble that stood near the Temple of Apollo at Delphi (see source 27). An inscription records that it was dedicated to celebrate a chariot victory at the Pythian Games, which were held every four years near Delphi in honor of Apollo.

The early dates of our first two pieces place them on the cusp of the classical period of Hellenic art, but our third piece is unmistakably classical. Known as the *Girl with Doves,* it is a grave *stele* (an upright stone monument) from the island of Paros. Its style places it squarely in mid century, around 450 B.C.E. Carved from Parian marble, this raised relief depicts a young girl who died unmarried (the doves symbolize virginity). The artist has created an especially poignant work of art by contrasting the subject's head with her body. The body is that of a child (note the arms and hands), but her stylishly coiffured head is that of the young woman she would never become. Note also how the sculptor has used the maiden's draped robe to give form to her figure.

QUESTIONS FOR ANALYSIS

1. "The art of fifth-century classical Hellas expressed the importance of the human person." Based on these three examples, do you agree or disagree? Be specific in articulating your reasons.
2. It has also been said that Hellenic artists created idealized human forms that conveyed a sense of serene balance without losing reality. Based on these three examples, do you agree or disagree? Be specific in articulating your reasons.
3. "Simplicity, dignity, and restraint were the hallmarks of classical Hellenic art, and all three qualities reflected the Greek vision of a world that was understandable and controllable." Based on these three examples, do you agree or disagree? Be specific in articulating your reasons.

A Maenad

The Bronze Charioteer of Delphi

Girl with Doves

Chapter 5

▼▼▼

Regional Empires and Afro-Eurasian Interchange

300 B.C.E.–500 C.E.

By 300 B.C.E. the cultural traditions of China, India, Southwest Asia, and Hellas were solidly in place and ready to expand beyond their original boundaries. Expand they did, but expansion followed no single pattern. Imperial aggrandizement, largely by means of military conquest, played a major role in spreading Chinese, Southwest Asian, and Hellenic cultural influences, but it was not a factor in the creation in Southeast Asia of a *Greater India* (as many historians term it).

As early as the first century C.E., people of the coastal areas of Southeast Asia accepted elements of Indian culture, including Hindu and Buddhist religious traditions, from merchants traveling across the Bay of Bengal. Colonists, including Indian priests and scholars, soon followed the merchants. Traffic, however, was not all one-way, as youths from various emerging Hindu and Buddhist kingdoms throughout Southeast Asia traveled to India for advanced religious instruction. Although the Hindu caste system failed to take root in Southeast Asia, other Indian traditions flourished there, including the Hindu cults of Shiva and Vishnu (Chapter 6, sources 41 and 42) and the notion of the *devaraja* (sacred king) — an idea embraced by native ruling elites.

Chinese cultural influences traveled south, northeast, and west as a consequence of both military adventure — the imperialistic expansionism of the Qin and *Han* dynasties — and more peaceful exchanges, especially the travels of merchants and the slow, steady southward migration of China's expanding peasant population. The armies of Han conquered Manchuria and northern Korea and established hegemony over non-Chinese peoples to the south in northern Vietnam and along the Himalayan foothills. To the west, the armies of Han China penetrated deeply into Central Asia. Wherever its soldiers went, its merchants were not too far behind. The roads that China opened to the West also served as conduits for the influx of new ideas into the Middle Kingdom, particularly Mahayana Buddhism (see Chapters 5, 6, and 9, sources 37–40 and 72–74), which flowed into China along its overland trade routes.

From the late sixth to the late fourth century B.C.E., the *Persian Empire,* centered in Southwest Asia, encompassed an area from the Nile to the Indus, from the Mediterranean to the Persian Gulf, from the Black Sea to the Red Sea. Although the Persians were respectful of local traditions, their massive empire was a fertile medium for the blending and transmission of many different cultures. Then, in the late fourth century, Persia and Greece were merged into a single empire for one brief but significant moment. The conquest of the Persian Empire by *Alexander the Great* (r. 336–323 B.C.E.) and his penetration as far east as Central Asia and the Indus Valley ushered in a new era for western Eurasia — the *Hellenistic Age.* Whereas the Hellenic World had been parochial, the Hellenistic World was cosmopolitan and culturally eclectic. The armies of Alexander and the state-builders who followed helped create a cultural amalgamation of Southwest Asian, Egyptian, and even some Indian elements, over which was laid a layer of Greek language, thought, and artistic expression. What emerged was, to use a Greek word, a cultural *ecumene* (a unity of diverse civilized peoples). This world culture stretched from western Central Asia and northwest India in the east to the regions of the central Mediterranean in the west, and much of it was Greek in form and inspiration.

Alexander's empire did not survive him, but the amalgamation of peoples and cultures that he forged laid the basis for Hellenistic successor states in Egypt, Southwest Asia, and the Mediterranean. Of these, the most impressive was the *Roman Empire*. To be sure, Romans spoke Latin and not Greek, and their civilization was as deeply influenced by the Etruscans of north-central Italy as it was by Greeks and other Hellenistic cultures. Moreover, their empire was centered on the Mediterranean Sea — far away from the heartland of the original Hellenistic Ecumene. Notwithstanding all of these realities, it is still reasonable to see the Roman Empire as the last and greatest of the Hellenistic states and as the carrier of Hellenistic culture into such faraway western regions as Gaul, Germany, and Britain.

Rome and Han China were certainly not Eurasia's only great empires. By the end of the first century B.C.E. four great regional empires linked China, India, Southwest Asia, and the Greco-

Roman Mediterranean in a chain of civilization from the Pacific to the Atlantic: Han China, Rome, the *Kushan Empire* of Central Asia, and the *Parthian Empire* of Southwest Asia.

The Kushans, who spoke an Indo-European language, were a confederation of nomadic peoples, many of whom had been pushed west from the borders of China in the second century B.C.E. Settling down in a region that was centered on what are today the nations of Afghanistan and Pakistan, they established a Central Asian empire that included the northern plains of India. Kushan history remains to be reconstructed, but our fragmentary sources indicate that their empire flourished from the early first century C.E. to the late third century and served as an important conduit for Indian goods on their way to China and the West. It is also clear that the Kushans adopted and transmitted some forms of Indian culture. Many of the Kushan aristocracy and their subjects became Buddhists, especially Mahayana Buddhists, and under Kushan rule a region of Pakistan known as *Gandhara* became the center of an exciting new form of Buddhist art (source 38).

Sometime in the first half of the third century B.C.E., the *Parni,* a tribe that inhabited lands just to the east of the Caspian Sea (modern Turkmenistan), expanded southwest into Parthia, an ancient Persian province in northern Iran, which they consolidated into a state around 200 B.C.E. The Parni were soon culturally absorbed by the settled peoples whom they conquered in Parthia and disappeared as a separate, identifiable people, but before their disappearance the Parni set Parthia on the road to empire. After 190 B.C.E. the Parni-Parthian state expanded westward at the expense of the Seleucid Empire, the most eastern of the Hellenistic states. Around 147 B.C.E. the Parthians conquered Babylon (Middle Mesopotamia) and were well on their way to carving out an empire that at its height stretched from the Caspian Sea to northern Syria and aggressively butted up against the Roman Empire. Not only did the Parthians fight the Romans, they also traded with them. Until its collapse around 224 C.E., when the empire was taken over by the Sassanians, the Parthian Empire served as an important intermediary along the network of caravan routes that linked the Mediterranean, India, Central Asia, and China and to which historians have given the romantic name the *Silk Road*.

Indeed, not only land routes, but sea lanes as well, were now joined in complex patterns to create the first age of Afro-Eurasian linkage.

Although most of the major trade routes traversed the lands and waters of Eurasia, Africa also shared in this unification to the extent that its northern regions were an integral part of the Roman Empire, and northern portions of its eastern coast were linked by regular trade with Arabia, India, and Southeast Asia.

This age of grand-scale linkage began to suffer retrenchment and shrinkage around 200 C.E., when both China and the Roman Empire entered periods of severe crisis. Despite political and economic disasters, however, trade across the Silk Road and along the sea lanes never totally ceased in the centuries that followed, even though it experienced periods of severe recession.

▼▼▼

The Greco-Roman World

Alexander the Great died in Babylon in 323 B.C.E. Tradition claims that when questioned as to whom he bequeathed his empire, he replied, "the best man." No single, would-be successor proved strong enough to seize the entire empire. Rather, rival generals divided the Hellenistic World into a number of successor states. The two mightiest and most brilliant were the kingdom of the *Seleucids,* centered on Anatolia, Mesopotamia, and Syria, and the kingdom of Egypt, which fell to the family of *Ptolemy,* one of Alexander's Macedonian generals.

Ptolemy and his successors lavished money on their capital, *Alexandria,* transforming this new city, located in Egypt's northern delta region, into the most impressive cosmopolitan setting in the Hellenistic World. The city's twin crowning glories, at least in the opinion of scholars and scientists, were the Museum, which functioned as a center of advanced research, and the Library, which represented an attempt to gather under one roof the entire Hellenistic World's store of written knowledge and contained perhaps as many as a half-million separate scrolls.

Both institutions enjoyed the continuous generous patronage of the Macedonian god-kings of Egypt and served as focal points for scientific and literary studies that were Greek in form and substance but cosmopolitan in scope and clientele. Educated Persians, Jews, Mesopotamians, Syrians, Italians, and members of many other ethnic groups flocked to Alexandria, where they formed an ecumenical community of scholars and artists whose common tongue and intellectual perspective were as Greek as that of their Ptolemaic hosts.

In 30 B.C.E. Cleopatra VII, the last Ptolemaic ruler of Egypt, died in Alexandria by her own hand, and Egypt passed under the direct control of the rising imperial power of Rome. By this time Rome had already seized control of Italy, Greece, major portions of Anatolia (which it termed *Asia Minor*), Syria, most of North Africa, all of the major Mediterranean islands, Spain, and the area north of the Alps and Pyrenees known as *Gaul.* The Mediterranean had truly become Rome's *Mare Nostrum* (Our Sea), and the Roman Empire now controlled a large portion of the

Hellenistic World. As inheritor by conquest of eastern Mediterranean lands and culture, Rome would disseminate a Greco-Roman form of Hellenistic culture throughout the western Mediterranean, as well as among various barbarian peoples living in European lands well beyond the Mediterranean coastline. Well before the end of the first century C.E., Roman legions would be erecting Greek-style temples to the Persian god Mithras along the Rhine and in Britain, and Greek literature would be studied in schools throughout lands recently wrested from Gallic tribes.

Images of the Hellenistic World
▼▼▼

29 ▾ *FOUR HELLENISTIC SCULPTURES*

The Hellenistic Ecumene was exceedingly cosmopolitan, but cosmopolitanism often carries a price. Parochial societies — such as fifth-century Hellas, which centered on small, fairly homogenous poleis — offer their inhabitants the security that comes from living in a friendly and understandable environment. Conversely, societies open to the world and filled with a bewildering array of different and often contradictory cultural stimuli can be frightening and alienating. Such alienation and confusion can have profound effects on artistic expression. But even when people are comfortable with cultural differences and at home in a *universal city* (which is the literal meaning of *cosmopolitan*) they tend to view the world and themselves differently from people whose horizons are more limited. This comfort with a wider world also finds expression in the arts.

As we saw in source 28, Hellenic artists of the fifth century B.C.E. idealized the human body and placed the human being securely in the center of an ordered world — a world that they saw reflected in the poleis in which they were citizens. As the following four sculptures suggest, later Hellenistic sculptors had different visions.

Our first item is a marble bust of King Euthydemos I of *Bactria* (r. ca. 235–200 B.C.E.), which dates from around 200 B.C.E. The Greek-speaking kings of Bactria had carved out a realm on the far horizon of the Hellenistic World, a wild mountainous region in western Central Asia shared by the modern nations of Turkmenistan, Tajikistan, Uzbekistan, and Afghanistan. A native of Anatolia, Euthydemos had risen to power by overthrowing his predecessor. Our second piece is a Roman marble copy of a bronze original that had been created around 230–220 B.C.E. Known as *The Gaul and Wife,* the original had served as one of a number of statues gracing a victory monument of King Attalos I of *Pergamon* (r. 241–197 B.C.E.) that celebrated his victories over invading Gallic, or Celtic, tribes. The kings of Pergamon, a city located near the northwestern coast of Anatolia, lavished money on their city's beautification, using art to trumpet their policies and achievements. Our third sculpture is *The Old Woman,* also known as *The Old Market Woman,* an original work in marble that dates from the late second or early first century B.C.E. One interpretation of the sculpture is that the woman is depicted in the act of calling out to potential customers, hoping that they purchase the chicken and basket of vegetables and fruits that she holds in her left hand. Another inter-

The Gaul and Wife

King Euthydemos I of Bactria

The Boxer

The Old Woman

129

pretation, which we favor, is that the laurel wreath on her head suggests she is offering the goods as part of a religious festival, possibly one in honor of Dionysus (see source 26). Our fourth sculpture is a bronze boxer by the Athenian sculptor Apollonius. Created around 60 B.C.E. in Italy, possibly for some rich fan of the Greek sport of pugilism, the work shows us a veteran boxer, whose broken nose, battered face and ears, muscular body, and leather gloves with bands of lead at the knuckles clearly indicate his profession.

In your study of the three full-body sculptures, pay particular attention to three artistic elements: facial expression, drapery, and *contrapposto* (the turning of the hip and leg away from the shoulders and the head). Hellenistic sculptors employed all three to add psychological insight, dramatic effect, and movement to their art.

QUESTIONS FOR ANALYSIS

1. Consider the bust of King Euthydemos. How does the sculptor present the king? What reaction do you think the sculptor desired to evoke from the viewer?
2. Compare the bust of Euthydemos with the face of the *Bronze Charioteer* in source 28. What conclusions follow from your study?
3. Compare the *Girl with Doves* (source 28) with *The Gaul and Wife*. Does it appear that the artists expected to elicit similar emotional responses from viewers? If so, what techniques did each employ? What conclusions follow from your answers?
4. Consider *The Old Woman* and *The Boxer*. How have their sculptors dealt with them? Compare them with the three Hellenic works of art in source 28. Which strike you as more significant, the similarities or the dissimilarities? What conclusions follow from your analysis?
5. Some commentators have characterized Hellenistic art as an attempt to create psychological portraits. Do any or all of these four works seem to fall into that category? If so, what was there about the Hellenistic World that might have led some artists to emphasize the individual human psyche?
6. If art is a window on the society that produces it, what do these four sculptures allow you to infer about the Hellenistic World?

Rome Viewed from the Underworld
▼▼▼

30 ▼ *Virgil, THE AENEID*

Due to its victory over Carthage in the Second Punic War (218–201 B.C.E.), the Roman Republic emerged as the major power in the Mediterranean and an empire in fact, if not in name. Rome's acquisition of an empire had major repercussions at home, and the resultant strains triggered more than a century of class discord and civil war. The civil wars ended in 30 B.C.E., when Octavian, the great-nephew and adopted son of Julius Caesar (ca. 100–44 B.C.E.), defeated Mark Antony and became sole master of the Roman World. In 27 B.C.E. the Senate accorded him the title *Augustus* (Revered One), implying he possessed divine authority. Posterity remembers Octavian as *Caesar Augustus* (63 B.C.E.–14 C.E.), Rome's first emperor and the man who created and presided over the first generation of the *Pax Romana,* or Roman Peace.

The significance of the *Pax Romana* was not lost on Augustus's contemporaries, not that there was much danger of anyone overlooking it given Augustus's policy of using his age's leading artists and intellectuals to trumpet his accomplishments. Of these publicists of the Roman Peace, none was more significant than Publius Vergilius Maro (70–19 B.C.E.), better known as *Virgil.* Virgil was simply classical Rome's greatest poet, and his most important creation, the *Aeneid,* was an epic that centered on nothing less than the divinely ordained destiny of Rome. The poem tells the story of the warrior-hero Aeneas, a refugee from Troy, whose settlement in Italy, following a long series of trials and troubled travels, would lead ultimately to the foundation of Rome. As the title and topic might suggest, Virgil borrowed liberally from Homer's *Iliad* and *Odyssey,* but he never slavishly imitated his Greek models. Rather, Virgil crafted a unique Latin masterpiece that deserves recognition on its own merits as one of the Ancient World's greatest epics. Virgil devoted the last ten years of his life to the *Aeneid,* but as he lay dying he left instructions that it should be burned, believing it needed three additional years of revision and polishing. Happily, Augustus countermanded the deathbed wishes of this poetic perfectionist.

Our source comes from Book 6, the pivotal point of this epic in twelve books. Aeneas has just reached Italy. There, accompanied by the Sibyl of Cumae, an inspired prophetess of the god Apollo, he enters the Underworld to consult the spirit of his father, Anchises. We begin with Aeneas and the Sibyl, having passed by Tartarus, the place of torment for the wicked, arriving at Elysium.

QUESTIONS FOR ANALYSIS

1. How does Virgil's Underworld differ from that of Gilgamesh (source 1)? From that of Homer (source 11)?
2. Can you discover any possible influences on Virgil's religious thought? Review Chapter 3 in addressing this question.
3. What does your answer to question 2 allow you to infer about cross-cultural influences in the Augustan Age?
4. What do the last two excerpts from this source suggest about the Roman self-image in the Age of Augustus?

They arrived at a land of joy, the green gardens and blessed abodes of the Blissful Groves. Here a fuller air clothes the meadows with a violet luminescence, and they have their own sun and starlight. Some exercise their limbs on the grassy playing fields, contend in sports, and wrestle on the yellow sand. Others beat out dances with their feet and sing songs. . . . Here is a band of men who incurred wounds fighting for their fatherland. Here are they who remained pure in their priesthood as long as they lived. Here are they who were true poets and who spoke in ways worthy of Phoebus.[1] And here are they who improved life by the arts of their inventions. Here are they who merited by their service remembrance before all others. The brows of all are encircled with snowy-white garlands. . . .

But Father Anchises, deep in the verdant valley, was surveying with intent mind the imprisoned souls that were to ascend to the light above, and by chance was counting numbers of men — his beloved descendants, their fates and their fortunes, their ways and their works.

And when he saw Aeneas coming toward him across the flowery meadow, he eagerly stretched out both hands, while tears flowed down his cheeks and a cry slipped from his mouth. "Have you come at last, and has the devotion that your father has expected of you[2] conquered the path of adversity? My son, is it given to me to gaze on your face and to hear and respond in familiar speech? . . ." Aeneas replied: "Your shade, Father, your sad shade, appearing to me so often drove me to steer toward these portals. My ships are at anchor on the Tyrrhenian Sea.[3] Grant that I might clasp your hand, grant it, Father, and do not withdraw from our embrace." While thus speaking, his face was drenched with copious tears. Three times there he tried to put his arms about his neck; three times the shade, embraced in vain, escaped out of his hands like weightless winds and even more so like a winged dream.

And now Aeneas sees within a hidden valley a secluded grove, rustling forest thickets, and the River Lethe flowing past peaceful dwellings. Around it hovered peoples and individuals beyond count. . . . Startled by this sudden vision, the uncomprehending Aeneas asks for an account: What is that river over there? Who are those people who throng on its banks in such great numbers? Father Anchises then answers: "Spirits to whom Fate owes another body drink the soothing waters of deep amnesia at the River Lethe's stream. Indeed, for quite a while I have wanted to tell you about these and show them to you face to face and to count the offspring of my descendants, so that you might rejoice with me the more for having reached Italy." "Father, must we think that some souls, soaring upwards, travel from here to the upper world and once again return to bodily fetters?"[4] Why do these sad souls have such a dreadful longing for the light of day?" "Surely, I will tell you, my son, and I will not hold you in suspense," replies Anchises, and he lays everything out in order, one by one.

"First of all, one intrinsic Spirit sustains the heavens and the Earth and the watery expanses, the shining globe of the moon and the Titanian stars,[5] and one Mind flows through all its parts, drives the entire entity, and mingles with the mighty structure. From them[6] are generated humanity and beasts, the lives of flying creatures, and those monsters that the sea contains beneath its marbled surface. Fire is their life force and their seeds originate in Heaven,[7] inasmuch as sinful bodies do not hamper them, and earthly frames and mortal limbs do not render them sluggish. Bodies are the cause of fear and desire, of sorrow and joy, and souls cannot discern the light of Heaven when shut up in the gloom of a dark dungeon.[8] Indeed, on the very last day when life has fled, all evil and all the ills of the body do not totally pass from these sad souls,[9] for it must be the case that many evils, long set hard, are deeply ingrained within them in ways beyond understanding. As a consequence, they are disci-

---

[1]Phoebus Apollo, the god of prophecy and of poetry (see source 27).

[2]Throughout this story Aeneas has consistently exhibited the virtue of *pietas,* or devotion to duty.

[3]That portion of the Mediterranean separating the islands of Corsica, Sardinia, and Sicily from the Italian Peninsula.

[4]These are the words of a world-weary Aeneas who has been exhausted by the trials he has undergone due to his devotion to duty.

[5]The sun and the stars.

[6]Spirit and Mind.

[7]Spirit and Mind spring from the primal element of fire (see note 10), and their seeds are particles of divine fire born out of heavenly air.

[8]The dungeon of the sinful, mortal body.

[9]Here Anchises picks up Aeneas's reference to "sad souls" and gives the term new meaning.

plined with punishments and pay the penalty for old evil ways. Some are hung, helplessly suspended before the winds; from others the stain of guilt is washed away under a swirling flood or burned off by fire.[10] Each of us endures his own ghost.[11] Then we are released to wander through wide Elysium. A few of us possess the Fields of Happiness until, once the cycle of time is completed, the passing days have removed the hardened stain and have left unsoiled the ethereal sentient spirit and the fire of pure air.[12] The god summons all these in a vast procession to the River Lethe once the wheel of time has revolved a full thousand years, so that they might revisit the vaulted world above[13] without memories and might begin to wish to return to bodily forms."[14]

Anchises finished speaking and drew his son, and the Sibyl along with him, into the midst of the crowded and murmuring throng. He took up a position on a knoll from where he could scan the entire long line and recognize their faces as they came.

"Come now, I will teach you about your destiny. I will make clear by my words what glory will eventually befall the progeny of Dardanus[15] and what sort of descendants will spring from Italian stock[16] — souls of renown who shall inherit our name. . . .

▷ Anchises begins to point out the souls of the great men, still awaiting rebirth, who will create Rome and bring it to glory. After describing Romulus, the son of Mars (the god of War) and founder of Rome, Anchises abandons a strict chronological sequence and jumps to Caesar Augustus, the second founder of Rome.

"This man, this is he whom so often you heard promised to you. This is Caesar Augustus, son of a god,[17] who shall again establish a Golden Age in Latium[18] amid the fields where Saturn once ruled.[19] He shall extend his rule beyond the Garamantians[20] and the Indians. His dominion will extend beyond the paths of the zodiac and of the sun.[21] . . . Even now, in anticipation of his coming as prophesied by the oracles, the kingdoms of the Caspian Sea[22] and the region around Lake Moeotis[23] shudder in horror, and the seven mouths of the Nile[24] tremble in terror.[25] Yes, not even Alcides[26] strode over such a space of earth. . . . Do we still hesitate to assert our valor by action, or does fear forbid our settling on Italian soil?[27]

---

[10]In other words, sinful souls are cleansed in this purgatory by air, water, or fire, three of the four primal elements of the universe (the other being earth). Irredeemably evil souls are condemned to eternal torment in Tartarus, the place that Aeneas just passed on his way to Elysium.

[11]Each soul suffers in accord with its unique imperfections. By using the term "we," Anchises implied he also has undergone this purgation.

[12]The soul (the sentient spirit) has been returned to its primal purity — the fire and air from which it was generated. See what Anchises says about the origins of Spirit and Mind (note 7).

[13]Earth, which is vaulted by the heavens.

[14]Were they to remember the miseries of life and the process of purgation they underwent after death, they would not want to return.

[15]The mythical founder of Troy.

[16]Aeneas' future descendants, who will bear both his Trojan blood and the blood of Lavinia, his Italian wife-to-be.

[17]Caesar Augustus was the great-nephew and adopted son of Julius Caesar, who had been declared a god after his death. Aeneas himself was half divine; his mother was Venus, the goddess of love.

[18]The region surrounding Rome, where the Latin people lived.

[19]According to Roman tradition, the Golden Age of Saturn was a primeval era of purity and simplicity — virtues that made Rome great. Saturn, originally an Italian god of agriculture, was deposed by his son Jupiter, king of the gods. Thereupon, Saturn fled to Latium, where he became its king, establishing a society that lacked weapons, money, walled cities, and all similar corrupting influences. During this era the fruits of the soil were gained without toil.

[20]A people of northeast Africa.

[21]Beyond the known world.

[22]The Parthian Empire ruled the region around the Caspian Sea.

[23]A reference to the steppe peoples north of the Black Sea.

[24]The Nile Delta.

[25]A reference to his victory over the forces of Cleopatra VII and Marc Antony at Actium.

[26]Another name for the legendary hero Hercules. Like Hercules, Augustus performed civilizing tasks and was a mortal who was destined to become a god.

[27]These two questions are directed to Aeneas: After seeing Augustus, can he have any hesitation as to following his destiny?

▷ Anchises returns to a chronological description of the shades of future Roman heroes, beginning with Numa, an ancient king of Rome and its first lawgiver. After pointing out Fabius Maximus, whose delaying tactics saved Rome in the dark days of the Second Punic War, Anchises sums up the essence of Rome's unique genius:

"Others,[28] for so I believe, shall hammer out more delicately breathing likenesses from bronze and draw forth living faces from marble. Others shall plead their causes better, plot with a gauge the movement of the heavens, and describe the rising of the stars. But, Roman, remember that you must rule nations by your dominion. These will be your arts: to crown peace with civilization, to show mercy to the conquered, and to tame the proud by war."

---

[28]Namely, the Greeks.

Queen Boudica and the *Pax Romana*
▼▼▼
31 ▼ *Tacitus, AGRICOLA and ANNALS*

Virgil portrayed the *Pax Romana* as a divinely ordained blessing for civilized humanity. The historian and statesman Publius Cornelius Tacitus (ca. 55 C.E. — after 116) presents another view. A prolific author, Tacitus composed the *Germania,* an ethnographic survey of the Germans; the *Agricola,* a biography of his father-in-law; and the *Dialogus,* a treatise on oratory. His reputation as Rome's greatest historian, however, rests on two other works, both of impressive scope, the *Histories* and the *Annals.* Together they survey the history of the empire from the death of Augustus in 14 C.E. to the assassination of Domitian in 96. Both survive only in fragmented form, but the more complete *Annals* contains detailed pictures of the period from 14 to 66, with some significant gaps.

Of the *Annals'* extant word pictures, one of the most famous is its description of a British rebellion against Roman authority in 60 or 61. Roman forces invaded Celtic Britain in 43 and encountered stiff resistance in their efforts to turn the island into a Roman province. They were never able to conquer the northern portions of the island (essentially Scotland), but by the mid second century the southern two-thirds of the island was pacified. Before that occurred, the Roman occupiers had to weather a number of rebellions. The most famous and destructive revolt took place in 60/61, led by the queen of the Iceni, Boudica (also known less correctly as Boudicca and Boadicea). Ironically, perhaps, her name meant "Victory."

Tacitus provides our only contemporary, or near-contemporary, evidence for this revolt in two of his works, the already-mentioned account in the *Annals,* which he completed around 116, and his earlier *Agricola,* which he finished in 98. Although Tacitus wrote about events that he never witnessed — he was a boy of about five and living in Italy when the revolt took place — he had access to two good sources: Roman imperial archives and the memories of his father-in-law, Gnaeus Julius Agricola, who had served as a high-ranking military officer in Britain during the rebellion. Agricola was later governor of the island province from 77 or 78 to 83 or 84.

QUESTIONS FOR ANALYSIS

1. Where do Tacitus's sympathies seem to lie? How does your answer help us evaluate the worth of his evidence?
2. Why did the Iceni rebel?
3. What enabled the Romans to suppress this rebellion?
4. What appear to have been the status and roles of women within British culture?
5. Compose Boudica's answer to Virgil's vision of the Roman Peace.

AGRICOLA

Suetonius Paulinus had two years of success.[1] Tribes were subdued and garrisons strengthened. Confident in these measures, he invaded the island of Mona, which served as a center of strength for the rebels,[2] but by doing so he laid himself open to attack from the rear.

With the governor absent, the Britons' fear was removed, and they complained among themselves about the evils of slavery. They compared grievances and inflamed one another's passions by their understanding of what this all meant: Patience would gain them nothing, except harsher treatment, which is so easy to impose on those who allow it. In the old days each tribe had a single king; now two were imposed upon them — a governor who savaged them with bloodshed and a procurator who preyed on their possessions.[3] For those subjugated, it was equally disastrous whether their overlords were at odds with one another or in harmony. One enjoyed the service of centurions,[4] the other of slaves[5] — a combination of violence and insult. Now nothing was exempt from greed and lust. In battle the spoils go to the braver, but now, more often than not, unwarlike cowards were tearing their homes away from them, abducting their children, and imposing conscription on them, as though Britons did not know how to die for their country. The body of soldiers that crossed over was quite small if compared to the numbers of Britons. That was how the Germans had shaken off the Roman yoke,[6] and the Germans were protected only by a river,[7] not by an ocean.[8] The Britons' reasons for fighting would be their homeland, their spouses, their parents; the Romans' reasons for fighting would be greed and luxury. They would retreat, as the deified Julius[9] had retreated,[10] if the Britons could emulate their ancestors' valor. They should also not be dismayed by the outcome of one or two battles. They who are prosperous might have more dash, but the oppressed have much more staying power. Now even the gods were taking pity on the Britons, for they were detaining the absent Roman governor and his army, far away on another island. Now, the Britons were doing that which was most difficult of all — deliberat-

---

[1]Gaius Suetonius Paulinus, already a celebrated general, arrived in Britain in late 58 or early 59 to serve as its governor. Thus, this account begins in either the year 60 or 61.

[2]The island of Anglesey, located just off the coast of Wales, was a place of special sanctity for the Britons. As such, it became the Druid priests' foremost stronghold in their resistance to the Romans. See the account in the *Annals* for further details.

[3]Power within an imperial province was divided between the governor, who commanded armies and acted as chief executive, and the procurator, who was chief financial officer. See the account in the *Annals* for more on the procurator.

[4]Roman commanders of bodies of 100 soldiers.

[5]Many of the clerks who served procurators were educated slaves.

[6]In the year 9 C.E. a German force led by Arminius wiped out three Roman legions in the Teutoburg Forest, far to the east of the Rhine. This defeat forced the Romans to abandon plans to occupy the lands between the Rhine and Elbe rivers, which would have substantially shortened Rome's northeastern frontier.

[7]The Rhine and Danube rivers largely separated the Roman Empire from the lands of the Germans.

[8]Actually, the English Channel.

[9]Julius Caesar (100–44 B.C.E.), who was declared a god after his death.

[10]In 55 B.C.E. and again the following year, Julius Caesar led expeditionary forces to Britain. British resistance, channel storms, and more pressing concerns in Gaul forced him to retire back to the continent on both occasions.

ing among themselves. For, in deliberations of this sort, detection is far more dangerous than boldness.

Having inspired one another with these and similar arguments and led by Boudica, a woman of royal lineage (for they do not discriminate in regard to sex when it comes to commanding armies), they took up arms in a general uprising. They moved swiftly against the troops dispersed among the outposts. Once they had overrun the garrisons, they then invaded the colony itself,[11] as the very seat of slavery. Their vengeance in this hour of victory overlooked no sort of barbarian cruelty. Had not Paulinus come to its aid with all due speed when he learned of the rising in the province, Britain would have been lost. As it was, the fortunes of a single battle restored it to its old state of submission.

ANNALS

In the consulship of Caesennius Paetus and Petronius Turpilianus[12] a terrible disaster beset Britain. . . . At the time, Suetonius Paulinus was in command of Britain. He was Corbulo's rival in military skill and in popular gossip, which allows no one to be without a rival, and he desired to match the glory that came with recovery of Armenia[13] with victories over enemies closer to home. For this reason, he prepared to attack the island of Mona, which was thickly settled and a haven for refugees from Roman authority. Because the channel is shallow and variable, he constructed flat-bottomed boats for the infantry. The cavalry followed by wading across or, when the water got deeper, by swimming alongside their horses.

Along the shore stood a hostile army, thickly packed with weapons and warriors and women who rushed here and there among the ranks. Very much like the Furies, the women were dressed in deathly black, had dishevelled hair, and brandished torches.[14] And all around there were Druids who, with their hands raised to the heavens, shouted out terrible incantations.[15] They so shocked the Roman troops with this extraordinary display that the soldiers acted as though their limbs were paralyzed and, without moving, exposed their bodies to wounds. At last, encouraged by their general and exhorting each other not to be terrified of an army of women and fanatics, they advanced behind their standards, cut down all who met them, and enveloped the enemy in his own flames. Next they set up a garrison over those whom they had conquered and the groves that were sacred to these savage superstitions were cut down. For the Britons considered it a pious duty to drench their altars with the blood of prisoners and to consult their gods by reading human entrails.[16] While he was engaged in these tasks, Suetonius was informed of a sudden rebellion in the province.

Prasutagus, king of the Iceni,[17] distinguished

---

[11]A colony of retired Roman army veterans had been established in Camulodunum (modern Colchester), the capital of the new province of Britain. See note 22 for more information.

[12]The chief magistrates of the Roman Republic were its two annually elected consuls, and each year was identified by reference to the serving consuls. The practice of naming consuls continued in the Age of Empire, even though power now resided in the hands of the emperor. These two consuls entered their offices in 61, but many historians, using other evidence, argue somewhat persuasively that the rebellion probably broke out in 60.

[13]Gnaeus Domitius Corbulo conquered Armenia (eastern Anatolia) in 59–60.

[14]The three Greco-Roman goddesses of retribution. They were clad in black, their hair consisted of poisonous snakes, and they carried torches, serpents, or knives in their hands.

[15]Druid priests came from the land-owning nobility, and their authority transcended tribal ties, making them pre-Roman Britain's sole unifying force. We know almost nothing about their rituals and teachings because of the secrecy in which they cloaked themselves.

[16]Presumed human sacrifice and the fact that the Druid priests were a rallying force for resistance to Roman authority in Britain and Gaul inspired the Romans to suppress this religion. Compare Chapter 7, sources 47 and 48.

[17]The Iceni inhabited what is today East Anglia in southeastern England and were accorded the status of a semi-independent client kingdom. Although considered subjects of the empire, they were not ruled directly by the governor or other Roman authorities in Britain. They also were allowed to retain their arms. Their king Prasutagus, who considered himself a friend of Rome, died in 59.

for his long and prosperous reign, had designated Caesar[18] as his heir, along with his two daughters. By this act of subservience he imagined his kingdom and his household would be spared injury.[19] But things turned out differently to the point that his kingdom was pillaged by centurions and his household by slaves, as though they were spoils of war.[20] First, his wife Boudica was flogged and his daughters were raped. All the leaders of the Iceni were stripped of their ancestral property, and the king's relatives were treated as if they were bound over into slavery.

Because of this outrageous conduct and fear of worse to come — for they had been reduced to the status of a province — they took up arms and incited to rebellion the Trinobantes[21] and others who, not yet broken by servitude, had secretly conspired together to regain their freedom.

Army veterans were the objects of their bitterest hatred. These men, recently settled in the colony at Camulodunum[22] and acting as though they had received the entire region as a gift, were driving them out of their homes, ejecting them from their farms, and calling them prisoners and slaves. The regular soldiers encouraged the veterans' violent behavior because they were men of similar habits, and they had hope of being granted the same license. In addition, the temple raised to the Deified Claudius[23] appeared to be very much like a citadel of perpetual slavery, and its chosen priests were pouring out fortunes under the guise of every sort of piety.[24]

It also did not seem to be an arduous task to wipe out a colony that lacked fortified walls —

something that our leaders had given little forethought to because they had more concern for amenities than utilities.

Just at this moment and with no apparent cause, the statue of Victory at Camulodunum fell down, with its back turned, as if it were retreating from the enemy. Women[25] who had been thrown into a frenzy prophesied imminent destruction, saying that strange noises had been heard in their senate house,[26] the theater had echoed with howls, and a vision of the destroyed colony had been seen in the estuary of the Thames. Moreover, the fact that the ocean appeared blood-red and the ebbing tide had left behind what seemed to be human corpses inspired hope in the Britons and fear in the veterans.

Because Suetonius was far away, the veterans appealed to the procurator, Catus Decianus, for help. He sent them not more than 200 men, without their proper armaments. In addition, there was a small body of troops stationed there. Trusting that the temple would protect them and misled by secret accomplices to the rebellion who interfered with their plans, they failed to place either a ditch or a rampart in front of their position. They also failed to evacuate women and the elderly and to leave only men of military age in place. Careless as if this were a time of peace, they were enveloped by huge numbers of barbarians. Except for the temple, where the troops had massed themselves, everything else was overrun in the first attack or set on flames. The temple withstood a siege for two days, but then was taken by storm.

---

[18]Caesar, or the emperor, at the time was Nero (r. 54–68).

[19]Prasutagus probably made the emperor one of his heirs in the hope of being able to pass on to his daughters at least half of his wealth and the kingdom.

[20]See the *Agricola,* where Tacitus mentions the centurions who serve the governor and the slaves who serve the procurator (notes 3–5).

[21]A tribe that inhabited lands just to the south of the Iceni.

[22]The Romans had settled retired soldiers there as pensioners and also to act as a reserve force, should they be needed to help quell any rebellion.

[23]The Roman occupation of Britain began with an invasion in 43 C.E. during the reign of Emperor Claudius (r. 41–54). Almost immediately, the Romans raised a temple to the

emperor, as a means of underscoring the divine authority of Rome.

[24]The Latin is ambiguous here. Tacitus probably means that the priests were wasting their own fortunes. Local nobles were expected to join the priesthoods of these imperial cults, as a way of binding them to Rome. In return for the prestige and certain privileges, they were required to expend their own wealth to support various public religious and civic enterprises. However, at least one modern historian has understood these words to mean that the priests were wasting the wealth of the entire country.

[25]It is not totally clear who these women were, but it seems probable that Tacitus meant they were Iceni.

[26]The senate house in Camulodunum.

The victorious Britons turned to meet Petilius Cerialis, commander of the Ninth Legion, who was advancing to the rescue, and routed his legion. They cut the infantry to pieces, but Cerialis escaped back to camp with the cavalry, where he found shelter behind its fortifications.[27] Unnerved by the disaster and the hatred for him throughout the province, which his greed had driven to war, the procurator Catus crossed over into Gaul.[28]

On his part, Suetonius, showing remarkable steadfastness, marched straight on through the midst of the enemy to Londinium, a place not dignified by the title of colony but, nevertheless, a busy place, mainly by reason of its throngs of merchants and numerous commodities.[29] Once there, he was uncertain about whether or not he should select it as his base of military operations. When he looked about and saw its small number of troops (and restrained by the overwhelming example afforded by Petilius's rashness), he decided to save the entire situation by sacrificing one town. He was unmoved by the laments and tears of those pleading for his aid. He gave the order to depart, and made room in his ranks for those who would accompany him. Those who were constrained to stay behind through weakness of sex, feebleness of age, or love of place were all massacred by the enemy. The same disaster befell the municipality of Verulamium,[30] because the barbarians, driven by a lust for plunder and a distaste for hard work, by-passed fortified positions and military garrisons and made straight for whichever place offered the richest booty and, at the same time, was indefensible. It has been established that up to 70,000 persons, Roman citizens and allies, were killed in the abovementioned locations. For they gave no thought to taking prisoners or selling captives into slavery or for any of the other commerce of war. Rather, they rushed full force ahead slaughtering, hanging victims on gibbets, burning, and crucifying, It was as if, with their day of punishment to come, they would first snatch revenge.

By now Suetonius had the Fourteenth Legion, along with veterans from the Twentieth and auxiliary troops from areas closest at hand, comprising almost 10,000 men-under-arms, when he decided to end delay and engage in battle. He chose a location in a narrow defile that was protected from the rear by woods, knowing full well that there was no trace of an enemy except to his front, where there was an open plain that offered no reason to fear ambushes. He therefore drew up the legionnaires in close order and on both of their flanks stationed his light-armed troops,[31] and he massed his cavalry on the far wings. On the other side, vast numbers of Britons ran riotously about here and there in masses of infantry and cavalry. Their numbers were greater than ever before, and their spirits had reached such a height of boldness that they even brought their wives with them to witness their victory and placed them in wagons, which they had positioned at the extreme edge of the battlefield.

Boudica, with her daughters standing in front of her, drove around in a chariot. As she reached each tribal contingent, she proclaimed:

> It was certainly customary for the Britons to be led into battle by women, but now she was not seeking vengeance for her lost kingdom and wealth, as someone descended from heroic ancestors. Rather, as a common woman of the people, she sought to avenge lost freedom, a body weakened by the lash, and the violated

---

[27]Quintus Petilius Cerialis lived to serve Rome on several fronts. In his *History,* Tacitus places into Cerialis's mouth an eloquent speech in defense of the benefits of Roman imperialism, which supposedly he delivered to rebel Gallic forces along the Rhine in 69–70. Cerialis supposedly argued that "victor and vanquished enjoy peace and imperial civilization under the same law and on an equal basis."

[28]Essentially modern France and the Low Countries. Like Britain, it was at this time inhabited by Celts. The Germans (Angles, Saxons, and Jutes) would not settle in Britain and Gaul until the fifth century.

[29]This famous passage is the first recorded description of London, which was founded as a Roman center of trade around the year 50.

[30]The modern town of St. Albans.

[31]Auxiliary troops, who wore lighter armor and carried lighter weapons than the legionnaires.

chastity of her daughters. The greed of the Romans had reached such a point that they did not leave undefiled the very bodies of the Britons, not even those of the old and of virgins. Yet, the gods were there with them to grant a just revenge. The legion that had dared to fight had perished. The others were hiding in their camps or looking around for a way to escape. They could never even face the roar and clamor of so many thousands, much less their assault and hand-to-hand combat. If they reflect upon the size of their armed force and the reasons for this war, they would realize that they must conquer or die on the field of battle. That was her resolve as a woman. Let the men live and be slaves!

On his part, Suetonius was not silent at this critical moment. Although confident of their courage, he still blended together exhortations and pleas to help them disregard the barbarians' noise and empty threats, saying:

There are more women than warriors to be seen over there. They are unwarlike and ill-armed and will immediately crack, as soon as they, who have been routed so often, recognize the iron weapons and valor of those who conquered them in the past. Even when forces numbered many legions, it was a few who turned the tide of battles won. What glory would be theirs when a modestly-sized band of soldiers attains the fame of an entire army! They should keep their ranks closed. Once they have thrown their

javelins, they should press forward behind their swords and shields butchering and slaughtering, without any thought of plunder. Once victory was achieved, everything would fall to them.

The general's words aroused tremendous ardor. With his veteran soldiers, who had a lot of battle experience, prepared to hurl their javelins, Suetonius, fully confident in the outcome, gave the signal for battle.

At first the legion stood its ground, using the narrowness of the defile as protection. When the enemy got closer, the legion discharged its javelins with unerring accuracy and then rushed forward in a wedge-like formation. The auxiliary troops made a similar charge, and the cavalry, with lances extended, shattered whatever serious opposition stood in their way. The rest of the Britons turned their backs, but escape was difficult because the circle of wagons blocked their flight.

The troops showed no mercy, not even to the women. Even baggage animals, their bodies studded with javelins, were added to the heap of corpses. The glory won that day was remarkable and equal to that of victories in days gone by. Indeed, there are those who claim that a bit fewer than 80,000 Britons were killed, while about 400 of our soldiers fell, with not many more than that number wounded. Boudica ended her life with poison.

Han China

In 2 C.E. an imperial census counted 12,233,062 families, or approximately 60 million people, residing in China. A Roman imperial census of 14 C.E. recorded 4,937,000 citizens of the empire. Assuming that full-fledged citizens of Rome constituted less than 10 percent of the empire's total population at that time, it is reasonable to conclude that the Roman Empire contained 50 to 60 million people in the early decades of the first century C.E. Therefore, as we survey Eurasia around the turn of the millennium, we see two massive empires of about equal size and population at the ends of this great land mass. For the next two centuries Han China and Rome dominated their respective regions, and although each experienced periods of crisis, each also offered its subjects fairly stable government and a degree of prosperity.

The Han Dynasty reigned during one of China's golden ages, creating a political and social order based on a synthesis of Legalist and Confucian principles. It expanded China's influence into Korea, Vietnam, and across the reaches of Central Asia. It presided over a general economic upswing, in spite of its expansionist policies, and witnessed a period of rich cultural productivity. Han China flourished for close to four centuries, but in the end, like the Roman Empire, the dynasty and its empire collapsed, the victim of internal instabilities and invasions.

The age of Han was not one period but two. From 202 B.C.E. to 9 C.E. the Former Han ruled China, and its most powerful and important emperor was *Han Wudi,* the Martial Emperor of Han, who reigned from 141 to 87 B.C.E. His domestic and foreign policies provided his successors for the next 2,000 years with *the* model of aggressive imperial greatness. Following an interlude in which Wang Mang (9–23 C.E.) managed to wrest the imperial throne temporarily from the Han family, the dynasty returned to power in the form of the Later, or Eastern, Han (25–220 C.E.). After the first century, however, domestic and frontier conditions deteriorated. From 88 C.E. onward, the family was plagued by a series of ineffective rulers.

By 220, when the Han Dynasty formally came to an end, local lords and invaders from the steppes ruled over a fragmented China. The stability and unity of earlier Han was only a memory as China was plunged into a social, economic, and political chaos that would last for about three and a half centuries. These more than 350 years of disruption following the collapse of Han have often been likened to the so-called Dark Ages that ensued after the disintegration of Roman imperial unity in the West, although the differences between the two are more significant than any superficial parallels.

Two Views on How to Deal with Empire
▼▼▼

32 ▼ *Huan Kuan,*
DISCOURSES ON SALT AND IRON

The *First Chinese Empire* can be said to have begun with the triumph of the Qin Dynasty in 221 B.C.E. and continued for four and a half centuries, until the collapse of the Han Dynasty in 220 C.E. As already noted, the two dynasties experienced vicissitudes but, by and large, China was *the* imperial power in East and Central Asia during these 441 years.

The reign of Emperor *Han Wudi* (r. 141–87 B.C.E.) was pivotal in China's drive toward empire. In 124 B.C.E. the emperor established an important precedent when he decreed that proven knowledge of one of the *Confucian Classics* would be a basis for promotion into the imperial civil service and created a rudimentary imperial academy for educating aspiring scholar-officials in the various fields of Confucian learning. By this act he set in motion a process whereby Confucianism was set on the road to become, centuries later, the empire's ideological framework. Although the principles of Confucius and his followers provided the First Chinese Empire with a façade of moralism and conformity to the ways of the past, its policies were Legalist.

The policies that Han Wudi pursued during his fifty-four-year reign were pragmatic and expansionistic. Beginning in 121, his armies began driving a fierce pastoral people, whom the Chinese called the *Xiongnu,* out of the Gansu (or Hexi) Corridor, a narrow defile bordered by desert and mountains that ran northwest for about 600 miles from the Han capital of Chang'an (modern Xi'an) in north central China. Once the Chinese gained control of the corridor, their armies, administrators, settlers, and merchants could begin moving farther west into the heart of Central Asia. The result was an empire whose influence stretched all the way to the Ferghana Valley in what is today eastern Uzbekistan. It also meant that the Silk Road, the network of caravan routes linking China with India and the Mediterranean, entered its first age of efflorescence.

Empire and long-distance trade have their rewards and their costs. Armies along an expanded western frontier demanded large outlays of money, and to raise sufficient funds Han Wudi's government turned the manufacture of two basic necessities, salt and iron, into government monopolies. It also placed liquor production under government supervision and taxed it heavily. All three were enterprises that previously had brought great wealth to private entrepreneurs. The government also took large-scale commerce in grain and other staple food products, another source of huge profits, out of the hands of individuals and turned it into a function of the state. Governmental control of food distribution, known as *equable marketing,* was designed to stabilize prices and to prevent famines by buying grain and similar commodities where and when they were plentiful and cheap and selling them at fair prices in places and times of scarcity. But it also turned the government into a market speculator.

In 81 B.C.E. Confucian scholars who disagreed with these policies were invited by Emperor Han Zhaodi (r. 87–74) to debate the issue with Sang Hongyang, the emperor's chief economic minister. Sometime between 74 and 49 B.C.E. an otherwise unknown scholar by the name of Huan Kuan preserved at least the essential elements of this debate in his *Discourses on Salt and Iron.* To his credit, although his sympathies lay with the Confucian critics, Huan Kuan impartially reported both sides of the debate. Because both parties put forth their best arguments in these discourses, we have a privileged insight into the differences that separated Confucians and Legalists in this age of empire.

QUESTIONS FOR ANALYSIS

1. What were the major points of disagreement in this debate?
2. What was the Confucian position? Was it consistent with the principles articulated in the *Analects* (source 21)?
3. Can you discover any Daoist principles (source 20) in the Confucians' arguments? What do you infer from your answer?

4. What was the Legalist position? Was it consistent with the principles articulated by Han Fei (source 22)?
5. Consider the styles and methods of argumentation employed by each side. Were they different or similar? What do you infer from your answer?
6. What does this document allow us to infer about the state of the Han Empire and its economy in the early first century B.C.E.? Be specific.

It so happened that in the sixth year of the Shiyuan era[1] an Imperial edict directed the Chancellor and the Lord Grand Secretary[2] to confer with the recommended Worthies and Literati,[3] and to enquire of them as to the rankling grievances among the people.[4]

The Literati responded as follows: It is our humble opinion that the principle of ruling men lies in nipping in the bud wantonness and frivolity, in extending wide the elementals of virtue, in discouraging mercantile pursuits, and in displaying benevolence and righteousness. Let profit never be paraded before the eyes of the people; only then will enlightenment flourish and folkways improve.

But now, with the system of the salt and iron monopolies, the liquor excise, and *equable marketing* established in the provinces and the demesnes,[5] the Government has entered into financial competition with the people, undermining their native honesty and simplicity and promoting selfishness and greed. As a result few among our people take up the fundamental pursuits of life,[6] while many flock to the non-essential.[7] Now sturdy natural qualities decay as artificiality thrives, and rural values decline when industrialism flourishes. When industrialism is cultivated, the people become frivolous; when the values of rural life are developed, the people are simple and unsophisticated. The people being unsophisticated, wealth will abound; when the people are extravagant, cold and hunger will follow. We pray that the salt, iron and liquor monopolies and the system of *equable marketing* be abolished so that the rural pursuits may be encouraged, people be deterred from entering the secondary occupations, and agriculture be materially and financially benefited.

The Lord Grand Secretary said: When the Xiongnu rebelled against our authority and frequently raided and devastated the frontier settlements, to be constantly on the watch for them was a great strain upon the soldiery of the Middle Kingdom;[8] but without measures of precaution being taken, these forays and depredations would never cease. The late Emperor,[9] grieving at the long suffering of the frontier settlers who live in fear of capture by the barbarians, caused consequently forts and signal stations[10] to be built, where garrisons were held ready against the nomads. When the revenue for the defense of the frontier fell short, the salt and iron monopoly was established, the liquor excise and the system of *equable marketing* introduced; goods were multiplied and wealth increased so as to furnish the frontier expenses.

Now our critics here, who demand that these measures be abolished, at home would have the

---

[1]The sixth year of Han Zhaodi's reign (81 B.C.E.).

[2]Sang Hongyang, the son of a shopkeeper, who rose to high office in 110 B.C.E. because of his mathematical abilities. Today he might be called a "number cruncher" or a "bean counter."

[3]Two grades of Confucian scholars.

[4]As the debate unfolds, it is obvious that it included much more than just the salt and iron monopolies.

[5]Administrative divisions of the empire.

[6]Agriculture.

[7]The Confucians considered manufacture and trade non-essential (or branch) pursuits in the sense that they were secondary in importance to agriculture.

[8]China.

[9]Han Wudi.

[10]These forts and signal towers, some of which were linked by steep but not very high earthen berms to hinder the progress of the nomads and their flocks of animals, constituted the original Great Wall of China. The massive stone wall that tourists visit today was largely built by the Ming Dynasty (1368–1644).

hoard of the treasury entirely depleted, and abroad would deprive the border of provision for its defense; they would expose our soldiers who defend the barriers and mount the walls to all the hunger and cold of the borderland. How else do they expect to provide for them? It is not expedient to abolish these measures!

The Literati: Confucius observed that *the ruler of a kingdom or the chief of a house is not concerned about his people being few, but about lack of equitable treatment, nor is he concerned about poverty, but over the presence of discontentment.*[11] Thus the Son of Heaven should not speak about *much and little,* the feudal lords should not talk about *advantage and detriment,* ministers about *gain and loss,* but they should cultivate benevolence and righteousness, to set an example to the people, and extend wide their virtuous conduct to gain the people's confidence. Then will nearby folk lovingly flock to them and distant peoples joyfully submit to their authority. Therefore *the master conqueror does not fight; the expert warrior needs no soldiers; the truly great commander requires not to set his troops in battle array.*[12] Cultivate virtue in the temple and the hall, then you need only to show a bold front to the enemy and your troops will return home in victory. The Prince who practices benevolent administration should be matchless in the world; for him, what use is expenditure?

The Lord Grand Secretary: The Xiongnu, savage and wily, boldly push through the barriers and harass the Middle Kingdom, massacring the provincial population and killing officers and officials along the northern frontier. They long deserve punishment for their unruliness and lawlessness. But Your Majesty[13] graciously took pity on the insufficiency of the multitude and did not allow his officials and soldiers to be exposed in the desert plains, yet unflinchingly You cherish the purpose of raising strong armies and driving the Xiongnu before You to their original haunts in the north. I again assert that the proposal to do

away with the salt and iron monopoly and *equable marketing* would grievously diminish our frontier supplies and impair our military plans. I can not consider favorably a proposal so heartlessly dismissing the frontier question.

The Literati: The ancients held in honor virtuous methods and discredited resort to arms. Thus Confucius said: *If remoter people are not submissive, civil culture and virtue are to be cultivated to attract them to be so; and when they have been so attracted, they must be made contented and tranquil.*[14] Now these virtuous principles are discarded and reliance put on military force; troops are raised to attack the enemy and garrisons are stationed to make ready for him. It is the long drawn-out service of our troops in the field and the ceaseless transportation for the needs of the commissariat that cause our soldiers on the marches to suffer from hunger and cold abroad, while the common people are burdened with labor at home. The establishment of the salt and iron monopoly and the institution of finance officials to supply the army's needs were not permanent schemes; it is therefore desirable that they now be abolished.

The Lord Grand Secretary: The ancient founders of this country made open the ways for both fundamental and branch industries and facilitated equitable distribution of goods. Markets and courts were provided to harmonize various demands; there people of all classes gathered together and all goods collected, so that farmer, merchant, and worker could each obtain what he desired; the exchange completed, everyone went back to his occupation. *Facilitate exchange so that the people will be unflagging in industry* says the Book of Changes.[15] Thus without artisans, the farmers will be deprived of the use of implements; without merchants, all prized commodities will be cut off. The former would lead to stoppage of grain production, the latter to exhaustion of wealth. It is clear that the salt and iron monopoly and *equable marketing* are really in-

---

[11]A quotation from the *Analects* (source 21).
[12]A quotation from some unknown source.
[13]Apparently the emperor was present at the debate.
[14]Another quotation from the *Analects.*

[15]The *Yijing,* a book of divination and one of the *Confucian Classics.* Today it is quite popular in the West among New Agers.

tended for the circulation of amassed wealth and the regulation of the consumption according to the urgency of the need. It is inexpedient to abolish them.

The Literati: Lead the people with virtue and the people will return to honest simplicity; entice the people with gain, and they will become vulgar.[16] Vulgar habits would lead them away from duty to follow after gain, with the result that people will swarm on the road and throng at the markets. *A poor country may appear plentiful, not because it possesses abundant wealth, but because wants multiply and people become reckless,* said Laozi.[17] Hence the true King promotes rural pursuits and discourages branch industries; he checks the people's desires through the principles of propriety and duty and provides a market for grain in exchange for other commodities, where there is no place for merchants to circulate useless goods, and for artisans to make useless implements. The purpose of merchants is to circulate and of artisans to provide tools; they should not become a major concern of the government.

The Lord Grand Secretary: Guanzi[18] is reported to have said: *A country may possess a wealth of fertile land and yet its people may be underfed — the reason lying in lack of an adequate supply of agricultural implements. It may possess rich natural resources in its mountains and seas and yet the people may be deficient in wealth — the reason being in the insufficient number of artisans and merchants.*[19] . . .

The Literati: The rulers of antiquity taxed the people but a tithe,[20] while they kept open the ponds and weirs according to season without restrictions. . . . This is how Yu and Tang[21] prepared against flood and drought and made the

people content. But if the grass and weeds are not cleared and the fields not regularly cultivated, there will be no sufficiency, even though a monopoly over the wealth of the mountains and seas is established and a hundred sorts of profit are developed. Hence the ancients honored manual labor and attended to the fundamental industry, so that they sowed and planted in abundance, everyone worked on the land according to season, and food and clothing were always sufficient. People did not suffer even in the face of several bad years. Agriculture should be the fundamental occupation of men, clothes and food being of primary necessity to the people. With both of these attended to, the country will be rich and the people at peace. In the words of the Book of Poetry: *Those hundred houses being full, the wives and children have a feeling of repose.*

The Lord Grand Secretary: The worthies and the sages did not found their families by means of one room,[22] nor did they enrich the state through one way. . . . If one must resort to agriculture alone to make a living and found a family, then Shun[23] would not have had to make pottery and Yi Yin[24] would not have had to be a cook. Hence, the Empire Builder acts according to the principle: *I honor what the whole world despises and value what the whole world slights.*[25] He would exchange the non-essential for the fundamental and secure the substantial with his own emptiness. . . . Thus, a piece of Chinese plain silk can be exchanged with the Xiongnu for articles worth several pieces of gold and thereby reduce the resources of our enemy. Mules, donkeys and camels enter the frontier in unbroken lines; horses, dapples and bays and prancing mounts, come

---

[16]See the *Analects* (source 21).

[17]This aphorism does not appear in any surviving text of the *Dao Dejing* (source 20).

[18]Guanzi was the seventh-century B.C.E. prime minister of the state of Qi who supposedly composed a book (the *Guanzi*) of Legalist-Daoist essays on society and politics. The essays were actually compiled between the mid fourth and mid second centuries B.C.E.

[19]This quotation does not appear in the surviving text of the *Guanzi*.

[20]According to legend, in China's earliest days agricultural fields were divided into nine equal squares. Eight were

given out to tenant farmers, who paid for their one-eighth portions by working together in the ninth portion, which belonged to the lord.

[21]The legendary founders, respectively, of the Xia and Shang dynasties.

[22]They were polygamists who had many wives and bedrooms.

[23]One of the legendary Five Sage Emperors who preceded the Xia Dynasty.

[24]A legendary minister of the Shang Dynasty. See source 5.

[25]A quotation from the *Guanzi* (see note 18).

into our possession. The furs of sables, marmots, foxes and badgers, colored rugs and decorated carpets fill the Imperial treasury, while jade and auspicious stones, corals and crystals, become national treasures. That is to say, products keep flowing in, while our wealth is not dissipated. Novelties flowing in, the government has plenty. National wealth not being dispersed abroad, the people enjoy abundance. So the Book of Poetry describes it: *Those hundred houses being full, the wives and children have a feeling of repose.*

The Literati: In ancient times merchants circulated goods without premeditation, artisans got their price without cheating. Therefore when the true gentleman farmed, hunted or fished he was in reality doing but one thing. Trade promotes dishonesty. Artisans provoke disputes. They lie in wait for their chance without a scruple. Thus avaricious men become cheats and honest men avaricious. In the olden time when Jie[26] filled the palace halls with singing girls in embroidered clothes, Yi Yin withdrew himself and went to Bao,[27] while the singing girls finally ruined his state. Now mules and donkeys are not as useful as cattle and horses. Sable and marmot furs, wool and felt goods do not add substance to silk. Beautiful jades and corals come from mount Kun.[28] Pearls and ivory are produced in Gui Lin.[29] These

places are more than ten thousand *li* distant from Han.[30] Calculating the labor for farming and silk raising and the costs in material and capital, it will be found that one article of foreign import costs a price one hundred times its value,[31] and for one handful, ten thousand weight of grain are paid. As the rulers take delight in novelties, extravagant clothing is adopted among the masses. As the rulers treasure the goods from distant lands, wealth flows outward. Therefore, a true King does not value useless things, so to set an example of thrift to his subjects; does not love exotic articles, so to enrich his country. Thus the principle of administering the people lies only in carefulness in expenditure, in honoring the primary occupation, and in distribution of land according to the "well tithe."[32]

The Lord Grand Secretary: From the capital,[33] east, west, north and south across the mountains and rivers and throughout the provinces and the demesnes, you will find that all of the prosperous, rich and great municipalities have streets extending in all directions, where the merchants gather and all commodities are exposed. Thus, the Sage utilizes nature's seasons and the Wise utilizes the wealth of the land. Superior men acquire through others. The mediocre burden their own bodies.

---

[26]The last Xia emperor. See source 5, note 3.
[27]He went into self-imposed exile.
[28]A mountain far to the west.
[29]The Kunlun Mountains, which lay far to the west of the heart of Han China. See the next note.
[30]A *li* is usually roughly computed as one-third of a mile,

but evidence suggests that a *li* at this time was about one-fifth of a mile. About 2,000 miles is a pretty good estimate.
[31]Compare this with a similar statement by Pliny the Elder (source 36).
[32]Described in note 20.
[33]From Chang'an.

A Woman's Place as Viewed by a Female Confucian
▼▼▼

33 ▼ *Ban Zhao, LESSONS FOR WOMEN*

Education in the *Confucian Classics* increasingly became one of several avenues to a position of social and political power in Han China. Confucian doctrine, however, did not accord women a status equal to that of men. In fact, the *Confucian Classics* say little about women, which suggests how little they mattered in the scheme of Confucian values. Most Confucians accepted women's subservience to men as natural and proper. In their view, failure to maintain a proper relationship between two such obviously unequal persons as husband and wife or brother and sister would result in a breakdown of all the rules of propriety and, as a consequence, lead to social disharmony.

Yet this was only part of the story. Confucian doctrine and Chinese society at large accorded women, as both mothers and mothers-in-law, a good deal of honor, and with that honor came power within the family structure. Moreover, there is plenty of evidence of literate, educated women of high status during the Han and Tang eras (202 B.C.E.–907 C.E.). Indeed, a handful of extraordinary women managed to acquire advanced literary educations and achieve positions of far-ranging influence and authority despite social constraints. The foremost female Confucian of the Age of Han was *Ban Zhao* (ca. 45–116 C.E.), sister of the court historian Ban Gu (32–92). Upon Gu's death, Zhao served as imperial historian under Emperor Han Hedi (r. 88–105) and completed her brother's *Han Annals,* a history of the Former Han Dynasty, which is regarded as one of China's historical masterpieces. Ban Zhao also served as an advisor on state matters to Empress Deng, who assumed power as regent for her infant son in 106.

Madame Ban was the daughter of the widely respected writer and administrator Ban Biao (3–54) and received her elementary education from her literate mother while still a child in her father's house. Otherwise her early life appears to have been quite conventional. She married at the age of fourteen, thereby becoming the lowest-ranking member of her husband's family, and bore children. Her husband died young, and Ban Zhao never remarried, devoting herself instead to literary pursuits and acquiring a reputation for scholarship and stylistic grace that brought her to the imperial court.

Among her many literary works, Ban Zhao composed a commentary on the popular *Lives of Admirable Women* by Liu Xiang (77–6 B.C.E.) and later in life produced her most famous work, the *Nü Jie,* or *Lessons for Women,* which purports to be an instructional manual on feminine behavior and virtue for her daughters. In fact, she intended it for a much wider audience. Realizing that Confucian texts contained little in the way of specific and practical guidelines for a woman's everyday life, Ban Zhao sought to fill that void with a coherent set of rules for women, especially young women.

QUESTIONS FOR ANALYSIS

1. What does Ban Zhao tell us about the status of daughters-in-law? How has she escaped from the fears of such servitude?
2. This essay contains several clues regarding a woman's role in maintaining a beneficial relationship with the family's ancestors. Find and comment on them. How significant, if at all, do you find this role?
3. According to Ban Zhao, what rules of propriety should govern a marriage?
4. What does Ban Zhao consider the principal duty of a husband? Of a wife? How and why are they complementary parts of the natural order of the universe? In addressing this last question, review source 23.

5. Consider her claim that she is inherently unintelligent. Does she mean it? Why do you think she makes such statements?

6. Why does Ban Zhao advocate that women be educated? Do her stated reasons strike you as her true motives? Be specific in defending your answer.

7. What was there about Ban Zhao's essay that caused it to be so highly regarded by Confucian scholars over the following centuries?

I, the unworthy writer, am unsophisticated, unenlightened, and by nature unintelligent, but I am fortunate both to have received not a little favor from my scholarly father, and to have had a cultured mother and instructresses upon whom to rely for a literary education as well as for training in good manners. More than forty years have passed since at the age of fourteen I took up the dustpan and the broom in the Cao family.[1] During this time with trembling heart I feared constantly that I might disgrace my parents, and that I might multiply difficulties for both the women and the men of my husband's family. Day and night I was distressed in heart, but I labored without confessing weariness. Now and hereafter, however, I know how to escape from such fears.

Being careless, and by nature stupid, I taught and trained my children without system. Consequently I fear that my son Gu may bring disgrace upon the Imperial Dynasty by whose Holy Grace he has unprecedentedly received the extraordinary privilege of wearing the Gold and the Purple, a privilege for the attainment of which by my son, I a humble subject never even hoped. Nevertheless, now that he is a man and able to plan his own life, I need not again have concern for him. But I do grieve that you, my daughters, just now at the age for marriage, have not at this time had gradual training and advice; that you still have not learned the proper customs for married women. I fear that by failure in good manners in other families you will humiliate both your ancestors and your clan. I am now seriously ill, life is uncertain. As I have thought of you all in so untrained a state, I have been uneasy many a

time for you. At hours of leisure I have composed . . . these instructions under the title, "Lessons for Women." In order that you may have something wherewith to benefit your persons, I wish every one of you, my daughters, each to write out a copy for yourself.

From this time on every one of you strive to practice these lessons.

HUMILITY

On the third day after the birth of a girl the ancients observed three customs: first to place the baby below the bed; second to give her a potsherd[2] with which to play; and third to announce her birth to her ancestors by an offering. Now to lay the baby below the bed plainly indicated that she is lowly and weak, and should regard it as her primary duty to humble herself before others. To give her potsherds with which to play indubitably signified that she should practice labor and consider it her primary duty to be industrious. To announce her birth before her ancestors clearly meant that she ought to esteem as her primary duty the continuation of the observance of worship in the home.

These three ancient customs epitomize a woman's ordinary way of life and the teachings of the traditional ceremonial rites and regulations. Let a woman modestly yield to others; let her respect others; let her put others first, herself last. Should she do something good, let her not mention it; should she do something bad, let her not deny it. Let her bear disgrace; let her even endure when others speak or do evil to her. Always let her seem

---

[1]The family into which she married.

[2]A piece of broken pottery.

to tremble and to fear. When a woman follows such maxims as these, then she may be said to humble herself before others.

Let a woman retire late to bed, but rise early to duties; let her not dread tasks by day or by night. Let her not refuse to perform domestic duties whether easy or difficult. That which must be done, let her finish completely, tidily, and systematically. When a woman follows such rules as these, then she may be said to be industrious.

Let a woman be correct in manner and upright in character in order to serve her husband. Let her live in purity and quietness of spirit, and attend to her own affairs. Let her love not gossip and silly laughter. Let her cleanse and purify and arrange in order the wine and the food for the offerings to the ancestors. When a woman observes such principles as these, then she may be said to continue ancestral worship.

No woman who observes these three fundamentals of life has ever had a bad reputation or has fallen into disgrace. If a woman fails to observe them, how can her name be honored; how can she but bring disgrace upon herself?

HUSBAND AND WIFE

The Way of husband and wife is intimately connected with *Yin* and *Yang*,[3] and relates the individual to gods and ancestors. Truly it is the great principle of Heaven and Earth, and the great basis of human relationships. Therefore the "Rites"[4] honor union of man and woman; and in the "Book of Poetry"[5] the "First Ode" manifests the principle of marriage. For these reasons the relationship cannot but be an important one.

If a husband is unworthy, then he possesses nothing by which to control his wife. If a wife is unworthy, then she possesses nothing with which to serve her husband. If a husband does not control his wife, then the rules of conduct manifesting his authority are abandoned and broken. If a wife does not serve her husband, then the proper relationship between men and women and the natural order of things are neglected and destroyed. As a matter of fact the purpose of these two [the controlling of women by men, and the serving of men by women] is the same.

Now examine the gentlemen of the present age. They only know that wives must be controlled, and that the husband's rules of conduct manifesting his authority must be established. They therefore teach their boys to read books and study histories. But they do not in the least understand that husbands and masters must also be served, and that the proper relationship and the rites should be maintained.

Yet only to teach men and not to teach women — is that not ignoring the essential relation between them? According to the "Rites," it is the rule to begin to teach children to read at the age of eight years, and by the age of fifteen years they ought then to be ready for cultural training. Only why should it not be that girls' education as well as boys' be according to this principle?

RESPECT AND CAUTION

As *Yin* and *Yang* are not of the same nature, so man and woman have different characteristics. The distinctive quality of the *Yang* is rigidity; the function of the *Yin* is yielding. Man is honored for strength; a woman is beautiful on account of her gentleness. Hence there arose the common saying: "A man though born like a wolf may, it is feared, become a weak monstrosity; a woman though born like a mouse may, it is feared, become a tiger."

Now for self-culture nothing equals respect for others. To counteract firmness nothing equals compliance. Consequently it can be said that the Way of respect and acquiescence is woman's most important principle of conduct. So respect may be defined as nothing other than holding on to that which is permanent; and acquiescence nothing other than being liberal and generous. Those

---

[3]See source 23.
[4]*The Book of Rites* (see the introduction to source 5).

[5]*The Book of Songs* (source 6).

who are steadfast in devotion know that they should stay in their proper places; those who are liberal and generous esteem others, and honor and serve them.

If husband and wife have the habit of staying together, never leaving one another, and following each other around within the limited space of their own rooms, then they will lust after and take liberties with one another. From such action improper language will arise between the two. This kind of discussion may lead to licentiousness. Out of licentiousness will be born a heart of disrespect to the husband. Such a result comes from not knowing that one should stay in one's proper place.

Furthermore, affairs may be either crooked or straight; words may be either right or wrong. Straightforwardness cannot but lead to quarreling; crookedness cannot but lead to accusation. If there are really accusations and quarrels, then undoubtedly there will be angry affairs. Such a result comes from not esteeming others, and not honoring and serving them.

If wives suppress not contempt for husbands, then it follows that such wives rebuke and scold their husbands. If husbands stop not short of anger, then they are certain to beat their wives. The correct relationship between husband and wife is based upon harmony and intimacy, and conjugal love is grounded in proper union. Should actual blows be dealt, how could matrimonial relationship be preserved? Should sharp words be spoken, how could conjugal love exist? If love and proper relationship both be destroyed, then husband and wife are divided.

WOMANLY QUALIFICATIONS

A woman ought to have four qualifications: (1) womanly virtue; (2) womanly words; (3) womanly bearing; and (4) womanly work. Now what is called womanly virtue need not be brilliant ability, exceptionally different from others. Womanly words need be neither clever in debate nor keen in conversation. Womanly appearance requires neither a pretty nor a perfect face and form. Womanly work need not be work done more skillfully than that of others.

To guard carefully her chastity; to control circumspectly her behavior; in every motion to exhibit modesty; and to model each act on the best usage, this is womanly virtue.

To choose her words with care; to avoid vulgar language; to speak at appropriate times; and not to weary others with much conversation, may be called the characteristics of womanly words.

To wash and scrub filth away; to keep clothes and ornaments fresh and clean; to wash the head and bathe the body regularly; and to keep the person free from disgraceful filth, may be called the characteristics of womanly bearing.

With whole-hearted devotion to sew and to weave; to love not gossip and silly laughter; in cleanliness and order to prepare the wine and food for serving guests, may be called the characteristics of womanly work.

These four qualifications characterize the greatest virtue of a woman. No woman can afford to be without them. In fact they are very easy to possess if a woman only treasure them in her heart. The ancients had a saying: "Is Love afar off? If I desire love, then love is at hand!" So can it be said of these qualifications. . . .

IMPLICIT OBEDIENCE

Whenever the mother-in-law says, "Do not do that," and if what she says is right, unquestionably the daughter-in-law obeys. Whenever the mother-in-law says, "Do that," even if what she says is wrong, still the daughter-in-law submits unfailingly to the command.

Let a woman not act contrary to the wishes and the opinions of parents-in-law about right and wrong; let her not dispute with them what is straight and what is crooked. Such docility may be called obedience which sacrifices personal opinion. Therefore the ancient book, "A Pattern for Women," says: "If a daughter-in-law who follows the wishes of her parents-in-law is like an echo and a shadow, how could she not be praised?"

▼▼▼

India in the Age of Empires

In its long history, India has been politically fragmented more often than not. Between the third century B.C.E. and the sixth century C.E., however, India witnessed the rise and flowering of two great native empires, each of which participated in the general interchange of goods, ideas, and peoples that characterized this age of Afro-Eurasian interchange.

First there was the mighty *Mauryan Empire* (ca. 315–183 B.C.E.), which controlled all but the most southern portions of the subcontinent. Centuries later the *Gupta Empire* (320–ca. 550 C.E.) arose, centered on the Ganges River in the northeast but exercising authority over most of northern and central India. Although neither equaled the Han and Roman empires in size, military power, or longevity, both Indian empires provided peace and general prosperity based, at least in part, on energetic administration and benign social intervention. At the height of the Gupta Empire under Chandragupta II (r. ca. 376–415), India was possibly the most prosperous and peaceful society in the Afro-Eurasian World. China was then immersed in an interdynastic time of troubles; Greco-Roman civilization was undergoing severe stresses at every level; and the powerful *Sassanian Empire* of Persia was embroiled in internal religious turmoil and wars on its frontiers.

Between these two homebred imperial periods, India underwent a series of invasions from the northwest that resulted in portions of northern India falling under the domination of alien rulers and being joined to important Central Asian kingdoms and empires. The first of these invaders were Greeks from Bactria (source 29), who came in the early second century B.C.E. and established a number of competing kingdoms in northern India. The Greco-Bactrians did not remain in India long. They soon gave way to various nomadic invaders from East and Central Asia, whose lives had been disrupted by the emergence of Chinese imperialism in the late third and second centuries B.C.E. and also by intertribal conflicts.

The most significant of the new invaders were a nomadic people the Chinese knew as the *Yuezhi,* who created the *Kushan Empire* toward the end of the first century B.C.E. The Kushans, whose imperial focus was always Central Asia, lasted into the late third century C.E., and during their centuries of empire provided India with connections to Southwest Asia, the Mediterranean, and China. Much of that interaction was the peaceful exchange of goods and ideas, but Chinese annals also tell how General Ban Chao, brother of the historians Ban Gu and Ban Zhao (source 33), destroyed a Yuezhi army in 90 C.E. when the Kushan emperor launched a retaliatory strike against the Chinese after he was refused the hand of a Han princess.

All of these important political developments should not blind us to the fact that the most significant developments taking place in India during the period 300 B.C.E.–500 C.E. were cultural. The Gupta Era is especially important in this regard and is rightly acknowledged as one of traditional India's golden ages.

The Softening Effects of Dharma
▼▼▼

34 ▼ *Asoka, ROCK AND PILLAR EDICTS*

As Alexander the Great and his Macedonian generals pulled back from northwest India, a local lord, Chandragupta Maurya (r. ca. 315–281 B.C.E.), began forming what would become the greatest of India's ancient empires. Under the founder and his son, Bindusara, the empire expanded and functioned with brutal efficiency. Around 269 B.C.E. Bindusara's son *Asoka* (r. ca. 269–232) inherited the throne and initially continued his family's tradition of foreign aggression and domestic repression.

In the eighth year of his reign, however, he underwent a spiritual conversion when he beheld the bloodshed and misery that resulted from his conquest of the land of Kalinga, along India's southeastern coast. As a consequence, Asoka embraced the teachings of the Buddha and embarked on a new policy of government. Probably inspired by the public monuments of the kings of Persia, Asoka publicized his change of heart and new imperial policies in a series of engraved rock and pillar inscriptions scattered throughout his lands.

QUESTIONS FOR ANALYSIS

1. Is there any evidence in this source that Asoka promoted Buddhist missionary activities? Be specific.
2. What was Asoka's attitude and policy toward all non-Buddhist religions and ceremonies?
3. Following his conversion, what did Asoka consider to be the purpose of good government? What structures and policies did he institute to achieve his vision?
4. Asoka saw himself as a follower of the Buddha's Law of Righteousness *(Dharma)*. Review sources 16 and 17. Based on your reading of these two lessons by the Buddha, respond to the following questions: Would the Buddha agree with any of Asoka's policies and beliefs? If so, which ones? Would the Buddha disagree with any of Asoka's policies and beliefs? If so, which ones? What would be the Buddha's overall evaluation of Asoka's understanding of Buddhist teachings?
5. Imagine that three Chinese travelers — a Confucian, a Legalist, and a Daoist — read these inscriptions. What would be their reactions?

ROCK EDICT XIII

The Kalinga country was conquered by King Priyadarsi,[1] Beloved of the Gods, in the eighth year of his reign. One hundred and fifty thousand persons were carried away captive, one hundred thousand were slain, and many times that number died.

---

[1] Asoka's throne name, it means "one who sees to the good of others."

Immediately after the Kalingas had been conquered, King Priyadarsi became intensely devoted to the study of Dharma,[2] to the love of Dharma, and to the inculcation of Dharma.

The Beloved of the Gods, conqueror of the Kalingas, is moved to remorse now. For he has felt profound sorrow and regret because the conquest of a people previously unconquered involves slaughter, death, and deportation.

But there is a more important reason for the King's remorse. The Brahmanas[3] and Sramanas[4] as well as the followers of other religions and householders — who all practiced obedience to superiors, parents, and teachers, and proper courtesy and firm devotion to friends, acquaintances, companions, relatives, slaves, and servants — all suffer from the injury, slaughter, and deportation inflicted on their loved ones. Even those who escaped calamity themselves are deeply afflicted by the misfortunes suffered by those friends, acquaintances, companions, and relatives for whom they feel an undiminished affection. Thus all men share in the misfortune, and this weighs on King Priyadarsi's mind. . . .

Therefore, even if the number of people who were killed or who died or who were carried away in the Kalinga war had been only one one-hundredth or one one-thousandth of what it actually was, this would still have weighed on the King's mind.

King Priyadarsi now thinks that even a person who wrongs him must be forgiven for wrongs that can be forgiven.

King Priyadarsi seeks to induce even the forest peoples[5] who have come under his dominion to adopt this way of life and this ideal. He reminds them, however, that he exercises the power to punish, despite his repentance, in order to induce them to desist from their crimes and escape execution.

For King Priyadarsi desires security, self-control, impartiality, and cheerfulness for all living creatures.

King Priyadarsi considers moral conquest the most important conquest. He has achieved this moral conquest repeatedly both here and among the peoples living beyond the borders of his kingdom, even as far away as six hundred *yojanas,*[6] where the Yona [Greek] king Antiyoka[7] rules, and even beyond Antiyoka in the realms of the four kings named Turamaya, Antikini, Maka, and Alikasudara,[8] and to the south among the Cholas and Pandyas[9] as far as Ceylon.[10]

Here in the King's dominion also, . . . everywhere people heed his instructions in Dharma.

Even in countries which King Priyadarsi's envoys have not reached, people have heard about Dharma and about his Majesty's ordinances and instructions in Dharma, and they themselves conform to Dharma and will continue to do so.

Wherever conquest is achieved by Dharma, it produces satisfaction. Satisfaction is firmly established by conquest by Dharma. Even satisfaction, however, is of little importance. King Priyadarsi attaches value ultimately only to consequences of action in the other world.

This edict on Dharma has been inscribed so that my sons and great-grandsons who may come after me should not think new conquests worth achieving. If they do conquer, let them take pleasure in moderation and mild punishments. Let them consider moral conquest the only true conquest.

---

[2]Sources 15 and 16 respectively provide definitions of Hindu *dharma* and Buddhist *Dharma.*
[3]Hindu ascetics who were members of the Brahmin, or priestly, caste. They were divided into many sects.
[4]Another group of ascetics. In the context of this edict, *Brahmanas and Sramanas* means all Hindu and Buddhist holy people.
[5]The primitive, largely uncivilized folk of the southern jungle.
[6]About 3,000 miles.

[7]Antiochus II Theos (r. 261–246 B.C.E.), a member of the Macedonian family of Seleucus and king of Syria.
[8]Ptolemy II Philadelphus of Egypt (r. 285–247 B.C.E.); Antigonos Gonatas of Macedonia (r. 278–239 B.C.E.); Magos of Cyrene in North Africa (r. 300–258 B.C.E.); and Alexander of Epirus in northwest Greece (r. ca. 272–258 B.C.E.).
[9]People of the southern tip of India.
[10]The major island off the southeast coast of India; today it is the nation of Sri Lanka.

This is good, here and hereafter. Let their pleasure be pleasure in morality. For this alone is good, here and hereafter.

PILLAR EDICT VII

King Priyadarsi, the Beloved of the Gods, speaks as follows: . . .

How can the people be induced to follow Dharma strictly? How can progress in morality be increased sufficiently? How can I raise them up by the promotion of Dharma? . . . This occurred to me. I shall issue proclamations on Dharma, and I shall order instruction in Dharma to be given to the people. Hearing these proclamations and instructions, the people will conform to Dharma; they will raise themselves up and will make progress by the promotion of Dharma. To this end I have issued proclamations on Dharma, and I have instituted various kinds of moral and religious instruction.

My highest officials, who have authority over large numbers of people, will expound and spread the precepts of Dharma. I have instructed the provincial governors, too, who are in charge of many hundred thousand people, concerning how to guide people devoted to Dharma. . . .

My officers charged with the spread of Dharma are occupied with various kinds of services beneficial to ascetics and householders, and they are empowered to concern themselves with all sects. I have ordered some of them to look after the affairs of the Sangha,[11] some to take care of the brahmin . . . ascetics, some to work among the Nirgranthas,[12] and some among the various other religious sects. Different officials are thus assigned specifically to the affairs of different religions, but my officers for spreading Dharma are occupied with all sects. . . .

These and many other high officials take care of the distribution of gifts from myself as well as from the queens. They report in various ways . . . worthy recipients of charity. . . . I also ordered some of them to supervise the distribution of gifts from my sons and the sons of other queens, in order to promote noble deeds of Dharma and conformity to the precepts of Dharma. These noble deeds and this conformity consist in promoting compassion, liberality, truthfulness, purity, gentleness, and goodness. . . .

Whatever good deeds I have done the people have imitated, and they have followed them as a model. In doing so, they have progressed and will progress in obedience to parents and teachers, in respect for elders, in courtesy to priests and ascetics, to the poor and distressed, and even to slaves and servants. . . .

The people can be induced to advance in Dharma by only two means, by moral prescriptions and by meditation. Of the two, moral prescriptions are of little consequence, but meditation is of great importance. The moral prescriptions I have promulgated include rules making certain animals inviolable,[13] and many others. But even in the case of abstention from injuring and from killing living creatures, it is by meditation that people have progressed in Dharma most.

This edict on Dharma has been inscribed in order that it may endure and be followed as long as my sons and great-grandsons shall reign and as long as the sun and moon shall shine. For one who adheres to it will attain happiness in this world and hereafter. . . .

This edict on morality should be engraved wherever stone pillars or stone slabs are available, in order that it may endure forever.

PILLAR EDICT II

King Priyadarsi says:

Dharma is good. But what does Dharma consist of? It consists of few sins and many good

---

[11]Buddhist monastic groups.
[12]Jain ascetics, who followed the teachings of the *Mahavira,* a rough contemporary of the Buddha who taught a doctrine of extreme asceticism and absolute nonviolence.

[13]Certain animals are not to be harmed.

deeds, of kindness, liberality, truthfulness, and purity.

I have bestowed even the gift of spiritual insight on men in various ways. I have decreed many kindnesses, including even the grant of life, to living creatures, two-footed and four-footed as well as birds and aquatic animals. I have also performed many other good deeds.

I have ordered this edict on Dharma to be inscribed in order that people may act according to it and that it may endure for a long time. And he who follows it completely will do good deeds.

ROCK EDICT IX

King Priyadarsi, the Beloved of the Gods, says:

People perform various ceremonies. Among the occasions on which ceremonies are performed are sicknesses, marriages of sons or daughters, children's births, and departures on journeys. Women in particular have recourse to many diverse, trivial, and meaningless ceremonies.

It is right that ceremonies be performed. But this kind bears little fruit. The ceremony of Dharma,[14] on the contrary, is very fruitful. It consists in proper treatment of slaves and servants, reverence to teachers, restraint of violence toward living creatures, and liberality to priests and ascetics. These and like actions are called the ceremonies of Dharma.

Therefore, a father, son, brother, master, friend, acquaintance, or even neighbor ought to say about such actions, "These are good; they should be performed until their purpose is achieved. I shall observe them."

Other ceremonies are of doubtful value. They may achieve their purpose, or they may not. Moreover the purposes for which they are performed are limited to this world.

The ceremony of Dharma, on the other hand, is not limited to time. Even if it does not achieve its object in this world, it produces unlimited merit in the next world. But if it produces its object in this world, it achieves both effects: the purpose desired in this world and unlimited merit in the next.

It has also been said that liberality is commendable. But there is no greater liberality than the gift of Dharma or the benefit of Dharma. Therefore, a friend, well-wisher, relative, or companion should urge one when the occasion arises, saying, "You should do this; this is commendable. By doing this you may attain Heaven." And what is more worth doing than attaining Heaven?

ROCK EDICT VII

King Priyadarsi wishes members of all faiths to live everywhere in his kingdom.

For they will seek mastery of the senses and purity of mind. Men are different in their inclinations and passions, however, and they may perform the whole of their duties or only part.

Even if one is not able to make lavish gifts, mastery of the senses, purity of mind, gratitude, and steadfast devotion are commendable and essential.

PILLAR EDICT IV

Impartiality is desirable in legal procedures and in punishments. I have therefore decreed that henceforth prisoners who have been convicted and sentenced to death shall be granted a respite of three days. During this period their relatives may appeal to the officials for the prisoners' lives; or, if no one makes an appeal, the prisoners may prepare for the other world by distributing gifts or by fasting.

For I desire that, when the period of respite has expired, they may attain happiness in the next world, and that various ways of practicing Dharma by self-control and the distribution of gifts may be increased among the people.

---

[14]*Ceremony* should be understood in a metaphorical sense — the good works of Dharma as encapsulated in the Holy Eightfold Path (source 16).

Sacred Law in Classical India
▼▼▼

35 ▼ *THE LAWS OF MANU*

Despite Asoka's promotion of the Buddhist principle of Dharma, or the Law of Righteousness, the majority of India's population remained true to more traditional Hindu ways and beliefs, which included acceptance of the caste system and the notion that dharma defines caste duties, as Lord Krishna taught in the *Bhagavad Gita* (source 15). For most Hindus, dharma became concrete in the innumerable rituals that Asoka found so useless and in Indian civilization's countless forms of mandated social behavior. Faith, worship, and social duty all sprang from dharma.

The earliest extant codification of the Sacred Law of dharma is the *Laws of Manu,* which was compiled between the first century B.C.E. and the second or third century C.E. In Hindu mythology *Manu* was the primeval human being, the father of humanity, and its first king. In the Vedas he appears as the founder of all human social order and the original teacher of dharma, having been instructed in the Sacred Law by Brahman. Tradition also regarded him as an Indian Utnapishtim or Noah, the sole survivor of a catastrophic flood, after which he created a woman, through whom he generated the human species. The anonymous compilers of the *Laws of Manu* claimed that the rules and regulations contained in this code were universal and timeless. Each law was a manifestation of dharma, passed down uncorrupted from Brahman through Manu. In reality, this collection mirrors 2,500 years of Indian social history and religious thought, and consequently contains what seem to the outside viewer to be numerous contradictions. These apparent discrepancies, however, are readily integrated in a cultural complex predicated on the idea that spiritual truth has infinite manifestations.

The selections here illustrate the two major determinants of classical Indian society: caste and gender. As far as we can ascertain, class and gender distinctions of one sort or another were common to all ancient civilizations, but the caste system was unique to India. The English word *caste* derives from the Portuguese *casta,* which means "pure." Hindus use two different Sanskrit words for caste: *varna* (color) and *jati* (birth). Varna refers only to the four major social-religious divisions that "The Hymn to Purusha" (source 10) enumerates: *Brahmins* (priests); *Kshatriyas* (warriors); *Vaisyas* (farmers, artisans, and merchants); *Sudras* (workers). These classifications of Indian society possibly resulted from the Aryans' attempt to separate themselves from the darker-skinned natives whom they conquered. The jati system, which today includes more than 3,000 identifiable groupings, was not fully developed until around the Gupta period, long after the Aryans had disappeared into India's general population. Jatis are hereditary occupations, each with its own dharma. Hindus generally classify jatis as subdivisions of the varna system and steps in the ladder of reincarnation.

QUESTIONS FOR ANALYSIS

1. The lowest-ranking jatis are composed of people known as *Untouchables*. Why are they called that, and what manner of life do they lead? What is there about their occupations that other Hindus find so offensive?
2. Under what circumstances might a person engage in work appropriate to a lower varna? How far may one go in this regard, and what are the consequences? May one legitimately assume the duties of a higher varna? Is intermarriage among the castes considered acceptable?
3. Each varna and jati has its own dharma. Can you find evidence of a universal dharma, common to all Hindus?
4. How might the caste system make political and social unification difficult?
5. Why are women denied access to ceremonies where the Vedic texts are recited? Notwithstanding this prohibition, do women perform any necessary religious functions? If so, what are they, and what do these functions suggest about the status of women?
6. What constraints are placed on women, and why? What freedoms, if any, does a woman enjoy? How and why, if at all, are women protected and honored? What are the duties of their fathers and husbands?
7. Compare the status of Hindu women with that of women in Han China (source 33). How are their respective situations reflections of the different cultures in which they live? Notwithstanding cultural differences, are their positions comparable, or does one seem to enjoy greater freedom and power? Is one better protected than the other? Be specific in your answers.

VARNA

The Brahmin, the Kshatriya, and the Vaisya castes are the twice-born ones,[1] but the fourth, the Sudra, has one birth only; there is no fifth caste. . . .

To Brahmins he[2] assigned teaching and studying the Vedas, sacrificing for their own benefit and for others, giving and accepting of alms.

The Kshatriya he commanded to protect the people, to bestow gifts, to offer sacrifices, to study the Vedas, and to abstain from attaching himself to sensual pleasures;

The Vaisya to tend cattle, to bestow gifts, to offer sacrifices, to study the Vedas, to trade, to lend money, and to cultivate land.

One occupation only the lord prescribed to the Sudra, to serve meekly . . . these other three castes.

JATIS

From a male Sudra are born an Ayogava, a Kshattri, and a Kandala, the lowest of men, by Vaisya, Kshatriya, and Brahmin females respectively, sons who owe their origin to a confusion of the castes.[3] . . .

Killing fish to Nishadas; carpenters' work to the Ayogava; to Medas, Andhras, Kunkus, and Madgus, the slaughter of wild animals. . . .

But the dwellings of Kandalas . . . shall be outside the village. . . .

---

[1]One's second birth is initiation into the recitation of the Vedas. Only men can be *twice-born*.
[2]Brahman.
[3]This explains the existence of certain low-born, or unclean, jatis; they originated in mythic time as the result of illicit unions between people of different castes. The greatest profanation of all was when a male Sudra defiled (had sexual intercourse with) a female Brahmin, and the consequence was the origin of the *Kandala* jati — the basest of all jatis.

Their dress shall be the garments of the dead, they shall eat their food from broken dishes, black iron shall be their ornaments, and they must always wander from place to place.

A man who fulfills a religious duty, shall not seek intercourse with them; their [Kandala] transactions shall be among themselves, and their marriages with their equals. . . .

At night they shall not walk about in villages and in towns.

By day they may go about for the purpose of their work, distinguished by marks at the king's command, and they shall carry out the corpses of persons who have no relatives; that is a settled rule.

By the king's order they shall always execute the criminals, in accordance with the law, and they shall take for themselves the clothes, the beds, and the ornaments of such criminals.

DHARMA

A king who knows the sacred law must inquire into the laws of castes [jatis], of districts, of guilds, and of families, and settle the peculiar law of each. . . .

Among the several occupations the most commendable are, teaching the Vedas for a Brahmin, protecting the people for a Kshatriya, and trade for a Vaisya.

But a Brahmin, unable to subsist by his peculiar occupations just mentioned, may live according to the law applicable to Kshatriyas; for the latter is next to him in rank. . . .

A man of low caste [varna] who through covetousness lives by the occupations of a higher one, the king shall deprive of his property and banish.

It is better to discharge one's own duty incompletely than to perform completely that of another; for he who lives according to the law of another caste is instantly excluded from his own.

A Vaisya who is unable to subsist by his own duties, may even maintain himself by a Sudra's

mode of life, avoiding however acts forbidden to him, and he should give it up, when he is able to do so. . . .

Abstention from injuring creatures, veracity, abstention from unlawfully appropriating the goods of others, purity, and control of the organs,[4] Manu has declared to be the summary of the law for the four castes.

THE NATURE OF WOMEN

It is the nature of women to seduce men in this world; for that reason the wise are never unguarded in the company of females. . . .

For women no rite is performed with sacred texts, thus the law is settled; women who are destitute of strength and destitute of the knowledge of Vedic texts are as impure as falsehood itself; that is a fixed rule.

HONORING WOMEN

Where women are honored, there the gods are pleased; but where they are not honored, no sacred rite yields rewards.

Where the female relations live in grief, the family soon wholly perishes; but that family where they are not unhappy ever prospers.

FEMALE PROPERTY RIGHTS

A wife, a son, and a slave, these three are declared to have no property; the wealth which they earn is acquired for him to whom they belong. . . .

What was given before the nuptial fire, what was given on the bridal procession, what was given in token of love, and what was received from her brother, mother, or father, that is called the six-fold property of a woman.

Such property, as well as a gift subsequent and what was given to her by her affectionate husband, shall go to her offspring, even if she dies in the lifetime of her husband. . . .

---

[4]Control of all the senses and especially one's sexual drives.

But when the mother has died, all the uterine[5] brothers and the uterine sisters shall equally divide the mother's estate.

A WOMAN'S DEPENDENCE

In childhood a female must be subject to her father, in youth to her husband, when her lord is dead to her sons; a woman must never be independent.

She must not seek to separate herself from her father, husband, or sons; by leaving them she would make both her own and her husband's families contemptible. . . .

Him to whom her father may give her, or her brother with the father's permission, she shall obey as long as he lives, and when he is dead, she must not insult his memory.

BETROTHAL

No father who knows the law must take even the smallest gratuity for his daughter; for a man who, through avarice, takes a gratuity, is a seller of his offspring. . . .

Three years let a damsel wait,[6] though she be marriageable,[7] but after that time let her choose for herself a bridegroom of equal caste and rank.

If, being not given in marriage, she herself seeks a husband, she incurs no guilt, nor does he whom she weds.

MARRIAGE AND ITS DUTIES

To be mothers were women created, and to be fathers men; religious rites, therefore, are ordained in the Vedas to be performed by the husband together with the wife. . . .

No sacrifice, no vow, no fast must be performed by women apart from their husbands; if a wife obeys her husband, she will for that reason alone be exalted in heaven.[8] . . .

By violating her duty towards her husband, a wife is disgraced in this world, after death she enters the womb of a jackal, and is tormented by diseases as punishment for her sin. . . .

Let the husband employ his wife in the collection and expenditure of his wealth, in keeping everything clean, in the fulfilment of religious duties, in the preparation of his food, and in looking after the household utensils. . . .

Drinking spirituous liquor, associating with wicked people, separation from the husband, rambling abroad, sleeping at unseasonable hours, and dwelling in other men's houses, are the six causes of the ruin of women. . . .

Offspring, religious rites, faithful service, highest conjugal happiness and heavenly bliss for the ancestors and oneself, depend on one's wife alone. . . .

"Let mutual fidelity continue until death" . . . may be considered as the summary of the highest law for husband and wife.

Let man and woman, united in marriage, constantly exert themselves, that they may not be disunited and may not violate their mutual fidelity.

DIVORCE

For one year let a husband bear with a wife who hates him; but after a year let him deprive her of her property and cease to cohabit with her. . . .

But she who shows aversion towards a mad or outcaste[9] husband, a eunuch,[10] one destitute of manly strength, or one afflicted with such dis-

---

[5]All natural siblings (born from her uterus).
[6]To be offered in marriage by her father or brother.
[7]Twelve was a common age of marriage for women; men tended to wait until their twenties.
[8]While waiting for the next incarnation on the karmic journey of release from the bonds of matter, a soul can be assigned to one of an infinite number of heavens or hells. Thus, depending on how well or poorly a person followed dharma, there was a double reward or punishment: a heaven

or a hell followed by incarnation into a higher or lower caste or even a lower life form. Compare this with Virgil's ideas regarding the afterlife and reincarnation (source 30).
[9]He has so egregiously violated the dharma of his caste (varna) that he has been made an *outcaste* — for example, a Brahmin who knowingly receives food or a gift from a Kandala or other unclean person.
[10]Sexually impotent.

eases as punish crimes,[11] shall neither be cast off nor be deprived of her property. . . .

A barren[12] wife may be superseded[13] in the eighth year, she whose children all die in the tenth, she who bears only daughters in the eleventh, but she who is quarrelsome without delay.

But a sick wife who is kind to her husband and virtuous in her conduct, may be superseded only with her own consent and must never be disgraced.

---

[11]A disease incurred by reason of a sin in a previous incarnation (the law of karma). Hindu society evolved complex and lengthy lists of diseases and their corresponding sins.

[12]Childless.
[13]Replaced as primary wife by a second wife.

▼▼▼

Long-Distance Travel and Exchange

At the beginning of the first millennium C.E., two major trade networks, one by water and the other by land, linked the First Afro-Eurasian Ecumene, making it possible for commodities and ideas to circulate from Southeast to Southwest Asia, from China to the Greco-Roman Mediterranean, from India to all of the above.

A series of sea routes extended from China and the lands of Southeast Asia in the east and from the Red Sea and the Persian Gulf in the west to India, which served as a central meeting point for merchants from both directions. There, for example, Western merchants exchanged gold for pepper and other spices, jewels, and muslin cloth, as well as for Chinese manufactured commodities, such as porcelains, lacquered boxes, ironware, and silk. The Hellenistic geographer Strabo (ca. 64 B.C.E.–25 C.E.) claimed that in his day 120 vessels made the annual voyage from Egypt to India. There is even a record of a group of supposedly Roman merchants (probably Syrians or Egyptians) who sailed from India to south China in the mid second century C.E., but such adventures were rare. For most merchant mariners, India was the main terminus and marketplace where East met West.

The other network connecting the East with the West was the so-called *Silk Road,* a series of linked caravan routes that ran on its east-west axis from northwestern China to the eastern shores of the Mediterranean, a distance of more than 4,000 miles, and on its north-south axis from China to India, by way of Afghanistan. As the name implies, Chinese silk was a major commodity along these roads, but many other trade items, including Central Asian horses and Baltic amber, moved along these overland routes. Because it was shorter, more direct, less costly, and safer, the Silk Road was the preferred route for long-distance exchange between China and the West — at least during the First Age of Afro-Eurasian Interchange. Yet very few Mediterraneans traveled all the way to China, and fewer Chinese ventured even to the borders of the Roman Empire. Instead, a series of merchant intermediaries passed along the silk, cotton, brocades, spices, plants and animals, manufactured goods, gold, ideas, and even killing diseases that traveled from one end of this great network to the other, with the *Parthian Empire* serving as a major site of exchange and interchange for east-west traffic. Aware of the profits to be gained from its strategic location, Parthia, which was centered in Mesopotamia and Iran, provided security by policing the roads that ran through its territories and guaranteed fair markets, but it also discouraged all direct commercial traffic through its regions. Merchants from East and West normally met in the lands of Parthia, exchanged their goods there, and returned home.

Although merchants from the Mediterranean traded some Western manufactured goods, such as colored glass vessels and bronze statues, for Eastern luxury items, their main form of payment was gold and silver, which meant that the Roman World suffered from a trade imbalance with the East. By the third century C.E. this trade imbalance contributed to the empire's overall economic miseries.

Rome's trade with Asia introduced other even more damaging miseries. From the mid second through the sixth centuries a series of new diseases, which appear to have traveled along the Silk Road from the east, devastated the Mediterranean. Each new disease, appearing as it did among an unprotected population, resulted in massive die-offs. The impact of the sudden deaths of tens of millions of Mediterraneans during these four and a half centuries significantly contributed to the eventual transformation of the Greco-Roman World.

Regardless of these tragic consequences, trade along the Silk Road continued after the empires of Rome and Han China had passed away. During the fifth and sixth centuries C.E. trade between China and the Mediterranean slowed to a trickle (if even that), but trade between India and China and between China and the states of Central Asia, especially a region known as *Sogdiana* (essentially modern Uzbekistan) remained at a high level. With the rise of the *Second Chinese Empire* (589–907), thanks to two dynasties, the *Sui* (589–618) and the *Tang* (618–907), the volume of Silk Road commerce rose dramatically. As we shall see in Chapter 9, during the first half of the Tang Era (618–750), China was open to the world and its front door was the Silk Road.

The riches that were available to those engaged in long-distance overland commerce drove many merchants to hazard their lives and fortunes along the Silk Road, despite bandits and natural obstacles such as deserts and mountains. The same was true for the merchant mariners plying the sea routes of the Indian Ocean. The dangers of pirates, storms, and other factors that often led to deadly shipwreck did not deter the brave, the foolhardy, and the avaricious from seeking riches in faraway lands. The pull of the Indian Ocean's currents and the push of its monsoon winds were too strong not to draw Africans, Arabs, Egyptians, Syrians, Persians, Indians, Malays, and Chinese into this rich trading complex, despite its dangers.

Our first source suggests the extent and limitations of the Roman World's participation in long-distance Afro-Eurasian commerce during the first century C.E. Our second source sheds light on the hazards and conditions of sea travel through the waters of the Indian Ocean and South China Sea in the early fifth century C.E. and suggests why overland travel was often preferred at this time. Our third source, a collection of five sculptures, suggests that more than just gold and goods traveled in the caravans of the Silk Road and the ships that sailed the Indian Ocean.

India and China Viewed from Rome
▼▼▼

36 ▼ Pliny the Elder, *NATURAL HISTORY*

Gaius Plinius Secundus (23–79 C.E.), known as Pliny the Elder, was a soldier, a lawyer, and a civil administrator, as well as the greatest Roman scholar of his day. His wide-ranging interests resulted in seven encyclopedic works, of which only the last, the *Natural History,* survives. Completed in the year 77, two years before Pliny died while trying to evacuate victims from the eruption of Mount Vesuvius that obliterated Pompeii, the work covers a wide range of natural phenomena in such fields as anthropology, astronomy, botany, geography, medicine, meteorology, mineralogy, and zoology. In his preface he claimed to present 20,000 items of importance carefully culled from the works of 100 selected authors, as well as his own observations.

The *Natural History,* which became a prime source of information for medieval European scholars, exhibits all the failings and virtues of late Greco-Roman science. Unsubstantiated myths abound and there is precious little evidence of systematic observation and even less of knowledge gained through experimentation. All of this is compounded by Pliny's own love of fantastic stories and his uncritical acceptance of outlandish accounts. Yet the work contains a good deal of practical knowledge and much wisdom. Pliny's description of human psychology and humanity's unique proclivity toward creating its own problems sounds as valid today as it did almost 2,000 years ago.

For our purposes, the *Natural History* provides insight into the Roman view of the world beyond its imperial borders in the late first century C.E. The following selections discuss Central Asia, the land of the Seres (China), Roman trade with India, and a wondrous people who lived at the far eastern end of Asia.

QUESTIONS FOR ANALYSIS

1. How does Pliny envision Central Asia? What do you infer from your answer?
2. How well does Pliny know China, the Chinese, and East Asia in general? What do you infer from your answer?
3. How does Pliny characterize Rome's balance of trade? What do you infer from your answer?
4. Describe and characterize the round trip between Alexandria and India. How difficult and long was it? What factors made it possible?
5. Why did mariners set sail at specific times of the year for either India or the Red Sea?

TRAVEL TO THE LAND OF THE SERES[1]

From the Caspian Sea and the Scythian Ocean,[2] our course bends toward the Morning Star, as the coast turns toward the east. The first part of the coast after the Scythian Promontory[3] is uninhabitable because of snow, and the neighboring region is uncultivated because of the savagery of its people. Here the Scythian cannibals live who feast on human bodies.[4] Consequently, the lands adjacent are vast wastelands inhabited by multitudinous wild beasts that lie in wait for humans who are no less bestial than the beasts themselves. Then we come to more Scythians and to more deserts teeming with beasts, until we come to a mountain range that runs up to the sea and is called Tabis.[5] It is not until we have traversed almost half the length of the coast that faces northeast that we come to a region that is inhabited. The first people we encounter are called the Seres. They are famous for the wool that is found in their forests.[6] After soaking it in water, they comb the white strands of the leaves and so give our women the double task of unraveling the threads and reweaving them again. Such is the substantial labor involved and from such a distant part of the globe is this material fetched — all so that a Roman matron might wear a transparent garment in public. Although the Seres are certainly a gentle people, they are like wild animals insofar as they flee the company of the rest of humanity and wait for trade to come to them.

COMMERCE WITH INDIA

It is appropriate to explain the entire journey from Egypt now that reliable knowledge of it is available for the first time. It is a worthy subject because in no year does India draw off less than fifty million sesterces[7] from our empire, sending back merchandise that is sold to us at one hundred times its original price.

Two miles from Alexandria[8] there is the town of Juliopolis. From there one sails up[9] the Nile to Coptos, a journey of 309 miles that takes twelve days when the midsummer trade winds blow. From Coptos the journey is made with camels, with watering stations located along the way. The first, located twenty-two miles along the way, is called Hydreuma.[10] The second is in the mountains, a day's journey away. The third is in another place called Hydreuma, eighty-five miles from Coptos. The next is in the mountains. Then we come to Apollo's Hydreuma, 184 miles from Coptos. Again there is one in the mountains. Then we get to New Hydreuma, 230 miles from Coptos. There is also another old Hydreuma, which is called Trogodyticum, where a garrison keeps watch over a caravansary that can accommodate 2,000 travelers. It lies seven miles from New Hydreuma. Then comes the town of Berenice, where there is a port on the Red Sea, 257 miles from Coptos. Because the major part of the journey is done at night on account of the heat and days are spent at the stations, the entire journey from Coptos to Berenice takes twelve days.

---

[1]This subtitle and the two that follow are editorial creations for the readers' ease of comprehension. They do not appear in any manuscript copies of the text.

[2]Pliny and geographers before him imagined that a great northern ocean, here called the Scythian Ocean, bordered Asia just a few degrees north of the Caspian Sea. Its shores were the presumed place of origin of the Scythians, a nomadic steppe people who inhabited the region north of the Black Sea, essentially modern Ukraine and southern Russia, in the sixth and fifth centuries B.C.E.

[3]Probably an imaginary place but possibly Siberia or northern Russia.

[4]Herodotus, a Greek historian of the mid fifth century B.C.E.,

reported that the Scythians allied with a tribe of cannibals in their fight against an invading Persian army. It is impossible to know with certainty if any nomadic people of this region actually practiced cannibalism.

[5]Possibly Tibet?

[6]This so-called wool probably is Chinese silk, but some commentators think it is cotton from Central Asia.

[7]The basic coin of the empire, made from either bronze or silver.

[8]A port city on Egypt's Mediterranean coast.

[9]Sails south. Because the Nile flows north, upriver lies to the south.

[10]Literally, "watering-place" in Greek.

Sea travel begins in midsummer before the Dog Star[11] rises or immediately after its rising. After about thirty days they arrive at Ocelis or else at Cane in the incense-producing region of Arabia.[12] There is also a third port named Muza, which is not called at on the voyage to India, not unless they are merchants trading in the incense and perfumes of Arabia. In the interior there is a town, the residence of the local king, which is called Sapphar. And there is another called Save.

The most advantageous route, however, for those intent on reaching India is to set out from Ocelis. If the Hippalus[13] is blowing, sailing time is forty days to the first trading station in India, Muziris, an undesirable port of call because of the pirates in the neighborhood who occupy a place called Nitrias. It is also not rich in trade articles. Furthermore, the place where ships anchor is located far from shore, and cargoes are brought in and ferried out in little boats. The person ruling there as I wrote this was Caelobothras. There is another, more serviceable port which is called Becare and belongs to the Neacyndi people. Pandion ruled there and dwelled in a town called Modura, which is located far inland, a long way from the market place. The region from which they transport pepper to Becare in boats made from a single tree is called Cottonara. All of these

names of peoples or ports or towns are not to be found in the work of earlier authors, which suggests that local conditions are changing. Those sailing home from India begin in the Egyptian month of Tybis (our December) or, at the latest, before the sixth day of the Egyptian Mechir, which works out to before our January 13. This makes it possible for them to return home in the same year. They set sail from India with a southeast wind and after entering the Red Sea, continue with a southwest or south wind.

THE PEOPLE OF THE FAR EAST

To the east, at the far end of the borders of India near the source of the Ganges, Megasthenes[14] places the Astomi,[15] a people who have no mouth and a body that is totally covered in hair. They dress in wool made from leaves[16] and subsist only by breathing and through the scent that they draw in through their nostrils. They have no food or drink except for the various aromas of the roots, flowers, and wild apples that they carry with them on their longer journeys, lest they lack a supply of scent. He writes that they can easily be killed by an odor that is a bit stronger than usual.

---

[11]Sirius, or the Dog Star, the brightest star in the heavens, rises and sets with the sun from early July to early September.
[12]Yemen in the southwestern corner of the Arabian Peninsula.
[13]The wind from the west.
[14]Megasthenes (ca. 350–290 B.C.E.), a Greek diplomat and scholar, served for ten years as ambassador to the Mauryan

court in India (source 34), representing the interests of Seleucus I, king of Hellenistic Syria. Megasthenes' *Indica,* a first-hand account of the geography, people, governments, religions, legends, and history of India, is lost, but fragments survive in the writings of later authors, such as Pliny.
[15]Literally, "mouthless" in Greek.
[16]Silk or cotton. See note 6.

Faxian's Homeward Voyage
▼▼▼

37 ▼ *Faxian, TRAVELS*

As Buddhism expanded in China (see Chapter 9, sources 72–74), devotees of the new religion, particularly monks, avidly sought to add to the available body of Buddhist literature, which meant tracking down various Buddhist holy books, or *sutras,* in India and translating them into Chinese. The search for a complete and authentic library of Buddhist scripture, together with the desire to make pilgrimages to sites made sacred by the Buddha and his early disciples, resulted in a steady but small stream of Chinese travelers to India during the age of the Gupta Empire and thereafter.

The earliest known Chinese pilgrim to travel to India and return with sacred books was the monk *Faxian*. In 399 C.E. he set out from North China, traveling by a difficult overland route to India, where he visited sacred shrines, learned Sanskrit, and immersed himself in the legends and lore of Buddhism. From India he sailed to the island of Ceylon (modern Sri Lanka), where he spent an additional two years and gathered more texts. From there Faxian traveled to Java and in 414 reached home, where he spent the rest of his days translating the texts he brought back to China.

In addition to the translations, Faxian left behind a record of his travels. In the following selection, Faxian describes his homeward voyage from Ceylon, thereby providing us with the earliest known account of travel through these waters. Faxian's plan was to reach the southern Chinese port of Guangzhou (Canton), but, as we shall see, when he finally set foot on Chinese soil, he found himself far up the northeast coast in Shandong Province, which lies across the Yellow Sea from Korea. His adventures and misadventures on his homeward voyage shed light on the interesting nature of early-fifth-century oceanic travel between India and China.

QUESTIONS FOR ANALYSIS

1. What does Faxian tell us about the voyage to Java-dvipa and the ship in which he sailed?
2. What does he tell us about the last leg of his journey from Java-dvipa to China and the ship in which he sailed?
3. Based on your answers to questions 1 and 2, describe the state of travel between India and China in the early fifth century C.E.
4. What does this account allow us to infer about cultural interchanges in this region?

Faxian abode in this country[1] two years. . . . Having obtained these Sanskrit works,[2] he took passage in a large merchantman, on board of which there were more than 200 men, and to which was attached by a rope a smaller vessel, as a provision against damage or injury to the large one from the perils of the navigation. With a favorable wind, they proceeded eastwards for three days, and then they encountered a great wind. The vessel sprang a leak and the water came in.

The merchants wished to go to the smaller vessel; but the men on board it, fearing that too many would come, cut the connecting rope. The merchants were greatly alarmed, feeling their risk of instant death. Afraid that the vessel would fill, they took their bulky goods and threw them into the water. Faxian also took his pitcher and washing-basin, with some other articles, and cast them into the sea; but fearing that the merchants would cast overboard his

---

[1]Ceylon.

[2]Four sutras to add to those he had collected in India.

books and images, he could only think with all his heart of Guanshiyin,[3] and commit his life to [the protection of] the Buddhist congregation of the land of Han,[4] [saying in effect], "I have travelled far in search of our Law. Let me, by your dread and supernatural [power], return from my wanderings, and reach my resting place!"

In this way the tempest continued day and night, till on the thirteenth day the ship was carried to the side of an island, where, on the ebbing of the tide, the place of the leak was discovered, and it was stopped, on which the voyage was resumed. On the sea [hereabouts] there are many pirates, to meet with whom is speedy death. The great ocean spreads out, a boundless expanse. There is no knowing east or west; only by observing the sun, moon, and stars was it possible to go forward. If the weather were dark and rainy, [the ship] went as she was carried by the wind, without any definite course. In the darkness of the night, only the great waves were to be seen, breaking on one another, and emitting a brightness like that of fire, with huge turtles and other monsters of the deep [all about]. The merchants were full of terror, not knowing where they were going. The sea was deep and bottomless, and there was no place where they could drop anchor and stop. But when the sky became clear, they could tell east and west, and [the ship] again went forward in the right direction. If she had come on any hidden rock, there would have been no way of escape.

After proceeding in this way for rather more than ninety days, they arrived at a country called Java-dvipa,[5] where various forms of error and Brahminism are flourishing, while Buddhism in it is not worth speaking of. After staying there for five months,[6] [Faxian] again embarked in an-

other large merchantman, which also had on board more than 200 men. They carried provisions for fifty days, and commenced the voyage on the sixteenth day of the fourth month.

Faxian kept his retreat on board the ship. They took a course to the north-east, intending to reach Guangzhou. After more than a month, when the night-drum sounded the second watch, they encountered a black wind and tempestuous rain, which threw the merchants and passengers into consternation. Faxian again with all his heart directed his thoughts to Guanshiyin and the monkish communities of the land of Han; and, through their awesome and mysterious protection, was preserved to day-break. After day-break, the Brahmins[7] deliberated together and said, "It is having this Sramana[8] on board that has occasioned our misfortune and brought us this great and bitter suffering. Let us land the bhikshu[9] and place him on some island-shore. We must not for the sake of one man allow ourselves to be exposed to such imminent peril." A patron of Faxian, however, said to them, "If you land the bhikshu, you must at the same time land me; and if you do not, then you must kill me. If you land this Sramana, when I get to the land of Han, I will go to the emperor, and inform against you. The emperor also reveres and believes the Law of Buddha, and honors the bhikshus." The merchants hereupon were perplexed, and did not dare immediately to land Faxian.

At this time the sky continued very dark and gloomy, and the sailing-masters looked at one another and made mistakes. More than seventy days passed [from their leaving Java], and the provisions and water were nearly exhausted. They used the salt-water of the sea for cooking,

---

[3]Literally, "Perceiver of the World's Sounds," or "One Who Hears the Cries of the World," this Bodhisattva is better known as *Guanyin*. (See Chapter 6, sources 39 and 40, for fuller treatment of this Mahayana Buddhist intermediary.)

[4]The Han Dynasty had collapsed in 220 C.E., but the Chinese still referred to China as the "land of Han."

[5]Apparently the western part of the island of Java, which lies to the east of the island of Sumatra. If Faxian wanted a direct voyage home, Java was off course, and his putting in there was probably an unforeseen consequence of the storm. Sumatra, which forms the southern coast of the narrow

Strait of Malacca, makes more sense as an intermediary stopping point. The strait connects the Indian Ocean with the South China Sea, and the ports along it became prosperous way stations on the oceanic trade route that joined India and Southeast Asia with China.

[6]Probably waiting for favorable trade winds.

[7]He might mean all Hindus on board, not just members of the Brahmin caste.

[8]A Buddhist monk.

[9]Another term for a Buddhist monk.

and carefully divided the [fresh] water, each man getting two pints. Soon the whole was nearly gone, and the merchants took counsel and said, "At the ordinary rate of sailing we ought to have reached Guangzhou, and now the time is passed by many days; — must we not have held a wrong course?" Immediately they directed the ship to the north-west, looking out for land; and after sailing day and night for twelve days, they reached the shore on the south of mount Lao,[10] . . . and immediately got good water and vegetables. They had passed through many perils and hardships, and had been in a state of anxious apprehension for many days together; and now suddenly arriving at this shore, . . . they knew indeed that it was the land of Han.

---

[10]On the Shandong Peninsula.

The Transit of Images along Trade Routes
▼▼▼

38 ▼ *FIVE ROBED STATUES*

The most visible manifestation of the First Age of Afro-Eurasian Interchange was the manner in which artistic motifs and styles traveled across the four major cultural pools, especially from west to east. As these ideas and forms moved from one region to another, they were reshaped and blended with native elements to produce striking examples of syncretic art. The first four sculptures that appear here illustrate the way in which a Greco-Roman artistic style traveled along the Silk Road from the Mediterranean to China. The fifth sculpture suggests how a northwest Indian art style, itself deeply influenced by Hellenistic models, traveled across the Indian Ocean to Southeast Asia.

As is evident in source 29, Hellenistic sculptors were masters at carving expressive faces and draped clothing in order to imbue each sculpted individual with a sense of personality and drama. They also used, to the point of making it a cliché, *contrapposto* to impart a sense of dynamism to their works. Our first statue portrays *Vibia Sabina,* the wife of the Roman emperor Hadrian. Created in 136 C.E., this statue presents the empress as a paragon of Roman feminine virtues. Her face, drapery, and even gentle turning of her foot evoke images of modesty, simplicity, dignity, and sobriety — all elements of the Roman self-image.

This particular statue was probably not seen outside of Italy, but its style was universal throughout the Greco-Roman World, and many examples of the style were exported beyond the boundaries of the Roman Empire, especially to Rome's immediate neighbor to the east — Parthia.

Our second sculpture — a woman in Southwest Asian dress — comes from Parthia and dates from the late second or early third century C.E. The work, which illustrates a typical Parthian blend of Greco-Roman and Southwest Asian components, is one of over 100 similar votive statues discovered at the many shrines of the city of Hatra in northern Mesopotamia. The unknown noblewoman it portrays offered it in devotion to an equally unknown deity. The statue, which is more than six feet high, affirms the importance of the donor, who stands with her hand raised in reverence.

Our third statue portrays the Buddha. Early Buddhists believed it was wrong to depict the Buddha artistically in human form because he had broken the chains of matter and had achieved Nirvana. For over 500 years Buddhist artists used such symbols as a wheel, a pipal tree (source 8), a throne, or a footprint to symbolize his last earthly body. Toward the end of the first century C.E., artists in the Kushan province of *Gandhara,* which today comprises Afghanistan and northwest Pakistan, began representing the Buddha as a human. The sculpture of the standing Buddha that appears here is typical of the many carvings that have survived from this period and place. The setting is the Buddha's first sermon on the Law of Righteousness. Many of the features are distinctively Buddhist. The knot on the top of the Buddha's head is known as the *ushnisha* and represents his cosmic consciousness, and it probably has no connection whatsoever with the stylish twist worn by Vibia Sabina. His pierced, distended earlobes symbolize his former royal life; the garment he wears is the *sanghati,* or monk's robe; the *halo,* or solar disk, that frames his head is typical of all Gandharan statues of the Buddha and represents his sanctity. His missing right hand probably was raised palm outward in the gesture of blessing. The lotuses, or water lilies, carved into the base of the statue are a Buddhist symbol of purity and peace, therefore Nirvana. But those lotuses are also an example of the syncretic nature of Buddhist art. The lotus first appeared in ancient Egyptian art as a symbol of rebirth, and it made its way to Gandhara and India through Mesopotamia and Iran. Therefore, it should not surprise us that many scholars claim that the style and majesty of the Greco-Roman imperial sculpture that emanated from the workshops of the Mediterranean deeply influenced the creators of the early Gandharan statues of the Buddha.

Our fourth sculpture depicts the Buddha standing on a lotus flower. Composed of gilded bronze, it was crafted in 477 in the region of China ruled by the Northern Wei Dynasty (386–535). The Northern Wei, Turkic invaders who had conquered and unified northern China during China's long period of political disunity following the collapse of the Han Empire, had adopted the trappings of Chinese aristocratic culture but added a new element. They were deeply devoted to Mahayana Buddhism (see Chapter 6) and patronized its rapid spread throughout northern China. The statue, missing only its original, attached halo, deals largely with the same theme and setting as the Gandharan Buddha, but artistically it is somewhat different. An excellent example of an emerging Chinese style of Buddhist art, the statue's face and spiraling hair style, as well as its formality, are distinctly Chinese. However, the sensuousness of the statue in which a well-formed body is revealed beneath diaphanous robes is quite new to Chinese art and an import from India.

Our fifth sculpture is a Buddha statue that was excavated in the remains of the Southeast Asian harbor of Oc Eo, a port city in the ancient kingdom of Funan. During the third century C.E. the kingdom of Funan, established by emigrant Hindus in an area that encompassed portions of modern Vietnam and Cambodia, was already deeply Indianized — at least as far as the culture of its rulers was concerned. The power and wealth of this kingdom attracted not only Indians and Chinese (the latter gave the region its name) but even sailors from the Sassanid Empire of Persia, which had replaced the Parthian Empire early in the third century. By the sixth century, however, due to successful competition from more southerly port areas, Funan's economic and political power was rapidly contracting.

QUESTIONS FOR ANALYSIS

1. Compare the first two sculptures. What moods are their respective artists trying to evoke?
2. Do you perceive any apparent Greco-Roman influences on the statue of the Parthian noblewoman? If so, what are they? How, if at all, have those influences been modified?

1

2

Vibia Sabina

Parthian Noblewoman

3. Consider the expressions, postures, and dress of the Gandharan and Chinese Buddhas. What responses do their respective sculptors hope to evoke from viewers?
4. Continue your comparative analysis of statues 3 and 4. In what ways are they similar? How do they differ? Which are more significant, the similarities or the differences? What do you conclude from your answer?

3

4

Gandharan Buddha   *Northern Wei Buddha*

5. Now compare statues 1 through 4. Do they share any common elements? Do any significant differences divide them? What conclusions follow from your answers?

6. Compare the Funan Buddha with the Gandharan Buddha. Do you see why scholars conclude that this was probably a local copy of a Gandharan original? Explain your answer.

5

Funan Buddha

Part Two

Faith, Devotion, and Salvation:
Great World Religions to 1500

By about 200 B.C.E. two overarching religious traditions had taken shape in Eurasia. Indian civilization produced a wide variety of cults and religions, most important of which were Buddhism and Brahminical Hinduism. Regardless of differences, all of India's home-grown religions denied the reality of this world and sought release from it. And in Southwest Asia two faiths emerged — Judaism and Zoroastrianism — each of which focused on a single God of righteousness, whose believers saw themselves as agents in the transformation of this world according to moral precepts decreed by their God.

During the next 1,500 years all four religions underwent significant changes. Zoroastrianism largely disappeared after the ninth century C.E., except for remnant communities in Iran, India, Central Asia, and China. Before it passed away as a major religion, however, Zoroastrianism had a profound impact on the teachings of several new faiths: Christianity, *Manichaeism,* and *Islam.* Judaism, which also exhibited some Zoroastrian influences, survived, continued its historical evolution, and served as a major source for two new religions: Christianity and Islam. Meanwhile, one school of Buddhist thought, the *Mahayana* sect, evolved into a faith that offered its believers personal salvation. Mainstream Brahminical Hinduism never developed a clearly articulated doctrine of heavenly salvation as it is understood in the religious traditions of Christianity and Islam, but it did evolve a form of worship centered on an intensely personal and deeply emotional devotion to a single, select deity.

Four faiths — Buddhism (largely in its Mahayana form), Christianity, Manichaeism, and Islam — became universal religions. That is, they found homes in a wide variety of cultural settings and claimed to offer salvation to all humanity. Of the four, Buddhism was the most regional, confined largely to the vast, heavily populated lands of South and East Asia. Islam became the most global, at least until around 1500. Islamic communities dominated the east coast of Africa and the trading empires of interior West Africa. Islam stretched across the entire breadth of North Africa, Southwest Asia, and the northern and central portions of India. It spread through much of Central Asia, the island and coastal regions of Southeast Asia, and touched many parts of China. It even penetrated Europe. Islamic rulers controlled much of the Iberian Peninsula from the early eighth to the early thirteenth century, and it was not until 1492 that Christian powers were able to conquer the final Islamic state in Spain. Meanwhile, during the fourteenth century Islam arrived in Europe's Balkan region, where it has remained a vital force down to today. Christianity in its various forms found homes in Ethiopia, in the lands that bordered the eastern rim of the Mediterranean, in Armenia and Georgia in the southern Caucasus, among the Slavs of Eastern and Central Europe, and throughout Western Europe. In addition, small groups of Christians inhabited portions of Central Asia, northern and western China, and the western shores of India. With the new age of European transoceanic explorations, which got underway in the fifteenth century, Westerners transplanted Christianity throughout the Americas, along the Atlantic and Indian Ocean coasts of Africa, and, in a limited way, in various parts of East and South Asia. Manichaeism, which had its origins in third-century Babylonia, penetrated both the Roman and Chinese empires but was never more than a minority movement in either area. Persecutions led to its ultimate disappearance in Southwest Asia and the Roman World, but it remained a vital force in Central Asia for a millennium more.

Meanwhile, Judaism and Hinduism also expanded beyond the confines of their ethnic and geographic origins. The most notable example of conversion to Judaism was when the ruling families of the *Khazars,* a Turkic people inhabiting the upper Volga region between the Black and Caspian seas, embraced Judaism toward the middle of the eighth century, possibly under the influence of Jewish refugees from Persia. Yet conversions of this sort were rare in Jewish history, and generally Jews did not attempt to spread their religion beyond their ethnic boundaries. Indian merchants and Brahmin teachers were more active disseminators of culture and religion than their Jewish counterparts. As we saw in Chapter 5, Indians traveled in significant numbers across the waters of the Bay of Bengal bringing Hindu culture, particularly that of southern India, to the coastal regions of Southeast Asia. The cults of *Shiva* and *Vishnu* were welcomed and patronized by local rulers in these lands across the sea, but in the process the cults were modified to fit their new host cultures. Despite this expansion, however, both Judaism and Hinduism remained far less universal in scope or appeal than Buddhism, Christianity, and Islam, and maybe even Manichaeism.

Chapter 6

▼▼▼

New Developments in Three Ancient Religions

During the first age of Afro-Eurasian interchange, Buddhism, Hinduism, and Judaism all experienced profound changes. The most far-reaching from the perspective of world history was a new form of Buddhist belief and devotion — the *Mahayana* sect. This school moved radically away from the Buddha's original teachings, which refused to consider such notions as immortality and deities (source 17), by offering the promise of salvation through the intermediacy of divine saviors. The message attracted many people suffering from the chaos of the breakdown of the first Afro-Eurasian Ecumene. Toward the middle of the first century B.C.E., Mahayana Buddhist ideas began to enter China from Central Asian lands as far away as Iran, and in the centuries that followed the Mahayana Doctrine swept through East Asia, becoming the dominant form of Buddhism in such lands as China, Tibet, Mongolia, Korea, and Japan.

Within Hinduism a new movement known as *bhakti,* or the Way of Devotion, challenged the caste system without rejecting it. At the same time, it was this new form of Hindu religion, not the caste system, that Indian merchants transplanted among the emerging civilizations of Southeast Asia in the early centuries C.E. Without the Way of Devotion, Hinduism probably would not have spread significantly beyond the Indian subcontinent.

Hinduism and Judaism have historically been family religions in the sense that each has been largely confined to the heirs of a single civilization. Normally, their adherents are born into these religious-social complexes and are not converts. At the same time, both religions have occasionally reached out beyond their cultural matrices. This was so in the case of *Rabbinical Judaism* because of the *Diaspora,* or Great

Dispersion, which scattered Jewish communities over much of the civilized Afro-Eurasian World. While Jews remained conscious of being a people apart from their *gentile,* or non-Jewish, neighbors, Jewish communities could not avoid cultural interchange with the societies within which they were settled.

▼▼▼

Mahayana Buddhism: A Religion of Infinite Compassion

Asoka's Buddhism was idealistic, but it was also practical. He endeavored to make the Law of Righteousness a living reality for his people. Withdrawal from the world to live the life of a mendicant monk who sought Nirvana through meditation was not for Asoka. While he revered and patronized Buddhist monks, he chose to practice social activism based on his understanding of Buddhist principles. Moreover, by sending missionaries to neighboring and distant regions he affirmed his belief in Buddhism's universality. As his edicts also indicate, unlike the Buddha, Asoka also did not consider the gods or a heavenly hereafter to be irrelevant concerns.

All of the qualities of Asoka's Buddhism became more pronounced in the generations that followed. Eventually they contributed to the emergence of a new interpretation of Buddhism known as *Mahayana,* or the Great Vehicle. The title is metaphorical: Mahayana sectarians picture their form of Buddhism as a great ferry which, under the guidance of enlightened pilots known as *Bodhisattvas,* carries all of humanity simultaneously across the river of life to salvation on the opposite shore.

Conversely, Mahayanists term the older, more traditional form of Buddhism *Hinayana,* or the Small Vehicle. The image is of a one-person raft because Hinayana Buddhism centers on the single *arahat,* or perfected disciple, who individually attains Enlightenment and Nirvana through solitary meditation, normally within a monastic setting. Followers of this form of Buddhism — which today predominates in the island nation of Sri Lanka and several countries of mainland Southeast Asia, especially Burma and Thailand — dislike the term *Hinayana,* because it implies inferiority, and call their sect *Theravada* (the Teaching of the Elders).

Evidence indicates that Mahayana Buddhism emerged in northwest India during the first or second century c.e. and was possibly affected by influences out of neighboring Southwest Asia, especially widespread belief in savior deities. According to Mahayana belief, the *Shakyamuni Buddha* (Siddhartha Gautama who came from the Shakya clan) was not unique. There have been many cosmic Buddhas who lived before and after Gautama and who now preside over countless heavens that serve as way stations to Nirvana. Additionally, there are infinite numbers of

Bodhisattvas. The title *Bodhisattva* means "an enlightened being." Although they have attained Enlightenment, these compassionate perfected beings delay Buddhahood and Nirvana in order to lead all humanity to salvation, drawing upon the countless merits they have accumulated in their perfect lives of selflessness to achieve this task. Those whom they save become, in turn, Bodhisattvas, who then delay their entry into Nirvana in order to help others. Through this pyramid of selfless compassion, ultimately all humanity will cross together into Nirvana, a state of perfect bliss. This comforting, nonexclusive doctrine was destined to become the basis of a world religion, and during the first millennium of the Common Era it spread throughout most of Central and East Asia.

Perceiver of the World's Sounds: A Bodhisattva for All Emergencies

▼▼▼

39 ▼ *TALES OF GUANSHIYIN*

When faced with disaster on the high seas, the Chinese monk Faxian sought the protection of *Guanshiyin* (source 37). Guanshiyin was the Chinese version of the Indian Bodhisattva *Avalokitesvara,* whose name in both Sanskrit and Chinese translation means "Perceiver of the World's Sounds," the sounds being both cries and prayers. The cult of Avalokitesvara/Guanshiyin entered China as early as 255 C.E. thanks to an early Chinese translation of the *Lotus Sutra.* In this Mahayana scripture the Shakyamuni Buddha promises that because of his infinite compassion and merit, Perceiver of the World's Sounds will miraculously intervene on behalf of anyone in distress who simply utters his name.

In the age of turmoil that followed the collapse of the Han regime this doctrine proved quite comforting, and devotion to Guanshiyin spread throughout China and beyond into Tibet, Korea, and Japan. In China, scriptures relating to him, such as the *Lotus Sutra* and the later *Guanshiyin Sutra,* were far and away the most popular of all Buddhist texts, and paintings of Guanshiyin's saving people from every sort of danger covered the walls of Buddhist shrines.

The period from the late fourth century to the late sixth century was particularly hard on the people of northern China. Various non-Chinese nomads, whom the Chinese called *caitiffs* (base and despicable people), invaded and exploited the region north of the Yangzi River. To make matters worse, periodic floods, famines, and plagues devastated the land, and rebellions and civil wars were endemic throughout all of China. In the midst of this chaos, a small number of pious monks and laypeople began to collect and record stories of Guanshiyin's miraculous interventions. They believed that by so doing they would earn merit by spreading the cult of a Bodhisattva who was available to all who called upon him.

Roughly 470 such stories exist in known manuscripts produced before the seventh century. The following six stories are part of that body of devotional literature.

QUESTIONS FOR ANALYSIS

1. What are the criteria for Guanshiyin's bestowing his mercy on a recipient? In other words, what does a person have to be or do?
2. What inferences do you draw from your answer to question 1.
3. What happens to some of the characters in these stories *after* they have been saved or blessed by Guanshiyin? What insight do you reach based on your answer?
4. Buddhism faced a good deal of opposition from Chinese traditionalists during these centuries (see Chapter 9, sources 73 and 74). Does knowing that help you place these stories into a fuller context? Explain your answer.

THE WIDOW LI

There was a widow surnamed Li who lived in Liang Province.[1] Her family had long been Buddhist; they faithfully kept every fast day and attended meetings. Each time she would listen to sutra readings; as soon as they were over, she could recite the sutra herself. Later, a [Chinese] woman who had been made a princess among the caitiffs suddenly [showed up and] sought refuge in Li's home. It was a moonless night, and Li could not bear to send her away. Soon officials came to register Li [on the population list], and their report stated that she was harboring a rebellious female slave.[2] Once this register was submitted [to the authorities], Li was jailed. Then with a perfect mind she recited the *Guanshiyin Sutra* and was able to keep reciting it continuously for over ten days.

Suddenly in the middle of the day she saw Guanshiyin. He asked her why she did not leave [her cell]; she replied that it was impossible. He then said: "Just get up." On doing so she found that her shackles were already unfastened, and then she quickly found herself back at home. The warden and the guards were all completely unaware of her departure. Later when the caitiffs learned of her escape, they sent someone to question her and find out how she had managed to return home. She told them everything that had happened. She was not rearrested.

TWO REBELS

Formerly, when the bandit Sun [En] stirred up rebellion,[3] many people living near the coast, both aristocrats and commoners, fled the destruction. A group of a dozen or so people were about to be executed in the eastern marketplace. Only one among them respected the Dharma, and this man began chanting [the name of] Guanshiyin with perfect sincerity. Another man who was sitting with him asked him what he was doing. He replied: "I have heard that the scriptures of the Buddha's Dharma mention a Bodhisattva Guanshiyin who saves people from distress. So I am taking refuge in him." The other man then followed his example. When the hour of execution arrived, the official list [of those to be executed] was found to be lacking just the names of these two people. This created shock and panic in the crowd, and everyone fled in different directions. These two men followed the crowd and were thus able to escape execution.

---

[1]Modern Gansu Province along China's northwestern border. The Gansu Corridor is a narrow defile between mountains and desert that served as an avenue of incursion for invading nomads from the western steppes.

[2]A rebel against the non-Chinese lords who controlled the area. See Chapter 9, source 72.

[3]Sun En led a Daoist-inspired peasant rebellion in 399–400 in the coastal regions of Zhenjiang and Fujian.

THE BIRTH OF A SON

Sun Daode, who lived during the Song, was a Daoist and a libationer.[4] He still had no son even after passing the age of fifty. In the year 423 a [Buddhist] monk who lived in a monastery nearby told Daode: "If you are determined to have a son, you must respectfully and with a perfect mind recite the *Guanshiyin Sutra.* You may then hope for success." Daode then gave up serving the Dao; with single-minded sincerity he took refuge in Guanshiyin. Within a few days he had a dream-response. His wife was indeed pregnant, and subsequently she gave birth to a boy.[5]

A DANGEROUS JOURNEY

The dharma-master[6] Shi Daowang was a native of Changle in northern Jizhou; his lay surname was Fan. He resided at Dragon Gorge Monastery in Yizhou,[7] where he attracted many disciples. My own grandfather Jianzi, while stationed in Yizhou on official assignment, greatly respected him. Daowang was once returning from Liangzhou[8] along the road to Shu[9] when he ran into an area controlled by a group of Qiang[10] rebels who had cut off the road and killed countless people. He had several dozen disciples with him, and they in turn were a part of a group of over three hundred travelers. When they met this trouble they had no idea what to do next. Daowang then single-mindedly fixed his thoughts on Guanshiyin, and he had his disciples call out [Guanshiyin's] name. They then walked almost a hundred miles through the hostile area, but all the while they remained concealed and so escaped harm.

Another group of a dozen or so had split off and taken another route. They were to meet [Daowang's group] at a certain point, but they missed the spot. So they turned back along the road, and as they approached the appointed place they saw Daowang pass by. But between them were several hundred bandits who had cut off access to the road, so that they were unable to rejoin his group. That day the bandits were particularly numerous, but Daowang and the others walked right along beside them without being seen, nor did Daowang and his group see the bandits. This was a great deed accomplished by divine power. All the followers [in the other group] were astonished [to see it].

A MIRACULOUS CURE

During the years 363–366 there flourished the monk Zhu Fayi, who dwelled in the mountains and was fond of study. He lived in the Bao Mountains in Shining.[11] In his travels he learned many scriptures and especially excelled in the *Lotus Sutra,* and he attracted many disciples— most of the time more than a hundred sat under him. In 372 he suddenly felt an illness localized in the region of his heart. For a long time he tried various preparations and techniques, but none cured him. After many attempts he gave up trying to heal himself and devoted himself exclusively to taking sincere refuge in Guanshiyin. After several days of devotional acts he fell asleep and saw, in a dream, a monk who came to attend him in his illness. To cure him, this monk cut him open, extracted his stomach and intestines, and washed them. He saw that there had been many impure objects inside him. After thor-

---

[4]He was a leader for communal affairs and rituals of a Daoist religious movement known as the *Way of the Celestial Masters.* During the second century C.E. several religious movements emerged based on Daoist principles and scriptures. This particular cult traced its origin to the prophet Zhang Daoling, who in 142 claimed a revelation from the Most High Lord Lao — the now-deified Laozi (source 20).
[5]Guanshiyin became increasingly associated with fertility

and childbirth and slowly metamorphosed into a female Bodhisattva. See source 40.
[6]A senior monk.
[7]In modern Sichuan Province.
[8]In modern Shanaxi Province.
[9]A dangerous road to Sichuan.
[10]Tibetan.
[11]Probably modern Yunnan Province.

oughly cleansing them, the monk replaced the organs and told Fayi: "Your sickness is now expelled." When Fayi woke up, all his symptoms were gone, and he soon felt like his old self again. It is said in the {Lotus} Sutra that sometimes he (Guanshiyin) appears in the form of a monk or brahmacarin.[12] Perhaps Fayi's dream was an instance of this.

A CONVERSION

Wang Tao came from the Zhaodu district of the capital. He was by nature violent and cruel, and in his youth he was leader of a band of young toughs. After reaching the age of thirty he settled down in a forest. Once he encountered a tiger eating its captured prey. He drew his bow and shot it, and it fled, injured; but there was another tiger that chased him down and crushed both his arms with its fangs, and still would not let him go. Tao suddenly remembered having once heard a monk speak of Guanshiyin, so he now took refuge in and meditated on [the Bodhisattva] with a perfect mind. The tiger at once let him go, and he was able to get up. But it was still angry and resentful, roaring as it circled around him. Tao once more tempered his heart and perfected his thoughts. The tiger then finally went away. Tao returned home and swore that if he did not die from his wounds he would revere the Buddha and undertake the [lay] precepts.[13] He soon recovered and so in the end became a devout man.

---

[12]Buddhist ascetic. According to the *Lotus Sutra,* the Shakyamuni Buddha states that Guanshiyin will assume whatever body or guise is needed to aid a living being in distress.

[13]He would live as a devout Buddhist layman. The precepts he vowed to follow included refraining from killing all living beings. (See source 16, note 8.)

Images of Compassion
▼▼▼

40 ▼ THREE BODHISATTVAS

As befit a religion that preached the message of universal salvation, Mahayana Buddhism developed a strong tradition of spreading the word through every available medium. In China this meant mass printing of the sacred texts during the era of the Tang Dynasty (618–907). The oldest extant printed book known today is a Chinese copy of the *Diamond Sutra,* which dates from 868. But sutras were not enough. People, especially the illiterate, needed artistic representations of the Bodhisattvas to whom they prayed. Statues and paintings of Bodhisattvas became fixtures throughout lands in which the Mahayana Doctrine took root, and as the following three statues demonstrate, images of the Bodhisattvas took many different forms.

The first statue is of Perceiver of the World's Sounds, whom we saw in source 39. Called *Avalokitesvara* in India, the home of his origin, this Bodhisattva took several different forms, one of which was an androgenous young man, and he carried that image to China, where he was initially known as *Guanshiyin,* but as time went on he became more commonly called *Guanyin.* In China Perceiver of the World's Sounds also underwent a sex change. Probably because Guanyin assumed the dual functions of making women fertile (especially so they could bear male children) and protecting them in childbirth, a few artists began, as early as the late sixth century, to portray this Bodhisattva as a woman. The two images, male and female, coexisted for quite a while, but the female was dominant by the beginning of the twelfth century and totally won out by the sixteenth century. Whether called Guanyin or *Kannon,* her Japanese name, she became the most widely beloved and prayed to Bodhisattva in East Asia. A pure and benevolent spirit, she was the gateway to the Pure Land, or Western Paradise, a heavenly way station of bliss on the road to Nirvana that the *Amitaba Buddha,* one of the great cosmic Buddhas, presided over.

This particular Guanyin is a gilded bronze statuette from the early years of the Sui Dynasty (589–618). Standing on a lotus blossom and wearing an ornate gown, jewelry, and a tasseled crown, she holds a flask of heavenly dew in her right hand. In her left hand Guanyin bears a willow sprig. A touch of the willow sprinkled with the dew cures all physical and spiritual disorders. The lotus, or water lily, which has iconographic origins in ancient Egyptian art, where it symbolized eternity, is one of the most common Buddhist symbols of Nirvana, chosen because this flower, rooted in mud, rises through stagnant water to free itself in purity and beauty.

The second statue comes from the *Khmer* kingdom (802–1406), located in the Southeast Asian land of Cambodia. The temple complexes in the Khmer capital at Angkor, which reached their heights of splendor in the twelfth and thirteenth centuries, show the profound influence of Hindu culture, but they also display strong Mahayanist elements. Our statue is a late-twelfth-century representation of the Bodhisattva *Hevajra* and displays the worldview of a branch of Mahayana Buddhism known as *Tantrism.* Tantrism, which originated in Hindu beliefs and practices, emphasizes magic and esoteric rituals. Beyond that it stresses the doctrine of *non-dualism,* a rejection of the notion that apparently contradictory elements — such as life and death, female and male, goodness and evil — are truly opposed to one another. Tantric Buddhism is particularly prevalent in Tibet, and this statue is markedly Tibetan in its overall form, but its Indian influences are equally apparent. Here we see an eight-faced Hevajra, with four legs (only seven faces and two legs are visible in the picture) and sixteen arms. In each hand he holds a skull, and he dances above a corpse. Significantly, that corpse lies on a lotus blossom.

The third statue, carved in 1343, is of *Arapacana* and comes from the island of Java in Southeast Asia. He sits in the lotus position of meditation (see source 8, seal 6) on a giant lotus flower. Wielding the sword of interior knowledge above his tiered crown, he clutches in his left hand the book of wisdom (the *Sutra of the Perfection of Insight*). Surrounding him are more lotuses and four lesser Bodhisattvas, who serve as his constant companions.

QUESTIONS FOR ANALYSIS

1. Consider Guanyin's dress, posture, facial expression, and implements. What do they combine to tell us about this Bodhisattva?
2. Review source 39. Is this statue true to the spirit and message of those tales of Guanshiyin? If so, how?
3. What do Hevajra's multiple limbs and faces seem to connote?

4. In what specific ways does the statue of Hevajra convey the doctrine of non-dualism?

5. Consider Arapacana. What does he appear to be doing? In answering this, consider his posture, his facial expression, his special sword, and the book that he holds.

6. Compare the three Bodhisattvas. What do their similarities and differences suggest about Mahayana beliefs and devotion?

Guanyin

Hevajra

Arapacana

Bhakti: The Way of Devotion

In one of the *Bhagavad Gita*'s most famous scenes (which does not appear in the excerpt quoted in source 15), Krishna, an incarnation of the god Vishnu, teaches Arjuna that *bhakti,* or unconditional devotion to a god, is one of several *yogas,* or paths of selfless, god-focused action, by which a person can win release from the cycle of rebirth. Such a path to liberation appealed to many low-caste and casteless persons (as well as many women), who found strict and selfless conformity to the laws of dharma (the *Yoga of Action*) unattractive. It also appealed to persons who lacked the temperament or leisure to attain release from the shackles of matter through asceticism, study of the sacred scriptures, and meditation (the *Yoga of Knowledge*). The *Yoga of Devotion,* in which one passionately adored a savior god, offered a promise of immediate liberation to everyone.

In the Gupta Age (320–ca. 550 C.E.) and thereafter there was an increasing tendency among many Hindus to reduce the myriad divine personifications of Brahman, the One, to three: *Brahma* the Creator, *Vishnu* the Preserver, and *Shiva* the Destroyer. Of this trinity, Brahma (not to be confused with Brahman) was the least widely worshiped because he was perceived as a remote kingly god who, after completing the process of creation, had retired from worldly affairs. Hindus widely adored Vishnu and Shiva, however, and they became two of the great gods of Asia. The cult of Shiva was especially popular in Southeast Asia, where he merged with several local native deities and was even adopted by some Buddhist sects.

Hindus who concentrated their worship on Vishnu or Shiva did not deny the existence of the many other divine and semidivine personalities who were part of the traditional pantheon of India. They simply chose Shiva or Vishnu as gods of special devotion because each, in his way, was a loving personification of the totality of Divine Reality. Vishnu's worshipers, for example, believed that he had selflessly blessed and taught humanity on a number of critical occasions in descents (*avataras*) from Heaven. On each occasion he took on either human or animal form and intervened on behalf of the forces of goodness to redress the equilibrium between good and evil. In fact, Vishnu's worshipers regarded the Buddha as one of Vishnu's nine chief avataras. Of all his various incarnations, however, the warriors Krishna and Rama enjoyed the widest devotional popularity. As Lord Krishna exemplified in the *Bhagavad Gita,* Vishnu's emergence into this world provided humanity with a model of divine perfection. By offering such a god exclusive and unqualified devotion, a worshiper hoped to share in that perfection.

The development of bhakti, which met so many of the needs of members of India's lower castes and social levels, helped Hinduism to counter successfully the challenge of Buddhism, especially that of the Mahayana school. Faxian, whom we saw in source 37, reported that Buddhist monasteries and festivals were an integral part of the cultural landscape of early-fifth-century India. A millennium later all that had changed. By 1500 C.E. Buddhism, as a religion with an identity separate from Hinduism, had largely disappeared from the land of its origin. Many factors contributed to its disappearance, but one important reason was a Hindu Renaissance during the Gupta Age that began and was strongest in the Tamil area of southern India. Tamil religious teachers and poets taught and sang about devotion to either Vishnu or Shiva, and their teachings and hymns traveled throughout India and across the waters of the Bay of Bengal to the coastal regions of Southeast Asia.

The Way of Supreme Love
▼▼▼

41 ▾ Narada, THE BHAKTI SUTRA

Between approximately 300 and 1000 C.E. many authors gave literary voice to bhakti in tracts, stories, and poems. The following sutra was composed at some unknown time by an anonymous author or authors but ascribed to *Narada,* a legendary sage who was said to have sprung from the forehead of Brahman (much as the Hellenic goddess of wisdom, Athena, sprang from Zeus's head). As you read the sutra, do not be misled by its reference to God. The author does not mean God as understood by Jewish, Christian, or Muslim monotheists. In this context, it means a god who encompasses in himself the fullness of Brahman — Divine Reality.

QUESTIONS FOR ANALYSIS

1. How does this sutra define bhakti?
2. How does one achieve bhakti?
3. What are the consequences of bhakti?
4. How, if at all, does this theological message represent a departure from the spirit that pervades *The Laws of Manu* (source 35)?
5. In what ways, if any, is bhakti consonant with the traditions and teachings of Brahminical Hinduism? To answer this question, review sources 10, 14, 15, and 35.
6. What elements made bhakti so attractive to Indians and non-Indians alike?
7. In what ways was bhakti a Hindu answer to Mahayana Buddhism?

Now then, we shall expound devotion. Devotion consists of supreme love for God. It also consists of immortality. On obtaining that, man has achieved everything, he becomes immortal,[1] he is completely satisfied. Having got it, he desires nothing else, he grieves not, he hates nothing, he delights not in anything else, he strives for nothing; having realized which, man becomes as if intoxicated, and benumbed; he delights in his own intrinsic bliss.

Devotion is not like ordinary passion, as it is the suppression of all other preoccupations. This suppression of preoccupations is the giving up of the activities of the world as well as those [namely, the rituals] ordained by the Vedas.

Devotion is complete and exclusive absorption in God and indifference to things opposed to Him. Completeness or exclusiveness of devotion to Him means the abandoning of anything else or anybody else as one's prop and support. And indifference to things opposed to Him means the doing and observance of only those things in the world or the Vedas which are conducive to devotion towards Him.

One may observe the scriptural ordinances after one's faith in God has been firmly estab-

---

[1]The person has thrown off the shackles of matter and rebirth and has achieved Moksha (release) and Brahma-Nirvana.

lished, for otherwise the devotee may be deemed to have fallen off from the standard of ordained conduct. Similarly, worldly activities, like taking food, should be kept up by the devotee only to the extent needed for keeping his body.

I shall set forth the characteristics of devotion according to different views: Sage Vyasa[2] says that devotion is the continuous desire one has to perform the worship, etc., of God. Sage Garga[3] opines that such a desire to listen to the stories, etc., of God is devotion. . . . But Narada [i.e., the present author] describes devotion as dedication of all acts to God and the intense anguish when one slips from his absorption in God. . . .

Devotion is superior to action, knowledge, or yogic contemplation; for devotion is itself its fruit,[4] and God loves the meek and dislikes those who are proud [of their attainments].

Some say that knowledge[5] alone is the means of acquiring devotion to God, but others opine that knowledge and devotion are interdependent. According to Narada, devotional love is itself its end. We can see this in cases like one's knowledge of a palace or a feast; certainly by one's knowledge of a palace one does not gain the satisfaction that he is a king or by one's knowledge of a feast one's hunger is not appeased. Therefore those desiring salvation should take to devotion alone.

Now, the means of acquiring devotion are set forth by teachers: 1) renunciation of sense pleasures and mundane associations; 2) ceaseless adoration of the Lord; 3) even when one is with others, engaging oneself in the listening to and the singing of the glory of the Lord; 4) chiefly the grace of the great souls[6] or a particle of divine grace itself.

The association of the great souls is hard to acquire, hard to be had completely, but is always fruitful. For gaining even that association, one requires God's blessing; for between God and His men there is no difference. So try to acquire the company of the holy souls; strive for that.

And, by all means, shun evil company; for that is responsible for passion, wrath, delusion, loss of the thought of the Lord, the loss of knowledge, in fact all kinds of loss; these evil traits swell up like an ocean by reason of bad company.

Who crosses over the illusion of phenomenal existence? He who gives up evil association, who waits upon the high-souled ones, who becomes freed of the ego; he who resorts to a secluded spot, uproots worldly bondage, transcends the three dispositions[7] and stops worrying himself about acquiring something or safeguarding something acquired; he who abandons the fruit of actions, renounces all action[8] and thereby transcends the pairs of joy and sorrow, gain and loss, and so on; he who lays aside even scriptures and cultivates solely uninterrupted love for God. He saves himself and becomes also the savior of the world.[9]

Devotion is something indescribable; it is like the taste that a dumb man enjoys. But it is occasionally revealed when there is somebody deserving of it. It is absolute, not vitiated by desire for anything, multiplying every minute of its existence, and is uninterrupted; it is a highly sublime form of experience. One who has it looks at it only, listens to it alone, and thinks of nothing else.

Devotion may also be qualified in these ways, by reason of the three dispositions, as of purity, of passion, and of darkness, or by reason of the condition of the devotee, namely, one in distress, one who is curious to know, and one who has an object in view. Of these three varieties, the preceding ones are superior to the succeeding ones.

---

[2]Another mythic teacher.
[3]An astronomer and teacher — apparently a historic person.
[4]Devotion is its own good karma.
[5]On the way of knowledge, see source 14.
[6]The saints, or *mahatman,* whose perfection brings grace and blessings to those whom they teach and with whom they come into contact.
[7]The three dispositions, or elements, of matter: purity, pas-

sion, and darkness. Somewhat like Yin and Yang (source 23), they are the three components of the material world. Of course, within the Hindu cosmology, they are unreal entities.
[8]On the Way of Action, see source 15.
[9]Compare this with the doctrine of Mahayana Buddhism (sources 39–40).

Compared to other paths, devotion is easiest. It stands in need of no external proof and it is its own proof; for it is of the very form of tranquillity and supreme bliss.

The devotee should have no anxiety if the world slips away from him; for has he not surrendered himself, the world, and the scriptures to the Lord? However, even when one is established in devotion, one should not voluntarily give up normal activities, but he should certainly give up the fruits of his actions and learn how to give them up.

The devotee should not listen to accounts of women's beauty, riches, and what unbelievers say; should cast away pride and vanity. Offering up all his activities to God, he should show his desire or pride only in activities on His behalf,

Transcending the tripartite distinction of love, lover, and object of love, one should develop that love which consists of continuous service and is like the yearning of a beloved for her lover. Those who are exclusive lovers are the chief devotees; with choked voices and streaming eyes, they commune among themselves; they are the souls who sanctify our homes and the world; they make holy spots holy, sanctify acts, and render scriptures sacred. For they are full of God. . . .

Among such devotees there is no distinction of birth, learning, appearance, pedigree, wealth, or profession;[10] for they belong to God.

A devotee should not get involved in discussion about God; for reasoning cuts in anyway and there is no finality about it. Texts which speak of devotion should be honored and the acts taught therein followed. Anxious to gain a time free from the preoccupation of pleasure or pain, desire or gain, one should not waste even a split second. One should observe nonviolence, truth, purity, compassion, faith, and other virtues.

Ever and with all heart, devotees should, without any other thought, worship only the Lord. When He is sung of, He hastens to present Himself and bestow on devotees His experience. Devotion to God is true for all times and is superior to everything else; it is superior.

Devotion, which is really one, yet takes eleven forms: attachment to the greatness of the Lord's qualities, to His form; being engrossed in His worship, and His thought; attachment to Him as a servant, as a friend, as a child or as toward a child, and as a beloved; surrendering oneself unto Him; seeing Him everywhere; and inability to bear the separation from Him.

So do they declare in one voice, without fear of what people say, the teachers of the path of devotion. . . . He who has faith in this wholesome teaching that Narada has given gains devotion and gains that most beloved object [God]; indeed he gains that Dearest Thing.

---

[10]Caste distinctions.

Shiva, Auspicious Destroyer
▼▼▼

42 ▼ *SHIVA NATARAJA*

Many people, especially those whose religions spring from the Southwest Asian tradition of ethical monotheism, might find it hard to accept the notion that a god whose primary function is destruction and death is regarded as a loving deity. Yet *Shiva,* the name of the Hindu god of destruction, means "auspicious." Indeed, contradiction is central to the cult of Shiva. He is celebrated as the divine patron of holy persons and is often portrayed as *Mahayogi* (the Great Ascetic) — deep in meditation, with matted hair and covered with ashes, all of which are signs of those who have renounced the pleasures of the world. At the same time, he is celebrated as a deity with an insatiable sexual appetite and is often portrayed as a sensuous lover.

The artifact illustrated here is a bronze statue of *Shiva Nataraja* (Lord of the Dance) from the Chola kingdom of southern India (ca. 850–1250), an area of fervent devotion to Shiva. The statue represents the god engaged in an ecstatic cosmic dance by which he brings to an end one of the cosmos's cycles of time and ushers in a new era. The statue's symbols offer numerous clues to how Shiva's worshipers perceive him. Here he is dancing within a circle of fire, but his face presents a countenance of absolute equanimity. His hair is piled up in a crownlike style; flowing from the sides of his head are strands of hair intertwined with flowers and forming the shape of wings. His upper-left hand holds a devouring flame; his upper-right hand clasps a drum for beating out the endless rhythm of the universe, for he is also Lord of Time. The lower-right arm is entwined by a cobra, but the hand is raised in the silent "fear not" *mudra,* or hand gesture. (Compare this with the Buddha's right hand in source 38.) The lower-left hand points to his raised left foot as a sign of release from the bonds of the material world. The other foot is planted firmly on the writhing body of *Apasamara,* the demon of ignorance and heedlessness.

QUESTIONS FOR ANALYSIS

1. What double function does fire serve, especially in an agricultural society?
2. Keeping in mind your answer to question 1 and also the fact that Shiva uses a drum to beat out the rhythm of the universe, what do you think the circle of fire and the flame in his left hand represent?
3. If fire presents a double message, what other symbols in this statue give a similar double message? Consider particularly Shiva's body language.
4. Consider Shiva's hair. According to one tradition, the sacred River Ganges, the Mother of India and the source of all life, flows from Shiva's head. What do this tradition and the manner in which the god's hair is represented suggest about this deity?
5. Why do you think the artist has depicted Shiva with four arms instead of the standard two?
6. One of the primary doctrines of the bhakti movement is that a chosen savior god, Vishnu or Shiva, exercises all of the primary functions of the Godhead — creation, destruction, regeneration, preservation, and release. Can you find the appropriate symbols in this statue that illustrate this belief?
7. Consider the demon of ignorance. How would an ignorant person regard death? What do you think Shiva's triumph over this demon represents?
8. Compare *Shiva Nataraja* and *Hevajra* (source 40). Which are more striking, the similarities or the differences? Be specific in addressing this issue. Now, what do you conclude from your answer?

Shiva Nataraja

▼▼▼

Rabbinical Judaism

In 66 C.E. the Jews of Palestine broke out in general rebellion against Roman occupation, and it took the Roman armies seven bloody years to root out the last vestiges of insurgency. In the process, Jerusalem and its Temple were destroyed in the year 70. Again in 132 another Jewish revolt against Roman authority flared up, and when it was finally suppressed in 135, the rebuilt remnants of ancient Jerusalem had been transformed into a Roman military camp that was closed to Jewish habitation. Long before the destruction of the Temple and their sacred city, Jews had established prosperous communities throughout the Greco-Roman, Persian, and Arabic worlds. After these two unsuccessful rebellions, however, the Jewish flight from Palestine reached the proportions of a folk migration, and the vast majority of Jews now resided outside of their ancestral lands. The Great Dispersion, or *Diaspora,* was underway. For 1,900 years, Jews would be strangers in a variety of foreign lands—a people without a homeland.

In spite of these travails, Judaism survived as a living faith and culture because wherever Jews settled, they remained faithful to the memory of their special Covenant with God and their dream of returning to the Promised Land. Moreover, despite its innate conservatism, born of a need to maintain contact with the ways of the past, Judaism continued to be flexible. Jews proved adaptable to a variety of alien settings, and over the centuries Judaism continued its historical development in response to the needs of its various scattered communities.

The primary agents responsible for cementing dispersed Jewish communities together and keeping alive Judaism's distinctive traditions were its religious teachers, or *rabbis.* The destruction of the Temple in Jerusalem occasioned a shift in religious emphasis and leadership. The old priesthood that had performed Temple sacrifices lost its primacy, giving way to rabbis who presided over congregations that met to pray and study in *synagogues.* Unlike the priests of old, rabbis did not inherit their positions by virtue of birth; they achieved prominence because of their reputations for piety and mastery of the Law. During the first six centuries of the Common Era, rabbis, especially groups of them residing in Palestine and Babylon, articulated a vision of Judaism that recognized only prayer and righteous conduct as legitimate forms of communication with the Divine. There were no heavenly saviors and no magical rituals. This was to become the core of mainstream Judaism down to the present.

A Defense of the Law
▼▼▼

43 ▼ *Flavius Josephus, AGAINST APION*

Joseph ben Matthias (37 or 38–ca. 100), known to his Roman patrons as *Flavius Josephus,* is the most important eyewitness to the history of the Jewish people during the first century C.E. Born into a distinguished priestly family in Jerusalem,

Josephus received a sound education in Jewish traditions and Greek culture. At the outbreak of the revolt against Roman occupation in 66, Josephus became leader of the Jewish forces in the north. Following an early defeat and capture at the hands of the Romans, Josephus went over to the enemy and became an advisor to two successive Roman generals, Vespasian and his son Titus. Vespasian became emperor in 69, leaving the final stages of the siege and capture of Jerusalem to Titus. Titus not only conquered and destroyed Jerusalem, he succeeded his father as emperor in 79. Following the war, Josephus was brought to Rome, where he was granted citizenship, lodged in the private household of his imperial patron, and provided with a generous pension. It was in this setting that he wrote, in Greek, a history of the Jewish War, a work flattering to the Romans but one that also attempted to present a sympathetic account of Jewish suffering and heroism. Following Titus's death in 81, Josephus found another Roman patron and continued to write on Jewish history and tradition. His *Jewish Antiquities* traces the story of his people from creation to the eve of the rebellion. More so than his earlier work, the *Antiquities* clearly rests on the argument that Judaism deserves an honored place within the Greco-Roman Ecumene. Josephus's last work was a spirited defense of Judaism entitled *Against Apion.* Written in the last decade of the first century, the work answered the anti-Jewish slanders made by many Greco-Roman critics, especially an Alexandrian grammarian named Apion. In our excerpt, which appears at the end of his tract, Josephus expounds on the Law of Moses. That Law is the body of religious regulations contained within the first five books of the Bible, books ascribed to the authorship of Moses and known collectively as the *Torah* (the Law).

QUESTIONS FOR ANALYSIS

1. How does Josephus compare the Law of Moses with Greek law and philosophy? What is his point? What is his apparent purpose?
2. What is his apparent reason for stating that Judaism is a *theocracy?*
3. According to Josephus, what role does the Law play in a Jew's life?
4. "Josephus compared the particularism of the Greeks with the universalism of the Jews, thereby implicitly arguing that Jews, more than Greeks, were true citizens of the Roman Commonwealth." Comment on and evaluate this statement.

Now, I maintain that our legislator[1] is the most ancient of all legislators in the record of the whole world. Compared with him, you Lycurguses[2] and Solons,[3] . . . and all who are held in such high esteem by the Greeks appear to have been born but yesterday. Why, the very word "law" was unknown in ancient Greece. Witness Homer, who nowhere employs it in his poems. In fact, there was no such thing in his day; the masses were governed by maxims not clearly defined and by the orders of royalty, and continued long afterwards the use of unwritten customs, many of

---

[1]Moses (see source 13).
[2]Lycurgus was the ninth-century B.C.E. lawgiver of Sparta.

[3]Solon (ca. 638–ca. 559 B.C.E.) was an Athenian constitutional reformer.

which were from time to time altered to suit particular circumstances. On the other hand, our legislator, who lived in the remotest past (that, I presume, is admitted even by our most unscrupulous detractors), proved himself the people's best guide and counselor; and after framing a code to embrace the whole conduct of their life, induced them to accept it, and secured, on the firmest footing, its observance for all time.

Let us consider his first magnificent achievement. When our ancestors decided to leave Egypt and return to their native land, it was he who took command of all those myriads and brought them safely through a host of formidable difficulties. . . . Throughout all this he proved the best of generals, the sagest of counselors, and the most conscientious of guardians. He succeeded in making the whole people dependent upon himself, and, having secured their obedience in all things, he did not use his influence for any personal aggrandizement. No; at the very moment when leading men assume absolute and despotic power and accustom their subjects to a life of extreme lawlessness, he, on the contrary, having reached that commanding position, considered it incumbent on him to live piously and to provide for his people an abundance of good laws, in the belief that this was the best means of displaying his own virtue and of ensuring the lasting welfare of those who had made him their leader. With such noble aspirations and such a record of successful achievements, he had good reason for thinking that he had God for his guide and counselor. Having first persuaded himself that God's will governed all his actions and all his thoughts, he regarded it as his primary duty to impress that idea upon the community; for to those who believe that their lives are under the eye of God all sin is intolerable. Such was our legislator; no charlatan or imposter, as slanderers unjustly call him, but one such as the Greeks boast of having had in Minos[4] and later legislators. . . .

There is endless variety in the details of the customs and laws which prevail in the world at large. To give but a summary enumeration: some peoples have entrusted the supreme political power to monarchies, others to oligarchies,[5] yet others to the masses. Our lawgiver, however, was attracted by none of these forms of polity, but gave to his constitution the form of what — if a forced expression be permitted — may be termed a "theocracy," placing all sovereignty and authority in the hands of God. To Him he persuaded all to look, as the author of all blessings, both those which are common to all mankind, and those which they had won for themselves by prayer in the crises of their history. He convinced them that no single action, no secret thought, could be hid from Him. He represented Him as One, uncreated and immutable to all eternity; in beauty surpassing all mortal thought, made known to us by His power, although the nature of His real being passes knowledge.

That the wisest of the Greeks learned to adopt these conceptions of God from principles with which Moses supplied them, I am not now concerned to urge; but they have borne abundant witness to the excellence of these doctrines, and to their consonance with the nature and majesty of God. In fact, Pythagoras, Anaxagoras, Plato, the Stoics[6] who succeeded him, and indeed nearly all the philosophers appear to have held similar views concerning the nature of God. These, however, addressed their philosophy to the few, and did not venture to divulge their true beliefs to the masses who had their own preconceived opinions; whereas our lawgiver, by making practice square with precept, not only convinced his own contemporaries, but so firmly implanted his belief concerning God in their descendants to all future generations that it cannot be moved. The cause of his success was that the very nature of his legislation made it [always] far more useful than any other; for he did not make religion a depart-

---

[4]A legendary king of Crete.
[5]Governments ruled by small factions.
[6]Pythagoras was a Greek philosopher and mathematician of the sixth century B.C.E. Anaxagoras (ca. 500–428 B.C.E.) was

a Greek philosopher and astronomer. For Plato, see source 27. The Stoics were a Hellenistic school of philosophy founded in Athens by Zeno (ca. 335–ca. 263 B.C.E.).

ment of virtue, but the various virtues — I mean, justice, temperance, fortitude, and mutual harmony in all things between the members of the community — departments of religion. Religion governs all our actions and occupations and speech; none of these things did our lawgiver leave unexamined or indeterminate.

All schemes of education and moral training fall into two categories; instruction is imparted in the one case by precept, in the other by practical exercising of the character. All other legislators, differing in their opinions, selected the particular method which each preferred and neglected the other. Thus the Lacedaemonians[7] and Cretans employed practical, not verbal, training; whereas the Athenians and nearly all the rest of the Greeks made laws enjoining what actions might or might not be performed, but neglected to familiarize the people with them by putting them into practice.

Our legislator, on the other hand, took great care to combine both systems. He did not leave practical training in morals inarticulate; nor did he permit the letter of the law to remain inoperative. Starting from the very beginning with the food of which we partake from infancy and the private life of the home, he left nothing, however insignificant, to the discretion and caprice of the individual. What meats a man should abstain from, and what he may enjoy; with what persons he should associate; what period would be devoted respectively to strenuous labor and to rest — for all this our leader made the Law the standard and rule, that we might live under it as under a father and master, and be guilty of no sin through wilfulness or ignorance.

For ignorance he left no pretext. He appointed the Law to be the most excellent and necessary form of instruction, ordaining, not that it should be heard once for all or twice or on several occasions, but that every week men should desert their other occupations and assemble to listen to

the Law and to obtain a thorough and accurate knowledge of it, a practice which all other legislators seem to have neglected. . . .

To this cause above all we owe our admirable harmony. Unity and identity of religious belief, perfect uniformity in habits and customs, produce a very beautiful concord in human character. Among us alone will be heard no contradictory statements about God, such as are common among other nations, not only on the lips of ordinary individuals under the impulse of some passing mood, but even boldly propounded by philosophers; some putting forward crushing arguments against the very existence of God, others depriving Him of His providential care for mankind. Among us alone will be seen no difference in the conduct of our lives. With us all act alike, all profess the same doctrine about God, one which is in harmony with our Law and affirms that all things are under His eye. Even our womenfolk and dependents would tell you that piety must be the motive of all our occupations in life. . . .

Our earliest imitators were the Greek philosophers, who, though ostensibly observing the laws of their own countries, yet in their conduct and philosophy were Moses' disciples, holding similar views about God, and advocating the simple life and friendly communion between man and man. But that is not all. The masses have long since shown a keen desire to adopt our religious observances; and there is not one city, Greek or barbarian, nor a single nation, to which our custom of abstaining from work on the seventh day has not spread, and where the fasts and the lighting of lamps and many of our prohibitions in the matter of food are not observed. Moreover, they attempt to imitate our unanimity, our liberal charities, our devoted labor in the crafts, our endurance under persecution on behalf of our laws. The greatest miracle of all is that our Law holds out no seductive bait of sensual pleasure,[8] but has

---

[7]The Spartans (see source 25).

[8]Jews and Christians alleged that pagan religious festivals were occasions for drinking, excessive eating, and sexual license. There was truth to the charge, especially in some forms of bacchic worship (but see source 26) and in fertility rites.

exercised this influence through its own inherent merits; and, as God permeates the universe, so the Law has found its way among all mankind. Let each man reflect for himself on his own country and his own household, and he will not disbelieve what I say. It follows, then, that our accusers must either condemn the whole world for deliberate malice in being so eager to adopt the bad laws of a foreign country in preference to the good laws of their own, or else give up their grudge against us.

Jacob's Seed
▼▼▼

44 ▾ *Maimonides, SELECTED WRITINGS*

Whenever rabbinical scholarship is the topic, one name always arises: Rabbi Moses ben Maimon (1135–1204), known in the West as *Maimonides*. Maimonides possessed the most comprehensive and original intellect of medieval Jewry and composed works that deeply influenced Jewish, Muslim, and Christian contemporaries. Maimonides's scholarship was immense; he composed works in Arabic and Hebrew on such topics as the Bible, Jewish law, astronomy, mathematics, medicine, ethics, and metaphysics. The sheer volume and scope of his writings earned him the sobriquet *The Great Eagle*.

The future rabbi was born in Cordoba, Spain, when the city was still a seat of Islamic power. Faced with persecution by a militant Islamic sect, Maimonides and his family fled across the Strait of Gibraltar to Morocco when he was a teenager. At age thirty he again had to take flight, this time from potential persecution in Morocco, and landed in Palestine, then the scene of the crusades. Finding the Promised Land bitterly disappointing, he migrated in 1167 to Islamic Egypt, where he could practice his faith freely and openly. There he became court physician to Sultan Saladin, the champion of Islam against crusader forces, and spent the rest of his life engaged in a ceaseless round of duties that would have destroyed a lesser person. For thirty years Maimonides served as head of the Jewish congregation of Cairo, one of Judaism's two most prosperous communities in the late twelfth century. (For the other, see Chapter 8, source 63.) The position brought him prestige among Jews throughout North Africa and Southwest Asia, but it also imposed on him the duties of a universally respected religious authority. His voluminous correspondence, in which he answered questions on a wide variety of issues, bears witness to his special place within the Jewish World.

The following selections from his treatises and letters, all written in response to burning issues of his day, reveal Judaism's dual sense of universality and exclusivity.

QUESTIONS FOR ANALYSIS

1. In Maimonides's view, how are Jews to treat one another?
2. According to Maimonides, why were Jews persecuted, and how were they to respond to that persecution? How would those persecutions affect Judaism?
3. Does Rabbi Moses consider a convert to Judaism to be fully a Jew? Why or why not?

4. According to Maimonides, what place does the Promised Land hold in a Jew's life?

5. In the rabbi's view, what will be the consequences of King Messiah's coming?

6. As Maimonides envisions it, what is the World-to-Come, and who will enjoy it?

7. Does Rabbi Moses agree with Second Isaiah (source 19) that, as a Chosen People, the Jews have a special role to play in human history? If so, what is that role?

8. Can you discover any evidence that suggests why Jews were able to maintain their cultural identity despite being so widely scattered?

RELATIONS AMONG JEWS

It is incumbent on every one to love each individual Israelite as himself, as it is said, "Thou shalt love thy neighbor as thyself." Hence a person ought to speak in praise of his neighbor and be careful of his neighbor's property as he is careful of his own property and solicitous about his own honor. Whoever glorifies himself by humiliating another person, will have no portion in the World-to-Come. . . .

The house of Israel that bears the name of Jacob[1] and upholds the religion of Moses our teacher, must be one united community. Nothing whatsoever should create dissension. You are wise and understanding people and you must know how serious are the consequences of discord and to what misfortunes it leads.

WHY ARE JEWS PERSECUTED?

The antagonism of the nations toward us is due to our unique position as a people of faith. This is why their kings oppress us and visit upon us hatred and hostility. But the Creator endowed us with confidence, so that whenever the fury of persecution arises against Israel, it will surely be endured. The power of the kings presses down upon us and they exercise a hard rule over us;

they persecute and torment us with oppressive decrees, but they cannot destroy us or wipe out our name. . . .

Therefore, brethren, be strong and of good courage. If persecutions arise, let them not disconcert you. Let not the mighty hand of the enemy and the weakness of our nation frighten you. These events are but trial and proof of your faith and your love. By holding firm to the law of truth in times like these, you prove that you belong to those of Jacob's seed who fear God and who are named "the remnant whom the Lord shall call."[2]

CONVERTS

I received the question of the master Obadiah, the wise and learned proselyte,[3] may the Lord reward him for his work, may a perfect recompense be bestowed upon him by the Lord of Israel, under whose wings he has sought cover.

You ask me if you, too, are allowed to say in the blessings and prayers you offer alone or in the congregation: "*Our* God" and "God of *our* Fathers," . . . "Thou who hast brought us out of the land of Egypt," Thou who hast worked miracles for our fathers," and more of this kind.

Yes, you may say all this in the described order and not change it in the least. In the same way as

---

[1]Jacob was the son of Isaac, who in turn was the son of Abraham, the father of the Hebrews. YHWH blessed Jacob, changed his name to Israel, and promised that he would be "the father of nations."

[2]The Bible, Joel 2:32. This biblical prophet of the fifth or

fourth century B.C.E. continued the theme of Second Isaiah and spoke of the coming *Day of the Lord,* when God would judge all humanity.

[3]A convert.

every Jew by birth says his blessing and prayer, you, too, shall bless and pray alike, whether you are alone or pray in the congregation. The reason for this is that Abraham, our father, taught the people, opened their minds, and revealed to them the truth, faith, and the unity of God; he rejected the idols and abolished their adoration; he brought many children under the wings of the Divine Presence; he gave them counsel and advice, and ordered his sons and the members of his household after him to keep the ways of the Lord forever. . . . Ever since then whoever adopts Judaism and confesses the unity of the Divine Name, as it is prescribed in the Torah,[4] is counted among the disciples of Abraham, our father, peace be with him. These men are Abraham's household, and he it is who converted them to righteousness. . . .

For the Creator, may He be extolled, has indeed chosen you and separated you from the nations and given you the Torah. For the Torah has been given to us *and* to the proselytes.

RIGHTEOUS GENTILES

As to your question about the nations,[5] know that the Lord desires the heart, and that the intention of the heart is the measure of all things. That is why our sages say, "The pious men among the Gentiles have a share in the World-to-Come," namely, if they have acquired what can be acquired of the knowledge of God, and if they ennoble their souls with worthy qualities. There is no doubt that every man who ennobles his soul with excellent morals and wisdom based on the faith in God, certainly belongs to the men of the World-to-Come.

THE PROMISED LAND

At all times one should live in Palestine even in a place the majority of whose population is heathen, and not live outside Palestine even in a place the majority of whose population is Jewish. . . .

It is forbidden to emigrate from Palestine and go abroad, unless one goes to study the Law, or to marry a wife, or to rescue property from heathens and then returns to Palestine.[6] So, too, one may leave on business. . . . But though one is permitted to emigrate, if one does, the act is not in conformity with the law of saintliness. . . .

When the Temple was destroyed, the Sages of the time ruled that a Jew should not build a painted and wainscoted house, but daub it with clay, wash it with lime, and leave about the entrance a square cubit's spot unwashed. The Sages likewise ordained: Whoever sets his table for a feast should let something be missing on it, and should leave one place empty without the service plate that otherwise would have been put there. When a woman orders ornaments of silver or gold, she should omit one of the details so that it should not appear perfect. When a man takes a wife, he should strew hearth-ashes on his head. All this one should do in remembrance of Jerusalem. As it is said: "If I forget thee, O Jerusalem, let my right hand forget her cunning. Let my tongue cleave to the roof of my mouth if I remember thee not; if I set not Jerusalem above my chiefest joy."

THE MESSIAH

King Messiah[7] will arise and restore the kingdom of David to its former state and original sover-

---

[4]The basic law of Judaism, comprising the first five books of the Bible.

[5]The nations of other (non-Jewish) peoples.

[6]Rabbi Moses left Palestine for Egypt because he concluded that it was intellectually and spiritually a wasteland, and in this age of the crusader Latin kingdom of Jerusalem, there was no place for Jews in Judea. He never returned.

[7]The Anointed One. The Messiah was the deliverer promised through the prophets. Christians believed Jesus Christ was the Messiah; Jews were still awaiting the deliverer's coming.

eignty. He will rebuild the sanctuary[8] and gather the dispersed of Israel. All the ancient laws will be reinstated in his days. . . .

He who does not believe in the restoration or does not look forward to the coming of the Messiah denies not only the teachings of the Prophets but also those of the Law of Moses, our teacher.

The ultimate and perfect reward, the final bliss which will suffer neither interruption nor diminution is the life in the World-to-Come. The Messianic Era, on the other hand, will be realized in this world; which will continue in its normal course except that independent sovereignty will be restored to Israel. The ancient Sages already said, "The only difference between the present and the Messianic Era is that political oppression will then cease." . . .

Let no one think that in the days of the Messiah any of the laws of nature will be set aside, or any innovations be introduced into creation. The world will follow its normal course. The words of Isaiah: And the wolf shall dwell with the lamb, and the leopard shall lie down with the kid are to be understood figuratively, meaning that Israel will live securely among the wicked of the heathens who are likened to wolves and leopards. . . .

They will all accept the true religion, and will neither plunder nor destroy, and together with Israel earn a comfortable living in a legitimate way.

Said the Rabbis: "The sole difference between the present and the Messianic days is deliverance from servitude to foreign powers." . . .

The Sages and Prophets did not long for the days of the Messiah that Israel might exercise dominion over the world, or rule over the heathens or be exalted by the nations, or that it might eat and drink and rejoice. Their aspiration was that Israel be free to devote itself to the Law and its wisdom, with no one to oppress or disturb it, and thus be worthy of the life of the world to come.

In that era will be neither famine nor war, neither jealousy nor strife. Blessings will be abundant, comforts within the reach of all. The one preoccupation of the whole world will be to know the Lord. Hence Israelites will be very wise; they will know the things that are now concealed, and will attain an understanding of their Creator to the utmost capacity of the human mind.

---

[8]The sanctuary of the Temple that was destroyed in 70 C.E.

Chapter 7

Christianity
Conquering the World for Christ

Mainstream Jewish thought perceived no meaningful distinction between church and state because Judaism's special Covenant with God bound it body and soul to the Lord of the Universe. Jews, therefore, believed that as God's people they had been given a sanctified homeland. When they were dispossessed of that inheritance and scattered among the gentiles, they believed it was because of their sins. They further believed that should they reform their ways and fully observe their holy Covenant with God, they would regain sovereign possession of Palestine. By right, this Holy Land and its Chosen People should be ruled according to the Law given them by God through Moses and interpreted by their rabbis.

Not all Jewish sects, however, accepted this interpretation of the Covenant. One dissident element was a small body of religious Jews who gathered around a prophet from Nazareth called *Joshua* or, in Greek, *Jesus* (ca. 4 B.C.E.–ca. 30 C.E.). The heart of Jesus' message was that the promised messianic Kingdom of God was at hand. The *Messiah* (the Anointed One) — God's promised deliverer — was generally expected to be a political and military leader, who would re-establish Israel as a free state. Jesus, to the contrary, expanding upon certain themes in the teachings of Second Isaiah (source 19), preached that the Messiah would usher in a spiritual age of judgment and redemption.

As his ministry developed, Jesus became convinced he was the Messiah. Although he claimed, "My kingdom is not of this Earth," local Roman and Jewish authorities were disquieted by the threat to the establishment that Jesus and his followers seemed to offer, and they conspired successfully to execute him by crucifixion. Jesus' followers believed, however, that he rose from the dead, appeared to a number of his friends, and then ascended to Heaven with the promise of returning soon to sit in judgment of all humanity. Believing that his resurrection proved Jesus' messiahship, his disciples proceeded to spread the *Gospel* (Good News) of redemption.

At first these disciples preached only to Palestinian Jews. Within a short time, however, they spread the faith throughout the entire Roman Empire and beyond, welcoming both Jew and gentile to receive the *New Covenant* proclaimed by Jesus. Before the end of the first century C.E., *Christians* (called so because of Jesus' title *Christos,* which is Greek for *Messiah*) had established the faith in every major city of the Roman Empire and had penetrated the Parthian Empire, non-Roman Africa, Arabia, and the west coast of India. In the early fourth century Christianity was adopted as the state religion in Armenia, Ethiopia, and Georgia, became the favored religion of the Roman Emperor Constantine I (r. 306–337), and took root among a number of German tribes beyond the northeast frontiers of the Roman Empire. In the seventh century a group of dissident Christians known as *Nestorians* established themselves in western China. This otherworldly faith was waging a successful campaign of spiritual conquest in a fair portion of the Afro-Eurasian World.

▼▼▼

The Foundations of Christianity

During Christianity's first century, its adherents had to define the religion to which they gave their allegiance. Just as important, they had to confront the issue of what Christianity *was not.* Were they Jews? Were they something else? If something else, what set their religion apart from Judaism and all of the other religions that flourished within the Greco-Roman World? In essence, what did they believe, and how should they organize themselves?

In resolving these issues, Christians had the guidance of several great teachers. First and foremost was Jesus himself. His call for spiritual perfection was the foundation of the Christian faith and has remained so for almost 2,000 years. Following Jesus' departure from the world, his followers had to grapple with many unresolved questions: Who was Jesus? What was his relationship with God and humanity? What was the nature of the community he had left behind? Among the many leaders who tried to answer these questions, none was more influential than *Paul of Tarsus,* who laid down the basic theological framework for this emerging church.

Becoming Spiritually Perfect

▼▼▼

45 ▾ *THE GOSPEL OF SAINT MATTHEW*

Tradition ascribes authorship of the *Gospels,* the four major accounts of Jesus of Nazareth's life and teachings, to authors known as Matthew, Mark, Luke, and John. The early Christian Church believed that Matthew had been one of Jesus' *Twelve Apostles,* or major companions, and accepted his Gospel as the authoritative re-membrances of a divinely inspired author. Modern scholarship dates the work to the period around 85 or 90, or approximately fifty-five to sixty years after Jesus' ministry. Its author appears to have been a Christian of Antioch in Syria and possi-bly a disciple of the Apostle Matthew, but probably not the apostle himself. The author clearly was trained in the Jewish rabbinical tradition but was equally com-fortable with the Greek language and Hellenistic culture, and he seems to have ad-dressed his Gospel to a cosmopolitan Christian community made up of former Jews and gentiles.

The central theme of the Gospel of Matthew is that Jesus is the Messiah, the ful-fillment of the promises made by God through Abraham, Moses, and the prophets. For Matthew, Second Isaiah was the greatest of the prophets, the one who had most clearly foretold Jesus' mission of salvation and who had preached that the universal reign of the Lord was imminent. In the following selection Matthew pre-sents what is commonly known as the *Sermon on the Mount*. Here Jesus instructs his followers about what the *Kingdom of God* requires of all its members. In all likelihood, what Matthew presents is not a verbatim account of a specific sermon that Jesus delivered on some mountainside but a distillation of Jesus' core moral and theological teachings. As you read this excerpt, keep in mind that Jesus lived in the environment that produced Rabbinical Judaism and was, himself, consid-ered a rabbi, or teacher.

QUESTIONS FOR ANALYSIS

1. Jesus establishes priorities for his followers. What are they?
2. In what ways does Jesus emphasize the spiritual relationship of each believer to God?
3. How does Jesus regard Judaism and especially the Law of Moses? In what ways does he claim that his teachings complete, or perfect, the Law of Moses?
4. What does Matthew mean when he states that Jesus taught with authority and was not like the scribes? Why does Jesus question the authority of the scribes and Pharisees? What is the presumed basis of Jesus' authority?
5. To whom would Jesus' message especially appeal?
6. Compare the message and spirit behind the Sermon on the Mount with that of the Buddha's first sermon, "Setting in Motion the Wheel of the Law" (source 16). Which strike you as more pronounced, their differences or similarities? What do you conclude from your answer?

Seeing the crowds, he went up on the mountain, and when he sat down his disciples came to him. And he opened his mouth and taught them, saying:

"Blessed are the poor in spirit, for theirs is the kingdom of Heaven.

"Blessed are those who mourn, for they shall be comforted.

"Blessed are the meek, for they shall inherit the Earth.

"Blessed are those who hunger and thirst for righteousness, for they shall be satisfied.

"Blessed are the merciful, for they shall obtain mercy.

"Blessed are the pure in heart, for they shall see God.

"Blessed are the peacemakers, for they shall be called sons of God.

"Blessed are those who are persecuted for righteousness' sake, for theirs is the kingdom of Heaven.

"Blessed are you when men revile you and persecute you and utter all kinds of evil against you falsely on my account. Rejoice and be glad, for your reward is great in Heaven, for so men persecuted the prophets who were before you. . . .

"Think not that I have come to abolish the law and the prophets; I have come not to abolish them but to fulfill them. For truly, I say to you, till Heaven and Earth pass away, not an iota, not a dot, will pass from the law until all is accomplished. Whoever then relaxes one of the least of these commandments and teaches men so, shall be called least in the kingdom of Heaven; but he who does them and teaches them shall be called great in the kingdom of Heaven. For I tell you, unless your righteousness exceeds that of the scribes and the Pharisees,[1] you will never enter the kingdom of Heaven.

"You have heard that it was said to the men of old, 'You shall not kill; and whoever kills shall be liable to judgment.' But I say to you that every one who is angry with his brother shall be liable to judgment; whoever insults his brother shall be liable to the council,[2] and whoever says, 'You fool!' shall be liable to the hell of fire. So if you are offering your gift at the altar, and there remember that your brother has something against you, leave your gift there before the altar and go; first be reconciled to your brother, and then come and offer your gift. . . . You have heard that it was said, 'An eye for an eye and a tooth for a tooth.' But I say to you, Do not resist one who is evil. But if any one strikes you on the right cheek, turn to him the other also. . . . You have heard that it was said, 'You shall love your neighbor and hate your enemy.' But I say to you, Love your enemies and pray for those who persecute you, so that you may be sons of your Father who is in Heaven; for he makes his sun rise on the evil and on the good, and sends rain on the just and on the unjust. For if you love those who love you, what reward have you? . . . You, therefore, must be perfect, as your heavenly Father is perfect. . . .

"And in praying do not heap up empty phrases as the Gentiles do; for they think that they will be heard for their many words. Do not be like them, for your Father knows what you need before you ask him. Pray then like this:

Our Father who art in Heaven.
Hallowed be thy name.
Thy kingdom come,
Thy will be done,
On Earth as it is in Heaven.

---

[1] The *scribes* were nonpriestly professionals who copied, interpreted, and applied the oral traditions that supplemented written biblical Law. The *Pharisees* were members of a Jewish religious party who stressed that all of this nonscriptural, oral law had to be observed as equally and as fully as the written Law of Moses. Eventually this *Oral Torah,* as it was often called, became codified in the *Talmud,* which was codified in two major editions between about 200 and 600 C.E.: an earlier and shorter one in Palestine and a later and fuller one in Babylonia. The Talmud has served as a major source for Rabbinical Judaism to the present.

[2] The *Sanhedrin,* Judaism's chief religious and judicial body.

Give us this day our daily bread;
And forgive us our debts,
    As we also have forgiven our debtors
And lead us not into temptation,
    But deliver us from evil.

For if you forgive men their trespasses, your heavenly Father also will forgive you; but if you do not forgive men their trespasses, neither will your Father forgive your trespasses. . . .

"Do not lay up for yourselves treasures on Earth, where moth and rust consume and where thieves break in and steal, but lay up for yourselves treasures in Heaven, where neither moth nor rust consumes and where thieves do not break in and steal. For where your treasure is, there will your heart be also. . . . Therefore do not be anxious, saying, 'What shall we eat?' or 'What shall we drink?' or 'What shall we wear?' For the Gentiles seek all these things; and your heavenly Father knows that you need them all. But seek first his kingdom and his righteousness, and all these things shall be yours as well. . . .

"Judge not, that you be not judged. For with the judgment you pronounce you will be judged, and the measure you give will be the measure you get. . . ."

And when Jesus finished these sayings, the crowds were astonished at his teaching, for he taught them as one who had authority, and not as their scribes.

The Path to Righteousness: The Law or Faith?

▼▼▼

46 ▾ *Saint Paul, EPISTLE TO THE ROMANS*

Our earliest Christian sources are not the Gospels but rather the *epistles,* or letters, that Saint Paul (ca. 3 B.C.E.–64 or 67 C.E.) wrote to a number of Christian communities. Paul, or to give him his Hebrew name, *Saul,* was a Hellenized Jew and rabbinical scholar from Tarsus in Asia Minor and has often been called *the second founder of Christianity.* Prior to his becoming a Christian, Paul was a member of the Jewish elite of the eastern Mediterranean. A Roman citizen, which was rare for Jews of his day, he studied under the leading pharisaical rabbi of his day, became a noted Pharisee himself, and probably was elevated to membership in the Sanhedrin, Judaism's supreme religious and judicial body. Converted dramatically to Christianity by a blinding revelation while traveling to Damascus in Syria in the pursuit of Christians whom he was persecuting, Paul became the leading opponent of certain Christian conservatives who wished to keep Christianity within the boundaries of Judaism. From roughly 47 to his death in Rome in either 64 or 67 (ancient authorities differ on the date), Paul was an indefatigable missionary, converting gentiles and Jews alike throughout the Mediterranean region. Most important of all, Paul transformed Jesus' messianic message into a faith centering on Jesus as Lord and Savior.

Paul developed his distinctive theology in his epistles, his only extant writings. Although each epistle was addressed to a specific group of Christians and often dealt with local issues, they were revered as authoritative pronouncements of general interest for all believers. As a result, copies were circulated, and in time some of his letters (as well as some Paul never composed but that were ascribed to him) were incorporated into the body of scriptural books known to Christians as the *New Testament* (the *Old Testament* being the pre-Christian, or Jewish, portion of the Bible).

Around 57, probably while residing in Corinth, Greece, Paul planned to establish a mission in Spain and decided to make Rome his base of operations. In preparation, he wrote to the Christians at Rome to inform them of his plans and to instruct them in the faith. The result was the *Epistle to the Romans,* the most fully articulated expression of Paul's theology of salvation.

QUESTIONS FOR ANALYSIS

1. According to Paul, who was Jesus?
2. This epistle centers on the issue of how one becomes righteous in the eyes of God. According to Paul, the former Pharisee and member of the Sanhedrin, can the Law of Moses or any other body of law put one right with God? Why or why not? What role does faith play in putting one right with God? Faith in what or whom?
3. For Paul, which two virtues, or qualities, must dominate a Christian's life?
4. What do you infer from the evidence about the role of women in the early Church?
5. Like Second Isaiah (source 19), Paul believes that God has a master plan for all humanity. How does Paul's understanding of that plan differ from that of his sixth-century B.C.E. predecessor?
6. Compare this epistle with the Sermon on the Mount. Do they agree, disagree, or complement one another? Be specific.
7. What parallels can you discover between Christian devotion to Jesus, as taught by Paul, and similar contemporary forms of piety and belief in the Hindu and Buddhist traditions? In answering this question, consider the sources in Chapter 6.

Paul, a servant of Jesus Christ, called to be an apostle,[1] set apart for the Gospel of God which he promised beforehand through his prophets in the holy scriptures, the Gospel concerning his Son, who was descended from David[2] according to the flesh and designated Son of God in power according to the Spirit of holiness by his resurrection from the dead, Jesus Christ our Lord, through whom we have received grace and apostleship to bring about obedience to the faith for the sake of his name among all the nations, including yourselves who are called to belong to Jesus Christ;

"To all God's beloved in Rome, who are called to be saints: . . . I am eager to preach the Gospel to you also who are in Rome.

For I am not ashamed of the Gospel: it is the power of God for salvation to every one who has faith, to the Jew first and also to the Greek.[3] For in it the righteousness of God is revealed through faith for faith; as it is written, "He who through faith is righteous shall live." . . . For we hold that

---

[1]Paul was not one of the original Twelve Apostles. He claimed apostolic status because he believed he had been miraculously called and converted by the Risen Christ, who appeared to him in a vision. Some of the close friends and earliest followers of Jesus were reluctant to recognize Paul as an apostle.

[2]The prophetic tradition maintained that the Messiah would be descended from the line of King David (see Maimonides, source 44). Consequently, Christian Jews stressed Jesus' Davidic lineage.

[3]*Greek* means any non-Jew, or gentile, because Greek was the common tongue of educated people in the eastern half of the Roman Empire.

a man is justified[4] by faith apart from works of law.[5] Or is God the God of Jews only? Is he not the God of gentiles also? Yes, of gentiles also, since God is one; and he will justify the circumcised[6] on the ground of their faith and the uncircumcised because of their faith. . . . The promise to Abraham[7] and his descendants, that they should inherit the world, did not come through the Law but through the righteousness of faith. If it is the adherents of the Law who are to be the heirs, faith is null and the promise is void. . . . That is why it depends on faith, in order that the promise may rest on grace and be guaranteed to all his descendants — not only to the adherents of the law but also to those who share the faith of Abraham, for he is the father of us all, as it is written, "I have made you the father of many nations." . . .

Therefore, since we are justified by faith, we have peace with God through our Lord Jesus Christ. Through him we have obtained access to this grace in which we stand, and we rejoice in our hope of sharing the glory of God. . . . God shows his love for us in that while we were yet sinners Christ died for us. Since, therefore, we are now justified by his blood, much more shall we be saved by him from the wrath of God. For if while we were enemies we were reconciled to God by the death of his Son, much more, now that we are reconciled, shall we be saved by his life. . . . There is therefore now no condemnation for those who are in Christ Jesus. For the law of the Spirit of life in Christ Jesus has set me free from the law of sin and death. . . .

If you confess with your lips that Jesus is Lord and believe in your heart that God raised him from the dead, you will be saved. For man believes with his heart and so is justified, and he confesses with his lips and so is saved. The scripture says, "No one who believes in him will be put to shame." For there is no distinction between Jew and Greek; the same Lord is Lord of all and bestows his riches upon all who call upon him. For, "every one who calls upon the name of the Lord will be saved." . . .

I appeal to you therefore, brethren, by the mercies of God, to present your bodies as a living sacrifice, holy and acceptable to God, which is your spiritual worship. . . . Let love be genuine; hate what is evil, hold fast to what is good; love one another with brotherly affection; outdo one another in showing honor. Never flag in zeal, be aglow with the Spirit, serve the Lord. Rejoice in your hope, be patient in tribulation, be constant in prayer. Contribute to the needs of the saints, practice hospitality.

Bless those who persecute you; bless and do not curse them. Rejoice with those who rejoice, weep with those who weep. Live in harmony with one another; do not be haughty, but associate with the lowly; never be conceited. Repay no one evil for evil, but take thought for what is noble in the sight of all. If possible, so far as it depends upon you, live peaceably with all. Beloved, never avenge yourselves, but leave it to the wrath of God; for it is written, "Vengeance is mine, I will repay, says the Lord." No, "if your enemy is hungry, feed him; if he is thirsty, give him drink; for by so doing you will heap burning coals upon his head." Do not be overcome by evil, but overcome evil with good. . . .

Owe no one anything, except to love one another; for he who loves his neighbor has fulfilled the Law. The commandments, "You shall not commit adultery, You shall not kill, You shall not steal, You shall not covet," and any other commandment, are summed up in this sentence, "You shall love your neighbor as yourself." Love does no wrong to a neighbor; therefore love is the fulfilling of the Law. . . .

I commend to you to our sister Phoebe, a deaconess of the church at Cenchreae,[8] that you may

---

[4]Made just, or righteous, in the eyes of God.

[5]The Law of Judaism.

[6]The Law of Moses prescribes circumcision for all Jewish males; gentiles are, therefore, *the uncircumcised*.

[7]The ancient patriarch from whom all Jews were descended and with whom YHWH entered into a covenant.

[8]A community in the Greek Peloponnesus. *Deaconesses* and their male counterparts, *deacons,* were assistants to the *presbyters* (elders) who supervised the various churches. The duties of these assistants consisted of baptizing, preaching, and dispensing charity.

receive her in the Lord as befits the saints, and help her in whatever she may require from you, for she has been a helper of many and of myself as well.

Greet Prisca and Aquila,[9] my fellow workers in Christ Jesus, who risked their necks for my life, to whom not only I but also all the churches of the gentiles give thanks; greet also the church in their house.

---

[9]A married couple of Hellenized Jewish-Christians who figured prominently in the Christian community of Rome. Prisca was the wife; Aquila the husband.

Christianity and the Roman World

Roman authorities were generally tolerant of the diverse deities and religious practices of the empire's subjects and tried to foster loyalty to the empire by merging these gods and goddesses into the Roman *pantheon,* or assemblage of recognized deities. Normally all that Romans required was that the various cults and their devotees not threaten public order or morality and that each religion help guarantee the gods' continued favor toward the state. Because, however, Roman officials perceived that Bacchism (source 26) violated all norms of decent social behavior and Druid priests (source 31) threatened the stability of Roman rule in Gaul and Britain, the Roman state acted vigorously to suppress both cults. The same was true of Christianity. As far as many Romans were concerned, Christianity was a threat to the state and civil order because of its uncompromising monotheism and its followers' extreme sense of exclusivity. Although Jews shared those characteristics, Judaism enjoyed the status of being the legally recognized religion of one of Rome's subject people. Once Christianity separated itself from the Jewish synagogues, it lost whatever protection it had enjoyed by reason of its Judaic heritage.

Although we possess no official state pronouncement concerning Christianity before the second century, it appears that the first imperial persecution of Christians took place in Rome under Emperor Nero (r. 54–68) around the year 64. Our source is the historian and moralist Tacitus (source 31). Writing more than four decades after the event, Tacitus noted that, following a massive fire that devastated the city, Christians became convenient targets of attack, because they were "hated for their abominations." Because of those putative abominations, Christianity became a prohibited cult, and adherence to it was technically a capital offense.

As the following four sources indicate, this was not the whole story. Indeed, the story of relations between Christianity and the Roman Empire is one of world history's most interesting and historically significant sagas.

Rome's Policy toward Christians
▼▼▼

47 ▾ *Pliny the Younger and Trajan,* LETTERS REGARDING CHRISTIANS

Despite a general attitude that Christians were an unsavory lot and deserved whatever sanctions were laid upon them, before the middle of the third century the Roman state was reluctant to prosecute Christians too vigorously. The following exchange of letters around the year 112 between Pliny the Younger (61/62–ca. 114), imperial deputy in Bithynia and Pontus, provinces that stretched along the Black Sea coast of Anatolia (modern Asiatic Turkey), and Emperor Trajan (r. 98–117) reveals the empire's attitude and policy toward Christians during the second-century *Pax Romana,* or Roman Peace.

If Pliny's name strikes a chord in your memory, it is because he was the nephew, namesake, and adopted son of Pliny the Elder (source 36).

QUESTIONS FOR ANALYSIS

1. What is Pliny's quandary regarding Christians? What does this confusion on the part of one of the empire's chief administrators suggest about early-second-century notions about these Christians?
2. As far as Pliny was concerned, what were the unquestionable errors and dangers of Christianity and similar cults? What does your answer suggest about second-century Roman attitudes and realities?
3. What procedures did Pliny follow when Christians were brought before him? What does this suggest about Roman attitudes toward cults such as Christianity?
4. What do Pliny's policies suggest about the legal differences between citizens and noncitizens?
5. What does Pliny's report tell us about early Christian practices?
6. What does Trajan's reply allow us to infer about second-century attitudes, imperial policies, and realities?

PLINY TO EMPEROR TRAJAN

It is my inviolable rule, my Lord, to refer all uncertain matters to you. For who is better able to guide my uncertainty or instruct me in my ignorance?

I never was present at the trials of Christians. Therefore, I am unacquainted with what is customary as to the method and extent of punishing and examining them. I am more than just a little uncertain on several points: Whether any dis-crimination is made for age; whether the weak are treated differently from the stronger; whether repentance earns a pardon; or whether, if someone was ever a Christian, his ceasing to be one does not gain him anything; whether the very name [of Christian] itself is punishable, even when it is not associated with any crimes; or whether crimes, which are associated with the name, are the punishable offenses.

Meanwhile, I have followed this procedure in regard to those who were brought before me as

Christians. I interrogated them as to whether they were Christians. If they confessed, I asked a second and a third time,[1] adding the threat of capital punishment. If they persevered, I ordered them executed. For I did not doubt that, whatever it might be that they believed, certainly their stubbornness and inflexible obstinacy merited punishment. There were others of similar madness, who, because they were Roman citizens, I directed to be remanded to the City.[2]

Soon, as is usually the case, accusations multiplied, simply because the matter was being investigated, and more forms of this phenomenon cropped up. An unsigned placard containing many names was put up. I thought it appropriate to dismiss those who denied they were or ever had been Christians, who repeated after me an invocation to the gods, who made supplication to Your statue with incense and wine, which I had ordered to be brought forward for that purpose, along with images of the gods, and who, furthermore, cursed Christ. For it is said that not one of these is an act that those who are truly Christians can be compelled to perform. Others who were named by the informer said they were Christians and afterwards denied it. In fact, they had been, but had forsaken it — some three years ago, others many years ago, a few even twenty-five years ago. They all venerated your statue and the images of the gods and cursed Christ.

They continued to affirm, moreover, that the sum total of their guilt or error was that they were in the habit of meeting before dawn on a certain fixed day of the week and to sing in alternating verses a hymn to Christ, as to a god, and bound themselves by sacred oath not to commit any impious action but that they would never perpetrate fraud, theft, or adultery nor would they bear false witness or, when called upon, refuse to deliver up anything entrusted to them. After this was over, they customarily dispersed and then reassembled to partake of food, but food of a common and innocent sort.[3] They had even ceased doing this after my edict was published in which, following your orders, I had forbidden secret associations. Given this, I believed it to be all the more necessary, in order to extract the truth, to question under torture two female slaves, who were called deaconesses.[4] I discovered, however, nothing more than a depraved and excessive superstition.

Consequently I suspended the proceedings and hastened to consult You. For the matter seemed to me well worth consultation, especially in light of the numbers at peril. For many of every age and rank, and even of both sexes, are and will be called into peril. For the contagion of this superstition has not only spread through the cities but even through villages and rural districts. It does, however, seem possible to contain and cure it. It is quite clear that the temples, which had been up to now almost deserted, have begun to be frequented, that the sacred festivals, after a long intermission, have been restored, and far and wide sacrificial victims,[5] which up until now very rarely had a buyer, are sold.[6] From this it is easy to judge what multitude of people might be set right, if there is room for repentance.

TRAJAN TO PLINY

You have acted properly, my dear Secundus,[7] in your handling of the cases of those denounced to you as Christians. For there is no general rule that

---

[1]Roman law required that a confession unsupported by external evidence had to be repeated in order for a person to be found guilty.
[2]They were sent to Rome, where they would be tried in an imperial court as citizens.
[3]See the next source by Tertullian for insight into the sort of uncommon and not-so-innocent food that many ascribed to Christians. The ceremony alluded to here is the *agape,* or love, feast — a communal meal in commemoration of Jesus' Last Supper with his apostles.

[4]See source 46, note 8.
[5]Cattle and other sacrificial animals.
[6]I prefer *passimque venire victimas* (sell sacrificial victims far and wide) rather than *pastumque venire victimarum* (sell the fodder for sacrificial victims), which appears in some editions of this letter.
[7]Pliny's full name was Gaius Plinius Caecilius Secundus.

can be set down as if it were a fixed standard for every case.[8] These people should not be sought out. If they are charged and convicted, they must be punished. Yet if someone denies being a Christian and provides proof in this matter, namely by praying to our gods, however much he might have been under suspicion in the past, he shall secure pardon by virtue of his repentance. Anonymous accusations have no place in a criminal proceeding. They are exceedingly bad precedents and do not conform to the standards of our age.

---

[8]Trajan avoids laying down an imperial rescript that would have the force of law throughout the empire. Rather, he offers Pliny practical advice for the situation at hand in these two provinces.

Why Are Christians Persecuted?
▼▼▼

48 ▼ *Tertullian, APOLOGIA*

Trajan's advice to Pliny the Younger did not end persecutions of Christians. In the next generation it fell to a native of Carthage in western North Africa, the home of one of the most vibrant Christian communities of the late second century, to plead for equality before the law for Christians.

Tertullian (ca. 160–after 220) was the first great Christian writer to use Latin, rather than Greek, as his chosen medium. His prolific outpouring of passionate, eminently quotable, and deliciously sarcastic writings in defense of his own rigorous vision of Christianity played a major role in forming a Western, or Latin, Christian culture. This was in distinction to the Hellenic modes of thought and expression articulated by the Christian Church's teachers in the Eastern Mediterranean, beginning with the authors of the books of the New Testament.

Born the pagan son of an army centurion, Tertullian initially enjoyed a brilliant career as a legal advocate and jurist. Around the year 195, he converted to Christianity and soon thereafter embarked on a new career as one of Christianity's most strident advocates. In reaction against his earlier education and life, he vigorously rejected Greco-Roman learning in all its forms and heaped abuse on most fellow Christians, whose lives, he believed, did not conform to the high standards of self-denial demanded by Christ.

Only about two years after his conversion, that is around 197, he composed one of his most famous works, the *Apologia*. The word means "defense," and in this work Tertullian, the lawyer turned Christian apologist, defended Christian practices and beliefs before the court of public opinion. Addressed to the empire's provincial governors, the *Apologia* develops the argument that persecution of Christians is inconsistent with the principles of Roman law, morality, and reason.

QUESTIONS FOR ANALYSIS

1. What were some of the heinous crimes Christians were accused of?
2. Why do you think these particular charges were leveled against them?
3. What does Tertullian think of the legality, internal consistency, and justice of Trajan's policy regarding Christians? What specific points does he make in his analysis of the policy?

4. According to Tertullian, why are Christians hated, and how rationally based is that hatred?
5. How would a reasonable, moderate pagan answer Tertullian's points?

Magistrates of the Roman Empire! You who are seated for the administration of justice in almost the highest position of the state[1] and under the gaze of everyone! If you are not allowed to conduct an open examination, face to face, into the truth regarding the Christians, if in this case alone you fear or are ashamed to exercise your authority to conduct a public investigation with the care that justice demands, if, finally, the extreme hatred shown this group (as happened recently in the domestic courts)[2] has been raised to such a level that it inhibits their defense, then let the truth reach your ears by the secret pathway of silent literature. . . .

If it is certain that we are the most criminal of people, why do you treat us differently from others of our kind, namely all other criminals? The same crime should receive the same treatment. When others are charged with the same crimes imputed to us, they are permitted to use their own mouths and the hired advocacy of others to plead their innocence. They have full freedom to answer the charge and to cross-examine. In fact, it is against the law to condemn anyone without a defense and a hearing. Only Christians are forbidden to say anything in defense of the truth that would clear their case and assist the judge in avoiding an injustice. All that they care about (and this by itself is enough to arouse public hatred) is a confession to bearing the name "Christian," not an investigation of the charge. Now, let us assume you are trying any other criminal. If he confesses to the crime of murder, or sacrilege, or sexual debauchery, or treason — to cite the crimes of which we stand accused — you are not content to pass sentence immediately. Rather, you weigh the relevant circumstances: the nature of the deed; how often, where, how, and when it was committed; the co-conspirators and the

partners-in-crime. Nothing of this sort is done in our case. Yet, whenever that false charge is brought against us, we should equally be made to confess: How many murdered babies has one eaten? How many illicit sexual acts has one performed under cover of darkness? Which cooks and which dogs were there? Oh, how great would be the glory of that governor who should bring to light a Christian who has already devoured 100 babies!

To the contrary, we find that it is forbidden to hunt us down. When Pliny the Younger was a provincial governor and had condemned some Christians to death and had intimidated others to abandon the steadfastness of their faith, he was still concerned by their sheer numbers and worried about what to do in the future. So he consulted Trajan, the reigning emperor. Pliny explained that, other than their obstinate refusal to offer sacrifice, he had learned nothing else about their religious ceremonies, except that they met before daybreak to sing hymns to Christ and God and to bind themselves by oath to a way of life that forbids murder, adultery, fraud, treachery, and all other crimes. Trajan then wrote back that people of this sort should not be hunted down, but, when brought to court, they should be punished.

What a decision! How inevitably self-contradictory! He declares that they should not be hunted down, as though they are innocent. Then he prescribes that they be punished, as though they are guilty. He spares them, yet he directs his anger upon them. He pretends to shut his eyes, yet he calls attention to them. Judges, why do you tie yourself up in knots? If you condemn them why not hunt them down? If you do not hunt them down, why not also find them innocent? Throughout all the provinces, soldiers are assigned by lot to hunt down bandits. When it

---

[1]The governors were second only to the emperor.
[2]This probably refers to some recent, now-unknown case in

which a slave had been indicted for introducing Christianity into a household.

comes to traitors and public enemies each person is a soldier. Inquiry extends even to one's associates and confederates. The Christian alone may not be hunted down, but he may be brought to court, as if hunting down led to anything other than being haled into court. So, you condemn someone who is haled into court, although no one wished to seek him out. He has not merited punishment, I suppose, because he is guilty, but because, forbidden to be looked for, he was found! . . .

A person shouts out, "I am a Christian." He says what he is. You want to hear what he is not. You preside to extort the truth, yet in our case alone you take infinite pains to hear a lie. "I am," he says, "what you ask if I am. Why torture me to twist the fact around? I confess, and you torture me. What would you do if I denied?" Clearly when others deny you do not readily believe them. In our case, when we deny, you immediately believe us. . . .

Inasmuch as you treat us differently from all other criminals, which you do by concentrating on disassociating us from that name (for we are cut off from the name "Christian" only if we do what non-Christians do), you must know that there is no crime whatsoever in our case. It is only a name. . . .

So much for my preface, as it were, which is intended to beat into submission the injustice of the public hatred felt for us. Now I take the stand to plead our innocence. . . .

We are said to be the worst of criminals because of our sacramental baby-killing and the baby-eating that accompanies it and the sexual license that follows the banquet, where dogs are our pimps in darkness when they overturn candles and procure a certain modesty for our impious lusts.[3] We are always spoken of in this way, yet you take no pains to investigate the charges that you have made against us for so long. If you believe them, investigate them. Otherwise, stop believing what you do not investigate. The fact that you look the other way suggests that the evil that you yourselves dare not investigate does not exist. . . .

You say, "You do not worship the gods, and you do not offer sacrifices for the emperors." It follows logically that we do not offer sacrifices for others because we do not do so even for ourselves. All of this is a consequence of our not worshipping the gods. So we are accused of sacrilege and treason.[4] This is the chief case against us. In fact, it is the whole case. . . . Your gods we cease to worship from the moment we recognize they are not gods. So that is what you ought to require us to prove — that those gods do not exist and for that reason should not be worshipped because they deserve worship only if they are gods.

---

[3]The story was that strings were tied to dogs' tails and to the candles that illuminated the room. When food was tossed to the dogs, they leaped at it, overturning the candles and plunging the room into darkness.

[4]Treason by virtue of denying the divine authority of the emperor and the divinely blessed majesty of the empire.

Persecution and Deliverance
▼▼▼

49 ▼ *Eusebius of Caesarea,* *ECCLESIASTICAL HISTORY*

Although some Christians were persecuted and executed by Roman authorities, between roughly the mid first and mid third centuries persecution of Christians was sporadic, local, and often halfhearted. When persecutions occurred, it was usually when provincial governors found themselves forced to bow to local senti-

ment in order to keep a discontented populace quiet. Crop failures and other natural disasters often seemed to demand a few Christian victims as propitiation to the gods, the theory being that the Christians were atheists and had angered the gods by their refusal to worship them. This policy of overlooking the Christians' supposed atheism and immorality changed around the year 250, when Emperor Decius embarked on a short but bitter empire-wide attack on Christians.

In 303 the empire launched its last and greatest persecution of Christianity; the attack continued until 311 when Emperor Galerius, in the grips of a frightening disease, decided to strike a bargain with the Christian god. His edict of toleration granted Christians freedom of worship, in exchange for their prayers for him. A few days after issuing the edict, Galerius was dead.

The following year, *Constantine I* (r. 306–337), a claimant to the imperial throne, was campaigning in Italy against a rival. According to a Christian source, prior to the battle Constantine had a vision in which the Christian god promised him victory, and shortly thereafter he won a decisive victory, thereby becoming uncontested emperor in the West. In gratitude, Constantine and the emperor of the eastern half of the empire met in 313 at Milan, in northern Italy, where they reached an agreement regarding freedom of worship for all persons in the empire and recognition of the full legal status of each local Christian church. Christianity had weathered the storm of Roman persecution.

After the meeting at Milan, Constantine never wavered in his patronage of Christianity, and the consequences were momentous for the empire, for Christianity, and for the subsequent civilizations of western Eurasia. A faith that commanded the belief of only about 10 percent of the empire's population in 313 was, by century's end, the religion of the vast majority of eastern Mediterranean urban dwellers and making rapid advances among the region's rural populations. In the western half of the empire the progress of conversion was slower but steady.

Our most important eyewitness to the revolution initiated by Constantine the Great is Eusebius (ca. 260–339 or 340), leader, or *bishop,* of the church of Caesarea in Palestine. Bishop Eusebius was a prolific writer, but his single enduring work is the *Ecclesiastical History,* which traces the fortunes of the Christian Church from its earliest days to the early fourth century. This history has rightly earned Eusebius the title *Father of Church history,* inasmuch as his history is the most complete and coherent account that we possess of the early Church's first three centuries.

Eusebius's careful scholarship, however, did not negate the *Ecclesiastical History*'s apologetical tone and theological message. Within its pages history is a cosmic contest between the forces of God and of the Devil. On one side are patriarchs, prophets, saints, and martyrs; on the other are pagans, persecutors, latter-day Jews, and *heretical,* or wrong-believing, Christians. Although the Devil and his minions always lose, the righteous suffer considerably as they struggle against evil.

More than simply a scholar, Eusebius was active in the affairs of the early fourth-century Church and suffered in the process. He had been imprisoned during the era of the Great Persecution and had seen many of his friends tortured and martyred. But he also lived to see the miracle of the Emperor Constantine's conversion to Christianity after the emperor's victory in 312. Following Eusebius's elevation to the bishopric of Caesarea around 313, he came to enjoy the Christian emperor's patronage and friendship.

Earlier, before the onslaught of the Great Persecution, Eusebius had begun a detailed history of the Church down to his own day, completing the work in seven volumes around 303. The events of 312 and following, however, necessitated that he update his work. Consequently, he enlarged the *Ecclesiastical History* to ten books in order to include the history of Christian fortunes down to 324, thereby demonstrating the manner in which Divine Providence had once again triumphed over the forces of evil.

Our three excerpts come from Book 5, an appendix to Book 8 entitled "The Martyrs of Palestine," and Book 10. Note the significant differences in tone and message between the first two excerpts and the third, which deals with Constantine's victory in 324 over Licinius, his former coemperor.

QUESTIONS FOR ANALYSIS

1. How did Eusebius distinguish between the history he wrote and the history that pagan Greeks and Romans wrote? Why did he make the distinction?
2. Consider the second excerpt. Why do you think Eusebius dwells on the punishments that Christian confessors bore?
3. What does his description of the heroism of the two female martyrs suggest about Christian notions of the place of women in the Church?
4. Compare your answer to the question above with your answer to question 4 of source 46. What conclusions do you reach?
5. Some see a dramatic difference in tone and message between what Eusebius writes in the first two excerpts and what he writes in the third excerpt. Do you see a difference? If so, how do you explain it?

BOOK 5

Other writers of history record the victories of war and trophies won from enemies, the skill of generals, and the manly bravery of soldiers, defiled with blood and with innumerable slaughters for the sake of children and country and other possessions. But our narrative of the government of God will record in ineffaceable letters the most peaceful wars waged in behalf of the peace of the soul, and will tell of men doing brave deeds for truth rather than country, and for piety rather than dearest friends. It will hand down to imperishable remembrance the discipline and the much-tried fortitude of the athletes of religion, the trophies won from demons, the victories over invisible enemies, and the crowns placed upon their heads.

THE MARTYRS OF PALESTINE

Up to the sixth year[1] the storm had been incessantly raging against us. Before this time there had been a very large number of confessors[2] of religion in the so-called Porphyry quarry in Thebais,[3] which gets its name from the stone found there.[4] Of these, one hundred men, lacking three, together with women and infants, were sent to the governor of Palestine. When they confessed

---

[1]The sixth year of the persecution, which began in the spring of 303.
[2]Those who confess, or proclaim and live, the faith in a heroic manner.

[3]The region around Thebes in Egypt.
[4]Slave labor in stone quarries and mines, which usually ended in death, was a common criminal penalty.

the God of the universe and Christ, Firmilianus, who had been sent there as a governor in the place of Urbanus, directed, in accordance with the imperial command, that they should be maimed by burning the sinews of the ankles of their left feet, and that their right eyes with the eyelids and pupils should first be cut out, and then destroyed by hot irons to the very roots. And he then sent them to the mines in the province to endure hardships with severe toil and suffering.

But it was not sufficient that these only who suffered such miseries should be deprived of their eyes, but those natives of Palestine also, who were mentioned just above as condemned to pugilistic combat,[5] since they would neither receive food from the royal storehouse nor undergo the necessary preparatory exercises. Having been brought on this account not only before the overseers, but also before Maximinus himself,[6] and having manifested the noblest persistence in confession by the endurance of hunger and stripes, they received like punishment with those whom we have mentioned, and with them other confessors in the city of Caesarea. Immediately afterwards others who were gathered to hear the Scriptures read, were seized in Gaza,[7] and some endured the same sufferings in the feet and eyes; but others were afflicted with yet greater torments and with most terrible tortures in the sides. One of these, in body a woman, but in understanding a man, would not endure the threat of rape, and spoke directly against the tyrant who entrusted the government to such cruel judges. She was first scourged and then raised aloft on the stake, and her sides lacerated. As those appointed for this purpose applied the tortures incessantly and severely at the command of the judge, another, with mind fixed, like the former, on virginity as her aim, — a woman who was altogether mean in form and contemptible in appearance, but, on

the other hand, strong in soul, and endowed with an understanding superior to her body, — being unable to bear the merciless and cruel and inhuman deeds, with a boldness beyond that of the combatants famed among the Greeks,[8] cried out to the judge from the midst of the crowd: "And how long will you thus cruelly torture my sister?" But he was greatly enraged and ordered the woman to be immediately seized. Thereupon she was brought forward and having called herself by the august name of the Savior, she was first urged by words to sacrifice, and as she refused she was dragged by force to the altar. But her sister continued to maintain her former zeal, and with intrepid and resolute foot kicked the altar, and overturned it with the fire that was on it. Thereupon the judge, enraged like a wild beast, inflicted on her such tortures in her sides as he never had on any one before, striving almost to glut himself with her raw flesh. But when his madness was satiated, he bound them both together, this one and her whom she called sister, and condemned them to death by fire. It is said that the first of these was from the country of Gaza; the other, by name Valentina, was of Caesarea, and was well known to many.

BOOK 10

Thanks for all things be given unto God the Omnipotent Ruler and King of the universe, and the greatest thanks to Jesus Christ the Savior and Redeemer of our souls, through whom we pray that peace may be always preserved for us firm and undisturbed by external troubles and troubles of the mind. Since in accordance with your wishes, my most holy Paulinus,[9] we have added the tenth book of the Church History to those which have preceded, we will inscribe it to you, proclaiming you as the seal of the whole work; and we will fitly add in a perfect number[10] the perfect pane-

[5]They were condemned to fight as boxing gladiators in the circus.
[6]Maximin Daia, emperor in the East from 305 to 313.
[7]The southern coastal region of Palestine.
[8]Professional wrestlers and boxers. See source 29.

[9]The bishop of Tyre, whom Eusebius especially admired.
[10]According to Pythagorean numerology, 10 is the perfect number because it is the sum of the four principal geometric numbers: 1, 2, 3, and 4.

gyric upon the restoration of the churches, obeying the Divine Spirit which exhorts us in the following words: "Sing unto the Lord a new song, for he hath done marvelous things. His right hand and his holy arm hath saved him. The Lord hath made known his salvation, his righteousness hath he revealed in the presence of the nations."[11] And in accordance with the utterance which commands us to sing the new song, let us proceed to show that, after those terrible and gloomy spectacles which we have described, we are now permitted to see and celebrate such things as many truly righteous men and martyrs of God before us desired to see upon Earth and did not see, and to hear and did not hear. But they, hastening on, obtained far better things, being carried to Heaven and the paradise of divine pleasure. But, acknowledging that even these things are greater than we deserve, we have been astonished at the grace manifested by the author of the great gifts, and rightly do we admire him, worshiping him with the whole power of our souls, and testifying to the truth of those recorded utterances, in which it is said, "Come and see the works of the Lord, the wonders which he hath done upon the earth; he removeth wars to the ends of the world, he shall break the bow and snap the spear in sunder, and shall burn the shields with fire."[12] Rejoicing in these things which have been clearly fulfilled in our day, let us proceed with our account.

The whole race of God's enemies was destroyed in the manner indicated, and was thus suddenly swept from the sight of men. So that again a divine utterance had its fulfillment: "I have seen the impious highly exalted and raising himself like the cedars of Lebanon; and I have passed by, and behold, he was not; and I have sought his place, and it could not be found."[13] And finally a bright and splendid day, overshadowed by no cloud, illuminated with beams of heavenly light the churches of Christ throughout the entire world. And not even those outside our communion[14] were prevented from sharing in the same blessings, or at least from coming under their influence and enjoying a part of the benefits bestowed upon us by God.

All men, then, were freed from the oppression of the tyrants, and being released from the former ills, one in one way and another in another acknowledged the defender of the pious to be the only true God. And we especially who placed our hopes in the Christ of God had unspeakable gladness, and a certain inspired joy bloomed for all of us, when we saw every place which shortly before had been desolated by the impieties of the tyrants reviving as if from a long and death-fraught pestilence, and temples again rising from their foundations to an immense height, and receiving a splendor far greater than that of the old ones which had been destroyed. But the supreme rulers also confirmed to us still more extensively the munificence of God by repeated ordinances in behalf of the Christians; and personal letters of the emperor were sent to the bishops, with honors and gifts of money. It may not be unfitting to insert these documents, translated from the Roman into the Greek tongue, at the proper place in this book, as in a sacred tablet, that they may remain as a memorial to all who shall come after us. . . .

To him, therefore, God granted, from Heaven above, the deserved fruit of piety, the trophies of victory over the impious, and he cast the guilty one with all his counselors and friends prostrate at the feet of Constantine. For when Licinius[15] carried his madness to the last extreme, the emperor, the friend of God, thinking that he ought no longer to be tolerated, acting upon the basis of

---

[11]The Bible, Psalms 98:1–2.

[12]Psalms 46:8–9.

[13]Psalms 37:35–36.

[14]Non-Christians and Christian heretics.

[15]Licinius had been coemperor since 308. In 313 he and Constantine allied, with Constantine taking the western half of the empire. In 316 Constantine attacked Licinius's lands, on the pretext that Licinius was persecuting Christians, and confiscated a major portion of the eastern half of the empire. In 324 Constantine returned to complete the job, on the same pretext. After capturing Licinius and uniting the entire empire under his control, Constantine had his former colleague murdered within a year. Circumstances thus forced Eusebius to excise earlier complimentary allusions to Licinius from his last edition of the *Ecclesiastical History*.

sound judgment, and mingling the firm principles of justice with humanity, gladly determined to come to the protection of those who were oppressed by the tyrant, and undertook, by putting a few destroyers out of the way, to save the greater part of the human race. For when he had formerly exercised humanity alone and had shown mercy to him who was not worthy of sympathy, nothing was accomplished; for Licinius did not renounce his wickedness, but rather increased his fury against the people that were subject to him, and there was left to the afflicted no hope of salvation, oppressed as they were by a savage beast. Wherefore, the protector of the virtuous, mingling hatred for evil with love for good, went forth with his son Crispus,[16] a most beneficent prince, and extended a saving right hand to all that were perishing. Both of them, father and son, under the protection, as it were, of God, the universal King, with the Son of God, the Savior of all, as their leader and ally, drew up their forces on all sides against the enemies of the Deity and won an easy victory; God having prospered them in the battle in all respects according to their wish. Thus, suddenly, and sooner than can be told, those who yesterday and the day before breathed death and threatening were no more, and not even their names were remembered, but their inscriptions and their honors suffered the merited disgrace. And the things which Licinius with his own eyes had seen come upon the former impious tyrants he himself likewise suffered, because he did not receive instruction nor learn wisdom from the chastisements of his neighbors, but followed the same path of impiety which they had trod, and was justly hurled over the same precipice. Thus he lay prostrate.

But Constantine, the mightiest victor, adorned with every virtue of piety, together with his son Crispus, a most God-beloved prince, and in all respects like his father, recovered the East which belonged to them; and they formed one united Roman empire as of old, bringing under their peaceful sway the whole world from the rising of the sun to the opposite quarter, both north and south, even to the extremities of the declining day. All fear therefore of those who had formerly afflicted them was taken away from men, and they celebrated splendid and festive days. Everything was filled with light, and those who before were downcast beheld each other with smiling faces and beaming eyes. With dances and hymns, in city and country, they glorified first of all God the universal King, because they had been thus taught, and then the pious emperor with his God-beloved children. There was oblivion of past evils and forgetfulness of every deed of impiety; there was enjoyment of present benefits and expectation of those yet to come. Edicts full of clemency and laws containing tokens of benevolence and true piety were issued in every place by the victorious emperor. Thus after all tyranny had been purged away, the empire which belonged to them was preserved firm and without a rival for Constantine and his sons alone. And having obliterated the godlessness of their predecessors, recognizing the benefits conferred upon them by God, they exhibited their love of virtue and their love of God, and their piety and gratitude to the Deity, by the deed which they performed in the sight of all men.

---

[16]Crispus was Constantine's eldest son and had held the title of *Caesar* (deputy emperor) since 317. He served with distinction in the war of 324, commanding Constantine's naval forces. For reasons unknown, Constantine ordered his execution in 326.

The Christian Emperor

▼▼▼

50 ▾ *THE BARBERINI IVORY*

Roman society consistently perceived its emperors as embodiments of the might of Roman sacred authority and of the divinely ordained destiny that Virgil had celebrated in the *Aeneid* (source 30). For this reason, since the days of Caesar Augustus, the Romans allowed the inhabitants of the empire's eastern provinces to revere the emperors as living gods, and even in the West, where divine kingship was not a well-rooted tradition, Romans deified their early emperors once they had shed the coils of mortal life. In a few extraordinary cases, Roman authorities even encouraged the worship of a still-living emperor in areas of the West, such as happened in Britain in an attempt to impose Roman order on a rebellious populace (source 31). During the late third century, however, Roman emperors instituted an empire-wide cult of emperor worship in an attempt to reinstitute public belief in the power and destiny of Rome amidst the terrible crises that threatened the very existence of the empire. Christian refusal to acknowledge the divinity of Rome's emperors played a major role in inciting Emperor Diocletian and his colleagues to institute the Great Persecution in 303. A few years later, however, Constantine the Great embraced Christianity, which worshiped only one god-man — Jesus Christ. How was the new Christian Empire to treat the emperor?

A sixth-century sculptural masterpiece known as the *Barberini Ivory* (named after later owners of the work) gives us insight into the way in which the Christian Roman World perceived its emperors. The sculpture consists of five interlocking panels and was probably crafted in *Constantinople,* the *New Rome* on the Bosporus that Constantine I had made the capital of the reunited empire in 330 (see Chapter 10). The carving portrays either Emperor Anastasius I (r. 491–518) or Emperor Justinian (r. 527–565) receiving the submission of various barbarian peoples. The triumphant emperor emerges on horseback out of the panel, while a female personification of Earth supports his right foot. Beneath the horse's hooves, Asiatic *Scythians* and Indians, led by a winged female spirit of Victory, offer tokens of submission. The Scythians, who no longer existed as an identifiable people, represented all of the pastoral peoples of Inner Asia who dwelt beyond the Black Sea. Behind the lance that the emperor holds, a soldier dressed in Scythian garments raises his hand in surrender. Farther to the emperor's right, a Roman general approaches, bearing a statuette of the spirit of Victory, who herself carries a laurel crown. A third winged Victory hovers over the mane of the emperor's horse. Crowning the whole composition is a bust of a youthful, beardless Christ in majesty, flanked by two angels. Within the *nimbus,* or halo, that surrounds Christ are symbols for the sun, the moon, and the stars. The Constantinopolitan artist has preserved Greco-Roman naturalism, particularly in regard to the bodies of humans and animals, and has also retained several traditional pagan symbols and motifs, such as the allegorical figures of Earth and Victory. At the same time, as we see in the figures of Christ and his flanking angels, the sculptor has transformed certain pre-Christian artistic types into figures representing Christian beliefs. This adaptation was certainly not new. Christians had been adapting pagan artistic conven-

The Barberini Ivory

tions to their own needs since the first century C.E., and by the sixth century, such *Christ in Majesty* scenes as we see at the top of the panel were quite common.

QUESTIONS FOR ANALYSIS

1. How do we know that the figures on the bottom left of the panel (our right) represent Indians?

2. What message is implied by portraying peoples from lands that lay outside of the empire?
3. What is the overall message of this sculpture? Be as complete as possible in answering this question.

▼▼▼

Beyond the Roman World

Christianity acquired a sense of universal mission quite early. According to the Gospel of Mark, composed probably sometime between 65 and 75 C.E. and written with a gentile, or non-Jewish, audience in mind, the Risen Jesus instructed his followers to "go out into the whole world and proclaim the Good News to all creation" (Mark 16:15–16).

According to tradition, the apostles divided up the known world by lot and went forth to preach in the regions that fell to each. Thomas, for example, went to India and Matthew to Ethiopia. Regardless of the historicity of this legend, given the steady commerce from the Roman Empire to the Horn of East Africa, southern Arabia, and India in the time of Pliny the Elder (source 36), it is more than likely that before the first century C.E. ended, Christian missionaries had followed the monsoon trade winds into the Indian Ocean. Likewise, the land routes of the so-called Silk Road that connected Han China with the Mediterranean World allowed missionaries to move east from Roman Syria and Anatolia into the heartland of the Parthian Empire and beyond. The Christian Church of the Anatolian city of Edessa (today Sanliurfa in Turkey), situated at the crossroads of two major trade routes and on the border between the Roman and Persian worlds, played a major role in the transmission of Christianity into the Caucasus, Mesopotamia, western Central Asia, and northern India by at least the end of the second century and maybe quite a bit earlier.

As the following two sources show, this was just the beginning. Our first source deals with the acceptance of Christianity as a state religion by a people of the Caucasuses known as the *Georgians;* the second source illustrates how Christianity traveled all the way to China along the Silk Road in the early seventh century. Of course, as we shall see in Chapter 10, during these same early centuries Christianity also moved west into lands that would later become known as Western Europe.

Georgia Becomes a Christian State
▼▼▼
51 ▼ *Rufinus of Aquileia, CHURCH HISTORY*

The distinction between Europe and Asia is a false one. Rather than being separate continents (an idea created by ancient Greek geographers), they are unequal parts of one great landmass that we call Eurasia. Nevertheless, western geographers have for centuries seen the region of the Caucasus Mountains — the area between the Black and Caspian seas that today includes southwest Russia, Azerbaijan, Armenia, and Georgia — as a rough boundary between Europe and Asia.

Christian grave sites dating from the second and third centuries indicate that Christianity made inroads into the Caucasus region fairly early, but it was only in the fourth century that two of its cultures, the Armenians and the Georgians, accepted the faith as a state religion. Indeed, the fourth century was pivotal in this regard. Early in the century Constantine I accepted Christianity as the new Roman imperial cult, and the Ethiopian kingdom of Axum adopted Christianity as the new religion of its kings sometime around 333, if traditional dates can be accepted. Armenia seems to have accepted Christianity as its official religion around 300. Neighboring Georgians, a people who speak a language that is unrelated to any known tongue of Eurasia, followed sometime probably between 325 and 355, during a period when Roman influence penetrated their land, thanks to a peace treaty between Rome and Persia.

Our earliest extant account of the Georgians' acceptance of Christianity comes from the pen of Tyrannius Rufinus (ca. 345–410/411), a Christian Roman from Aquileia in northeast Italy. Rufinus resided in the Eastern Mediterranean, the home- and heartland of Christianity, from 373 to 397, and it was there that he became imbued with its monastic spirituality and also mastered Greek. Following his return to Italy, Rufinus undertook to translate Eusebius of Caesarea's *Ecclesiastical History* from Greek into Latin around the year 402. In that year Gothic warriors under the leadership of Alaric had marched into Italy and laid siege to Milan. Eusebius's history, which had been completed in 325, presented a triumphalist vision of Christian history, and the consolation that it offered the Christians of Italy in this time of trials was sorely needed. In 402 or 403 Rufinus completed an abridged translation of Eusebius's history with an additional two books of his own composition that brought the story down to 395.

Rufinus's history is also triumphalist, ending on an upbeat note with the reception into Heaven of the pious emperor Theodosius I (r. 379–395) and the Christian Roman Empire established on a firm foundation. Unhappily for Rufinus, he lived long enough to learn of the sack of the city of Rome by Alaric's Goths in 410.

QUESTIONS FOR ANALYSIS

1. Is there anything about this story that seems to have the ring of pagan legend dressed up in Christian clothing? What and why? Be specific.
2. Is there anything in this story that seems to have the ring of authenticity? What and why? Be specific.
3. What might we infer about gender roles in fourth-century Georgia?
4. What does this story suggest about Roman-Georgian relations in the fourth century?
5. Based on clues contained within this story, what factors and motives do you think were behind the Georgian royal family's acceptance of Christianity? Support your inferences with specific reference to the evidence.

It was at this time[1] too that the Georgians, who dwell in the region of Pontus,[2] accepted the word of God and faith in the kingdom to come. The cause of this great benefit was a woman captive[3] who lived among them and led such a faithful, sober, and modest life, spending all of her days and nights in sleepless supplications to God, that the very novelty of it began to be wondered at by the barbarians. Their curiosity led them to ask what she was about. She replied with the truth: that in this manner she simply worshiped Christ as God. This answer made the barbarians wonder only at the novelty of the name, although it is true, as often happens, that her very perseverance made the common women wonder if she were deriving some benefit from such great devotion.

Now it is said that they have the custom that, if a child falls sick, it is taken around by its mother to each of the houses to see if anyone knows of a proven remedy to apply to the illness. And when one of the women had brought her child around to everyone, according to custom, and had found no remedy in any of the houses, she went to the woman captive as well to see if she knew of anything. She answered that she knew of no human remedy, but declared that Christ her God, whom she worshiped, could give it the healing despaired of by humans. And after she had put the child on her hair shirt and poured out above it her prayer to the Lord, she gave the infant back to its mother in good health. Word of this got around to many people, and news of the wonderful deed reached the ears of the queen, who was suffering from a bodily illness of the gravest sort and had been reduced to a state of absolute despair. She asked for the woman captive to be brought to her. She declined to go, lest she appear to pretend to more than was proper to her sex. The queen ordered that she herself be brought to the captive's hovel. Having placed her likewise on her hair shirt and invoked Christ's name, no sooner was her prayer done than she had her stand up healthy and vigorous, and taught her that it was Christ, God and Son of God most high, who had conferred healing upon her, and advised her to invoke him whom she should know to be the author of her life and well-being, for he it was who allotted kingdoms to kings and life to mortals. She returned joyfully home and disclosed the affair to her husband,[4] who wanted to know the reason for this sudden return to health. When he in his joy at his wife's cure ordered gifts to be presented to the woman, she said, "O king, the captive deigns to accept none of these things. She despises gold, rejects silver, and battens on fasting as though it were food. This alone may we give her as a gift, if we worship as God the Christ who cured me when she called upon him."

But the king was not then inclined to do so and put it off for the time, although his wife urged him often, until it happened one day when he was hunting in the woods with his companions that a thick darkness fell upon the day, and with the light removed there was no longer any way for his blind steps through the grim and awful night. Each of his companions wandered off a different way, while he, left alone in the thick darkness which surrounded him, did not know what to do or where to turn, when suddenly there arose in his heart, which was near to losing hope of being saved, the thought that if the Christ preached to his wife by the woman captive were really God, he might now free him from this darkness so that he could from then on abandon all the others and worship him. No sooner had he vowed to do so, not even verbally but only mentally, than the daylight returned to the world

---

[1]The establishment of a Christian Church in India during the reign of Constantine I. Contrary to the more popular tradition, Rufinus does not credit the Apostle Thomas with bringing Christianity to India in the first century. Rather, he credits Frumentius, a captive-turned-missionary, with having planted the seeds of Christianity in India in the early fourth century.

[2]The Black Sea.
[3]A later Georgian tradition accords her the name Nino.
[4]Legend identifies him as Mirian, and he is usually identified with King Meribanes, a contemporary of Emperor Constantine I.

and guided the king safely to the city. He explained directly to the queen what had happened. He required that the woman captive be summoned at once and hand on to him her manner of worship, insisting that from then on he would venerate no god but Christ. The captive came, instructed him that Christ is God, and explained, as far as it was lawful for a woman to disclose such things,[5] the ways of making petition and offering reverence. She advised that a church be built and described its shape.

The king therefore called together all of his people and explained the matter from the beginning, what had happened to the queen and him, taught them the faith, and before even being initiated into sacred things became the apostle of his nation. The men believed because of the king, the women because of the queen, and with everyone desiring the same thing a church was put up without delay. The outer walls having quickly been raised, it was time to put the columns in place. When the first and second had been set up and they came to the third, they used all the machines and the strength of men and oxen to get it raised halfway up to an inclined position, but no machine could lift it the rest of the way, not even with efforts repeated again and again; with everyone exhausted, it would not budge. Everyone was confounded, the king's enthusiasm waned, and no one could think what to do. But when nightfall intervened and everyone went away and all mortal labors ceased, the woman captive remained inside alone, passing the night in prayer.

And when the worried king entered in the morning with all his people, he saw the column, which so many machines and people had been unable to move, suspended upright just above its base: not placed upon it, but hanging about one foot in the air. Then indeed all the people looking on glorified God and accepted the witness of the miracle before them that the king's faith and the captive's religion were true. And behold, while everyone was still in the grip of wonder and astonishment, before their very eyes the column, with no one touching it, gradually and with perfect balance settled down upon its base. After that the remaining columns were raised with such ease that all that were left were put in place that day.

Now after the church had been magnificently built and the people were thirsting even more deeply for God's faith, on the advice of the captive an embassy of the entire people was sent to the emperor Constantine,[6] and what had happened was explained to him. They implored him to send priests who could complete God's work begun among them. He dispatched them with all joy and honor, made far happier by this than if he had annexed to the Roman empire unknown peoples and kingdoms. That this happened was related to us by that most faithful man Bacurius, the king of that nation who in our realm held the rank of *comes domesticorum*[7] and whose chief concern was for religion and truth; when he was *dux limitis*[8] in Palestine he spent some time with us in Jerusalem in great concord of spirit.[9]

---

[5]In other words, she was not a (male) priest.
[6]Many scholars point out that Rufinus tended to ascribe to Constantine and his time events that actually took place during the reign of his son Constantius II (r. 337–361).
[7]Overseer of household attendants — he was in charge of the imperial court garrison.

[8]General of the frontier — he commanded troops in a frontier district.
[9]The Roman historian Ammianus Marcellinus places Bacarius at the disastrous Battle of Adrianople of 378, where he commanded Roman archers and lightly armed footsoldiers.

Christianity Comes to China
▼▼▼

52 ▼ Bishop Adam, *THE CHRISTIAN MONUMENT*

The Silk Road provided missionaries, as well as merchants, with a convenient route into the heart of China. During the early years of the Tang Dynasty (618–907), roughly down to 750, China was open to the outside world and its influences (see Chapter 9). As evidence of that, in 635 a *Nestorian* Christian bishop from Persia named Aluoben (Abraham?) arrived in Chang'an, China's capital city.

In the fifth century the Nestorian Christians of Syria, who drew a sharp distinction between the human and divine natures of Jesus, had been declared *heretics* (deviant believers) by the imperial Roman Church. The charges of heresy were motivated more by political considerations than theological doctrine, but the result was no less devastating. The Nestorians were effectively denied a place within the imperial Christian Church that looked to Constantinople and Rome as its twin centers of authority (see Chapter 10). Moving east, the Nestorians found a home in the Sassanid Empire of Persia. The Sassanid *shahs,* or emperors, had persecuted Persian Christians between 340 and 401, mainly because Persia's traditional enemy, the Roman Empire, had accepted the Christian faith, and Christianity was now identified, in Sassanid eyes, with a menacing power to the west. However, probably because the Nestorians were themselves identified as enemies of the imperial Roman Church, Nestorianism enjoyed Sassanid imperial protection and flourished in Persia's two major cultural centers: Mesopotamia (also called *Babylonia*) and Iran.

From Persia, Nestorian Christian ideas traveled farther east to the Turkic peoples of Inner Asia and finally to China. Bishop Aluoben was not the first Nestorian to reach China, but he is the first of whom we have any record.

Aluoben was fortunate that he arrived in the reign of *Tang Taizong* (r. 626–649), the second Tang emperor. Of mixed Chinese and Turko-Mongol descent, Tang Taizong was open to novelties from the western steppes, including Buddhism, Manichaeism (source 54), and Nestorian Christianity. Under the emperor's protection, Aluoben established a monastery, which initially housed twenty-one monks, probably all of them Persians.

In 781 a scholar-bishop named Adam, who also bore the Chinese name Jing Jing, composed a short history of the early fortunes of the Nestorian Church in China. Under the patronage of a prominent Chinese-born Nestorian of Persian descent named Yazdbozid, whose Chinese name was Yisi, Adam's history was then inscribed on a nine-foot-high stone memorial that bears the heading "A Monument Commemorating the Propagation of the Daqin (Syrian) Luminous Religion in the Middle Kingdom (China)." Interestingly, Yazdbozid, who apparently was Adam's father, was an assistant bishop in the Nestorian Church and had formerly served as a high-ranking general in the Chinese army and an imperial civil official. The career of this Christian priest, warrior, and civil servant of Persian heritage nicely illustrates the cosmopolitanism of early Tang, in which non-Chinese were called to the imperial service. Yazdbozid is also a symbol of the Nestorian Church's eighth-century political connections, which gave it a measure of influence in Tang China.

That good fortune did not last, however. By tying its fortunes to the patronage of the Tang emperors, this minor foreign religion suffered irreversible losses when the empire waged an assault on foreign religions between 840 and 846. Although some small communities possibly survived, Nestorian Christianity essentially disappeared in China by the late tenth century. It would only reappear in the twelfth and thirteenth centuries, brought in from Central Asia by various Turkic tribes that had adopted the faith. But it would suffer a second eclipse in the fourteenth century with the rise of the anti-foreign Ming Dynasty.

Regardless of future reverses, the Nestorian community's *Christian Monument* celebrates an age when China was open to foreign innovations, including this faith from Southwest Asia.

QUESTIONS FOR ANALYSIS

1. Review source 20. How does Adam borrow Daoist imagery and terms to describe Nestorian Christianity? Why do you think he does so?
2. Can you find any Buddhist and Confucian overtones in this memorial? How and why does Adam use them?
3. What reasons did Emperor Tang Taizong give for allowing this new religion into his empire? What does your answer suggest about the man and his reign?
4. How does the memorial deal with the issue of Christianity's reverses under Empress Wu? What do you infer from your answer?
5. What do those assaults on Nestorian Christianity suggest to you?
6. How does the memorial describe Christianity's imperial patrons? What do you infer from your answer?
7. At the apex of the monument is an ornate engraved cross, which rises from a white cloud, a symbol of Daoism, and beneath the cloud is a Buddhist lotus blossom. In light of the text of the memorial, what do you think this carved image means?
8. This and the preceding source show us how Christian missionaries used monarchs and their families in their attempts to propagate the faith. What were the advantages and disadvantages of that tactic?

"The *Way*" would not have spread so widely had it not been for the Sage,[1] and the Sage would not have been so great were it not for "The *Way*." Ever since the Sage and "The *Way*" were united together as the two halves of an indentured deed would agree,[2] then the world became refined and enlightened.

When the accomplished Emperor Taizong began his magnificent career in glory and splendor over the (recently) established dynasty[3] and ruled his people with intelligence, he proved himself to be a brilliant Sage.

And behold there was a highly virtuous man named Aluoben in the Kingdom of Daqin.[4] Au-

---

[1]Emperor Tang Taizong.
[2]Just as the two copies of a legal contract executed in duplicate would agree in all respects.
[3]A great warrior even in his teens, Tang Taizong (his given name was Li Shimin) was a driving force in the war that toppled the short-lived *Sui Dynasty* (589–618) and placed

his father, Li Yuan, on the throne as first Tang emperor. His father later abdicated the throne in Li Shimin's favor.
[4]Syria. We should not take it literally. Aluoben came from the west with a religion that was shaped in Syria. Thus Iran, Mesopotamia, and Syria are all lumped together under this term.

guring (of the Sage, i.e., Emperor) from the azure sky,[5] he decided to carry the true Sutras[6] (of the True Way) with him, and observing the course of the winds, he made his way (to China) through difficulties and perils. Thus in the ninth year of the period named Zhenguan (635 C.E.) he arrived at Chang'an.[7] The Emperor dispatched his Minister, Duke Fang Xuanling, with a guard of honor, to the western suburb to meet the visitor and conduct him to the Palace. The Sutras (Scriptures) were translated in the Imperial Library. (His Majesty) investigated "The *Way*" in his own forbidden apartments,[8] and being deeply convinced of its correctness and truth, he gave special orders for its propagation.

In the twelfth year of the Zhenguan Period (638 C.E.) in the seventh month of Autumn, the following Imperial Rescript was issued: —

"'The Way' had not, at all times and in all places, the selfsame name; the Sage had not, at all times and in all places, the selfsame human body. (Heaven) caused a suitable religion to be instituted for every region and clime so that each one of the races of mankind might be saved. Bishop Aluoben of the kingdom of Daqin, bringing with him the Sutras and Images,[9] has come from afar and presented them at our Capital. Having carefully examined the scope of his teaching, we find it to be mysteriously spiritual and of silent operation. Having observed its principal and most essential points, we reached the conclusion that they cover all that is most important in life. Their language is free from perplexing expressions; their principles are so simple that they 'remain as the fish would remain even after the net (of the language) were forgotten.' This Teaching

is helpful to all creatures and beneficial to all men. So let it have free course throughout the Empire."

Accordingly, the proper authorities built a Daqin monastery in the Yining Ward[10] in the Capital and twenty-one priests were ordained and attached to it. The virtue of the honored House of Zhou had died away;[11] (the rider on) the black chariot had ascended to the West.[12] But (virtue revived) and "The *Way*" was brilliantly manifested again at the moment when the Great Tang began its rule, whilst the breezes of the Luminous (Religion) came eastward to fan it.[13] Immediately afterwards, the proper officials were again ordered to take a faithful portrait of the Emperor, and to have it copied on the walls of the monastery. The celestial beauty appeared in its variegated colors, and the dazzling splendor illuminated the Luminous "portals" (i.e., congregation). The sacred features (lit., foot-prints) (thus preserved) conferred great blessing (on the monastery), and illuminated the Church for evermore. . . .

The great Emperor Gaozong (650–683 C.E.) succeeded most respectfully to his ancestors; and giving the True Religion the proper elegance and finish, he caused monasteries of the Luminous Religion to be founded in every prefecture. Accordingly, he honored Aluoben by conferring on him the office of the Great Patron and Spiritual Lord of the Empire. The Law (of the Luminous Religion) spread throughout the ten provinces, and the Empire enjoyed great peace and concord. Monasteries were built in many cities, whilst every family enjoyed the great blessings (of Salvation).

---

[5]He discovered in the heavens signs of the Sage Emperor.
[6]The Bible.
[7]Tang China's capital, Chang'an (modern Xi'an), was probably the largest and richest city in the world in the seventh century.
[8]The private imperial chambers.
[9]Artistic representations, or *icons,* of Jesus and the saints.
[10]The name of a street in the western part of the city.
[11]Rule by virtue, as established in the early Zhou Dynasty and later taught by Confucius, had departed long before the rise of Tang.

[12]According to one tradition, when the Eastern Zhou Dynasty (770–256 B.C.E.) lost its virtue, Laozi, the founder of Daoism, abandoned China in disgust. He went west (or ascended to the Western Heaven) in a chariot drawn by a black ox, thereby leaving China without a moral guide. The Tang Dynasty shared Laozi's family name, Li, and claimed descent from him.
[13]Laozi had gone west (note 12); now the Way was returning from that direction.

During the period of Shengli (698–699 C.E.),[14] the Buddhists, taking advantage of these circumstances, and using all their strength raised their voices (against the Luminous Religion) in the Eastern Zhou,[15] and at the end of the Xiandian Period (712 C.E.)[16] some inferior scholars[17] ridiculed and derided it, slandering and speaking against it in the Western Hao.[18] But there came the Head-priest (or Archdeacon) Luohan,[19] Bishop Jilie,[20] and others, as well as Noblemen from the "Golden" region[21] and the eminent priests who had forsaken all worldly interests. All these men co-operated in restoring the great fundamental principles and united together to re-bind the broken ties.

The Emperor Xuanzong,[22] who was surnamed "the Perfection of the Way," ordered the Royal prince, the King of Ningguo and four other Royal princes to visit the blessed edifices (i.e., monastery) personally and to set up altars therein. Thus the "consecrated rafters," which had been temporarily bent, were once more straightened and strengthened, whilst the sacred foundation-stones which for a time had lost the right position were restored and perfected. In the early part of the period Tianbao (742 C.E.) he gave orders to his general Gao Lishi to carry the faithful portraits of the Five Emperors[23] and to have them placed securely in the monastery, and also to take the Imperial gift of one hundred pieces of silk

with him. Making the most courteous and reverent obeisance to the Imperial portraits, we feel as though "we were in a position to hang on to the Imperial bow and sword, in case the beard of the Dragon should be out of reach."[24] Although the solar horns[25] shine forth with such dazzling brilliance, yet the gracious Imperial faces are so gentle that they may be gazed upon at a distance less than a foot.

In the third year of the same period (744 C.E.) there was a priest named Jihe[26] in the Kingdom of Daqin. Observing the stars, he decided to engage in the work of conversion; and looking toward the sun (i.e., eastward), he came to pay court to the most honorable Emperor. The Imperial orders were given to the Head-priest (Archdeacon) Luohan, priest Pulun[27] and others, seven in all, to perform services to cultivate merit and virtue with this Bishop Jihe in the Xingqing Palace. Thereupon the monastery-names, composed and written by the Emperor himself, began to appear on the monastery gates; and the front-tablets to bear the Dragon-writing (i.e., the Imperial hand-writing).[28] The monastery was resorted to by (visitors) whose costumes resembled the shining feathers of the king-fisher bird whilst all (the buildings) shone forth with the splendor of the sun. The Imperial tablets hung high in the air and their radiance flamed as though vying with the sun. The gifts of the Imperial favor are

[14]One of several periods in the reign of Empress Wu, who ruled the empire in her own name from 690 to 705. She gained effective control over the state around 654, but at first used several puppet emperors to mask her power.
[15]Empress Wu changed the name of her short-lived dynasty to *Zhou* and moved her primary capital east to Luoyang, the capital city of the ancient Eastern Zhou Dynasty (770–256 B.C.E.). She declared Buddhism the official state religion in 691 and seems to have encouraged persecution of Christianity, although persecution did not become an articulated state policy. In 698 a mob sacked the Nestorian church in Luoyang.
[16]The last year of disorder following Empress Wu's retirement in 705.
[17]Probably Confucians, but possibly Daoists. Maybe both.
[18]*Hao* was the name of Chang'an when it was the capital of the Western Zhou Dynasty (ca. 1050–771 B.C.E.). Hostile crowds attacked and violated the monastery in the Yining Ward, which Tang Taizong had patronized.

[19]Abraham.
[20]Gabriel?
[21]From the West, the source of so much gold and silver that flowed into Tang China by virtue of China's favorable balance of trade across the Silk Road.
[22]Under Emperor Xuanzong (r. 712–756) Tang China reached the heights of its greatness and prosperity.
[23]The legendary Five Sage Emperors, who established the foundations of Chinese civilization in predynastic times.
[24]Although the emperor (the dragon) might be far away, his power extends to the monastery.
[25]The radiance emanating from the faces of the Five Sage Emperors.
[26]George.
[27]Paul?
[28]The emperor composed an inscription to be fixed above the monastery's door. Almost all public buildings in China had similar inscriptions.

immense like the highest peak of the highest mountains in the South, and the food of its rich benevolence is as deep as the depths of the Eastern sea.

There is nothing that "The *Way*" cannot effect (through the Sage); and whatever it effects, it is right of us to define it as such (in eulogy). There is nothing that the Sage cannot accomplish (through "The *Way*"); and whatever He accomplishes, it is right we should proclaim it in writing (as the Sage's work).

▼▼▼

Religious Exchange and Interchange

The Judaic roots of Christianity are clear. Less obvious, but equally important, are the influences of late antiquity's *mystery religions* on Christian belief and expression. The Hellenistic and Roman Eras witnessed large numbers of people turning to religions that scholars categorize as the mystery religions, or the mystery cults. What they had in common was psychic comfort in an often hostile world and the promise of relief, both on Earth and in the hereafter, from the ills and sorrows that attend all humans. The attraction of these religions, which largely originated in the eastern Mediterranean and Southwest Asia but spread throughout the Roman Empire, became pronounced in the first century C.E., when the Greco-Roman World became increasingly vast and complex, thereby contributing to a high level of anxiety and alienation. As the empire began to undergo frightening challenges from the late second century onward, conversions to the empire's many mystery religions multiplied many times over.

Members of the various mystery religions believed that, through a process of conversion and ritual initiation, a devotee was transformed into a new person. By virtue of that transformation, or rebirth, the new member was admitted to the religion's mysteries, or secret knowledge, that led to everlasting tranquility. Membership in this select body of initiates provided a believer with the immediate support of a cohesive community of like-minded individuals and the promise of personal salvation. The various savior deities who offered such aid to their worshipers included *Mithras,* an Iranian sun god whose cult was open only to men; *Cybele,* or the Great Mother, a fertility goddess from Anatolia; and Dionysus, whose cult we saw in source 26. Most popular of all was the goddess *Isis,* whose temples could be found throughout the empire. Isis originated more than 2,500 years earlier in Egypt's Old Kingdom as the consort of Osiris (sources 3 and 9), but in the Hellenistic Era she assimilated the religious identities and functions of many foreign goddesses to emerge transformed into an ecumenical loving mother of all humanity. In the first of our two sources we shall explore the impact on early Christianity of a family of related mystery religions known as *Gnosticism.*

Equally often overlooked is Christianity's impact on other religions of salvation. In our second source we will examine some of the ways in which *Manichaeism* borrowed from Christian teachings. As both sources illustrate, cultural syncretism was a two-way street during Christianity's formative years.

Gnostic Christianity:
The Secret Knowledge of Jesus
▼▼▼

53 ▼ *THE GOSPEL OF THOMAS*

In 1945 two Egyptian farmers unearthed a jar containing fifty-two early Christian texts written in Coptic, the common tongue of late ancient Egypt. Known collectively as the *Nag Hammadi Library,* the texts, most of which were previously unknown, shed new light on an important but little understood branch of early Christianity known as the *Gnostics*.

Gnosticism is an all-encompassing term for a widespread, Hellenistic religious philosophy that was based on the belief that salvation is attainable through a secret, mystical knowledge, which is called *gnosis* in Greek. Gnosticism predated Christianity, and it manifested itself in many different varieties. There was no single, all-encompassing Gnostic Church. Rather, there were many different Gnostic sects, most of which were pagan, but there were even Jewish Gnostics. Notwithstanding its largely pagan associations, Gnosticism made inroads into early Christianity and influenced its development. Ultimately rejected as *heretics,* or wrong believers, by the mainstream Christian Church, Gnostic Christians suffered the fate of having their core teachings condemned and their books largely destroyed.

For that reason alone, the discovery of the Nag Hammadi Library excited scholarly interest. Of all the recovered texts, the one that drew the most attention was the *Gospel of Thomas*. Ascribed to the authorship of Jesus' twin brother, the Apostle Judas Thomas, it was composed during the second century C.E. or earlier, possibly about the same time that the *Gospel of Saint John,* the last of the four canonical, or officially approved, Gospels of the New Testament, was completed. One theory recently put forward by a leading scholar in the field is that the Gospel of John, the only Gospel that unambiguously presents Jesus as God incarnate (a unique being who was both God and human), was written in refutation of the teachings of the so-called Thomas Christians.

The Gospel of Thomas has no narrative; it simply consists of 113 sayings of Jesus. The reader who knows the four canonical Gospels of Matthew, Mark, Luke, and John will recognize some familiar passages. Many of the sayings, however, will seem foreign, possibly even strange. Cumulatively, the sayings portray Jesus as a purely spiritual, noncorporeal savior who imparts to a select few a secret wisdom that will enable them to discover within themselves the divine spark of heavenly light. Although the Gnostic vision did not become mainstream Christian theology, Gnosticism was one of many forces that left a mark on Christianity as it took shape within the late Hellenistic world.

QUESTIONS FOR ANALYSIS

1. What does saying 22 seem to say? Does it help to compare it with the statues of *Hevajra* and *Shiva Nataraja* (sources 40 and 42)?

2. Sayings 49 and 50 are overtly Gnostic. What do they suggest about Gnostic beliefs?
3. What does saying 70 mean? What about saying 75? Compare these sayings with the *Upanishads* (source 14). What conclusions follow from this comparative analysis?
4. How and where does one gain this knowledge, or *gnosis,* and how difficult is it to attain it?
5. What is there about the teachings of the *Gospel of Thomas* that contradicts the *Gospel of John*'s claim that "God sent His Son into the world . . . so that through Him the world might be saved. No one who believes in Him shall be judged, but whoever does not believe is already judged because that person does not believe in God's only Son" (John 3:17–18)?
6. Compare these sayings with the biblical passages cited in the notes. What do you infer from this comparison?

Prologue

These are the secret sayings that the living Jesus[1] spoke and Judas Thomas the Twin[2] recorded.

Saying 1

He said, "Whoever finds the interpretation of these sayings will not taste death."

Saying 2

Jesus said, "Let one who seeks not stop seeking until one finds.
    When one finds, one will be disturbed.
    When one is disturbed, one will be amazed, and will reign over all."

Saying 3

Jesus said, "If your leaders say to you, 'Behold, the kingdom is in the sky,' then the birds in the sky will get there before you. If they say to you, 'It is in the sea,' then the fish will get there before you.
    "Rather, the kingdom is inside you and outside you.[3] When you know yourselves, then you will be known, and will understand that you are children of the living Father. But if you do not know

yourselves, then you live in poverty, and embody poverty." . . .

Saying 9

Jesus said, "Behold, the sower went out, took a handful of seeds, and scattered them. Some fell on the road, and the birds came and ate them. Others fell on rock, and they did not take root in the soil or produce any heads of grain. Others fell among thorns, and the thorns choked the seeds and worms consumed them. Still others fell on good soil, and brought forth a good crop: it yielded sixty per measure and one hundred twenty per measure."[4] . . .

Saying 22

Jesus saw some babies nursing. He said to his disciples, "These nursing babies are like those who enter the kingdom."[5]
    They said to him, "Then shall we enter the kingdom as babies?"
    Jesus said to them,
        "When you make the two into one,
        when you make the inner like the outer
            and the outer like the inner,
            and the upper like the lower,

---

[1]Jesus who offered the life of *gnosis.*
[2]According to a Syriac Christian tradition, Jesus had a twin brother, Judas Thomas.
[3]The Kingdom of God begins with knowledge of self and of God.

[4]Compare this with Matthew 13:3–9; Mark 4:3–9; and Luke 8:5–8.
[5]Compare this with Matthew 18:1–5; Mark 9:33–37; and Luke 9:46–48; also compare Matthew 19:13–15; Mark 10:13–16; and Luke 18:15–17.

when you make male and female into a
   single one,
   so that the male will not be male
   and the female will not be female,
when you make eyes replacing an eye,
   a hand replacing a hand,
   a foot replacing a foot,
   and an image replacing an image,
then you will enter the kingdom." . . .

Saying 36
Jesus said, "Do not worry, from morning to evening and from evening to morning, about what you will wear."[6] . . .

Saying 39
Jesus said, "The Pharisees and the scribes have taken the keys to knowledge and have hidden them. They have not entered, nor have they allowed those who want to enter to do so. As for you, be as clever as snakes and as innocent as doves." . . .

Saying 49
Jesus said,
   "Blessed are those who are alone and chosen:
      you will find the kingdom.[7]
   For you have come from it, and you will
      return there again."

Saying 50
Jesus said, "If some say to you, 'Where have you come from?' say to them, 'We have come from the light,
   where the light came into being by itself,
   established itself,
   and appeared in an image of light.'
"If they say to you, 'Are you the light?' say,
   'We are its children,
   and we are the chosen of the living Father.'
"If they ask you, 'What is the evidence of your Father in you?' tell them,
   'It is motion and rest.'" . . .

Saying 54
Jesus said,
   "Blessed are the poor:
      yours is the kingdom of Heaven."[8] . . .

Saying 58
Jesus said,
   "Blessed is one who has suffered:
      that one has found life."[9] . . .

Saying 68
Jesus said,
   "Blessed are you when you are hated and
      persecuted,
   and no one will discover the place where
      you have been persecuted."

Saying 69
Jesus said,
   "Blessed are those who have been persecuted
      in their hearts:
      they truly know the Father.
   "Blessed are those who are hungry,
      for the stomach of the famished will be
      filled."[10]

Saying 70
Jesus said,
   "If you bring forth what is within you,
      what you have will save you.
   If you do not have that within you,
      what you do not have within you will
        kill you." . . .

Saying 75
Jesus said,
   "I am the light that is over all things.
   I am all:
      all came forth from me,
      and all attained to me.
   Split a piece of wood,
      and I am there.
   Pick up a stone,
      and you will find me there." . . .

---

[6]Compare this with the Sermon on the Mount.
[7]Compare this with the Sermon on the Mount.
[8]Compare this with the Sermon on the Mount.
[9]Compare this with the Sermon on the Mount.
[10]Compare sayings 68 and 69 with the Sermon on the Mount.

Saying 113

Simon Peter[11] said to them, "Let Mary[12] leave us, because women are not worthy of life."

Jesus said, "Behold, I shall guide her so as to make her male, that she too may become a living spirit like you men.[13] For every woman who makes herself male will enter the kingdom of heaven."

---

[11]The Apostle Peter. Prior to being given the name *Peter* (Greek for "rock") by Jesus, his name was Simon.
[12]Several of Jesus' closest and most loyal female friends were named Mary. This might refer to *Mary Magdalene,* one of Jesus' inner circle of followers.

[13]The male (heavenly) principle must replace totally the female (earthly) principle.

Manichaeism: Enlightening the World
▼▼▼

54 ▼ *THE PARABLE ABOUT THE WORLD-OCEAN*

Gnosticism and mainstream, or *orthodox,* Christianity parted ways, but the Gnostic search for spiritual knowledge did not end there. In the third century C.E. a Persian prophet from Babylonia named *Mani* (216–276) founded a Gnostic religion that claimed a worldwide mission. Drawing deeply from Christian, Jewish, Hindu, Buddhist, and Zoroastrian sources, Mani articulated a *Religion of Light* whose message was aimed not at a small group of select initiates but at all of humanity. Indeed, *Manichaeism* became a major world religion, despite attempts to suppress it. Initially Manichaeism made major inroads into the Greco-Roman World, but the Christian Roman Empire fought back and largely ousted this Gnostic faith from the West before the sixth century was over. Manichaeism likewise enjoyed early success in Mesopotamia and Iran, but persecution by the Zoroastrian Sassanid Empire and the later triumph of Islam combined to produce a similar eclipse of Manichaeism in the land of its birth.

Regardless of these setbacks, Manichaeism did not die an early death. It traveled east along the Silk Road, making deep inroads in Central Asia and gaining a firm foothold in China, where it proved to be a strong rival to Buddhism and lasted into early modern times. By the late seventeenth century, however, very few living vestiges of Manichaeism remained in Central and East Asia, but certainly it had enjoyed a long life in those areas touched by the eastern portions of the Silk Road. This longevity was due in large part to Manichaean missionaries who were willing and able to take this religion, which had sprung largely from Christian, Jewish, and Zoroastrian roots, and translate it into terms understandable to Central and East Asians. For example, Manichaeism's *Jesus the Messiah,* a savior who will return to Earth, became identified with the *Buddha Maitreya,* a messianic Buddha of the future who was the focus of devotion in a number of Mahayana cults.

Babylonia was a religiously complex region in the third century. The fact that Mani was raised in a Gnostic Christian sect that maintained strong connections with Judaism hints at the religious syncretism that pervaded Mesopotamia. At age twenty-four Mani began his public preaching. Claiming direct revelation from

Jesus of Light, the divine, supreme revealer of the truth of the Light, Mani maintained that his revelation completed the revelations of three predecessors who had preached true religion: the Buddha, Zoroaster, and Jesus the Messiah, a fully divine historical being who was separate from Jesus of Light.

The essence of Mani's teaching was that there are two coeternal and coequal principles, Light and Darkness: *Light* is harmony and peace; *Darkness* is disorder and strife. Originally separated from one another, Light and Darkness came into conflict when Darkness attempted to possess Light for itself. Darkness's swallowing of part of the realm of Light led to the creation of the universe and humanity, in whom sparks of divine light reside within bodies that are ruled by Darkness. Humanity is now called upon to take part in the cosmic struggle. Once all the lost light is recovered, Darkness will be reduced to impotence, Light will reign supreme, and the universe will end.

The following document was written in the language of the people of the Central Asian region that the Chinese knew as *Kangju* and the Greco-Roman West called *Sogdiana* — an Iranian steppe culture located southeast of the Aral Sea (largely modern Uzbekistan and Tajikistan). Sogdian merchants were *the* major commercial travelers on the Silk Road in the period ca. 200–700. Although most Sogdians were Zoroastrians, some had converted to Manichaeism and introduced their religion to several Turkish tribes far to the east. One of these was the *Uighurs,* who moved from the Mongolian steppes to the oasis towns along the branch of the Silk Road that skirted the northern fringes of the forbidding Taklamakan Desert (also called the Tarim Basin). In the mid ninth century the Uighurs established a partially Manichaean state centered on the caravan city of Turfan, and it was probably there that some Uighur scribe copied this text, which was discovered at Turfan in the early twentieth century.

The text takes the form of a *parable,* or extended metaphor. In it Mani's revelation is likened to the *World-Ocean* into which all other rivers (previous religions) flow. If we read the parable carefully, we can discover several of Manichaeism's more important doctrines. Please note that words in parentheses are editorial explanations; words in brackets have been supplied by the editor to fill in the broken text.

QUESTIONS FOR ANALYSIS

1. According to the parable, is salvation possible outside of the Manichaean Church?
2. What does the Manichaean Church demand of all its members?
3. What is especially demanded of the *elect?*
4. Which of these articles reveal(s) the gnostic elements within Manichaeism?
5. What is the daily work of the Manichaean Church?

And the wonderful Religion of the Apostle [is similar] to the world-ocean [in ten ways].

{First}: It is wise (full of wisdom), and no one knows nor can estimate its wisdom . . . , nor the quantity and [number] of its sermons and explanations; and no one can comprehend it. The former religions are similar to the small waters which arise in [different places]. . . . [But] the religion of the Apostle which [is similar] to the great world-ocean can be [seen] in the whole world and in every place. And it is ripe to be presented in [the darkness] in a most open manner and to be proclaimed in all languages. And [one can] find the explanation and systematization (?) of all wisdom in it.

Second: The other shore that no one [knows] is the fragrant, wonderful Paradise that the living beings [on Earth], apart from the elect and the [auditors],[1] do not perceive and will never comprehend.

Third: The [waters] of the world-ocean have one taste, and the other waters have different tastes and appearances, but its own taste does not change. That is [the] deep wisdom of the Law and the commandments of the Religion, and the sweet, wonderful words that are preached. The fine parables and [their] explanations [and] interpretations, the rich and wholly pure [practice] of [its] mode of life, the noble exercise of its good customs, the humble . . . change of mind which the Religion shows (suggests) to [men], teaching and instructing (them). . . . But it itself has not been instructed by anyone in anything.

Fourth: The world-ocean absorbs the bodies . . . and does not reject anyone. These are the mighty [spirits?] and men; and [whoever] of these comes to the Church of the Apostle is absorbed [by the Church], for it does not reject anyone. Rather, according to the order of its Law and commandments, it gives them their [places]. And as many as approach it [repeatedly], in order to enter it, [all] of them have their places either amongst the auditors or the elect. And they all do their works according to their rank, their zeal and their strength. And [the Religion] does not make . . . and honor . . . , and out of love it does not shout out loud. And however many of these people may be mighty, nothing takes it by surprise, nor does it rejoice, for it remains placid and tranquil at all times. [Thus] it is like the world-ocean.

Fifth: The Religion of the Apostle [is] without stain, (being) clean and pure and holy; and it immediately refuses to retain those men who are confused and immoral and [have] filthy thoughts, men who are like corpses, excrements and diverse (forms of) pollution. It tosses them back onto the shore.

Sixth: When an elect one sees another elect one face to face, or an auditor sees [another] auditor, then the pure, loving gaze gives rise to great joy among them. And [so] great blessing comes upon them, and like light it appears in the faces of the light gods and becomes visible.

Seventh: The many great, strong bipeds and otherwise fashioned wonderful beings and animals [that are born] in the world-ocean are [like] the elect that behave quite differently from the world. And [they] bear the burden and the heavy load of the Law and endure great pain and suffering. And they always accept personally, what no man in the whole world would bear or take upon himself.

Eighth: In the world-ocean, . . . varied priceless pearls and beautiful, miraculous jewels are born which are not born in [any] deep [place] (in the Earth). Never can this be comprehended and never can it be seen. This reflects the difference between the two places, the good and the evil one, and the self-realization of the soul which is not

---

[1]The Manichaean Church divided its members into the *elect* and the *auditors,* or hearers. The elect were the chosen few who led lives of great asceticism and provided leadership in the Church. Because of their purity they were the earthly agents for the release of captive Light. The hearers were the mass of Manichaean believers who served the elect. Whereas the soul of the elect returns directly to the Kingdom of Light upon death, the soul of the hearer must still go through a series of reincarnations, first in a series of luminous fruits and then in the form of an elect. How soon this last incarnation happens depends on the quality of the hearer's service to the elect.

born in a learned place.[2] It (that wisdom) can never be attained except in [the Religion] and in the Law and in the commandments of the Apostle.

Ninth: The strong one[3] and the demon[4] of the world-ocean that shakes the whole world-ocean when it rises (in the tide) is the Nous[5] of the Religion, which is in the [whole] Church, shaking the bodies (of men). It (the Nous) seizes (them) mightily and draws out [the light] (they have accumulated), this being the daily work (of the men) of the Religion. [That light] ascends daily from the whole body of the elect to the light [chariots] (the Sun and the Moon); and the gods in command of these chariots draw it up [and]

constantly send it on to the world of Paradise.

Tenth: All roaring and thundering waters that flow into the ocean, that then become still and stop roaring, are the adherents of [other] religions and men of worldly wisdom [and] eloquent men who remain [mere] creators of words, believing themselves to be wise. But when they come to the door of the Religion of the Apostle, they all become silent and their (own) words silence them. And now they do [not] exalt themselves (any more), and henceforth they do not dare to make any more speeches [and] dare not say anything.

[Here] ends the story about the Religion and the world-ocean.

---

[2]Worldly learning stands in contrast to the knowledge of the soul that one receives from the Manichaean religion.

[3]A metaphorical term for the *tide*.

[4]According to Manichaean cosmology, the tide, or *ocean giant*, arises as a consequence of demonic substances poured into the ocean. This is positive, however, because the turbulence purifies the waters of the ocean.

[5]A Greek term that means *Divine Intelligence. Nous* is an emanation of Jesus of Light and carries out his redemptive role. Nous is the father of all true religious leaders and enters the world through their teachings. It is Nous that imparts knowledge of the divine origin of the soul, and this knowledge brings with it liberation from Darkness.

Chapter 8

▼▼▼

Islam

Universal Submission to God

The last of the great monotheistic faiths to arise in Southwest Asia was Islam, which emerged in Arabia during the early seventh century. *Islam* means "submission" in Arabic, and a *Muslim* is anyone who submits to the Will of God.

The Prophet of Islam was a merchant of Mecca known as *Muhammad ibn (son of) Abdullah* (ca. 571–632), who around 610 began to receive visions in which he was called to be the Messenger of *Allah* — a divinity whose Arabic name (al-Llah) means "*the* God." Muhammad's mission was to preach the Oneness of God ("there is no god but the God"), the imminence of the Resurrection of the Dead, the coming of a divine Day of Judgment, and the existence of an all-consuming hell fire for the unjust and unbelievers and a paradise of bliss for the faithful. Muhammad believed that, just as Jews and Christians had their divine revelations from God, now the Arabs were receiving the full and final word of God through him, the last and greatest of the prophets but still only a man. Abraham, Moses, Jesus, and the other prophets had been earlier messengers of God. Muhammad was the *seal* of these forerunners.

Most Meccans, including almost all of his own kinsmen, were initially unmoved by Muhammad's message, so in 622 Muhammad and the majority of his small band of converts journeyed over 200 miles northeast to an oasis settlement that would become known as *Medinat al-Nabi* (City of the Prophet) or, more simply, *Medina*. By this act, known as the *hijra* (breaking of ties), these first Muslims abandoned their tribal bonds — bonds that defined traditional Arabic society — and opted for membership in an Islamic community of faith, or *umma*. This migration was so pivotal in the history of Islam that Muslims later chose the year 622 to mark the beginning of the era of Islam — the Year 1 of the Islamic calendar.

It was at Medina that circumstances forced Muhammad to add the duties of statesman and warrior to that of prophet, and he proved successful at all three. After more than seven years of struggle, Muhammad and a reputed 10,000 followers were able to enter Mecca in triumph in January 630. The Messenger of Allah was now the most powerful chieftain in Arabia, and most of the tribes of the peninsula soon were united under his leadership. When Muhammad died in 632, his closest friend, *Abu Bakr,* assumed the title and office of *caliph* (deputy of the Prophet), thereby accepting leadership over the family of Islam. Abu Bakr did not claim to be a prophet; God's revelation had ceased with Muhammad's death. As caliph, Abu Bakr served as head of the umma — the community of God's people. Thanks to Abu Bakr's efforts at destroying secessionist elements that arose after Muhammad's death, Islam under his stewardship (632–634) remained a unified community ready to explode out of its homeland, which it did under the second caliph, Umar (r. 634–644).

Both the Sassanian Persian and Byzantine empires had exhausted each other in a series of destructive wars that ran from 503 to 627. In addition, the Byzantine Empire was rent by ethnic and religious dissension, especially in Syria-Palestine and Egypt. So, when Muslims began raiding the territories of these neighboring empires, they discovered lands ripe for conquest. Before Umar's death the Byzantines had lost all of Syria-Palestine and Egypt to the green flag of Islam, and the Arab conquest of the Sassanian Empire was virtually completed. By the year 750, lands under Islamic domination reached from the Pyrenees and Atlantic coast in Spain to the Indus Valley of India and to Tang China's far-western borders.

Originally the Arabs considered Islam their special revelation and had little interest in sharing the faith with their non-Arab subjects, but several factors combined to attract large numbers of converts. These included Islam's uncompromising monotheism and the straightforwardness of its other central doctrines; its attractive ethical code; the psychic and social security offered by membership in a totally integrated Muslim community, where one's entire life is subject to God's Word; and the desire to escape the second-class status of Islam's non-Muslim subjects. When the Abbasid caliphs (r. 750–1258) established their court at Baghdad on the Tigris in 762, they claimed dominion over a multiethnic ecumene bound together by one of the fastest growing religions in the history of humanity. The culture of this world community was a combination of many elements, of which the most important were Arabic, Persian, and Hellenistic.

Later other peoples, especially the Turks, would convert to Islam and carry it farther afield, especially into the heart of India and deep into Central Asia. Arab and East African merchants would transport the faith across the Indian Ocean to the ports of Southeast Asia, and Berbers from North Africa would introduce Islam into western sub-Saharan Africa.

▼▼▼

The Foundations of Islamic Life

Like the Buddha and Jesus, Muhammad was a teacher who spoke rather than wrote his message, but also like Buddhism and Christianity, following its Messenger's death, Islam quickly became a religious culture centered on a body of sacred texts, and it has remained so to the present. Islam's text without equal is *al-Quran* (the Recitations), which Muslims believe contains, word for word, absolutely everything that God revealed to Muhammad and nothing else. In Muslim eyes, the Quran is the full and final revelation of God and coeternal with Him. Its verses, each a poetically perfect proclamation from Heaven, are both doctrine and law, governing every aspect of a Muslim's life. Islam without the Quran is unimaginable.

A second source of guidance for most Muslims is *al-Hadith* (Tradition), a vast body of transmitted stories and sayings attributed to the Prophet and his Companions. Unlike the Quran, these stories, individually known as *hadiths* (tales or instructions), are not assembled in a single, absolutely accepted text. Rather, there are many collections of Hadith, some more authoritative than others, some even largely dismissed as spurious. The majority of Muslims believe that authentic hadiths enshrine the *sunna* (the beaten track), or valid traditions, of the Prophet and the first Islamic community at Medina and thereby provide perfect models for behavior in all aspects of life, especially those not expressly covered in the precepts of the Quran.

A third source that provides inspiration and guidance is the earliest extant biography of the Prophet of God. Because Muslims regard Muhammad as only a man, Islam has no Gospels in the sense that Christianity does — divinely inspired and infallible accounts of its Teacher's miracles and salvific deeds. Islam does have, however, the recorded remembrances of the Messenger of God's Companions from Mecca and his earliest converts at Medina, which document portions of Muhammad's life and actions. Collected and arranged into a coherent biography in eighth-century Baghdad, this work has served through the centuries as a model for devout Muslims who desire to follow the path of Allah's perfect servant.

Like the Jewish Torah, the Quran provides its believers with a total way of life. The dichotomy between church and state that the European West developed has no meaning in Islam, at least as it emerged in the seventh century. Indeed, Islam has no Church in the Christian sense, and it has no separate secular polity — at least in the ideal. In the ideal, there is only God's *umma,* which is governed by God's Holy Law, or *Sharia.* The study and application of Sharia is one of the highest callings in Islamic life and stands at the center of its civilization.

The Word of God
▼▼▼

55 ▼ *THE QURAN*

As long as the Prophet was alive, there was no compelling reason to set his messages down in some definitive form. However, following Muhammad's death in 632, Caliph Abu Bakr ordered one of the Prophet's Companions, Zayd ibn Thabit, to collect from both oral and written sources all of Muhammad's inspired utterances. Subsequently, Caliph Uthman (r. 644–656) promulgated an official collection of these Recitations and ordered all other versions destroyed.

This standard text became the basis of every pious Muslim's education. As Islam spread beyond Arab ethnic boundaries, Muslims all over the world continued to learn Arabic in order to study and recite (usually from memory) the sacred *surahs* (chapters) of this holy book. Because of the Quran's centrality to Islam, Arabic literacy became the hallmark of Muslims from sub-Saharan West Africa to Southeast Asia.

The following excerpts come from the second of the Quran's 114 surahs. Known as "The Cow" (*al-Baqarah*) because portions of it tell the story of how the ancient Israelites sacrificed a cow to God, this surah dates to the first year after the *hijra* from Mecca to Medina, or around 623. Our selections illustrate several of Islam's major doctrinal tenets, religious obligations, and moral principles and also shed light on the connections between Islam and the faiths of Judaism and Christianity.

QUESTIONS FOR ANALYSIS

1. What evidence is there that Muhammad was experiencing difficulty converting Jewish, Christian, and pagan Arabs?
2. How does the Quran portray Jews and Christians, and what is Islam's relationship with these two faiths?
3. What are the basic tenets of faith enjoined on all Muslims?
4. What are a Muslim's basic moral obligations?
5. What specific religious rites and practices must every observant Muslim perform?
6. How are Muslims to deal with those who attack them?
7. "For members of the Islamic community, there is no distinction between what one believes and the manner in which one lives and conducts one's affairs." After reading these passages from the Quran, do you agree or disagree that this is a central Islamic principle?

8. Compare these passages with the Sermon on the Mount (source 45). Which strike you as more significant, the similarities or the differences in message and tone? What do you conclude from your answer?

Those unbelievers of the People of the Book[1]
and the idolaters[2] wish not that any good
should be sent down upon you from your
    Lord;
but God singles out for His mercy whom he
    will;
      God is of bounty abounding. . . .

Many of the People of the Book wish they
    might
restore you as unbelievers, after you have
    believed,
in the jealousy of their souls, after the truth
has become clear to them; yet do you pardon
and be forgiving, till God brings His
    command;
truly God is powerful over everything.
And perform the prayer, and pay the alms;[3]
whatever good you shall forward to your souls'
    account,
you shall find it with God; assuredly God
      sees the things you do.
And they say, "None shall enter Paradise
except that they be Jews or Christians."
Such are their fancies. Say: "Produce your
    proof, if you speak truly."
Nay, but whosoever submits his will to God,
being a good-doer, his wage is with his Lord,
and no fear shall be on them, neither shall
    they sorrow.

The Jews say, "The Christians stand not on
    anything";
the Christians say, "The Jews stand not on
    anything";
yet they recite the Book. So too the ignorant
say the like of them. God shall decide
between them on the Day of Resurrection
    touching their differences.
And who does greater evil than he who bars
God's places of worship, so that His Name
be not rehearsed in them, and strives to
    destroy them?
Such men might never enter them, save in
    fear;
for them is degradation in the present world,
and in the world to come a mighty
    chastisement. . . .

Children of Israel,[4] remember My blessing
wherewith I blessed you, and that I have
preferred you above all beings. . . .

And when his Lord tested Abraham[5]
with certain words, and he fulfilled them.
He said, "Behold, I make you a leader
for the people." Said he, "And of my seed?"
He said, "My covenant shall not reach
    the evildoers."[6]
And when We appointed the House[7] to be
a place of visitation for the people,
    and a sanctuary,

---

[1]People who have their own sacred scriptures from God through such prophets as Moses and Jesus. Elsewhere, this surah identifies three such peoples: Jews, Christians, and Sabeans (a Gnostic sect with Jewish and Christian roots that inhabited the borderlands of Syria, Iraq, and Iran; see source 53 for Gnosticism).

[2]Pagans who worship idols.

[3]The *zakat,* or obligatory alms-payment, which supports the poor within the Islamic community.

[4]Jews — the offspring of Israel, or Jacob, the son of Isaac and grandson of Abraham (note 5).

[5]According to both Arabic and Jewish traditions, Abraham (ca. 1800 B.C.E.) was the father of both the Arabic and Jewish people, through, respectively, his sons Ishmael and Isaac.

[6]Jews who have abandoned God's Word and are not submissive to the Divine Will.

[7]The Kaaba, a cube-shaped shrine at the heart of the Great Mosque of Mecca.

and: "Take to yourselves Abraham's station
for a place of prayer." And We made covenant
with Abraham and Ishmael,[8] "Purify
My House[9] for those that shall go about it
and those that cleave to it, to those who bow
    and prostrate themselves."[10]. . .

When his Lord said to him, "Surrender,"
he said, "I have surrendered me to
    the Lord of all Being."
And Abraham charged his sons with this
and Jacob[11] likewise: "My sons, God has
  chosen for you the religion;
see that you die not
    save in surrender."[12]

Why, were you witnesses, when death came
to Jacob? When he said to his sons,
"What will you serve after me?" They said,
"We will serve thy God and the God of thy
    fathers
Abraham, Ishmael, and Isaac, One God,
    to Him we surrender."
That is a nation that has passed away;[13]
there awaits them that they have earned,
and there awaits you that you have earned;
you shall not be questioned concerning
    the things they did.

And they say, "Be Jews or Christians and
you shall be guided." Say thou: "Nay, rather
the creed of Abraham, a man of pure faith;
    he was no idolater."
Say you: "We believe in God, and
in that which has been sent down on us

and sent down on Abraham, Ishmael,
Isaac and Jacob, and the Tribes,[14]
and that which was given to Moses and Jesus
and the Prophets, of their Lord; we
make no division between any of them, and
    to Him we surrender."
And if they believe in the like of that you
believe in, then they are truly guided; but if
they turn away, then they are clearly in schism;[15]
God will suffice you for them; He is
    the All-hearing, the All-knowing;
the baptism of God; and who is there
that baptizes fairer than God?[16]
    Him we are serving.
Say: "Would you then dispute with us
concerning God, who is our Lord
and your Lord? Our deeds belong to us,
and to you belong your deeds; Him
    we serve sincerely. . . .

It is not piety, that you turn your faces
    to the East and to the West.[17]
    True piety is this:
to believe in God, and the Last Day,
the angels, the Book, and the Prophets,
to give of one's substance, however cherished,
  to kinsmen, and orphans,
the needy, the traveler, beggars,
  and to ransom the slave,
to perform the prayer,[18] to pay the alms.
And they who fulfill their covenant
when they have engaged in a covenant,
  and endure with fortitude
  misfortune, hardship, and peril,

---

[8]See notes 5 and 9.

[9]According to this surah, Abraham and his elder son, Ishmael, were commanded by God to cleanse the Kaaba of its idols, whose worship Muslims consider to be the worst of all possible sins. Muhammad cleansed the same sanctuary of idols following his triumphant reentry into Mecca in 630.

[10]Associated with Adam, Abraham, and Ishmael, the Kaaba is the focal point of a Muslim's daily prayer and the sacred spot around which pilgrims on *hajj* (note 21) circulate in a series of ritual ceremonies.

[11]Notes 4 and 5.

[12]By surrendering to God, Abraham and his sons and grandsons were Muslims.

[13]Jews (the progeny of Jacob) who surrender to God, and are Muslims by reason of that submission, no longer exist.

[14]The Twelve Tribes of the Israelites whom Moses led out of Egypt.

[15]Schism means separation. They have separated themselves from Islam.

[16]Here the Quran juxtaposes the Christian sacrament of baptism, the ceremony of initiation into the Christian faith, with God's baptism of the Word.

[17]In prayer.

[18]The ritual prayer performed five times daily by all observant Muslims.

these are they who are true in their faith,
    these are the truly godfearing. . . .

O believers, prescribed for you is
the Fast,[19] even as it was prescribed for
those that were before you — haply you
        will be godfearing —
for days numbered; and if any of you
be sick, or if he be on a journey,
then a number of other days. . . .

And fight in the way of God with those
who fight with you, but aggress not: God
        loves not the aggressors.
And slay them wherever you come upon them,
and expel them from where they expelled you;
persecution is more grievous than slaying.
But fight them not by the Holy Mosque[20]
until they should fight you there;
then, if they fight you, slay them —
such is the recompense of unbelievers —
but if they give over, surely God is
All-forgiving, All-compassionate.
Fight them, till there is no persecution
and the religion is God's; then if they
give over, there shall be no enmity
        save for evildoers.
The holy month for the holy month;
holy things demand retaliation.
Whoso commits aggression against you,
do you commit aggression against him
like as he has committed against you;
and fear you God, and know that God is
        with the godfearing.

And expend in the way of God;
and cast not yourselves by your own hands
into destruction, but be good-doers; God
        loves the good-doers.

Fulfill the Pilgrimage[21] and the Visitation
unto God; but if you are prevented,

then such offering as may be feasible. . . .
And when you have performed your holy rites
remember God, as you remember your fathers
or yet more devoutly. . . .

                    God
        there is no god but He, the
        Living, the Everlasting.
Slumber seizes Him not, neither sleep;
                to Him belongs
all that is in the heavens and the earth.
Who is there that shall intercede with Him
        save by His leave?
He knows what lies before them and
        what is after them,
and they comprehend not anything of
        His knowledge save such as He
        wills.
His Throne comprises the heavens and
        earth;
the preserving of them oppresses Him not;
He is the All-high, the All-glorious.

No compulsion is there in religion.
Rectitude has become clear from error.
So whosoever disbelieves in idols
and believes in God, has laid hold of
the most firm handle, unbreaking; God is
        All-hearing, All-knowing.

God is the Protector of the believers;
He brings them forth from the shadows
        into the light. . . .

Those who believe and do deeds of
    righteousness,
and perform the prayer, and pay the alms —
their wage awaits them with their Lord,
and no fear shall be on them, neither shall
    they sorrow. . . .

---

[19]The annual fast during the month of *Ramadan* when observant Muslims refrain from all food, drink, and other physical pleasures from sunrise to sunset.
[20]The Great Mosque of Mecca (see note 7).

[21]All adult Muslims who are able to make the journey must embark on the *hajj,* or pilgrimage to Mecca, at least once before death. See sources 58 and 60.

God charges no soul save to its capacity;
standing to its account is what it has earned,
and against its account what it has merited.

Our Lord,
take us not to task
if we forget, or make mistake.
Our Lord,
charge us not with a load such
as Thou didst lay upon those before us.

Our Lord,
do Thou not burden us
beyond what we have the strength to bear.
And pardon us,
and forgive us,
and have mercy on us;
Thou art our Protector.
And help us against the people
of the unbelievers.

The Tales of Tradition
▼▼▼

56 ▾ *Imam Nawawi,*
GARDENS OF THE RIGHTEOUS

Although earlier Muslims, such as Malik ibn-Anas (d. 795), collected stories about the Prophet, it was not until about two centuries after Muhammad's death that Muslim scholars began to catalogue systematically the traditions that circulated about the Prophet and his Companions. The most important individual in this effort was the Persian legal scholar Ismail al-Bokhari (810–870), who reportedly collected some 600,000 tales (undoubtedly many were variations of common themes) and memorized more than 200,000 of them. From this vast body of material he identified a little over 7,000 tales as genuine, which he then preserved. The second great editor of Hadith was Bokhari's younger contemporary, Abul Husain Muslim (819–875), whose collection is almost identical to Bokhari's. Slightly less important than the work of these two scholarly giants were the collections of Abu Daud (d. 889), al-Tirmidhi (d. 892), Ibn Majah (d. 896), and al-Nisai (d. 915). The combined efforts of these six individuals are known as the *Sahih Sitta* (*The Six Authentic Compilations*).

The sheer bulk of these canonical texts, as well as the discrepancies among them and the existence of many other less universally accepted compendia of such tales, necessitated continued editing and digesting of Islamic tradition by legions of jurists and religious scholars in every generation. One of the most significant of these later scholars was the Syrian *imam* (religious teacher) Nawawi (1233–1278), whose *Gardens of the Righteous* provided an analytical digest of the spiritual values enshrined in *The Six Authentic Compilations* and several lesser collections of Hadith.

As the following texts show, Nawawi's usual method of exposition was to set out a relevant passage or series of passages from the Quran and then to list a number of variant stories and sayings, largely as remembered by the Prophet's Companions, that illustrate the spiritual message contained in that quranic text.

QUESTIONS FOR ANALYSIS

1. Which virtues do these selections emphasize?
2. The Arabic word used for *striving* in both the Quran and Hadith is *jihad,* which is often translated as "holy war." In the light of these excerpts, does this translation seem correct and complete?
3. What gives Hadith its authority, since, unlike the Quran, Muslims do not regard it as the literal word of God?
4. How does Hadith allow for a certain diversity within the context of religious uniformity?

ON MAKING PEACE BETWEEN PEOPLE

Allah, the Exalted, has said:

> Most of their conferrings together are devoid of good, except such as enjoin charity, or the promotion of public welfare or of public peace (4.115).
> Reconciliation is best (4.129).
> Be mindful of your duty to Allah and try to promote accord between yourselves (8.2).
> All believers are brothers; so make peace between your brothers (49.11).

Abu Hurairah relates that the Honorable Prophet said: Charity is incumbent upon every human limb every day on which the sun rises. To bring about just reconciliation between two contestants is charity. Helping a person to mount his animal, or to load his baggage on to it is charity. A good word is charity. Every step taken towards the mosque for *salat*[1] is charity. To remove anything from the street that causes inconvenience is charity (Bokhari and Muslim).

Umm Kulthum relates that she heard the Honorable Prophet say: He who brings about peace between people and attains good or says that which is good is not a liar (Bokhari and Muslim). . . .

ON THE SUPERIORITY OF THE POOR AND WEAK AMONG MUSLIMS

Allah, the Exalted, has said:

> Continue thy companionship with those who call on their Lord, morning and evening, seeking His pleasure, and look not beyond them (18.29).

Haritha ibn Wahb relates that he heard the Honorable Prophet say: Shall I tell you who are the dwellers of Paradise? It is every weak one who is accounted weak and is looked down upon, who if he takes an oath relying upon Allah He would fulfill it. Now shall I tell you who are the denizens of the Fire? It is every ignorant, impertinent, prideful, and arrogant one (Bokhari and Muslim). . . .

Usamah relates that the Honorable Prophet said: I stood at the gate of Paradise and observed that the generality of those who entered it were the lowly. The wealthy had been held back from it. Then those condemned to the Fire were ordered to it and I stood at the gate of the Fire and observed that the generality of those who entered it were women (Bokhari and Muslim).

---

[1]Ritual prayer performed five times daily; on Fridays Muslims gather in the mosque around noon for community prayer. See sources 57 and 58 for more on *salat*, or ritual prayer.

ON KIND TREATMENT OF ORPHANS, GIRLS, THE WEAK, THE POOR, AND THE LOWLY

Allah, the Exalted, has said:

> Continue to be kindly gracious towards the believers (15.89).
>
> Continue thy companionship with those who call on their Lord, morning and evening, seeking His pleasure, and look not beyond them, for if thou dost that thou wouldst be seeking the values of this life (18.29).
>
> Oppress not the orphan and chide not him who asks (93.10–11).
>
> Knowest thou him who rejects the faith? That is the one who drives away the orphan and urges not the feeding of the poor (107.2–4). . . .

Abu Hurairah relates that the Honorable Prophet said: He who exerts himself on behalf of widows and the indigent is like one who strives[2] in the cause of Allah; and the narrator thinks he added: and like the guardian who never retreats, and like one who observes the fast and does not break it (Bokhari and Muslim). . . .

Anas relates that the Honorable Prophet said: He who brings up two girls through their childhood will appear on the Day of Judgment attached to me like two fingers of a hand (Muslim). . . .

Ayesha[3] relates: A poor woman came to me with her two daughters. I gave her three dates. She gave one to each girl and raised the third to her own mouth to eat. The girls asked her for it. So she broke it into two parts and gave one to each of the girls. I was much struck by her action and mentioned what she had done to the Honorable Prophet. He said: Allah appointed Paradise for her in consequence of it; or he said: Allah freed her from the Fire[4] on account of it.

Abu Shuraih Khuwailad ibn Amr Khuza'i relates that the Honorable Prophet said: Allah, I declare sinful any failure to safeguard the rights of two weak ones; orphans and women (Nisai).

ON A HUSBAND'S RIGHT CONCERNING HIS WIFE

Allah, the Exalted, has said:

> Men are appointed guardians over women, because of that in respect of which Allah has made some of them excel others, and because the men spend their wealth. So virtuous women are obedient and safeguard, with Allah's help, matters the knowledge of which is shared by them with their husbands (4.35). . . .

Ibn Umar relates that the Honorable Prophet said: Every one of you is a steward and is accountable for that which is committed to his charge. The ruler is a steward and is accountable for his charge, a man is a steward in respect of his household, a woman is a steward in respect of her husband's house and his children. Thus everyone of you is a steward and is accountable for that which is committed to his charge (Bokhari and Muslim). . . .

Umm Salamah relates that the Honorable Prophet said: If a woman dies and her husband is pleased with her she will enter Paradise (Tirmidhi).

Mu'az ibn Jabal relates that the Honorable Prophet said: Whenever a woman distresses her husband his mate from among the *houris*[5] of Paradise says to her: Allah ruin thee, do not cause him distress for he is only thy guest and will soon part from thee to come to us (Tirmidhi).

Usamah ibn Zaid relates that the Honorable Prophet said: I am not leaving a more harmful trial for men than woman (Bokhari and Muslim).

---

[2]Jihad (see question 2).
[3]The daughter of Abu Bakr, the first caliph; she was the Prophet's favorite wife and a major source for Sunni hadiths.
[4]Hell.
[5]Beautiful virgins who serve the saved in Paradise.

ON STRIVING IN THE CAUSE OF ALLAH

Allah, the Exalted, has said:

Fight the idolators all together, as they fight you all together, and know that Allah is with the righteous (9.36). . . .

Allah has purchased of the believers their persons and their belongings in return for the promise that they shall have Paradise, for they fight in the cause of Allah and they slay the enemy or are themselves slain. This is a promise that He has made incumbent upon Himself as set out in the Torah, and the Gospel and the Quran; and who is more faithful to his promises than Allah? Rejoice, then, in the bargain that you have made with Him; that indeed is the supreme triumph (9.111). . . .

O ye who believe, shall I guide you to a commerce that will deliver you from a painful chastisement? It is that you believe in Allah and His Messenger, and strive in the cause of Allah with your belongings and your persons, that is the better for you, did you but know. He will forgive you your sins and will admit you to gardens beneath which rivers flow, and to pure and pleasant dwellings in Gardens of Eternity. That is the supreme triumph (61.11–14). . . .

Anas relates that the Honorable Prophet said: To be occupied in the cause of Allah a morning or evening is better than the world and all it contains (Bokhari and Muslim). . . .

Sahl ibn Saad relates that the Honorable Prophet said: Patroling the frontier for a day is better than the world and all it contains. Your being allotted a strip in Paradise no wider than your horse-whip is better than the world and all it contains. Being occupied with striving in the cause of Allah for a morning or an evening is better than the world and all it contains (Bokhari and Muslim). . . .

Fuzalah ibn Ubaid relates that the Honorable Prophet said: Death puts an end to all action, except in the case of one who patrols the frontier in the cause of Allah, for his activity continues to grow till the Day of Judgment and he is shielded against the trials of the grave (Abu Daud and Tirmidhi).

Uthman relates that he heard the Honorable Prophet say: Patroling the frontier for a day in the cause of Allah is better than a thousand days of other good works (Tirmidhi). . . .

Abu Bakr ibn Abu Musa Ashari relates that he heard his father say in the face of the enemy: The Honorable Prophet said: The gates of Paradise are under the shadow of swords. Thereupon a man of lowly condition stood up and inquired: Abu Musa, did you indeed hear the Honorable Prophet say that? He answered: Yes. The man then turned towards his companions and saluted them in farewell. He then broke the scabbard of his sword and threw it away and walked with his sword into the enemy ranks and fought till he was killed (Muslim). . . .

Anas relates that the Honorable Prophet said: He who supplicates sincerely for martyrdom is granted it, even though he is not slain (Muslim).

Abu Hurairah relates that the Honorable Prophet said: A martyr does not suffer when he is slain any more than one of you suffers from being bitten by an ant (Tirmidhi). . . .

Abu Hurairah relates that the Honorable Prophet said: He who observes the fast for a day in the cause of Allah will find that Allah has dug a moat between him and the Fire as wide as the distance between Heaven and Earth (Tirmidhi).

Abu Hurairah relates that the Honorable Prophet said: He who dies without having fought in the cause of Allah and without having thought of it in his mind dies with one characteristic of hypocrisy within him (Muslim). . . .

Abu Hurairah relates that a man asked the Honorable Prophet's permission to travel and he told him: The travel for my people is striving in the cause of Allah, the Lord of honor and glory (Abu Daud). . . .

Anas relates that the Honorable Prophet said: Strive against the idolators with your belongings, your persons and your tongues (Abu Daud).

Muhammad's Night Journey
and Ascent to Heaven

▼▼▼

57 ▼ *Muhammad ibn Ishaq,*
THE LIFE OF THE MESSENGER OF GOD

An ambiguous passage in the Quran proclaims: "Glory be to Him who carried His servant by night from the sacred shrine to the distant shrine, whose surroundings We have blessed, that We might show him some of Our signs" (Surah 17:1). Most Muslims interpret the *sacred shrine* to mean Mecca's *Kaaba,* a temple sacred to the pre-Islamic polytheists of Arabia and, once Muhammad cleansed it of its 360 idols, a shrine that has remained a focal point of Islamic devotion down to our day. Many Muslims further interpret the *distant shrine* to signify Jerusalem's *Temple Mount,* the site of the destroyed Jewish Temple. According to a tradition not specifically recorded in the Quran, one night, around the year 620, while asleep within the Kaaba's stone porch, Muhammad was transported to Jerusalem and from there to Heaven on a mythical beast known as *Buraq.* Actually, the tradition is not and never was that simple. Many variations of the story existed (and exist) side by side, even in the Prophet's own day. Apparently, Muhammad had a mystical vision which he was reluctant or unable to discuss in detail

Around the mid eighth century, Muhammad ibn Ishaq (ca. 704–ca. 767), the author of the first and most influential biography of the Prophet, faced the problem of trying to reconcile the often contradictory stories that he had collected regarding the Messenger of God's Night Journey. What follows is his attempt to balance and evaluate these variant accounts.

QUESTIONS FOR ANALYSIS

1. Where does Ibn Ishaq seem to stand on the question of whether Muhammad's Night Journey was a physical one or a purely spiritual one?
2. How do these various accounts use the Night Journey to explain some of Islam's values, practices, and attributes? Be specific.
3. Compare this account of Heaven and Hell with the other visions of the Afterworld that we saw in *The Epic of Gilgamesh* (source 1), the *Odyssey* (source 11), and the *Aeneid* (source 30). What conclusions follow from this comparative analysis?

Then the apostle was carried by night from the mosque at Mecca to the Masjid al-Aqsa,[1] which is the temple of Aelia.[2] . . .

The following account reached me from Abdullah b. Masud and Abu Said al-Khudri, and Aisha the prophet's wife, and Muaiya b. Abu Sufyan, and al-Hasan b. Abul-Hasan al-Basri, and Ibn Shihab al-Zuhri and Qatada and other traditionists. . . . It is pieced together in the story that follows, each one contributing something of what he was told about what happened when he was taken on the night journey. The matter of the place of the journey and what is said about it is a searching test and a matter of God's power and authority wherein is a lesson for the intelligent; and guidance and mercy and strengthening to those who believe. It was certainly an act of God by which He took him by night in what way He pleased to show him His signs which He willed him to see so that he witnessed His mighty sovereignty and power by which He does what He wills to do.

According to what I have heard Abdullah b. Masud used to say: Buraq, the animal whose every stride carried it as far as its eye could reach on which the prophets before him used to ride was brought to the apostle[3] and he was mounted on it. His companion[4] went with him to see the wonders between Heaven and Earth, until he came to Jerusalem's temple. There he found Abraham the friend of God, Moses, and Jesus assembled with a company of prophets, and he prayed with them. Then he was brought three vessels containing milk, wine, and water respectively. The apostle said: 'I heard a voice saying when these were offered to me: If he takes the water he will be drowned and his people also; if he takes the wine he will go astray and his people also; and if he takes the milk he will be rightly

guided and his people also. So I took the vessel containing milk and drank it. Gabriel said to me, You have been rightly guided and so will your people be, Muhammad.'[5]

I was told that al-Hasan said that the apostle said: 'While I was sleeping in the Hijr[6] Gabriel came and stirred me with his foot. I sat up but saw nothing and lay down again. He came a second time and stirred me with his foot. I sat up but saw nothing and lay down again. He came to me the third time and stirred me with his foot. I sat up and he took hold of my arm and I stood beside him and he brought me out to the door of the mosque and there was a white animal, half mule, half donkey, with wings on its sides with which it propelled its feet, putting down each forefoot at the limit of its sight and he mounted me on it. Then he went out with me keeping close to me. . . .

In his story al-Hasan said: 'The apostle and Gabriel went their way until they arrived at the temple at Jerusalem. There he found Abraham, Moses, and Jesus among a company of the prophets. The apostle acted as their imam[7] in prayer. Then he was brought two vessels, one containing wine and the other milk. The apostle took the milk and drank it, leaving the wine. Gabriel said: "You have been rightly guided to the way of nature and so will your people be, Muhammad. Wine is forbidden you." Then the apostle returned to Mecca and in the morning he told Quraysh[8] what had happened. Most of them said, "By God, this is a plain absurdity! A caravan takes a month to go to Syria and a month to return and can Muhammad do the return journey in one night?" Many Muslims gave up their faith; some went to Abu Bakr and said, "What do you think of your friend now, Abu Bakr? He alleges that he went to Jerusalem last night and

---

[1]The Farther Shrine. The Mosque of al-Aqsa, which stands on Jerusalem's Temple Mount, is believed by many Muslims to be the location from which Muhammad physically rose to Heaven.
[2]The Roman name for Jerusalem.
[3]Muhammad.
[4]The angel Gabriel.
[5]Many Islamic commentators interpret this as meaning that

Muhammad rejected the extremes of asceticism (water) and hedonism (wine).
[6]The Kaaba's stone porch.
[7]Prayer leader.
[8]The dominant tribe of Mecca, which controlled the city's commerce. Although Muhammad was of that tribe, most of its members rejected his prophecies at this time.

prayed there and came back to Mecca." He replied that they were lying about the apostle; but they said that he was in the mosque at that very moment telling the people about it. Abu Bakr said, "If he says so then it is true. And what is so surprising in that? He tells me that communications from God from Heaven to Earth come to him in an hour of a day or night and I believe him, and that is more extraordinary than that at which you boggle!" He then went to the apostle and asked him if these reports were true, and when he said they were, he asked him to describe Jerusalem to him.' Al-Hasan said that he was lifted up so that he could see the apostle speaking as he told Abu Bakr what Jerusalem was like.[9] Whenever he described a part of it he said, 'That's true. I testify that you are the apostle of God' until he had completed the description, and then the apostle said, 'And you, Abu Bakr, are the *Siddiq.*'[10] This was the occasion on which he got this honorific. . . .

One of Abu Bakr's family told me that Aisha the prophet's wife used to say: 'The apostle's body remained where it was but God removed his spirit by night.'

Yqub b. Utba b. al-Mughira b. al-Akhnas told me that Muawiya b. Abu Sufyan when he was asked about the apostle's night journey said, 'It was a true vision from God.' What these two latter said does not contradict what al-Hasan said, seeing that God Himself said, 'We made the vision which we showed thee only for a test to men;' nor does it contradict what God said in the story of Abraham when he said to his son, 'O my son, verily I saw in a dream that I must sacrifice thee,'[11] and he acted accordingly. Thus, as I see it, revelation from God comes to the prophets waking or sleeping.

I have heard that the apostle used to say, 'My eyes sleep while my heart is awake.' Only God knows how revelation came and he saw what he saw. But whether he was asleep or awake, it was all true and actually happened. . . .

One whom I have no reason to doubt told me on the authority of Abu Said al-Khudri: I heard the apostle say, 'After the completion of my business in Jerusalem a ladder was brought to me finer than any I have ever seen. It was that to which the dying man looks when death approaches. My companion mounted it with me until we came to one of the gates of Heaven called the Gate of the Watchers. An angel called Ismail was in charge of it, and under his command were twelve thousand angels each of them having twelve thousand angels under his command.' As he told this story the apostle used to say, 'and none knows the armies of God but He.' When Gabriel brought me in, Ismail asked who I was, and when he was told that I was Muhammad he asked if I had been given a mission, and on being assured of this he wished me well. . . .

In his tradition Abu Said al-Khudri said that the apostle said: 'When I entered the lowest heaven I saw a man sitting there with the spirits of men passing before him. To one he would speak well and rejoice in him saying: "A good spirit from a good body" and of another he would say "Faugh!" and frown, saying: "An evil spirit from an evil body." In answer to my question Gabriel told me that this was our father Adam reviewing the spirits of his offspring; the spirit of a believer excited his pleasure, and the spirit of an infidel excited his disgust so that he said the words just quoted.

'Then I saw men with lips like camels; in their hands were pieces of fire like stones which they used to thrust into their mouths and they would come out of their posteriors. I was told that these were those who sinfully devoured the wealth of orphans. . . .

'Then I saw men with good fat meat before them side by side with lean stinking meat, eating of the latter and leaving the former. These are those who forsake the women which God has permitted and go after those he has forbidden.

---

[9]Al-Hasan was a child at the time in which he witnessed this.

[10]Testifier to the Truth.

[11]Surah, 37:10.

'Then I saw women hanging by their breasts. These were those who had fathered bastards on their husbands.' . . .

To continue the tradition of Said al-Khudri: "Then I was taken up to the second heaven and there were the two maternal cousins Jesus, Son of Mary, and John, son of Zakariah.[12] Then to the third heaven and there was a man whose face was as the moon at the full. This was my brother Joseph, son of Jacob. Then to the fourth heaven and there was a man called Idris.[13] And we have exalted him to a lofty place." Then to the fifth heaven and there was a man with white hair and a long beard, never have I seen a more handsome man than he. This was the beloved among his people Aaron son of Imran.[14] Then to the sixth heaven, and there was a dark man with a hooked nose. . . . This was my brother Moses, son of Imran. Then to the seventh heaven and there was a man sitting on a throne at the gate of the immortal mansion. Every day seventy thousand angels went in not to come back until the resurrection day. Never have I seen a man more like myself. This was my father Abraham.[15] Then he took me into Paradise and there I saw a damsel with dark red lips and I asked her to whom she belonged, for she pleased me much when I saw her, and she told me "Zayd b. Haritha." The apostle gave Zayd the good news about her.'[16]

From a tradition of Abdullah b. Masud from the prophet there has reached me the following: When Gabriel took him up to each of the heavens and asked permission to enter he had to say whom he had brought and whether he had received a mission and they would say 'God grant him life, brother and friend!' until they reached the seventh heaven and his Lord. There the duty of fifty prayers a day was laid upon him.

The apostle said: 'On my return I passed by Moses and what a fine friend of yours he was! He asked me how many prayers had been laid upon me and when I told him fifty he said, "Prayer is a weighty matter and your people are weak, so go back to your Lord and ask him to reduce the number for you and your community." I did so and He took off ten. Again I passed by Moses and he said the same again; and so it went on until only five prayers for the whole day and night were left. Moses again gave me the same advice. I replied that I had been back to my Lord and asked him to reduce the number until I was ashamed, and I would not do it again. He of you who performs them in faith and trust will have the reward of fifty prayers.'[17]

---

[12]Known to Christians as John the Baptist.
[13]Known to Jews and Christians as Enoch, the father of Methuselah.
[14]Islam reveres the memory of two men named *Imran:* the father of the Prophet Moses and Moses' brother Aaron; and the father of Mary, the mother of Jesus. Clearly, the reference is to the former Imran.

[15]See source 55, notes 5, 9, and 12.
[16]Zayd was a former slave whom Muhammad freed and then received into his house as a foster son. Muhammad arranged the marriage between Zayd and the beautiful Zaynab bint Jahsh. Later, when Zayd divorced Zaynab, Muhammad married her.
[17] See source 56, note 1.

The First Formulation of *Sharia*, God's Law

▼▼▼

58 ▼ *Malik ibn Anas, THE SMOOTHED PATH*

Because Muslims believe that Allah imparted to His community of believers a body of revelation that encompasses every aspect of their being, the study and application of Sacred Law, or *Sharia*, became and remains one of Islam's most revered religious professions. Among *Sunni,* or mainstream, Muslims, four major schools of interpretive jurisprudence, or *fiqh*, emerged: the *Shafii*, the *Hanafi*, the *Hanbali*, and the *Maliki* — each named after an early master of the law.

Although the schools differ in some matters of juristic interpretation and emphasis, they agree on fundamental legal principles and are largely divided along regional, rather than ideological, lines. All four schools recognize "the four roots of jurisprudence." First and foremost, there is the *Quran*. Second, there is the *sunna,* or correct pathway, of the Prophet and his Companions as preserved in *Hadith* (source 56). Third, there is the consensus and tradition (also the *sunna*) of the *umma,* or universal body of Muslims, which cannot err because it is God's community. Finally, there is a measure of personal interpretation based on analogy, reason, and good sense.

Jurists belonging to the *Shia* branch of Islam revere the same Quran but have their own, distinctive collections of Hadith and reject the consensus of the majority Sunni community as a valid root of the law because they view Sunni Muslims as misguided. They rely, instead, on the infallible teachings of their *imams,* or religious teachers. For more on the these imams and the Shia-Sunni schism, see source 59.

The first significant Sunni scholar to set his hand to codifying Islamic Sacred Law was *Malik ibn Anas* (ca. 716–ca. 796), after whom the Maliki School was later named. The great-grandson of a contemporary of the Prophet, Malik devoted himself to the rational application of Holy Law in all aspects of life and worship. As a legal authority, he rejected the strict and narrow traditionalism of contemporaries such as Ibn Ishaq (source 57) and opted instead for the collective customs of Medina, the City of the Prophet and his own home town, as the standard by which he applied Sharia to those everyday concerns and activities that are not dealt with in the Quran. Put another way, when Hadith and the practices of the Muslims of Medina conflicted, Malik normally gave preference to the latter. What is more, he was not reticent to lay down his own interpretations and judgments when he thought an issue demanded clarification.

Malik's masterwork, *Al-Muwatta (The Smoothed Path),* Islam's earliest significant lawbook, survives in fifteen different versions, of which only two are complete. The reason for these variant forms is that "the Imam of Medina" (as he was and is known) spent his long lifetime lecturing rather than writing. This form of communication lends itself to constant revision. Of the two complete versions of his work, the most authoritative was transmitted by Yahya ibn Yahya al-Masmudi (d. 848), who studied with the imam.

In the following selections from Yahya's version of *The Smoothed Path* we see Malik focus on Islam's Five Pillars: the *shahadah,* or act of bearing witness to the Oneness and Uniqueness of God and the Messengership of Muhammad; daily prayer (*salat*); alms-giving (*zakat*); fasting (*al-Sawm*); and pilgrimage to Mecca (*al-Hajj*).

QUESTIONS FOR ANALYSIS

1. According to this lawbook, what above all else identifies a person as a Muslim?
2. Is zakat a private or a public function? What does your answer suggest about Islam?

3. What is so special about the Five Pillars of Islam? What do they collectively tell us about the religion and its ideals?

4. "Sharia exists to aid imperfect people in becoming holy." Please comment on this statement in light of this source. Be specific in your response.

5. "Sharia demands nothing impossible or unreasonable." Please comment on this statement in light of this source. Be specific in your response.

6. Why do you think this work is known as *The Smoothed Path?*

PRAYER

The Times of Prayer

Yahya related to me from Malik from Nafi, the *mawla*[1] of Abdullah ibn Umar,[2] that Umar ibn al-Khattab[3] wrote to his governors, saying, "The most important of your affairs in my view is the prayer. Whoever protects it and observes it carefully is protecting his *deen,*[4] while whoever is negligent about it will be even more negligent about other things."

Then he added, "Pray Dhuhr[5] any time from when the afternoon shade is the length of your forearm until the length of your shadow matches your height. Pray Asr[6] when the sun is still pure white, so that a rider can travel two or three *farsakhs*[7] before the sun sets. Pray Maghrib[8] when the sun has set. Pray Isha[9] any time from when the redness in the western sky has disappeared until a third of the night has passed — and a person who sleeps, may he have no rest, a person who sleeps, may he have no rest. And pray Subh[10] when all the stars are visible and like a haze in the sky."

▾▾▾

Yahya related to me from Malik that Zayd ibn Aslam said, "The Messenger of Allah, may Allah bless him and grant him peace, stopped for a rest one night on the way to Makka[11] and appointed Bilal[12] to wake them up for the prayer. Bilal slept and everyone else slept and none of them woke up until the sun had risen. When they did wake up they were all alarmed. The Messenger of Allah, may Allah bless him and grant him peace, ordered them to ride out of the valley, saying that there was a shaytan[13] in it. So they rode out of the valley and the Messenger of Allah, may Allah bless him and grant him peace, ordered them to dismount and do wudu[14] and he told Bilal either to call the prayer or to give the *iqama.*[15] The Messenger of Allah, may Allah bless him and grant him peace, then led them in prayer. Noticing their uneasiness, he went to them and said, 'O people!. Allah seized our spirits and if He had wished He would have returned them to us at a time other than this. So if you sleep through the time for a prayer or forget it and then are anxious about it, pray it as if you were praying it in its time.' The Messenger of Allah, may Allah bless him and grant him peace, turned to Abu Bakr[16] and said, 'Shaytan came to Bilal when he was

---

[1] A freed slave.

[2] The son of (*ibn*) Caliph Umar I, Abdullah, who was noted for his piety and scrupulous adherence to the precepts of Islam, is one of the most frequently cited sources for hadiths. He died in 693, well over the age of 80.

[3] Caliph Umar I (r. 634–644), Islam's second caliph, is credited with a large number of religious and civil ordinances.

[4] The contract between Allah and His believers.

[5] The noon prayer.

[6] The afternoon prayer.

[7] One *farsakh* is about three miles.

[8] *Maghrib* means "the West," or the direction in which the sun sets. It is the prayer just after sunset.

[9] The evening or night prayer.

[10] The morning prayer, which is offered between false dawn (first light) and sunrise.

[11] Mecca.

[12] A slave of Ethiopian descent, he was purchased by Abu Bakr (note 16) and freed because of his deep faith. He accompanied Muhammad to Medina and there was appointed Islam's first *muezzin,* the person who calls the Faithful to prayer.

[13] A satan, or devil.

[14] Ritual ablution. See "How to Do Wudu."

[15] The call announcing that prayer is about to begin.

[16] Muhammad's close friend and Islam's first caliph (r. 632–634).

standing in prayer and made him lie down and lulled him to sleep like a small boy.' The Messenger of Allah, may Allah bless him and grant him peace, then called Bilal and told him the same as he had told Abu Bakr. Abu Bakr declared, 'I bear witness that you are the Messenger of Allah.'"

How to Do Wudu

Yahya related to me from Malik from Amr ibn Yahya al-Mazini that his father once asked Abdullah ibn Zayd ibn Asim, who was the grandfather of Amr ibn Yahya al-Mazini and one of the companions of the Messenger of Allah, may Allah bless him and grant him peace, if he could show him how the Messenger of Allah, may Allah bless him and grant him peace, did *wudu*. Abdullah ibn Zayd ibn Asim agreed to do so and asked for water to do *wudu*. He poured some out on to his hand and washed each hand twice and then rinsed his mouth and snuffed water up his nose and blew it out three times. Then he washed his face three times and both of his arms up to the elbows twice. He then wiped his head with both hands, taking his hands from his forehead to the nape of his neck and then bringing them back to where he had begun. Then he washed his feet.

▼▼▼

Yahya said that Malik was asked what a man should do if, when he did *wudu,* he forgot and washed his face before he had rinsed his mouth, or washed his forearms before he had washed his face. He said, "If someone washes his face before rinsing his mouth, he should rinse his mouth and not wash his face again. If someone washes his forearms before his face, however, he should wash his forearms again so that he has washed them after his face. This is if he is still near the place (of *wudu*)."

Yahya said that Malik was asked about what a man should do if he does not remember that he has not rinsed his mouth and nose until after he has prayed. He said, "He does not have to repeat the prayer, but should rinse his mouth and nose if he wishes to do any more prayers after that."

▼▼▼

Yahya related to me from Malik from Nafi that Abdullah ibn Umar used to say that men and their wives used to do *wudu* together in the time of the Messenger of Allah

Tayammum[17]

Yahya related to me from Malik from Abd ar-Rahman ibn al-Qasim from his father that Aisha,[18] *Umm al-Muminin,*[19] said, "We went out on a journey with the Messenger of Allah, may Allah bless him and grant him peace, and, when we came to Bayda or Dhat al-Jaysh, a necklace of mine broke. The Messenger of Allah, may Allah bless him and grant him peace, stopped to look for it and the people stopped with him. There was no water nearby and the people were not carrying any with them, so they came to Abu Bakr as-Siddiq[20] and said, 'Don't you see what Aisha has done? She has made the Messenger of Allah, may Allah bless him and grant him peace, and the people stop when there is no water nearby and they are not carrying any with them.'"

Aisha continued, "Abu Bakr came and the Messenger of Allah, may Allah bless him and grant him peace, had fallen asleep with his head on my thigh. Abu Bakr said, 'You have made the Messenger of Allah, may Allah bless him and grant him peace, and the people stop when there is no water nearby and they are not carrying any with them.'"

She continued, "Abu Bakr remonstrated with me and said whatever Allah willed him to say,

---

[17]Purification before prayer with clean earth or stone, if water is not available or is polluted and detrimental to health.

[18]The third and favorite wife of Muhammad, she was born ca. 614 and was married in 623 or 624. Left a childless widow at age 18 in 632, she became the source for many hadiths. She died in 678.

[19]Mother of the Believers, a title given to each of the Prophet's wives.

[20]Aisha's father. *As-Siddiq,* which means "the most righteous," is his honorific title. See also note 16.

and began to poke me in the waist. The only thing that stopped me from moving was that the Messenger of Allah, may Allah bless him and grant him peace, had his head on my thigh. The Messenger of Allah, may Allah bless him and grant him peace, slept until morning found him with no water. Allah, the Blessed and Exalted, sent down the *ayat*[21] of *tayammum* and so they did *tayammum*. Usayd ibn Hudayr said, 'This is not the first *baraka*[22] from you, O family of Abu Bakr.' "

Aisha added, "We roused the camel I had been on and found the necklace under it."

Malik was asked whether someone who did *tayammum* for one prayer should do *tayammum* when the time of the next prayer came or whether the first *tayammum* was enough. He said, "No, he does *tayammum* for every prayer, because he has to look for water for every prayer. If he looks for it and does not find it then he does *tayammum*."

Malik was asked whether a man who did *tayammum* could lead others in prayer if they were in *wudu*. He said, "I prefer that someone else should lead them. However, I see no harm in it if he does lead them in prayer."

Yahya said that Malik said that a man who did *tayammum* because he could not find any water, and then stood and said the *takbir*[23] and entered into the prayer, and then someone came with some water, did not stop his prayer but completed it with *tayammum* and did *wudu* for future prayers.

Yahya said that Malik said, "Whoever rises for prayer and does not find water and so does what Allah has ordered him to do of *tayammum* has obeyed Allah. Someone who does find water is neither purer than him nor more perfect in prayer, because both have been commanded and each does as Allah has commanded. What Allah has commanded as far as *wudu* is concerned is for the one who finds water, and *tayammum* is for the one who does not find water before he enters into the prayer.

Prayer in General

Yahya related to me from Malik from Ibn Shihab from Ata ibn Yazid al-Laythi that Ubaydullah ibn Adi ibn al-Khiyar said, "Once when the Messenger of Allah, may Allah bless him and grant him peace, was sitting with some people, a man came to him and spoke secretly to him. Nobody knew what he had said until the Messenger of Allah, may Allah bless him and grant him peace, disclosed that he had asked for permission to kill one of the hypocrites. When he disclosed this, the Messenger of Allah, may Allah bless him and grant him peace, said, 'Doesn't he testify that there is no god but Allah and that Muhammad is the Messenger of Allah?' The man replied, 'Of course, but he hasn't really done so.' He said, 'Doesn't he do the prayer?' and the man replied, 'Of course, but he doesn't really do the prayer.' He said, may Allah bless him and grant him peace, Those are the ones whom Allah has forbidden me (to kill).' "

ZAKAT[24]

Things Subject to Zakat

Yahya related to me from Malik from Muhammad ibn Abdullah ibn Abd ar-Rahman ibn Abi Sasaa al-Ansari from al-Mazini from his father from Abu Said al-Khudri that the Messenger of Allah, may Allah bless him and grant him peace, said, "There is no *zakat* on less than five *awsaq*[25] of dates, there is no *zakat* on less than five *awsaq* of silver and there is no *zakat* on less than five camels."

Yahya related to me from Malik that he had heard that Umar ibn Abd al-Aziz[26] wrote to his governor in Damascus about *zakat* saying,

---

[21]A sign or revelation.
[22]A beneficial spiritual energy that flows from a person, place, or thing.
[23]The gesture and proclamation that begins each prayer. The worshiper raises hands to ears and proclaims "*Allahu Akbar*" (God is great).

[24]Two and one-half percent of a Muslim's income that is annually given for charity and support of the *umma*.
[25]An *awsaq* equaled 123 grams of silver. See note 27.
[26]Umar II, the fifth Umayyad caliph (r. 717–720).

"*Zakat* is paid on the produce of cultivated land, on gold and silver, and on livestock." Malik said, "*Zakat* is only paid on three things: the produce of cultivated land, gold and silver, and livestock."

The Zakat on Gold and Silver Coin

Malik said, "The agreed *sunna* with us is that *zakat* has to be paid on twenty dinars[27] (of gold coin) in the same way as it has to be paid on two hundred dirhams[28] (of silver)."

▼▼▼

Malik said, "What we are agreed upon (here in Medina) regarding income from hiring out slaves, rent from property, and the instalments received when a slave buys his freedom, is that no *zakat* is due on any of it, whether great or small, from the day the owner takes possession of it until a year has elapsed over it from the day when the owner takes possession of it."

Non-Zukatable Fruits, Animal Fodder and Vegetables

Malik said, "The *sunna* that we are all agreed upon here (in Medina) and which I have heard from the people of knowledge, is that there is no *zakat* on any kind of fresh (soft) fruit, whether it be pomegranates, peaches, figs or anything that is like them or not like them as long as it is fruit."

He continued, "No *zakat* has to be paid on animal fodder or herbs and vegetables of any kind, and there is no *zakat* to pay on the price realised on their sale until a year has elapsed over it from the day of sale when the seller receives the sum, as long as it reaches the *nisab*."[29]

Zakat on Slaves and Horses

Yahya related to me from Malik from Abdullah ibn Umar from Sulayman ibn Yasar from Irak ibn Malik from Abu Hurayra[30] that the Messenger of Allah, may Allah bless him and grant him peace, said, "A Muslim does not have to pay any zakat on his slave or his horse."

FASTING

Kaffara (Making Amends) for Breaking the Fast in Ramadan[31]

Yahya related to me from Malik from Ibn Shihab from Hunayd ibn Abd ar-Rahman ibn Awf from Abu Hurayra that a man broke the fast in Ramadan and the Messenger of Allah, may Allah bless him and grant him peace, ordered him to make *kaffara* by freeing a slave, or fasting two consecutive months, or feeding sixty poor people, and he said, "I can't do it." Someone brought a large basket of dates to the Messenger of Allah, may Allah bless him and grant him peace, and he said, "Take this and give it away as *sadaqa*."[32] He said, "Messenger of Allah, there is no-one more needy than I am." The Messenger of Allah, may Allah bless him and grant him peace, laughed until his eyeteeth appeared and then said, "Eat them."

The Fidya (Compensation) for Breaking the Fast in Ramadan from Weakness

Yahya related to me from Malik that he had heard that Anas ibn Malik[33] used to pay *fidya* when he had grown old and was no longer able to fast.

Malik said, "I do not consider that to do so is obligatory, but what I like most is that a man does the fast when he is strong enough. Whoever pays compensation gives one *mudd*[34] of food in place of every day, using the *mudd* of the Prophet, may Allah bless him and grant him peace."

Yahya related to me from Malik that he had heard that Abdullah ibn Umar was asked about what a pregnant woman should do if the fast be-

---

[27]One *dinar* was 4.4 grams of gold.

[28]One *dirham* was 3.08 grams of silver. Hence, 200 dirhams equaled five *awsaq* of silver.

[29]The minimum amount of wealth subject to *zakat*.

[30]A Companion of the Prophet and a prolific source of hadiths. Some 3,500 were attributed to him.

[31]The ninth month of the Islamic calendar, when Muslims must abstain from all food and drink from sunrise to sunset.

[32]A gift given in the name of Allah.

[33]The servant of the Prophet in Medina, he died around 709–711 at the age of either 97 or 107.

[34]A measure of volume, approximately one double-handled scoop.

came difficult for her and she feared for her child, and he said, "She should break the fast and feed a poor man one *mudd* of wheat in place of every day missed, using the *mudd* of the Prophet, may Allah bless him and grant him peace."

Malik said, "The people of knowledge consider that she has to make up for each day of the fast that she misses as Allah, the Exalted and Glorified, says, 'And whoever of you is sick or on a journey should fast an equal number of other days,' and they consider this pregnancy as a sickness, in addition to her fear for her child."

The Fast in General

Yahya related to me from Malik from Abuz-Zinad from al-Araj from Abu Hurayra that the Messenger of Allah, may Allah bless him and grant him peace, said, "By the One in Whose hand my self is, the smell of the breath of a man fasting is better with Allah than the scent of musk. Allah says, 'He leaves his desires and his food and drink for My sake. Fasting is for Me and I reward it. Every good action is rewarded by ten times its kind, up to seven hundred times, except fasting, which is for Me, and I reward it.'"[35]

HAJJ

Clothes Forbidden in Ihram[36]

Yahya related to me from Malik from Nafi from Abdullah ibn Umar that a man once asked the Messenger of Allah, may Allah bless him and grant him peace, what clothes some one in *ihram* could wear, and the Messenger of Allah, may Allah bless him and grant him peace, said, "Do not wear shirts, turbans, trousers, burnouses, or leather socks except if you cannot find sandals. In that case you can wear leather socks, but cut them off below the ankles. Do not wear any clothes that have been touched by saffron or yellow dye."

Veiling the Face in Ihram

Yahya related to me from Malik from Nafi that Abdullah ibn Umar used to say that a woman in *ihram* should wear neither a veil nor gloves.

Yahya related to me from Malik from Hisham ibn Urwa that Fatima bint al-Mundhir said, "We used to veil our faces when we were in *ihram* in the company of Asma bint Abi Bakr as-Siddiq."[37]

Wearing Perfume during Hajj

Yahya related to me from Malik from Abd ar-Rahman ibn al-Qasim from his father that Aisha, the wife of the Prophet, may Allah bless him and grant him peace, said, "I perfumed the Messenger of Allah, may Allah bless him and grant him peace, for his *ihram* before he entered *ihram,* and when he came out of *ihram* before he did *tawaf* of the House."[38]

▾▾▾

Yahya related to me from Malik from Nafi from Aslam, the *mawla* of Umar ibn al-Khattab, that Umar ibn al-Khattab noticed the smell of perfume while he was at ash-Shajara, and he asked, "Who is this smell of perfume coming from?" Muawiya ibn Abi Sufyan answered, "From me, *Amir al-Muminin.*"[39] Umar said, "From you? By the life of Allah!" Muawiya explained, "Umm Habiba perfumed me, *Amir al-Muminin.*" "Umar then said, "You must go back and wash it off."

Things That Someone in Ihram Is Allowed to Do

Yahya related to me from Yahya ibn Said from Muhammad ibn Ibrahim ibn al-Harith al-Taymi from Rabia ibn Abr Abdullah ibn al-Hudayr that he saw Umar ibn al-Khattab taking the ticks off a camel of his at as-Suqya while he was in *ihram.*

---

[35]Its rewards are unlimited.
[36]The state of consecration of a pilgrim on *hajj;* its external signs include ritual cleansing of the hair and body, wearing a special garment, and restrictions on behavior.
[37]A sister of Aisha (note 18).
[38]The circumambulation of the Kaaba (also known as the House of God) at the center of the Grand Mosque in Mecca. On two separate occasions pilgrims walk around it seven times in a counterclockwise manner. Aisha refers to the second, which ends the *Hajj.*
[39]Commander of the Believers, a title that Caliph Umar I adopted for himself.

Malik said that he disapproved of that.

Yahya related to me from Malik from Alqama ibn Abi Alqama that his mother said, "I heard Aisha, the wife of the Prophet, may Allah bless him and grant him peace, being asked whether someone in *ihram* could scratch their body or not, and she said, 'Yes, he can scratch it and do so as hard as he pleases. I would scratch even if my hands were tied and I could only use my feet.'"

▼▼▼

Yahya related to me from Malik that Muhammad ibn Abdullah ibn Abi Maryam once asked Said ibn al-Musayyab about (what to do with) one of his nails that had broken while he was in *ihram* and Said said, "Cut it off."[40]

Malik was asked whether someone in *ihram* who had an ear-complaint could use medicinal oil which was not perfumed for dropping into his ears, and he said, I do not see any harm in that, and even if he were to put it into his mouth I still would not see any harm in it."

Malik said that there was no harm in someone in *ihram* lancing an abscess that he had, or a boil, or cutting a vein, if he needed to do so.

Doing the Hajj for Somebody Else

Yahya related to me from Malik from Ibn Shihab from Sulayman ibn Yasar that Abdullah ibn Abbas said, "Al-Fadl ibn Abbas was riding behind the Messenger of Allah, may Allah bless him and grant him peace, when a woman from the Khathama tribe came to him to ask him for a *fatwa*.[41] Al-Fadl began to look at her, and she at him, and the Messenger of Allah, may Allah bless him and grant him peace, turned Fadl's face away to the other side. The woman said, 'Messenger of Allah, Allah's making the *hajj* obligatory finds my father a very old man, unable to stay firm on his riding-beast. Can I do *hajj* for him?', and he said, 'Yes.' This was during the Farewell Hajj."[42]

---

[40]Normally the pilgrim cannot cut hair or nails while in *ihram*.

[41]An authoritative legal opinion.
[42]The Prophet's last *hajj*, at which he gave a farewell sermon.

▼▼▼

Variety and Unity within Islam

Ideally, Islam is a single community united in submission and service to God. In fact, however, as is true of every world religion, it has historically fragmented into a wide variety of sects and schools. The single greatest split within the community of Islam is the division between *Sunnis* and *Shias,* which we shall explore in source 59. The schism between these two branches has often been bitter and violent, as events in contemporary Iraq and other nations of the Islamic Middle East bear witness.

For every act of animosity, however, one can find many instances of understanding and solidarity binding together members of the various factions of Islam. Certainly the centrality of the Quran in the life of every practicing Muslim, regardless of sect, plays a large role in this regard. So also does the fact that almost all Muslims accept as basic religious obligations the Five Pillars of Islam, which we explored in source 58. Of these, the *hajj,* or pilgrimage to Mecca, has served as the single most

important vehicle for bringing Muslims of every identity together in a common religious exercise of transcendental importance. Source 60 provides further insight
into the ways in which the *hajj* has helped unify Muslims from all corners of the
umma.

Two chief purposes behind the *hajj* are reconciliatory: to reconcile Muslims with
God and with one another. Another phenomenon within Islam that has served
these same ends is *Sufi* mysticism. Sunnis and Shias alike have had and continue to
have their Sufi saints, and despite sectarian differences, both sets of Sufi teachers
have preached the primacy of love. Source 61 introduces us to the great thirteenth-
century Sufi mystic, *al-Rumi,* a poet whose voice is as alive today as it was seven
centuries ago.

God's Martyrs: The Party of Ali
▼▼▼
59 ▼ *Ibn Babawayh al-Saduq,*
CREED CONCERNING THE IMAMS

The Six Authentic Compilations preserve traditions sacred to that majority element
of Islam known as *Sunni* Muslims, who claim to follow the correct path *(sunna)* of
tradition as it evolved from the day of the Prophet and his Companions to the present. Underlying the Sunni self-image is the belief that God's community is *infallible,* which means that it can never err. Consequently, the practices and institutions
of mainstream Islam are always correct. Another major faction of Islam, which
claims its own Hadith as the authentic record of the words and actions of the
Prophet and his closest Companions, is the *Shiat Ali* (Party of Ali). Members of this
branch of Islam, known popularly as *Shias,* today comprise almost all of Iran's
population, are a majority in Iraq, and also inhabit portions of Syria, Lebanon, and
the Indian subcontinent.

The Shia break with other Muslims dates back to the mid seventh century. Par-
tisans of Ali, Muhammad's cousin and son-in-law, managed to have him installed
as fourth caliph (r. 656–661) following the murder of Caliph Uthman (r. 644–656).
Many of Uthman's followers did not recognize Ali, however, and civil war ensued.
The result was Ali's assassination in 661, establishment of the rival *Umayyad Dynasty* in the caliphate (r. 661–750), and the martyrdom of Ali's son, *al-Husayn,* the
Prophet's sole surviving grandson, in 680. Supporters of the family of Ali, who included many of the original Muslims of the first Islamic community at Medina, refused to accept the Umayyads as rightful successors of the Prophet. Following the
patriarchal traditions of the desert, they claimed that only a member of Muhammad's family could succeed him as *imam,* or religious leader, of Islam. The result
was a schism in Islam, and to this day the annual commemoration of al-Husayn's
martyrdom at Karbala is the most sorrowful event on the Shia religious calendar.

Often persecuted as religious dissidents and driven underground, the Shias
evolved a theology of history. They not only traced the rightful succession of leadership over the community of Islam from Muhammad and Ali through a number
of subsequent imams, whom the Sunnis did not accept as legitimate, but they also

developed the notion of a messianic *hidden imam,* or *Mahdi* (the Guided One). According to this religious vision, the imams who followed Muhammad were infallible teachers who spoke with the same authority as the Prophet. This line of earthly imams ended, however, at an early point in time (here the various Shia sects disagree as to who was the last visible imam). The imamate, however, was not destroyed. Rather, the last visible imam had, through the power of God, withdrawn from human sight into a state of *occultation,* or spiritual concealment. There he would remain until some future time when he would reappear as the Mahdi to gather his faithful, persecuted followers around him, usher in an Islamic holy age, and herald the Last Judgment.

The largest of all Shia sects is the *Twelver Shia,* which developed around the year 900. These Shias, who predominate in Iran, accept a line of twelve infallible imams, divinely appointed from birth, and believe that the twelfth and last of these visible imams disappeared in the late ninth century.

The following selection from the *creed,* or statement of belief, of Muhammad ibn Ali ibn Babawayh, known as *Sheik al-Saduq* (d. 991), one of the greatest of the early Twelver theologians, illustrates several major Twelver beliefs.

QUESTIONS FOR ANALYSIS

1. Who is Muhammad al-Qaim, and what will he accomplish?
2. What happened to the Prophet Muhammad and each of the first eleven imams?
3. What is *taqiya,* and why is it obligatory for a Shia? In what ways does a follower of the imams follow the model of al-Qaim by practicing taqiya?
4. Can you find any suggestion that Shias believe they possess a secret religious truth denied Sunnis? What is the source of the truth?
5. Shias are said to see themselves as the persecuted, righteous remnant of Islam. Is there any evidence to support such a conclusion in this document? Explain your answer.
6. Will this persecution end? If so, how?
7. How does al-Saduq view Sunnis? Please be specific.

Our belief concerning the number of the prophets is that there have been one hundred and twenty-four thousand prophets and a like number of plenipotentiaries. Each prophet had a plenipotentiary to whom he gave instructions by the command of God. And concerning them we believe that they brought the truth from God and their word is the word of God, their command God's command, and obedience to them obedience to God. . . .

The leaders of the prophets are five (on whom all depends): Noah, Abraham, Moses, Jesus, and Muhammad. Muhammad is their leader . . . he confirmed the (other) apostles.

It is necessary to believe that God did not create anything more excellent than Muhammad and the Imams. . . . After His Prophet,[1] the proofs of God for the people are the Twelve Imams. . . .

We believe that the Proof of Allah in His earth and His viceregent among His slaves in this age

---

[1]The Prophet Muhammad.

of ours is the Upholder {al-Qaim} [of the law of God], the Expected One, Muhammad ibn al-Hasan al-Askari.[2] He it is concerning whose name and descent the Prophet was informed by God, and he it is who WILL FILL THE EARTH WITH JUSTICE AND EQUITY JUST AS IT IS NOW FULL OF OPPRESSION AND WRONG. He it is whom God will make victorious over the whole world until from every place the call to prayer is heard and religion will belong entirely to God, exalted be He. He is the rightly guided *Mahdi* about whom the prophet gave information that when he appears, Jesus, son of Mary, will descend upon the earth and pray behind him.[3] We believe there can be no other *Qaim* than him; he may live in the state of occultation[4] (as long as he likes); were it the space of the existence of this world, there would be no *Qaim* other than him.

Our belief concerning prophets, apostles, Imams, and angels is that they are infallible . . . and do not commit any sin, minor or major . . . he who denies infallibility to them in any matter . . . is a *kafir,* an infidel. . . .

Our belief concerning the Prophet [Muhammad] is that he was poisoned by Jews during the expedition to Khaybar. The poison continued to be noxious until he died of its effects.

1. Imam: And the Prince of Believers [Ali], on whom be peace, was murdered by . . . Ibn Muljam al-Muradi, may God curse him, and was buried in Ghari.
2. Imam: Hasan ibn Ali,[5] on whom be peace, was poisoned by his wife Jada bint Ashath of Kinda, may God curse her and her father.

3. Imam: Husayn ibn Ali[6] was slain at Karbala. His murderer was Sinan ibn-Anal al-Nakhai, may God curse him and his father. . . .

▷　Al-Saduq then lists the fourth through eleventh imams and identifies the murderer of each.

And verily the Prophet and Imams, on whom be peace, had informed the people that they would be murdered. He who says that they were not has given them the lie and has imputed falsehood to God the Mighty and Glorious.

Our belief concerning *taqiya* [permissible dissimulation of one's true beliefs] is that it is obligatory, and he who forsakes it is in the same position as he who forsakes prayer. . . . Now until the time when the Imam al-Qaim appears, *taqiya* is obligatory and it is not permissible to dispense with it. He who does . . . has verily gone out of the religion of God. And God has described the showing of friendship to unbelievers as being possible only in the state of *taqiya.*

And the Imam Jafar[7] said, "Mix with enemies openly but oppose them inwardly, so long as authority is a matter of question."[8] . . . And he said, "He who prays with hypocrites [Sunnis], standing in the first row, it is as though he prayed with the Prophet standing in the first row." And he said, "Visit their sick and attend their funerals and pray in their mosques." . . .

Our belief concerning the Alawiya [descendants of Ali] is that they are the progeny of the Messenger of God and devotion to them is obligatory.

---

[2]The twelfth imam. Al-Hasan al-Askari, the eleventh imam, died around January 1, 874. Twelvers believe that he was succeeded by a young son Muhammad ibn (son of) al-Hasan al Askari, known as *al-Qaim* (the Upholder [of God's Law]), who went into concealment around 878.
[3]Sunni and Shia Muslims believe that the return to Earth in Jerusalem of the prophet and Messiah Jesus will signal the Last Judgment.

[4]Invisible to earthly eyes.
[5]Hasan, the elder son of Ali and Fatima, the Prophet's daughter and sole surviving offspring.
[6]Al-Husayn, Ali and Fatima's younger son.
[7]The sixth imam.
[8]As long as there are Sunni rulers.

An African Pilgrim to Mecca
▼▼▼

60 ▼ Mahmud Kati,
THE CHRONICLE OF THE SEEKER

Despite their differences, all Muslims accept certain basic beliefs, such as the One-ness of God, and perform a number of common religious obligations that serve as powerful forces for Islamic unification. Among these is the pilgrimage, or *hajj,* to Mecca. Every Muslim adult is expected, unless it is impossible, to travel once in a lifetime to Mecca, arriving during the sacred month of *Dhu-al-Hijja,* and join a vast multitude of other pilgrims in a mass celebration of devotional activities. Here Muslims of all sects, races, and social levels mingle without distinction and join in affirming the unity of the family of Islam.

The following document describes the famous pilgrimage that Mansa (King) Musa (Moses) of Mali (r. 1312–1327) made to Mecca in 1324–1325. The sheer size of Mansa Musa's entourage and the generosity this king of sub-Saharan West Africa exhibited to Muslims along the route guaranteed that the memory of his pilgrim-age would not be lost. Several written accounts exist. This particular record is as-cribed to the family of Mahmud Kati (1468?–1593), a native scholar and Islamic judge of Timbuktu. Kati, who according to tradition lived for 125 years, began to compose his history around 1519 and continued it until his death almost 75 years later. His sons and grandsons carried on his labors, bringing the story of Islam in West Africa down to 1655. As was the case with all contemporary writers in that region of the world, Kati and his family composed the work in Arabic.

QUESTIONS FOR ANALYSIS

1. What does Mansa Musa's alleged reason for undertaking the pilgrimage suggest about the hajj and pilgrimages in general?
2. How did his going on pilgrimage make Mansa Musa a better Muslim? What does this suggest about the role of hajj?
3. Is there any evidence in this story to suggest that Islam, though a world religion, still retained strong Arabic connections and flavor? Please explain your answer.
4. What impact did Mansa Musa's hajj have on the traditions and shared histori-cal memory of Mali?
5. What role did oral tradition apparently play in sub-Saharan West African society?

We shall now relate some of what we have been able to discover about the history of the Mali-koy Kankan Musa.[1]

This Mali-koy was an upright, godly, and de-vout sultan.[2] His dominion stretched from the limits of Mali as far as Sibiridugu, and all the

---

[1]Titles meaning "King of Mali, Lord Musa."

[2]An Arabic term meaning "one who wields authority."

peoples in these lands, Songhay[3] and others, obeyed him. Among the signs of his virtue are that he used to emancipate a slave every day, that he made the pilgrimage to the sacred house of God,[4] and that in the course of his pilgrimage he built the great mosque of Timbuktu[5] as well as the mosques of Dukurey, Gundam, Direy, Wanko, and Bako.

His mother Kankan was a native woman, though some say she was of Arab origin. The cause of his pilgrimage was related to me as follows by the scholar Muhammad Quma, may God have mercy on him, who had memorized the traditions of the ancients. He said that the Mali-koy Kankan Musa had killed his mother, Nana Kankan, by mistake. For this he felt deep regret and remorse and feared retribution. In expiation he gave great sums of money in alms and resolved on a life-long fast.

He asked one of the ulama[6] of his time what he could do to expiate this terrible crime, and he replied, "You should seek refuge with the Prophet of God, may God bless and save him. Flee to him, place yourself under his protection, and ask him to intercede for you with God, and God will accept his intercession. That is my view."

Kankan Musa made up his mind that very day and began to collect the money and equipment needed for the journey. He sent proclamations to all parts of his realm asking for supplies and support and went to one of his shaykhs[7] and asked him to choose the day of his departure. "You should wait," said the shaykh, "for the Saturday which falls on the twelfth day of the month. Set forth on that day, and you will not die before you return safe and sound to your residence, please God."

He therefore delayed and waited until these two coincided, and it was not until nine months later that the twelfth of the month fell on a Saturday. He set forth when the head of his caravan had already reached Timbuktu, while he himself was still in his residence in Mali.

Since that time travelers of that people believe it is lucky to set out on a journey on a Saturday which falls on the twelfth of a month. It has become proverbial that when a traveler returns in a bad state, they say of him, "Here is one who did not set out on the Mali-koy's Saturday of departure!"

Kankan Musa set out in force, with much money and a numerous army. A scholar told me that he heard from our shaykh, the very learned qadi[8] Abul-Abbas Sidi Ahmad ibn Ahmad ibn Anda-ag-Muhammad, may God have mercy on him and be pleased with him, that on the day when the pasha[9] Ali ibn al-Qadir[10] left for Twat, announcing that he was going on the pilgrimage to Mecca, he asked how many persons were going with him and was told that the total number of armed men the pasha had with him was about eighty. "God is great! Praise be to God!," said the qadi. "Everything in the world grows less. When Kankan Musa left here to go on pilgrimage he had with him 8,000 men. The Askia Muhammad[11] made the pilgrimage later with 800 men, that is, one-tenth of that. Third after them came Ali ibn Abd al-Qadir, with 80 men, one-tenth of

---

[3]Songhay lay to the east of Mali and centered on the trading city of Gao. Mansa Musa's armies conquered Gao around 1325, and Mali maintained control over Songhay until about 1375. By the late fifteenth century Songhay had replaced Mali as West Africa's major sub-Saharan trading kingdom and held this position of primacy until it was conquered in 1591 by invaders from Morocco.
[4]The *Kaaba* in Mecca, Islam's holiest site. See sources 57 and 58.
[5]Timbuktu was the major trading city of the kingdom of Mali from 1325 to 1433. Its mosque school became the chief center of Islamic learning in sub-Saharan West Africa.

[6]A term that means "the Learned." Islam has no priests but, very much like Rabbinical Judaism, its religious authorities attain and hold their position by virtue of their learning.
[7]An Arabic title of respect meaning "elder."
[8]An Islamic judge who interprets and administers Sharia.
[9]A Turkish title meaning "chief."
[10]Governor of Timbuktu, 1628–1632.
[11]Askia (Emperor) Muhammad Ture the Great (r. 1492–1528), Lord of Songhay. The askia undertook his pilgrimage in 1495–1496, accompanied by Mahmud Kati, who was one of his chief advisors.

800." And he added, "Praise be to God, other than Whom there is no God! Ali ibn Abd al-Qadir did not even achieve his purpose."

Kankan Musa went on his journey, about which there are many stories. Most of them are untrue and the mind refuses to accept them. One such story is that in every town where he stopped on Friday between here and Egypt he built a mosque on that very day. It is said that the mosques of Gundam and Dukurey were among those he built. Both at lunch and at dinner, from when he left his residence until he returned, he ate fresh fish and fresh vegetables.

I was told that his wife, called Inari Konte, went with him, accompanied by 500 of her women and serving women.

Our shaykh, the Mori Bukar ibn Salih, . . . may God have mercy on him, told me that Kankan Musa took forty mule-loads of gold with him when he went on his pilgrimage and visited the tomb of the Prophet [12]

It is said that he asked the Shaykh of the noble and holy city of Mecca, may Almighty God protect it, to give him two, three, or four *sharifs*[13] of the kin of the Prophet of God, may God bless him and save him, to go with him to his country, so that the people of these parts might be blessed by the sight of them and by the blessing of their footsteps in these lands. But the shaykh refused, it being generally agreed that such things should be prevented and refused out of respect and regard for the noble blood of the *sharifs* and for fear lest one of them fall into the hands of the infidels and be lost or go astray. But he persisted in his request and urged them very strongly, until the shaykh said, "I will not do it, but I will neither command nor forbid it. If anyone wishes, let him

follow you. His fate is in his own hands, I am not responsible."

The Mali-koy then sent a crier to the mosques to say, "Whoever wishes to have a thousand *mithqals*[14] of gold, let him follow me to my country, and the thousand is ready for him." Four men of the tribe of Quraysh[15] came to him, but it is claimed that they were freedmen[16] of Quraysh and not real Qurayshis. He gave them 4,000, 1,000 each,[17] and they followed him, with their families, when he returned to his country.

When the Mali-koy reached Timbuktu on his way back, he collected ships and small boats on which he transported their families and luggage, together with his own women, as far as his country, for the riding animals were too exhausted to use. When the ships, carrying the *sharifs* from Mecca, reached the town of Kami, the Dienne-koy[18] . . . attacked the ships and plundered all that they contained. They took the *sharifs* ashore and revolted against the Mali-koy. But when the people of the ships told them about the *sharifs* and informed them of their high station, they attended them, and installed them in a nearby place called Shinshin. It is said that the *sharifs* of the town of Kay are descended from them.

This is the end of the story of the pilgrimage of the Mali-koy Kankan Musa. . . .

As for Mali, it is a vast region and an immense country, containing many towns and villages. The authority of the Sultan of Mali extends over all with force and might. We have heard the common people of our time say that there are four sultans in the world, not counting the supreme sultan,[19] and they are the Sultan of Baghdad,[20] the Sultan of Egypt, the Sultan of Bornu,[21] and the Sultan of Mali.

---

[12]The Prophet's tomb is in Medina.
[13]An Arabic title meaning "exalted one."
[14]A weight of precious metal that varied by region.
[15]The tribe of the Prophet.
[16]Freed former slaves, therefore Qurayshis by adoption, not birth.
[17]He gave each of four men 1,000 mithqals of gold.

[18]The lord of Dienne, technically one of Mansa Musa's vassals.
[19]The Ottoman sultan of Constantinople.
[20]The last Abbasid caliph of Baghdad died in 1258.
[21]A West African trading rival of Songhay located in the region of Lake Chad, along the border of modern Chad and Nigeria.

The Sufi Path

▼▼▼

61 ▼ *Jalaluddin al-Rumi, POEMS, and Ahmed al-Aflaki, THE VIRTUES OF THOSE WHO KNOW*

Islam enjoins all its faithful to live a life centered on God. Those who have taken this injunction most literally, to the point of seeking mystical union with the Divine, are known as *Sufis*. The term might derive from the rough wool *(suf)* clothes worn by many Sufis; it could also refer to the reputed purity *(safa)* of their lives. Whatever the origin of their name, Sufis have been an important force within Islam from its early days.

Despite their emphasis on interior spirituality, Sufis accept the dogmas, rituals, traditions, and practices of Islam, all of which emphasize a balanced, moderate life and worship within a community of believers. This means that although Sufis form themselves into religious brotherhoods, or orders, devoted to prayer and study, most opt not to cut themselves off from the world. Rather, after initiation into an order, most Sufis return to the world to marry, earn a livelihood, and serve the community. At the same time, the movement has produced numerous saints and teachers who have given their entire lives to finding God and leading all who would listen to that Divine Reality. While alive, these Sufi masters have enjoyed widespread popularity among the masses, and in death their tombs serve as sites of pilgrimage.

One of the most popular Sufi pilgrimage sites for over 700 years has been the mausoleum raised over the body of *Mevlana Jalaluddin al-Rumi* (1207–1273) in Konya, a city in Turkey. *Al-Rumi,* as he is generally known in the West, has enjoyed widespread popularity outside of the Islamic World during the past half century because of his poetry, which has been translated out of Persian into a wide variety of modern languages. Sufism has produced many great poets, but none is more beloved than al-Rumi, whose passionate, even eccentric style of ecstatic lyricism has struck respondent chords in millions of Muslims and non-Muslims alike.

Born in Balkh, Afghanistan, the son of a renowned religious teacher, the young Jalaluddin (Keeper of the Faith) left in advance of the Mongol destruction of the city. After wandering from city to city for sixteen years, during which time Jalaluddin married, the young man and his father reached Konya in 1226, where they settled down for life. Konya, the capital of the Seljuk Turkish state of Rum (Rome), so called because it was carved out of Anatolian lands that had once been part of the East Roman, or Byzantine, Empire, gave Jalaluddin not only a home but an identity. He became al-Rumi, "the man from Rum."

Thirteenth-century Konya was a richly cosmopolitan city, with a large Jewish community and a Christian population that outnumbered its resident Muslims. Under its Turkish sultan, the city was also noted for its arts, letters, and religious scholarship. For two years, until his death in 1228, Jalaluddin's father served as the city's leading Islamic teacher. Upon his father's death, the young Jalaluddin continued his studies for an additional eleven years, until, at the age of thirty-two, he was ready to take his place as Konya's preeminent religious teacher. As such, he earned the title *Mevlana* (Our Master).

During the years that followed, until his death on December 17, 1273, al-Rumi wrote and taught prolifically, became his city's most revered figure, and inspired the founding of the *Mevlevi order of Sufis,* which takes its name from his honorific title — Mevlana. Today this order, which can be found throughout Turkey and beyond, is popularly known in the West as the Whirling Dervishes. The term *dervish* is a Turkish variant of the Persian word *darvish,* which means "the sill of a door" and is used to describe someone on the threshold of reaching God. The term *whirling* refers to this brotherhood's distinctive devotional dance in which members whirl about rhythmically to the accompaniment of music while they utter over and over in prayer the name "Allah." Through this dance and prayer they reach a state of transcendence whereby, they believe, they are able to leave behind all earthly concerns and to touch the Divine.

What follow are two of al-Rumi's many poems and a story told about him in the years following his death, a death we are told that was mourned throughout Konya by Muslims, Jews, and Christians alike. The story is contained in a collection of tales of Mevlevi saints compiled between 1318 and 1354 by a disciple of al-Rumi's grandson.

QUESTIONS FOR ANALYSIS

1. What are the key elements of al-Rumi's message and vision as articulated in *The Shepherd's Care* and *From self to Self?*
2. Consider the story reported by Ahmed al-Aflaki. Leaving aside the question of whether or not it is believable (an issue that does not concern historians), what does it suggest about the roles that Sufi saints, such as al-Rumi, have played in Islamic culture?
3. Compose a commentary by a Sufi follower of al-Rumi on one of the following: Ibn Ishaq's treatment of the Prophet's Night Journey; Malik ibn Anas's commentary on Sharia; or al-Saduq's treatise on the Shia.
4. "Sufism transcends sect, class, sex, and all other categories." Please comment on this statement in light of these two sources.
5. Sufis proved to be effective messengers of Islam in India after around the year 1000 (Chapter 9). What was there about Sufis and their approach to religion that might have made it easy for some Indians to convert to Islam?

THE SHEPHERD'S CARE

Join the community of saints and know the delight of your own soul.
Enter the ruins of your heart and learn the meaning of humility.

Drain the cup of passion and walk steadfast on the path of Truth.
Close both eyes and see the mysteries with your inner eye.

Open your arms if you want the Beloved's embrace.

Break your bonds with this body if you want to
see His pure and radiant Face.

Would you marry an old woman to gain a dowry
of a few pennies?
Would you face the threat of swords and spears
for three loaves of bread?

The *Saaqi*[1] is not a tyrant.
So come and sit within her circle.
How long will you stay outside and watch her
dance the way you watch the circling night
sky?

God's creation is vast —
Why do you sit all day in a tiny prison?

Look! He's giving you a real bargain —
Give up one and get a hundred.
Stop running around like a wolf or a dog — stay
and receive the Shepherd's care.

You say, *He stole away my sweetheart!*
Forget it — twenty more sweethearts will come

Thoughts of the Beloved will feed your soul.
How can your hunger be satisfied by thoughts of
bread alone?

Speak little,
Learn the words of eternity.

Go beyond your tangled thoughts and find the
splendor of Paradise.
Go beyond your little world and find the
grandeur of God's world.

FROM self TO SELF

If a tree could run or fly it would not suffer from
the teeth of a saw or the blows of an axe.
If the Sun did not run across the sky the world
would not see the colors of morning.

If water did not rise from the sea plants would
not be quickened by rivers or rain.
It's only when a drop leaves the ocean — and
returns — that it can find an oyster and
become a pearl.

When Joseph left his father both were weeping.
Didn't he gain a kingdom and a fortune in the
end?[2]
Didn't the Prophet gain the world and a
hundred empires by traveling to Medina?[3]

But you have no need to go anywhere —
journey within yourself
Enter a mine of rubies and bathe in the splendor
of your own light.

O great one,
Journey from self to Self and find the mine of
gold.
Leave behind what is sour and bitter — move
toward what is sweet.
Be like the thousand different fruits that grow
from briny soil.

This is the miracle —
Every tree becomes beautiful when touched by
sunlight;
Every soul becomes God when touched by the
Sun of Tabriz.[4]

---

[1]The female cupbearer at a feast or in a tavern. She is a
metaphor for Allah who intoxicates the soul by pouring
forth grace and love.
[2]According to the story of Joseph as told in the Quran
(Joseph also appears as a major figure in the Bible's Book of
Genesis), he was taken from his father and sold into slavery.
Due to his virtues, however, he was released, raised to high
office, and later reunited with his family.

[3]The *hijra* of July 622.
[4]This is one of a number of poems that al-Rumi composed in
memory of his spiritual teacher *Shamsuddin al-Tabrizi*.
Known as "The Glorious Sun of Tabriz," Shamsuddin traveled to Konya from the Iranian city of Tabriz in 642 and immediately captivated Rumi with his mystical message. He
vanished mysteriously in 643, apparently murdered by some
of al-Rumi's jealous disciples, who felt neglected.

FAKHRU-N NISA'S HAJJ

One of Jalal's disciples was a holy woman named Fakhru-n Nisa, "The Glory of Women." She was well known among all the holy men as a woman possessing unsurpassed sanctity. She always attended the meetings at Jalal's house, and he occasionally visited her.

One day her friends suggested that she go on a Pilgrimage to Mecca.[5] She agreed but would not begin her journey without first consulting her master. And so she went to see him. As she entered his presence, before she was even able to speak, Jalal called out to her: "O, most wonderful idea! May thy journey bring you the fortune of both worlds! God willing, we shall be there together." She bowed, said nothing, and left the room. All the disciples who saw this were puzzled.

That night she stayed at Jalal's house, praying with him till midnight. At midnight he went up to the terraced roof to perform the divine vigil. When the service was over, he fell into an ecstatic state, shouting and proclaiming the glory of God. Then he called to the room below, where the lady was, and invited her to come up on the roof and join him.

When she arrived, he told her to look upward, saying that her wish was about to be granted. On looking up, she beheld the sacred black stone of Mecca[6] suspended in the air. It was circling Jalal's head, and spinning round like a whirling darvish. It was so plain and distinct as to leave no room for doubt or uncertainty. She fell into a deep trance, which lasted for a short time, but which felt like an eternity. When she came to, she abandoned ideas of making a pilgrimage to Mecca. For she saw that Jalal was her Mecca. What need had she to go anywhere else?

---

[5]The *hajj.* See sources 58 and 60.
[6]The sacred black stone contained in the Kaaba at Mecca, a cubic building in the heart of the Great Mosque at Mecca and one of the chief objects of veneration during the *hajj.*

Islam and Unbelievers

The Quran reminds Muslims of the heritage that they share with *People of the Book* — namely, Jews, Christians, and Sabeans. Yet the Quran also threatens eternal hell fire for all who perversely refuse to become Muslims, including Jews and Christians who remain obstinate in their rejection of the Prophet's revelations. For those who embrace Islam there is God's peace because they reside in *Dar al-Islam,* the *House of Submission* (or Peace). Many of the stories that comprise Hadith remind Muslims that the followers of Islam share the security of belonging to a community that, at least in the ideal, is fully integrated and supportive of all its members, even the poorest and weakest. Yet Hadith also enjoins upon this community's members the service of *jihad,* or holy struggle, in the name of God. As we have seen in source 56, jihad is a complex obligation that embraces many forms of religious and spiritual struggle. But it does include struggling against unbelievers who do not belong to that community but who reside, rather, in *Dar al-Harb,* the *House of Chaos* (or War). Most classical Islamic jurists from the late eighth century on agreed that while there might be momentary truces between Muslims and those who reside in the House of Chaos, the two Houses could never be permanently at peace with one another. Conflict was inevitable, and consequently jurists crafted treatises on the law of jihad, in which they set out rules governing the calling and prosecution of a jihad of the sword.

But what about unbelievers, or *infidels,* who submit to Islam's secular authority but remain outside of the community of Muslim faithful? How should and, more important, *did* Islamic rulers deal with their non-Muslim subjects, both People of the Book and those outside of the Judaeo-Christian tradition? As the following sources suggest, the answer is not a simple one.

The Dhimma

▼▼▼

62 ▾ *IBN MUSLAMA'S PACT WITH THE CHRISTIANS OF TIFLIS and THE PACT OF UMAR*

One question that faced conquering Islamic armies was how to deal with their non-Muslim subjects, particularly Jews and Christians. Contrary to one popular image, the Muslim conquerors of the seventh and eighth centuries did not, as a matter of general policy, force their new, non-Arab subjects to convert to Islam (although there is evidence of some forced conversions and even massacres of non-Muslim populations during this first age of expansion). Indeed, the Quran expressly forbids forced conversion, and the Prophet's own actions underscored that prohibition. In 628 Muhammad entered into a contract, or *dhimma,* with an Arabic Jewish tribe at the oasis of Khaybar, whereby he guaranteed to defend them and to respect their religious practices in return for their submission, assistance, and payment of tribute. This contract of protection became the paradigm for Islam's generals and statesmen as Arab armies exploded out of the peninsula, but the manner in which Muslims understood and applied the *dhimma* differed from age to age, place to place, and ruler to ruler. The following two documents show us two varieties of the *dhimma* and also reflect some of the ways that the pact tended to change over time.

Our first document records a pact of peace offered to the Christian inhabitants of the city of Tiflis (modern Tbilisi) around 653 by Habib ibn Muslama (617–662), the military commander responsible for the conquest of Christian Armenia and Georgia in the region between the Black and Caspian seas south of the Caucasus Mountains. Ibn Muslama's pact with the Christians of Tiflis is a good example of the earliest form of the *dhimma.*

The second document purports to be the pact of peace offered by Caliph Umar I (r. 634–644) to the Christians of Syria around 637, but scholars generally agree it is a later creation — crafted probably in the early ninth century when the new Abbasid Dynasty of caliphs (r. 750–1258) was occupied with crushing local revolts and needed historical support for policies that were more repressive than those of the earlier Umayyad caliphs (r. 661–750).

However their pacts of protection might differ, the non-Muslims who lived under these compacts were known as *dhimmis* and paid a *jizya,* or poll tax (a tax levied on persons rather than on property), as a token of their submission to the authority of Islam.

QUESTIONS FOR ANALYSIS

1. Exactly what does Ibn Muslama's pact guarantee the Christians, and what obligations does it place on them?
2. What hints are there in Ibn Muslama's pact that strongly suggest it was crafted during the first generation of Islamic expansion?
3. How does the Pact of Umar differ from Ibn Muslama's pact? Please be specific and thorough in your answer.
4. What do the differences that you discovered in answering question 3 suggest about the realities of the era of the Early Abbasids?
5. Large numbers of people living in regions conquered by Islam ultimately converted to that faith. Do these pacts suggest to you any possible reasons for some of those conversions? Please be specific.

THE PACT OF IBN MUSLAMA

In the name of Allah, the compassionate, the merciful. This is a statement from Habib ibn-Muslama to the inhabitants of Tiflis, . . . securing them safety for their lives, churches, convents,[1] religious services and faith, provided they acknowledge their humiliation and pay tax to the amount of one *dinar* on every household. You are not to combine more than one household into one in order to reduce the tax, nor are we to divide the same household into more than one in order to increase it. You owe us counsel and support against the enemies of Allah and his Prophet to the utmost of your ability, and are bound to entertain the needy Muslim for one night and provide him with that food used by "the people of the Book" and which it is legal for us to partake of.[2] If a Muslim is cut off from his companions and falls into your hands, you are bound to deliver him to the nearest body of the "Believers," unless something stands in the way. If you

return to the obedience of Allah and observe prayer, you are our brethren in faith, otherwise poll-tax is incumbent on you. In case an enemy of yours attacks and subjugates you while the Muslims are too busy to come to your aid, the Muslims are not held responsible, nor is it a violation of the covenant with you. The above are your rights and obligations to which Allah and his angels are witness and it is sufficient to have Allah for witness.

THE PACT OF UMAR

In the name of God, the Merciful, the Compassionate! This is a writing to Umar from the Christians of *such and such a city.* When you[3] marched against us,[4] we asked of you protection for ourselves, our posterity, and our co-religionists; and we made this stipulation with you that we will not erect in our city or the suburbs any new monastery, church, cell, or hermitage;[5] that we

[1]Places that house religious communities, such as monks.
[2]Islam prohibits the consumption of certain foods and drink, most notably pork and alcohol.

[3]Muslims.
[4]The Christians of Syria.
[5]The dwelling of a Christian hermit or monk.

will not repair any of such buildings that might fall into ruins, or renew those that might be situated in the Muslim quarters of the town; that we will not refuse the Muslims entry into our churches either by night or by day; that we will open the gates wide to passengers and travelers; that we will receive any Muslim traveler into our houses and give him food and lodging for three nights; that we will not harbor any spy in our churches or houses or conceal any enemy of the Muslims.

That we will not teach our children the Quran; that we will not make a show of the Christian religion or invite anyone to embrace it; that we will not prevent any of our kinsmen from embracing Islam, if they so desire. That we will honor the Muslims and rise up in our assemblies when they wish to take their seats; that we will not imitate them in our dress, either in the cap, turban, sandals, or parting of the hair; that we will not make use of their expressions of speech[6] or adopt their surnames; that we will not ride on saddles or gird on swords or take to ourselves arms or wear them or engrave Arabic inscriptions on our rings; that we will not sell wine;[7] that we

will shave the front of our heads; that we will keep to our own style of dress, wherever we might be; that we will wear belts around our waists.[8]

That we will not display the cross[9] upon our churches or display our crosses or our sacred books in the streets of the Muslims or in their marketplaces; that we will strike the clappers in our churches lightly;[10] that we will not recite our services in a loud voice when a Muslim is present; that we will not carry palm-branches[11] or our images[12] in procession in the streets; that at the burial of our dead we will not chant loudly or carry lighted candles in the streets of the Muslims or their marketplaces; that we will not take any slaves who have already been in the possession of Muslims or spy into their houses; and that we will not strike any Muslim.

All this we promise to observe, on behalf of ourselves and our co-religionists, and receive protection from you in exchange; and if we violate any of the conditions of this agreement, then we forfeit your protection and you are at liberty to treat us as enemies and rebels.

---

[6]Muslims greet one another with certain quranic verses and other affirmations of their faith.
[7]See note 2.
[8]Dhimmis wore leather or cord belts; Muslims wore silk and other types of cloth belts.
[9]Although they greatly revere Jesus as the Messiah, Muslims deny he died on the cross.
[10]Christian churches could not ring bells; the faithful were summoned to prayer by wooden clappers.

[11]On Palm Sunday, the Sunday that precedes Easter. This public procession commemorates Jesus' triumphal entry into Jerusalem.
[12]Islam has traditionally looked upon the use of sacred images as *idolatry* (the worship of idols) and, therefore, a grave offense against God.

The Jewish Community of Twelfth-Century Baghdad

▼▼▼

63 ▼ *Benjamin of Tudela, BOOK OF TRAVELS*

Around 1159 a Jewish traveler, Benjamin ben Jonah of Tudela, departed his native northern Spain and spent the next thirteen or fourteen years visiting several hundred Jewish communities from the Mediterranean to possibly as far east as India. Wherever he traveled he took notes on the Jewish communities that he visited and even some that he only heard about. For example, he informs us that scattered remnants of Israel were flourishing in China. This preoccupation with the location and condition of Jewish communities suggests that Benjamin was seeking to discover places where Jews lived in peace and prospered.

In the following account Benjamin describes the quality of life for Jews under Islamic rule in Baghdad, the capital of the Abbasid caliphate. Despite what Benjamin implies, the twelfth-century caliphs exercised no real civil or military power, having surrendered those powers in the eleventh century to a variety of *sultans* and other so-called subordinates. What is more, the lands that owed the caliphs even nominal obedience had shrunk dramatically in number and size from the days of Abbasid greatness in the early ninth century.

We must keep this in mind as we read Benjamin's enthusiastic account and ask ourselves: By exaggerating the position of the caliph, has Benjamin also exaggerated the position of the *Exilarch* (the leader of the Jewish Community in Exile)? If so, why? An answer suggests itself. Benjamin's book of travels falls into a special genre of Jewish writing known as *consolation literature*. His purpose was to offer his coreligionists the consolation of hope by showing them that, regardless of the Diaspora, the Jewish people prospered because they remained faithful to the Covenant. Given such faithful service, the day of their return to Israel was not far away. If he wanted to highlight Jewish prosperity and strict adherence to the Law, where would be a better place than in the capital of Islam?

This purpose and the possible exaggerations that followed from it do not, however, mean that Benjamin's account is so distorted as to be worthless. Other portions of his book strongly suggest that he attempted to give a true account of Jewish fortunes as he discovered them. For example, he noted that the Jewish community of Christian Constantinople, despite all of the wealth and goodness of the members of this small community of about 2,500, suffered constant public humiliation from the city's inhabitants. Presumably he visited both Constantinople and Baghdad and was able to compare the relative situations of the Jewish populations in these two imperial capitals — the two richest cities in the world, according to Benjamin.

QUESTIONS FOR ANALYSIS

1. Who was Daniel the son of Hisdai, and what function did he serve under the caliph?
2. According to Benjamin of Tudela, what was the status of Jews within the lands ruled by the caliph, and how does he characterize Muslim-Jewish relations in the reign of al-Abbasi?
3. The Jews of Baghdad referred to their leader as *Head of the Captivity,* a term that brings to mind the earlier Babylonian Captivity and the prophecies of Second Isaiah (source 19). What does this term suggest about the Jews' vision of their present status and their hopes for the future?
4. Which aspects of Baghdad's Jewish community most interested Rabbi Benjamin, and what does his interest in them suggest about the reasons why Diaspora Judaism managed to flourish as a religion and a culture?
5. The introduction to this document suggests that Benjamin possibly exaggerated the position and status of the Jews of Baghdad. Which elements of this account strike you as believable? Which strike you as unbelievable or suspicious? Defend your answers.

Baghdad [is] . . . the royal residence of the Caliph Emir al-Muminin al-Abbasi[1] of the family of Muhammad.[2] He is at the head of the Muslim religion, and all the kings of Islam obey him; he occupies a similar position to that held by the pope over the Christians.[3] He has a palace in Baghdad three miles in extent, wherein is a great park with all varieties of trees, fruit-bearing and otherwise, and all manner of animals. . . . There the great king, al-Abbasi the Caliph holds his court, and he is kind unto Israel, and many belonging to the people of Israel are his attendants; he knows all languages, and is well versed in the Law of Israel. He reads and writes the holy language [Hebrew]. . . . He is truthful and trusty, speaking peace to all men. . . .

In Baghdad there are about forty thousand Jews, and they dwell in security, prosperity, and honor under the great Caliph, and among them are great sages, the heads of Academies engaged in the study of the Law.[4] In this city there are ten Academies. . . . And at the head of them all is Daniel the son of Hisdai, who is styled "Our Lord the Head of the Captivity of all Israel." He possesses a book of pedigrees going back as far as David, King of Israel.[5] The Jews call him "Our Lord, Head of the Captivity," and the Muslims call him "Saidna ben Daoud,"[6] and he has been invested with authority over all the congregations of Israel at the hands of the Emir al-Muminin, the Lord of Islam. For thus Muhammad[7] commanded concerning him and his descendants; and he granted him a seal of office over all the congrega-

tions that dwell under his rule, and ordered that every one, whether Muslim or Jew, or belonging to any other nation in his dominion, should rise up before him and salute him, and that any one who should refuse to rise up should receive one hundred stripes.[8]

And every fifth day when he goes to pay a visit to the great Caliph, horsemen, gentiles as well as Jews, escort him, and heralds proclaim in advance, "Make way before our Lord, the son of David, as is due unto him," the Arabic words being "Amilu tarik la Saidna ben Daud." He is mounted on a horse, and is attired in robes of silk and embroidery with a large turban on his head. . . . Then he appears before the Caliph and kisses his hand, and the Caliph rises and places him on a throne which Muhammad had ordered to be made for him, and all the Muslim princes who attend the court of the Caliph rise up before him. And the Head of the Captivity is seated on his throne opposite to the Caliph, in compliance with the command of Muhammad. . . . The authority of the Head of the Captivity extends over all the communities of Shinar,[9] Persia, Khurasan[10] and Sheba which is El-Yemen,[11] and Diyar Kalach[12] and the land of Aram Naharaim,[13] and over the dwellers in the mountains of Ararat[14] and the land of the Alans.[15] . . . His authority extends also over the land of Siberia,[16] and the communities in the land of the Togarmim[17] unto the mountains of Asveh and the land of Gurgan, the inhabitants of which are called Gurganim who dwell by the river Gihon, and these are the Gir-

---

[1]Also known as *al-Mustanjid* (r. 1160–1170).
[2]The Abbasids claimed descent from the Prophet's uncle Abbas.
[3]The bishop of Rome who served as head of the Christian Church in the West. See Chapter 10.
[4]Academies for the study of scripture and postbiblical law (see note 21). These scholars served as the rabbis, or religious teachers and judges, of their community.
[5]King of Israel around 1000 B.C.E.
[6]The Lord son of David.
[7]Not the Prophet Muhammad but possibly al-Abbasi's predecessor, Muhammad el-Moktafi.
[8]A public flogging in which the person receives 100 blows.
[9]Southern Mesopotamia (ancient Sumer and Akkad).
[10]Northeastern Iran.

[11]Southern Arabia. This was the presumed land of the tenth-century B.C.E. queen of Sheba, who visited Israel's King Solomon (the Bible, 1 Kings 10:1–13).
[12]Anatolia (modern Asiatic Turkey).
[13]Northern Mesopotamia (modern northern Syria).
[14]Armenia.
[15]An Indo-European people inhabiting the southern Caucasus Mountain region of Georgia.
[16]He probably means *Iberia* not Siberia. If the reference is to Iberia, he does not mean the Iberian Peninsula, where the modern nations of Spain and Portugal are located, but rather the land that today roughly corresponds to the nation of Georgia (source 51).
[17]One of a number of people of the central Euphrates in biblical times (the Bible, Genesis 10:3).

gashites who follow the Christian religion.[18] Further it extends to the gates of Samarkand,[19] the land of Tibet, and the land of India. In respect of all these countries the Head of the Captivity gives the communities power to appoint Rabbis and Ministers who come unto him to be consecrated and to receive his authority. They bring him offerings and gifts from the ends of the earth. He owns hospices, gardens, and plantations in Babylon,[20] and much land inherited from his fathers, and no one can take his possessions from him by force. He has a fixed weekly revenue arising from the hospices of the Jews, the markets and the merchants, apart from that which is brought to him from far-off lands. The man is very rich, and wise in the Scriptures as well as in the Talmud,[21] and many Israelites dine at his table every day.

At his installation, the Head of the Captivity gives much money to the Caliph, to the Princes, and to the Ministers. On the day that the Caliph performs the ceremony of investing him with au-

thority, he rides in the second of the royal carriages, and is escorted from the palace of the Caliph to his own house with timbrels and fifes. The Exilarch[22] appoints the Chiefs of the Academies by placing his hand upon their heads, thus installing them in their office. The Jews of the city are learned men and very rich.

In Baghdad there are twenty-eight Jewish Synagogues, situated either in the city itself or in al-Karkh on the other side of the Tigris; for the river divides the metropolis into two parts. The great synagogue of the Head of the Captivity has columns of marble of various colors overlaid with silver and gold, and on these columns are sentences of the Psalms[23] in golden letters. And in front of the ark are about ten steps of marble; on the topmost step are the seats of the Head of the Captivity and of the Princes of the House of David. The city of Baghdad is twenty miles in circumference, situated in a land of palms, gardens and plantations, the like of which is not to be found in the whole land of Shinar.

---

[18]Apparently he means the African Christian civilizations of Nubia (modern Sudan) and Ethiopia. Gihon was one of the four biblical rivers of the Garden of Eden and usually refers to the Nile. The Girgashites were one of the seven people who inhabited Canaan before its conquest by the Hebrews under Joshua.
[19]A major commercial city that today is located in Uzbekistan, in Central Asia.
[20]The region around Baghdad.

[21]The *Talmud* (Instruction or Learning) is a collection of postbiblical laws, customs, moral teachings, and edifying stories compiled in Palestine and Mesopotamia during the first six centuries C.E. So far as Rabbinical Judaism is concerned, it is second in authority only to the Tanakh, or Bible.
[22]The ruler of the exile — Daniel, the son of Hisdai.
[23]Sacred hymns that constitute one of the books of the Bible.

Fourteenth-Century Hindu Dhimmis

▼▼▼

64 ▼ *THE DEEDS OF SULTAN FIRUZ SHAH*

As the armies of Islam moved out of Arabia, they came into contact with cultures that practiced religions other than Judaism and Christianity, such as Zoroastrianism in Iran and Hinduism and Buddhism in India. Although Muslims initially viewed these religions as polytheistic faiths that deserved no consideration or protection, necessity demanded that Islamic leaders make the same accommodations with them that they made with the People of the Book.

Actually Zoroastrianism had sacred books that drew the admiration of Islamic religious teachers, once they learned of them, and it held many doctrines, such as a belief in a Last Judgment, that were quite close to those of Islam. Indeed, many of Zoroastrianism's religious tenets had deeply influenced the development of certain

Judaic, Christian, and Islamic articles of faith. So it is somewhat ironic that Zoroastrianism largely disappeared from its native land following the Islamic conquest of Iran in the mid seventh century. Although Zoroastrianism was not outlawed, the social and economic pressures placed on its priests, or *magi,* and its adherents led to the eventual conversion to Islam of most Zoroastrians who opted to remain in their homeland. The situation for Hindus under Islam was not so clear cut.

In 711 Islamic forces out of Iraq and Syria secured the extreme northwest coastal corner of the Indian subcontinent along the mouth of the Indus River, but they advanced no farther. The next Islamic advance into India came from another direction and was carried forward by Muslims from another ethnic culture. Around the year 1000, Turkish Muslims out of Afghanistan began pushing into northwest India, where they set up a base of operations in Lahore, which is located in the modern Islamic nation of Pakistan. Around the year 1200, another Islamic-Turkish group of warlords, also out of Afghanistan, swept through north central India. In the course of the next 150 years this second wave of Turks established the *Sultanate of Delhi.* At its height in the early fourteenth century, this Islamic state controlled, in varying degrees, almost the entire Indian subcontinent, except for the southernmost areas.

Firuz Shah Tughluq, who reigned from 1351 to 1388, enjoyed the reputation of being the most pious, humane, and generous of the sultans of Delhi. Toward the end of his life he prepared an account of the accomplishments in which he took the greatest pride. In the following excerpts from that account he details the manner in which he carried out his duties toward his subjects, of whom only a minority were Muslims.

QUESTIONS FOR ANALYSIS

1. How did Firuz Shah see his responsibilities toward Sunni Muslims? How did he treat Shias?
2. How did Firuz Shah treat his Hindu subjects? Did he seem to have any sense of responsibility on their behalf? If so, what sort of responsibility?
3. Study Firuz Shah's treatment of his Hindu subjects in light of the two pacts in source 62. What conclusions follow from your analysis?
4. Compare Firuz Shah's treatment of Hindus with the way in which he dealt with Shias. What conclusions follow from your analysis?
5. What did Firuz Shah believe were his greatest responsibilities and achievements? What conclusions follow from your answer?
6. Reconsider your answer to question 5 of source 62 in the light of this document. Has the present document confirmed your earlier inferences or caused you to modify them?

Praises without end, and infinite thanks to that merciful Creator who gave to me his poor abject creature Firuz. . . . His impulse for the maintenance of the laws of His religion, for the repression of heresy, the prevention of crime, and the prohibition of things forbidden; who gave me also a disposition for discharging my lawful duties and my moral obligations. My desire is that, to the best of my human power, I should recount and pay my thanks for the many blessings He has bestowed upon me, so that I may be found among the number of His grateful servants. First I would praise Him because when irreligion and sins opposed to the Law prevailed in Hindustan,[1] and men's habits and dispositions were inclined towards them, and were averse to the restraints of religion, He inspired me His humble servant with an earnest desire to repress irreligion and wickedness, so that I was able to labor diligently until with His blessing the vanities of the world, and things repugnant to religion, were set aside, and the true was distinguished from the false.

In the reigns of former kings[2] the blood of many Muslims had been shed, and many varieties of torture employed. Amputation of hands and feet, ears and noses; tearing out the eyes, pouring molten lead into the throat, crushing the bones of the hands and feet with mallets, burning the body with fire, driving iron nails into the hands, feet, and bosom, cutting the sinews, sawing men asunder; these and many similar tortures were practiced. The great and merciful God made me, His servant, hope and seek for His mercy by devoting myself to prevent the unlawful killing of Muslims, and the infliction of any kind of torture upon them or upon any men. . . .

By God's help I determined that the lives of Muslims and true believers should be in perfect immunity, and whoever transgressed the Law should receive the punishment prescribed by the book[3] and the decrees of judges. . . .

The sect of Shias . . . had endeavored to make proselytes.[4] They wrote treatises and books, and gave instruction and lectures upon the tenets of their sect, and traduced and reviled the first chiefs of our religion (on whom be the peace of God!). I seized them all and I convicted them of their errors and perversions. On the most zealous I inflicted punishment, and the rest I visited with censure and threats of public punishment. Their books I burnt in public, and so by the grace of God the influence of this sect was entirely suppressed. . . .

The Hindus and idol-worshipers had agreed to pay the money for toleration, and had consented to the poll tax, in return for which they and their families enjoyed security. These people now erected new idol temples in the city and the environs in opposition to the Law of the Prophet which declares that such temples are not to be tolerated. Under Divine guidance I destroyed these edifices, and I killed those leaders of infidelity who seduced others into error, and the lower orders I subjected to stripes and chastisement, until this abuse was entirely abolished.[5] . . . I forbade the infliction of any severe punishment on the Hindus in general, but I destroyed their idol temples, and instead thereof raised mosques. . . . Where infidels and idolaters worshiped idols, Muslims now, by God's mercy, perform their devotions to the true God. Praises of God and the summons to prayer are now heard there, and that place which was formerly the home of infidels has become the habitation of the faithful, who there repeat their creed and offer up their praises to God. . . .

In former times it had been the custom to wear ornamented garments, and men received robes as tokens of honor from kings' courts. Figures and devices were painted and displayed on saddles, bridles, and collars, on censers, on goblets and cups, and flagons, on dishes and ewers, in tents, on curtains and on chairs, and upon all articles and utensils. Under Divine guidance and favor I ordered all pictures and portraits to be removed from these things, and that such articles only should be made as are approved and recognized by the Law. Those pictures and portraits which were painted on the doors and walls of palaces I ordered to be effaced.[6]

---

[1]The north central region of India inhabited largely by Hindus.

[2]Muhammad ben Tughluq (r. 1325–1351), his predecessor, had been noted for his cruelty.

[3]Sharia according to the dictates of the Quran.

[4]Converts.

[5]Compare this with the *Pact of Umar.*

[6]Most Muslims regard the representation of human or animal figures to be blasphemy.

Formerly the garments of great men were generally made of silk and gold brocades, beautiful but unlawful. Under Divine guidance I ordered that such garments should be worn as are approved by the Law of the Prophet, and that choice should be made of such trimmings of gold brocade, embroidery, or braiding as did not exceed four inches in breadth. Whatever was unlawful and forbidden by, or opposed to, the Law was set aside.

Among the gifts which God bestowed upon me, His humble servant, was a desire to erect public buildings. So I built many mosques and colleges[7] and monasteries, that the learned and the elders, the devout and the holy, might worship God in these edifices, and aid the kind builder with their prayers. The digging of canals, the planting of trees, and the endowing with lands are in accordance with the directions of the Law. The learned doctors of the Law of Islam have many troubles; of this there is no doubt. I settled allowances upon them in proportion to their necessary expenses, so that they might regularly receive the income. . . .

For the benefit of travelers and pilgrims resorting to the tombs of illustrious kings and celebrated saints,[8] and for providing the things necessary in these holy places, I confirmed and gave effect to the grants of villages, lands, and other endowments which had been conferred upon them in olden times. In those cases where no endowment or provision has been settled, I made an endowment, so that these establishments might for ever be secure of an income, to afford comfort to travelers and wayfarers, to holy men and learned men. May they remember those ancient benefactors and me in their prayers.

I was enabled by God's help to build a . . . hospital, for the benefit of every one of high or low degree, who was suddenly attacked by illness and overcome by suffering. Physicians attend there to ascertain the disease, to look after the cure, to regulate the diet, and to administer medicine. The cost of the medicines and the food is defrayed from my endowments. All sick persons, residents and travelers, gentle and simple, bond and free, resort thither; their maladies are treated, and, under God's blessing, they are cured. . . .

I encouraged my infidel subjects to embrace the religion of the Prophet, and I proclaimed that every one who repeated the creed[9] and became a Muslim should be exempt from the jizya, or poll-tax. Information of this came to the ears of the people at large, and great numbers of Hindus presented themselves, and were admitted to the honor of Islam. Thus they came forward day by day from every quarter, and, adopting the faith, were exonerated from the jizya, and were favored with presents and honors. . . .

Whenever a person had completed the natural term of life and had become full of years, after providing for his support, I advised and admonished him to direct his thoughts to making preparation for the life to come, and to repent of all things which he had done contrary to the Law and religion in his youth; to wean his affections from this world, and to fix them on the next. . . .

My object in writing this book has been to express my gratitude to the All-bountiful God for the many and various blessings He has bestowed upon me. Secondly, that men who desire to be good and prosperous may read this and learn what is the proper course. There is this concise maxim, by observing which, a man may obtain God's guidance: Men will be judged according to their works, and rewarded for the good that they have done.

---

[7]*Madrasas* — religious academies for boys.
[8]The tombs of Sufi saints around whom cults of veneration had grown.

[9]"There is no god but *the* God; Muhammad is the Messenger of God."

Part Three

▼▼▼

Continuity, Change, and Interchange:
500–1500

Hinduism, Buddhism, Confucianism, Greek rationalism, imperial systems of government and bureaucracy, Christianity, and many other major world traditions were firmly in place by 500 C.E., and despite vicissitudes, they remained integral elements of global history for the next 1,000 years and beyond. The continuity of culture, especially in China and India, is one of the major features of the period 500–1500. A Chinese of the Han Dynasty would find much that was familiar in *Ming* China (1368–1644), and even while Islam was making an important impact on northern India after 1000, Hindu culture continued to flourish and develop along lines that reached back at least to Indo-Aryan antiquity. At the same time, this millennium witnessed radical changes from which even the essentially conservative societies of China and India were not immune.

Many of the changes were due to the movement and interchange of peoples. Germans and other fringe groups infiltrated the Roman Empire and became a major factor in the radical transformation of society in the empire's western regions. The rise and spread of Islam in the seventh and eighth centuries created a new cultural bloc that stretched from western North Africa and Spain to Central Asia. The later movements of Turkish and Mongol nomads out of Central Asia resulted in empires that severely strained but also richly cross-pollinated almost all of Eurasia's older civilized societies. Hindu, Chinese, and Arab merchants deeply influenced the development of civilization in Southeast Asia, their common meeting ground. It is almost impossible to exaggerate the impact that China had on the development of Korean and Japanese cultures, but regardless of their debts to China, both evolved distinctive cultures that were anything but slavish copies of Chinese civilization. The Byzantine World, centered on Constantinople, became the model and civilizer of Eastern and Southern Slavs, most notably the Russians and the Serbs. Western Christian Europe expanded into Ireland, Germany, Scandinavia, Iceland, Greenland, the lands of the Baltic Sea, Poland, and Hungary. It even established a brief presence in North America around the year 1000 and, more significantly, set up overseas colonies in the Eastern Mediterranean and Black Sea during the Age of the Crusades. By 1500 Christianity, in both its Latin and Byzantine forms, provided spiritual direction to Europeans from Iceland to the Volga. Well before 1500, major portions of sub-Saharan Africa had become integral parts of the Islamic World, and toward the end of the fifteenth century Europeans were making their presence known along the African coast.

Of all of Eurasia's civilizations, Western Europe underwent the most radical changes during this thousand-year period. Out of the chaos that ensued following the collapse of Roman society in the West, a new civilization emerged: Western Christian Europe. By 1100 it was an aggressive, expansionistic power, as the crusades bear witness. Despite a number of crises in the fourteenth century, which occasioned a momentary retrenchment, Western Europe never abandoned its spirit of expansion. In 1492 it was ready to resume explorations across the Atlantic. One consequence of this transoceanic expansion was the virtual destruction of almost all Amerindian cultures and their absorption into the fabric of Western European civilization.

Chapter 9

Asia
Change in the Context of Tradition

Asia was home to the world's oldest and most complex civilizations, and as such, its deeply rooted cultures were the most tradition bound. Even Asia's newer civilizations, such as Japan, exhibited an innate conservatism, in part because they had borrowed so heavily from their well-established neighbors.

Change, of course, comes to all societies, old and new, and Asia was no exception. Occasionally, it arrived in dramatic fashion, as in the destruction of the Abbasid caliphate in 1258 or the establishment of the hated *Yuan* Dynasty (1264–1368) in China. More often than not, however, change arrived clothed in the guise of tradition. Even *Khubilai Khan,* Mongol emperor of China (r. 1260–1294), adopted a Chinese name for his dynasty, performed the Confucian imperial rites, and tried to re-establish the civil service examination system. When in 1192 Minamoto Yoritomo (1147–1199) transferred all real political and military power to himself as *shogun,* he left Japan's imperial court and structure in place and allowed local lords to retain a good measure of their old feudal autonomy.

A reverence for tradition did not mean a lack of dynamism. The great urban centers of Asia — Baghdad, Cambay, Chang'an, Delhi, Hangzhou, Nara — were prosperous and cosmopolitan. China in the eleventh century had several cities with populations of a million or more, and the volume of commerce in those urban centers eventually necessitated the creation of imperially guaranteed paper money. Economic prosperity also meant artistic patronage, and as a result artistic expression flourished from Southwest Asia to Japan. As European travelers learned, the riches of Asia were no empty fable.

▼▼▼

Japan: Creating a Distinctive Civilization

Composed of four main islands, Japan's closest continental neighbor is Korea, which at its closest point is still about 120 miles away across a stretch of often tempestuous water. This insularity has benefited Japan to the point that it is close enough to the East Asian mainland to receive the stimulation of foreign ideas but far enough away to be free to choose what it wishes to adopt from abroad. The result is a culturally homogenous Japanese civilization that has its distinctive identity but which also clearly has been the beneficiary of influences from across the Sea of Japan.

The Japanese spoken language is distantly related to Korean but unrelated to Chinese, suggesting that the ancestors of the historical Japanese originated in lands northeast of China and migrated down into the Korean Peninsula, from where they sailed into the archipelago of islands that make up Japan. There they slowly displaced the islands' original inhabitants, including the *Ainu,* who are physically quite different from the Japanese. It is not at all clear when this migration took place, but sometime after 300 B.C.E. the Japanese emerged as an identifiable culture. It was only in the period around the end of the fourth century B.C.E. that agriculture based on rice cultivation arrived from South China, probably by way of Korea. Given Korea's proximity and earlier historical development, it is not at all surprising that the peninsula proved to be a major conduit for cultural imports from mainland East Asia. Around 200 C.E. the Japanese were working iron, a Chinese process received from Korea.

Japan's first identifiable state arose no earlier than the third century C.E. when the chieftains of a clan devoted to the Sun Goddess established their hegemony on the Yamato Plain in the western regions of the island of Honshu. To the Chinese, Japan in this period was the rustic land of *Wa,* which they represented by an ideograph that meant "dwarf." The Japanese themselves were illiterate until, as the story goes, a Korean scribe named Wani arrived in 405 C.E. to offer instruction in Chinese script, which the Japanese quickly adapted to their language. In the mid sixth century a Chinese form of Mahayana Buddhism made its way to Japan from Korea, and in 646 it was officially acknowledged as the religion of the aristocracy. The coming of Buddhism sharpened the desire of Japan's leaders to adopt Chinese culture, and during the seventh and eighth centuries the imperial court of Japan dispatched numerous sons of noblemen to China's imperial court at *Chang'an,* where they could observe firsthand the governmental system of the *Tang Dynasty* (618–907) before returning home to assume important official positions. These visitors to Chang'an brought back with them not only the forms of Chinese government but also some of the spirit that infused Chinese culture. Confucianism, Buddhism, and Daoism were woven into the fabric of Japanese civilization during these centuries of tutelage. What is more, many Chinese tastes, artistic styles, and artifacts were adopted.

Never, however, did these Chinese influences destroy native Japanese culture. The religion of *Shinto* (the way of the gods), Japan's original animistic religion, is a good example. Shinto remained a vital force within Japanese culture despite attempts by some Japanese leaders to suppress it as a backward religion. Just as important, clan descent and inherited status remained vital social and political determinants in Japan. Unlike China, whose tightly organized government was increasingly in the hands of a professional class of scholars, Japan's society and government remained in the control of feudal clan lords and hereditary aristocrats. Japan experimented with but chose not to adopt the Chinese civil service examinations.

In 794 Emperor Kammu moved his capital from *Heijo* (known today as *Nara*), which had been modeled physically upon the Tang capital at Chang'an, to *Heiankyo* (later known as *Kyoto*) in order to end what seemed to him to be a slavish imitation of everything Chinese. Tang China was now in turmoil, and it was a good time to modify and even discard some aspects of Chinese culture that earlier Japanese Sinophiles (lovers of all things Chinese) had adopted so enthusiastically. During the *Heian Period* (794–1185) the culture of the imperial court soared to unprecedented levels of refinement, and Japanese civilization reached a level of mature independence it would never relinquish. The Japanese became more selective in their assimilation of Chinese influences and increasingly discovered inspiration for creative expression in their own land and people.

The Constitution of Prince Shotoku
▼▼▼
65 ▼ *CHRONICLES OF JAPAN*

Japan is unique in the fact that a single imperial dynasty has reigned over the land and its people for the past 1,700 years. This family, known as the *Sun Line,* claims descent from the sun goddess Ameterasu through her great-great-grandson *Jimmu Tennu* (Divine Warrior), the mythic first emperor of Japan who, according to legend, began to rule in 660 B.C.E. The historical truth is less grand. The *Yamato* clan, which became the Sun Line, seems to have established its dominance in western Japan no earlier than the third century C.E. Whatever the origins of their dynasty, the range of the Yamato clan's authority grew in the course of its first several centuries of state building, thanks to fortunate alliances, conquests, and the development of a literate bureaucracy. By the sixth century the Yamato emperors and empresses had become living symbols of Japanese religious and cultural unity. However, even though it claimed divine origins, the Yamato family could not control several of Japan's powerful clan chieftains. Indeed, the opposite was more the case. Several powerful clans vied to control the imperial family.

One of the most powerful of Japan's late-sixth-century clans, or *uji*, was the *Soga family* headed by *Soga no Umako.* In addition to struggling successfully against the rival Nakatomi and Mononobe clans for influence over the imperial court, Soga no Umako also supported the policy of actively welcoming Chinese influences on a massive scale into Japan as a way of extending the authority of the imperial family that it controlled and increasing the overall prosperity and power of this island empire.

After engineering the assassination of one emperor, Soga no Umako chose a woman, *Empress Suiko* (r. 592–628), as nominal ruler. To guide her along lines that he considered correct, Soga designated an imperial prince to serve as regent. Under the direction of this crown prince, known as *Shotoku* (Sovereign Moral Power), Japan embarked on a course of deliberate cultural borrowing that was unprecedented in history. In 604 Prince Shotoku issued the *Constitution of Seventeen Articles,* which laid out the ideological basis for the reforms that he, Empress Suiko, and Soga no Umako were championing.

Our knowledge of Shotoku's constitution comes from the *Nihongi* or *Chronicles of Japan,* one of Japan's two oldest collections of legend and history. Composed in its final form in 720, the *Nihongi* traces the history of Japan back to the mythological age of the gods. By the time the *Nihongi* reaches the sixth century C.E., its narrative has largely left the realm of myth and become more reliable history.

QUESTIONS FOR ANALYSIS

1. What kind of constitution is this? Is it a code of institutional rules and regulations, or is it something else? What does your answer suggest?
2. What does this constitution allow you to infer about Shotoku's ideals and goals?
3. Review sources 5–6, 20–22, and 32–33. What Confucian principles do you find in this document? Can you find any Daoist ideas? What about Legalist elements?
4. What native, or non-Chinese, elements do you find in this document? What do they suggest about Japanese society?

The Prince Imperial in person prepared for the first time laws. There were seventeen clauses as follows: —

1. Harmony is to be valued, and an avoidance of wanton opposition to be honored. All men are influenced by class-feelings, and there are few who are intelligent. Hence there are some who disobey their lords and fathers, or who maintain feuds with the neighboring villages. But when those above are harmonious and those below are friendly, and there is concord in the discussion of business, right views of things spontaneously gain acceptance. Then what is there which cannot be accomplished!

2. Sincerely reverence the three treasures. The three treasures: the Buddha, the Law, and the Priesthood,[1] are the final refuge . . . and are the supreme objects of faith in all countries. What man in what age can fail to reverence this law? Few men are utterly bad. They may be taught to follow it. But if they do not go to the three treasures, how shall their crookedness be made straight?

3. When you receive the Imperial commands, fail not scrupulously to obey them. The lord is Heaven, the vassal is Earth.[2] Heaven overspreads, and Earth upbears. When this is so, the four seasons follow their due course, and the powers of Nature obtain their efficacy. If the Earth at-

---

[1]The Buddha, the Law of Dharma, and the Sangha, or order of male and female monks, are the three treasures, or key elements, of Buddhism.

[2]Lord and vassal mean in this context not just emperor and subject but local clan chieftains and their retainers.

tempted to overspread, Heaven would simply fall in ruin. Therefore is it that when the lord speaks, the vassal listens; when the superior acts, the inferior yields compliance. Consequently when you receive the Imperial commands, fail not to carry them out scrupulously. Let there be a want of care in this matter, and ruin is the natural consequence.

4. The Ministers and functionaries should make decorous behavior their leading principle, for the leading principle of the government of the people consists in decorous behavior. If the superiors do not behave with decorum, the inferiors are disorderly: if inferiors are wanting in proper behavior, there must necessarily be offenses. Therefore it is that when lord and vassal behave with propriety, the distinctions of rank are not confused: when the people behave with propriety, the Government of the Commonwealth proceeds of itself. . . .

6. Chastise that which is evil and encourage that which is good. This was the excellent rule of antiquity. Conceal not, therefore, the good qualities of others, and fail not to correct that which is wrong when you see it. Flatterers and deceivers are a sharp weapon for the overthrow of the State, and a pointed sword for the destruction of the people. Sycophants are also fond, when they meet, of speaking at length to their superiors on the errors of their inferiors; to their inferiors, they censure the faults of their superiors. Men of this kind are all wanting in fidelity to their lord, and in benevolence toward the people. From such an origin great civil disturbances arise.

7. Let every man have his own charge, and let not the spheres of duty be confused. When wise men are entrusted with office, the sound of praise arises. If unprincipled men hold office, disasters and tumults are multiplied. In this world, few are born with knowledge: wisdom is the product of earnest meditation. In all things, whether great or small, find the right man, and they will surely be well managed: on all occasions, be they

urgent or the reverse, meet but with a wise man, and they will of themselves be amenable. In this way will the State be lasting and the Temples of the Earth and of Grain[3] will be free from danger. Therefore did the wise sovereigns of antiquity seek the man to fill the office, and not the office for the sake of the man. . . .

10. Let us cease from wrath, and refrain from angry looks. Nor let us be resentful when others differ from us. For all men have hearts, and each heart has its own leanings. Their right is our wrong, and our right is their wrong. We are not unquestionably sages, nor are they unquestionably fools. Both of us are simply ordinary men. How can any one lay down a rule by which to distinguish right from wrong? For we are all, one with another, wise and foolish, like a ring which has no end. Therefore, although others give way to anger, let us on the contrary dread our own faults, and though we alone may be in the right, let us follow the multitude and act like them.

11. Give clear appreciation to merit and demerit, and deal out to each its sure reward or punishment. In these days, reward does not attend upon merit, nor punishment upon crime. You high functionaries who have charge of public affairs, let it be your task to make clear rewards and punishments. . . .

15. To turn away from that which is private, and to set our faces toward that which is public — this is the path of a Minister. Now if a man is influenced by private motives, he will assuredly feel resentments, and if he is influenced by resentful feelings, he will assuredly fail to act harmoniously with others. If he fails to act harmoniously with others, he will assuredly sacrifice the public interest to his private feelings. When resentment arises, it interferes with order, and is subversive of law. . . .

16. Let the people be employed [in forced labor] at seasonable times. This is an ancient and excellent rule. Let them be employed, therefore, in the winter months, when they are at leisure.

---

[3]Shinto shrines dedicated to the *kami,* or spirits, of agriculture — probably a metaphor for prosperity in this context.

But from Spring to Autumn, when they are engaged in agriculture or with the mulberry trees,[4] the people should not be so employed. For if they do not attend to agriculture, what will they have to eat? If they do not attend to the mulberry trees, what will they do for clothing?

17. Decisions on important matters should not be made by one person alone. They should be discussed with many. But small matters are of less consequence. It is unnecessary to consult a number of people. It is only in the case of the discussion of weighty affairs, when there is a suspicion that they may miscarry, that one should arrange matters in concert with others, so as to arrive at the right conclusion.

---

[4]The cultivation of silk worms that ate mulberry leaves. The technique of silk production was an import from China.

Lives and Loves at the Heian Court
▼▼▼

66 ▼ *Sei Shonagon, THE PILLOW BOOK*

The centralized administrative system modeled on Tang China's imperial structure that Japanese reformers tried to establish during the seventh and eighth centuries failed to function as intended. By the mid ninth century true power in the provinces rested in the hands of local clan chiefs and a new element, Buddhist monasteries (see source 67). The imperial government continued to appoint provincial governors, who theoretically administered their regions in the name of the emperor, but most governors resided in the imperial court at *Kyoto,* far away from their areas of nominal responsibility. The court itself became an increasingly elegant setting for emperors and empresses, who were regarded as sacred beings and theoretically stood at the summit of all power. The elaborate ceremony that surrounded these people, who claimed to rule the world, masked, at least at close hand, the fact that effective power lay elsewhere.

While the imperial court was increasingly losing touch with the center of political authority, a group of aristocratic women at court were developing Japan's first native literature. Unlike Japan's male Confucian scholars, who continued to study the Chinese classics along fairly rigid lines established a millennium earlier in a foreign land, the court women gave free play in their prose and poetry to their imaginations, emotions, and powers of analysis.

Among Japan's great female literary artists of the Heian Period, *Sei Shonagon* (ca. 965–after 1000), a lady-in-waiting to Empress Sadako (r. 990–1000), deserves a special place of honor. Her masterpiece is *The Pillow Book,* a collection of observations that she began while serving at the imperial court. The title of the work probably derives from the fact that the author composed miscellaneous notes at night, after retiring to her room, on paper that she kept in a drawer of her wooden pillow. Although the book appears to be a hodgepodge of random observations that lack order and cohesion, it is a carefully polished work of literature that the author began around 994 and continued to refine well after the year 1000 when she left the court following the young empress's death in childbirth.

Many of the imperial ladies-in-waiting at Heian composed memoirs and diaries with an eye toward publication, but Sei Shonagon's contribution to this genre is special because of the beauty of her prose and the human face that she puts on upper-class Heian society, with all its virtues, foibles, and flaws. Although we know almost nothing about the details of her life, even the casual reader comes away from *The Pillow Book* feeling that Sei Shonagon has revealed her complex personality in an especially intimate way.

QUESTIONS FOR ANALYSIS

1. Consider the role of ceremony at the Heian court. How significant does it appear to have been? What do you infer from your answer?
2. *The Pillow Book* has been said to be a complex collection of apparently contradictory elements. What are those apparently contradictory strands, and what do they suggest to you about life and values at the late-tenth-century Heian court?
3. How well or poorly does Sei Shonagon measure up to the stereotype of East Asian women? Be specific. What do you infer from your answer?
4. Compose a commentary on *The Pillow Book* by Ban Zhao (source 33).

ESPECIALLY DELIGHTFUL IS THE FIRST DAY

Especially delightful is the first day of the First Month, when the mists so often shroud the sky. Everyone pays great attention to his appearance and dresses with the utmost care. What a pleasure it is to see them all offer their congratulations to the Emperor and celebrate their own new year![1]

I also enjoy the seventh day, when people pluck the young herbs that have sprouted fresh and green beneath the snow. It is amusing to see their excitement when they find such plants near the Palace, by no means a spot where one might expect them.

This is the day when members of the nobility who live outside the Palace arrive in their magnificently decorated carriages to admire the blue

horses.[2] As the carriages are drawn over the ground-beam of the Central Gate, there is always a tremendous bump, and the heads of the women passengers are knocked together; the combs fall out of their hair, and may be smashed to pieces if the owners are not careful. I enjoy the way everyone laughs when this happens. . . .

The fifteenth day is the festival of the full-moon gruel,[3] when a bowl of gruel is presented to His Majesty. On this day all the women of the house carry gruel-sticks, which they hide carefully from each other. It is most amusing to see them walking about, as they await an opportunity to hit their companions. Each one is careful not to be struck herself and is constantly looking over her shoulder to make sure that no one is stealing up on her. Yet the precautions are useless, for before long one of the women manages to score a hit. She is extremely pleased with herself

---

[1]Because of their lunar calendar, which was borrowed from China, Japanese New Year's Day is a movable date, falling between January 21 and February 19 in the Western, or Gregorian, calendar. The first day of the New Year was also a sort of birthday because on that day the Japanese added a year to their age.

[2]In the early eighth century, Japan imported from Tang China the annual ceremony of parading twenty-one steel-

gray (blue) horses before the emperor. Because such horses are rare and white is the color of purity in Shinto rituals, white horses were substituted in the tenth century, even though the ceremony's name remained unchanged.

[3]In the Japanese lunar calendar, the fifteenth was the day of the full moon. At the full moon of the First Month a special gruel was eaten.

and laughs merrily. Everyone finds this delightful — except, of course, the victim, who looks very put out.

In a certain household a young gentleman had been married during the previous year to one of the girls in the family. Having spent the night with her, he was now, on the morning of the fifteenth, about to set off for the Palace. There was a woman in the house who was in the habit of lording it over everyone. On this occasion she was standing in the back of the room, impatiently awaiting an opportunity to hit the man with her gruel-stick as he left. One of the other women realized what she had in mind and burst out laughing. The woman with the stick signalled excitedly that she should be quiet. Fortunately the young man did not notice what was afoot and he stood there unconcernedly.

'I have to pick up something over there,' said the woman with the stick, approaching the man. Suddenly she darted forward, gave a great whack, and made her escape. Everyone in the room burst out laughing; even the young man smiled pleasantly, not in the least annoyed. He was not too startled; but he did blush a little, which was charming.

Sometimes when the women are hitting each other the men also join in the fun. The strange thing is that, when a woman is hit, she often gets angry and bursts into tears; then she will upbraid her assailant and say the most awful things about him — most amusing. Even in the Palace, where the atmosphere is usually so solemn, everything is in confusion on this day, and no one stands on ceremony.

▼▼▼

WHEN I MAKE MYSELF IMAGINE

When I make myself imagine what it is like to be one of those women who live at home, faithfully serving their husbands — women who have not a single exciting prospect in life yet who believe that they are perfectly happy — I am filled

with scorn. Often they are of quite good birth, yet have had no opportunity to find out what the world is like. I wish they could live for a while in our society . . . so that they might come to know the delights it has to offer.

I cannot bear men who believe that women serving in the Palace are bound to be frivolous and wicked. Yet I suppose their prejudice is understandable. After all, women at Court do not spend their time hiding modestly behind fans and screens, but walk about, looking openly at people they chance to meet. Yes, they see everyone face to face, not only ladies-in-waiting like themselves, but even Their Imperial Majesties (whose august names I hardly dare mention), High Court Nobles, senior courtiers, and other gentlemen of high rank. In the presence of such exalted personages the women in the Palace are all equally brazen, whether they be the maids of ladies-in-waiting, or the relations of Court ladies who have come to visit them, or housekeepers, or latrine-cleaners, or women who are of no more value than a roof-tile or a pebble. Small wonder that the young men regard them as immodest! Yet are the gentlemen themselves any less so? They are not exactly bashful when it comes to looking at the great people in the Palace. No, everyone at Court is much the same in this respect.

Women who have served in the Palace, but who later get married and live at home, are called Madam and receive the most respectful treatment. To be sure, people often consider that these women, who have displayed their faces to all and sundry during their years at Court, are lacking in feminine grace. How proud they must be, nevertheless, when they are styled Assistant Attendants, or summoned to the Palace for occasional duty, or ordered to serve as Imperial envoys during the Kamo Festival![4] Even those who stay at home lose nothing by having served at Court. In fact they make very good wives. For example, if they are married to a provincial governor and their daughter is chosen to take part in the Gosechi dances,[5] they do not have to disgrace

---

[4]The main Shinto festival, observed in the middle of the Fourth Month.

[5]Court dances performed in the Eleventh Month by four young girls from high-ranking families.

themselves by acting like provincials and asking other people about procedure. They themselves are well versed in the formalities, which is just as it should be.

▾▾▾

HATEFUL THINGS

One is in a hurry to leave, but one's visitor keeps chattering away. If it is someone of no importance, one can get rid of him by saying, 'You must tell me all about it next time'; but, should it be the sort of visitor whose presence commands one's best behavior, the situation is hateful indeed. . . .

A man who has nothing in particular to recommend discusses all sorts of subjects at random as though he knew everything. . . .

I hate the sight of men in their cups who shout, poke their fingers in their mouths, stroke their beards, and pass on the wine to their neighbours with great cries of 'Have some more! Drink up!' They tremble, shake their heads, twist their faces, and gesticulate like children who are singing, 'We're off to see the Governor.' I have seen really well-bred people behave like this and I find it most distasteful.

To envy others and to complain about one's own lot; to speak badly about people; to be inquisitive about the most trivial matters and to resent and abuse people for not telling one, or, if one does manage to worm out some facts, to inform everyone in the most detailed fashion as if one had known all from the beginning — oh, how hateful!

One is just about to be told some interesting piece of news when a baby starts crying. . . .

An admirer has come on a clandestine visit, but a dog catches sight of him and starts barking. One feels like killing the beast.

One has been foolish enough to invite a man to spend the night in an unsuitable place — and then he starts snoring. . . .

One is in the middle of a story when someone butts in and tries to show that he is the only clever person in the room. Such a person is hateful, and so, indeed, is anyone, child or adult, who tries to push himself forward.

One is telling a story about old times when someone breaks in with a little detail that he happens to know, implying that one's own version is inaccurate — disgusting behaviour! . . .

Some children have called at one's house. One makes a great fuss of them and gives them toys to play with. The children become accustomed to this treatment and start to come regularly, forcing their way into one's inner rooms and scattering one's furnishings and possessions. Hateful! . . .

A man with whom one is having an affair keeps singing the praises of some woman he used to know. Even if it is a thing of the past, this can be very annoying. How much more so if he is still seeing the woman! (Yet sometimes I find that it is not as unpleasant as all that.)

A person who recites a spell himself after sneezing.[6] In fact I detest anyone who sneezes except the master of the house.

Fleas, too, are very hateful. When they dance about under someone's clothes, they really seem to be lifting them up.

The sound of dogs when they bark for a long time in chorus is ominous and hateful.

I cannot stand people who leave without closing the panel behind them. . . .

I hate people whose letters show that they lack respect for worldly civilities, whether by discourtesy in the phrasing or by extreme politeness to someone who does not deserve it. This sort of thing is, of course, most odious if the letter is for oneself, but it is bad enough even if it is addressed to someone else.

As a matter of fact, most people are too casual, not only in their letters but in their direct conversation. Sometimes I am quite disgusted at noting how little decorum people observe when talking to each other. It is particularly unpleasant

---

[6]Saying the equivalent of "Bless you" or "Gesundheit" to counter the evil omen that sneezing represents.

to hear some foolish man or woman omit the proper marks of respect when addressing a person of quality; and, when servants fail to use honorific forms of speech in referring to their masters, it is very bad indeed. No less odious, however, are those masters who, in addressing their servants, use such phrases as 'When you were good enough to do such-and-such' or 'As you so kindly remarked.' No doubt there are some masters who, in describing their own actions to a servant, say, 'I presumed to do so-and-so'!

Sometimes a person who is utterly devoid of charm will try to create a good impression by using very elegant language; yet he only succeeds in being ridiculous. No doubt he believes this refined language to be just what the occasion demands, but, when it goes so far that everyone bursts out laughing, surely something must be wrong.

It is most improper to address high-ranking courtiers, Imperial Advisers, and the like simply by using their names without any titles or marks of respect; but such mistakes are fortunately rare. . . .

A lover who is leaving at dawn announces that he has to find his fan and his paper.[7] 'I know I put them somewhere last night,' he says. Since it is pitch dark, he gropes about the room, bumping into the furniture and muttering, 'Strange! Where on earth can they be?' Finally he discovers the objects. He thrusts the paper into the breast of his robe with a great rustling sound; then he snaps open his fan and busily fans away with it. Only now is he ready to take his leave. What charmless behaviour! 'Hateful' is an understatement.

Equally disagreeable is the man who, when leaving in the middle of the night, takes care to fasten the cord of his headdress. This is quite unnecessary; he could perfectly well put it gently on his head without tying the cord. And why must he spend time adjusting his cloak or hunting costume? Does he really think someone may see him

at this time of night and criticize him for not being impeccably dressed?

A good lover will behave as elegantly at dawn as at any other time. He drags himself out of bed with a look of dismay on his face. The lady urges on: 'Come, my friend, it's getting light. You don't want anyone to find you here.' He gives a deep sigh, as if to say that the night has not been nearly long enough and that it is agony to leave. Once up, he does not instantly pull on his trousers. Instead he comes close to the lady and whispers whatever was left unsaid during the night. Even when he is dressed, he still lingers, vaguely pretending to be fastening his sash.

Presently he raises the lattice, and the two lovers stand together by the side door while he tells her how he dreads the coming day, which will keep them apart; then he slips away. The lady watches him go, and this moment of parting will remain among her most charming memories.

Indeed, one's attachment to a man depends largely on the elegance of his leave-taking. When he jumps out of bed, scurries about the room, tightly fastens his trouser-sash, rolls up the sleeves of his Court cloak, over-robe, or hunting costume, stuffs his belongings into the breast of his robe and then briskly secures the outer sash — one really begins to hate him.

▾▾▾

EMBARRASSING THINGS

While entertaining a visitor, one hears some servants chatting without any restraint in one of the back rooms. It is embarrassing to know that one's visitor can overhear. But how to stop them?

A man whom one loves gets drunk and keeps repeating himself.

To have spoken about someone not knowing that he could overhear. This is embarrassing even if it be a servant or some other completely insignificant person.

---

[7]Colored paper that gentlemen carried in the folds of their robe for notes and use as tissue.

To hear one's servants making merry. This is equally annoying if one is on a journey and staying in cramped quarters or at home and hears the servants in a neighboring room.

Parents, convinced that their ugly child is adorable, pet him and repeat the things he has said, imitating his voice.

An ignoramus who in the presence of some learned person puts on a knowing air and converses about men of old.

A man recites his own poems (not especially good ones) and tells one about the praise they have received — most embarrassing.

Lying awake at night, one says something to one's companion, who simply goes on sleeping.

In the presence of a skilled musician, someone plays a zither just for his own pleasure and without tuning it.

A son-in-law who his long since stopped visiting his wife runs into his father-in-law in a public place.

The Ideal Samurai
▼▼▼
67 ▼ *CHRONICLE OF THE GRAND PACIFICATION*

While imperial court women at Kyoto devoted their talents to crafting new forms of literature, Japan's warlords engaged their energies in carving out independent principalities backed by the might of their private armies of *samurai* (they who serve). Between 1180 and 1185 a conflict known as the *Gempei War* devastated the heartland of the main island of Honshu as the mighty Taira and *Minimoto* clans fought for control of the imperial family and its court. In 1185 the Minimoto house destroyed the Taira faction, thereby becoming the supreme military power in Japan.

Rather than seizing the imperial office for himself, the leader of the victorious Minimoto family accepted the title of *shogun,* or imperial commander in chief, and elected to rule over a number of military governors from his remote base at *Kamakura,* while a puppet emperor reigned at Kyoto. This feudal system, known as the *bakufu* (tent headquarters), shaped the politics and culture of Japan for centuries to come.

Toward the early fourteenth century the *Kamakura Shogunate* began to show signs of weakening, which in turn encouraged *Emperor Go-Daigo* (r. 1318–1336) to lead a coup in an attempt to destroy the shogunate and re-establish the primacy of the emperor. This rebel emperor became the nucleus of a full-scale feudal uprising by a wide number of dissatisfied warlords, samurai, and warrior-monks. The warrior-monks were members of great landholding Buddhist monasteries, which already for many centuries had been centers of independent political, economic, and military power. The rebellion resulted in the destruction of Kamakura and the death of its last shogun.

Go-Daigo's victory was brief, however. Within a few years he was deposed by another warlord, who installed his own emperor and received back from him the title of shogun, thereby establishing the *Ashikaga Shogunate* (1338–1573). Japanese government and society, therefore, continued to be dominated by its feudal warriors.

The story of the last several years of the Kamakura Shogunate is recorded in the pages of the *Taiheiki,* or *Chronicle of the Grand Pacification.* Composed by a number of largely anonymous Buddhist monks between about 1333 and maybe as late as 1370, this chronicle recounts the battles and intrigues of the period 1318–1333. Its title refers to Go-Daigo's momentarily successful attempt to destroy, or "pacify," the shogunate.

Our excerpt tells the story of the defense in 1331 of Akasaka castle by *Kusunoki Masashige,* one of the emperor's most fervent supporters. This was a dark moment for the imperial forces. The emperor, along with many followers, had recently been captured at Kasagi, a fortified monastic temple. The imperial cause needed a victory, even a moral one, and this heretofore obscure warrior was about to provide new hope with his inspired defense of this stronghold.

Killed in 1333 in a battle he knew he could not win, Masashige has been revered through the centuries as a paragon of samurai virtues. The *kamikaze* (divine wind) suicide pilots whom Japan launched against the U.S. Navy in 1945 were called "chrysanthemum warriors" in reference to the Kusunoki family's flowered crest.

QUESTIONS FOR ANALYSIS

1. Why do the warriors assaulting Akasaka hope that Kusunoki will be able to hold out for at least one day? What does your answer suggest?
2. Bravery is naturally expected of all warriors, but which other samurai virtues does Kusunoki Masashige exemplify?
3. Which samurai virtues do his foes exhibit? In what ways did they show themselves to be less than ideal warriors?
4. Thinking their enemy dead, the shogun's warriors pause to remember Kusunoki Masashige. What does this suggest?
5. Based on this account, what picture emerges of the ideals and realities of fourteenth-century Japanese feudal warfare?

No man of the mighty host from the distant eastern lands was willing to enter the capital, so sorely were their spirits mortified because Kasagi castle had fallen.[1] . . . All took their way instead toward Akasaka castle, where Kusunoki Hyoe Masashige was shut up. . . .

When these had passed beyond the Ishi River, they beheld the castle. Surely this was a stronghold of hasty devising! The ditch was not a proper ditch, and there was but a single wooden wall, plastered over with mud. Likewise in size the castle was not more than one hundred or two hundred yards around, with but twenty or thirty towers within, made ready in haste. Of those who saw it, not one but thought:

"Ah, what a pitiable spectacle the enemy presents! Even if we were to hold this castle in one hand and throw, we would be able to throw it! Let us hope that in some strange manner Kusunoki will endure for at least a day, that by taking booty and winning honor we may obtain future rewards."

---

[1] This force of Kamakura supporters from the east was dispirited because it had arrived too late to participate in the capture of Kasagi.

Drawing near, the three hundred thousand riders[2] got down from their horses, one after another, jumped into the ditch, stood below the towers, and competed to be the first to enter the castle.

Now by nature Masashige was a man who would "scheme in his tent to defeat an enemy a thousand leagues distant," one whose counsels were as subtle as though sprung from the brain of Chenping or Zhang Liang.[3] Wherefore had he kept two hundred mighty archers within the castle, and had given three hundred riders to his brother Shichiro and Wada Goro Masato outside in the mountains. Yet the attackers, all unwitting, rushed forward together to the banks of the ditch on the four sides, resolved to bring down the castle in a single assault.

Then from tower tops and windows the archers shot furiously with arrowheads aligned together, smiting more than a thousand men in an instant. And greatly amazed, the eastern warriors said:

"No, no! From the look of things at this castle, it will never fall in a day or two. Let us take time before going against it, that we may establish camps and battle-offices and form separate parties."

They drew back from the attack a little, took off their horses' saddles, cast aside their armor, and rested in their camps.

In the mountains Kusunoki Shichiro and Wada Goro said, "The time is right." They made two parties of the three hundred horsemen, came out from the shelter of the trees on the eastern and western slopes with two fluttering banners, whereon were depicted the chrysanthemum and water crest of the Kusunoki house, and advanced quietly toward the enemy, urging their horses forward in the swirling mist.

The attackers hesitated doubtfully.

"Are they enemies or friends?" they thought.

Then suddenly from both sides the three hundred attacked, shouting, in wedge-shaped formations. They smote the center of the three hundred thousand horsemen spread out like clouds or mist, broke into them in all directions, and cut them down on every side. And the attackers' hosts were powerless to form to give battle, so great was their bewilderment.

Next within the castle three gates opened all together, wherefrom two hundred horsemen galloped forth side by side to let fly a multitude of arrows from bows pulled back to the utmost limits. Although the attackers were a mighty host, they were confounded utterly by these few enemies, so that they clamored aloud. Some mounted tethered horses and beat them with their stirrups, seeking to advance; others fixed arrows to unstrung bows and tried vainly to shoot. Two or three men took up a single piece of armor and disputed it, pulling against each other. Though a lord was killed, his vassals knew nothing of it; though a father was killed, his sons aided him not, but like scattered spiders they retreated to the Ishi River. For half a league along their way there was no space where a foot might tread, by reason of their abandoned horses and arms. To be sure, great gains came suddenly to the common folk of Tojo district![4]

Perhaps the proud eastern warriors thought in their hearts that Kusunoki's strategy could not be despised, since blundering unexpectedly they had been defeated in the first battle. For though they went forth against Handa and Narahara,[5] they did not seek to attack the castle again quickly, but consulted together and made a resolution, saying:

"Let us remain awhile in this place, that led by men acquainted with the home provinces we may cut down trees on the mountains, burn houses, and guard thereby against warriors wait-

---

[2]The *Taiheiki* grossly exaggerates the number of pro-Kamakura fighters.
[3]Two ministers of the first Han emperor of China. The quotation is from Ban Gu and Ban Zhao's *History of the Former Han Dynasty*.

[4]Commoners scavenged battlefields.
[5]Settlements near Akasaka.

ing in reserve to fall upon us. Then may we attack the castle with tranquil spirits."

But there were many . . . who had lost fathers and sons in the fighting. These roused themselves up, saying:

"What is the use of living? Though we go alone, let us gallop forth to die in battle!"

And thereupon all the others took heart as well, and galloped forward eagerly.

Now Akasaka castle might not be attacked easily on the east, where terraced rice fields extended far up the mountainside. But on three sides the land was flat; likewise there was but a single ditch and wall. All the attackers were contemptuous, thinking, "No matter what demons may be inside, it cannot be much of an affair." When they drew near again, they went forward quickly into the ditch to the opposite bank, pulled away the obstacles and made ready to enter. Yet within the castle there was no sound.

Then the attackers thought in their hearts:

"As it was yesterday, so will it be today. After wounding many men with arrows to confuse us, they will send other warriors to fight in our midst."

They counted out a hundred thousand riders to go to the mountains in the rear, while the remaining two hundred thousand compassed the castle round about like thickly growing rice, hemp, bamboo, or reeds. Yet from within the castle not an arrow was released, nor was any man seen.

At last the attackers laid hold of the wall on the four sides to climb over it, filled with excitement. But thereupon men within the castle cut the ropes supporting that wall, all at the same time, for it was a double wall, built to let the outside fall down. More than a thousand of the attackers became as though crushed by a weight, so that only their eyes moved as the defenders threw down logs and boulders onto them. And in this day's fighting more than seven hundred of them were slain.

Unwilling to attack again because of the bitterness of the first two days of fighting, for four or five days the eastern hosts merely besieged the castle from camps hard by. Truly were they without pride, to watch thus idly from a nearby place! How mortifying it was that men of the future would make a mock of them, saying, "Although the enemy were no more than four or five hundred persons shut up in a flatland castle not five hundred yards around, the hosts of the eight eastern provinces would not attack them, but shamefully laid down a siege from a distance!"

At last the attackers spoke among themselves, saying:

"Previously we attacked in the fierceness of our valor, not carrying shields or preparing weapons of assault, wherefore we suffered unforeseen injury. Let us go against them now with a different method."

All commanded the making of shields with toughened hide on their faces, such as might not be smashed through easily, and with these upheld they went against the castle once more, saying:

"There can be no difficulty about jumping across to the wall, since the banks are not high, nor is the ditch deep. Yet will not this wall also drop down upon us?"

They spoke with fearful hearts, reluctant to seize upon the wall lightly. All went down into the water of the ditch, laid hold upon the wall with grapnels, and pulled at it. But when the wall was about to fall, those within the castle took ladles with handles ten or twenty feet long, dipped up boiling water, and poured it onto them. The hot water passed through the holes in their helmet tops, ran down from the edges of their shoulder-guards, and burned their bodies so grievously that they fled panic-stricken, throwing down their shields and grapnels. How shameful it was! Although no man of them was slain, there were as many as two or three hundred persons who could not stand up from the burns on their hands and feet, or who lay down with sick bodies.

So it was that whenever the attackers advanced with new devisings, those within the castle defended against them with changed stratagems. Wherefore in consultation together the attackers said, "From this time on, let us starve them, for we can do no other." They forbore utterly to do battle, but only built towers in their camps, lined up obstacles, and laid down a siege.

Soon the warriors in the castle grew weary of spirit, since there was no diversion for them. Nor was their food sufficient, since Kusunoki had built the castle in haste. The battle having begun and the siege commenced, within twenty days the stores were eaten up; nor did food remain for more than four or five days.

Then Masashige spoke a word to his men, saying:

"In various battles of late have we overreached the foe, whose slain are beyond counting, but these things are as nothing in the eyes of so mighty a host. Moreover, the castle's food is eaten up, and no other warriors will come to deliver us.

"Assuredly I will not cherish life in the hour of need, from the beginning having been steadfast for His Majesty's sake. . . . But the true man of courage 'is cautious in the face of difficulties, and deliberates before acting.'[6] I will flee this castle for a time, causing the enemy to believe that I have taken my life, so that they may go away rejoicing. When they are gone I will come forward to fight; and if they return I will go deep into the mountains. When I have harassed the eastern hosts four or five times in this manner, will they not grow weary? This is a plan for destroying the enemy in safety. What are your views?"

All agreed, "It ought to be so."

Then quickly within the castle they dug a mighty hole seven feet deep, filling it with twenty or thirty bodies of the slain (who were fallen down dead into the ditch in great numbers), whereon they piled up charcoal and firewood. And they awaited a night of pouring rain and driving wind.

Perhaps because Masashige had found favor in the sight of Heaven, suddenly a harsh wind came raising the sand, accompanied by a rain violent enough to pierce bamboo. The night was exceedingly dark, and all the enemy in their camps were sheltered behind curtains. This indeed was the awaited night!

Leaving a man in the castle to light a blaze when they were fled away safely five or six hundred yards, the defenders cast off their armor, assumed the guise of attackers, and fled away calmly by threes and fives, passing in front of the enemy battle-offices and beside enemy sleeping places.

It came about that the eyes of an enemy fell upon Masashige, where he passed before the stables of Nagasaki. The man challenged him, saying, "What person passes before this battle-office in stealth, not announcing himself?"

In haste Masashige passed beyond that place, calling back, "I am a follower of the grand marshal who has taken the wrong road."

"A suspicious fellow indeed!" thought the man. "Assuredly he is a stealer of horses! I shall shoot him down."

He ran up close and shot Masashige full in the body. But although the arrow looked to have driven deep at the height of the elbow-joint, it turned over and flew back again without touching the naked flesh.

Later, when that arrow's track was observed, men saw that it had struck an amulet wherein was preserved the *Kannon Sutra*,[7] which Masashige had trusted and read for many years. Its arrowhead had stopped in the two-line poem, "Wholeheartedly praising the name."[8] How strange it was!

When in this manner Masashige had escaped death from a certain-death arrowhead, he fled to a safe place more than half a league distant. And looking back he saw that the warrior had lighted fires in the castle's battle-offices, faithful to his covenant.

---

[6]A quotation from Confucius' *Analects.*
[7]Known in its Chinese original as the *Guanshiyin Sutra,* this Buddhist holy book was dedicated to the Bodhisattva Guanyin (sources 39 and 40), who in Japan was known as *Kannon.*

[8]Compare this with the miracle stories in the *Tales of Guanshiyin* (source 39).

The hosts of the attackers were seized with amazement at the sight of the flames.

"Aha! The castle has fallen!" they shouted exultantly. "Let no man be spared! Let none escape!"

When the flames died away, they saw a mighty hole inside the castle, piled up with charcoal, wherein lay the burned bodies of many men. And then not a man of them but spoke words of praise, saying:

"How pitiful! Masashige had ended his life! Though he was an enemy, his was a glorious death, well befitting a warrior."

▼▼▼

China: The Ages of Tang and Song

The period from 500 to 1500 witnessed a variety of momentous developments in China: renewed imperial greatness, philosophical and technological innovation, economic expansion and a rapidly growing population, new modes of artistic expression, rebellions, invasions by various nomadic peoples, conquest by Mongol invaders, and recovery and retrenchment. Through it all, Chinese civilization managed to retain intact its basic institutions and way of life.

The Time of Troubles that followed the fall of the House of Han was over by the end of the sixth century, and under the *Tang Dynasty* (618–907) China was again a great imperial power, with a restored Confucian civil service firmly in power. At the end of the seventh century China's borders reached to Korea and Manchuria in the northeast, to Vietnam in the south, and to the Aral Sea in the western regions of Central Asia, where China met and was checked by the new Islamic Empire at the Battle of the Talas River in 751. The almost simultaneous creation of these two massive empires, which together once again connected the Atlantic with the Pacific, resulted in a dramatic increase of traffic along the Silk Road and through the waters of South Asia. Foreign goods, precious metals, peoples, and ideas flowed into China's cities. As a consequence, Tang China enjoyed the richest, most cosmopolitan culture on the face of the Earth, until its empire began to deteriorate after the mid eighth century. Between 755 and 763 China was torn apart by a rebellion initiated by An Lushan, a military governor of Turkic descent. In the wake of the devastation, Tang imperial strength rapidly disintegrated, and with it went an earlier openness of spirit to outside influences. Fifty-three years of disunity followed Tang's official collapse in 907, but, in fact, the previous half century of nominal Tang rule had been equally anarchic.

In 960 the *Song Dynasty* (960–1279) reunited most of China, which it ruled over from its northern capital at Kaifeng. In 1126, however, Kaifeng, along with all of North China, fell to invaders from the steppes. A younger brother to the former Song emperor escaped to the south, where he re-established a truncated Song Empire centered on the so-called temporary capital of *Hangzhou.*

For almost one half of its more than 300-year-long reign the Song Dynasty was cut off from the Yellow River. Despite this, Song Era China reached and maintained levels of economic prosperity, technological advancement, and cultural maturity that were unequaled anywhere else on Earth at the time. By the mid eleventh century, for example, the production of printed books had become such an important industry that artisans were experimenting with movable type — 400 years before the introduction of a similar printing process in Europe. The thousands of books and millions of pages printed in Song China before and after 1126/1127 are evidence that a remarkably high degree of its population was literate.

In addition to this dramatic rise in basic lieracy, there were significant developments in advanced philosophy. Intellectuals reinvigorated Confucian thought by injecting into it metaphysical concepts borrowed from Buddhism and Daoism. This new Study of the Way, or *Neo-Confucianism,* provided fresh philosophical insights clothed in traditional forms and enabled Confucianism to topple Buddhism from its position of intellectual preeminence.

The fine arts also reached new levels of achievement. Landscape painting, particularly during the era of Southern Song, expressed in two dimensions the mystical visions of Daoism and Chan Buddhism. On a three-dimensional plane, the craft of porcelain-making became a high art, and large numbers of exquisitely delicate pieces of fine *chinaware* were traded from Japan to East Africa.

Advanced ships and navigational aids enabled Chinese traders to take to the sea in unprecedented numbers, especially in the direction of Southeast Asia, thereby transforming their homeland into the world's greatest merchant marine power of its day. Rapid-maturing strains of rice were introduced from Champa in Southeast Asia, making it possible to feed a population that exceeded one hundred million, about double that of the Age of Tang. Although most of this massive population was engaged in traditional, labor-intensive agriculture, some Chinese were employed in industries (such as mining, iron and steel production, and textile manufacture) that used advanced technologies unequaled anywhere else in the world.

Song's age of greatness was brought to a close by *Mongol* invaders, who by 1279 had joined all of China to the largest land empire in world history. Mongol rule during what is known as the *Yuan Dynasty* (1264–1368) was unmitigated military occupation. Both the Mongols and the many foreigners whom they admitted into their service exploited and oppressed the Chinese. Although the Mongols encouraged agriculture and trade, few Chinese benefited from a prosperity that was largely confined to a small circle of landlords.

By the mid fourteenth century China was in rebellion, and in 1368 a commoner, Zhu Yuanzhang, re-established native rule in the form of the *Ming Dynasty* (1368–1644). This new imperial family restored Chinese prestige and influence in East Asia to levels enjoyed under Tang and provided China with stability and prosperity until the late sixteenth century. Under the Ming traditional Chinese civilization attained full maturity. Toward the middle of the Age of Ming, however, China reluctantly established relations with seaborne western European merchants and missionaries, and the resultant challenge of the West would result, centuries later, in major transformations in Chinese life.

Chapters 12 and 13 will deal with the Yuan and Ming eras. In this chapter we will concentrate on the Tang and Song eras.

Imperial Greatness and Disaster
in Eighth-Century China
▼▼▼

68 ▼ *Du Fu, POEMS*

The first half of the eighth century was dominated by the seesaw reign of Emperor *Tang Xuanzong* (r. 713–756), known more popularly as *Tang Ming Huang* (Brilliant Emperor of Tang). In these forty-three years China's empire went from heights of grandeur to debasement and disaster. A gifted artist and generous patron of the arts, he created a court known for refined elegance. Continuing the expansionistic policies of his predecessors, he drove his armies to overextension along China's far western and southwestern frontiers. His passionate love for a young concubine, *Yang Guifei,* finally led him to neglect imperial duties. One result was the rebellion of General *An Lushan* in 755 and the seizure and sacking of the capital cities of Luoyang and Chang'an. In the confusion that followed, the grieving emperor was forced to order his lover's death, and shortly thereafter he abdicated, a broken man. Although An Lushan was killed in 757, the rebellion continued to rage across China. Tang rule was nominally restored in 763, but for the next 144 years Tang power remained weak.

One witness to these events was *Du Fu* (712–770), a Confucian man of letters who is generally regarded as China's greatest poet. Born a year before Xuanzong assumed the throne, Du Fu enjoyed the peace and prosperity of an apparently successful empire during his youth. By the late 740s and early 750s, however, Du Fu became increasingly aware of the cracks and imperfections in the imperial system. The Great Rebellion, which broke the back of Tang power, brought numerous hardships to Du Fu and family. Despite intermittent impoverishment, constant wandering in search of employment and security, and poor health, he composed some of his greatest poems during this time of trials. Far from home, he died in late 770 but not before leaving behind works of poetry that provide vivid insights into the vicissitudes of fortune that China experienced during his eventful life.

Our first selection is a poem composed around 741. Our second was composed in 748 or 749 when Du Fu was at the imperial capital of Chang'an. In it he thanks a high-ranking official, Wei Ji, for his patronage and hints at his desire for continued assistance. The third poem, written around 750, describes the consequences of China's border conflicts with such peoples as the Tibetans and the Uighurs (see source 69). The fourth poem was composed in the autumn of 756, when Du Fu was detained in Chang'an after it had been captured by rebel forces. The last poem was composed in 759.

QUESTIONS FOR ANALYSIS

1. What is the tone and message of *Officer Fang's Barbarian Steed?*
2. In *Twenty-two Rhymes Presented to Assistant Secretary of the Left Wei* Du Fu recounts, with some self-deprecating humor, the history of his disappoint-

ments in search for advancement in the civil service. What is the overall tone and message of the poem? Has Du Fu lost confidence in the system?

3. The *Ballad of the War Wagons* deals with the conscription of peasants to fight Emperor Xuanzong's border wars. What is its tone and message?
4. Who is the prince in *Pitying the Prince,* and what does he represent?
5. What is the tone and overall message of this fourth poem? Has Du Fu lost all hope?
6. *Lovely Lady* might describe the situation of a particular woman whom Du Fu met, but it is certainly also an extended metaphor. Who is the lady? Who is the husband? Who is the "new girl"?

OFFICER FANG'S BARBARIAN STEED

Barbarian steed, pride of Ferghana,[1]
all jags and angles, well-knit bones;
two ears cocked, like bamboo tubes split
    sideways;
four hoofs fleet, as though buoyed on the wind.
Wherever headed, no distance too challenging,
fit indeed for a life-or-death charge.
With a mount superlative as this,
ten-thousand-mile sorties are at your command![2]

TWENTY-TWO RHYMES PRESENTED TO ASSISTANT SECRETARY OF THE LEFT WEI

Those in silk underpants rarely die of hunger,
but a scholar's cap can bring its wearer much
    mishap.
Kind sir, please listen attentively
while a humble man states his case.
In the past, when I was still young,
already chosen a candidate for the exam,

reading books, I polished off ten thousand
    volumes,
wielded my writing brush like a god,
in rhyme-prose hailed the rival of Yang Xiong,[3]
in poetry rated akin to Cao Zhi;[4]
Li Yong[5] desired to make my acquaintance,
Wang Han[6] begged to move in next door.
I too thought myself quite exceptional,
fit at once to climb to high office,
to lift my ruler higher than Yao and Shun,[7]
restore the purity of the people's ways.
Those hopes ended in bleak despair,[8]
though I go on singing, no hider from the
    world.
Thirty years astride a donkey,
I take what there is to eat in the springtime
    capital,
mornings rapping at some rich fellow's gate,
evenings trailing the dust of his fat horses.
Leftover wine, a bit of cold roast,
and everywhere this sorrow I bear in silence.
Not long ago the sovereign held a levy;
suddenly here was my chance for advancement!
But in the blue sky my wings failed me;[9]

---

[1]The Ferghana Valley in what is today Uzbekistan and adjacent lands was the breeding ground for the most highly prized horses out of Central Asia.

[2]As you read this poem be aware that Tang China had an absolute love affair with the superior horses of the Ferghana Valley — horses that the Chinese called, in admiration, "heavenly horses." Horses and equestrian sports (including polo, a game that came into China from northwest India in the Tang Era) were favorite subjects of Tang artists, particularly its ceramic sculptors.

[3]Yang Xiong (53 B.C.E.–18 C.E.) was a noted poet.

[4]Cao Zhi (192–232) was also an eminent poet.

[5]Li Yong was a contemporary of Du Fu's father and a highly respected literary figure.

[6]Wang Han was also a member of the generation of Du Fu's father and a noted man of letters.

[7]The last two of the legendary Five Sage Emperors.

[8]In 735 Du Fu failed the examination which would have made him a Presented Scholar and eligible for a post in the imperial administration.

[9]In 747 Du Fu took a special examination given by Emperor Tang Xuanzong. All candidates failed it because of the chief minister's fear of competition.

I couldn't swim as fast as others in the shoal,
so ashamed to betray your generosity,
so certain, however, that you truly understand.
Always among the host of officials
you deign to recite the newest of my fine lines.
Like Gong Yu, I dare to delight in a friend's
    success,[10]
but find it hard to endure Yuan Man's poverty.[11]
How, with a mind so darkly downcast,
can I go on merely hopping this way and that?
My wish now is to retire to eastern seas,
leave this western land of Qin,[12]
though still I long for the Zhongnan hills,[13]
turn my head toward the banks of the clear
    Wei.[14]
Always I try to repay even small favors;
how not regret parting from my high official
    friend?
White gull in the vastness of the waves —
ten thousand miles away, who can tame him?'

BALLAD OF THE WAR WAGONS

Rumble-rumble of wagons,
horses whinnying,
war-bound, bow and arrows at each man's waist,
fathers, mothers, wives, children running
    alongside,
dust so thick you can't see Xianyang Bridge,[15]
snatching at clothes, stumbling, blocking the
    road, wailing,
wailing voices that rise straight up to the clouds.
From the roadside, a passer-by, I question the
    recruits;
all they say is, "Again and again men drafted!
Some sent north at fifteen to guard the Yellow
    River,

at forty still manning garrison farms out west.
When they set out, the village headman tied
    their turbans for them;
they come home white-haired and draw border
    duty again!
Border posts washed in blood, enough to make a
    sea,
but the Martial Sovereign's not yet done
    'expanding his borders.'[16]
You've never seen them?
Our Han land's two hundred districts east of the
    mountains,
a thousand villages, ten thousand hamlets gone
    to thorns and brambles!
Sturdy wives can handle plow and mattock,
but the rows of grain never come up quite right.
What's worse, we men of Qin,[17] renowned as
    tough fighters,
they herd us into the ranks like dogs and
    chickens!
You, sir, ask these questions,
but recruits like us hardly dare grumble out
    loud.
Still, in winter this year,
troops from here, West of the Pass,[18] not yet
    disbanded,
officials started pressing for taxes —
tax payments — where would they come from?
Now you know why it's no good to have sons,
much better have daughters instead!
Sire a daughter, you can marry her to a neigh-
    bor;
sire a son and he ends buried under a hundred
    grasses.
You've never seen what it's like in Koko Nor?[19]
Years now, white bones no one gathers up,
new ghosts cursing fate, old ghosts wailing,

[10]When Gong Yu's friend was appointed to an office, Gong Yu perceived it as an omen that he also would receive an appointment.
[11]One of Confucius' students who was noted for his poverty.
[12]Land that once comprised the ancient state of Qin, in which Chang'an was now located.
[13]Hills south of Chang'an.
[14]The Wei River, which is north of the capital.
[15]A bridge that spans the Wei River (note 14). The troops are on their way to a western border.

[16]Here Tang Xuanzong is identified with Han Wudi (r. 141–87 B.C.E.), the "Martial Emperor of Han," whose aggressive policies expanded the First Chinese Empire deep into Central Asia.
[17]Men from the capital area around Chang'an. See note 12.
[18]Another term for the area around Chang'an.
[19]A lake on the border between China and Tibet. Tibet at this time was an enemy and competitor for hegemony over major routes of the Silk Road.

skies dark, drizzly rain, the whimpering,
  whimpering voices."

PITYING THE PRINCE

Over Chang'an city walls white-headed crows[20]
fly by night, crying above Greeting Autumn
  Gate.
Then they turn to homes of the populace,
  pecking at great mansions,
mansions where high officials scramble to flee
  the barbarians.
Golden whips broken, royal steeds dropping
  dead,
even flesh and blood of the ruler can't all get
  away in time.
How pathetic — costly disc of green coral at his
  waist,
this young prince standing weeping by the
  roadside!
I ask, but he won't tell me his name or surname,
says only that he's tired and in trouble, begs me
  to make him my servant.
A hundred days now, hiding in brambles and
  thorns,
not a spot on his body where the flesh is untorn.
Sons and grandsons of the founder all have high-
  arched noses;
heirs of the Dragon line[21] naturally differ from
  plain people.
"Wild cats and wolves in the city, dragons in the
  wilds,
prince, take care of this body worth a thousand
  in gold![22]
I dare not talk for long, here at the crossroads,
but for your sake, prince, I stay a moment
  longer.
Last night, east winds blew rank with the smell
  of blood,

from the east came camels[23] crowding the old
  Capital.[24]
Those Shuofang troops, good men all —
why so keen, so brave in the past, so ineffectual
  now?[25]
I've heard the Son of Heaven has relinquished
  his throne,
but in the north his sacred virtue has won the
  Uighur khan to our side.[26]
The Uighurs slash their faces,[27] beg to wipe out
  our disgrace.
Take care, say nothing of this — others wait in
  ambush!
I pity you, my prince — take care, do nothing
  rash!
Auspicious signs over the five imperial graves
  never for a moment cease."[28]

LOVELY LADY

Lovely lady, fairest of the time,
hiding away in an empty valley;
daughter of a good house, she said,
fallen now among grasses of the wood.
"There was tumult and death within the passes
  then;
my brothers, old and young, all killed.
Office, position — what help were they?
I couldn't even gather up my brothers' bones!
The world despises you when your luck is down;
all I had went with the turn of the flame.
My husband was a fickle fellow,
his new girl as fair as jade.
Blossoms that close at dusk keep faith with the
  hour,
mandarin ducks will not rest apart;
but he could only see the new one laughing,
never hear the former one's tears —"
Within the mountain the stream runs clear;

---

[20]White-headed crows are harbingers of evil.
[21]The Tang family. The dragon is a symbol of imperial power.
[22]As ransom, should he be captured.
[23]The rebels used Bactrian camels as transport animals.
[24]Chang'an.
[25]Troops from north of Chang'an who had fought successful-

ly against the Tibetans but were defeated by the rebels in 756.
[26]Emperor Tang Suzong had recently concluded an alliance with the Uighurs. See source 69.
[27]A sign of Uighur sincerity. See source 69.
[28]Omens of good fortune still linger around the gravesites of Emperor Tang Suzong's greatest imperial ancestors.

out of the mountain it turns to mud.
Her maid returns from selling a pearl,
braids vines to mend their roof of thatch.
The lady picks a flower but does not put it in
  her hair,

gathers juniper berries, sometimes a handful.
When the sky is cold, in thin azure sleeves,
at dusk she stands leaning by the tall bamboo.

The Bartered Bride:
China and the Uighurs in an Age of Civil War
▼▼▼

69 ▼ *THE OLD TANG HISTORY*

Following the collapse of the Tang Dynasty, China passed into a period of turmoil
known as the Era of the Five Dynasties (907–960). Even in the midst of troubles,
what passed for an imperial court took pains to recover and record the past. In 941
Emperor Gaozu, a non-Chinese, Turkic adventurer, ordered the compilation from
extant records of the history of the previous Tang Era. Completed in 945, the work
eventually became known as *The Old Tang History,* to distinguish it from a later
version, *The New Tang History,* which was compiled in the Song Era.

In the story excerpted here we learn about relations between the short-lived but
important Uighur Empire (744–840) and Tang China. The time period is 758–759,
and China is torn apart by the An Lushan Rebellion. In desperation, Emperor Tang
Suzong (r. 756–762), the son and successor of Tang Xuanzong, turns to the
Uighurs, a Turkic people who dominated the Mongolian steppes, having recently
emerged as the major force along China's northwestern border. Traditionally pastoral nomads, the Uighurs were in the process of settling down as agriculturalists
and establishing several cities, but they maintained much of their nomadic culture,
especially their warrior traditions. Until recently, in fact, they had been at war with
the Chinese.

Our story begins in June 758 with the arrival of an embassy at the Chinese capital city of Chang'an, which imperial forces, with the help of a Uighur detachment
of about 4,000 cavalry, had reoccupied in November 757. Indeed, Uighurs had
been fighting alongside loyalist Chinese forces since December 756.

QUESTIONS FOR ANALYSIS

1. What did each side, the Chinese and the Uighur, hope to gain by this marriage
    alliance?
2. Were the goals achieved?
3. This story is told from a Chinese perspective. How did the Chinese interpret
    or explain their relations with the Uighurs?
4. Retell the story from the Uighur perspective.
5. Retell it from the princess's perspective.
6. What does this story suggest about China's relations with the nomadic peoples
    along its borders?

On the day *renshen,* the first day of the fifth month of the first year of Qianyuan (June 11, 758), eighty Uighur envoys . . . and six Abbasid Arab chiefs[1]. . . came simultaneously to court to have an audience. When they arrived at the pavilion gate, they argued over who should go in first. The visitors-and-audience officials separated them into right and left and they entered at the same time through the east and west gates.

In the sixth month, on the day *wuxu* (July 7, 758), there was a banquet in honor of some Uighur envoys in front of the Zichen Hall.[2]

In the autumn, on the day *dinghai* of the seventh month (August 25, 758), the emperor issued an edict that one of his young daughters[3] should be installed as the Princess of Ningguo and that she should go out and be married [to the Uighur khaghan].[4] On the day of her departure for the Uighur territory, the emperor's younger cousin on his father's side, who was the Prefectural Prince of Hanzhong, Yu, was to be specially promoted to be Trial President of the Court of Imperial Sacrifices, was to hold temporarily the rank of President of the Censorate, and was to fill the office of Commissioner Who Appoints and Names "Brave and Warlike, Aweing the Distant Lands, the Turkic Khaghan." The emperor's nephew on his father's side, the Left Secretary Sun, as Secretary of the Ministry of War, was to be given temporarily the rank of Vice President of the Censorate and President of the Court of Diplomatic Reception, and to act as deputy to Yu. Concurrently, [Sun] was to be made the Commissioner for the Rites and Entertainments of the [Wedding of the] Princess of Ningguo. . . .

On the day *guiwu* (August 31, 758), the emperor appointed and set up "Brave and Warlike,

Aweing the Distant Lands, the Turkic Khaghan of the Uighurs." He (the emperor) sat in the Grand Audience Hall, and the Prince of Hanzhong received from him the imperial diploma [of appointment].

On the day *jiawu* (September 1, 758), the Emperor Suzong, escorting the Princess of Ningguo, arrived at the Cimen Postal Station in Xianyang.[5] The princess wept and spoke to him saying, "The affairs of our state are serious. Even should I die, I shall not regret going." The emperor shed tears and returned.

When Yu reached his royal camp, the Turkic khaghan, dressed in a yellow-ocher robe and a barbarian hat, was sitting in his tent on a bed. His insignia and body-guards were extremely abundant. They led Yu before him, standing outside the tent. The khaghan spoke to Yu saying, "Prince, what relation are you to the Heavenly Khaghan?"[6] Yu said, "I am the cousin of the Son of Heaven of Tang." Again the khaghan asked, "Who is it who is standing above you, the prince?" Yu replied, "It is the palace eunuch Lei Lujun." The khaghan again declared thus, "The palace eunuch is a slave in status. How is it that he can stand above you, who are of noble birth?" Lei Lujun was afraid, he stepped aside and made himself lower.

Everybody was in his proper place. But Yu would not bow and remained standing. The khaghan declared thus, "The leaders, nobility and subjects of both our states observe a rite. How can you not bow?" Yu said, "The Son of Heaven of Tang considered you, the khaghan, to have merit, and therefore he is having his daughter brought here and given to you in marriage. He is tying together a friendship through this

---

[1]The Abbasids, who had seized the caliphate from the Umayyads in 750, had beaten Chinese forces rather badly at the Battle of the Talas River in 751, which meant a loss of China's westernmost areas of influence and the beginning of the Tang Dynasty's downward slide. Despite these earlier hostilities, the Arab ambassadors were in Chang'an to discuss rendering military assistance in the fight against the rebels.

[2]A hall in the heart of the imperial palace complex, which was known as the Daming Palace.

[3]The second of Emperor Tang Suzong's seven daughters. She had been married previously.

[4]Moyanchuo (r. 747–759), second *khaghan,* or leader, of the Uighur confederation. He consolidated the empire begun by his father and also built the Uighur capital city and palace.

[5]A city about twenty miles northwest of Chang'an.

[6]Emperor Tang Suzong. The Uighurs also used this title for their own khaghan.

marriage with you, the khaghan. Recently the women whom China has given to outside barbarians as wives have in all cases been [merely] daughters of members of the imperial clan and have been named "princesses." The present Princess of Ningguo is the true daughter of the Son of Heaven.[7] Also she has talents and a becoming appearance and has come 10,000 *li*[8] to be married to the khaghan. The khaghan is to be the son-in-law of the Son of Heaven of the Tang family. He should know the differences in grades of the rites. How can he conceivably remain seated on his bed while receiving the diploma of such an edict? At that the khaghan stood up to take the edict and immediately received the imperial diploma of his appointment.

The following day the princess was appointed the khatun.[9] The barbarian chief rejoiced over it and said, "The Son of Heaven of the Tang state is most high and has had his true daughter brought here." The state seals, the silken fabrics, the multi-colored clothes and garments and the gold and silver dishes which Yu had brought, the khaghan distributed down to the last one among his officials, chiefs and others. When Yu was on the point of going home, the khaghan presented him with 500 horses and 100 pieces of sable fur.

In the eighth month,[10] the Uighurs sent their prince, Prince Guchuo, and their Chief Minister, Dide, and other brave men at the head of 3,000 troops to help China in her fight against the rebels. Suzong commended them for having come from so far, and gave them a banquet. He ordered that they be attached to the Expeditionary Camps of the Shuofang Army and made Pugu Huaien[11] supervise them. On the day *ji-ashen* of the ninth month (October 21, 758), the Uighurs sent the great chief, General Gai, and others to give thanks for the granting of the Princess [of Ningguo] in marriage. At the same time a memorial was set up to the effect that they had destroyed [an army of] 50,000 Kirghiz.[12]

There was a banquet in the Zichen Hall and the emperor gave gifts according to rank.

On the day *jiazi* of the twelfth month (January 29, 759?), the Uighurs sent three ladies to give thanks for the marriage of the Princess of Ningguo. The emperor gave them a banquet in the Zichen Hall.

In the second year of Qianyuan (759), the Uighurs, Prince Guchuo and others led their armies, following Guo Ziyi[13] and the nine military governors to [positions] outside the walls of Xiangzhou. There was a battle,[14] [the outcome of which] was not favorable [for government forces]. . . . [T]he Uighur prince, Prince Guchuo, the Chief Minister, Dide, and thirteen others fled from Xiangzhou to the Western Capital.[15] Suzong gave them a banquet in the Zichen Hall and rewarded them according to rank.

On the day *gengyin* of the same month (April 25, 759), the Uighur prince took his farewell and was about to take home his expeditionary camps. The emperor gave them a banquet in the Zichen Hall and made presentations according to rank.

▷   After receiving several imperial offices and titles, the prince and his troops return home.

In the summer, in the fourth month (May 2–30, 759), the Uighur Turkic khaghan died.[16] . . .

---

[7]The princess was the first daughter of a Tang emperor to be married to a foreign ruler.

[8]Later one *li* was about one-third of a mile, but evidence (as well as measurement of the distance from Chang'an to the heart of Mongolia) suggests that one *li* in the Tang Era was about one-fifth of a mile.

[9]Wife of the khaghan.

[10]The period from September 7 through October 6, 758.

[11]One of Tang China's leading generals, he was a member of the Turkic Pugu tribe, which was one of the nine tribes that made up the Uighur confederation.

[12]In an unrelated battle. The Kirghiz were a Turkic enemy of the Uighurs who eventually destroyed the Uighur Empire in 840.

[13]China's most important and successful general of the time, he was responsible, more than anyone else, for the successful suppression of the rebellion and for defending China from two Tibetan invasions.

[14]On April 7, 759.

[15]Chang'an. They arrived on April 19, 759.

[16]Sometime between May 2 and May 30, word arrived in Chang'an of his death. It had occurred a bit earlier.

When the Turkic khaghan died, his court officials, governors-general and others had wanted the Princess of Ningguo to be buried with him. The princess said, "In our Chinese law, when a woman's husband dies, she immediately observes mourning. She weeps in the morning and evening, and for a period approaching three years she dons mourning clothes. That [the khaghan of] the Uighurs took me as his wife must mean that he admired the rites of the Middle Kingdom. If he had still been following the laws of his own country, why was it necessary for him to marry a wife from 10,000 *li* away?" However, the princess also observed Uighur custom by slashing her face and weeping loudly. Finally, since she had no sons, she obtained permission to go home, and in the autumn, in the eighth month (August 27–September 25, 759), the Princess of Ningguo came back from Uighur territory to China.[17] There was an edict that all the officials should welcome her outside the Mingfeng Gate.

---

[17]She arrived on September 18, 759.

The Dao of Agriculture in Song China
▼▼▼

70 ▾ Chen Pu, THE CRAFT OF FARMING

China has continually faced the problem of producing sufficient food to meet the needs of an expanding population. During the Song Era the Chinese met this challenge with reasonable success, despite a steep increase in population, whereby China's probable 50 to 60 million in the early 700s grew to about 120 million by about 1200. This success was partially due to an activist agenda by the central government, which encouraged land reclamation through tax incentives and published illustrated handbooks that promoted up-to-date agricultural technology. The following selections from a popular treatise written in 1149 by the otherwise unknown Chen Pu provide insight into the manner in which Song China approached the problem of feeding itself adequately.

QUESTIONS FOR ANALYSIS

1. What does Chen Pu assume is more scarce, and consequently more valuable, labor or land? What do you infer from your answer?
2. Chen Pu focuses on several key elements that contributed to Song China's success in feeding its people. What are they?
3. According to Chen Pu, which qualities set the superior farmer apart from all others?
4. It has been said that this treatise focuses more on producing a superior farmer than a superior farm. What does this mean, and do you agree? If you agree, what do you find so distinctly Chinese about such a goal?
5. In what way is this treatise a combination of agricultural science, folk wisdom, Confucian learning, and Daoist ideology? Can you find any Legalist elements in the essay?

FINANCE AND LABOR

All those who engage in business should do so in accordance with their own capacity. They should refrain from careless investment and excessive greed, lest in the end they achieve nothing. . . . In the farming business, which is the most difficult business to manage, how can you afford not to calculate your financial and labor capacities carefully? Only when you are certain that you have sufficient funds and labor to assure success should you launch an enterprise. Anyone who covets more than he can manage is likely to fall into carelessness and irresponsibility. . . . Thus, to procure more land is to increase trouble, not profit.

On the other hand, anyone who plans carefully, begins with good methods, and continues in the same way can reasonably expect success and does not have to rely on luck. The proverb says, "Owning a great deal of emptiness is less desirable than reaping from a narrow patch of land." . . . For the farmer who is engaged in the management of fields, the secret lies not in expanding the farmland, but in balancing finance and labor. If the farmer can achieve that, he can expect prosperity and abundance. . . .

PLOWING

Early and late plowing both have their advantages. For the early rice crop,[1] as soon as the reaping is completed, immediately plow the fields and expose the stalks to glaring sunlight. Then add manure and bury the stalks to nourish the soil. Next, plant beans, wheat, and vegetables to ripen and fertilize the soil so as to minimize the next year's labor. In addition, when the harvest is good, these extra crops can add to the yearly income. For late crops, however, do not plow until spring. Because the rice stalks are soft but tough,

it is necessary to wait until they have fully decayed to plow satisfactorily. . . .

THE SIX KINDS OF CROPS

There is an order to the planting of different crops. Anyone who knows the right timing and follows the order can cultivate one thing after another, and use one to assist the others. Then there will not be a day without planting, nor a month without harvest, and money will be coming in throughout the year. How can there then be any worry about cold, hunger, or lack of funds?

Plant the nettle-hemp in the first month. Apply manure in intervals of ten days and by the fifth or sixth month it will be time for reaping. The women should take charge of knotting and spinning cloth out of the hemp.

Plant millet in the second month. It is necessary to sow the seeds sparsely and then roll cart wheels over the soil to firm it up; this will make the millet grow luxuriantly, its stalks long and its grains full. In the seventh month the millet will be harvested, easing any temporary financial difficulties.

There are two crops of oil-hemp. The early crop is planted in the third month. Rake the field to spread out the seedlings. Repeat the raking process three times a month and the hemp will grow well. It can be harvested in the seventh or the eighth month.

In the fourth month plant beans. Rake as with hemp. They will be ripe by the seventh month.

In mid-fifth month plant the late oil-hemp. Proceed as with the early crop. The ninth month will be reaping time.

After the 7th day of the seventh month, plant radishes and cabbage.

In the eighth month, before the autumn sacrifice to the god of the Earth, wheat can be planted. It is advisable to apply manure and remove

---

[1]Rice became a central part of the Chinese diet in the Song Era, thanks to the introduction of early-ripening, drought-resistant strains from Southeast Asia. These new seeds made it possible to grow the crop in areas that previously had been unsuitable for rice cultivation.

weeds frequently. When wheat grows from the autumn through the spring sacrifices to the god of the Earth, the harvest will double and the grains will be full and solid.

The *Book of Poetry*[2] says, "The tenth month is the time to harvest crops." You will have a large variety of crops, including millet, rice, beans, hemp, and wheat and will lack nothing needed through the year. Will you ever be concerned for want of resources? . . .

FERTILIZER

At the side of the farm house, erect a compost hut. Make the eaves low to prevent the wind and rain from entering it, for when the compost is exposed to the moon and the stars, it will lose its fertility. In this hut, dig a deep pit and line it with bricks to prevent leakage. Collect waste, ashes, chaff, broken stalks, and fallen leaves and burn them in the pit; then pour manure over them to make them fertile. In this way considerable quantities of compost are acquired over time. Then, whenever sowing is to be done, sieve and discard stones and tiles, mix the fine compost with the seeds, and plant them sparsely in pinches. When the seedlings have grown tall, again sprinkle the compost and bank it up against the roots. These methods will ensure a double yield.

Some people say that when the soil is exhausted, grass and trees will not grow; that when the qi[3] is weak, all living things will be stunted; and that after three to five years of continuous planting, the soil of any field will be exhausted. This theory is erroneous because it fails to recognize one factor: by adding new, fertile soil, enriched

with compost, the land can be reinforced in strength. If this is so, where can the alleged exhaustion come from?

WEEDING

The *Book of Poetry* says, "Root out the weeds. Where the weeds decay, there the grains will grow luxuriantly." The author of the *Record of Ritual* also remarks, "The months of midsummer are advantageous for weeding. Weeds can fertilize the fields and improve the land." Modern farmers, ignorant of these principles, throw the weeds away. They do not know that, if mixed with soil and buried deep under the roots of rice seedlings, the weeds will eventually decay and the soil will be enriched; the harvest, as a result, will be abundant and of superior quality. . . .

CONCENTRATION

If something is thought out carefully, it will succeed; if not, it will fail; this is a universal truth. It is very rare that a person works and yet gains nothing. On the other hand, there is never any harm in trying too hard.

In farming it is especially appropriate to be concerned about what you are doing. Mencius said, "Will a farmer discard his plow when he leaves his land?" Ordinary people will become idle if they have leisure and prosperity. Only those who love farming, who behave in harmony with it, who take pleasure in talking about it and think about it all the time will manage it without a moment's negligence. For these people a day's work results in a day's gain, a year's work in a year's gain. How can they escape affluence?

[2]Also known as *The Book of Songs* (source 6).
[3]Vital energy, or material force. *Qi* was a construct of *Neo-Confucian* philosophers during the Song Era. They envi-

sioned a cosmos in which all entities are composed of *li* (an infinite moral Principle) and *qi* (its driving force).

Thirteenth-Century Hangzhou
▼▼▼

71 ▾ A RECORD OF MUSINGS ON THE EASTERN CAPITAL

When *Ruzhen* steppe-people overran all of northern China in the early twelfth century and established the rival *Jin Dynasty* (1115–1234) with its capital at Beijing, the Song imperial court fled from its capital at Kaifeng to the port city of *Hangzhou,* just south of the Yangzi River. From here the Song ruled over the southern remnants of their mutilated empire until Mongols captured the city in 1276.

Southern Song (1127–1279) presided over territory that was now China's most densely populated region and the newest hub of Chinese culture. Its heart was Hangzhou, which was more than merely an administrative center. In the thirteenth century it was home to well over one million people (some estimates reach as high as two and one-half million), who inhabited an area of seven to eight square miles, making it the largest and richest city in the world. Marco Polo, who visited the city on several occasions in the late thirteenth century, knew Hangzhou by the name *Kinsai,* which he translated as "City of Heaven." According to Polo, travelers to the city were so captivated by it that they could scarcely wait to return.

The following account, composed anonymously in 1235, describes the city and its residents.

QUESTIONS FOR ANALYSIS

1. Describe and characterize Hangzhou's economy. Be as specific as possible.
2. Which adjectives would you use to characterize this city? Defend each one.
3. Compare life in Hangzhou with that in a modern metropolis, such as New York City or Los Angeles. What would a modern urban dweller or visitor recognize as familiar in this thirteenth-century city?

MARKETS

During the morning hours, markets extend from Tranquility Gate of the palace all the way to the north and south sides of the New Boulevard. Here we find pearl, jade, talismans, exotic plants and fruits, seasonal catches from the sea, wild game — all the rarities of the world seem to be gathered here. The food and commodity markets at the Heavenly-View Gate, River Market Place, Central Square, Ba Creek, the end of Superior Lane, Tent Place, and Universal Peace Bridge are all crowded and full of traffic.

In the evening, with the exception of the square in front of the palace, the markets are as busy as during the day. The most attractive one is at Central Square, where all sorts of exquisite artifacts, instruments, containers, and hundreds of varieties of goods are for sale. In other market-places, sales, auctions, and exchanges go on constantly. In the wine shops and inns business also thrives. Only after the fourth drum[1] does the city gradually quiet down, but by the fifth drum, court officials already start preparing for audiences and merchants are getting ready for the morning market again. This cycle goes on all year round without respite. . . .

On the lot in front of the wall of the city building, there are always various acting troupes performing, and this usually attracts a large crowd. The same kind of activity is seen in almost any vacant lot, including those at the meat market of the Great Common, the herb market at Charcoal Bridge, the book market at Orange Grove, the vegetable market on the east side of the city, and the rice market on the north side. There are many more interesting markets, such as the candy center at the Five Buildings, but I cannot name them all.

COMMERCIAL ESTABLISHMENTS

In general, the capital attracts the greatest variety of goods and has the best craftsmen. For instance, the flower company at Superior Lane does a truly excellent job of flower arrangement, and its caps, hairpins, and collars are unsurpassed in craftsmanship. Some of the most famous specialties of the capital are the sweet-bean soup at the Miscellaneous Market, the pickled dates of the Ge family, the thick soup of the Guang family at Superior Lane, the fruit at the Great Commons marketplace, the cooked meats in front of Eternal Mercy Temple, Sister Song's fish broth at Penny Pond Gate, the juicy lungs at Flowing Gold Gate, the "lamb rice" of the Zhi family at Central Square, the boots of the Peng family, the fine clothing of the Xuan family at Southern Com-mons, the sticky rice pastry of the Zhang family, the flutes made by Gu the Fourth, and the Qiu family's Tatar whistles at the Great Commons.

WINE SHOPS

Among the various kinds of wine shops, the tea-and-food shops sell not only wine, but also various foods to go with it. However, to get seasonal delicacies not available in these shops, one should go to the inns, for they also have a menu from which one can make selections. The pastry-and-wine shops sell pastries with duckling and goose fillings, various fixings of pig tripe, intestines and blood, fish fat and spawn; but they are rather expensive. The mansion-style inns are either decorated in the same way as officials' mansions or are actually remodeled from such mansions. The garden-style inns are often located in the suburbs, though some are also situated in town. Their decoration is usually an imitation of a studio-garden combination. Among other kinds of wine shops are the straight ones which do not sell food. There are also the small retail wine shops which sell house wine as well as wine from other stores. Instead of the common emblem — a painted branching twig — used by all other winehouses, they have bamboo fences and canvas awnings. To go drinking in such a place is called "hitting the cup," meaning that a person drinks only one cup; it is therefore not the most respectable place and is unfit for polite company.

The "luxuriant inns" have prostitutes residing in them, and the wine chambers are equipped with beds. At the gate of such an inn, on top of the red gardenia lantern, there is always a cover made of bamboo leaves. Rain or shine, this cover is always present, serving as a trademark. In other inns, the girls only keep the guests company. If a

---

[1]The night was divided into five *watches,* each of which was signaled by a drumbeat.

guest has other wishes, he has to go to the girl's place. . . .

The expenses incurred on visiting an inn can vary widely. If you order food, but no drinks, it is called "having the lowly soup-and-stuff," and is quite inexpensive. If your order of wine and food falls within the range of 100–5,000 cash,[2] it is called a small order. However, if you ask for female company, then it is most likely that the girls will order the most expensive delicacies. You are well advised to appear shrewd and experienced, so as not to be robbed. One trick, for instance, in ordering wines is to give a large order, of say, ten bottles, but open them one by one. In the end, you will probably have used only five or six bottles of the best. You can then return the rest. . . .

TEAHOUSES

In large teahouses there are usually paintings and calligraphies by famous artists on display. In the old capital,[3] only restaurants had them, to enable their patrons to while away the time as the food was being prepared, but now it is customary for teahouses as well to display paintings and the like. . . .

Often many young men gather in teahouses to practice singing or playing musical instruments. To give such amateur performances is called "getting posted."

A "social teahouse" is more of a community gathering place than a mere place that sells tea. Often tea-drinking is but an excuse, and people are rather generous when it comes to the tips.

There is a special kind of teahouse where pimps and gigolos hang out. Another kind is occupied by people from various trades and crafts who use them as places to hire help, buy apprentices, and conduct business. These teahouses are called "trade heads."

"Water teahouses" are in fact pleasure houses, the tea being a cover. Some youths are quite will-

ing to spend their money there, which is called "dry tea money." . . .

SPECIALTY STORES

The commercial area of the capital extends from the old Qing River Market to the Southern Commons on the south and to the border on the north. It includes the Central Square, which is also called the Center of Five Flowers. From the north side of the Five Buildings to South Imperial Boulevard, there are more than one hundred gold, silver, and money exchanges. On the short walls in front of these stores, there are piles of gold, silver, and copper cash: these are called "the money that watches over the store." Around these exchanges there are also numerous gold- and silversmiths. The pearl marts are situated between the north side of Cordial Marketplace and Southtown Marketplace. Most deals made here involve over 10,000 cash. A score of pawnshops are scattered in between, all owned by very wealthy people and dealing only in the most valuable objects.

Some famous fabric stores sell exquisite brocade and fine silk which are unsurpassed elsewhere in the country. Along the river, close to the Peaceful Ford Bridge, there are numerous fabric stores, fan shops, and lacquerware and porcelain shops. Most other cities can only boast of one special product; what makes the capital unique is that it gathers goods from all places. Furthermore, because of the large population and busy commercial traffic, there is a demand for everything. There are even shops that deal exclusively in used paper or in feathers, for instance.

WAREHOUSES

In Liu Yong's (ca. 1045) poem on Qiantang, we read that there were about ten thousand families residing here; but that was before the Yuanfeng

---

[2]The basic unit of currency was the *cash*, a copper coin with a square hole in the middle. These were strung together in groups of hundreds and thousands. Late in the century, the

government was circulating bank notes, backed by gold and silver, ranging in value from 1,000 to 100,000 cash coins.
[3]Kaifeng, which was captured in 1126.

reign (1078–1085). Today, having been the "temporary capital" for more than a hundred years,[4] the city has over a million households. The suburbs extend to the south, west, and north; all are densely populated and prosperous in commerce as well as in agriculture. The size of the suburbs is comparable to a small county or prefecture, and it takes several days to travel through them. This again reflects the prosperity of the capital.

In the middle of the city, enclosed by the Northern Pass Dam, is White Ocean Lake. Its water spreads over several tens of *li*.[5] Wealthy families have built scores of warehouse complexes along this waterfront. Each of these consists of several hundred to over a thousand rooms for the storage needs of the various businesses in the capital and of traveling merchants. Because these warehouses are surrounded by water, they are not endangered by fires or thieves, and therefore they offer a special convenience.

HUSTLERS

Some of these hustlers are students who failed to achieve any literary distinction. Though able to read and write, and play musical instruments and chess, they are not highly skilled in any art. They end up being a kind of guide for young men from wealthy families, accompanying them in their pleasure-seeking activities. Some also serve as guides or assistants to officials on business from other parts of the country. The lowliest of these people actually engage themselves in writing and delivering invitation cards and the like for brothels. . . .

There are also professional go-betweens, nick-named "water-treaders," whose principal targets are pleasure houses, where they flatter the wealthy young patrons, run errands for them, and help make business deals. Some gather at brothels or scenic attractions and accost the visitors. They beg for donations for "religious purposes," but in fact use the money to make a living for themselves and their families. If you pay attention to them, they will become greedy; if you ignore them, they will force themselves on you and will not stop until you give in. It requires art to deal with these people appropriately.

---

[4]The Song emperors never gave up hope of recovering Kaifeng and the northern part of the empire. Kaifeng thus remained the official capital, and Hangzhou was designated only *temporary capital*.

[5]A *li* is a bit more than a third of a mile (but see source 69, note 8).

▼▼▼

Buddhism in East Asia: Acceptance, Rejection, and Accommodation

Buddhism spread out of India and into East Asia about the same time that the Mahayana Doctrine was transforming the teachings of the Buddha into a popular religion. Following branches of the Silk Road out of northwest India, Mahayana Buddhism traveled through Central Asia and into the heartland of northern China, reaching the Middle Kingdom as early as the reign of Emperor Han Mingdi (58–75 C.E.). Initially, however, Buddhism made little progress in China because some of its practices, such as monasticism and celibacy (rejection of marriage), and its basic otherworldliness ran counter to two primary Chinese qualities: emphasis on the centrality of the family and preoccupation with this world. The few early inroads Buddhism made in China occurred largely because some Chinese initially were able to equate it with Daoism, whereby they perceived Nirvana to be the equivalent of the Daoist principle of active nonaction *(wuwei)*, and they translated *Dharma* (the Law of Righteousness) as *Dao* (the Way). In the time of troubles that followed the collapse of Later Han in 220, however, Buddhism, especially in its Mahayana form, achieved its own place in China as a religious doctrine offering comfort in the face of affliction.

From China, Buddhist ideas were introduced into Korea by the fourth century, into Japan in the sixth, and later into Tibet, Mongolia, and northern regions of Southeast Asia. In each of these regions Mahayana Buddhism took deep root and became a living part of its host civilization. As the following sources suggest, however, the story of Buddhism's spread through East Asia was not a simple one. As it traveled, Buddhism absorbed local ideas and styles, which in turn were passed on to a neighboring culture, which then adapted the received ideas and styles to suit its own needs and perceptions. Yet even when adapted to a preexisting culture, Buddhist ideas and ways could and did face local resistance, especially in China. Despite resistance, even solidly secular China was forced to come to grips with Buddhist metaphysics, and despite several attempts to suppress the religion, China assimilated Buddhism's basic concepts, deities, rituals, artistic motifs, and festivals into its everyday culture. Along with Confucianism, Daoism, and Legalism, Buddhism became one of the major pillars of Chinese civilization.

Buddhism Comes to China:
The Story of the Nun An Lingshou
▼▼▼

72 ▼ *Shi Baochang, LIVES OF THE NUNS*

The following story, which is from a collection of sixty-five biographies of eminent Buddhist nuns who lived between the fourth and sixth centuries, illustrates the inherent tension between traditional Chinese social principles and Buddhist beliefs. It also shows us how Buddhist missionaries were able to accommodate Mahayana Buddhism to China's prevailing values.

The nun *An Lingshou* lived 200 years before Shi Baochang completed his work in or around 516. Because of the time gap and because of the compiler's avowed purpose to offer these holy women as models of Buddhist virtue, we would be naive if we did not wonder about the authenticity of the story, or at least the truth of its details. Yet there are aspects of the story that ring true. Even if the reported debate between An Lingshou and her father never took place, it certainly reflects opinions that were voiced during this era of Buddhist infiltration.

QUESTIONS FOR ANALYSIS

1. What is the evidence for concluding that An Lingshou adopted a Mahayana form of Buddhism? If you have questions regarding Mahayana Buddhism, review sources 39 and 40.
2. What was the classic Chinese objection to Buddhism?
3. How did Buddhists answer this objection?
4. Review the teachings of the Buddha (sources 16 and 17). What was there about Buddhism, and maybe especially its Mahayana forms, that attracted women and provided support for female monasticism?

An[1] Lingshou's secular surname was Xu. Her family was originally from Donghuan.[2] Her father Xu Chong served the non-Chinese dynasty of Latter Zhao[3] as an undersecretary of the provincial forces.

When she was young, Lingshou was intelligent and fond of study.[4] Her speech was clear and beautiful; her nature modest and unassuming. Taking no pleasure in worldly affairs, she was at ease in secluded quiet. She delighted in the Buddhist teachings and did not wish for her parents to arrange her betrothal.

Her father said, "You ought to marry. How can you be so unfilial?"

Lingshou said, "My mind is concentrated on the work of religion, and my thought dwells exclusively on spiritual matters. Neither blame nor praise moves me; purity and uprightness are sufficient in themselves. Why must I submit three times before I am considered a woman of propriety?[5]

Her father said, "You want to benefit only one person — yourself. How can you help your father and mother at the same time?"

Lingshou said, "I am setting myself to cultivate the Way exactly because I want to free all living beings from suffering. How much more, then, do I want to free my two parents!"

Xu Chong consulted the Buddhist magician monk[6] from Kucha,[7] Fotudeng,[8] who said, "You return home and keep a vegetarian fast, and after three days you may come back to see me again." Xu Chong obeyed him. At the end of the three days, Fotudeng spread Xu Chong's palm with the oil of sesame ground together with safflower. When he ordered Xu Chong to look at it, Chong saw a person who resembled his daughter dressed in Buddhist monastic robes preaching the Buddhist teachings in the midst of a large assembly.

When he told all of this to Fotudeng, the monk said, "This is a former incarnation of your daughter, in which she left the household life and benefited living beings — such were her deeds. If you consent to her plan, she indeed shall raise her family to glory and bring you blessings and honor; and she shall guide you [to Nirvana] on the far shore of the great ocean of suffering known as the incessant round of birth and death."

---

[1]Her religious surname, An, indicates that she traced her spiritual lineage back to a Parthian Buddhist missionary.
[2]In northeastern China.
[3]Literally, "the illegitimate dynasty of Latter Zhao." Between 304 and 431, sixteen kingdoms, largely dominated by foreigners of Mongol and Turkic ethnicity, emerged and vied with one another in northern China. Latter Zhao, which lasted from 319 to 350, instituted a reign of terror (see notes 12–14).
[4]High-born women in Han and for centuries thereafter tended to be well educated.

[5]Submit first to her father and elder brother, then to her husband, and after his death to her son.
[6]A number of Buddhist missionary monks in China enjoyed reputations as healers, magicians, seers, interpreters of dreams, and miracle workers.
[7]An oasis city that was the center of a Central Asian kingdom along the Silk Road.
[8]Zhu Fotudeng (232–348) was a Central Asian of Indian ancestry who arrived in northern China in 310. His disciples are considered the founding parents of Chinese Buddhism.

Xu Chong returned home and permitted his daughter to become a nun.[9] Lingshou thereupon cut off her hair, discarded secular ornaments, and received the rules of monastic life from Fotudeng and the nun Jingjian.[10] She established Founding of Wisdom Convent, and Fotudeng presented her with a cut-flower embroidered vestment, a seven-strip monastic robe.[11] and an elephant-trunk-shaped water ewer that Shiluo, first emperor of the Latter Zhao Dynasty, had given him.[12]

Lingshou widely perused all kinds of books, and, having read a book through only once, she was always able to chant it by heart. Her thought extended to the depths of the profound; her spirit intuited the subtle and divine. In the religious communities of that time there was no one who did not honor her. Those who left the household life because of her numbered more than two hundred. Furthermore, she built five or six monastic retreats. She had no fear of hard work and brought her projects to completion.

The Emperor Shihu,[13] nephew of the late Emperor Shiluo,[14] honored her and promoted her father Xu Chong to the official court position of undersecretary of the Yellow Gate and administrator of the Qinghe Commandery.

---

[9]Buddhist monastic rules mandated parental consent for minors and young women who wished to enter the *Sangha,* or monastic community.

[10]The subject of the first biography in this collection, Zhu Jingjian (ca. 292–ca. 361), whose secular name was Zhong Lingyi, was a well-educated widow. She is credited with founding China's first female Buddhist monastery, Bamboo Grove Convent, in 317 in the city of Chang'an.

[11]Traditionally, a garment made out of rags and scraps that symbolized rejection of worldly wealth.

[12]Shiluo reigned 319–333. Fotudeng's magical powers gained him entry to the court of Latter Zhao, and he was able to use his influence to ameliorate somewhat its brutality (note 3).

[13]Reigned 335–349, he had a reputation for psychopathic viciousness.

[14]Shihu gained the throne by killing off Shiluo's son.

A Conflict of Values: Buddhism in Late Tang China
▼▼▼

73 ▾ *Han Yu, MEMORIAL ON BUDDHISM*

Chinese Buddhism reached its high point of popularity and influence during the early years of the Tang Dynasty. Buddhist monasteries and sects proliferated, and the Tang imperial court often patronized Buddhism in one form or another during its first two centuries of power. However, because so many aspects of Buddhism were at variance with the traditional culture of China, especially Confucian values, conflict was almost inevitable. One of the leaders in the Confucian counterattack on Buddhism was the classical prose stylist and poet Han Yu (768–824), who in 819 composed a polemic against Buddhism. Presented as a memorandum, or *memorial,* to Emperor Tang Xianzong on the subject of the emperor's veneration of a relic of the Buddha's finger, Han Yu's elegant and witty essay so enraged the emperor that initially he wanted to execute the author. Eventually, the emperor contented himself with banishing his impudent civil servant to a frontier outpost.

QUESTIONS FOR ANALYSIS

1. How does Han Yu imply that emperors who have espoused Buddhism have lost the Mandate of Heaven?
2. Which aspect of Buddhism most repels Han Yu?
3. In Han Yu's mind, what are the social, cultural, and political dangers of Buddhism?
4. Compose Han Yu's rejoinder to the story of the nun An Lingshao.

MEMORIAL ON BUDDHISM

Your servant submits that Buddhism is but one of the practices of barbarians which has filtered into China since the Later Han. In ancient times there was no such thing. . . . In those times the empire was at peace, and the people, contented and happy, lived out their full complement of years. . . . The Buddhist doctrine had still not reached China, so this could not have been the result of serving the Buddha.

The Buddhist doctrine first appeared in the time of the Emperor Ming[1] of the Han Dynasty, and the Emperor Ming was a scant eighteen years on the throne. Afterwards followed a succession of disorders and revolutions, when dynasties did not long endure. From the time of the dynasties Song, Qi, Liang, Chen, and Wei,[2] as they grew more zealous in the service of the Buddha, the reigns of kings became shorter. There was only the Emperor Wu of the Liang who was on the throne for forty-eight years. First and last, he thrice abandoned the world and dedicated himself to the service of the Buddha. He refused to use animals in the sacrifices in his own ancestral temple. His single meal a day was limited to fruits and vegetables. In the end he was driven out and died of hunger. His dynasty likewise came to an untimely end. In serving the Buddha

he was seeking good fortune, but the disaster that overtook him was only the greater. Viewed in the light of this, it is obvious that the Buddha is not worth serving.

When Gaozu[3] first succeeded to the throne of the Sui,[4] he planned to do away with Buddhism, but his ministers and advisors were short-sighted men incapable of any real understanding of the Way of the Former Kings, or of what is fitting for past and present; they were unable to apply the Emperor's ideas so as to remedy this evil, and the matter subsequently came to naught — many the times your servant has regretted it. I venture to consider that Your Imperial Majesty, shrewd and wise in peace and war, with divine wisdom and heroic courage, is without an equal through the centuries. When first you came to the throne, you would not permit laymen to become monks or nuns or Daoist priests,[5] nor would you allow the founding of temples or cloisters. It constantly struck me that the intention of Gaozu was to be fulfilled by Your Majesty. Now even though it has not been possible to put it into effect immediately, it is surely not right to remove all restrictions and turn around and actively encourage them.

Now I hear that by Your Majesty's command a troupe of monks went to Fengxiang[6] to get the Buddha-bone, and that you viewed it from a

---

[1]Han Mingdi (57–75 C.E.).

[2]Five fairly short-lived dynasties of the troubled fourth through sixth centuries. The Wei, who were foreign conquerors, apparently used Buddhism's universal message as an ideological buttress for their rule.

[3]Literally "high (or great) ancestor," an honorific title bestowed posthumously on several Chinese emperors. This high ancestor was Li Yuan, the first Tang emperor.

[4]The Sui Dynasty (581–618) reunited China in 589 and began a period of expansion that some characterize as the *Second Chinese Empire* (589–ca. 755).

[5]By the second century C.E., a polytheistic Daoist Church, which practiced congregational worship, preached physical immortality, and used drugs and magic to achieve that immortality, had emerged as a significant force.

[6]A western city.

tower as it was carried into the Imperial Palace; also that you have ordered that it be received and honored in all the temples in turn. Although your servant[7] is stupid, he cannot help knowing that Your Majesty is not misled by this Buddha, and that you do not perform these devotions to pray for good luck. But just because the harvest has been good and the people are happy, you are complying with the general desire by putting on for the citizens of the capital this extraordinary spectacle which is nothing more than a sort of theatrical amusement. How could a sublime intelligence like yours consent to believe in this sort of thing?

But the people are stupid and ignorant; they are easily deceived and with difficulty enlightened. If they see Your Majesty behaving in this fashion, they are going to think you serve the Buddha in all sincerity. All will say, "The Emperor is wisest of all, and yet he is a sincere believer. What are we common people that we still should grudge our lives?" Burning heads and searing fingers by the tens and hundreds, throwing away their clothes and scattering their money, from morning to night emulating one another and fearing only to be last, old and young rush about, abandoning their work and place; and if restrictions are not immediately imposed, they will increasingly make the rounds of temples and some will inevitably cut off their arms and slice their flesh in the way of offerings. Thus to violate decency and draw the ridicule of the whole world is no light matter.

Now the Buddha was of barbarian origin. His language differed from Chinese speech; his clothes were of a different cut; his mouth did not pronounce the prescribed words of the Former Kings,[8] his body was not clad in the garments prescribed by the Former Kings. He did not recognize the relationship between prince and subject, nor the sentiments of father and son. Let us suppose him to be living today, and that he come to court at the capital as an emissary of his country. Your Majesty would receive him courteously. But only one interview in the audience chamber, one banquet in his honor, one gift of clothing, and he would be escorted under guard to the border that he might not mislead the masses.

How much the less, now that he has long been dead, is it fitting that his decayed and rotten bone, his ill-omened and filthy remains, should be allowed to enter in the forbidden precincts of the Palace? Confucius said, "Respect ghosts and spirits, but keep away from them."[9] The feudal lords of ancient times, when they went to pay a visit of condolence in their states, made it their practice to have exorcists go before with rush-brooms and peachwood branches to dispel unlucky influences. Only after such precautions did they make their visit of condolence. Now without reason you have taken up an unclean thing and examined it in person when no exorcist had gone before, when neither rush-broom nor peachwood branch had been employed. But your ministers did not speak of the wrong nor did the censors call attention to the impropriety; I am in truth ashamed of them. I pray that Your Majesty will turn this bone over to the officials that it may be cast into water or fire, cutting off for all time the root and so dispelling the suspicions of the empire and preventing the befuddlement of later generations. Thereby men may know in what manner a great sage acts who a million times surpasses ordinary men. Could this be anything but ground for prosperity? Could it be anything but a cause for rejoicing?

If the Buddha has supernatural power and can wreak harm and evil, may any blame or retribution fittingly fall on my person. Heaven be my witness: I will not regret it. Unbearably disturbed and with the utmost sincerity I respectfully present my petition that these things may be known.

Your servant is truly alarmed, truly afraid.

---

[7]Han Yu.
[8]The legendary predynastic Sage Emperors.

[9]From *The Analects* (source 21).

A Japanese Monk in China

▼▼▼

74 ▼ TALES FROM UJI

A champion of rationalism, Han Yu wished to suppress religious Daoism as well as Buddhism. Stimulated by the example of Buddhism and by the same political turmoil that had aided the rise in popularity of the Mahayana faith in China, Daoism had evolved during the early centuries C.E. into an organized religion that promised physical immortality through magic. Ironically, it was due in part to the influence of Daoist priests that Emperor Tang Wuzong (r. 840–846) initiated in 842 a policy of state suppression of foreign religious establishments. These included Manichaean, Zoroastrian, and Nestorian Christian (source 52) shrines, temples, churches, and monasteries, but hardest hit of all were China's thousands of Buddhist monasteries. The most severe of the emperor's edicts, published in 845, required the confiscation of 4,600 Buddhist monasteries and 40,000 private temples, as well as the secularization of 260,500 Buddhist monks and nuns and the emancipation of 150,000 of their slaves. In contrast, the same edict ordered a total of 3,000 Zoroastrian and Christian monks to return to the lay life. Neither faith had ever been a serious challenge to Buddhism's primacy.

The emperor died in 846, from a Daoist elixir that he consumed in hope of achieving eternal life, and with his death the full force of the edict was relaxed. Substantial damage, however, had already been done to the institutional structures of Chinese Buddhism, as well as Nestorian Christianity and other foreign faiths that had infiltrated the Middle Kingdom during the cosmopolitan reign of Early Tang.

Buddhist monasteries were hard hit by the state-ordered closures, and never again would they wield the economic power and political influence that they enjoyed before 842. But this was not the end of Chinese Buddhism. Buddhist monasticism revived under the last Tang emperors. Just as significant, Buddhist beliefs and practices remained strong at the popular level, where they increasingly merged with folk magic, Daoism, and Confucianism to become part of a uniquely Chinese religious complex. None of this was true for Nestorian Christianity and other faiths from the Far West, which were too shallowly rooted to survive the impact of this state-sponsored assault.

Across the sea in Japan, which received much of its Buddhism from China (source 65), the religion of the Middle Path, especially in its many Mahayana forms, remained a strong and vital force. In the following Japanese folktale, which was set down in its current form sometime after 1070 (and possibly as late as the thirteenth century) by an unknown editor, we see Emperor Tang Wuzong's attempted suppression of Buddhism as remembered two to four centuries after the fact. The story revolves around an important historical individual, the Japanese Buddhist monk Ennin (793–864), who traveled in northern China between 838 and 847 in search of deeper insights into his sect of the Mahayana Doctrine. Upon his return home he served as abbot of the *Tendai Sect* monastery on Mount Hiei, high above the capital city of Kyoto. As Japan's most respected Buddhist master, he introduced new Chinese forms of the faith into his native land, and played a key role in promoting Buddhism as a dominant force throughout Japan.

When reading this source, be aware that it is a folktale. Even though it revolves around a historic person during a period of actual crisis, many of its details do not conform to the facts as we know them.

QUESTIONS FOR ANALYSIS

1. Leaving aside its historical errors, what does this story suggest to you about the impact that Ennin and Buddhism had on Japanese culture and folk memory?
2. Compare Ennin's adventures with the Chinese *Tales of Guanshiyin* (source 39). What do you conclude?
3. Write Han Yu's rejoinder to this story.

HOW THE GREAT TEACHER JIKAKU[1] WENT TO TIE-DYEING CASTLE

Long ago, while the Great Teacher Jikaku was over in China studying Buddhism, he was caught up in the disorders which occurred when the Tang Emperor Wuzong, in the Huizhang period, persecuted Buddhism, destroying temples and pagodas, arresting and executing monks and nuns,[2] or forcing them to return to lay life. The Great Teacher himself was on the point of being arrested, but fled and took refuge inside a chapel. When his pursuers came in to look for him, he had no choice but to hide among the statues, meanwhile praying to Fudo.[3] The searchers found a new Fudo among the statues, which they suspiciously lifted down to examine. Jikaku now

changed back to his original form, much to the surprise of his pursuers, who reported the matter to the emperor and were told, 'He is a holy man from a foreign land. Send him away at once.' Jikaku was then released.

Thankfully, he escaped to another country,[4] where, far away over the mountains, he came to a house that was surrounded by a high earth wall, with a gateway in which someone was standing. Greatly relieved, Jikaku asked where he was. 'This house belongs to a rich man,' the other replied. 'Who are you?' 'I am a monk here from Japan to study Buddhism,' answered Jikaku, 'but I have been caught up in these dreadful disorders and wish to go into hiding for a time.' 'This is not a place that people can easily get to,' said the man. 'You are welcome to stay here for a while and go out to continue your Buddhist studies

---

[1]Ennin's posthumous title, *Jikaku Daishi* (Great Teacher of Compassion and Understanding), bestowed on him by imperial decree in 866.

[2]Some Buddhist monks and nuns were killed in the suppression, but this was not the intention or policy of the emperor. As his edict of 845 shows, his main aim was to break the economic power of the rich Buddhist monasteries and temples, which were untaxed and draining wealth and human resources from the state. Consequently, lands and buildings were confiscated, slaves were emancipated, and Buddhist

monks and nuns were forced to return to useful secular pursuits and to pay taxes.

[3]One of the Five Great Guardian Kings of Japanese Buddhism who is portrayed with a sword in his right hand and a rope in his left. He is particularly important in the *Shingon* sect of Buddhism (see note 10).

[4]Not true. Ennin left China in 847 and sailed back home to Japan, which he reached fifteen days later. The fact that he took refuge in a Korean Buddhist community in China in 845 might be a basis for this story.

when the world is in a more settled condition.' Very pleased, the Great Teacher went inside. The man locked the gate and walked to the other end of the compound. Following him, Jikaku came to rows of houses of different kinds and noisy crowds of people. He was put in a house at one side of the compound.

Now when he walked around to see if there was any place where he could pursue his Buddhist studies, he could find no trace of sutras or monks. At the farther end of the compound, there was a building close to the mountainside, and when he went up to it he could hear a number of people groaning. Puzzled, he peeped through a gap in the fence and saw some trussed-up human bodies, suspended off the ground with vessels placed beneath them into which their blood was being drained. In horror, he asked what was going on, but there was no reply. Greatly perturbed, he listened in another spot, and again he heard groaning. When he peered in he saw a number of people sprawled on the ground, ghastly pale and terribly emaciated. He beckoned one of them over and asked, 'What is happening here? How do you come to be in this appalling condition?' The other took a scrap of wood and stretching out his thin arm, wrote on the ground: 'This is Tie-Dyeing Castle. Anyone who comes here is first given a drug which deprives him of speech, then one which makes him fat. After this, he is strung up off the ground, several cuts are made on his body and his blood is drained off. The blood is used to dye variegated cloth,[5] which is then sold. People are unaware of the fate in store for them and this is how they end up. You will find some blackish things, like sesame seeds, in your food. They are the drugs which deprive people of speech. If you are offered anything of that sort, pretend to eat it but throw it away. And if anyone speaks to you, just give a groan. Then make ready to escape somehow, and

get away. The gates are securely locked, so getting away will not be easy.' Now that he had been given all this information, the Great Teacher returned to the quarters assigned to him.

After a while someone brought him some food in which, just as the man had said, there were some suspicious-looking objects. Jikaku made a show of eating them, but hid them inside his robe and later threw them away. When someone came and asked him a question, he groaned and said nothing. Thinking that he had been successfully dealt with, his captors fed him different kinds of drugs to make him fat, which he likewise pretended to swallow but did not. At a moment when they had left him alone, he turned towards the north-east and joining his hands in prayer called upon the Three Treasures of his mountain[6] to save him. A big dog now appeared which took his sleeve in its teeth and pulled him along. Confident that this was not mere chance, he followed where the dog pulled him, and it dragged him out through a drain which happened all unexpectedly to be at hand. Once outside the castle, the dog vanished.

Now at last Jikaku felt safe and ran off, letting his legs take him where they might. He had gone a long way, over the mountains, when he reached a village, where someone came up to him and asked, 'Where have you come from, sir, running like this?' Jikaku explained where he had been and how he had escaped. 'Why, that's amazing!' he was told, 'that is Tie-Dyeing Castle. No one who goes there ever comes away again. There is no way out, unless some Buddha performs a miracle to help you. What a marvel! You must be a very holy man indeed, sir.' And the man bowed reverently as he walked away.

Leaving this village, Jikaku continued his flight, until he once again entered the capital,[7] where he lay low. In the sixth year of Huizhang (846) Wuzong died, and in the following year

---

[5]The blood collected there was used for a dyeing process in which the coloring does not touch or permeate all of the fabric, thereby creating a variegated, or motley, effect.

[6]The Three Buddhist Treasures (the Buddha, the Law, and the Sangha) of Mount Hiei, site of his home monastery.
[7]Chang'an.

(the first of the Dazhong period) Xuanzong[8] succeeded to the throne and stopped the persecution of Buddhism.[9] As a result, Jikaku is said to have been able to study the Buddhist Law without

hindrance, until, after some ten years in China, he returned to Japan and spread the doctrine of Shingon.[10]

---

[8]Emperor Tang Xuanzong (r. 846–859), who should not be confused with the earlier Xuanzong mentioned in the introduction to source 68.

[9]Although a Daoist, he reversed the policy of suppressing Buddhism, allowed a limited reconstruction of Buddhist temples, and revived Buddhist services. His son and succes-

sor, Tang Yizong, was a Buddhist and lavished gifts and favors on its monks and monasteries, large numbers of which he allowed to be rebuilt.

[10]A school of esoteric, or tantric, Buddhism (source 40). Actually, Ennin belonged to another esoteric sect, the Tendai, which was a rival of Shingon.

▼▼▼

Southwest Asia:
Crossroads of the Afro-Eurasian World

Of all the significant developments that took place in Southwest Asia during the thousand-year period from 500 to 1500, the two most far-reaching were the rise and spread of Islam and the arrival of Turkish, European, and Mongol invaders after the year 1000. By approximately 750 Islam was firmly in control of most of Southwest Asia, except for the Anatolian Peninsula, which remained the heart of the East Roman, or *Byzantine,* Empire until late in the eleventh century, when Islamic Turkish forces began the process of transforming this land into Turkey. Seljuk and Ottoman Turks, European crusaders, Mongols, and the armies of Timur the Lame (Tamerlane; see Chapter 12, source 106) would invade and contest Southwest Asia for much of the period from 1000 to 1500.

Around the early sixteenth century a clear pattern emerged. Most of Europe's Christian crusaders had been expelled from the eastern Mediterranean, except for their precarious possession of a handful of island strongholds, such as Cyprus and Crete; the Mongol empire was only a fading memory; and Timur the Lame's empire had crumbled upon his death in 1405. Two Turkish Islamic empires dominated Southwest Asia — the Shia Safavids of Persia and the Sunni Ottomans, whose base of power was Anatolia, but who also controlled Syria-Palestine, Egypt, and western Arabia and were driving deeply into Europe's Balkan Peninsula. Although these two empires would quarrel viciously for control of Islam, and Sunnis and Shias would continue to shed one another's blood, Turkish domination of Southwest Asia was secure for the foreseeable future. European attempts to counter the Turkish menace by launching new crusades in the eastern Mediterranean generally proved feeble, and the Ottomans' and Safavids' pastoral cousins on the steppes of Inner Asia were becoming less of a threat to the stability of Eurasia's civilizations.

The Arrival of the Turks
▼▼▼

75 ▼ Al-Jahiz,
THE MERITS OF THE TURKS AND
OF THE IMPERIAL ARMY AS A WHOLE

Early in the ninth century the caliphs of Baghdad addressed the problem of creating a loyal army by enlisting foreign slaves and mercenaries, many of whom came from various tribes of Turkic-speaking, pastoral peoples across the frontier in the steppes of Inner Asia. As aliens, the Turks had no ties to the various factions that threatened the caliph's power. To the contrary, they were initially dependent upon the caliph, their lord and paymaster. In a short time, however, these Turkish warriors converted to Islam and became powers behind the throne. As early as the mid ninth century some Turkish officers were playing important roles in the selection of caliphs. From that point on the caliphs and their ministers became increasingly dependent on various Turkish elements in the army, and it was almost an anticlimax when Tughril-Beg, leader of a tribe of Turks known as the *Seljuks,* entered Baghdad on December 19, 1055, to be recognized formally as *sultan* (governor) and to have his name mentioned in Friday prayers after that of the caliph. Civil and military authority now lay in the hands of Turkish sultans, and the caliph retained only religious and ceremonial functions. Under the Seljuks, Islam quickly expanded into Byzantine Anatolia, thereby precipitating a Western Christian response — the crusades.

   Two centuries earlier, a resident of the port city of Basra in southern Iraq, Abu Uthman Amr ibn Bahr (776–869) — better known by his nickname *al-Jahiz* (the Goggle-Eyed) — composed a study of the Turks, in which he attempted to place these recent converts to Islam in a favorable light. Many cultivated Arabs and Persians despised the Turks, whom they considered to be barbarians, and resented their growing power. Al-Jahiz, one of the most popular and gifted essayists of his day and always a voice of reason and moderation, attempted to counter those attitudes. A person of largely African lineage, al-Jahiz was possibly influenced to take this public stand by the prejudice he had apparently suffered because of his dark skin.

QUESTIONS FOR ANALYSIS

1. What does al-Jahiz's essay tell us about the equestrian and military qualities of the Turks and, by extension, of other pastoral peoples from Central Asia? Does this portrait help explain the role played in Eurasian history by the horse nomads?
2. How, according to the essayist, do the Turks resemble the Arabs of the Prophet's day?
3. Given these qualities, what special value do the Turks offer Islamic society?

4. Does al-Jahiz seem to believe that the Turks are capable of being civilized and becoming more than just warriors? If so, what? On what do you base your answer?

5. How, if at all, does this essay reveal the cosmopolitan perspective of ninth-century Iraq?

THE TURK AS A HORSEMAN

A Kharijite[1] at close quarters relies entirely on his lance. But the Turks are as good as the Kharijites with the lance, and in addition, if a thousand of their horsemen are hard-pressed they will loose all their arrows in a single volley and bring down a thousand enemy horsemen. No body of men can stand up against such a test.

Neither the Kharijites nor the Bedouins[2] are famous for their prowess as mounted bowmen. But the Turk will hit from his saddle an animal, a bird, a target, a man, a couching animal, a marker post or a bird of prey stooping on its quarry. His horse may be exhausted from being galloped and reined in, wheeled to right and left, and mounted and dismounted: but he himself goes on shooting, loosing ten arrows before the Kharijite has let fly one. He gallops his horse up a hillside or down a gully faster than the Kharijite can make his go on the flat.

The Turk has two pairs of eyes, one at the front and the other at the back of his head. . . .

They train their horsemen to carry two or even three bows, and spare bowstrings in proportion. Thus in the hour of battle the Turk has on him everything needful for himself, his weapon and the care of his steed. As for their ability to stand trotting, sustained galloping, long night rides and cross-country journeys, it is truly extraordinary. In the first place the Kharijite's horse has not the staying-power of the Turk's pony; and the Kharijite has no more than a horseman's knowl-

edge of how to look after his mount. The Turk, however, is more experienced than a professional farrier,[3] and better than a trainer at getting what he wants from his pony. For it was he who brought it into the world and reared it from a foal; it comes when he calls it, and follows behind him when he runs. . . .

If the Turk's daily life were to be reckoned up in detail, he would be found to spend more time in the saddle than on the ground.

The Turk sometimes rides a stallion, sometimes a brood mare. Whether he is going to war, on a journey, out hunting or on any other errand, the brood mare follows behind with her foals. If he gets tired of hunting the enemy he hunts waterfowl. If he gets hungry, jogging up and down in the saddle, he has only to lay hands on one of his animals. If he gets thirsty, he milks one of his brood mares. If he needs to rest his mount, he vaults on to another without so much as putting his feet to the ground.

Of all living creatures he is the only one whose body can adapt itself to eating nothing but meat. As for his steed, leaves and shoots are all it needs; he gives it no shelter from the sun and no covering against the cold.

As regards ability to stand trotting, if the stamina of the border fighters, the posthorse outriders,[4] the Kharijites and the eunuchs[5] were all combined in one man, they would not equal a Turk.

The Turk demands so much of his mount that only the toughest of his horses is equal to the

---

[1]One of the earliest sects to break off from the main body of Islam, the Kharijites were noted as fierce warriors.

[2]Arab nomads of Arabia, North Africa, and the eastern Mediterranean.

[3]A blacksmith.

[4]Mounted attendants who rode alongside a carriage and, as needed, exchanged horses at post stations along the route.

[5]Castrated slaves who performed domestic services. According to ninth-century Arabic folklore, eunuchs endured long horse rides especially well — possibly as a consequence of their mutilation.

task; even one that he had ridden to exhaustion, so as to be useless for his expeditions, would outdo a Kharijite's horse in staying power, and no Tukhari pony could compare with it.

The Turk is at one and the same time herdsman, groom, trainer, horse-dealer, farrier and rider: in short, a one-man team.

When the Turk travels with horsemen of other races, he covers twenty miles to their ten, leaving them and circling around to right and left, up on to the high ground and down to the bottom of the gullies, and shooting all the while at anything that runs, crawls, flies or stands still. The Turk never travels like the rest of the band, and never rides straight ahead. On a long, hard ride, when it is noon and the halting-place is still afar off, all are silent, oppressed with fatigue and overwhelmed into weariness. Their misery leaves no room for conversation. Everything round them crackles in the intense heat, or perhaps is frozen hard. As the journey drags on, even the toughest and most resolute begin to wish that the ground would open under their feet. At the sight of a mirage or a marker post on a ridge they are transported with joy, supposing it to be the halting-place. When at last they reach it, the horsemen all drop from the saddle and stagger about bandy-legged like children who have been given an enema, groaning like sick men, yawning to refresh themselves and stretching luxuriously to overcome their stiffness. But your Turk, though he has covered twice the distance and dislocated his shoulders with shooting, has only to catch sight of a gazelle or an onager[6] near the halting-place, or put up a fox or a hare, and he is off again at a gallop as though he had only just mounted. It might have been someone else who had done that long ride and endured all that weariness.

At the gully the band bunches together at the bridge or the best crossing-place; but the Turk, digging his heels into his pony, is already going up the other side like a shooting star. If there is a steep rise, he leaves the track and scrambles straight up the hillside, going where even the ibex[7] cannot go. To see him scaling such slopes anyone would think he was recklessly risking his life: but if that were so he would not last long, for he is always doing it. . . .

NATIONAL CHARACTERISTICS

Know that every nation, people, generation or tribe that shows itself outstanding in craftsmanship or pre-eminent in eloquence, the various branches of learning, the establishment of empires or the art of war, only attains the peak of perfection because God has steered it in that direction and given it the means and the special aptitudes appropriate to those activities. Peoples of varying habits of thought, different opinions and dissimilar characters cannot attain perfection unless they fulfill the conditions needed to carry on an activity, and have a natural aptitude for it. Good examples are the Chinese in craftsmanship, the Greeks in philosophy and literature, the Arabs in fields that we mean to deal with in their proper place . . . and the Turks in the art of war. . . .

The Chinese for their part are specialists in smelting, casting and metalworking, in fine colors, in sculpture, weaving and drawing; they are very skillful with their hands, whatever the medium, the technique or the cost of the materials. The Greeks are theoreticians rather than practitioners, while the Chinese are practitioners rather than theoreticians; the former are thinkers, the latter doers.

The Arabs, again, were not merchants, artisans, physicians, farmers — for that would have degraded them —, mathematicians or fruit-farmers — for they wished to escape the humiliation of the tax; nor were they out to earn or amass money, hoard possessions or lay hands on other people's; they were not of those who make their living with a pair of scales; . . . they were not poor enough to be indifferent to learning, pursued neither wealth, that breeds foolishness,

---

[6]A speedy wild ass of Central Asia.

[7]An Asiatic mountain goat.

nor good fortune, that begets apathy, and never tolerated humiliation, which was dishonor and death to their souls. They dwelt in the plains, and grew up in contemplation of the desert. They knew neither damp nor rising mist, neither fog nor foul air, nor a horizon bounded by walls. When these keen minds and clear brains turned to poetry, fine language, eloquence and oratory, to physiognomy and astrology, genealogy, navigation by the stars and by marks on the ground, . . . to horse-breeding, weaponry and engines of war, to memorizing all that they heard, pondering on everything that caught their attention and discriminating between the glories and the shames of their tribes, they achieved perfection beyond the wildest dreams. Certain of these activities broadened their minds and exalted their aspirations, so that of all nations they are now the most glorious and the most given to recalling their past splendors.

It is the same with the Turks who dwell in tents in the desert and keep herds: they are the Bedouins of the non-Arabs. . . . Uninterested in craftsmanship or commerce, medicine, geometry, fruit-farming, building, digging canals or collecting taxes, they care only about raiding, hunting, horsemanship, skirmishing with rival chieftains, taking booty and invading other countries. Their efforts are all directed towards these activities, and they devote all their energies to these occupations. In this way they have acquired a mastery of these skills, which for them take the place of craftsmanship and commerce and constitute their only pleasure, their glory and the subject of all their conversation. Thus have they become in the realm of warfare what the Greeks are in philosophy, the Chinese in craftsmanship, and the Arabs in the fields we have enumerated.

Muslims and Franks in the Crusader States
▼▼▼

76 ▼ Ibn Jubayr, TRAVELS

In 1095 Pope Urban II (r. 1088–1099) set in motion a movement that became known as the *crusades* — close to 500 years of Western Christian involvement in the lands of the *Levant,* or eastern Mediterranean. Between March 1098 and July 1109 the armies of the *First Crusade* (1096–1101) and adventurers building upon the gains of their predecessors carved out four *crusader states* in lands that had recently been under Muslim domination: the *county of Edessa* (1098–1150); the *principality of Antioch* (1098–1268); the *kingdom of Jerusalem* (1099–1291); and the *county of Tripoli* (1109–1289). In some respects they were Europe's first overseas colonies, but each was a state answerable to no mother country in Europe.

Western European settlers, known as *Franj,* or *Franks,* to the natives of the region, were a decided minority in the land they called *Outremer* (the land across the sea). Edessa had a large Armenian Christian majority, and Antioch's population was dominated by Greek (Byzantine) and Syrian Christians. Both states also had significant Muslim minorities who probably outnumbered the resident Franks several times over. Probably 80 percent or more of the populations of Tripoli and Jerusalem was divided about equally between Muslims and Eastern Christians of various sorts, with Western, or *Latin,* Christian settlers constituting the remainder — no more than 20 percent and probably far less. The only places where Franks probably outnumbered indigenous Eastern Christians and Muslims were key coastal towns, such as *Acre,* and the holy city of Jerusalem. These realities meant that the Frankish lords of the crusader states had to find ways of governing the indigenous populations of their states that took into account this overall numerical imbalance.

In 1184 Abu al-Husayn Muhammad ibn Ahmad ibn Jubayr, a native of Valencia in Muslim Spain, on his way home after having completed the *hajj* to Mecca, spent thirty-two days in crusader territory. Throughout his two-year journey from Spain to the East and back, Ibn Jubayr kept an almost-daily journal of his travels, which provides us with vivid pictures of late-twelfth-century life and culture in Egypt, Iraq, Arabia, Syria-Palestine, and other stopping places along the way.

QUESTIONS FOR ANALYSIS

1. Does Ibn Jubayr like the Franks? Support your answer.
2. What does he think is the worst aspect of Frankish rule?
3. What arguments can you adduce to support the proposition that Ibn Jubayr's testimony is solid and trustworthy?
4. What counterarguments can you adduce that cast doubt on his testimony?
5. Where do you stand on the issue? Be specific in explaining your position.
6. Based on all your study of this source, what do you conclude you can say with some degree of certainty about Frankish-Muslim relations in the Latin kingdom of Jerusalem around 1184?

We left Damascus[1] on the evening of Thursday . . . , which was the 13th of September, in a large caravan of merchants travelling with their merchandise to Acre. One of the strangest things in the world is that Muslim caravans go forth to Frankish lands, while Frankish captives enter Muslim lands.[2] . . . We ourselves went forth to Frankish lands at a time when Frankish prisoners were entering Muslim lands. Let this be evidence enough to you of the temperateness of the policy of Saladin.[3] . . . We left, on the morning of Saturday, for the city of Banyas. Halfway on the road, we came upon an oak-tree of great proportions and with widespreading branches. We learnt that it is called 'The Tree of Measure,' and when we enquired concerning it, we were told that it was the boundary on this road between security and danger, by reason of some Frankish brigands

who prowl and rob thereon. He whom they seize on the Muslim side, be it by the length of the arms or a span, they capture; but he whom they seize on the Frankish side at a like distance, they release. This is a pact they faithfully observe and is one of the most pleasing and singular conventions of the Franks.

A Note on the City of Banyas {Belinas}

God Most High defend it

This city is on the frontier of the Muslim territories. It is small, but has a fortress below the walls of which winds a river that flows out from one of the gates of the city. A canal leading from it turns the mills. The city had been in the hands of the Franks, but Nur al-Din[4] — may God's mercy rest upon his soul — recovered it [in 1165]. It has a wide tillage in a contiguous vale. It is com-

---

[1]Damascus was the center of Islamic power in southern Syria.

[2]The several thousand Franks who had been captured and enslaved during the successful campaign of 1184 against the crusader city of Nablus and its environs conducted by Saladin, sultan of Egypt and Syria.

[3]Ibn Jubayr seems to be arguing here that Saladin's reputa-

tion for fair-dealing and temperate behavior, even with the Franks, made this commerce possible.

[4]Nur al-Din, Turkish ruler of Syria (r. 1146–1174), initiated the first real *jihad* against the crusader states. Saladin continued his religious war, but both Nur al-Din and Saladin were willing to enter into periodic but time-limited truces with the Franks when it suited their needs.

manded by a fortress of the Franks called Hunin[5] three parasangs[6] distant from Banyas. The cultivation of the vale is divided between the Franks and the Muslims, and in it there is a boundary known as 'The Boundary of Dividing.' They apportion the crops equally, and their animals are mingled together, yet no wrong takes place between them because of it.

We departed from Banyas on the evening of the same Saturday for a village called al-Masiyah, near to the Frankish fort we have mentioned. We passed the night in it, and removed on Sunday at daybreak. Between Hunin and Tibnin[7] we passed a valley thick with trees. . . . Marvelling at the place, we passed it, travelling close beside, and came to one of the biggest fortresses of the Franks, called Tibnin. At this place customs dues are levied on the caravans. It belongs to the sow known as Queen[8] who is the mother of the pig who is the Lord of Acre[9] may God destroy it.[10]

We camped at the foot of this fortress. The fullest tax was not exacted from us. . . . No toll was laid upon the merchants, since they were bound for the place of the accursed king [Acre], where the tax is gathered.[11] The tax there is a qirat in every dinar[12] (worth of merchandise), the dinar having twenty-four qirat.[13] The greater part of those taxed were Maghribis,[14] those from all other Muslim lands being unmolested. This was because some earlier Maghribis had annoyed the Franks. A gallant company of them had attacked one of their strongholds with Nur al-Din

— may God have mercy upon him — and by its taking they had become manifestly rich and famous. The Franks punished them by this tax, and their chiefs enforced it. Every Maghribi therefore paid this dinar for his hostility to their country. The Franks declared: 'These Maghribis came and went in our country and we treated them well and took nothing from them. But when they interfered in the war, joining with their brother Muslims against us, we were compelled to place this tax upon them.' In the payment of this tax, the Maghribis are pleasingly reminded of their vexing of the enemy, and thus the payment of it is lightened and its harshness made tolerable.

We moved from Tibnin — may God destroy it[15] — at daybreak on Monday. Our way lay through continuous farms and ordered settlements, whose inhabitants were all Muslims,[16] living comfortably with the Franks. God protect us from such temptation. They surrender their crops to the Franks at harvest time, and pay as well a poll-tax[17] of one and five qirat for each person. Other than that, they are not interfered with, save for a light tax on the fruits of trees. Their houses and all their effects are left to their full possession. All the coastal cities occupied by the Franks are managed in this fashion, their rural districts, the villages and farms, belonging to the Muslims. But their hearts have been seduced, for they observe how unlike them in ease and comfort are their brethren in the Muslim re-

---

[5]Better known to the Franks as *Chastel Neuf,* the fortress commanded the headwaters of the Jordan River and the fertile plain around Banyas, which is located in the Upper Galilee (today northern Israel).

[6]An ancient Persian unit of measurement — about 3.5 miles.

[7]Better known as *Toron,* this was one of the strongest crusader castles in the Galilee.

[8]Queen Agnes of Courtenay, widow of King Amalric. In a state noted for its powerful and strong-willed women, Agnes was one of the Latin kingdom of Jerusalem's most powerful and controversial queens.

[9]King Baldwin IV (r. 1174–1185).

[10]Acre, a city on the Bay of Haifa in northern Israel, was the kingdom of Jerusalem's premier port. Initially captured by crusaders in 1104, it was recaptured by Saladin in 1187. The armies of the Third Crusade retook the city in 1191, and it remained in Frankish hands until 1291 when the

Mamluk sultan of Egypt captured and razed the city's defenses. With its fall, crusader presence along the Mediterranean coast of Southwest Asia was essentially ended.

[11]The laws of the kingdom of Jerusalem specified 111 items on which tax was due at Acre.

[12]A gold coin weighing 4.72 grams.

[13]A *qirat* was a twenty-fourth of anything. In this case, of a dinar.

[14]Muslims from the western Mediterranean, either western North Africa or *al-Andalus* (Muslim Spain).

[15]Toron held out until 1291.

[16]Frankish, Eastern Christian, and Muslim farmers normally inhabited villages separate from one another.

[17]A head tax. This was a Frankish variation on the *jizya,* or head tax, that Islamic law prescribed for *dhimmis,* or tolerated People of the Book (source 62). Under Frankish law, Muslims were now the dhimmis.

gions under their (Muslim) governors. This is one of the misfortunes afflicting the Muslims. The Muslim community bewails the injustice of a landlord of its own faith, and applauds the conduct of its opponent and enemy, the Frankish landlord, and is accustomed to justice from him. He who laments this state must turn to God. There is comfort and consolation enough for us in the exalted Book: 'It is nothing but a trial; Thou makest to err with it whom Thou pleasest, and guidest whom Thou pleasest.[18]

On the same Monday, we alighted at a farmstead a parasang distant from Acre. Its headman is a Muslim, appointed by the Franks to oversee the Muslim workers in it. He gave generous hospitality to all members of the caravan, assembling them, great and small, in a large room in his house, and giving them a variety of foods and treating all with liberality. We were amongst those who attended this party, and passed the night there. On the morning of Tuesday . . . , which was the 18th of September, we came to the city of Acre — may God destroy it. We were taken to the custom-house, which is a khan[19] prepared to accommodate the caravan. Before the door are stone benches, spread with carpets, where are the Christian[20] clerks of the Customs with their ebony ink-stands ornamented with gold. They write Arabic, which they also speak. Their chief is the Sahib al-Diwan [Chief of the Customs], who holds the contract to farm the customs.[21] He is known as al-Sahib [the Director or Master], a title bestowed on him by reason of his office, and which they apply to all respected persons, save the soldiery, who hold office with them. All the dues collected go to the contractor for the customs, who pays a vast sum (to the

Government). The merchants deposited their baggage there and lodged in the upper storey. The baggage of any who had no merchandise was also examined in case it contained concealed (and dutiable) merchandise, after which the owner was permitted to go his way and seek lodging where he would. All this was done with civility and respect, and without harshness and unfairness. We lodged beside the sea in a house which we rented from a Christian woman, and prayed God Most High to save us from all dangers and help us to security.

A Note on the City of Acre

May God exterminate (the Christians in) it and restore it (to the Muslims)

Acre is the capital of the Frankish cities in Syria,[22] the unloading place of 'ships reared aloft in the seas like mountains,'[23] and a port of call for all ships. In its greatness it resembles Constantinople. It is the focus of ships and caravans, and the meeting-place of Muslim and Christian merchants from all regions. Its roads and streets are choked by the press of men, so that it is hard to put foot to ground. Unbelief and unpiousness there burn fiercely, and pigs[24] and crosses abound. It stinks and is filthy, being full of refuse and excrement. The Franks ravished it from Muslim hands in the first decade of the sixth century,[25] and the eyes of Islam were swollen with weeping for it; it was one of its griefs. Mosques became churches and minarets bell-towers, but God kept undefiled one part of the principal mosque, which remained in the hands of the Muslims as a small mosque where strangers could congregate to offer the obligatory prayers. Near its mihrab[26] is the tomb of the prophet

---

[18]The Quran, 7:155.

[19]Another term for *caravanserai* — a place set aside for caravan traffic.

[20]Syrian Christians whose native language was Arabic.

[21]As Ibn Jubayr makes clear below, a person who farms taxes pays the state a set fee for the contract. Whatever is collected in excess of the payment is profit.

[22]It only became the capital of the kingdom of Jerusalem upon its recapture by Christian forces in 1191 (note 10) because Jerusalem, the former capital, had been captured by

Saladin in 1187. This anachronism might suggest later editing. More likely, it is due to Ibn Jubayr's misunderstanding, but see note 31.

[23]The Quran, 55:24.

[24]The pig is the most unclean of animals in Islamic tradition. Here he uses the term to mean Christians.

[25]Actually, the last decade of the fifth century of the Islamic calendar (March 24, 1104).

[26]The decorated niche in the mosque that indicates the direction of Mecca.

Salih[27] — God bless and preserve him and all the prophets. God protected this part (of the mosque) from desecration by the unbelievers for the benign influence of this holy tomb.

To the east of the town is the spring called Ayn al-Baqar [the Spring of the Cattle], from which God brought forth the cattle for Adam[28] — may God bless and preserve him. The descent to this spring is by a deep stairway. Over it is a mosque of which there remains in its former state only the mihrab, to the east of which the Franks have built their own mihrab[29]; and Muslim and infidel assemble there, the one turning to his place of worship, the other to his. In the hands of the Christians its venerableness is maintained, and God has preserved in it a place of prayer for the Muslims.

Two days we tarried at this place, and then, on Thursday . . . the 20th of September, we set forth across country to Sur [Tyre].[30] . . . And so we alighted at this town on the evening of that same Thursday, for the distance between the two cities (of Acre and Tyre) is thirty miles. We lodged in a khan in the town prepared for the reception of pilgrims.

A Note on the City of Sur {Tyre}

May God Most High destroy it

This city has become proverbial for its impregnability, and he who seeks to conquer it will meet with no surrender or humility.[31] The Franks prepared it as a refuge in case of unforeseen emergency, making it a strong point for their safety. Its roads and streets are cleaner than those of Acre. Its people are by disposition less stubborn in their unbelief, and by nature and habit they are kinder to the Muslim stranger. Their manners, in other words, are gentler. Their dwellings are larger and more spacious. The state of the Muslims in this city is easier and more peaceful.

Acre is a town at once bigger, more impious, and more unbelieving. But the strength and impregnability of Tyre is more marvellous. . . . The beauty of the site of this port is truly wonderful. Acre resembles it in situation and description, but cannot take the large ships, which must anchor outside, small ships only being able to enter. The port of Tyre is more complete, more beautiful, and more animated. Eleven days we tarried in the city, entering it on Thursday, and leaving it on Sunday . . . , which was the last day of September; this was because the ship in which we had hoped to sail we found to be too small, so that we were unwilling to set forth in it.

An alluring worldly spectacle deserving of record was a nuptial procession which we witnessed one day near the port in Tyre. All the Christians, men and women, had assembled, and were formed in two lines at the bride's door. Trumpets, flutes, and all the musical instruments, were played until she proudly emerged between two men who held her right and left as though they were her kindred. She was most elegantly garbed in a beautiful dress from which trailed, according to their traditional style, a long train of golden silk. On her head she wore a golden diadem covered by a net of woven gold, and on her breast was a like arrangement. Proud she was in her ornaments and dress, walking with little steps of half a span, like a dove, or in the manner of a wisp of cloud. God protect us from the seduction of the sight. Before her went Christian notables in their finest and most splendid clothing, their trains falling behind them. Behind her were her peers and equals of the Christian women, parading in their richest apparel and proud of bearing in their superb ornaments. Leading them all were the musical instruments. The Muslims and other Christian onlookers formed two ranks along the route, and gazed on

---

[27]A prophet and messenger (*rasul*) of God who is only mentioned in the Quran (7:73 and following). Like the biblical Jonah, he was sent to warn an errant people.
[28]The Quran, 20:115.
[29]Possibly an altar niche facing Jerusalem.
[30]Tyre (in modern Lebanon) was held continuously by the

Franks from 1124 to 1291. It was the most northerly and deepest of the kingdom of Jerusalem's ports.
[31]Either this is prophetic or it was composed after Saladin failed to take the city — one of his few failures — during his campaign of 1187–1188 when he almost (momentarily) swept the Franks out of Syria-Palestine. See note 22.

them without reproof. So they passed along until they brought her to the house of the groom; and all that day they feasted. We thus were given the chance of seeing this alluring sight, from the seducement of which God preserve us.

We then returned by sea to Acre and landed there on the morning of Monday . . . , being the first day in October. We hired passages on a large ship, about to sail to Messina on the island of Sicily. My God Most High, in His power and strength, assure the easing and lightening (of our way).

During our stay in Tyre we rested in one of the mosques that remained in Muslim hands. One of the Muslim elders of Tyre told us that it[32] had been wrested from them in the year 518[33] . . . after a long siege and after hunger had overcome them. We were told that it had brought them to such a pass — we take refuge in God from it — that shame had driven them to propose a course from which God had preserved them. They had determined to gather their wives and children into the Great Mosque and there put them to the sword, rather than that the Christians should possess them. They themselves would then sally forth determinedly, and in a violent assault on the enemy, die together. But God made His irreversible decree, and their jurisprudents[34] and some of their godly men prevented them. They thereupon decided to abandon the town, and to make good their escape. So it happened, and they dispersed among the Muslim lands. But there were some whose love of native land impelled them to return and, under the conditions of a safeguard which was written for them, to live amongst the infidels. . . .

There can be no excuse in the eyes of God, for a Muslim to stay in any infidel country, save when passing through it, while the way lies clear in Muslim lands. They will face pains and terrors such as the abasement and destitution of the capitation and more especially, amongst their base and lower orders, the hearing of what will distress the heart in the reviling of him [Muhammad] whose memory God has sanctified, and whose rank He has exalted; there is also the absence of cleanliness, the mixing with the pigs, and all the other prohibited matters too numerous to be related or enumerated. Beware, beware of entering their lands. May God Most High grant His beneficent indulgence for this sin into which (our) feet have slipped, but His forgiveness is not given save after accepting our penitence. Glory to God, the Master. There is no Lord but He. . . .

By an unhappy chance, from the evils of which we take refuge in God, we were accompanied on our road to Acre from Damascus by a Maghribi. . . . In one of his patron's caravans he had come to Acre, where he had mixed with the Christians, and taken on much of their character. The devil increasingly seduced and incited him until he renounced the faith of Islam, turned unbeliever, and became a Christian in the time of our stay in Tyre. We left to Acre, but received news of him. He had been baptised and become unclean, and had put on the girdle of a monk, thereby hastening for himself the flames of hell, verifying the threats of torture, and exposing himself to a grievous account and a long-distance return (from hell). We beg Great and Glorious God to confirm us in the true word in this world and the next, allowing us not to deviate from the pure faith and letting us, in His grace and mercy, die Muslims. . . .

The cities of Acre and Tyre have no gardens around them, and stand in a wide plain that reaches to the shores of the sea. Fruits are brought to them from the orchards that are in the neighbourhood. They possess broad lands and the nearby mountains are furnished with farmsteads from which fruits are brought to them. They are very rich cities. At the eastern extremity of Acre is a torrent course, along the banks of which extending to the sea is a sandy plain, than which I have seen no more beautiful sight. As a course for

---

[32]The city.
[33]June 27, 1124.

[34]*Qadis,* or Islamic jurists.

horses there is none to compare with it. Every morning and evening the Lord of the town rides over it, and there the soldiers parade — destroy them, God. Beside Tyre's landward gate is a fresh spring down to which a stairway leads. The wells and cisterns of the town are many, and there is no house without one. May God Most High, in His grace and favour, restore to it and to its sister (cities) the word of Islam.

On Saturday . . . , being the 6th of October, with the favor of God towards the Muslims, we embarked on a large ship, taking water and pro-

visions. The Muslims secured places apart from the Franks. Some Christians called 'bilghriyin'[35] came aboard. They had been on the pilgrimage to Jerusalem, and were too numerous to count, but were more than two thousand. May God in His grace and favor soon relieve us of their company and bring us to safety with His hoped-for assistance and beneficent works; none but He should be worshipped. So, under the will of Great and Glorious God, we awaited a favoring wind and the completion of the ship's stowing.

---

[35]From the Italian *pellegrini* — pilgrims.

Sinbad's First Voyage
▼▼▼
77 ▼ *A THOUSAND AND ONE ARABIAN NIGHTS*

Reading sources 75 and 76 in isolation might give us the impression that invasion and war were the primary realities of this thousand-year period of Southwest Asian history. That would be an incorrect conclusion. It is true that many different empire builders and invaders marched across this crossroad of the Afro-Eurasian World, and in the process they destroyed and altered much. Equally true, however, was the fact that villages, towns, and cities prospered in large numbers, fed by the productive activities of peasants, artisans, and merchants alike. Farming, craft production, and even large-scale industrial manufacture contributed to a healthy economy, but all these activities paled in comparison with the economic impact of commerce, particularly transit trade. Evidence suggests that Southwest Asian production of commodities for export declined from the eleventh century onward, whereas trade in manufactured goods produced elsewhere, primarily China, India, and Western Europe, rose appreciably. Added to this was a booming trade in the raw materials of Africa and Southeast Asia, including slaves, ivory, and gold from Africa and exotic woods and spices from the eastern islands of the Indian Ocean. Merchants who engaged in long-distance commerce could become rapidly wealthy and rise to positions of eminence within their cities.

This was especially the case with the merchants of Iraq. One ninth-century Arab geographer described Iraq as "the center of the world, the navel of the Earth." Iraq's centrality, and its consequent prosperity, was a function of its lying at the head of the Persian Gulf. The Persian Gulf afforded the merchants of Baghdad and Basra access to the Indian Ocean and the rich markets of the Indian Ocean and the South China Sea. The potential for wealth was great for any Iraqi merchant who was sufficiently enterprising, courageous, skilled, and lucky. Danger, however, lay around every corner, as the following tale from *A Thousand and One Arabian Nights* suggests.

A Thousand and One Arabian Nights is one of the most celebrated collections of stories in the world. Loosely arranged around the theme of a series of nightly stories — told by Shahrazad in order to forestall decapitation by the order of her disturbed husband, Shahriyar, king of India and China — *The Arabian Nights* is a rich pastiche of Persian, Arabic, Greco-Roman, Indian, and Egyptian fables and legends. Its core is a now-lost ancient Persian collection known as *A Thousand Tales,* which tenth-century Arab commentators tell us was similarly structured around Queen Shahrazad's ingenious filibuster. This Persian work served as the matrix around which numerous anonymous Arab storytellers wove additional tales, especially out of the rich folk traditions of Iraq and Egypt, to create, by the fourteenth century, *The Arabian Nights* as we more or less know it today.

A major Arab addition to this constantly changing treasury of tales was the Sinbad cycle — seven stories that related the merchant voyages of one of literature's most celebrated adventurers. In the course of his seven voyages into the Indian Ocean, Sinbad narrowly escaped death at the hands of pirates and cannibals, monster birds and huge serpents, storms and whirlpools, and the murderous one-eyed Cyclops and the Old Man of the Sea. In his travels he discovered such fabled places as the valley of diamonds, the land where living people were buried alive with their deceased spouses, and the ivory-rich elephant burying ground. Not only did he survive to tell his tales, but each voyage left him wealthier than before.

Doubtless the professional storytellers who recounted the adventures of this fictional merchant-sailor deliberately employed hyperbolic flights of fancy because their purpose was to present thrilling entertainment. Yet the more fantastic elements within the stories also hint at some of the ways in which the world of the Indian Ocean was viewed from the perspective of Iraq.

QUESTIONS FOR ANALYSIS

1. How did an Arab merchant of modest means undertake the expense of outfitting a ship and filling it with cargo?
2. What do the goods that Sinbad brought back with him suggest about the nature of commerce in the Indian Ocean?
3. Consider the wonders that Sinbad reported. What do they suggest about the level of Arab knowledge of the more distant regions of the Indian Ocean? What do they suggest about Arab attitudes toward the eastern Indian Ocean?
4. It has been said that this tale illustrates the ambivalence of the Iraqi World toward the vast region of the Indian Ocean? Do you agree? Why or why not?
5. What might we infer from this story about the role and status of merchants in Arabic society?

I dissipated the greatest part of my paternal inheritance in the excesses of my youth; but at length, seeing my folly, I became convinced that riches were not of much use when applied to such purposes as I had employed them in; and I moreover reflected that the time I spent in dissipation was of still greater value than gold, and that nothing could be more truly deplorable than poverty in old age. I recollected the words of the wise Solomon, which my father had often repeated to me, that it is better to be in the grave than poor. Feeling the truth of all these reflections, I resolved to collect the small remains of my patrimony and to sell my goods by auction. I then formed connections with some merchants who had negotiations by sea, and consulted those who appeared best able to give me advice. In short, I determined to employ to some profit the small sum I had remaining, and no sooner was this resolution formed than I put it into execution. I went to Basra,[1] where I embarked with several merchants in a vessel which had been equipped at our united expense.

We set sail and steered toward the East Indies by the Persian Gulf, which is formed by the coast of Arabia on the right, and by that of Persia on the left, and is commonly supposed to be seventy leagues[2] in breadth in the widest part; beyond this gulf the Western Sea, or Indian Ocean, is very spacious, and is bounded by the coast of Abyssinia,[3] extending in length four thousand five hundred leagues to the island of Vakvak.[4] I was at first rather incommoded with what is termed sea-sickness, but I soon recovered my health; and from that period I have never been subject to that malady. In the course of our voyage we touched at several islands, and sold or exchanged our merchandise. One day, when in full sail, we were unexpectedly becalmed before a small island appearing just above the water, and which, from its green color, resembled a beautiful meadow. The captain ordered the sails to be lowered, and gave permission to those who wished it to go ashore, of which number I formed one. But during the time that we were regaling ourselves with eating and drinking, by way of relaxation from the fatigues we had endured at sea, the island suddenly trembled, and we felt a severe shock.

They who were in the ship perceived the earthquake in the island, and immediately called to us to re-embark as soon as possible, or we should all perish, for what we supposed to be an island was no more than the back of a whale. The most active of the party jumped into the boat, whilst others threw themselves into the water to swim to the ship: as for me, I was still on the island, or, more properly speaking, on the whale, when it plunged into the sea, and I had only time to seize hold of a piece of wood which had been brought to make a fire with. Meantime the captain, willing to avail himself of a fair breeze which had sprung up, set sail with those who had reached his vessel, and left me to the mercy of the waves. I remained in this situation the whole of that day and the following night; and on the return of morning I had neither strength nor hope left, when a breaker happily dashed me on an island. The shore was high and steep, and I should have found great difficulty in landing, had not some roots of trees, which fortune seemed to have furnished for my preservation, assisted me. I threw myself on the ground, where I continued, more than half dead, till the sun rose.

Although I was extremely enfeebled by the fatigues I had undergone, I tried to creep about in search of some herb or fruit that might satisfy my hunger. I found some, and had also the good luck to meet with a stream of excellent water, which contributed not a little to my recovery. Having in a great measure regained my strength, I began to explore the island, and entered a beautiful plain, where I perceived at some distance a horse that was grazing. I bent my steps that way, trembling

---

[1]Basra, located at the northern tip of the Persian Gulf and connected to Baghdad by the Tigris River, is Iraq's entryway to the Persian Gulf and Indian Ocean.
[2]A league is three miles.

[3]The horn of Africa: the region of the modern nations of Ethiopia and Somalia.
[4]Possibly a reference to Sumatra.

between fear and joy, for I could not ascertain whether I was advancing to safety or perdition. I remarked, as I approached, that it was a mare tied to a stake: her beauty attracted my attention; but whilst I was admiring her, I heard a voice underground of a man, who shortly after appeared, and coming to me, asked me who I was. I related my adventure to him; after which he took me by the hand and led me into a cave, where there were some other persons, who were not less astonished to see me than I was to find them there.

I ate some food which they offered me; and having asked them what they did in a place which appeared so barren, they replied that they were grooms to King Mihrage, who was the sovereign of that isle, and that they came every year about that time with some mares belonging to the king, for the purpose of having a breed between them and a sea-horse which came on shore at that spot. They tied the mares in that manner, because they were obliged almost immediately, by their cries, to drive back the sea horse, otherwise he began to tear them in pieces. As soon as the mares were with foal they carried them back, and these colts were called sea-colts, and set apart for the king's use. To-morrow, they added, was the day fixed for their departure, and if I had been one day later I must certainly have perished, because they lived so far off that it was impossible to reach their habitations without a guide.

Whilst they were talking to me, the horse rose out of the sea as they had described, and immediately attacked the mares. He would then have torn them to pieces, but the grooms began to make such a noise that he let go his prey, and again plunged into the ocean.

The following day they returned to the capital of the island with the mares, whither I accompanied them. On our arrival, King Mihrage, to whom I was presented, asked me who I was, and by what chance I had reached his dominions; and when I had satisfied his curiosity, he expressed pity at my misfortune. At the same time, he gave orders that I should be taken care of and have everything I might want. These orders were executed in a manner that proved the king's generosity, as well as the exactness of his officers.

As I was a merchant, I associated with persons of my own profession. I sought, in particular, such as were foreigners, as much to hear some intelligence of Baghdad, as with the hope of meeting with some one whom I could return with; for the capital of King Mihrage is situated on the sea-coast, and has a beautiful port, where vessels from all parts of the world daily arrive. I also sought the society of the Indian sages, and found great pleasure in their conversation; this, however, did not prevent me from attending at court very regularly, nor from conversing with the governors of provinces, and some less powerful kings, tributaries of Mihrage, who were about his person. They asked me a thousand questions about my country; and I, on my part, was not less inquisitive about the laws and customs of their different states, or whatever appeared to merit my curiosity.

In the dominions of King Mihrage there is an island called Cassel. I had been told that in that island there was heard every night the sound of cymbals, which had given rise to the sailors' opinion, that al-Dajjal[5] had chosen that spot for his residence. I felt a great desire to witness these wonders, and during my voyage I saw some fish of one and two hundred cubits in length,[6] which occasion much fear, but do no harm; they are so timid that they are frightened away by beating on a board. I remarked also some other fish that were not above a cubit long, and whose heads resembled that of an owl.

After I returned, as I was standing one day near the port, I saw a ship come toward the land; when they had cast anchor, they began to unload its goods, and the merchants, to whom they belonged, took them away to their warehouses.

---

[5]The *deceiver*, or *imposter*, al-Dajjal is the false messiah who, according to Islamic belief, will appear shortly before Jesus returns to Earth to usher in the end of time. Jesus will destroy al-Dajjal, and the Day of Judgment will follow.

[6]A cubit varies from seventeen to twenty-two inches.

Happening to cast my eyes on some of the packages, I saw my name written, and, having attentively examined them, I concluded them to be those which I had embarked in the ship in which I left Basra. I also recollected the captain; but as I was persuaded that he thought me dead, I went up to him, and asked him to whom those parcels belonged. "I had on board with me," replied he, "a merchant of Baghdad, named Sinbad. One day, when we were near an island, at least such it appeared to be, he, with some other passengers, went ashore on this supposed island, which was no other than an enormous whale, that had fallen asleep on the surface of the water. The fish no sooner felt the heat of the fire they had lighted on its back, to cook their provisions, than it began to move and flounce about in the sea. The greatest part of the persons who were on it were drowned, and the unfortunate Sinbad was one of the number. These parcels belonged to him, and I have resolved to sell them, that, if I meet with any of his family, I may be able to return them the profit I shall have made of the principal." "Captain," said I then, "I am that Sinbad, whom you supposed dead, but who is still alive, and these parcels are my property and merchandise."

When the captain of the vessel heard me speak thus, he exclaimed, "Great God! whom shall I trust? There is no longer truth in man. I with my own eyes saw Sinbad perish; the passengers I had on board were also witnesses of it; and you have the assurance to say that you are the same Sinbad? what audacity! At first sight you appeared a man of probity and honor, yet you assert an impious falsity to possess yourself of some merchandise which does not belong to you." "Have patience," replied I, "and have the goodness to listen to what I have to say." "Well," said he, "what can you have to say? speak, and I will attend." I then related in what manner I had been saved, and by what accident I had met with King

Mihrage's grooms, who had brought me to his court.

He was rather staggered at my discourse, but was soon convinced that I was not an impostor; for some people arriving from his ship knew me, and began to congratulate me on my fortunate escape. At last he recollected me himself, and embracing me, "Heaven be praised," said he, "that you have thus happily avoided so great a danger; I cannot express the pleasure I feel on the occasion. Here are your goods, take them, for they are yours, and do with them as you like." I thanked him, and praised his honorable conduct, and by way of recompense I begged him to accept part of the merchandise, but that he refused.

I selected the most precious and valuable things in my bales, as presents for King Mihrage. As this prince had been informed of my misfortunes, he asked me where I had obtained such rare curiosities. I related to him the manner in which I had recovered my property, and he had the complaisance to express his joy on the occasion; he accepted my presents, and gave me others of far greater value. After that, I took my leave of him, and re-embarked in the same vessel, having first exchanged what merchandise remained with that of the country, which consisted of aloes and sandal-wood,[7] camphor,[8] nutmegs, cloves, pepper, and ginger. We touched at several islands, and at last landed at Basra, from whence I came here, having realized about a hundred thousand dinars.[9] I returned to my family, and was received by them with the joy which a true and sincere friendship inspires. I purchased slaves of each sex, and bought a magnificent house and grounds. I thus established myself, determined to forget the disagreeable things I had endured, and to enjoy the pleasures of life. . . .

I had resolved after my first voyage, to pass the rest of my days in tranquility at Baghdad. . . . But I soon grew weary of an idle life; the desire of

---

[7]Both are woods noted for their aromatic and medicinal properties.

[8]A medicinal drug and aromatic made from camphor wood.
[9]A gold coin weighing 4.72 grams.

seeing foreign countries, and carrying on some negotiations by sea returned: I bought some merchandise, which I thought likely to answer in the traffic I meditated; and I set off a second time with some merchants, upon whose probity I could rely. We embarked in a good vessel, and having recommended ourselves to the care of the Almighty, we began our voyage. . . .

▷ And so the second voyage begins.

▼▼▼

India: Continuity and Change

Invasions from Central Asia by a nomadic people known as the *Hunas,* or White Huns, precipitated the collapse of the Gupta Empire around the middle of the sixth century. Northern India was again politically fragmented, but Indian culture, having reached maturity in the Gupta Age, continued to develop vigorously. Hinduism took on new vitality, thanks in large part to the bhakti movement out of southern India (sources 41 and 42), and Buddhism was still a significant force, although it was steadily losing ground to a Hindu Renaissance. Although transcendental spirituality has always been a primary concern of Indian culture, India's cultural developments were not confined to religion. There was a significant literary revival both in the sacred language of Sanskrit and in such vernacular tongues as Pali and Tamil, and Indian comic drama emerged as a major art form. Music, dance, sculpture, and painting all flowered. In astronomy and mathematics India was second to none. Indian astronomers borrowed and built upon Greek observations and theories, and Indian mathematicians formulated the principal of *zero* as a positive numerical value. India's Arab neighbors happily adopted the base-ten concept, turned it into a tool of the marketplace, and passed it on. For that reason, Indian decimal mathematics became mistakenly known as the Arabic system of numeration in the European West. If India received scant or no recognition for its cultural brilliance in the Far West, the same was not true of Asia, especially South and East Asia. Just as merchants from elsewhere in Asia and from East Africa flocked to its markets, so scholars and religious persons sought out its schools, monasteries, and temples.

It is no exaggeration to say that the history of classical India is largely the story of cultural continuity and evolution, in which political events and their chronology, although important, are less central to the story. The one significant exception to this rule in the period 500–1500 was the coming of Islam. Its impact was profound and permanent.

Early in the eighth century, Arabs conquered the northwest corner of the Indian subcontinent, a region known as *Sind,* but advanced no farther. While Hindu civilization moved to its own rhythms, neighboring Muslims traded with it and freely borrowed whatever they found useful and non-threatening to their Islamic faith.

Islam did not make a significant impact on Indian life until the appearance of the Turks. These recent converts to the faith, whose origins lay in Central Asia, conducted a series of raids out of Afghanistan between 986 and 1030. After a respite of about 150 years, they turned to conquest. In 1192 the army of *Muhammad of Ghor* crushed a coalition of Indian princes, and the whole Ganges basin lay defenseless before his generals. By 1206 the Turkish *sultanate of Delhi* dominated all of northern India, and by 1327 it had extended its power over virtually the entire peninsula. Although these Turkish sultans lost the south to the Hindu state of *Vijayanagar* (1336–1565), they controlled India's northern and central regions until the arrival of other Islamic conquerors: first, *Timur the Lame*'s (Tamerlane's) plundering horde in 1398; then *Babur,* who established the great *Mughal Dynasty* (1526–1857), which ruled most of India until the mid-eighteenth century.

As the modern Islamic states of Pakistan and Bangladesh bear witness, Islam became an important element in Indian society, but in the end Hinduism prevailed as the way of life for the majority of the Indian subcontinent's people. The coming and going of armies all but destroyed Buddhism in mainland India by 1400. Many factors contributed to the decline of Buddhism in its homeland since the Gupta Era, but Islamic armies delivered the final blow. The heart of Buddhism, its monasteries, were easy targets for marauders, especially Muslim raiders out to destroy every visible vestige of polytheism. At the same time, because Ceylon (Sri Lanka) escaped the ravages of Islamic attack, Buddhism continued to flourish there, as it does even today. Despite similar attacks on Hindu shrines on the mainland, no amount of destruction could root out the hold that the many varieties of Hindu belief and custom had upon Indian life. In the final analysis, Hinduism is rooted not in temples and not in any class of specially trained clerics, but in family traditions and practices.

Nalanda: Center of Spirituality and Learning
▼▼▼

78 ▼ Huili,
A BIOGRAPHY OF THE TRIPITAKA MASTER

India was a magnet for overland and seafaring merchants, scholars in search of its ancient wisdom, and persons seeking spiritual enlightenment, especially Buddhists from China and Central Asia and devotees of Shiva and Vishnu from the coastal regions of Southeast Asia. In September 629, a young Chinese monk named *Xuanzang* (ca. 602–664) left Chang'an, the capital city of Tang China, and began an adventure that lasted sixteen years. Very much like Faxian two centuries earlier (source 37) and Ennin two centuries later (source 74), he desired to obtain Buddhist sutras that would fill in major gaps in the sacred texts then available in his homeland. Also like Faxian, he longed to study and worship at sites in India sacred to the memory of the Buddha. Consequently, this Mahayana monk headed west. When he reached Samarkand he turned south, crossed the Hindu Kush Mountains, and entered India in the early autumn of 630.

He returned home in 645, carrying with him 657 sacred sutras, which he proceeded to translate into Chinese, with the help of other scholars. During the time he was away from China, Xuanzang traveled approximately 10,000 miles along various routes of the Silk Road and encountered a wide variety of peoples and cultures in Central Asia and India. At the command of Emperor Tang Taizong (r. 626–649), Xuanzang rendered a written account of his travels, *The Great Tang Dynasty Record of the Western Regions,* and he also served as the living source for a biographical travelogue that the monk *Huili,* a friend and collaborator, composed in 648–649.

In the following selection, which focuses on Xuanzang's initial visit to the monastery of *Nalanda* in 637, Huili describes the size, wealth, and scope of activities of this great complex in northeastern India, which was a major center of Buddhist worship and study down to 1199, when it was destroyed by Turkish Muslim invaders out of Afghanistan. During his years in India, Xuanzang spent two extended periods at Nalanda. Initially he was a student, applying himself to the study of a wide number of Buddhist texts, some Brahminical sacred books, logic, and Sanskrit. Later he lectured at the monastery and engaged in a public debate with several Theravada monks.

QUESTIONS FOR ANALYSIS

1. Should Huili's description of Nalanda be accepted at face value? Defend your answer.
2. Regardless of your answer to the first question, what do you think we can say with a reasonable degree of certainty about Nalanda and its activities in the seventh century?
3. Some modern commentators have described Nalanda as a "university." Does this ascription seem warranted?
4. What does Huili's description of Nalanda suggest about the vitality of Buddhism in seventh-century northern India?

Nalanda Monastery means the monastery of Insatiability in Almsgiving. It was said by old tradition that to the south of the monastery there had been a pond in a mango grove in which lived a dragon named Nalanda. As the monastery was built beside the pond, it was named so. It was also said that when the Tathagata was practising the Bodhisattva path in one of his former lives,[1] he was a great king and founded his capital at this place. As he had pity on the poor and the lonely, he often gave alms to them; and in memory of his beneficence the people called the place Insatiability in Almsgiving. This place was originally a garden of the Elder Amra. Five hundred merchants purchased it with ten *koti*[2] of golden coins and offered it to the Buddha, who preached the Dharma at this place for three months. Most of the merchants attained sainthood.

---

[1] According to Mahayanist doctrine, the historical Buddha (the *Tathagata,* or the *Buddha Shakyamuni*) was a Bodhisattva in his previous incarnations.

[2] A *koti* was normally a unit of 10 million, but it could also be a unit of one million.

After the Buddha's nirvana, Sakraditya (meaning Indra Sun), a former king of this country, built this monastery in respectful memory of the Buddha. After the demise of the king, his son, King Buddhagupta (meaning Enlightenment Protection), repeated his great deed and built another monastery to the south. His son, King Tathagata (meaning Thus Come), also built a monastery to the east. His son, Baladitya (meaning Morning Sun), built another monastery to the northeast. Afterward, when he saw a holy monk coming from China to receive his offerings, he was so pleased that he abdicated and became a monk himself. His son, Vajra (meaning Diamond), succeeded to the Throne and also built a monastery to the north. Later a king of Central India built another monastery beside it. Thus six kings built as many monasteries one after the other, and an enclosure was made with bricks to merge them all into one monastery with one common entrance.

There were separate courtyards divided into eight departments. Precious terraces ranged like stars in the sky and jade storeyed pavilions spired like lofty peaks. The temples stood high in the mist, and the shrines hovered over the rosy clouds. Breeze and fog rose from the doors and windows, and the sun and moon shone alternately at the eaves of the buildings. Moreover, brooks of clear water meandered through the compounds, with blue lotuses and water lilies growing in them. The flowers of sandalwood trees glowed inside the enclosure, and outside it there was a dense mango grove. All the monks' chambers in the different departments had four storeys. The ridgepoles were carved with little dragons, the beams were painted all the colors of the rainbow, and green beam-supporters contrasted with crimson pillars. The frontal columns and railings had ornamental engravings and

hollowed-out carvings. The plinths were made of jade, and the tips of the rafters were adorned with drawings. The ridges of the roofs stood high in the sunlight, and the eaves were connected with ropes from which hung colored silk pendants. In India there were thousands of monasteries, but this was the most magnificent and sublime of them all.

Ten thousand monks always lived there, both hosts and guests. They studied Mahayana teachings and the doctrines of the eighteen schools,[3] as well as worldly books such as the Vedas.[4] They also learned about works on logic, grammar, medicine, and divination. Those who could understand twenty scriptures and commentaries amounted to over a thousand persons. More than five hundred persons had mastered thirty works, while ten persons, including the Master,[5] were experts on fifty works. The Venerable Silabhadra[6] was the only person who had thoroughly mastered all the texts; and being a scholar of advanced age and unusual virtue, he was a great teacher of all the monks. Lectures were given at more than a hundred places in the monastery every day, and the students studied diligently without wasting a single moment. As all the monks who lived there were men of virtue, the atmosphere in the monastery was naturally solemn and dignified. For more than seven hundred years since its establishment, none of the monks had committed any offense. Out of respect for them, the king gave more than a hundred villages for their sustenance. Each village had two hundred families, who daily provided several hundred *shi*[7] of polished nonglutinous rice, butter, and milk. Thus the students could enjoy sufficient supplies of the four requisites[8] without the trouble of going to beg for them. It was because of this effort of their supporters that the scholars could gain achievements in learning.

---

[3]Eighteen schools of Theravada Buddhism.
[4]Source 10.
[5]Xuanzang.
[6]Known by the title "Treasury of the Righteous Law," he was Nalanda's leading master and became Xuanzang's teacher.

[7]A measure of unknown quantity.
[8]The four minimal requisites of a Buddhist monk: clothing, food, bedding, and medicine.

Islam and Hindu Civilization: Cultures in Conflict
▼▼▼

79 ▼ Abul Raihan al-Biruni, *DESCRIPTION OF INDIA*

At the end of the tenth century, Sultan Mahmud of Ghazana (r. 998–1030), who proudly bore the titles the *Sword of Islam* and the *Image Breaker,* began a series of seventeen raids through the Khyber Pass and into India from his base just south of Kabul in modern Afghanistan. This Turkish lord made no serious attempt at conquering all of India, but he incorporated into his lands part of the subcontinent's northwestern region of Punjab (an area that today is part of the Islamic state of Pakistan). For a century and a half after Mahmud's death, Islam penetrated no farther into India, but the precedent of Islamic jihad against infidel Hindus had been established.

The riches that Mahmud accumulated from his plunder and destruction of Hindu temples (he is reputed to have carried off six and one-half tons of gold from one expedition alone) enabled him to turn his otherwise remote, mountain-ringed capital of Ghazana into a major center of Islamic culture. Scholars and artists from all over Southwest Asia gathered at Mahmud's court. Many came willingly; others were forced to come. In 1017 Mahmud conquered the Central Asian Islamic state of Khwarazm, located west of Ghazana and just south of the Aral Sea. The conqueror brought back many of Khwarazm's intellectuals and artisans to his capital, including the Iranian scholar *Abul Raihan al-Biruni* (973–ca. 1050).

Known to subsequent generations as *al-Ustadh* (the Master), al-Biruni was primarily an astronomer, mathematician, and linguist, but his wide-ranging interests and intellect involved him in many other fields of inquiry. For thirteen years following his capture, al-Biruni served Mahmud, probably as court astrologer, and traveled with him into India's Punjab region. Shortly after his lord's death in 1030, al-Biruni completed his *Description of India,* an encyclopedic account of Indian civilization, especially Hindu science. The following excerpts come from the book's opening pages, in which the author deals with the essential differences that separate Hindus from Muslims.

QUESTIONS FOR ANALYSIS

1. According to al-Biruni, what separates Muslims from Hindus?
2. Where in previous sources have we seen the Hindu notions of purity and *mleccha?* By what other names or terms do you know this phenomenon?
3. What impact did eighth-century Islam have on India?
4. What impact did Mahmud and his father have on India?
5. Al-Biruni presents a critique of Hindu science and compares it with Greek science (and implicitly with Islamic science). In so doing, he faults Hindu scientists for certain basic failings. What are they?

6. What basic Hindu vision of reality might have influenced a scientific tradition that followed a path different from that of the Greeks and the Muslims?
7. What is the general tone of this entire excerpt, and what do you infer from it?

ON THE HINDUS IN GENERAL, AS AN INTRODUCTION TO OUR ACCOUNT OF THEM.

Before entering on our exposition, we must form an adequate idea of that which renders it so particularly difficult to penetrate to the essential nature of any Indian subject. The knowledge of these difficulties will either facilitate the progress of our work, or serve as an apology for any shortcomings of ours. For the reader must always bear in mind that the Hindus entirely differ from us in every respect, many a subject appearing intricate and obscure which would be perfectly clear if there were more connection between us. The barriers which separate Muslims and Hindus rest on different causes.

First, they differ from us in everything which other nations have in common. And here we first mention the language, although the difference of language also exists between other nations. . . .

Secondly, they totally differ from us in religion, as we believe in nothing in which they believe, and *vice versa*. On the whole, there is very little disputing about theological topics among themselves; at the utmost, they fight with words, but they will never stake their soul or body or their property on religious controversy. On the contrary, all their fanaticism is directed against those who do not belong to them — against all foreigners. They call them *mleccha, i.e.* impure, and forbid having any connection with them, be it by intermarriage or any other kind of relationship, or by sitting, eating, and drinking with them, because thereby, they think, they would be polluted. They consider as impure anything which touches the fire and the water of a foreigner; and no household can exist without these two

elements. Besides, they never desire that a thing which once has been polluted should be purified and thus recovered, as, under ordinary circumstances, if anybody or anything has become unclean, he or it would strive to regain the state of purity. They are not allowed to receive anybody who does not belong to them, even if he wished it, or was inclined to their religion. This, too, renders any connection with them quite impossible, and constitutes the widest gulf between us and them.

In the third place, in all manners and usages they differ from us to such a degree as to frighten their children with us, with our dress, and our ways and customs, and as to declare us to be devil's breed, and our doings as the very opposite of all that is good and proper. By the way, we must confess, in order to be just, that a similar depreciation of foreigners not only prevails among us and the Hindus, but is common to all nations towards each other. I recollect a Hindu who wreaked his vengeance on us for the following reason: —

Some Hindu king had perished at the hand of an enemy[1] of his who had marched against him from our country. After his death there was born a child to him, which succeeded him, by the name of Sagara. On coming of age, the young man asked his mother about his father, and then she told him what had happened. Now he was inflamed with hatred, marched out of his country into the country of the enemy, and plentifully satiated his thirst of vengeance upon them. After having become tired of slaughtering, he compelled the survivors to dress in our dress, which was meant as an ignominious punishment for them. When I heard of it, I felt thankful that he was gracious enough not to compel us to Indi-

---

[1] Apparently a Hindu enemy who had used the land beyond the Khyber Pass as a refuge and point from which to attack.

anise ourselves and to adopt Hindu dress and manners. . . .

But then came Islam;[2] the Persian empire perished, and the repugnance of the Hindus against foreigners increased more and more when the Muslims began to make their inroads into their country; for Muhammad Ibn al-Qasim entered Sind[3] . . . and conquered the cities of Bahmanwa and Mulasthana, the former of which he called *Al-mansura,* the latter *Al-mamura.* He entered India proper, and penetrated even as far as Kanauj, marched through the country of Gandhara, and on his way back, through the confines of Kashmir,[4] sometimes fighting sword in hand, sometimes gaining his ends by treaties, leaving to the people their ancient belief, except in the case of those who wanted to become Muslims. All these events planted a deeply rooted hatred in their hearts.

Now in the following times no Muslim conqueror passed beyond the frontier of Kabul and the river Sind until the days of the Turks, when they seized the power in Ghazna under the Samani dynasty, and the supreme power fell to the lot of Sabuktagin. This prince chose the holy war as his calling, and therefore called himself *al-Ghazi.*[5] In the interest of his successors he constructed, in order to weaken the Indian frontier, those roads on which afterwards his son Mahmud marched into India during a period of thirty years and more. God be merciful to both father and son! Mahmud utterly ruined the prosperity of the country, and performed there wonderful exploits, by which the Hindus became like atoms of dust scattered in all directions, and like a tale of old in the mouth of the people. Their scattered remains cherish, of course, the most inveterate aversion towards all Muslims. This is the reason, too, why Hindu sciences have retired far away from those parts of the country conquered by us, and have fled to places which our hand cannot yet

reach, to Kashmir, Benares,[6] and other places. And there the antagonism between them and all foreigners receives more and more nourishment both from political and religious sources.

In the fifth place, there are other causes, the mentioning of which sounds like satire — peculiarities of their national character, deeply rooted in them, but manifest to everybody. We can only say, folly is an illness for which there is no medicine, and the Hindus believe that there is no country but theirs, no nation like theirs, no kings like theirs, no religion like theirs, no science like theirs. They are haughty, foolishly vain, self-conceited, and stolid. They are by nature niggardly in communicating that which they know, and they take the greatest possible care to withhold it from men of another caste among their own people, still much more, of course, from any foreigner. According to their belief, there is no other country on earth but theirs, no other race of man but theirs, and no created beings besides them have any knowledge of science whatsoever. . . . If they traveled and mixed with other nations, they would soon change their mind, for their ancestors were not as narrow-minded as the present generation is. One of their scholars, Varahamihira,[7] in a passage where he calls on the people to honor the Brahmins, says: *"The Greeks, though impure, must be honored, since they were trained in sciences and therein excelled others. What, then, are we to say of a Brahmin, if he combines with his purity the height of science?"* In former times, the Hindus used to acknowledge that the progress of science due to the Greeks is much more important than that which is due to themselves. But from this passage of Varahamihira alone you see what a self-lauding man he is, while he gives himself airs as doing justice to others. . . .

The heathen Greeks, before the rise of Christianity, held much the same opinions as the Hindus; their educated classes thought much the

---

[2]The initial rise of Islam in the seventh century.
[3]In 711.
[4]The mountainous northwestern region that separates the modern nations of Pakistan and India and which today is disputed territory.

[5]The holy warrior.
[6]A city on the Ganges River in central northeast India, it is a sacred site of both Hindu and Buddhist pilgrimage.
[7]An astronomer and astrologer of the early sixth century (ca. 505), he was one of Gupta India's greatest scientists.

same as those of the Hindus; their common people held the same idolatrous views as those of the Hindus. Therefore I like to confront the theories of the one nation with those of the other simply on account of their close relationship, not in order to correct them. For that which is not *the truth*[8] does not admit of any correction and all heathenism, whether Greek or Indian, is in its heart and soul one and the same belief, because it is only a deviation *from the truth*. The Greeks, however, had philosophers who, living in their country, discovered and worked out for them the elements of science, not of popular superstition, for it is the object of the upper classes to be guided by the results of science, while the common crowd will always be inclined to plunge into wrong-headed wrangling, as long as they are not kept down by fear of punishment. Think of Socrates when he opposed the crowd of his nation as to their idolatry and did not want to call the stars gods! At once eleven of the twelve judges of the Athenians agreed on a sentence of death, and Socrates died faithful to the truth.[9]

The Hindus had no men of this stamp both capable and willing to bring sciences to a classical perfection. Therefore you mostly find that even the so-called scientific theorems of the Hindus are in a state of utter confusion, devoid of any logical order, and in the last instance always mixed up with the silly notions of the crowd, *e.g.* immense numbers, enormous spaces of time, and all kinds of religious dogmas, which the vulgar belief does not admit of being called into question. . . . I can only compare their mathematical and astronomical literature, as far as I know it, to a mixture of pearl shells and sour dates, or of pearls and dung, or of costly crystals and common pebbles. Both kinds of things are equal in their eyes, since they cannot raise themselves to the methods of a strictly scientific deduction.[10]

---

[8]The true faith of Islam.
[9]See source 27. Al-Biruni's facts regarding the trial of Socrates are not correct.
[10]That is, logical argumentation, especially according to the system created by Aristotle, a Greek scientist-philosopher of the fourth century B.C.E. Aristotle's logic, which had a profound impact on both Islamic and Western science and philosophical thought, was based on the *principle of contradiction:* An entity either *is* or *is not;* it cannot simultaneously be both. The spiritual principle of *nondualism* (sources 40 and 42) rejects the principle of contradiction.

A Sati's Sacrifice
▼▼▼

80 ▾ *VIKRAMA'S ADVENTURES*

One of the many myths regarding premodern Indian history is that a majority of widows performed ritual suicide by self-immolation on their late husbands' funeral pyres, and those who refused to go willingly to their deaths were forced into the flames. In point of fact, it was rare for widows to join their recently deceased husbands in death in ancient India. It was only during the Gupta Era, when female remarriage began to be discouraged and even prohibited, that the practice began to become something of a tradition. Even then, death by burning was not the fate of the vast majority of widows in that or any subsequent period. There were, however, enough incidents of widow suicide and murder to shock British colonial administrators, who took over direct management of India in the mid nineteenth century and managed to suppress the practice fairly effectively.

Another myth shared by Western observers is that Indians call this practice *suttee.* There is no such word. Suttee is a British misunderstanding and mispronunciation of *sati,* which means "a virtuous woman." According to the social-religious traditions that supported the practice of widow burning, a widow, no matter her caste, could not remarry, for this would entail her breaking her marriage vow and endangering her husband's spiritual welfare. She was expected to live out her life in severe austerity, shunned by all but her children, in the hope of remarrying her husband in some future incarnation. If she were especially virtuous, she would choose to join her deceased husband sooner rather than later and end her present life on his funeral day. Undoubtedly some satis committed suicide willingly. Probably far more were forced by their husbands' relatives, for social and economic reasons, to perform this ultimate act of loyalty.

Our text, which sheds some light on this act of sacrifice, comes from an anonymous collection of stories recounting the adventures and wisdom of the semi-legendary King Vikrama, or Vikramaditya, who might have lived around 58 B.C.E. The stories, as we have received them, were probably collected between the eleventh and thirteenth centuries.

QUESTIONS FOR ANALYSIS

1. Can a widow who refuses to immolate herself achieve moksha (release)?
2. What proprietary interest do the families to which the sati belongs have in her sacrifice?
3. What impact does her act have on her husband's soul? On her own?
4. What social and psychological factors make suicide appear so attractive?
5. "By her perfect selflessness, a sati perfects and redeems her husband." What does this anonymous statement mean? How, if at all, does this story illustrate that attitude?
6. Some commentators have argued that this story is predicated upon the assumption that wives and husbands fulfill one another, and without the other each is incomplete. Do you agree with this analysis? Why or why not? In addressing this question, you might want to review the *Laws of Manu* (source 35).

Once King Vikrama, attended by all his vassal princes, had ascended his throne. At this time a certain magician came in, and blessing him with the words "Live forever!" said: "Sire, you are skilled in all the arts; many magicians have come into your presence and exhibited their tricks. So today be so good as to behold an exhibition of my dexterity." The king said: "I have not time now; it is the time to bathe and eat. Tomorrow I will behold it." So on the morrow the juggler came into the king's assembly as a stately man, with a mighty beard and glorious countenance, holding a sword in his hand, and accompanied by a lovely woman; and he bowed to the king. Then the ministers who were present, seeing the stately man, were astonished, and asked: "O hero, who are you, and whence do you come?" He said: "I am a servant of Great Indra;[1] I was cursed once by my lord, and was cast down to Earth; and now I dwell here. And this is my wife. Today a great

---

[1]Source 10.

battle has begun between the gods and the Daityas [demons], so I am going thither. This King Vikramaditya treats other men's wives as his sisters, so before going to the battle I wish to leave my wife with him." Hearing this the king also was greatly amazed. And the man left his wife with the king and delivered her over to him, and sword in hand flew up into Heaven. Then a great and terrible shouting was heard in the sky: "Ho there, kill them, kill them, smite them, smite them!" were the words they heard. And all the people who sat in the court, with upturned faces, gazed in amazement. After this, when a moment had passed by, one of the man's arms, holding his sword and stained with blood, fell from the sky into the king's assembly. Then all the people, seeing it, said: "Ah, this great hero has been killed in battle by his opponents; his sword and one arm have fallen." While the people who sat in the court were even saying this, again his head fell also; and then his trunk fell too. And seeing this his wife said: "Sire, my husband, fighting on the field of battle, has been slain by the enemy. His head, his arm, his sword, and his trunk have fallen down here. So, that this my beloved may not be wooed by the heavenly nymphs, I will go to where he is. Let fire be provided for me." Hearing her words the king said: "My daughter, why will you enter the fire? I will guard you even as my own daughter; preserve your body." She said: "Sire, what is this you say? My lord, for whom this body of mine exists, has been slain on the battlefield by his foes. Now for whose sake shall I preserve this body? Moreover, you should not say this, since even fools know that wives should follow their husbands. For thus it is said:

1. Moonlight goes with the moon, the lightning clings to the cloud, and women follow their husbands; even fools know this.

And so, as the learned tradition has it:

2. The wife who enters into the fire when her husband dies, imitating Arundhati [a star, regarded as the wife of one of the Seven Rishis (the Dipper), and as a typical faithful spouse] in her behavior, enjoys bliss in Heaven.

3. Until a wife burns herself in the fire after the death of her husband, so long that woman can in no way be permanently freed from the body.

4. A woman who follows after her husband shall surely purify three families: her mother's, her father's, and that into which she was given in marriage.

And so:

5. Three and a half crores[2] is the number of the hairs on the human body; so many years shall a wife who follows her husband dwell in Heaven.

6. As a snake-charmer powerfully draws a snake out of a hole, so a wife draws her husband upward [by burning herself] and enjoys bliss with him.

7. A wife who abides by the law of righteousness [in burning herself] saves her husband, whether he be good or wicked; yes, even if he be guilty of all crimes.

Furthermore, O king, a woman who is bereft of her husband has no use for her life. And it is said:

8. What profit is there in the life of a wretched woman who has lost her husband? Her body is as useless as a banyan tree in a cemetery.

9. Surely father, brother, and son measure their gifts; what woman would not honor her husband, who gives without measure?

Moreover:

10. Though a woman be surrounded by kinsfolk, though she have many sons, and be endowed with excellent qualities, she is a miserable, poor wretched creature, when deprived of her husband.

---

[2]One *crore* is 10 million, therefore, 35 million.

And so:

11. What shall a widow do with perfumes, garlands, and incense, or with manifold ornaments, or garments and couches of ease?

12. A lute does not sound without strings, a wagon does not go without wheels, and a wife does not obtain happiness without her husband, not even with a hundred kinsfolk.

13. Woman's highest refuge is her husband, even if he be poor, vicious, old, infirm, crippled, outcast, and stingy.

14. There is no kinsman, no friend, no protector, no refuge for a woman like her husband.

15. There is no other misery for women like widowhood. Happy is she among women who dies before her husband.

Thus speaking she fell at the king's feet, begging that a fire be provided for her. And when the king heard her words, his heart being tender with genuine compassion, he caused a pyre to be erected of sandalwood and the like, and gave her leave. So she took leave of the king, and in his presence entered the fire together with her husband's body.

Chapter 10

Two Christian Civilizations

Byzantium and Western Europe

Contrary to popular belief, the Roman Empire was not a European civilization, and the Romans did not think of themselves as Europeans. Yes, the city of Rome was located in Italy, which is a European peninsula, and a portion of its empire lay in lands that later became part of the community known as Europe. Nevertheless, the Roman Empire was a Mediterranean civilization that encompassed the coastlands and peoples of three continents: Africa, Asia, and Europe. Given this fact, it is best to think of the Roman Empire as the last and largest of the Hellenistic empires, with all of the cultural variety that the term connotes.

During the period from roughly 235 to 600, this Mediterranean civilization underwent a transformation. Many modern historians have characterized this era as the period of "the decline and fall of the Roman Empire," but the phrase and all that it suggests misses the mark. Rome and its empire did not fall in the sense of a sudden collapse. What happened was more subtle and profound. The Roman Empire, which embraced the cultures of so many diverse peoples, was metamorphosed over a period of centuries into three new civilizations: Byzantium, Europe, and Islam.

Islam originated in Arabia, a land beyond the boundaries of the Roman Empire, and in the mid eighth century it established its capital at Baghdad, in the heart of the former Persian Empire. Nevertheless, by conquering the lands of Syria-Palestine, all of North Africa, and most of the Iberian Peninsula, Islam inherited a good deal of Hellenistic culture, including Greek science and philosophy, and in that sense it was an heir of the Roman Empire. We have already studied Islam in Chapters 8 and 9, and it needs no further comment here. Byzantium and Europe, Rome's other two heirs, are another matter. It is to these two new civilizations that we now must turn.

The civilization that we term *Byzantium* receives its name from the eastern Mediterranean city of that name (*Byzantion* in Greek; *Byzantium* in Latin), which Emperor Constantine the Great transformed into the capital of the newly Christianized Roman Empire in 330. The fact that Constantine chose to locate *New Rome,* as he styled the city, in the East is testimony to the increasing unimportance of the West to the fourth-century empire. Although the city came to be called *Constantinople* (Constantine's city), modern scholars have favored using the older name — Byzantium — to delineate the civilization that centered on this East Roman capital. Actually, the Byzantines never called themselves anything other than *Romaioi* (Romans). From the early fourth century to 1453, when the city and its empire finally succumbed to the advances of the Ottoman Turks, Constantinople was the center of an empire and a civilization whose members viewed it as the legitimate heir of Roman imperial traditions. In fact, however, already by the late sixth century, Byzantium had become a distinctive civilization — a Greek-speaking civilization that retained many Hellenistic qualities but which also developed many new forms of expression and organization.

Byzantine civilization resulted from the fusion of three key elements. First there were the traditions of the late Roman Empire in which the emperor had been transformed into an autocratic ruler along the lines of the Persian *shahs,* or emperors. Then there was *Eastern Orthodox Christianity. Orthodox* is a Greek term that means "correct thinking," and in this context it means the time-honored traditions of Eastern Mediterranean Christianity, which included folk practices as well as the teachings of theologians and church councils. The third element was the cultural heritage of the Hellenistic past, itself a fusion of Greek, western Asiatic, and Egyptian elements.

Although Byzantium was an empire, with definite boundaries that expanded and contracted over the centuries, as a civilization it transcended political boundaries. Byzantine traditions deeply influenced the cultures of a number of neighboring peoples, especially the Russians, Bulgars, and Serbs. In a real sense, even after the Byzantine Empire collapsed in the face of Ottoman Turkish assaults, its civilization lived on, in somewhat altered form, among such Orthodox Christian cultures as Russia, Bulgaria, and Serbia.

The story in the western half of the Roman Empire was different. Continuities were less evident, and dramatic changes were more the norm. Whereas the empire's eastern half evolved somewhat gently into a new cultural synthesis, the western half experienced a painful process of political breakdown and sweeping cultural transformation.

Toward the end of the fourth century C.E., pressures on Rome's western frontiers become intolerable, and the western portion of the empire rapidly slid toward its unforeseen end, defeated and transformed by fringe peoples who came from beyond the borders of the Rhine and Danube rivers. By the end of the sixth century, precious little of the western half of the Roman World was still ruled by imperial Roman authority. More profoundly, these newcomers played a key role in transforming culture in the West, thereby helping to usher out the old Greco-Roman order and to lay the basis for a new civilization that many historians call the *First Europe,* or *Latin Europe.*

One of the enduring clichés favored by writers of history textbooks is that Europe emerged out of a fusion of three elements: the remnants of Greco-Roman civilization; Latin, or Western, Christianity; and the culture and vigor of the fringe peoples who migrated into the western regions of the late Roman Empire. As is true of so many commonplace notions, there is a good deal of truth to this statement, but it is not the complete story. These three elements differed radically from one another in many essential ways, and it took centuries for them to fuse into something resembling a coherent civilization. Even when they had achieved a level of integration, their differences continued to infuse into an emerging European civilization tensions that became identifying characteristics of the new order developing in the West. That dynamism eventually drove Europe into competition with Islam and Byzantium — a competition that would have global consequences.

▼▼▼

Justinian the Great: The First Byzantine Emperor

Some eighteenth-century European historians considered Byzantine civilization merely an unoriginal and degenerate fossilization of late antiquity, but nothing could be farther from the truth. Although the Byzantines saw their state as a living continuation of the Roman Empire, by the late sixth century Constantinople had become the matrix of a new civilization that persisted and largely flourished down to 1453, when finally the city of Constantinople fell to Ottoman Turkish forces.

The history of Byzantium is one of peaks and troughs. The pattern of triumph, decline, and recovery repeated itself continuously until Byzantium's collapse in the mid fifteenth century. One key to understanding this cycle is the power invested in the emperor (and occasionally the empress). Rarely does an individual single-handedly alter in a radical way the historical course of an empire or any other large institution, but autocratic monarchs could and did play inordinately important roles in the unfolding of Byzantine fortunes. The following sources shed light on the person and reign of Justinian the Great (r. 527–565), arguably the Eastern Roman Empire's first Byzantine emperor.

Two Imperial Portraits: Justinian and Theodora
▼▼▼

81 ▼ THE MOSAICS OF SAN VITALE

The age of Justinian I (r. 527–565) was pivotal in the history of the Eastern Roman Empire. The last of the emperors of Constantinople to speak Latin as his native tongue, Justinian attempted to reconquer the West from the various Germanic tribes that had divided it into competing kingdoms. Justinian's forces invaded Italy in 535 in order to wrest it from the Ostrogoths, who had controlled the peninsula since the late fifth century. The war that ensued was protracted, bitter, and destructive. When fighting finally ceased in 553, the Ostrogoths had been eliminated as a recognizable culture, and Rome's aristocratic families likewise had disappeared from the historical record. Cities, towns, and countryside alike were in ruin. Fifteen years later, in 568, new Germanic invaders, the Lombards, carved out their own kingdom in northern Italy and several smaller, semi-independent states in parts of central and southern Italy, thereby denying Byzantium control over the entire peninsula. In effect, Justinian's attempt at reconquest enjoyed only limited, short-term success. Its major accomplishment was transforming Rome and much of Italy into a war-ravaged backwater and stripping the eastern empire of much-needed resources. After Justinian's age, the Greek-speaking emperors and people of Constantinople were forced to look less to the West and more toward their eastern, southern, and northern borders, thereby accelerating the impact of Asian influences on Byzantium's cultural development.

For all of his large-scale miscalculations, however, Justinian ranks as one of Byzantium's greatest emperors; indeed, he often is referred to as *Justinian the Great,* the last Roman and first Byzantine emperor. A measure of that greatness is seen in the portrait mosaics of Justinian and Empress Theodora at the Church of San Vitale in Ravenna, Italy.

Created in 548 following the capture of Ravenna by imperial troops, the two mosaics flank the altar of the church. High above the altar is a mosaic of *Christ in Glory.* Below and to Christ's right is Justinian's mosaic; opposite and to Christ's left is Theodora's mosaic. In Justinian's mosaic we see the crowned emperor, his head surrounded by a *nimbus,* or *halo,* a sign of sacred power. He wears imperial purple and gold and carries, as an offering, the eucharistic bread, which a priest will transform at mass into the Body of Christ. On his left are four individuals: three churchmen and what appears to be a court official (the person in the background). The clerics are Maximian, archbishop of Ravenna (his name appears over his head, he holds a cross, and he wears around his shoulders an archbishop's *pallium,* a long white cloth with an embroidered cross), and two priests. One priest holds a book of Gospels (every mass has a Gospel reading from the same side of the altar on which Justinian's mosaic is located); the other holds an incense burner. On the emperor's right stand two high-ranking imperial officials and six members of the imperial bodyguard, known as the Praetorian Guard. One of the guardsmen displays a shield with the *chi-rho* monogram: the Greek letters *X* (chi) and *P* (rho), which when combined represent the word *Christos* (Christ). Empress Theodora, Justinian's wife, also appears with a crown, imperial purple and gold robes, and a halo. The hem of her robe has an image of the Three Kings bearing gifts to the Christ child. In her hands is a golden, bejeweled cup containing the eucharistic wine, which a priest will transform at mass into the Blood of Christ. On her left are seven court ladies, in descending order of rank; the one closest to her wears the purple of the imperial family. Two high-ranking civil officials stand on her right. One pulls back a curtain to reveal a baptismal font, the fountain in which persons are baptized into the Church.

QUESTIONS FOR ANALYSIS

1. Theodora's mosaic places her into a definite space: an imperial palace (or possibly a church). Justinian's mosaic lacks any spatial points of reference. Does this seem significant? If so, how do you interpret the emperor's lack of specific place?

2. Based on these two mosaics, please describe the place that Empress Theodora apparently held within the empire. What was her theoretical position? What do you think were her actual powers? As always, be as specific as possible.

3. "The Byzantine emperor was perceived as the living image of God on Earth, insofar as his imperial majesty was a pale reflection of the Glory of God. As such, he was the link between the Roman Christian people and their God." In light of these mosaics, please comment in depth on this anonymous statement.

4. First study the *Barberini Ivory* (source 50). Now address the following problem: Two titles borne by the emperor of Constantinople were *isapostolos* (peer of the apostles) and *autokrator* (sole ruler of the world). Do the *Barberini Ivory* and the San Vitale mosaic of Justinian symbolize either or both of these titles? Please be specific in your answer.

Emperor Justinian and His Court

Empress Theodora and Her Court

Justinian: God's Deputy or a Devil?
▼▼▼

82 ▼ *Procopius, ON THE BUILDINGS and THE SECRET HISTORY*

Justinian's largely unsuccessful attempt to reconquer the West was not his only misstep. A sincerely but narrowly pious man who took seriously his duties as God-anointed emperor, Justinian also promoted the cause of Christian *Orthodoxy* (correct thinking) in a cosmopolitan empire that contained many variant Christian beliefs and ways of interpreting the faith. The result was deep alienation, especially among Egyptian and Syrian subjects of the empire, and a consequent weakness that Islamic Arab forces exploited in the next century.

Regardless of his failures, Justinian achieved many successes. Among his accomplishments, he ordered and saw to completion the codification of imperial Roman law, and he commissioned the rebuilding of many of Constantinople's churches and public buildings following an especially destructive urban riot in 532. The greatest of all these edifices was the massive domed church of *Hagia Sophia* (Holy Wisdom), the first great example of a distinctly Byzantine style of architecture.

To celebrate Justinian's building projects, a Palestinian courtier named Procopius (d. after 562?) composed a work entitled *On the Buildings* around 553–554. Earlier he had composed the first seven books of his *History in Eight Books*, also known as *The Wars*, a largely eyewitness account of Justinian's wars against the Persians, Vandals, and Goths, which he waged between 527 and 553. Both of these works were meant for widespread distribution and praised the emperor's actions and character in a most obsequious manner. Unknown to Justinian and the imperial censors, Procopius also wrote, probably in the year 550, a work he never intended to be seen in his own lifetime. Known today as *The Secret History,* this work purports to be a corrective to the laudatory *Wars,* the inside story of court life and policy-making, and a true description of the characters of the emperor and his empress, Theodora.

Our two excerpts come respectively from the *Buildings* and the slightly earlier *Secret History.* Together they illustrate how and why Justinian the Great was and still is such a controversial ruler and individual.

QUESTIONS FOR ANALYSIS

1. According to *On the Buildings,* what were Justinian's greatest accomplishments?
2. According to *The Secret History,* what specific evils was Justinian guilty of?
3. Consider Justinian's supposed character flaws and vices. How would a partisan of Justinian interpret those qualities?
4. How useful does *The Secret History* appear to be as a source? What about *On the Buildings?* Please be specific in your answer.

5. Assume the *Barberini Ivory* (source 50) represents Justinian (as it probably does). Compose Procopius's commentary on it — first in the spirit of *On the Buildings* and then in the spirit of *The Secret History*.

ON THE BUILDINGS

In our time Justinian became emperor. He took over the state when it was tottering dangerously. He increased its size and made it far more glorious by driving from it the barbarians who had violated it from ancient times, as I have described in detail in my work on the wars. . . . Justinian did not refuse to acquire other states as well. At any rate, he won over many which in his time were already foreign to the Roman Empire, and he built innumerable new cities. And finding doctrine about God before his time wavering and being forced into many directions, he checked all the pathways leading to error and caused the faith to stand on one secure foundation. Besides this, he found that the laws were obscure because they had been multiplied unnecessarily and were in confusion because of their obvious contradiction. So he purified them of the mass of quibbles, and by greatly strengthening them, preserved them from contradiction.[1] By using his own initiative to remove possible causes of conspiracy and by satisfying those in need of a livelihood with gifts of money and by forcibly removing the fate which threatened them, he brought the state to blessedness. Further, he strengthened the Roman Empire, which was subject everywhere to barbarians, with large numbers of soldiers and fortified all its furthest points by building strongholds. As for the rest, most of it has been recorded in my other works: The good that was done by his building shall be my present subject. . . .

As I have just said, he more than doubled the state in area and increased its power in other ways: And those who plotted against him, even to the extent of wanting his death, have not only lived to this day in the enjoyment of their property, even though they were openly caught, but actually still serve as Roman generals and enjoy the rank of consuls.[2] But now, as I said, I must go on to the buildings of this emperor, so that it may not come about that those who look upon them in the future may fail to believe because of their number and size that they are the work of one man. For many achievements of our ancestors are discredited because of their outstanding merits, if they have not been recorded in writing. The buildings in Byzantium will naturally be the foundation of the record. . . .

At one period some of the common people and the dregs of the mob rose against the Emperor Justinian in Byzantium and caused the so-called Nika Revolt,[3] as I have described in detail without hiding anything in my work on the wars. Showing that they had taken up arms, not only against the emperor, but just as much against God in their wickedness, they dared to burn the Christian church (the Byzantines call this temple Wisdom,[4] thinking this name most appropriate to God), and God allowed them to accomplish this impiety in the foreknowledge of the beauty which this shrine was destined to attain when restored. So the whole church was burned down and lay in ruins. Not long after, the Emperor Justinian rounded it off so beautifully that if anyone had asked the Christians earlier whether they

---

[1]Justinian's *Corpus Iuris Civilis* (Body of Civil Law), which codified and clarified imperial Roman law.
[2]Consuls were originally the two annually elected chief magistrates of the Roman Republic. In the age of the empire, the rank became honorific.
[3]January 532. The riot received its name from the fact that

the rioters cried out *"Nika"* (Win!), the traditional chant of the crowds at the chariot races in the Hippodrome, where the riot began and ended. See note 33 for further information.
[4]Hagia Sophia.

wanted the church to be destroyed and rebuilt like this, and had shown them the outlines of what can now be seen, I think they would have immediately prayed to see the church in ruins so that it could be changed into its present form. In the event, the Emperor proceeded with all haste to the building, with no heed to expense, and collected all the craftsmen from all over the world. . . . This, too, was a sign of the honor in which God held the Emperor, in that he procured in advance those who would be best to help him in his undertakings. One might reasonably admire the Emperor's own good sense also, in that he was able to select from all men those best adapted for the most serious tasks. . . .

And whenever anyone enters this church to pray, he perceives at once that this edifice has been so finely crafted not by any human power or skill but by the agency of God. Therefore his mind is lifted up toward God and exalted.

THE SECRET HISTORY

Deceptive Affability and Piety of a Tyrant

Justinian, while otherwise of such character as I have shown, did make himself easy of access and affable to his visitors; nobody of all those who sought audience with him was ever denied: even those who confronted him improperly or noisily never made him angry. On the other hand, he never blushed at the murders he committed. Thus he never revealed a sign of wrath or irritation at any offender, but with a gentle countenance and unruffled brow gave the order to destroy myriads of innocent men, to sack cities, to confiscate any amount of properties.

One would think from this manner that the man had the mind of a lamb. If, however, anyone tried to propitiate him and in suppliance beg him to forgive his victims, he would grin like a wild beast, and woe betide those who saw his teeth thus bared!

The priests he permitted fearlessly to outrage their neighbors, and even took sympathetic pleasure in their robberies, fancying he was thus shar-

ing their divine piety. When he judged such cases, he thought he was doing the holy thing when he gave the decision to the priest and let him go free with his ill-gotten booty: justice, in his mind, meant the priests' getting the better of their opponents. When he himself thus illegally got possession of estates of people alive or dead, he would straightway make them over to one of the churches, gilding his violence with the color of piety — and so that his victims could not possibly get their property back. Furthermore he committed an inconceivable number of murders for the same cause: for in his zeal to gather all men into one Christian doctrine, he recklessly killed all who dissented, and this too he did in the name of piety. For he did not call it homicide, when those who perished happened to be of a belief that was different from his own. . . .

He was untiring; and hardly slept at all, generally speaking; he had no appetite for food or drink, but picking up a morsel with the tips of his fingers, tasted it and left the table, as if eating were a duty imposed upon him by nature and of no more interest than a courier takes in delivering a letter. Indeed, he would often go without food for two days and nights, especially when the time before the festival called Easter enjoins such fasting. Then, as I have said, he often went without food for two days, living only on a little water and a few wild herbs, sleeping perhaps a single hour, and then spending the rest of the time walking up and down.

If, mark you, he had spent these periods in good works, matters might have been considerably alleviated. Instead, he devoted the full strength of his nature to the ruin of the Romans, and succeeded in razing the state to its foundation. For his constant wakefulness, his privations and his labors were undergone for no other reason than to contrive each day ever more exaggerated calamities for his people. For he was, as I said, unusually keen at inventing and quick at accomplishing unholy acts, so that even the good in him transpired to be answerable for the downfall of his subjects. . . .

How Justinian Killed a Trillion People

That Justinian was not a man, but a demon, as I have said, in human form,[5] one might prove by considering the enormity of the evils he brought upon mankind. For in the monstrousness of his actions the power of a fiend is manifest. Certainly an accurate reckoning of all those whom he destroyed would be impossible, I think, for anyone but God to make. Sooner could one number, I fancy, the sands of the sea than the men this emperor murdered. Examining the countries that he made desolate of inhabitants, I would say he slew a trillion people. For Libya,[6] vast as it is, he so devastated that you would have to go a long way to find a single man, and he would be remarkable. Yet eighty thousand Vandals[7] capable of bearing arms had dwelt there, and as for their wives and children and servants, who could guess their number? Yet still more numerous than these were the Mauretanians,[8] who with their wives and children were all exterminated. And again, many Roman soldiers and those who followed them to Constantinople, the Earth now covers; so that if one should venture to say that five million men perished in Libya alone, he would not, I imagine, be telling the half of it.

The reason for this was that after the Vandals were defeated,[9] Justinian planned, not how he might best strengthen his hold on the country, nor how by safe-guarding the interests of those who were loyal to him he might have the good-will of his subjects: but instead he foolishly recalled Belisarius[10] at once, on the charge that the latter intended to make himself king (an idea of which Belisarius was utterly incapable),[11] and so that he might manage affairs there himself and be able to plunder the whole of Libya. Sending commissioners to value the province, he imposed grievous taxes where before there had been none. Whatever lands were most valuable, he seized, and prohibited the Arians[12] from observing their religious ceremonies. Negligent toward sending necessary supplies to the soldiers, he was overstrict with them in other ways; wherefore mutinies arose resulting in the deaths of many. For he was never able to abide by established customs, but naturally threw everything into confusion and disturbance.

Italy, which is not less than thrice as large as Libya,[13] was everywhere desolated of men, even worse than the other country,[14] and from this the count of those who perished there may be imagined. The reason for what happened in Italy I have already made plain.[15] All of his crimes in Libya were repeated here; sending his auditors to Italy, he soon upset and ruined everything.

The rule of the Goths, before this war, had extended from the land of the Gauls to the boundaries of Dacia.[16] . . . The Germans held Cisalpine Gaul[17] and most of the land of the Venetians,[18] when the Roman army arrived in Italy. Sirmium and the neighboring country was in the hands of the Gepidae.[19] All of these he utterly depopulated. For those who did not die in battle perished

---

[5]Procopius did not mean this in a metaphorical sense. Contemporary Christians believed that demons in human form inhabited the world.

[6]Western North Africa.

[7]A Germanic people who had occupied the western regions of North Africa.

[8]The people of western North Africa.

[9]This war lasted from 533 to 534.

[10]Constantinople's best general, Belisarius (ca. 505–565) had suppressed the Nika riot, conquered North Africa, and captured Rome in 536.

[11]Procopius had served as Belisarius's secretary and was quite loyal to the man. Apparently, he is correct. Despite contrary rumors, Belisarius was totally loyal to Justinian.

[12]The Vandals belonged to the *Arian* branch of Christianity. Named after Arius, a priest of Alexandria, this sect believed Jesus was God only by divine adoption and was not coeternal with God the Father. Their doctrine was declared heretical in 325 at the Council of Nicaea, which Constantine I convened to settle the issue of Christ's divinity and several other problems confronting the new imperial Church.

[13]Hardly.

[14]The Italian, or Gothic, War began in 536 and dragged on to 561.

[15]In his earlier history of the Gothic War.

[16]From eastern Gaul (today southeastern France, western Switzerland, and western Germany) to the region that is today Romania (Dacia).

[17]Literally, "Gaul this side of the Alps." This refers to Italy north of the Po River, especially northwestern Italy, which ancient Celtic tribes had inhabited.

[18]Northeastern Italy.

[19]A Gothic people.

of disease and famine, which as usual followed in the train of war. Illyria[20] and all of Thrace,[21] that is, from the Ionian Gulf[22] to the suburbs of Constantinople, including Greece and the Chersonese,[23] were overrun by the Huns,[24] Slavs[25] and Antes,[26] almost every year, from the time when Justinian took over the Roman Empire; and intolerable things they did to the inhabitants. For in each of these incursions, I should say, more than two hundred thousand Romans were slain or enslaved, so that all this country became a desert like that of Scythia.[27]

Such were the results of the wars in Libya and in Europe. Meanwhile the Saracens[28] were continuously making inroads on the Romans of the East, from the land of Egypt to the boundaries of Persia; and so completely did their work, that in all this country few were left, and it will never be possible, I fear, to find out how many thus perished. Also the Persians under Chosroes[29] three times invaded the rest of this Roman territory, sacked the cities, and either killing or carrying away the men they captured in the cities and country, emptied the land of inhabitants every time they invaded it. . . .

For neither the Persians nor the Saracens, the Huns or the Slavs or the rest of the barbarians, were able to withdraw from Roman territory undamaged. In their inroads, and still more in their sieges of cities and in battles, where they prevailed over opposing forces, they shared in disastrous losses quite as much. Not only the Romans, but nearly all the barbarians thus felt Justinian's

bloodthirstiness. For while Chosroes himself was bad enough, as I have duly shown elsewhere, Justinian was the one who each time gave him an occasion for the war. For he took no heed to fit his policies to an appropriate time, but did everything at the wrong moment: in time of peace or truce he ever craftily contrived to find pretext for war with his neighbors; while in time of war, he unreasonably lost interest, and hesitated too long in preparing for the campaign, grudging the necessary expenses; and instead of putting his mind on the war, gave his attention to stargazing and research as to the nature of God.[30] Yet he would not abandon hostilities, since he was so bloodthirsty and tyrannical, even when thus unable to conquer the enemy because of his negligence in meeting the situation.

So while he was emperor, the whole Earth ran red with the blood of nearly all the Romans and the barbarians. Such were the results of the wars throughout the whole empire during this time. But the civil strife in Constantinople and in every other city, if the dead were reckoned, would total no smaller number of slain than those who perished in the wars, I believe. Since justice and impartial punishment were seldom directed against offenders, and each of the two factions[31] tried to win the favor of the emperor over the other, neither party kept the peace. Each, according to his smile or his frown, was now terrified, now encouraged. Sometimes they attacked each other in full strength, sometimes in smaller groups, or even lay in ambush against the first single man of

---

[20]The western, or Adriatic, shore of the Balkans.
[21]The eastern, or Black Sea, region of the Balkans.
[22]The Mediterranean region between southern Italy and Greece.
[23]A narrow peninsula in Thrace that extends along the European side of the Dardanelles, the strait that separates modern European Turkey from Asiatic Turkey.
[24]The so-called Cotrigur Huns and also the Avars, both of whom were Turkic horsepeople out of the steppes of Central Asia.
[25]Various Slavic-speaking pagan peoples who were moving into the northern Balkans.
[26]A conglomeration of people, possibly Indo-Iranians or Slavs, from north of the Black Sea. Justinian made them allies in 545; they disappear from history after 602.

[27]The desolate steppes of Central Asia.
[28]Arabs.
[29]Chosroes I (r. 531–578/579), king of kings of the Sassanian Empire of Persia, which encompassed Mesopotamia and Iran. He inherited a war with Justinian that had been raging since 527. In 532 he and Justinian negotiated an Eternal Peace. Chosroes broke the peace in 540 when he invaded Byzantine Mesopotamia and Syria. In 561 both exhausted parties concluded a fifty-year truce.
[30]Justinian was avidly interested in subtle points of theology and believed himself to be a theologian.
[31]The two major circus factions — the Blues and the Greens. They were much more than just fans of chariot-racing teams. Their rivalries and, at times, mutual frustrations often resulted in mob violence.

the opposite party who came along. For thirty-two years, without ever ceasing, they performed outrages against each other, many of them being punished with death by the municipal prefect.[32]

However, punishment for these offenses was mostly directed against the Greens.[33]

Furthermore the persecution of the Samaritans[34] and the so-called heretics filled the Roman realm with blood. Let this present recapitulation suffice to recall what I have described more fully a little while since. Such were the things done to all mankind by the demon in flesh for which Justinian, as emperor, was responsible. But what evils he wrought against men by some hidden power and diabolic force I shall now relate.

During his rule over the Romans, many disasters of various kinds occurred: which some said were due to the presence and artifices of the Devil, and others considered were effected by the Divinity, Who, disgusted with the Roman Empire, had turned away from it and given the country up to the Old One.[35] The Scirtus River flooded Edessa,[36] creating countless sufferings among the inhabitants, as I have elsewhere written. The Nile, rising as usual, but not subsiding in the customary season, brought terrible calamities to the people there, as I have also previously recounted. . . .

Earthquakes destroyed Antioch,[37] the leading city of the East; Seleucia, which is situated nearby; and Anazarbus, most renowned city in Cilicia. Who could number those that perished in these metropoles? Yet one must add also those who lived in Ibora; in Amasea, the chief city of Pontus; in Polybotus in Phrygia, called Polymede by the Pisidians; in Lychnidus in Epirus; and in Corinth: all thickly inhabited cities from of old. All of these were destroyed by earthquakes during this time, with a loss of almost all their inhabitants.[38] And then came the plague, which I have previously mentioned, killing half at least of those who had survived the earthquakes.[39] To so many men came their doom, when Justinian first came to direct the Roman state and later possessed the throne of autocracy.

---

[32]Constantinople's chief municipal official.

[33]See note 31. The Greens were especially troublesome for Justinian. They precipitated the Nika riot of 532 (note 3) when they staged a demonstration in the Hippodrome in which they complained of the arbitrary actions of imperial authorities, including the emperor.

[34]A nonorthodox Jewish sect with settlements in Palestine, Syria, Egypt, and Constantinople, they were centered in the hills of Samaria in central Israel. Rebelling against Byzantine authority in 529, they were ruthlessly crushed.

[35]The Devil.

[36]A city in what is today southeast Turkey.

[37]The chief city of northern Syria.

[38]These cities were located throughout the eastern empire. Nine major earthquakes are recorded in this entire region during the period 526–557. The death toll was staggering.

[39]A Mediterranean-wide pandemic of bubonic plague broke out in Egypt in 541 and reached Constantinople by May 542. Justinian himself contracted the plague but survived. Justinian's invading armies introduced the plague into Italy, where it proved quite devastating. By 600 the plague had essentially burnt itself out, but only after reducing the total population of the Mediterranean to 60 percent or less of its preplague numbers.

▼▼▼

Charles the Great: Europe's First Emperor

Although Byzantine cultural influences spread beyond the territorial limits of the Eastern Roman Empire, Byzantium was largely a civilization centered upon a single empire. In the West, to the contrary, a new civilization arose that was not identified with any single political entity, even though the West created its own empire in the year 800 and then recreated it in 962. Despite having its own *Holy Roman*

Empire, as it was later called, European civilization was politically pluralistic and was never tied to any single state.

In many respects youthful, dynamic Europe was an everexpanding culture in the period from roughly 500 to 1500. Yet this dynamism was certainly not obvious during the early centuries in which European civilization was taking shape. With the passing of Roman imperial order, Western Europeans were thrown back on their own resources and forced to create new social and political structures and a new civilization. In fashioning this civilization, Westerners melded together three elements: the vestiges and memories of Roman civilization; the moral and organizational leadership of the Roman Catholic Church; and the vigor and culture of the various fringe peoples who carved out kingdoms in Europe from the fifth century onward. The single act that most vividly symbolizes the new order that emerged from that fusion was Pope Leo III's coronation of Charles the Great as Roman emperor on Christmas Day, 800. The following sources shed light on the person and reign of Charlemagne, a man whom the West styled *Roman emperor* but who was less and much more than that.

A Papal Portrait: Leo III and Charles the Great
▼▼▼

83 ▼ POPE LEO III'S LATERAN MOSAIC

With the deposition of Romulus Augustulus in 476, the western half of the Roman Empire lost its last resident Roman emperor. Although the emperor at Constantinople remained, in theory, ruler of the western, as well as the eastern, regions of the Roman Empire, in reality, the West was divided into a number of Germanic kingdoms — a process that had begun well before 476. If any single entity commanded the loyalties of all or most Europeans, it was the *Roman Church,* which was centered upon the person and office of the *pope* of Rome. The pope, whose title means "father" in Latin, was bishop of the city of Rome and claimed authority over all of Christendom, not just the Western Church, by virtue of being the heir of Saint Peter. According to arguments first put forward in the fourth century, Christ had given Saint Peter, the leader of the apostles, "the keys of the Kingdom of Heaven" and, therefore, authority over the entire Church. Peter later became the first bishop of Rome, and it was as bishop of Rome that he exercised his God-given authority over Christendom. When he died in office, all his power passed to his successor, and it continued to be handed on to each successive bishop of Rome. This vision of church history, which received a fair amount of acceptance in the West, failed to convince Christians in the East, including those who looked to Constantinople for spiritual guidance.

Although the Western Church considered the bishop of Rome to be the successor of Saint Peter and, therefore, the *holy father,* the actual power that popes exercised over Western Christendom was severely limited, especially before the twelfth century. Certainly Pope Leo III (r. 795–816), a contemporary of Charles the Great, had a vision of papal authority that far exceeded the bounds of political and even ecclesiastical reality. In point of fact, he had very little authority outside of Rome

Lateran Palace Mosaic

and its environs, and even in Rome he was beset by enemies, some of whom plotted his deposition and maybe even his assassination.

In search of a protector, Leo III turned to the most powerful man of the day, Charles, king of the Franks and of the Lombards, whose lands covered much of western continental Europe by the late eighth century. Protection, however, usually comes with a price, and perhaps Pope Leo had that in mind when he commissioned the mosaic that appears here.

Leo was lavish in the money he spent beautifying papal Rome, and one of his more ambitious building projects was adding two massive state reception halls to the papal residence known as the *Lateran Palace.* In the fashion of the day, the interiors of each hall were covered with mosaics. One of the mosaics pictured a seated Saint Peter flanked by two kneeling figures: Pope Leo and King Charles.

Inasmuch as the mosaic was completed sometime between 798 and April 799, Charles undoubtedly saw this artistic interpretation of papal-Frankish relations on his fateful last visit to Rome in 800/801, when the pope crowned him emperor. One can only wonder what Charles thought of the mosaic.

Time badly deteriorated the mosaic, and a heavy-handed attempt at restoration in 1743 completed the process of destruction. What we see in this mid-eighteenth-century replacement copy is Saint Peter, the keys to the Kingdom of Heaven on his lap, handing a *pallium* (see source 81) to Pope Leo and a lance with attached battle standard to King Charles. The pallium that Leo receives is the sign of authority worn by popes and archbishops. Note that Peter, who is dressed in clerical robes, wears one. Both the pope and the king have square nimbuses, or haloes, conventional signs that they are especially sanctified or powerful people who are still living; Peter has a round nimbus, a sign of canonized sainthood. The four Latin inscriptions read, from top to bottom and left to right as we view the mosaic: "Saint Peter"; "Most Holy Lord Pope Leo"; "To Lord King Charles"; and "Blessed Peter, You Give Life to Pope Leo and You Give Victory to King Charles."

QUESTIONS FOR ANALYSIS

1. Is there anything significant about Leo's position on Saint Peter's right and Charles's position on his left? Explain your answer.
2. What do you make of the fact that it is *Peter* who gives Charles the lance and not Jesus or some other manifestation of God?
3. What is the message of this mosaic?
4. Review source 81. Now compose a Byzantine commentary on the mosaic.

A Carolingian Vision of Reality
▼▼▼

84 ▼ Charles the Great, *THE CAPITULARY ON SAXONY* and *A LETTER TO POPE LEO III*

Charlemagne ruled a major portion of continental Europe for close to half a century (768–814). During his lifetime, Charles's efforts to expand the boundaries of Christendom and impose an order based on his understanding of Christian principles won him a reputation that extended all the way to the court of Caliph Harun al-Rashid in Baghdad. His *Carolingian* (the family of Charles) successors, however, were less fortunate and probably less able. In 843, Charles's three grandsons divided the empire into three kingdoms, signaling continental Europe's return to political pluralism — a pluralism that proved permanent and one of the major driving forces in European history.

Before the collapse of the Carolingian Empire, however, Charlemagne established at least a sense of order and unity, if not its total reality, that served as an inspiration for many of Europe's later emperors and kings. These included the king of Germany, Otto I, who laid the basis for the Germanic *Holy Roman Empire* with his imperial coronation in 962, and Napoleon, who in the early nineteenth century attempted to create a pan-European empire centered on France.

The following two sources, both of which were composed in Charlemagne's name by his counselors and secretaries, illustrate the ideals of Charles's court and the realities that faced it. The first document is a *capitulary,* so called because it consists of a number of regulatory chapters (*capitula* in Latin), which King Charles issued in 785. Known as the *Capitulary on Saxony,* it set down regulations regarding the Saxons and the Christian Church of Saxony that Charles was attempting to establish. From 772 to 804 Charles's armies waged a series of campaigns of conquest against the Saxons, a pagan Germanic people who lived just beyond the Franks' northeastern frontier. Although the Saxons resisted Charles's attempts to impose Carolingian order and Christianity upon them, in the end Charles's tenacity won out. By 804 all resistance had collapsed (thanks in large part to the forced resettlement of many Saxons, who were moved into the Frankish heartland). Saxony was incorporated into the Carolingian Empire, and the Saxons were at least nominal Christians. The second document is a letter to Pope Leo III written in 796, shortly after King Charles received word of the pope's accession to the papal throne — some four years before Charles's imperial coronation.

QUESTIONS FOR ANALYSIS

1. Consider the Capitulary on Saxony. What tactics does Charles employ to win over the Saxons to Christianity?
2. What does this document allow us to infer regarding Saxon pagan practices?
3. Does the Capitulary on Saxony distinguish between crimes and sins? Does it punish one type of infraction more than another? If yes, what type of infractions are most severely punished? What inferences do you draw from your answers?
4. Consider Charles's letter to Pope Leo III. What role(s) does Charles claim for himself? What role(s) does he assign the pope?
5. After a careful reading of both documents, what do you infer was Charles's vision of his duties as king?
6. On one of his campaigns in Italy, King Charles visited the Church of San Vitale and viewed the mosaic of Justinian (source 81). He subsequently constructed a palace chapel at Aachen, his favorite residence, that was roughly modeled on San Vitale. Compose King Charles's commentary on the mosaic of Justinian.
7. Compose Charles's commentary on Pope Leo III's *Lateran Mosaic* (source 83).
8. The introduction to this chapter mentions special tensions that were built into the fabric of European civilization. Do sources 83 and 84 provide evidence of any of those tensions? Explain. Be specific in your answer.

CAPITULARY ON SAXONY

First, concerning the greater chapters[1] it has been enacted:

1. It is pleasing to all that the churches of Christ, which are now being built in Saxony and consecrated to God, should not have less, but greater and more illustrious honor than the shrines of the idols have had.

2. If any one shall have fled to a church for refuge, let no one presume to expel him from the church by violence, but he shall be left in peace until he shall be brought to the judicial assemblage; and on account of the honor due to God and the saints, and the reverence due to the church itself, let his life and all his members be granted to him. Moreover, let him plead his cause as best he can and he shall be judged; and so let him be led to the presence of the lord king, and the latter shall send him where it shall seem fitting to his clemency.

3. If any one shall have entered a church by violence and shall have carried off anything in it by force or theft, or shall have burned the church itself, let him be punished by death.

4. If any one, out of contempt for Christianity, shall have despised the holy Lenten fast[2] and shall have eaten flesh, let him be punished by death. But, nevertheless, let it be taken into consideration by a priest lest perhaps any one from necessity has been led to eat flesh.

5. If any one shall have killed a bishop or priest or deacon[3] let him likewise be punished capitally.

6. If any one, deceived by the devil, shall have believed, after the manner of the pagans, that any man or woman is a witch and eats men, and on this account shall have burned the person, or shall have given the person's flesh to others to eat, or shall have eaten it himself, let him be punished by a capital sentence.

7. If any one, in accordance with pagan rites, shall have caused the body of a dead man to be burned, and shall have reduced his bones to ashes, let him be punished capitally.

8. If any one of the race of the Saxons hereafter, concealed among them, shall have wished to hide himself unbaptized, and shall have scorned to come to baptism, and shall have wished to remain a pagan, let him be punished by death.

9. If any one shall have sacrificed a man to the devil, and, after the manner of the pagans, shall have presented him as a victim to the demons, let him be punished by death.

10. If any one shall have formed a conspiracy with the pagans against the Christians, or shall have wished to join with them in opposition to the Christians, let him be punished by death; and whosoever shall have consented fraudulently to this same against the king and the Christian people, let him be punished by death.

11. If any one shall have shown himself unfaithful to the lord king, let him be punished with a capital sentence. . . .

13. If any one shall have killed his lord or lady, let him be punished in a like manner.

14. If, indeed, for these mortal crimes secretly committed any one shall have fled of his own accord to a priest, and after confession[4] shall have wished to do penance, let him be freed by the testimony of the priest from death.[5] . . .

18. On the Lord's day no meetings or public judicial assemblages shall be held, unless perchance in a case of great necessity, or when war compels it, but all shall go to church to hear the word of God, and shall be free for prayers or good works. Likewise, also, on the special festivals they shall devote themselves to God and to the services of the Church, and shall refrain from secular assemblies.

19. Likewise, it has been pleasing to insert in these decrees that all infants shall be baptized

---

[1]The greater chapters concerned offenses that involved capital punishment; the lesser chapters dealt with noncapital offenses.

[2]The forty-day fast preceding Easter during which meat and many other foods were prohibited.

[3]A Greek term meaning "minister" or "administrator." A deacon ranked just below a priest and performed such functions as preaching and dispensing alms.

[4]The sacrament in which a person confesses sins to a priest and receives absolution and a penance.

[5]From this point on the capitulary deals with lesser chapters.

within a year; we have decreed this, that if any one shall have refused to bring his infant to baptism within the course of a year, without the advice or permission of the priest, if he is a noble he shall pay 120 *solidi*[6] to the treasury; if a freeman, 60; if a *litus,*[7] 30. . . .

21. If any one shall have made a vow at springs or trees or groves,[8] or shall have made an offering after the manner of the heathen and shall have partaken of a repast in honor of the demons, if he shall be a noble, 60 *solidi;* if a freeman, 30; if a *litus,* 15. If, indeed, they have not the means of paying at once, they shall be given into the service of the Church[9] until the *solidi* are paid.

22. We command that the bodies of Saxon Christians shall be carried to the church cemeteries, and not to the mounds of the pagans.

23. We have ordered that diviners and soothsayers shall be handed over to the churches and priests.

24. Concerning robbers and malefactors who shall have fled from one county to another, if any one shall receive them into his protection and shall keep them with him for seven nights, except for the purpose of bringing them to justice, let him pay our ban.[10] Likewise, if a count[11] shall have concealed them, and shall be unwilling to bring them forward so that Justice may be done,

and is not able to excuse himself for this, let him lose his office. . . .

34. We have forbidden that Saxons shall hold public assemblies in general, unless perchance our *missus*[12] shall have caused them to come together in accordance with our command; but each count shall hold judicial assemblies and administer justice in his jurisdiction. And this shall be cared for by the priests, lest it be done otherwise.[13]

A LETTER TO POPE LEO III

Charles, by the grace of God king of the Franks[14] and Lombards,[15] and patrician of the Romans,[16] to his holiness, Pope Leo, greeting. . . . Just as I entered into an agreement with the most holy father, your predecessor,[17] so also I desire to make with you an inviolable treaty of mutual fidelity and love; that, on the one hand, you shall pray for me and give me the apostolic benediction,[18] and that, on the other, with the aid of God I will ever defend the most holy seat[19] of the holy Roman Church. For it is our part to defend the holy Church of Christ from the attacks of pagans and infidels[20] from without, and within to enforce the acceptance of the Catholic faith. It is your part, most holy father, to aid us in the good fight by

---

[6]A weight, not a coin, a *solidus* (plural *solidi*) was 1/72 of a pound of gold.

[7]A *litus,* or *leet,* was someone whose class was midway between a free person and a slave.

[8]Places sacred to Saxon deities. Pagan Germans believed in the sacredness of nature and conducted all of their religious rites in the open air, having no enclosed temples.

[9]As indentured servants.

[10]The fine assessed by the king for breaking the peace or, in this case, harboring a fugitive criminal.

[11]Charles's local secular lords and representatives of his authority. Counties tended to be coterminous with episcopal dioceses, meaning that the local count and the local bishop were the two leading individuals of the region. Counts raised troops, made public Charles's capitularies, collected revenues, and kept the peace.

[12]A *missus* (plural *missi*) was a lay or an ecclesiastical lord who exercised a special commission to inquire into the activities of local counts, bishops, and monasteries. Often working in pairs of one layman and one churchman, they traveled to a region, examined the state of affairs in their assigned area, corrected minor irregularities, and reported major crimes and misdemeanors to the emperor.

[13]Priests, and here he probably means local bishops and abbots (heads of monasteries), had the responsibility of supervising local government, in order to assure that it was just and proper.

[14]In 768 Charles and his brother Carloman had divided the kingdom of the Franks between them upon the death of their father, King Pepin. When Carloman died in 771, Charles seized his deceased brother's half of the kingdom.

[15]In 774 Charles seized control of the Lombard Kingdom in northern and central Italy. The Lombards, a Germanic people, had invaded Italy in 568.

[16]A title bestowed on King Pepin and his sons Charles and Carloman by Pope Stephen II in 754.

[17]Pope Hadrian I (r. 772–795).

[18]The blessing of the pope, the *apostolic* successor of Saint Peter, prince of the apostles, whom each pope claims as his predecessor and the source of papal authority.

[19]The *see,* or church, where the pope resides — this is a metaphor for the papacy itself.

[20]The unfaithful who do not believe in the teachings of the Church.

raising your hands to God as Moses did,[21] so that by your intercession the Christian people under the leadership of God may always and everywhere have the victory over the enemies of His holy name, and the name of our Lord Jesus Christ may be glorified throughout the world. Abide by the canonical law[22] in all things and obey the precepts of the Holy Fathers always, that your life may be an example of sanctity to all, and your holy admonitions be observed by the whole world, and that your light may so shine before men that they may see your good works and glorify your father who is in Heaven.[23] May omnipotent God preserve your holiness unharmed through many years for the exalting of His holy Church.

---

[21]The Bible, Exodus 17:11.
[22]*Canon law* is the law of the Church; the word *canon* means "standard of measurement" in Greek.

[23]The Bible, Matthew 5:16.

▼▼▼

Byzantium and the West in the Age of Otto the Great

Internal weaknesses, irresistible tendencies toward the creation of regional power blocs, and multiple invasions by non-Christian outsiders — Vikings from the north, Hungarian horsemen from the east, and Saracen raiders from North Africa — precipitated the collapse of Carolingian unity during the later ninth century. We would be very mistaken, however, if we viewed the 800s and the two centuries that followed as an era of unmitigated disasters, unremitting invasions, universal political fragmentation, and total social dislocation. Between roughly 850 and 1050, Western Europe rose to the challenge of meeting its crises and emerged quite the stronger for it.

Ironically, the power that took the lead in this effort was Germany, led by its Saxon kings. The Saxons, whom Charles the Great had violently introduced to Christianity, became the new champions of Western Christendom and inheritors of the imperial crown.

Following the death of the king of Italy, Berengar I (r. 915–923), who enjoyed the title but not the authority of emperor, the imperial title died out in the West for lack of anyone strong enough to claim it. On February 2, 962, however, Pope John XII (r. 955–964) anointed the Saxon king of Germany, *Otto I* (r. 936–973), as emperor, thereby resurrecting the Western imperial office. Much like Charlemagne, upon whom he modeled himself, Otto was the most powerful monarch of his day in Western Europe and was remembered by posterity as worthy of the title "the Great," but unlike Charles the Great, Otto carved out an empire in Germany and Italy that lived on for centuries after his death.

Under Otto and his son and grandson, Otto II (r. 973–983) and Otto III (r. 983–1002), Germany pushed out the boundaries of Latin Christianity as it subjugated and colonized Slavic lands to its immediate east and converted its new subjects in the process. What is more, imperially sponsored missionaries ranged into Poland, Bohemia, Croatia, and Hungary — all of which officially accepted Latin forms of the Christian faith by the year 1000. Meanwhile, Anglo-Saxon England was taking the lead in the conversion of Scandinavia, especially Denmark and Norway.

At the same time that Western Europe was extending its cultural boundaries, Byzantium's missionaries were bringing Byzantine forms of Christian culture to the Bulgars, Serbs, and Rus' in the Balkans and Eastern Europe. By the year 1000 the Rus' of Kiev, a people of mixed Slavic and Scandinavian origin, had officially accepted the ecclesiastical leadership of the Church of Constantinople, and the foundations for the Russian and Ukrainian Orthodox Churches had been laid. Farther south in the Balkans, Latin Christian Croats lived alongside Byzantine Christian Serbs.

At times the Churches of Rome and Constantinople cooperated in these missionary ventures; at times they competed. This same ambivalent spirit of a shared Christianity tempered by a realization of their differences and competing claims is manifested in their religious art and diplomatic exchanges, as the following two sources indicate.

A Western Ambassador to Constantinople
▼▼▼

85 ▼ Liudprand of Cremona,
A REPORT ON THE EMBASSY
TO CONSTANTINOPLE

Liudprand (ca. 920–972) was born into one of wealthiest and most learned families of northern Italy, whose members had a long history of service to the kings of Italy. His father, for example, represented King Hugh of Arles at the imperial court of Constantinople in 927. Liudprand became a partisan of Otto I sometime before 960, and in return for that loyalty, Otto installed Liudprand as bishop of Cremona in 961. In 962 Pope John XII crowned Otto Western emperor, thus resurrecting the imperial title that had fallen into disuse in the West during the late ninth century.

In 968 Emperor Otto endeavored to lessen tensions with Byzantium, after an unsuccessful attack on Byzantine lands south of Rome, by arranging a marriage alliance between his son and heir, the future Otto II, and a Byzantine princess. His natural choice of ambassador to the court of Emperor Nicephorus II Phocas was Liudprand. Liudprand not only spoke and read Greek, he had already served as an ambassador to Constantinople for King Berengar II in 949 and possibly also visited Constantinople for Otto as recently as 960.

Liudprand had gained an appreciation for the imperial city and its people, as he showed in an early work of his, the *Antapodosis (Tit-for-Tat),* where he stated that

Constantinople's inhabitants surpassed all of their Eastern neighbors in wealth and wisdom. His experiences in 968–969 changed his opinion.

Liudprand's embassy was a failure, and what was worse, he felt insulted by the way he and other Westerners were treated by the Byzantines. Before leaving the city, Liudprand witnessed a tiff between the emperor and envoys from Pope John XIII. The envoys arrived in Constantinople bearing a papal letter addressed to the "emperor of the Greeks," and for that unintentional provocation, they were tossed into prison. Liudprand also had to endure the indignity of having precious purple cloth that he had secured and tried to carry back home confiscated by Byzantine authorities who deemed it wrong for foreigners to wear this imperial color. If we can believe Liudprand, he retorted that at home such garments were worn by prostitutes and magicians.

Following his return to the West, the bishop composed the *Report on the Embassy to Constantinople,* in which he vented his anger. When reading the excerpt that appears below, we should keep Liudprand's indignation in mind; he was not an objective reporter.

Despite his bitterness, Liudprand returned to Constantinople in 971 and was successful on that occasion, returning with the princess Theophano for young Otto.

Our excerpt from Liudprand's account of his misadventures in Byzantium begins with him sick and feeling quite mistreated by the emperor, with whom he has dined and exchanged insults (if we can believe the bishop had the courage to do so). In that mood, he writes to Nicephorus's brother from the lodgings to which he has been banished.

QUESTIONS FOR ANALYSIS

1. Emperor Otto I secured the deposition of two popes (John XII and Benedict V) and arranged the appointment of three other popes, including the current John XIII. Despite this close imperial control over the Roman papacy, how does Liudprand view and treat the papal office?
2. How do the Byzantines view the pope? Other churchmen?
3. Does Liudprand consider the Byzantines to be fellow Christians in communion with the West?
4. How do the Byzantines look upon the Western Church?
5. What was the real reason why the Bulgarian envoy was accorded more honor than Liudprand? (Hint: Locate the land of the Bulgars on a map.) What does your answer to this question suggest about cultural-political realities at this time?
6. What does the emperor imply by his remark concerning the synod of Saxony?
7. How does Liudprand answer these charges, and what does his answer imply?
8. What does this excerpt suggest about Western-Byzantine relations toward the end of the tenth century?

Weakened therefore by my own tribulations and those of my companions, I called in our warden, or rather my persecutor, and by prayers and bribes induced him to take the following letter to the emperor's brother:

> Bishop Liudprand to Leo, chancellor and marshal of the palace.
>
> If his serene highness the emperor intends to grant the request for which I came, then the sufferings I am now enduring shall not exhaust my patience; my master, however, must be informed by letter and messenger that my stay is not useless. On the other hand, if a refusal is contemplated, there is a Venetian merchantman in the harbor here just about to start. Let him permit me as a sick man to go on board, so that, if the time of my dissolution is at hand, my native land may at least receive my corpse.

Leo read my letter and gave me an audience four days later. In accordance with their rule, their wisest men, strong in Attic[1] eloquence sat with him to discuss your request, namely Basil the chief chamberlain, the chief secretary, the chief master of the wardrobe, and two other dignitaries. They began their discourse as follows: "Tell us, brother, the reason that induced you to take the trouble to come here." When I told them that it was on account of the marriage which was to be the ground for a lasting peace, they said: "It is unheard of that a daughter born in the purple of an emperor born in the purple[2] should contract a foreign marriage. Still, great as

is your demand, you shall have what you want, if you give what is proper: Ravenna,[3] namely, and Rome with all the adjoining territories from thence to our possessions. If you desire friendship without the marriage, let your master permit Rome to be free,[4] and hand over to their former lord[5] the princes of Capua and Benevento,[6] who were formerly slaves of our holy empire and are now rebels."

To this I answered: "Even you cannot but know that my master rules over Slavonian princes[7] who are more powerful than Peter, king of the Bulgarians, who has married the daughter of the emperor Christopher."[8] "Ah," said they, "but Christopher was not born in the purple."[9]

"As for Rome," I went on, "for whose freedom you are so noisily eager; who is her master? To whom does she pay tribute? Was she not formerly enslaved to harlots? And while you were sleeping, nay powerless, did not my master the august emperor free her from that foul servitude?[10] Constantine, the august emperor who founded this city and called it after his name, as ruler of the world made many offerings to the holy Roman apostolic Church, not only in Italy but in almost all the western kingdoms, as well as those in the east and south, in Greece, Judaea, Persia, Mesopotamia, Babylonia, Egypt, Libya, as his own special regulations testify that are preserved in our country. In Italy, in Saxony, in Bavaria, and in all my master's realms, everything that belongs to the Church of the blessed apostles has been handed over to the vicar of those holy apostles.[11] And if my master has kept back a single city,

---

[1]Athenian Greek — the purest form of classical Greek.

[2]The daughter of an emperor (born in the purple, the imperial color), who himself was born the son of a reigning emperor.

[3]A city in northeastern Italy that had been the seat of Byzantine power in Italy until it was captured by the Lombards (Liudprand's ancestors) in the eighth century.

[4]From Otto's control.

[5]Emperor Nicephorus.

[6]Lordships in south central Italy.

[7]In the northern Balkan region, where both empires also clashed.

[8]In 927 King Peter (r. 927–969) married Maria, daughter of Christopher, the eldest son and crowned coemperor of Romanus I (r. 920–944). Christopher died in 931 before he could assume the imperial throne on his own.

[9]When Christopher was born, his father, Romanus, was not a member of the imperial family. Romanus I rose from humble origins and achieved the throne by virtue of his military and diplomatic abilities and the marriage of his daughter, Helena, to the young emperor Constantine VII (r. 913–959). In 920 Romanus was crowned coemperor, and he dominated his son-in-law until his death in 944.

[10]According to the Ottonian vision of history, Rome had been under the control of immoral men and women, including the evil Pope John XII, until Otto I liberated the city and the papacy from this scourge.

[11]The pope is the vicar, or deputy, of Saint Peter, prince of the apostles.

farm, vassal or slave, then I have denied God. Why does not your emperor do the same? Why does he not restore to the apostolic Church what lies in his kingdoms and thereby himself increase the richness and freedom that it already owes to my master's exertions and generosity?"

"He will do so," said the chief chamberlain Basil, "when Rome and the Roman Church shall be so ordered as he wishes." Then said I: "A certain man having suffered much injury from another, approached God with these words: 'Lord, avenge me upon my adversary.' To whom the Lord said: 'I will do so on the day when I shall render to each man according to his works.' 'How late that day will be!' the man replied."

At that everyone except the emperor's brother burst into laughter. Then they broke off the discussion and ordered me to be taken back to my detestable dwelling place and to be carefully guarded until the day of the apostles, a feast that all religious persons duly observe.[12] At the ceremony the emperor commanded me, though I was very ill at the time, together with the Bulgarian envoys who had arrived the day before, to meet him at the Church of the Holy Apostles.[13] After some verbose chants had been sung and mass celebrated, we were invited to table, where I found placed above me on my side of the long narrow board the Bulgarian envoy. He was a fellow with his hair cut in the Hungarian[14] fashion, girt about with a brazen chain and, as I fancy, just admitted into the Christian faith. The preference given to him over me was plainly meant as an insult to you, my august masters.[15] On your account I was despised, rejected, and scorned. I thank the Lord Jesus Christ, whom you serve with all your heart, that I have been considered worthy to suffer insults for your sake. However, my masters, I considered that the insult was done to you, not to me, and I therefore left the table. I

was just going indignantly away when Leo, the emperor's brother and marshal of the court, and Simeon, the chief secretary, came after me, howling: "When Peter, king of the Bulgarians, married Christopher's daughter, a mutual agreement was sworn to on both sides to the effect that envoys of the Bulgarians should with us be preferred, honored, and esteemed above the envoys of all other nations. What you say is true: the Bulgarian envoy over there has his hair cut short, he has not washed himself, and his girdle consists of a brass chain. But nevertheless he is a patrician, and we are definitely of the opinion that it would be wrong to give a bishop, especially a Frankish[16] bishop, preference over him. We have noticed your show of indignation, and we are not going to allow you to return to your lodgings, as you suppose; we shall force you to take food with the emperor's servants in an inn."

My mental anguish was so unparalleled that I could not answer them back but did what they ordered, judging that table no fit place for me, seeing that a Bulgarian envoy was preferred, I will not say to myself personally, that is, to Bishop Liudprand, but to your representative. But my indignation was appeased by a handsome present! The sacred emperor sent me one of his most delicate dishes, a fat goat, of which he himself had partaken, richly stuffed with garlic, onion, and leeks and swimming in fish sauce. I wish, sires, that you could have had it on your table. The sight of it, I am sure, would have banished any incredulity you have felt concerning the sacred emperor's luxurious ways.

When eight days had passed and the Bulgarians had left the city, Nicephorus, thinking that I esteemed his table highly, compelled me, in spite of my ill health, to dine with him again in the same place. The patriarch[17] with several other bishops was present, and before them he pro-

---

[12]One of the many holy days shared by the Churches of Constantinople and Rome.
[13]The Church of the Holy Apostles was one of the city's grandest structures and served as the model for many Byzantine-style churches in the East and the West (e.g., San Marco in Venice and Saint Basil's Cathedral in Moscow).
[14]The Hungarians, whom Otto I had crushed in battle in 955, were still considered barbaric pagans. Their leader,

Duke Vajik (renamed Stephen upon his conversion), accepted Latin Christianity and was crowned as their first king on Christmas Day 1000 with a crown sent him by Pope Sylvester II (r. 999–1003).
[15]Otto I and his son.
[16]All Westerners were *Franks* to the Byzantines.
[17]Polyeuctus, patriarch of Constantinople (r. 956–970), was the chief bishop of the Byzantine Church.

pounded to me many questions concerning the Holy Scriptures, which, under the inspiration of the Holy Spirit, I elegantly answered. Finally, wishing to make merry of you, he asked which synods[18] we recognized. Those of Nicaea, Chalcedon, Ephesus, Carthage, Antioch, Ancyra, and Constantinople,[19] I replied. "Ha, ha," he said, "you have forgotten to mention Saxony.[20] If you ask me, the reason why our books do not mention it either is that the Christian faith there is too young. . . ."[21]

I answered: "On that member of the body where the malady has its seat a cautery must be used. All the heresies[22] have emanated from you and among you have flourished; by our Western peoples they have been either strangled or killed. Synods have often been held at Rome or Pavia,[23] but I do not count them here. It was a Roman cleric, he whom you call Dialogus, who afterwards became the universal Pope Gregory,[24] who freed the heretic Eutychius, patriarch of Constantinople, from his error.[25] Eutychius said, and not only said but in his teachings, sermons, and writings proclaimed, that at the Resurrection[26] we should put on not the real flesh that we have

here but a certain fantastic substance of his own imagination.[27] The book that set forth this heresy was burned in the interests of orthodoxy by Gregory. Moreover, Ennodius, bishop of Pavia, was sent here, that is, to Constantinople, by the patriarch of Rome[28] to deal with a certain other heresy, which he repressed, and he restored the orthodox catholic doctrine.[29] As for the Saxon people, ever since they received holy baptism and the knowledge of God, they have not been stained by any heresy which rendered a synod necessary for its correction; of heresies we have had none. You declare that our Saxon faith is young, and I agree. Faith in Christ is always young and not old among people whose faith is seconded by works. Here faith is old, not young; works do not accompany it, and by reason of its age it is held in light esteem like a worn-out garment. I know for certain of one synod held in Saxony where it was enacted and decreed that it was more seemly to fight with the sword than with the pen, and better to face death than to fly before a foe. Your own army is finding that out now." And in my own mind I said: "May it soon find out by experience how warlike our men are."

---

[18]Councils of the Church's leaders at which orthodox church doctrine was defined under the inspiration of the Holy Spirit.

[19]With the exception of Carthage in western North Africa, all of these major councils were held in the East.

[20]Saxony, the northern German homeland of Emperor Otto I, was never the site of a major church council.

[21]As we saw in source 84, Christianity came to Saxony around the year 800 with the conquering armies of Charlemagne.

[22]Heresy is false religious doctrine.

[23]Pavia was Liudprand's native city.

[24]Pope Saint Gregory I the Great (r. 590–604). Liudprand possibly refers to Gregory as "universal pope" because during Gregory's pontificate the patriarch of Constantinople, John IV the Faster, began the practice of referring to himself

as "ecumenical (universal) patriarch," and Gregory took exception with this novelty. The term stuck, however, and became part of the normal patriarchal title.

[25]Patriarch Eutychius (r. 552–565 and 577–582) is venerated as a saint by the Eastern Orthodox Church. His confrontation with Gregory took place while Gregory served as papal emissary to Constantinople in the years 579–586.

[26]The Resurrection of everyone at the End of Time and the Final Judgment.

[27]Because Eutychius's book is lost, we do not know exactly what he taught.

[28]The pope is also the patriarch of Rome.

[29]Saint Ennodius's two missions to Constantinople in 515 and 517 failed to resolve the so-called Acacian Schism (484–519).

Two Representations of the Virgin
▼▼▼

86 ▾ *A BYZANTINE ICON OF THE KOIMESIS and A DORMITION MINIATURE*

By the year 1000 Eastern and Western Christians disagreed over a number of issues, but they equally regarded Mary, the mother of Jesus, as the most lovable and
loving of all God's saints. Both Byzantine and Latin Christians revered Mary as the
fully human yet sinless Mother of God who served as advocate for all humanity before her Son's throne.

The cult of Mary resulted in a massive volume of religious artwork in East and
West centering on the Virgin Mother. One of the more popular themes, which originated in Byzantium (possibly influenced by somewhat similar representations of
the Buddha's *parinirvana,* or passing into Nirvana at death) was the "Falling
Asleep" of Mary, known in Greek as the *Koimesis.* According to a tradition equally
accepted in the East and the West, when Mary died, her incorruptible body was assumed into Heaven. With body and soul reunited, she was crowned Queen of
Heaven. In the West, the same moment in sacred history was referred to as the
Dormition. By whichever name they knew it, both Byzantines and Western Christians celebrated the feast day of that event as one of the most holy days in the religious calendar.

Illustrated below are two images of the *Falling Asleep.* The first is a carved icon,
or sacred image, from Byzantium, dating from the second half of the tenth century. Here we see the sleeping Virgin, who could not die because she was sinless. She
is surrounded by mourning apostles and disciples, including Mary Magdalene (in
the far left corner covering her lower face with a veil). Saint Paul stands at the foot
of her bed and Saint Peter is at the head, incensing her body. Her son, Jesus, has
taken her soul in his hands, and two angels prepare to receive it into Heaven. Our
second illustration is a miniature (a small manuscript painting) from the German
monastery at Reichenau. This work, which dates to around the year 1000, varies
somewhat from the Byzantine icon. Saint Paul is still at the foot of the bed, but
Saint Peter has been replaced at the head of the bed to stand just behind the beardless Saint John, to whom Jesus commended the care of his mother as he was dying
on the cross. (In the Byzantine icon John is half hidden behind Peter's censer and
has his hand on the Virgin's bed.)

As you study these two masterpieces, see if you can find any iconographical and
artistic connections between them.

QUESTIONS FOR ANALYSIS

1. List all of the similarities and dissimilarities between these two works of art.
2. The artistic motif of the Virgin's Falling Asleep originated in the East, where
   popular veneration of Mary was deep and widespread. What do the similarities in these two works of art suggest to you?

3. Discuss the dissimilarities. Do they suggest anything about differences between these two Christian cultures?
4. Which seem to you the more significant, the similarities or dissimilarities? Why? Be specific in your answer.

A Byzantine Icon of the Koimesis

A Dormition Miniature

▼▼▼

Byzantium and the West in the Age of the Crusades: The Dividing of Christendom

Many history textbooks continue to perpetuate the myth that the Churches of Constantinople and Rome entered into clear and permanent *schism,* or separation, in 1054 when the patriarch of Constantinople and representatives of the pope hurled mutual curses of damnation and excommunication at one another's Church. In fact, nothing of the sort happened. It is true that, following a heated argument, several papal envoys laid a sentence of excommunication on the patriarch and his supporters. But they did so on their own initiative, and their attack was largely aimed at one man — Patriarch Michael Cerularius. It is also true that Byzantine church officials responded in kind by excommunicating the offending Western churchmen. But the Byzantine Church officially refused to believe that the legates were true representatives of the pope or the Western Church. The point is that this celebrated incident of 1054 was not the *cause* of a visible rift between these two branches of Christendom. It was, however, one of many *symptoms* of a growing alienation between the two Christian cultures.

The factors that led to the division between the Churches of Catholic Rome and Orthodox Constantinople were rooted in centuries of political separation and cultural estrangement. The process began as early as the fourth century and accelerated as time went on. Not until the latter half of the eleventh century, however, when the papacy promoted an agenda of transforming Christian society under papal leadership, did the differences between the Byzantine and Western visions of the world and the Church begin to become apparent.

One expression of the new papal self-confidence was its attempt to marshal the military vigor of the West in a series of holy wars known as the *crusades.* As early as 1074, news of Seljuk Turkish victories over Byzantine forces moved Pope Gregory VII to propose publicly that he lead an army of 50,000 volunteers to rescue these Christian siblings in the East. The Investiture Controversy prevented him from realizing this dream, but the papacy never forgot the project. His successor once-removed, Pope Urban II, responded to overtures from Emperor Alexius I for help in raising troops for the Byzantine army by calling upon the warrior class of the West, and especially of the pope's own French homeland, to march eastward to rescue their fellow Christians from Islam and to liberate Jerusalem from the infidel. The pope's appeal, which he enunciated for the first time on November 27, 1095, provided the impetus for the First Crusade (1096–1101).

By transforming this simple request from Emperor Alexius for assistance in raising mercenary soldiers for the imperial army into a call for a mass expedition of holy warriors, Pope Urban unleashed the vigor of emerging Europe upon an unsuspecting Eastern Mediterranean World.

An Appeal to Christian Charity
▼▼▼

87 ▼ Baldric of Dol, *THE JERUSALEM HISTORY*

The crusades had many underlying causes but only one parent: Pope Urban II. Western Christians had been fighting Muslims off and on since the eighth century, and in the eleventh century two fronts, Spain and Sicily, became quite hot. In Spain, Christian forces, with papal encouragement, had been battling Almoravids from Morocco since late 1086 in one of the early rounds of the *Reconquista,* or Christian reconquest of the Iberian Peninsula — a war that did not end until 1492. In a series of papally supported campaigns that began in 1061 and ended in 1091, Norman French forces conquered Sicily, an island that had been under Muslim domination since 948. In a sense, therefore, Urban II's call for a crusade to Jerusalem in 1095 was simply one more stage in a papal program of counterattack against Islam. And yet, Urban set into motion something quite new — a phenomenon that would leave a lasting imprint on the culture of Western Civilization and deeply affect the civilizations of Islam and Byzantium.

A *crusade* is a holy war, but a special sort of holy war. The term means "to bear a cross." In its most basic sense, a crusade is a papally sanctioned war fought against an enemy of the Church by persons — crusaders — who have sworn sacred vows to carry out this mission and who wear the sign of the cross as a symbol of their commitment. By virtue of their vow and sacrifice, they are promised spiritual rewards and are accorded a special protected status by the Church. Very much like the Islamic jihad, the crusade is seen as a positive spiritual act that brings with it the promise of salvation for those who fight with the right intention and purity of heart against a perceived evil.

What began as an idealistic call for warriors to fight an enemy of Christendom in the Holy Land soon grew into institutionalized holy war fought on many fronts over many centuries. The Spanish *Reconquista* soon received crusade status, as did wars of conquest against various pagan (and later Christian) peoples in the Baltic. By the early thirteenth century the papacy was also calling crusades against heretics in southern France and against political enemies in Italy and Germany. So far as crusades against Islam were concerned, the beat went on and on. Although Jerusalem was securely back in Muslim hands in 1244 and all four crusader states in the East were lost to Islam by 1291 (source 76), Western Christian Europe continued to launch crusades against Muslim foes well into the late seventeenth century. Arguably, the crusading spirit also drove the Spanish *conquistadors* in the Americas. What is more, the ideal of the crusade — the use of sanctified violence to combat evil — has remained an integral part of the Western mindset down to today.

Space precludes our tracing the long, convoluted history of the crusades, but in this and the following two sources we can see how the crusades affected relations between the Latin West and the Byzantine East.

Our first document comes from the pen of Baldric of Dol, abbot of the monastery of Saint-Pierre-de-Bourgueil (1089–1107) and elected archbishop of Dol in Brittany in 1107. Baldric had been at the Council of Clermont in 1095 when

Pope Urban called for the liberation of Jerusalem. In his history of the First Crusade, which he composed around 1108, Baldric presents his version of Pope Urban's sermon.

We do not have a transcript of that sermon. Rather, we have five versions contained in histories of the First Crusade, most composed by eyewitnesses and all set down at least several years after the event. Although they contain some similarities, their differences are striking. And this should not surprise us. The authors were not attempting to give accurate, word-for-word reports of what the pope had said. They felt free to exercise their own rhetorical skills in crafting their versions of the pope's sermon, and each emphasized those aspects of the speech that most captivated or interested him. Clearly, all of the authors were influenced by the crusade's success and wrote from a postcrusade perspective. This surely influenced how they remembered Urban's speech. Moreover, as was the case with Baldric and at least one other churchman, several of the reporters tried to place the crusade sermon into a theological context. Nevertheless, despite the fact that we will never know exactly what Urban II said that day, it does seem clear that Baldric and the other four reporters did a pretty good job, individually and collectively, in conveying many of the major points that the pope made in one of the most significant speeches in world history.

QUESTIONS FOR ANALYSIS

1. According to Baldric's account of the speech, why did Pope Urban II call for this expedition?
2. How does he portray Eastern Christians?
3. What appeals does he use to attract knights to this cause?

"We have heard, most beloved brethren, and you have heard what we cannot recount without deep sorrow — how, with great hurt and dire sufferings our Christian brothers, members in Christ, are scourged, oppressed, and injured in Jerusalem, in Antioch,[1] and the other cities of the East. Your own blood-brothers, your companions, your associates (for you are sons of the same Christ and the same Church) are either subjected in their inherited homes to other masters, or are driven from them, or they come as beggars among us; or, which is far worse, they are flogged and exiled as slaves for sale in their own land. Christian blood, redeemed by the blood of Christ, has been shed, and Christian flesh, akin to the flesh of Christ, has been subjected to unspeakable degradation and servitude. Everywhere in those cities there is sorrow, everywhere misery, everywhere groaning (I say it with a sigh). The churches in which divine mysteries were celebrated in olden times are now, to our sorrow, used as stables for the animals of these people! Holy men do not possess those cities; nay, base and bastard Turks hold sway over our brothers. The blessed Peter first presided as bishop at Antioch;[2] behold, in his own church the Gentiles[3] have established their superstitions, and the Christian religion, which they ought rather to

---

[1] The major city of northern Syria, it had been captured by Muslims in 638 but recovered by Byzantine forces in 969. In 1084 it was lost to the Seljuk Turks. Most of its population was Byzantine Christian.

[2] According to tradition, Peter, prince of the apostles, had been initially bishop of Antioch before moving to Rome.
[3] Muslim Turks.

cherish, they have basely shut out from the hall dedicated to God! The estates given for the support of the saints and the patrimony of nobles set aside for the sustenance of the poor are subject to pagan tyranny, while cruel masters abuse for their own purposes the returns from these lands. The priesthood of God has been ground down into the dust. The sanctuary of God (unspeakable shame!) is everywhere profaned. Whatever Christians still remain in hiding there are sought out with unheard of tortures.

"Of holy Jerusalem, brethren, we dare not speak, for we are exceedingly afraid and ashamed to speak of it. This very city, in which, as you all know, Christ Himself suffered for us, because our sins demanded it, has been reduced to the pollution of paganism and, I say it to our disgrace, withdrawn from the service of God. Such is the heap of reproach upon us who have so much deserved it! Who now serves the church of the Blessed Mary in the valley of Josaphat, in which church she herself was buried in body?[4] But why do we pass over the Temple of Solomon,[5] nay of the Lord, in which the barbarous nations placed their idols[6] contrary to law, human and divine? Of the Lord's Sepulcher[7] we have refrained from speaking, since some of you with your own eyes have seen to what abominations it has been given over. The Turks violently took from it the offerings which you brought there for alms in such vast amounts, and, in addition, they scoffed much and often at your religion. And yet in that place (I say only what you already know) rested the Lord; there He died for us; there He was buried. How precious would be the longed-for, incomparable place of the Lord's burial, even if God failed there to perform the yearly miracle! For in the days of His Passion all the lights in the Sepulcher and round about in the church, which

have been extinguished, are relighted by divine command.[8] Whose heart is so stony, brethren, that it is not touched by so great a miracle? Believe me, that man is bestial and senseless whose heart such divinely manifest grace does not move to faith! And yet the Gentiles see this in common with the Christians and are not turned from their ways! They are, indeed, afraid, but they are not converted to the faith; nor is it to be wondered at, for a blindness of mind rules over them. With what afflictions they wronged you who have returned and are now present, you yourselves know too well, you who there sacrificed your substance and your blood for God.

"This, beloved brethren, we shall say, that we may have you as witness of our words. More suffering of our brethren and devastation of churches remains than we can speak of one by one, for we are oppressed by tears and groans, sighs and sobs. We weep and wail, brethren, alas, like the Psalmist, in our inmost heart! We are wretched and unhappy, and in us is that prophecy fulfilled: 'God, the nations are come into thine inheritance; thy holy temple have they defiled; they have laid Jerusalem in heaps; the dead bodies of thy servants have been given to be food for the birds of the heaven, the flesh of thy saints unto the beasts of the Earth. Their blood have they shed like water round about Jerusalem, and there was none to bury them.' Woe unto us, brethren! We who have already become a reproach to our neighbors, a scoffing, and derision to them round about us, let us at least with tears condone and have compassion upon our brothers! We who have become the scorn of all peoples, and worse than all, let us bewail the most monstrous devastation of the Holy Land! This land we have deservedly called holy in which there is not even a foot-step that the body or spirit of the Savior did

---

[4]The Church of Mary, believed to be the site where her body was laid before her Assumption into Heaven (source 86), lies just outside the walls of Jerusalem.

[5]The site of the Mosque of al-Aqsa (source 57).

[6]The misperception that Muslims are idol worshipers was rampant in the West at this time.

[7]The empty tomb of Jesus. Christendom's holiest site, it lies within the Church of the Holy Sepulcher in Jerusalem.

[8]This is a presumed miraculous ceremony that is still conducted annually by a combined group of Greek, Armenian, and Syrian Christian church leaders. On Holy Saturday afternoon a Holy Fire is believed to miraculously burst forth from within the *edicule,* the small domed shrine that houses the tomb of Jesus. The flames are then passed around to the faithful so that the entire Church of the Holy Sepulcher is illuminated.

not render glorious and blessed; which embraced the holy presence of the mother of God, and the meetings of the apostles, and drank up the blood of the martyrs shed there. How blessed are the stones which crowned you, Stephen, the first martyr! How happy, O, John the Baptist, the waters of the Jordan which served you in baptizing the Savior! The children of Israel, who were led out of Egypt, and who prefigured you in the crossing of the Red Sea, have taken that land by their arms, with Jesus[9] as leader; they have driven out the Jebusites[10] and other inhabitants and have themselves inhabited earthly Jerusalem, the image of celestial Jerusalem.[11]

"What are we saying? Listen and learn! You, girt about with the badge of knighthood, are arrogant with great pride; you rage against your brothers and cut each other in pieces. This is not the [true] soldiery of Christ which rends asunder the sheep-fold of the Redeemer. The Holy Church has reserved a soldiery for herself to help her people, but you debase her wickedly to her hurt. Let us confess the truth, whose heralds we ought to be; truly, you are not holding to the way which leads to life. You, the oppressers of childen, plunderers of widows; you, guilty of homicide, of sacrilege, robbers of another's rights; you who await the pay of thieves for the shedding of Christian blood — as vultures smell fetid corpses, so do you sense battles from afar and rush to them eagerly. Truly, this is the worst way, for it is utterly removed from God! If you wish to be mindful of your souls, either lay down the belt of such knighthood, or advance boldly, as knights of Christ, and rush as quickly as you can to the defense of the Eastern Church. For she it is from whom the joys of your whole salvation have come forth, who poured into your mouths the milk of divine wisdom, who set before you the holy teachings of the Gospels.[12] We say this, brethren, that you may restrain your murderous

hands from the destruction of your brothers, and in behalf of your relatives in the faith oppose yourselves to the Gentiles. Under Jesus Christ, our Leader, may you struggle for your Jerusalem, in Christian battle-line, most invincible line, even more successfully than did the sons of Jacob[13] of old — struggle, that you may assail and drive out the Turks, more execrable than the Jebusites, who are in this land, and may you deem it a beautiful thing to die for Christ in that city in which He died for us. But if it befall you to die this side of it, be sure that to have died on the way is of equal value, if Christ shall find you in His army. God pays with the same coin, whether at the first or eleventh hour.[14] You should shudder, brethren, you should shudder at raising a violent hand against Christians; it is less wicked to brandish your sword against Saracens. It is the only warfare that is righteous, for it is charity to risk your life for your brothers. That you may not be troubled about the concerns of tomorrow, know that those who fear God want nothing, nor those who cherish Him in truth. The possessions of the enemy, too, will be yours, since you will make spoil of their treasures and return victorious to your own; or empurpled with your own blood, you will have gained everlasting glory. For such a Commander you ought to fight, for One who lacks neither might nor wealth with which to reward you. Short is the way, little the labor, which, nevertheless, will repay you with the crown that fadeth not away. Accordingly, we speak with the authority of the prophet: 'Gird thy sword upon thy thigh, O mighty one.' Gird yourselves, everyone of you, I say, and be valiant sons; for it is better for you to die in battle than to behold the sorrows of your race and of your holy places. Let neither property nor the alluring charms of your wives entice you from going; nor let the trials that are to be borne so deter you that you remain here."

---

[9]Joshua, who led the Israelites across the Jordan and into Canaan after Moses' death (source 13). Jesus is the Greek version of the name Joshua, and the medieval Church saw Joshua as a prefiguration of Jesus the Savior, who led humanity to salvation.

[10]One of several groups of people living in Canaan when the Israelites invaded.

[11]Earthly Jerusalem prefigures the Heavenly Jerusalem.

[12]Christianity was born in the East.

[13]The Israelites.

[14]A reference to Jesus' parable of the workers in the vineyard: Matthew 20:1–16.

The West and the First Crusade
from a Byzantine Perspective

▼▼▼

88 ▼ *Anna Comnena, THE ALEXIAD*

The response to Pope Urban II's idealistic appeal was astounding. Between 1096 and 1101 three major waves of crusaders left Europe for the Holy Land; altogether, maybe as many as 130,000 men, women, and children participated, of whom probably only about 10 percent were professional warriors. Urban set in motion a phenomenon that was to engage much of Europe's energy for the next several centuries and would touch all levels of European society. What is more, the crusades would have a profound impact on the immediate and long-range histories of Islam, Byzantium, and, ultimately, the world. Arguably, their effects are still being felt today.

The following document, which reflects a twelfth-century Byzantine view of Western Europe and its crusaders, comes from the pen of Anna Comnena (1083– after 1148), daughter of Emperor Alexius I (r. 1081–1118). Anna, who had received an extensive education in classical Greek literature and thought, undertook to write the history of her father's eventful reign following the death of her husband in 1137. The fact that she entitled the work the *Alexiad,* in imitation of Homer's epic poem the *Iliad,* clearly indicates the view she held of her father's place in history. Anna's protestations of historical objectivity notwithstanding, this is partisan history, but its very partisanship allows us to see the world through Byzantine eyes.

In the first selection Anna comments on the *Investiture Controversy,* a struggle that provided the domestic background to the First Crusade. Waged from 1075 to 1122 between two successive emperors, Henry IV and Henry V, and a reformed and revitalized papacy that claimed unique authority within and over Christendom because it had inherited the full powers of Saint Peter, the controversy centered on one issue: Who, pope or emperor, is the supreme, God-anointed head of Christendom on Earth? In 1122 the exhausted parties entered into a peace treaty known as the *Concordat of Worms,* which settled some peripheral issues but did not resolve the core ideological disagreement. Popes and emperors and popes and kings would continue to wrestle with this question for several more centuries, and out of that controversy Western European political thinkers slowly and hesitantly evolved a radical idea: There are two separate spheres of authority, each with its own legitimate interests and powers. But that was in the future. Although it was much more than just an instance of papal muscle flexing, on one important level Urban's call for the First Crusade was an assertion of papal moral supremacy over Emperor Henry IV (r. 1056–1106), with whom the pope was locked in ideological battle.

The second selection deals with the arrival on Byzantine soil in 1096 of the lead elements of the First Crusade.

Anna's history contained more than just a few errors, misconceptions, and polemical diatribes whenever she wrote about the West and Westerners, but these very flaws add to its worth, inasmuch as they reveal how at least one high-born Byzantine viewed the papacy and the West in the first half of the twelfth century.

QUESTIONS FOR ANALYSIS

1. What does Anna Comnena think of Pope Gregory VII's actions in the Investiture Controversy?
2. What does she think of the Roman papacy's claims?
3. To her mind, who is the Church's chief priest, and what is the source of his authority?
4. What was Princess Anna's view of the Western crusaders?
5. Despite Urban II's hopes and idealism, the Age of the Crusades witnessed a growing estrangement between the societies of Western Europe and Byzantium. Judging from Anna's account, what do you think contributed to that rift?

THE INVESTITURE CONTROVERSY

Meanwhile, an event occurred which is worth relating, as it, too, contributed to this man's [Emperor Alexius] reputation and good fortune. . . . Now it happened that the pope of Rome[1] had a difference with Henry, king of Germany.[2] . . . The pope is a very high dignitary, and is protected by troops of various nationalities. The dispute between the king and the pope was this: the latter accused Henry of not bestowing livings[3] as free gifts, but selling them for money,[4] and occasionally entrusting archbishoprics to unworthy recipients,[5] and he also brought further charges of a similar nature against him. The king of Germany on his side indicted the pope of usurpation, as he had seized the apostolic chair without his consent.[6] Moreover, he had the effrontery to utter reckless threats against the pope, saying that if he did not resign his self-elected office, he should be expelled from it. . . . When these words reached the pope's ears, he vented his rage upon Henry's ambassadors;[7] first he tortured them inhumanly,

then clipped their hair with scissors, and sheared their beards with a razor, and finally committed a most indecent outrage upon them, which transcended even the insolence of barbarians, and so sent them away. My womanly and princely dignity forbids my naming the outrage inflicted on them, for it was not only unworthy of a high priest, but of anyone who bears the name of a Christian. I abhor this barbarian's idea, and more still the deed, and I should have defiled both my pen and my paper had I described it explicitly.[8] But as a display of barbaric insolence, and a proof that time in its flow produces men with shameless morals, ripe for any wickedness, this alone will suffice, if I say, that I could not bear to disclose or relate even the tiniest word about what he did. And this was the work of a high priest. Oh, justice! The deed of the supreme high priest! nay, of one who claimed to be the president of the whole world, as indeed the Latins assert and believe, but this, too, is a bit of their boasting. For when the imperial seat was transferred from Rome hither to our native Queen of Cities, and

---

[1]Pope Gregory VII (r. 1073–1085).

[2]Henry IV. As king of Germany, Henry was also emperor-elect of the Western Roman Empire.

[3]A *living,* also known as a *prebend,* was the income a cleric received to support him in his clerical office and duties.

[4]The papacy claimed that lay rulers, such as Henry, were guilty of the sin of *simony* — the selling of sacred clerical offices and other holy items.

[5]According to the papal reformers, this was another abuse of

the system known as *lay investiture,* and some radical reformers, such as Gregory VII, called upon pious lay people to throw out unworthy clerics who had been invested in their offices by lay rulers.

[6]By tradition, the pope-elect applied for imperial approval of his election.

[7]There is no evidence for the abuse that she recounts in the account that follows.

[8]Anna seems to imply that Gregory had the envoys castrated.

the senate, and the whole administration, there was also transferred the arch-hieratical primacy.[9] And the emperors from the very beginning have given the supreme right to the episcopacy[10] of Constantinople, and the Council of Chalcedon emphatically raised the bishop of Constantinople to the highest position, and placed all the dioceses of the inhabited world under his jurisdiction.[11] There can be no doubt that the insult done to the ambassadors was aimed at the king who sent them; not only because he scourged them, but also because he was the first to invent this new kind of outrage. For by his actions, the pope suggested, I think, that the power of the king was despicable, and by this horrible outrage on his ambassadors that he, a demi-god, as it were, was treating with a demi-ass! The pope consequently, by wreaking his insolence on the ambassadors, and sending them back to the king in the state I have mentioned, provoked a very great war.

THE ARRIVAL OF THE FRANKS

Before he[12] had enjoyed even a short rest, he heard a report of the approach of innumerable Frankish[13] armies. Now he dreaded their arrival for he knew their irresistible manner of attack, their unstable and mobile character and all the peculiar natural and concomitant characteristics which the Frank retains throughout; and he also knew that they were always agape for money, and seemed to disregard their truces readily for any reason that cropped up. For he had always heard

this reported of them, and found it very true. However, he did not lose heart, but prepared himself in every way so that, when the occasion called, he would be ready for battle. And indeed the actual facts were far greater and more terrible than rumor made them. For the whole of the West and all the barbarian tribes which dwell between the further side of the Adriatic and the pillars of Heracles,[14] had all migrated in a body and were marching into Asia through the intervening Europe, and were making the journey with all their household. . . . And they were all so zealous and eager that every highroad was full of them. And those Frankish soldiers were accompanied by an unarmed host more numerous than the sand or the stars, carrying palms and crosses on their shoulders; women and children, too, came away from their countries.[15] And the sight of them was like many rivers streaming from all sides, and they were advancing towards us through Dacia[16] generally with all their hosts.

The incidents of the barbarians' approach followed in the order I have described, and persons of intelligence could feel that they were witnessing a strange occurrence. The arrival of these multitudes did not take place at the same time nor by the same road (for how indeed could such masses starting from different places have crossed the straits of Lombardy all together?). Some first, some next, others after them and thus successively all accomplished the transit, and then marched through the continent. Each army was preceded, as we said, by an unspeakable number of locusts; and all who saw this more than once recognized them as forerunners of the Frankish armies.

---

[9]Chief *patriarch* of the universal Church (see note 10).

[10]Another term for *bishopric.* A *bishop* was the chief priest of a city or large town and its surrounding lands. An *archbishop* was the bishop of a major city and exercised authority over a number of subordinate, or suffragan, bishops. A *patriarch* was the bishop of such an exceptionally important city that he claimed authority over vast areas and a large number of subordinate archbishops and bishops. The question was: Who was the chief patriarch of the Church — the bishop of Rome or the bishop of Constantinople?

[11]Wrong. The Ecumenical Council of Chalcedon of 451

stipulated in canon (regulation) 28 that the bishop of Constantinople enjoyed a primacy of honor second only to that of the bishop of Rome because Constantinople was the *New Rome.*

[12]Emperor Alexius.

[13]*Frank* was a term used in the eastern Mediterranean to refer to any Westerner (see source 76).

[14]The Strait of Gibraltar.

[15]This, the first wave of the crusade, was the so-called (and misnamed) *Peasants' Crusade of 1096.*

[16]Hungary and Romania.

The Fourth Crusade from a Byzantine Perspective
▼▼▼

89 ▼ Nicetas Choniates, ANNALS

As Anna Comnena's account suggests, from the Byzantine perspective, the crusades were nothing less than barbarian invasions from the West. Before the First Crusade ended, Latin and Greek Christians had already clashed on the field of battle, although these initial skirmishes were not terribly serious (except to the people who died in them). During the twelfth century, as Latin fortunes suffered a number of reverses in the Holy Land, two additional major crusades were sent eastward: the Second Crusade (1147–1149) and the Third Crusade (1189–1192). Each further exacerbated Latin-Byzantine relations by engendering increasingly sharp conflicts and misunderstandings.

Following Saladin's recapture of Jerusalem in 1187 and the failure of the Third Crusade to retake the holy city, the West was eager to strike back at Islam. In the early thirteenth century, a force made up largely of French warriors and Venetian sailors planned to strike at Islam by capturing Alexandria in Egypt, thereby relieving pressure on the embattled Latin settlements in the Holy Land. That particular assault never took place. Rather, circumstances led the army and fleet of the Fourth Crusade (1202–1204) to Constantinople, where the crusaders became embroiled in a dynastic power struggle between rival imperial claimants. Eventually the crusaders attacked Constantinople on April 12, 1204, and captured it the following day. After three days of brutal looting, the crusaders settled down and established the Latin Empire of Constantinople (1204–1261).

The Byzantines regained their capital city in 1261, but their empire was by then largely a shadow of its former self. Just as significant, the events of 1204 caused the final and, until today, irreconcilable rupture between the Roman Catholic and Eastern Orthodox branches of Christianity.

The Byzantine nobleman, court official, and historian Nicetas Choniates (ca. 1155–ca. 1216) included a vivid account of the Fourth Crusade in his *Annals,* a history that traces Byzantine imperial fortunes from 1118 to 1207. His account is especially telling inasmuch as he was an eyewitness to and victim of the crusaders' capture and pillage of Constantinople. The following selection begins early on the morning of April 13. On the previous day, after bloody and bitter fighting, the crusaders had managed to penetrate the walls of the city and set up a small armed camp within hostile territory. With the situation still in doubt, they spent a sleepless night, wondering what the morning would bring.

QUESTIONS FOR ANALYSIS

1. According to Nicetas, how do the crusaders show themselves to be hypocrites?
2. According to Nicetas, what is the crusaders' greatest sin?

3. What, does he imply, could Constantinople expect if it were captured by Muslims?

The enemy, who had expected otherwise, found no one openly venturing into battle or taking up arms to resist; they saw that the way was open before them and everything there for the taking. The narrow streets were clear and the crossroads unobstructed, safe from attack, and advantageous to the enemy. The populace, moved by the hope of propitiating them, had turned out to greet them with crosses and venerable icons[1] of Christ as was customary during festivals of solemn processions. But their disposition was not at all affected by what they saw, nor did their lips break into the slightest smile, nor did the unexpected spectacle transform their grim and frenzied glance and fury into a semblance of cheerfulness. Instead, they plundered with impunity and stripped their victims shamelessly, beginning with their carts. Not only did they rob them of their substance but also the articles consecrated to God; the rest fortified themselves all around with defensive weapons as their horses were roused at the sound of the war trumpet.

What then should I recount first and what last of those things dared at that time by these murderous men? O, the shameful dashing to earth of the venerable icons and the flinging of the relics[2] of the saints, who had suffered for Christ's sake, into defiled places! How horrible it was to see the Divine Body and Blood of Christ[3] poured out and thrown to the ground! These forerunners of Antichrist,[4] chief agents and harbingers of his anticipated ungodly deeds, seized as plunder the precious chalices and patens;[5] some they smashed, taking possession of the ornaments embellishing them, and they set the remaining vessels on their tables to serve as bread dishes and wine goblets. Just as happened long ago, Christ was now disrobed and mocked, his garments were parted, and lots were cast for them by this race; and although his side was not pierced by the lance, yet once more streams of Divine Blood poured to the earth.

The report of the impious acts perpetrated in the Great Church[6] are unwelcome to the ears. The table of sacrifice, fashioned from every kind of precious material and fused by fire into one whole — blended together into a perfection of one multicolored thing of beauty, truly extraordinary and admired by all nations — was broken into pieces and divided among the despoilers, as was the lot of all the sacred church treasures, countless in number and unsurpassed in beauty. They found it fitting to bring out as so much booty the all-hallowed vessels and furnishings which had been wrought with incomparable elegance and craftsmanship from rare materials. In addition, in order to remove the pure silver which overlay the railing of the bema,[7] the wondrous pulpit and the gates, as well as that which covered a great many other adornments, all of which were plated with gold, they led to the very sanctuary of the temple itself mules and asses with packsaddles; some of these, unable to keep their feet on the smoothly polished marble floors, slipped and were pierced by knives so that the excrement from the bowels and the spilled blood defiled the sacred floor. Moreover, a certain silly woman laden with sins . . . the handmaid of demons, the workshop of unspeakable spells and reprehensible charms, waxing wanton against

---

[1]Sacred pictures.
[2]Highly revered body parts and other items associated with the lives of saints and of Jesus.
[3]Consecrated eucharistic bread and wine, which both Western and Eastern Christians believed was the actual body and blood of Jesus.

[4]An evil false Christ who will momentarily reign prior to Jesus' Second Coming.
[5]Vessels used in the sacrifice of the Mass.
[6]Hagia Sophia (see source 82).
[7]The sanctuary where Mass is performed.

Christ, sat upon the synthronon[8] and intoned a song, and then whirled about and kicked up her heels in dance.

It was not that these crimes were committed in this fashion while others were not, or that some acts were more heinous than others, but that the most wicked and impious deeds were perpetrated by all with one accord. Did these madmen, raging thus against the sacred, spare pious matrons and girls of marriageable age or those maidens who, having chosen a life of chastity, were consecrated to God? Above all, it was a difficult and arduous task to mollify the barbarians with entreaties and to dispose them kindly towards us, as they were highly irascible and bilious and unwilling to listen to anything. Everything incited their anger, and they were thought fools and became a laughingstock. He who spoke freely and openly was rebuked, and often the dagger would be drawn against him who expressed a small difference of opinion or who hesitated to carry out their wishes.

The whole head was in pain. There were lamentations and cries of woe and weeping in the narrow ways, wailing at the crossroads, moaning in the temples, outcries of men, screams of women, the taking of captives, and the dragging about, tearing in pieces, and raping of bodies heretofore sound and whole. They who were bashful of their sex were led about naked, they who were venerable in their old age uttered plaintive cries, and the wealthy were despoiled of their riches. Thus it was in the squares, thus it was on the corners, thus it was in the temples, thus it was in the hiding places; for there was no place that could escape detection or that could offer asylum to those who came streaming in.

O Christ our Emperor, what tribulation and distress of men at that time! The roaring of the sea, the darkening and dimming of the sun, the turning of the moon into blood, the displacement of the stars — did they not foretell in this way the last evils? Indeed, we have seen the abomination of desolation stand in the holy place, rounding off meretricious and petty speeches and other things which were moving definitely, if not altogether, contrariwise to those things deemed by Christians as holy and ennobling the word of faith.

Such then, to make a long story short, were the outrageous crimes committed by the Western armies against the inheritance of Christ. Without showing any feelings of humanity whatsoever, they exacted from all their money and chattel, dwellings and clothing, leaving to them nothing of all their goods. Thus behaved the brazen neck, the haughty spirit, the high brow, the ever-shaved and youthful cheek, the bloodthirsty right hand, the wrathful nostril, the disdainful eye, the insatiable jaw, the hateful heart, the piercing and running speech practically dancing over the lips. More to blame were the learned and wise among men, they who were faithful to their oaths, who loved the truth and hated evil, who were both more pious and just and scrupulous in keeping the commandments of Christ than we "Greeks."[9] Even more culpable were those who had raised the cross to their shoulders, who had time and again sworn by it and the sayings of the Lord to cross over Christian lands without bloodletting, neither turning aside to the right nor inclining to the left, and to take up arms against the Saracens and to stain red their swords in their blood; they who had sacked Jerusalem, and had taken an oath not to marry or to have sexual intercourse with women as long as they carried the cross on their shoulders, and who were consecrated to God and commissioned to follow in his footsteps.

In truth, they were exposed as frauds. Seeking to avenge the Holy Sepulcher,[10] they raged openly against Christ and sinned by overturning the Cross with the cross they bore on their backs, not even shuddering to trample on it for the sake of a

---

[8]The patriarch's throne.
[9]A sarcastic reference to Western clerics who maintained they were better Christians than these degenerate *Greeks.*

[10]The Tomb of Christ, which is in Jerusalem.

little gold and silver. By grasping pearls, they rejected Christ, the pearl of great price, scattering among the most accursed of brutes the All-Hallowed One. The sons of Ismael[11] did not behave in this way, for when the Latins overpowered Sion[12] the Latins showed no compassion or kindness to their race.[13] Neither did the Ismaelites neigh after Latin women, nor did they turn the cenotaph of Christ[14] into a common burial place of the fallen, nor did they transform the entranceway of the life-bringing tomb into a passageway leading down into Hades, nor did they replace the Resurrection with the Fall.

Rather, they allowed everyone to depart in exchange for the payment of a few gold coins; they took only the ransom money and left to the people all their possessions, even though these numbered more than the grains of sand. Thus the enemies of Christ dealt magnanimously with the Latin infidels, inflicting upon them neither sword, nor fire, nor hunger, nor persecution, nor nakedness, nor bruises, nor constraints.[15] How differently, as we have briefly recounted, the Latins treated us who love Christ and are their fellow believers, guiltless of any wrong against them.

---

[11]Muslims. Arabs claim descent from Abraham through his son Ishmael.

[12]Jerusalem.

[13] The army of the First Crusade captured Jerusalem in a blood bath in July 1099.

[14]A *cenotaph* is a monument. This is a reference to the crusader Church of the Holy Sepulcher in Jerusalem, which stands over the presumed sites where Jesus was crucified, buried, and arose from the dead.

[15]Nicetas contrasts Saladin's treatment of the defeated Latins, after he captured Jerusalem on October 2, 1187, with the crusaders' actions at Jerusalem on July 15, 1099 and in Constantinople.

Chapter 11

▼▼▼

Africa and
the Americas

As we saw in Chapter 5, toward the end of the first century B.C.E. the dominant civilizations of Eurasia and North Africa were loosely linked through a series of trade networks and imperialistic adventures. The result was the first *Afro-Eurasian Ecumene,* or universal community, whose heyday extended down to about 200 C.E. The term itself is somewhat misleading, however, because most of Africa south of the Sahara Desert lay outside of this first ecumene of the so-called Old World.

The cultures of the so-called New World — the Americas — also did not participate in that first age of Afro-Eurasian linkage, nor in the second, which peaked between 1250 and 1350. Granted all of this, the question remains: Were there any meaningful contacts between the Eastern and Western hemispheres before 1492?

A few adventurers and lost sailors from Africa and Eurasia undoubtedly reached the lands of America prior to Columbus. This certainly was the case with a handful of Vikings who set up a short-lived colony in northern Newfoundland around 1000 C.E. but departed without having made any appreciable impact on the culture of the American Indians whom they encountered. We can only speculate how many more ancient mariners made it all the way to the Americas alive. Did any of them leave behind cultural footprints? Several sober specialists have pointed to certain striking similarities between the classic 260-day calendar of Mesoamerica and the lunar zodiacs of East Asia and have suggested that coincidence does not adequately explain the parallels. One scholar has also made a study of the tools and means used to fashion bark paper all around the Pacific Basin and concluded that the technique traveled from Indonesia to Mesoamerica at an early date. These clues, if interpreted correctly, as well as some interesting parallels in certain artistic styles and motifs around the

Pacific Basin (for example, both Polynesians and the American Indians of the Northwest carved wooden totems) suggest that there might have been some cultural exchange before 1492.

Even if we grant these exchanges, we still are left with the conclusion that no American Indian culture was a derivative of any culture from across the oceans. At the most, a few ideas and techniques might have made their way across the waters, but once in the Americas they were grafted onto essentially indigenous cultures and civilizations. The fact that American Indian agriculture was based on fruits, vegetables, and cereals unknown in the Old World seems evidence enough of that. What is more, the fact that European and African diseases caused such massive depopulation in the Americas after 1492 is convincing evidence that occasional pre-Columbian visitors established no meaningful or long-term links between the Americas and the outside world.

Isolated though they might have been from the rest of the world before 1492, most American Indian peoples were linked, although loosely, in an *American Ecumene* that made possible the spread of goods and cultural influences over vast expanses. Maize, for example, initially domesticated as early as 5000 B.C.E. in the highlands of south central Mexico, had spread to Peru by 2000 B.C.E. or earlier and to Canada by 1000 C.E.

Sub-Saharan Africa also had its early cultural and trade networks, which made possible a widespread diffusion of such technologies as agriculture and iron metallurgy and such ideas as the faith of Islam. Moreover, despite the continued growth of the Sahara Desert from around 2500 B.C.E. to the present, interior Africa has never been totally cut off from the rest of the Afro-Eurasian World, even in the most ancient times. However, the volume of traffic across the Sahara only began to achieve significant proportions after the introduction into North Africa of the Arabian, or single-humped, camel as a beast of burden during the early centuries C.E. Conquest of western North Africa by Muslim Arabs in the seventh century provided another major boost to trans-Saharan trade, so that by about the year 1000, four major commercial routes connected the north with western sub-Saharan Africa. Gold, more than any other single item, drew the camel caravans of Berber and Arab traders to the inland kingdoms of West Africa's grasslands, but large numbers of slaves were also sold for transportation northward to markets throughout the Mediterranean and beyond. In return, western sub-

Saharan Africans received salt, raw copper, fine horses, and such manufactured goods as tempered steel and even glassware from Venice.

Trade and the development of trade-based Islamic states in the western sub-Saharan grasslands constitute a major chapter in Africa's history, but they are not the whole story of what was happening during the millennium 500–1500 C.E. in this richly diverse continent. East Africa, especially its coastal region from Somalia to Tanzania, was linked to a shipping network of monsoon-driven vessels that sailed throughout the Indian Ocean and its adjacent waters — all the way to China. Commodities such as ivory and gold made their way from the interior of East Africa to ports on the Indian Ocean, where they joined such coastal raw materials as ambergris (a resin used in the production of perfumes) and mangrove timber. At these emporia, which dotted the islands off the eastern coast, East Africa's goods were exchanged for ceramics from China, glassware, and Indian textiles. In addition, captives taken in war and by raiding parties were brought to the coast, where they were sold to Arab slavers for exportation to the mines and plantations of Iraq. For better and for worse, Africa was increasingly becoming linked to the Eurasian World between 500 and 1500.

▼▼▼

Africa

During the millennium from 500 to 1500 Africa witnessed a number of important historical developments. Chief among them were the last stages of the *Bantu Expansion,* the coming of Islam, the creation of trade empires in the western Sudan, the rise of a *Swahili* culture in East Africa, and the arrival of Europeans toward the end of this period.

The approximately 450 languages belonging to the *Bantu* linguistic family that are spoken today throughout most of the southern half of the continent are traceable to a common place of origin in West Africa, probably in present eastern Nigeria. Bantu speakers probably began spreading out of their ancestral homeland as early as 3,000 or 4,000 years ago, aided by their skills in fishing and agriculture. In its later stages, this slow, almost imperceptible movement was aided by their iron-working skills. As they spread east and south, the Bantu-speaking peoples introduced wherever they settled the crafts of farming and iron metallurgy. By the early centuries C.E. Bantu speakers had pushed as far south as the region today occupied by the nation of Zimbabwe, where by the late thirteenth century they constructed a gold-trade civilization centered on the now famous Great Zimbabwe stone citadel, from which the modern state took its name in 1979.

Another great migration that profoundly influenced Africa's history was the influx of Islam in the wake of the conquering Arab armies that swept through North Africa in the seventh century. These conquests and the conversions that followed transformed what had been Christian North Africa into an integral part of the Islamic World, thereby wrenching it out of the orbits of Constantinople and Rome and tying it culturally to Mecca, Damascus, and Baghdad.

From North Africa the faith and culture of Islam penetrated into the trade empires of the western grassland states south of the Sahara after 1000 C.E. The empires of *Ghana, Mali,* and *Songhai* became progressively more Islamic and, therefore, more closely tied to North Africa and the greater Islamic World beyond Africa by reason of a shared religious culture, as well as by commercial interests.

On the east coast of Africa a similar phenomenon was at work. In the ninth and tenth centuries Arab sailor-merchants established trading settlements far down the coast of East Africa. The culture that emerged from the interchange between the Arab and East African peoples who traded and intermarried here is known as *Swahili* (from the Arabic word for "coast" — *sahil*). Like *Kiswahili,* the language of the region, Swahili culture was a coastal trade culture consisting of an indigenous Bantu base with strong Arabic influences. From about 1200 to the early sixteenth century, the port city of *Kilwa,* today located in the nation of Tanzania, served as the Swahili coast's main emporium.

Kilwa's commercial prominence along Africa's eastern shore ended with its sack and destruction by the Portuguese in 1505. With the arrival in force of the Portuguese, first on Africa's west coast in the fifteenth century and then on the east coast in the early sixteenth century, the age of direct European contact with sub-Saharan Africa had begun, with all of the consequences that would follow from that interchange.

Despite the impact of Islam and Europe on Africa south of the Sahara, older ways of life proved usually resilient to influences from outside. *Ethiopia,* for example, successfully resisted Islamic and later Portuguese attempts at conquest and conversion, retaining its autonomy and ancient Christian culture. Likewise, the coastal states of West Africa retained their core cultural features, even as their leaders accepted the faith of Islam. Moreover, they maintained autonomy, extensive political authority, and widespread economic interests, even in the face of the European presence along their coastline.

The Land of Zanj: Tenth-Century East Africa
▼▼▼

90 ▼ Abul-Hasan Ali al-Masudi,
   MEADOWS OF GOLD

To ancient Greek and Roman geographers, the coastal region of East Africa was known as *Azania.* The Arabs who traded along this coast knew it as the *Land of Zanj,* a name that survives in *Zanzibar,* an island that comprises part of the modern nation of Tanzania. Following the monsoon winds of the Indian Ocean, which blow toward East Africa between November and March, Arab merchants sailed from Oman and other regions of the Arabian Peninsula and visited trading ports that stretched southward from Mogadishu in Somalia to Sofala, which is located in the modern nation of Mozambique. At these trading centers, the Arabs met sailors from India and the islands of Southeast Asia, as well as colonists from Arabia and Persia, many of whom had intermarried with Africans. Because of the presence of Arabic speakers along this coast, the Arab merchants who visited the region found little difficulty in conducting commerce, apart from the normal hazards of venturing long distances across treacherous ocean waters in small vessels. After acquiring their desired raw materials, Arab merchants returned home or else sailed to India, driven by monsoon winds that blow northeastward between April and October.

One of the earliest Arabic accounts of East African society and its trade comes from the pen of Abul-Hasan Ali al-Masudi (ca. 890–956), who visited the region in 915/916. In his masterwork of history and geography, *Meadows of Gold,* which he composed in 943, al-Masudi informs his reader of the Indian Ocean trade network into which the Land of Zanj was interwoven and of the people of interior East Africa, who fed that trade. How much of what he tells us about the people of Zanj is fact and how much is the stuff of distorted legend is open to question. What is clear and undisputed is the picture that al-Masudi draws of the importance of Africa's east coast to foreign merchants.

QUESTIONS FOR ANALYSIS

1. What evidence does al-Masudi provide of the evolving Swahili culture of this region?
2. What are the dangers of the voyage to the Land of Zanj? What are the rewards?
3. Describe the ivory trade that originated in East Africa.
4. What does al-Masudi tell us about the culture of the Bantu people of the interior? Which elements seem the most believable? Why? Which seem the least believable? Why?
5. Review the story of Sinbad (source 77). Does al-Masudi's account place the story into a clearer context?
6. The Indian Ocean has been described as the heart of the Afro-Eurasian World. To what extent does al-Masudi's account support or call into question that judgment?

The pilots of Oman[1] pass by the channel [of Berbera] to reach the island of Kanbalu,[2] which is in the Zanj sea.[3] It has a mixed population of Muslims and Zanj idolaters.[4] . . . The aforesaid Kanbalu is the farthest point of their voyages on the Zanj sea, and the land of Sofala and the

---

[1]The region of southeast Arabia that stretches along the entrance to the Persian Gulf.
[2]The island of Pemba.

[3]The region of the Indian Ocean that washes the central portion of Africa's eastern coast.
[4]Worshipers of idols. People who follow traditional religions.

Waqwaq,[5] on the edge of the Zanj mainland and at the end of this branch of the sea. The people of Siraf[6] also make this voyage, and I myself have sailed on this sea, setting off from Sanjar, the capital of Oman, in company with a number of Omani shipowners, among whom were Muhammad ibn al-Zaidbud and Jawhar ibn Ahmad surnamed Ibn Sirah, who was later lost at sea with his ship. My last voyage from Kanbalu to Oman was in A.H. 304[7] on the ship belonging to Ahmad and Abd al-Samad, who were the brothers of Abd al-Rahim ibn Jafar al-Sirafi, a native of Mikan, which is a quarter of Siraf. They were both lost at sea with all their goods later on. The Amir[8] of Oman at the time of my last voyage was Ahmad ibn Hilal, son of a sister of al-Qital. I have sailed much on the seas, . . . but I do not know of one more dangerous than that of the Zanj, of which I have just spoken. . . .

The land of Zanj produces wild leopard skins. The people wear them as clothes, or export them to Muslim countries. They are the largest leopard skins and the most beautiful for making saddles. The sea of Zanj and that of Abyssinia[9] lie on the right of the sea of India, and join up. They also export tortoise-shell for making combs, for which ivory is likewise used. . . . As we have said, the Zanj and other Abyssinian peoples are spread about on the right bank of the Nile,[10] as far as the end of the Abyssinian sea. The Zanj are the only Abyssinian people[11] to have crossed the branch which flows out of the upper stream of the Nile into the sea of Zanj. They settled in that area,

which stretches as far as Sofala, which is the farthest limit of land and the end of the voyages made from Oman and Siraf on the sea of Zanj. In the same way that the sea of China ends with the land of Japan, the sea of Zanj ends with the land of Sofala and the Waqwaq, which produces gold and many other wonderful things. It has a warm climate and is fertile. The Zanj capital is there[12] and they have a king called the *Mfalme*. This is the ancient name of their kings, and all the other Zanj kings are subject to him: he has 300,000 horsemen. The Zanj use the ox as a beast of burden, for they have no horses, mules or camels in their land, and do not know of their existence. Like all Abyssinians they do not know of snow or hail. Some of their tribes sharpen their teeth and are cannibals. The land of Zanj begins with the branch which leaves the upper Nile[13] and continues to the land of Sofala and Waqwaq. The villages stretch for 700 parasangs[14] and the same distance inland: the country is cut up into valleys, mountains and stony deserts. There are many wild elephants but no tame ones. The Zanj do not use them for war or anything else, but only hunt and kill them. When they want to catch them, they throw down the leaves, bark and branches of a certain tree which grows in their country: then they wait in ambush until the elephants come to drink. The water burns them and makes them drunk. They fall down and cannot get up: their limbs will not articulate. The Zanj rush upon them armed with very long spears, and kill them for their ivory. It is from

---

[5]Arabs normally used this term to refer only to the people of Malaysia, who speak a language that is related to the Malagasy tongue of Madagascar. Madagascar is a large island off the coast of East Africa and opposite Sofala; Malaysia is across the Indian Ocean in Southeast Asia (see note 19). In the present context, however, the term seems to refer to the people of interior Africa.

[6]A port on the Iranian shore of the Persian Gulf.

[7]A.H. is an abbreviation for a Latin term that translates as *in the year of the Hijra.* Muhammad's *hijra* from Mecca to Medina, which took place in 622, is the starting point of the Islamic calendar. Because the Islamic year is lunar, one cannot simply subtract 622 years from a date in the common calendar to arrive at its equivalent in the Islamic calendar. A.H. 304 equates to 915/916 C.E.

[8]An Arabic term that means "commander." Here it means "prince" or "governor."

[9]Usually the term refers only to Ethiopia, but al-Masudi seems to use it here to refer to a substantial portion of the northeastern coast of Africa (see note 11).

[10]Not the Nile. Maybe he means the Sabi River, which flows out of the Zimbabwe Plateau and reaches the ocean in the modern state of Mozambique.

[11]Apparently all dark-skinned Africans are Abyssinians (see note 9).

[12]Probably the site, far up the Sabi River Valley, where the Shona state would construct the massive enclosures of Great Zimbabwe between 1200 and 1450.

[13]Al-Masudi is wrong again (see note 10). Several major rivers run into the Indian Ocean, but not one of them is the Nile. This river, which delineates the northern boundary of the Land of Zanj, might be the Juba River.

[14]A *parasang,* an ancient Persian unit of measurement, was roughly three and one-half miles.

this country that come tusks weighing fifty pounds and more. They usually go to Oman, and from there are sent to China and India. This is the chief trade route, and if it were not so, ivory would be common in Muslim lands.

In China the kings and military civil officers use ivory palanquins:[15] no officer or notable dares to come into the royal presence in an iron palanquin, and ivory alone can be used. Thus they seek after straight tusks in preference to the curved, to make the things we have spoken of. They also burn ivory before their idols and cense their altars with it, just as Christians use the Mary incense[16] and other perfumes. The Chinese make no other use of the elephant, and consider it unlucky to use it for domestic purposes or war. This fear has its origin in a tradition about one of their most ancient military expeditions. In India ivory is much sought after.[17] It is used for the handles of daggers called *harari* or *harri* in the singular: and also for the curved sword-scabbards called *kartal*, in the plural *karatil*, but the chief use of ivory is making chessmen and backgammon pieces. . . .

In the land of Zanj the elephant lives about 400 years, according to what the people say, and they speak with certainty of having met an elephant so tall that it was impossible to kill it. . . . It is only in the land of Zanj and in India that elephants reproduce. . . .

Now let us return to our subject of the beginning of the chapter, the Zanj, the description of their country and of the other peoples of Abyssinia. The Zanj, although always busied hunting the elephant and collecting its ivory, make no use of it for domestic purposes. They use iron instead of gold and silver, just as they use oxen, as we said

before, both for beasts of burden and for war. These oxen are harnessed like a horse and run as fast. . . .

To go back to the Zanj and their kings, these are known as *Wafalme*,[18] which means son of the Great Lord, since he is chosen to govern them justly. If he is tyrannical or strays from the truth, they kill him and exclude his seed from the throne; for they consider that in acting wrongfully he forfeits his position as the son of the Lord, the King of Heaven and Earth. They call God *Maliknajlu,* which means Great Lord.

The Zanj have an elegant language and men who preach in it. One of their holy men will often gather a crowd and exhort his hearers to please God in their lives and to be obedient to him. He explains the punishments that follow upon disobedience, and reminds them of their ancestors and kings of old. These people have no religious law: their kings rule by custom and by political expediency.

The Zanj eat bananas,[19] which are as common among them as they are in India; but their staple food is millet[20] and a plant called *kalari* which is pulled out of the earth like truffles. It is plentiful in Aden[21] and the neighboring part of Yemen[22] near to the town. It is like the cucumber of Egypt and Syria. They also eat honey and meat. Every man worships what he pleases, be it a plant, an animal or a mineral. They have many islands where the coconut grows: its nuts are used as fruit by all the Zanj peoples. One of these islands, which is one or two days' sail from the coast, has a Muslim population and a royal family. This is the island of Kanbalu of which we have already spoken.

---

[15]A covered litter carried on the shoulders of two or four persons.

[16]Incense (also known as *frankincense*) was a fragrant resin from Yemen in the southwestern corner of the Arabian Peninsula that Christians, Muslims, Jews, Zoroastrians, and many others burned in their places of worship. Here the author seems to refer to a particular grade of incense that was burned in Christian churches in honor of Mary, the mother of Jesus.

[17]Despite the presence of elephants in India, Indian artisans preferred African ivory because of its texture and size.

[18]Apparently these are the kings mentioned earlier in this excerpt who are subordinate to the *Mfalme.*

[19]Migrants from Malaysia in Southeast Asia settled in Madagascar around the first century C.E. (see note 5) and brought with them plants and seeds from their homeland, including the banana. From Madagascar the banana traveled into the tropical rain forests of continental Africa, where it flourished as a domesticated crop.

[20]A cereal.

[21]An Arabian port city that commands the entrance to the Red Sea.

[22]See note 16.

The Land of Ghana:
Eleventh-Century Western Sudan
▼▼▼

91 ▼ Abu Ubaydallah al-Bakri,
THE BOOK OF ROUTES AND REALMS

Located south of the Sahara Desert is a broad expanse of grasslands, or *savanna*, that stretches across the breadth of the African continent from the Atlantic Ocean to the Red Sea. To the Arabs this region was known as *Bilad al-Sudan* (the country of the blacks). Arab and Berber merchants were especially interested in West Africa's Sudan because its inhabitants were advantageously located between the markets of North Africa and cultures farther south toward the tropical rain forests of the coast. From the southern peoples of the Niger and Senegal river valleys the inhabitants of the savanna obtained gold and slaves, which they traded for manu-factured goods, horses, and salt with Berber and Arab merchants, who arrived in camel caravans from the north. Over time, this trans-Saharan commerce stimulat-ed development of a series of large trading states in the region that connected West Africa's gold fields with the cities of Mediterranean North Africa.

One of the earliest important trading empires to emerge was *Ghana* (not to be confused with its modern namesake, the nation of Ghana), which was located es-sentially in territory encompassed today by the nations of Mauritania and Mali. The origins of Ghana as an organized entity are lost in the shadows of the past but go back at least as far as the fifth century C.E., when the introduction of the *dromedary,* or single-humped Arabian camel, made it easier for outsiders to penetrate across the Sahara into the land of the *Soninke* people. Coming as traders and as raiders, the *Berber* people of the western Sahara apparently helped stimulate the formation of a Soninke kingdom organized for commerce and defense. Eventually that king-dom became known as *Ghana* — a term that originated as a royal title. During the course of the eighth and ninth centuries Arab merchants inhabiting the coastal cities of North Africa began to enter the lucrative trans-Saharan trading system, thereby gaining direct access to the region they called *the land of gold* — a land now dominated by the well-established state of Ghana.

In 1067/1068 Abu Ubaydallah al-Bakri (d. 1094), a resident of the city of Cordo-ba in what is today Spain but was then the Muslim land of *al-Andalus,* composed a detailed description of this fabled region. Although he never traveled to nearby Africa and probably never even left his native land, al-Bakri provides us with one of the most important sources for the early history of the western Sudan. As was the accepted practice among Islamic geographers of his era, al-Bakri drew heavily from the writings of predecessors, many of whose works are now otherwise lost, and he also interviewed merchants who had traveled to the area. These interviews made it possible for al-Bakri to present up-to-date information on Ghana at a cru-cial moment in its history.

During the latter portion of the eleventh century the rulers and leading families of Ghana were increasingly adopting the faith and attendant culture of Islam. However, Muslims from the north brought not only the peaceful message of universal submission to the Word of God, they also brought war. A fundamentalist Islamic group of Berbers, from Morocco, known as the *Almoravids,* waged holy war, or *jihad,* against the Soninke of Ghana. It is unclear whether or not the Almoravids prevailed in this war, but apparently the conflict disrupted trade and weakened Ghana's economic base. In addition, the heartland of Ghana was becoming far less able to support its population due to an environmental crisis brought about by overfarming and excessive grazing. Large numbers of farmers and townspeople were forced to move away. With these combined losses, the recently converted monarchs of Ghana lost their ability to hold together their loosely organized and still predominantly non-Islamic empire. By the early thirteenth century Ghana had disintegrated. Hegemony over the markets of the western Sudan briefly passed to the kingdom of *Sosso* and then to the state of *Mali,* which reached its greatest territorial extent under Mansa Musa (r. 1312–1327), whom we saw in source 60. We shall see Mali again in Chapter 12.

QUESTIONS FOR ANALYSIS

1. To whom did a monarch pass his royal power? What does this tradition of royal succession suggest about Ghanian society?
2. Describe the city of Ghana. What does its physical environment, especially its two centers, suggest about eleventh-century Ghanian culture?
3. How do we know that the empire of Ghana was not the only state in the western Sudan?
4. How would you characterize the authority and sources of power of the rulers of Ghana?
5. What role did Islam play in Ghanian society? What does your answer suggest about the way in which Islam entered the western Sudan?
6. What does the story of the conversion of the king of Malal suggest about the process of Islamization in the western Sudan?

Ghana is a title given to their kings; the name of the region is Awkar, and their king today, namely in the year 460,[1] is Tunka Manin. He ascended the throne in 455.[2] The name of his predecessor was Basi and he became their ruler at the age of 85. He led a praiseworthy life on account of his love of justice and friendship for the Muslims. At the end of his life he became blind, but he concealed this from his subjects and pretended that he could see. When something was put before him he said: "This is good" or "This is bad." His ministers deceived the people by indicating to the king in cryptic words what he should say, so that the commoners could not understand. Basi was a maternal uncle of Tunka Manin. This is their custom and their habit, that the kingship is inherited only by the son of the king's sister. He has no doubt that his successor is a son of his sister, while he is not certain that his son is in fact his own, and he is not convinced of the genuine-

---

[1]1067/1068 C.E. (see source 90, note 7).   [2]1063 C.E.

ness of his relationship to him. This Tunka Manin is powerful, rules an enormous kingdom, and possesses great authority.

The city of Ghana consists of two towns situated on a plain.[3] One of these towns, which is inhabited by Muslims, is large and possesses twelve mosques, in one of which they assemble for the Friday prayer. There are salaried imams and muezzins,[4] as well as jurists and scholars. In the environs are wells with sweet water, from which they drink and with which they grow vegetables. The king's town is six miles distant from this one and bears the name of Al-Ghaba.[5] Between these two towns there are continuous habitations. The houses of the inhabitants are of stone and acacia wood. The king has a palace and a number of domed dwellings all surrounded with an enclosure like a city wall. In the king's town, and not far from his court of justice, is a mosque where the Muslims who arrive at his court pray. Around the king's town are domed buildings and groves and thickets where the sorcerers of these people, men in charge of the religious cult, live. In them too are their idols and the tombs of their kings. These woods are guarded and none may enter them and know what is there. In them also are the king's prisons. If somebody is imprisoned there no news of him is ever heard. The king's interpreters, the official in charge of his treasury and the majority of his ministers are Muslims. Among the people who follow the king's religion[6] only he and his heir apparent (who is the son of his sister) may wear sewn clothes. All other people wear robes of cotton, silk, or brocade, according to their means. All of them shave their beards, and women shave their heads. The king adorns himself like a woman, wearing necklaces round his neck and bracelets on his forearms, and he puts on a high cap decorated with gold and wrapped in a turban of fine cotton. He sits in audience or to hear grievances against officials in a domed pavilion around which stand ten horses covered with gold-embroidered materials. Behind the king stand ten pages holding shields and swords decorated with gold, and on his right are the sons of the vassal kings[7] of his country wearing splendid garments and their hair plaited with gold. The governor of the city sits on the ground before the king and around him are ministers seated likewise. . . . When people who profess the same religion as the king approach him they fall on their knees and sprinkle dust on their heads, for this is their way of greeting him. As for the Muslims, they greet him only by clapping their hands.

Their religion is paganism and the worship of idols. When their king dies they construct over the place where his tomb will be an enormous dome of wood. Then they bring him on a bed covered with a few carpets and cushions and place him beside the dome. At his side they place his ornaments, his weapons, and the vessels from which he used to eat and drink, filled with various kinds of food and beverages. They place there too the men who used to serve his meals. They close the door of the dome and cover it with mats and furnishings. Then the people assemble, who heap earth upon it until it becomes like a big hillock and dig a ditch around it until the mound can be reached at only one place.

They make sacrifices to their dead and make offerings of intoxicating drinks.

On every donkey-load of salt when it is brought into the country their king levies one

---

[3]The city consisted of two separate walled towns connected by a long, unwalled strip of private dwellings. Known as *Koumbi-Saleh,* its ruins are located in the southern region of the modern nation of Mauritania. At its eleventh-century height, this double city probably held some 20,000 people.
[4]*Imams* are religious teachers and prayer leaders; *muezzins* are the chanters who ascend the minarets, or towers, of the mosques and call the faithful to prayer five times daily.

[5]The term means "the forest," and refers to the sacred grove mentioned later in this source. (For more on sacred groves, see source 93.)
[6]The king, who was not a Muslim, followed the ancient religious ways of the Soninke people.
[7]Subordinate kings, or lords.

golden dinar,[8] and two dinars when it is sent out. From a load of copper the king's due is five mithqals,[9] and from a load of other goods ten mithqals. The best gold found in his land comes from the town of Ghiyaru, which is eighteen days' traveling distant from the king's town over a country inhabited by tribes of the Sudan whose dwellings are continuous.

The nuggets found in all the mines of his country are reserved for the king, only this gold dust being left for the people. But for this the people would accumulate gold until it lost its value. The nuggets may weigh from an ounce to a pound. It is related that the king owns a nugget as large as a big stone. . . .

The king of Ghana, when he calls up his army, can put 200,000 men[10] into the field, more than 40,000 of them archers. . . .

On the opposite bank of the Nil[11] is another great kingdom, stretching a distance of more than eight days' marching, the king of which has the title of *Daw.* The inhabitants of this region use arrows when fighting. Beyond this country lies another called Malal,[12] the king of which is known as *al-musulmani.*[13] He is thus called because his country became afflicted with drought one year following another; the inhabitants prayed for rain, sacrificing cattle till they had exterminated almost all of them, but the drought and the misery only increased. The king had as his guest a Muslim who used to read the Quran and was acquainted with the Sunna.[14] To this man the king complained of the calamities that

assailed him and his people. The man said: "O King, if you believed in God (who is exalted) and testified that He is One, and testified as to the prophetic mission of Muhammad (God bless him and give him peace) and if you accepted all the religious laws of Islam, I would pray for your deliverance from your plight and that God's mercy would envelop all the people of your country and that your enemies and adversaries might envy you on that account." Thus he continued to press the king until the latter accepted Islam and became a sincere Muslim. The man made him recite from the Quran some easy passages and taught him religious obligations and practices which no one may be excused from knowing. Then the Muslim made him wait till the eve of the following Friday,[15] when he ordered him to purify himself by a complete ablution, and clothed him in a cotton garment which he had. The two of them came out towards a mound of earth, and there the Muslim stood praying while the king, standing at his right side, imitated him. Thus they prayed for a part of the night, the Muslim reciting invocations and the king saying "Amen." The dawn had just started to break when God caused abundant rain to descend upon them. So the king ordered the idols to be broken and expelled the sorcerers from his country. He and his descendants after him as well as his nobles were sincerely attached to Islam, while the common people of his kingdom remained polytheists. Since then their rulers have been given the title of *al-musulmani.*

---

[8]A standard gold coin in the Islamic world that weighed 4.72 grams, or one *mithqal* (see note 9).

[9]A standard of weight equaling 4.72 grams.

[10]An apparent exaggeration. There was no regular standing Ghanian army; the various districts of the empire sent warriors as the occasion warranted.

[11]Islamic geographers of this era mistakenly believed that the Niger River was the western source of the Nile.

[12]A *Mandike* kingdom that was the nucleus of the later empire of Mali.

[13]"The Muslim."

[14]The traditions of Islam.

[15]The beginning of the Islamic day of rest and community worship.

The Land of Seyon:
Fourteenth-Century Ethiopia
▼▼▼

92 ▼ *ETHIOPIAN ROYAL CHRONICLE*

Ethiopia, a kingdom to the southeast of ancient Kush (or Nubia) in Africa's northeast highlands, looks out across the Red Sea to Yemen, the southwestern portion of the Arabian Peninsula. Settlers from Yemen, known as the *Sabeans,* crossed these waters, perhaps as early as the seventh century B.C.E., and mixed with the indigenous inhabitants to produce a hybrid civilization whose language, *Geez,* was essentially Semitic but contained significant Kushitic elements. Because of its strategic location astride a trade route that linked Egypt and the Mediterranean World with the markets of East Africa, Arabia, and India, Ethiopia flourished. A Greek shipping manual of the first century C.E. notes that Adulis, Ethiopia's port on the Red Sea, was northeast Africa's premier center for the ivory trade.

The Ethiopian Church claims that Christianity came to the land and its people in the first century C.E., at the time of the apostles. Given Ethiopia's commercial importance, this is credible, but Christianity only became the state-sponsored religion of Ethiopia in the early fourth century, when *King Ezana* (r. 320?–350?) converted to Christianity around 333. In the years that followed the Ethiopian people gradually adopted the new faith. Under the influence of Egyptians and Nubians to their north, Ethiopians embraced a type of Christianity known as *Monophysitism* (from the Greek words for "one nature"). This form of Christian belief, which arose in the fifth century, centered on a doctrine that deemphasized Jesus' humanity to the point of maintaining that he had a single, divine nature. When the Churches of Constantinople and Rome condemned Monophysite teachings as heresy in 451, the Ethiopian Church was doctrinally cut off from these two Mediterranean centers of Christianity. The Arab-Muslim conquest of Egypt in the 640s further cut Ethiopia off from its Christian coreligionists in Byzantium and the West. In time, most of previously Christian Egypt converted to Islam, although its native Christians, known as *Coptic Christians,* remained a significant minority, as they are today. Egypt, the land that had introduced Christianity to Nubia and Ethiopia, was now an Islamic stronghold. On their part, Nubians and Ethiopians vigorously fought to retain their political autonomy and Christian identity in the face of Islamic pressure from Egypt. After the mid thirteenth century, however, Nubian resistance to Islam weakened. By the mid fourteenth century Nubia no longer had an independent Christian monarchy, and the Christian faith was fast losing out to Islam. By the sixteenth century, Nubia's Christian population was a minority and would remain so down to the present. (Nubia today is the nation of Sudan.)

Farther to the south, Ethiopia, fairly secure in its mountain strongholds, continued to hold out against Islam. The following document, a fourteenth-century royal chronicle, tells the story of how King *Amda Seyon I* (r. 1312–1342), whose throne name was *Gabra Masqal* (Servant of the Cross), resisted an invasion in 1329 by Sabr ad-Din, the ruler of Ifat, an Islamic emirate on the coast. More than simply a monarch on the defensive, Amda Seyon was a militant expansionist, who in his thirty-year reign undertook a series of offensive operations against neighboring Islamic states in his drive to control access routes to the Red Sea and Gulf of Aden. Between 1320 and 1340 he managed to bring Ifat and other Islamic states of the highland plateau under the control of his expanding kingdom. As the chronicle points out, Sabr ad-Din was actually a tributary prince who revolted against Amda Seyon's authority.

QUESTIONS FOR ANALYSIS

1. What picture emerges of Muslim-Christian relations in fourteenth-century Ethiopia?
2. The Christian Ethiopian attitude toward Jews and Judaism has been characterized as ambivalent. Do you find in this source any evidence to support such a judgment? Please be specific in your answer.
3. Reread Eusebius of Caesarea's *Ecclesiastical History* (source 49). Do you see any parallels between the tone and message of that source and this document? What are they? What conclusions do you draw?

Let us write, with the help of our Lord Jesus Christ, of the power and the victory which God wrought by the hands of Amda Seyon king of Ethiopia, whose throne-name is Gabra Masqal. . . . Now the king of Ethiopia . . . heard that the king of the Rebels[1] had revolted, and in his arrogance was unfaithful to him, making himself great, like the Devil who set himself above his creator and exalted himself like the Most High. The king of the Rebels, whose name was Sabra-din, was full of arrogance towards his lord Amda Seyon, and said, "I will be king over all the land of Ethiopia; I will rule the Christians according to my law, and I will destroy their churches." And having said this, he arose and set out and came to the land of the Christians, and killed some of them; and those who survived, both men

and women, he took prisoner and converted them to his religion.

And after this he said, "I will nominate governors over the provinces of Ethiopia." . . . And he appointed governors over all the provinces of Ethiopia, even those which he had not been able to reach.

But the feet cannot become the head, nor the Earth the sky, nor the servant the master. That perverse one, the son of a viper, of the seed of a serpent, the son of a stranger from the race of Satan, thought covetously of the throne of David[2] and said, "I will rule in Seyon,"[3] for pride entered into his heart, as into the Devil his father. He said, "I will make the Christian churches into mosques for the Muslims, and I will convert to my religion the king of the Christians together

---

[1] The word *elwan,* translated here as "rebels," can also be translated as "infidels," or nonbelievers.

[2] The Ethiopian royal family, known as the *Solomonid Dynasty* (1270–1974), claimed descent from the union of the Queen of Sheba and King Solomon of Israel (r. ca. 962–922 B.C.E.), son of King David. See the Bible, 1 Kings 10:1–13, and 2 Chronicles 9:1–12, for an account of the queen's visit to King Solomon. According to Ethiopian tradition, *Menelik,* son of the Queen of Sheba and Solomon and first king of

Ethiopia, stole the Ark of the Covenant from Jerusalem and brought it to Ethiopia, where it is still revered as the country's most sacred relic.

[3] The Geez transliteration of *Zion,* one of Jerusalem's hills and a common symbolic term for Jerusalem and even the entire Holy Land. Here *Seyon* refers to Ethiopia because the Ethiopians claim partial Hebraic descent (note 2). Amda Seyon means *Pillar of Zion.*

with his people, and I will nominate him governor of one province, and if he refuses to be converted to my religion I will deliver him to the herdsmen . . . that they make him a herder of camels. As for the queen Zan Mangesa, the wife of the king, I will make her work at the mill." . . .

Saying this, he collected all the troops of the Muslims, and chose from among them the ablest and most intelligent. These in truth were not able and intelligent, but fools, men full of error, impostors who foretell the future by means of sand and take omens from the sun and moon and stars of Heaven, who say, "We observe the stars," but they have knowledge only of evil, they have no knowledge of God, their knowledge is of men which fades and perishes, for as Saint Paul says, "God hath made foolish the wisdom of this world."[4]

Let us return to the original subject. This evil man then questioned the diviners, saying, "Now tell me, I pray you, shall we conquer when we fight with the king of the Christians?" And one of them rose, a prophet of darkness. . . .

When Sabradin the king of the Rebels examined him, this diviner answered him persuasively, saying, "Behold, the kingdom of the Christians is finished; it shall be given to us, and you shall reign in Seyon. Rise, make war on the king of the Christians, and conquering you shall rule him and his people." And all the diviners said likewise. So the Rebel king sent into all the lands of the Muslims and called together his troops, and formed them into three divisions: one division set out for the land of Amhara, another set out for the land of Angot, and he himself prepared for war and set out to invade Shoa where the king was, — the slave of slaves against the prince of princes, the tail of the dog against the head of the lion, trusting in the false prediction that the Christian kingdom was come to an end.

As for us, we have heard and we know from the Holy Scriptures that the kingdom of the Muslims, established for but seven hundred years,

shall cease to be at the proper time. But the kingdom of the Christians shall continue till the second coming of the Son of God, according to the words of Holy Scripture; and above all we know that the kingdom of Ethiopia shall endure till the coming of Christ, of which David prophesied saying "Ethiopia shall stretch her hands unto God."[5]

The messengers whom the king had sent to that Rebel returned to him the whole answer of the renegade, that rebel against righteousness. Hearing the insults of the evil man, the king called together his commanders. . . . He sent them forth to war against the evil Sabradin on the 24th day of Yakatit,[6] saying to them, "May God give you strength and victory, and may He help you." . . . And they fought with him and forced him out of his residence; and he fled before them. And they defeated him through the power of God. . . . And they pursued him till sunset; but he escaped them, going by a different road. God threw him down from his glory. . . .

Then the army of the king set forth and attacked the camp of the Rebel. They looted the rebel king's treasure houses and took gold and silver and fine clothes and jewels without number. They killed men and women, old men and children; the corpses of the slain filled a large space. And those who survived were made prisoners, and there were left none but those who had escaped with that evil man. But the soldiers could not find a place to camp because of the foul smell of the corpses; and they went to another place and made their camp there. . . .

The king, hearing that the Rebel had escaped, went into the tabernacle[7] and approached the altar; seizing the horns of the altar[8] he implored mercy of Jesus Christ saying, "Hear the petition of my heart and reject not the prayer of my lips, and shut not the gates of Thy mercy because of my sins, but send me Thy good angel to guide me on my road to pursue mine enemy who has set himself above Thy sheep and above Thy holy

---

[4]The Bible, 1 Corinthians 1:20.
[5]The Bible, Psalms 68:31.
[6]February 18, 1329.
[7]A tent used as a chapel in the king's camp.

[8]As was the fashion in ancient Israel, Ethiopian altars had horns on all four corners. Suppliants would grasp one while praying.

name." And having said this, he gave an offering to the church of colored hangings for the altar, and went out. Then he sent other troops, . . . cavalry and foot-soldiers, strong and skilled in war, powerful without comparison in warfare and battle; he sent their commander . . . to make war in the land of the renegades who are like Jews, the crucifiers,[9] . . . Because like the Jews, the crucifiers, they denied Christ, he sent troops to destroy and devastate them and subject them to the rule of Christ. . . .

The Rebel was filled with fear, and not knowing where to turn, for fear had taken possession of him, he sent to the queen[10] saying, "I have done wrong to my lord the king, I have wrought injustice against him, and it is better that I fall into his hands than into the hands of a stranger. I will come myself and surrender to him, that he may do what he will to me." Thereupon the queen went to tell the king the whole of the message from that Rebel Sabradin, whose acts, like his name 'broken judgment,'[11] consist of insults, mad rage, errors, contentions, and arrogance. When the king heard this message which the Rebel had sent to the queen, he was exceedingly angry, and said to the queen, "Do you send him a message and say: 'If you come, or if you do not come, it will not trouble me; but if you go to a distant country I will pursue you through the power of God. And if you go into a cave, or if you just run away, I will not leave you alone nor will I return to my capital till I have taken you.'"

Now when he received this message, Sabradin set out and came to the king, and stood before him. And the king asked him, saying, "Why have you behaved thus to me? The gifts which you formerly sent to me you have given to your servants; and the multitude of goods of silver and gold which I gave to the poor you have taken away. Those who traded with me you have bound in chains; and what is worse, you have aspired to the throne of my kingdom, in imitation of the Devil your father who wished to be the equal of his creator." When that Rebel heard these words of the king he was at a loss for an answer in the greatness of his fear, for he was afraid of the king's presence; and he answered, "Do with me according to your will." And immediately the soldiers who were on the left and right of the king stood forth in anger and said, "This man is not worthy of life, for he has burnt the churches of God, he has slain Christians, and those whom he did not kill he has compelled to accept his religion. Moreover he desired to ascend the high mountain of the kingdom." And some said, "Let us slay him with the edge of the sword"; others said, "Let us stone him to death"; and others again, "Let us burn him with fire that he may disappear from the Earth." And they said to the king, "Think not, O king, that he comes to you honestly and freely, for he trusts in his magic art." And so saying, they lifted from his bosom and arm a talisman and revealed the form of his magic. Then said the king, "Can your talismans deliver you from my hands in which God has imprisoned you?" And he gave orders for his two hands to be bound with iron chains; he did not wish him to be killed, for he is merciful and forbearing. Thus was taken the Rebel in the net which he himself had woven, and in the snare which he himself had set. . . . After this the king sent news to the capital . . . of his kingdom. . . . "There is good news for you: with the help of your prayers I have defeated my enemy who is also the enemy of Christ."

---

[9]The *Falashas,* or Ethiopian Jews, are Kushitic people whose ancestors had intermarried with Jewish immigrants from Yemen. They are termed *crucifiers* here because of the notion that the Jews were responsible for Jesus' crucifixion.

[10]Queen Mangesa, wife of King Amda Seyon.

[11]A pun. In Geez *sabara* means "break" and *dayn* means "judgment." Actually, the Arabic name Sabr ad-Din means "Constant in the Faith."

A Yoruba Woman of Authority?

▼▼▼

93 ▼ SEATED FEMALE FIGURE

Like the Ethiopians, the *Yoruba*-speaking peoples of West Africa, who inhabit the forestlands that stretch from the edge of the savanna to the coast, trace their ancestry back to Southwest Asia, specifically Mecca. Such oral traditions are suspect as historical evidence and probably arose from a desire on the part of people converted to Islam well after 1200 to create for themselves an Arabic lineage. Whatever their origins, by the late fourteenth century the Yoruba people had established a number of independent kingdoms in a region encompassed today by the nations of Nigeria and Benin. One of the most important of these Yoruba kingdoms was *Oyo*. Although it reached its apogee as a regional power in the period 1600–1830, Oyo's foundations as a city-state go back much earlier. Its first capital city, Old Oyo, located near the Niger River, was founded sometime between 800 and 1000.

The Yoruba of Oyo and elsewhere were great artists as well as state builders. The town of Esie in Nigeria is the site of a collection of over 1,000 soapstone carvings of human figures that have lain for centuries in a grove (see source 91 for a description of Ghana's sacred groves). Each carving is an individual portrait, and it seems reasonable to infer that each represents a prominent, probably deceased, individual. The sculptures date to somewhere between 1100 and 1500 and seem to have come from either Old Oyo or the equally powerful Yoruba city-state of *Ife*.

The sculpture pictured here is twenty-six inches high and represents a seated woman holding a cutlass that rests against her right shoulder. Note her elaborate hairstyle, whose height equals that of her face, the three-stringed necklace, and the scarification of her face. This arrangement of scars is found equally on male and female effigies in the collection. The figure probably represents an *Iyalode* (mother in charge of external affairs), an important officer among the Yoruba. Although the specific functions of Iyalodes differed from kingdom to kingdom and from era to era, it is clear that they enjoyed wide-ranging political, social, economic, and even military powers. Simply stated, the Iyalode was a chief in her own right and one of the monarch's main lieutenants.

QUESTIONS FOR ANALYSIS

1. List and comment on all of the clues that lead us to infer that this figurine represents a woman of authority. What do you think each symbol of authority represents?
2. Compare this statue with the five statues in source 38. What do all six statues have in common? What do those common characteristics suggest about the way in which authority is perceived and portrayed across cultures and time?

A Yoruba Woman of Authority?

▼▼▼

The Americas

Recently reported genetic evidence based on a study of living Siberian and American Indian populations strongly suggests that migrants from East Asia reached the Western Hemisphere no more than 18,000 years ago. Datable artifacts in two widely separated archaeological sites, Cactus Hill in southeastern Virginia and Monte Verde in Chile, further indicate that hunter-gatherers inhabited both North and South America at least as far back as 15,000 years ago. The Monte Verde site is about 15,000 years old, and the earliest materials found at Cactus Hill are 15,000–17,000 years old. As the picture now stands, and it will likely be revised as new evidence comes in, the First Americans arrived in a series of waves, but of these, there were probably two periods of major migration. The first occurred sometime soon after 18,000 years ago when a land bridge, known as *Beringia,* connected Siberia and Alaska. Rising waters from melting glaciers toward the end of the last ice age wiped out that bridge about 11,000 years ago. The second major wave of migration probably occurred about 8,000 years ago as various newcomers traveled from northeastern Asia in small boats, stopping at various locations along the western shores of the Americas.

Whenever it began and however it occurred, the initial peopling of the Americas was an epochal event (or, better, series of events) rivaled only in magnitude by the demographic shifts that took place following the arrival in force of Europeans and Africans after 1492. With the advent of European and African peoples and their diseases, the whole population structure of the Americas underwent massive changes.

During the many years that separated these two eras, the Americas witnessed a variety of other only slightly less monumental developments. One of the most consequential was the indigenous development of agriculture based on the cultivation of over 100 different crops unknown to the peoples of Africa and Eurasia. Chief among them were *maize* (*corn* in American English), potatoes, avocados, sweet potatoes, tomatoes, peanuts, manioc, and various types of beans, peppers (especially chilies), and squashes. By the time the Europeans arrived, agriculture was practiced from the woodlands of eastern North America to the rain forests of the Amazon tropics. As elsewhere, agriculture imposed restrictions on the behavior and social patterns of the cultivators and also produced enough food in a sufficiently regular manner to allow for the growth of dense populations. One result was the rise of civilizations, first in South America, Mexico, and Central America, and later in regions that are today part of the United States.

Three of the major civilizations of North America were the *Mississippian Mound Culture,* the *Hohokam,* and the *Anasazi.* Between 1050 and 1200 C.E. the Mississippian Mound Builders created the city of Cahokia at a site that today is in East St. Louis, Illinois. At its height, Cahokia supported a population of at least 11,000 people and possibly as many as 30,000. The Hohokam (those who have vanished) of the Sonoran Desert produced a complex urban society based upon their ability to construct and maintain some 300 miles of irrigation canals in the region of what is today Phoenix, Arizona. During the twelfth and thirteenth centuries the Anasazi (the ancient ones) of the Four Corners region of the American Southwest built cities in Chaco Canyon, New Mexico, and at Mesa Verde in Colorado, which today stand as silent testimony of their engineering skills. All three civilizations participated in widespread trade networks and were influenced by the earlier civilizations of Mexico. All three also passed away as urban cultures long before the arrival of Europeans, who could only marvel at the ruins they left behind.

Because they left no written records behind and abandoned their urban centers so long ago, these North American civilizations remain largely mysterious, despite the considerable work of archaeologists over the past half century. The *Maya, Aztec,* and *Inca* peoples of farther south, however, were still identifiable cultures when European conquerors and missionaries arrived on the scene. Despite the best attempts of many Europeans to efface totally the presumed devilish cultures that they had discovered, the Maya, Aztec, and Inca civilizations would not be forgotten.

The sources that follow — the products of American Indian and European crafters and authors — combine to shed light on four important American cultures that flourished between 500 and 1500 C.E.

Mayan Faces and Figures
▼▼▼

94 ▾ *THREE MAYAN CERAMIC SCULPTURES*

The *Maya,* one of Ancient America's most brilliant civilizations, inhabited an area that today encompasses all of Mexico's Yucatan Peninsula and parts of the states of Tabasco and Chiapas, all of Guatemala and Belize, and the western regions of Honduras and El Salvador. Indeed, the Maya, today more than 6 million strong, continue to inhabit these lands and to maintain their traditions and related but often mutually incomprehensible Mayan languages. Far from being a vanished people, they are a vital culture, despite often violent attempts since the sixteenth century and down to today to repress and acculturate them.

The Maya did not create the first civilization in pre-Spanish *Mesoamerica* (Mexico and Central America). That distinction belongs to a people we know as the *Olmec,* who formed a civilization around 1500 B.C.E. along Mexico's Gulf Coast and fashioned many of the distinguishing cultural characteristics shared by all Mesoamerican civilizations, including a complex calendar and massive ceremonial complexes.

A distinctive Mayan civilization began to flourish in what is known as the Late Preclassical Age (300 B.C.E.–250 C.E.), when the Maya constructed a number of monumental temple complexes. In the subsequent Classical Age (300–925) Mayan genius soared, but very much like the Classical Age of Ancient Greece, it was accompanied by turmoil and uneven fortunes. Between around 800 to 925, Mayan civilization witnessed glory, tragic decline, and triumph as some areas of the Mayan World suffered profound political, social, and demographic dislocation. In the southern lowlands thrones were toppled and cities abandoned, whereas in the Yucatan Peninsula, the northernmost area of Mayan civilization, there was prosperity. During the tenth century, however, there was a second Mayan collapse, and most cities in the Yucatan were abandoned, apparent victims of overpopulation and environmental degradation. Perhaps as a consequence of their own failings, the Maya of the north now fell under the domination of the militaristic Toltecs from the highlands of Central Mexico. Mayan civilization was not snuffed out, but its days of glory and independence were over.

Today's visitor to the lands of the Maya is awed by the recovered remains of their cities, such as Palenque. But Mayan artistic genius was not confined to the construction of great temples and so-called pyramids. The Maya also excelled in all of the representational arts, including crafting ceramic figurines of human and divine beings. The following three ceramic pieces, all from Jaina, a tiny island in the Bay of Campeche off the western shore of the Yucatan Peninsula, date from the Late Classical Period (700–925). The island was a religious sanctuary and necropolis (city of the dead), where important Mayans of the period were buried. All statuettes discovered there are hollow and fitted with whistles at their backs. We can only guess at their ceremonial use. Whatever their purposes, they are vivid portraits of flesh-and-blood Maya who lived over 1,000 years ago, and also provide us with some tantalizing clues regarding Mayan life, beliefs, and practices.

QUESTIONS FOR ANALYSIS

1. Our first two statuettes depict ballplayers. One of the players is a captive who will be sacrificed at the end of the game. How do we know or infer that?
2. The other ballplayer is a Mayan aristocrat on the home team, as it were. How do we know or infer that?
3. The third piece, showing a woman and a man, has been variously interpreted. Some see it as the union of the moon goddess and the sun god. Others view it as evidence of the sophistication of Mayan society that could depict a common aspect of human life and love. What might that be? A third interpretation is that this is also a comic scene. What is the joke?
4. Based on these three statuettes, what do you conclude about Mayan interest in the human face and form? You might want to compare these works with the Hellenic and Hellenistic statues in sources 28 and 29.

Ballplayer

Ballplayer

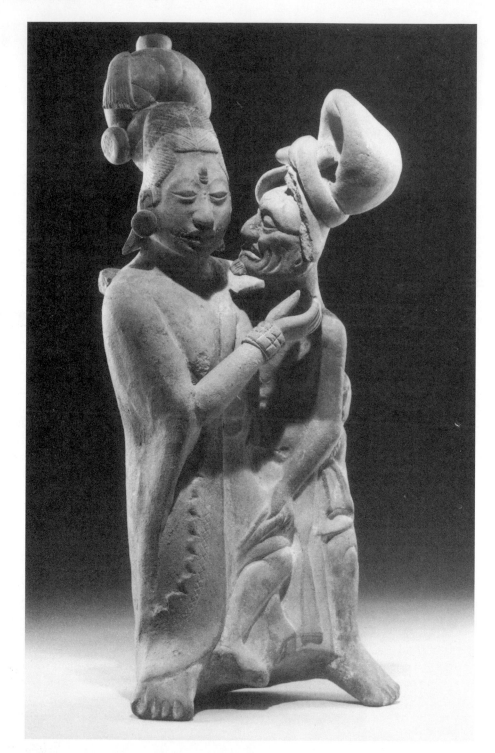

A Woman and a Man

The Sacred Marketplace:
Aztec Commerce and Religion
▼▼▼

95 ▼ *Diego Durán,*
BOOK OF THE GODS AND RITES

Father Diego Durán (1537–1588) was born in Seville, Spain, but moved with his family to New Spain while a young boy. In 1556 he entered the Dominican Order in Mexico City and served as a priest throughout Central and Southern Mexico until his death. Like a number of other Dominican and Franciscan friars, Durán became a strong advocate of the native American Indians and a student of their history and culture. He mastered *Nahuatl,* the language of the Aztecs, and explored indigenous beliefs and religious practices by talking with elders and studying available native records. As his studies progressed, he became increasingly convinced that apparent parallels between his own Catholic faith, moral code, and rituals and those of his native friends pointed to a diffusion of Judaism or Christianity or both into the New World at some unknown time or times in the past. He further concluded that the bloody human sacrifices that were an integral part of Mesoamerican religion were evidence of the intervention of the Devil, who had succeeded in perverting the True Religion among the Mesoamericans prior to the arrival of the Spaniards. He also believed that he and his fellow missionaries would never succeed in rooting out these erroneous beliefs and satanic practices until they first understood the ancient religion.

In order to aid this missionary work (and probably also because of his innate curiosity), Durán produced three books: the *Book of the Gods and Rite*s (ca. 1576–1579), which is excerpted here; *The Ancient Calendar* (1579), which is a guide to the Mesoamerican calendar; and *The History of the Indies of New Spain* (1580?–1581), which traces the Aztecs from their legendary origins in the ninth century up to their conquest in 1521. The encyclopedic nature and apparent accuracy of his work places Durán, along with several other Spanish missionary-scholars, in the ranks of the pioneers of Mesoamerican ethnohistory, and his books are invaluable texts for modern students of both pre- and early post-Conquest Mexico. Much of the information he supplies is not found in any other extant documentary source, but quite a bit has been confirmed by other means, especially through archaeological evidence.

In the following excerpts Durán deals with the intimate connections in Aztec society between commerce and religion and the manner in which the supposedly converted Mexicans of his day retained some of the old customs. Durán also drew or commissioned illustrations for his book, and one of those, a drawing of an Aztec market, accompanies these excerpts. Its overall composition suggests that it was copied from a pre-Conquest original.

QUESTIONS FOR ANALYSIS

1. Where did merchants fit into the Mesoamerican class system? How did they raise their status?
2. What religious and economic roles did the *tianguiz,* or local marketplace, play in pre-Conquest Mexico?
3. How did religious taboos help stimulate the Aztec economy?
4. What roles did slavery and human sacrifice play in the dynamics of the marketplace?
5. What religious functions did slavery and human sacrifice serve?
6. In what ways had the customs of the marketplace survived, despite the imposition of Christianity?
7. Based on Durán's description of a *tianguiz,* describe and explain all of the activities, persons, and elements in the accompanying illustration. Do not neglect to take into account the sexes of the nine people. If you wish, compose a short story or journalistic report revolving around this scene.

In this land in pagan times the ancient kings and princes took very special care and caution in rewarding and honoring the upright, the virtuous, and the brave so that the rest might find heart to imitate their strength, when they saw the reward given. . . . There were three established and honored ways in all the nations[1] [for obtaining these rewards]. The first and principal path which the kings designated was soldiery — to make oneself known in war through valiant feats, to be outstanding in killing, taking prisoners, to destroy armies and squadrons, to have directed these things. These [warriors] were given great honors, rewards, weapons, and insignia which were proof of their splendid deeds and valor. . . .

The second way in which men rose was through religion, entering the priesthood. After having served in the temples in a virtuous, penitential, and cloistered way of life, in their old age they were sent out to high and honorable posts (which exist to this day) in the different nations. They were given high-sounding names and titles, which in our language today, to judge by the respect and reverence they enjoyed and still do, can be considered to have been the equivalent of

counts, dukes, or marquises; bishops or archbishops; and so forth. They were present when the government councils were held, their opinions and advice were listened to, and they were part of the ruling boards and juntas. Without their council and opinion kings did not dare act. . . .

The third and least glorious manner of [rising in the world] was that of becoming a merchant or trader, that of buying and selling, going forth to all the markets of the land, bartering cloth for jewels, jewels for feathers, feathers for stones, and stones for slaves, always dealing in things of importance, of renown, and of high value. These [men] strengthened their social position with their wealth. We have seen many men of low birth and worse blood rise to a state which has permitted them to marry daughters of dukes, counts, and marquises and to form magnificent and rich family estates, mixing their humble blood with that of the highest of Spain. The same was true of these Indian merchants. They acquired wealth and obtained slaves to sacrifice to this their god.[2] And so they were considered among the magnates of the land, just as the valorous soldier brought sacrificial captives from

---

[1] In other words, not just the Aztecs, but also all other tribes and states in pre-Conquest Mexico.

[2] *Quetzalcoatl,* the feathered serpent. He was the chief deity of the *Choultecs,* or people of *Cholula,* a people noted for their

mercantile skills and wealth. One of the gods of creation, as well as inventor of writing and the calendar, Quetzalcoatl also served as the god of all merchants. See note 3.

war, gaining fame as a brave. He received people and prepared a banquet with the flesh of the man he had brought back as an offering to god, all the lords and chieftains granting him in return insignia and high privileges — the same was true of the merchants. They offered one or two sacrificial slaves with the usual ceremonies of eating and dancing, presenting gifts of mantles, breechcloths, and sandals to all the lords, preparing different dishes for all the guests. [These merchants] were given the title of noblemen and were honored with the same pomp as the warriors. [Each one] was given an appropriate name, different from the rest, which indicated the way in which he had gained his honors. . . .

The merchants celebrated the feast in honor of their god because their divine patron had been the most excellent, the richest merchant in his time, and possibly the one who gave them the patterns and rules of their trade. . . .

I wish to give warning that even today there is a diabolical custom among the natives, especially in Cholula,[3] where the god [Quetzalcoatl] was worshiped; peddlers will traffic for ten, twelve, and even twenty years, earning and saving up to two or three hundred pesos. And after all their toil, wretched eating and sleeping — without aim or reason — they offer a most lavish banquet. There they spend all their savings. What I most regret is that they follow the ancient custom of holding that memorial feast in order to celebrate their [ancient] titles and set themselves on high. This would not be wrong except that for their celebration they await the day on which the god [Quetzalcoatl] was honored. . . .

We have already dealt with all the main deities to whom men were sacrificed, with all the rites and ceremonies performed in their honor. Though briefly, in order not to be tiring, it is now timely and correct to tell something about the people who died as offerings to the gods, who were sacrificed and slain. Before we deal with this subject, though, first it will be necessary to say that in

olden times there was a god of markets and fairs. This deity had his place upon a *momoztli,* which is like a roadside shrine or a pillory block. These were used in ancient times, and later we boys called them places of idle gossip. Many of these stood along the roads, on street corners, and in the market.

In the shrines at the market places were fixed round carved stones as large as shields, each one bearing a round figure like that of the sun with flowers and circles carved around it. Some were carved with other images, depending upon the feeling of the priests and the importance of the market place and the town. The gods[4] of these market places threatened terrible ills and made evil omens and auguries to the neighboring villages which did not attend their market places. There were clearly set limits regarding how many leagues[5] could be traveled to attend the markets to honor their gods. Also a law and commandment forced the people to attend unless excused by some just impediment. . . .

Thus they came from all parts, from two, from three, from four and more leagues away, to the market places. From all of this has survived the strange custom of attending the market before going to mass. Since the ancient custom of holding the market every five days still exists, occasionally this falls on Sunday, and no one hears mass in the area of the town where the market is held. . . .

The markets were so inviting, pleasurable, appealing, and gratifying to these people that great crowds attended, and still attend, them, especially during the big fairs, as is well known to all. I suspect that if I said to a market woman accustomed to going from market to market: "Look, today is market day in such and such a town. What would you rather do, go from here right to Heaven or to that market?" I believe this would be her answer: "Allow me to go to the market first, and then I will go to Heaven." She would be happier to lose those minutes of glory to visit the

---

[3]A city in central Mexico noted for its commerce (note 2) and which also served as a special religious sanctuary because of its association with Quetzalcoatl's cult.

[4]In addition to Quetzalcoatl, the god of commerce, each marketplace had its local deity.
[5]A *league* is three miles.

market place and walk about hither and thither without any gain or profit, to satisfy her hunger and whim to see the *tianguiz*.[6]

Regarding these opinions of mine, I wish to tell an anecdote which confirms my beliefs. While I was living in a town not too far from the City of Mexico, an old woman dwelt there, ninety or more years of age, who was accused more than once by the catechists of not attending mass. She constantly gave her advanced age as an excuse for her absence, and was brought to confession by force. She never missed a market day, however, or those held in the entire region. It so happened that on a Friday she walked two leagues from her house to a market place, and on the way back, as she was carrying a small bundle of scrawny ears of corn, she fainted because of the burning sun, her strength failed her, and she fell dead on the path. Her children and grandchildren, frightened by the sudden death, brought her body to the church. There they lost their fear, and all confessed that she had never missed a *tianguiz* [but that] there had been no way of getting her to mass. It was then agreed that she would be buried in the market place so that the place which had served her well in life and which she so loved, in death would not be denied her. . . .

The markets in this land were all enclosed by walls and stood either in front of the temples of the gods or to one side. Market day in each town was considered a main feast in that town or city. And thus in that small shrine where the idol of the market stood were offered ears of corn, chili, tomatoes, fruit, and other vegetables, seeds, and breads — in sum, everything sold in the *tianguiz*. Some say that [these offerings] were left there until they spoiled; others deny this, saying that all was gathered up by the priests and ministers of the temples.

But, to return to what I said about the market day being a feast day, the following is the truth. One day I was informed in a personal way, and now I shall tell what took place between me and a lord of a certain village.[7] When I begged him to

finish a part of the church that was under construction, he answered: "Father, do you not know that tomorrow is a great feast in this town? How can you expect them to work? Leave it for another day." Then, very carefully, I looked at the calendar to see which saint's day it was, and I found none. Laughing at me, [the lord] said: "Do you not know that tomorrow is the feast of the *tianguiz* of this town? [Do you not know] that not a man or a woman will fail to pay it its due honor?" From these words I realized [how important] a feast and solemnity the market is for them. . . .

Furthermore, a law was established by the state prohibiting the selling of goods outside the market place. Not only were there laws and penalties connected with this, but there was a fear of the supernatural, of misfortune, and of the ire and wrath of the god of the market. No one ventured, therefore, to trade outside [the market limits], and the custom has survived until these days. Many a time have I seen a native carry two or three hens or a load of fruit for sale in the market. On the road he meets a Spaniard who wants to buy them from him. The Spaniard offers the price which he would have received in the market. The native refuses and is unwilling to sell, even though he would save himself a league or two of walking. He begs the Spaniard to go to the market place to buy them there. . . . Even today, though they are Christians, the awe and fear of their ancient law is still strong. It must also be said that the planting of this awe and nonsense in these people brought a certain income from all that which was sold in the markets [in the form of taxes], which was divided between the lord and the community.

In this land the sovereigns had set up a regulation regarding the markets: they were to take the form of fairs or markets specializing in the selling of certain things. Some markets, therefore, became famous and popular for these reasons: it was commanded that slaves were to be sold at the fair in Azcapotzalco and that all the people of the land who had slaves for sale must go there and to

---

[6]Durán has already explained that this word means "marketplace."

[7]Probably a native lord, or local ruler, who was allowed to continue in office after the Conquest.

no other place to sell. The same can be said of Itzocan. Slaves could be sold in these two places only. It was at these two fairs that slaves were sold so that those who needed them would go there and to no other place to buy. In other places, such as Cholula, it was ordered that the merchandise must consist of jewels, precious stones, and fine featherwork. At others, such as Tetzcoco, cloth and fine gourds were sold, together with exquisitely worked ceramics, splendidly done in the native way. . . .

I would like to say some things regarding the slaves sold in the two markets I have mentioned, Azcapotzalco and Itzocan. Some things worthy of remembering can be said about these slaves. In the first place, it should be known that in honor of the gods (as has been noted) men and women were slain on all the feast days. Some of these were slaves bought in the market place for the special purpose of representing gods. When they had performed the representation, when those slaves had been purified and washed — some for an entire year, others for forty days, others for nine, others for seven — after having been honored and served in the name of the god they impersonated, at the end they were sacrificed by those who owned them.

Captives of another type were those taken as prisoners in war. These served exclusively as sacrifices for the man who had impersonated the god whose feast was being celebrated.[8] Thus these were called the "delicious food of the gods." I do not have to deal with all of these, but only with the slaves who were sold in the market place for having broken the law or for the reasons I shall describe later. These were bought by rich merchants and by important chieftains, some to

glorify their own names and others to fulfill their customary vows.[9]

The masters took the slaves to the *tianguiz*: some took men, others women, others boys or girls, so that there would be variety from which to choose. So that they would be identified as slaves, they wore on their necks wooden or metal collars with small rings through which passed rods about one yard long. In its place I shall explain the reason for putting these collars on them. At the site where these slaves were sold (which stood at one side of the *tianguiz*, according to market regulations) the owners kept [the slaves] dancing and singing so that merchants would be attracted by the charm of their voices and their [dance] steps and buy them quickly. If one possessed this facility, therefore, he found a master immediately. This was not the case for those who lacked grace and were inept in these things. Thus they were presented many times at market places without anyone paying attention to them, though [occasionally] some bought them to make use of them [in some way],[10] since they were unfit to represent the gods. Singers and dancers were in demand because when they were garbed in the raiment of the gods they went about singing and dancing in the streets and the houses during the time of their impersonation. They entered [the houses] and the temples and [climbed to] the flat roofs of the royal houses and those of their masters. They were given all the pleasures and joys of the world — foods, drink, feasts — as if they had been the gods themselves. So it was that the merchants wished that, aside from being good dancers and singers, they were healthy, without blemish or deformity. . . . [These slaves] were therefore made to strip, and were

---

[8]Prisoners were sacrificed to the gods and to the impersonators of the gods. The feasts of important deities involved a sacrifice that assumed the level of death, ritual resurrection, and some sort of communion. Flawless slaves, as described later in the reading, became impersonators of the deity and lived a life of splendor and glory for a stipulated period of time. The impersonator of Quetzalcoatl, for example, served forty days. On the feast day, the impersonator was sacrificed. For some feasts the body was cooked and consumed in a ritual meal. For other feasts the body was flayed and the skin worn by a priest.

[9]Once when Durán asked why the people were not content to sacrifice animals, he was told that the sacrifice of humans was the honored offering of a great lord. For the feast of Quetzalcoatl, which was held on February 3, the merchants of Cholula purchased a slave without blemish to serve as the impersonator. Later they were the ones who consumed his body.

[10]They were kept as domestic servants.

A Tianguiz, *or Marketplace.*

examined from head to foot, member by member. They were forced to extend their hands and lift their feet [as is done today with] Negro [slaves], to determine whether they were crippled. If one was found healthy, he was bought; otherwise, no. For it was desired that the slaves to be purified to represent the gods (this ceremony belonging to their rites, religion, and precepts) were healthy and without blemish, just as we read in the Holy Writ about the sacrifices of the Old Testament which were to be without blemish. These slaves were not strangers or foreigners or prisoners of war, as some have declared, but were natives of the same town. . . .

▷   Durán then enumerates the reasons for which a
person could be enslaved.

We have digressed from our theme (but not too far, because what we have told is related to the slaves and is worthy of note). Now that the way in which one became a slave has been described, it would be interesting to note how one was freed. It should be known that there was a law in this land of New Spain: whenever the masters of slaves took them out for sale, they were weighed down with collars and with rods one yard long across their backs. One reason [for these collars and rods] was so that these [slaves] might be easily recognized; furthermore, if they tried to escape, the rod was an obstacle and hindrance to fleeing in a crowd. For it was decreed that if the slave could escape from his master in the *tianguiz* after having entered it and could pass the limits of the market before his master caught him, having passed these limits, he could step upon human excrement and in this way become free. Thus soiled, he went to the purifiers of slaves, showed himself to them, and said: "O lords, I was a slave, and, according to what your laws decree,

I fled today from the market place, from the hands of my master! I escaped like a bird from a cage and stepped upon the offal as is the law. And so I have come to you to purify me and to free me from my servitude." The authorities removed the fetters, stripped him, and washed him from head to foot. Having washed him, they garbed him in new clothing and presented him to the lord; they told him that [this man] had been a slave but had been liberated according to law. The law praised him for his skill and enterprise and gave him complete freedom. Thenceforth he was to be honored and given insignia as a free and spirited man. Often he was kept in the palace as a servant of the house. . . .

Slaves were exchanged for cloths, which were called *cuachtli,* jewels of gold and stones, and rich feathers. Some [slaves], depending upon their disposition and quality, were worth more than others.

Regarding the second [type of slaves], men captured in war, no more can be added to what has been said. It was certain and sure that such captives were to serve as victims in sacrifice (unless they escaped), because they had been brought exclusively to be sacrificed to the gods.

Governing the Inca Empire
▼▼▼

96 ▼ Pedro de Cieza de León, CHRONICLES

In addition to accounts composed by scholar-missionaries such as Diego Durán, we have written records, engraved on stone and written on parchment, from the hands of pre-Conquest Mesoamericans. Needless to say, they are invaluable for filling out our picture of the cultures of this region. The same is not true for South America.

Until recently, scholars believed that no indigenous civilization of South America produced a system of writing. A book published in 2003 challenges that notion and argues that the Inca Empire's *quipus,* knotted strings used for record-keeping, constituted a highly complex system of three-dimensional writing that Spanish colonists (as well as almost all modern scholars) failed to recognize as more than just abacus-like devices that allowed Inca functionaries to perform numerical calculations. The failure by Spaniards and historians alike to look beyond the apparently obvious was due to their shared assumption that writing can only be two-dimensional. This new theory needs further study and testing, especially through computer analysis of extant *quipus,* before it can be accepted or rejected. Whatever the truth, as the situation currently stands, even if the *quipus* were a form of writing, we cannot yet decipher them. Furthermore, there is no evidence that any other culture of South America had anything even approaching a system of writing.

This absence of decipherable written records for the peoples of South America prior to the arrival of the Spaniards means that our only current sources for their pre-Conquest history are archaeological artifacts and accounts composed by sixteenth- and early seventeenth-century American Indian and Spanish writers who labored to preserve the memory of a past in imminent danger of being lost forever.

One such ethnohistorian was Pedro de Cieza de León (1520–1554). In 1535 he arrived in the Americas as a teenage soldier-adventurer and spent the next seventeen years trekking throughout South America, falling increasingly under the spell of the continent and its native peoples. As he traveled and fought, he took detailed notes of all he observed and experienced. Believing, as he noted, that "we and the Indians have the same origin," Cieza wrote with great sympathy for the many different American Indian cultures he encountered, even though he seems never to have doubted the righteousness of the Spanish conquest and conversion of these peoples. Indeed, one of his primary reasons for recording his observations was that he considered it "right that the world know how so great a multitude of these Indians were brought into the sanctity of the Church."

Cieza's *Chronicles* describe many different native South American cultures, but their greatest value to modern historians is the wealth of detail they provide of the Inca Empire and the *Quechua* Indians who created it. Like the Aztecs of Mexico, the Quechuas were recent arrivals on the scene who fashioned a civilization that borrowed heavily from a variety of preceding cultures. Also like the Aztec Empire, the Inca Empire was young, having taken shape during the reigns of Pachacuti (1438–1471) and his son Topac Yupanqui (1471–1493). As was also true in Mexico, the Inca Empire's life was prematurely cut short by *conquistadores.*

In the following selection Cieza describes how the Inca monarchs governed an empire that covered about 500,000 square miles, stretched some 2,500 miles from end to end, and included anywhere from 6 to 13 million people of different ethnic origins and languages.

QUESTIONS FOR ANALYSIS

1. What devices did the Incas use to govern their vast empire?
2. From Cieza's perspective, what were the most admirable qualities of this empire?
3. What appear to have been the strengths of this empire? Can you perceive any weaknesses? Were the Incas aware of these shortcomings, and, if so, how did they attempt to counter them?
4. Consider the theory that the quipus constituted a writing system. Does León's testimony seem to support or contradict this new theory? Be specific.

It is told for a fact of the rulers of this kingdom that in the days of their rule they had their representatives in the capitals of all the provinces, . . . for in all these places there were larger and finer lodgings than in most of the other cities of this great kingdom, and many storehouses. They served as the head of the provinces or regions, and from every so many leagues[1] around the tributes were brought to one of these capitals, and from so many others, to another. This was so well organized that there was not a village that did not know where it was to send its tribute. In all these capitals the Incas had temples of the sun, mints, and many silversmiths who did nothing but work rich pieces of gold or fair vessels of silver; large garrisons were stationed there, and, as I have said, a steward or representative who was in command of them all, to whom an accounting of

---

[1] One *league* is three miles.

everything that was brought in was made, and who, in turn, had to give one of all that was issued. And these governors could in no way interfere with the jurisdiction of another who held a similar post, but within his own, if there were any disorder or disturbance, he had authority to punish it[s perpetrators], especially if it were in the nature of a conspiracy or a rebellion, or failure to obey the Inca,[2] for full power resided in these governors. And if the Incas had not had the foresight to appoint them and to establish the *mitimaes*,[3] the natives would have often revolted and shaken off the royal rule; but with the many troops and the abundance of provisions, they could not effect this unless they had all plotted such treason or rebellion together. This happened rarely, for these governors who were named were of complete trust, all of them *Orejones*,[4] and most of them had their holdings, or *chacaras*, in the neighborhood of *Cuzco*,[5] and their homes and kinfolk. If one of them did not show sufficient capacity for his duties, he was removed and another put in his place.

When one of them came to Cuzco on private business or to see the Inca, he left a lieutenant in his place, not one who aspired to the post, but one he knew would faithfully carry out what he was ordered to do and what was best for the service of the Inca. And if one of these governors or delegates died while in office, the natives at once sent word to the Inca how and of what he had died, and even transported the body by the post road if this seemed to them advisable. The tribute paid by each of these districts where the capital was situated and that turned over by the natives, whether gold, silver, clothing, arms, and all else they gave, was entered in the accounts of

. . . [those] who kept the *quipus* and did everything ordered by the governor in the matter of finding the soldiers or supplying whomever the Inca ordered, or making delivery to Cuzco; but when they came from the city of Cuzco to go over the accounts, or they were ordered to go to Cuzco to give an accounting, the accountants themselves gave it by the quipus, or went to give it where there could be no fraud, but everything had to come out right. Few years went by in which an accounting of all these things was not made. . . .

Realizing how difficult it would be to travel the great distances of their land where every league and at every turn a different language was spoken, and how bothersome it would be to have to employ interpreters to understand them, these rulers, as the best measure, ordered and decreed, with severe punishment for failure to obey, that all the natives of their empire should know and understand the language of Cuzco, both they and their women. This was so strictly enforced that an infant had not yet left its mother's breast before they began to teach it the language it had to know. And although at the beginning this was difficult and many stubbornly refused to learn any language but their own, the Incas were so forceful that they accomplished what they had proposed, and all had to do their bidding. This was carried out so faithfully that in the space of a few years a single tongue was known and used in an extension of more than 1,200 leagues, yet, even though this language was employed, they all spoke their own [languages], which were so numerous that if I were to list them it would not be credited. . . .

As the city of Cuzco was the most important in all Peru, and the Incas lived there most of the

---

[2]*Inca* means "sovereign lord." In its strictest sense it should be used only to refer to this civilization's god-kings. Today, however, historians customarily use the term loosely to refer to the civilization, its empire, and the Quechua people who created them.
[3]Literally, "those moved from one land to another." This was the systematic practice of resettling groups from one area of the empire to another. These resettled people would serve as a check on the loyalties of the natives of the region to which they had been transferred and would, in turn, be kept in check by their new neighbors. This helped keep down rebel-

lions and broke down regional and ethnic differences within the empire; it also was a means of cultivating land that needed settlers.
[4]Literally in Spanish, "big-ears." They were members of the ruling class, often of royal blood, who were distinguished by the large earplugs they wore. Earplugs can be seen in two of the Mayan figurines in source 94. Earplugs were a token of high status for many American Indian societies from South America to the Mound Cultures of the Ohio Valley.
[5]The capital city of the empire.

time, they had with them in the city many of the leading men of the country, the most intelligent and informed of all, as their advisers. For all agree that before they undertook anything of importance, they discussed it with these counselors, and submitted their opinion to that of the majority. And for the administration of the city, and that the highways should be safe and nowhere should offenses or thefts be committed, from among the most highly esteemed of them he [the Inca] appointed those whose duty it was to punish wrongdoers, and to this end they were always traveling about the country. The Incas took such care to see that justice was meted out that nobody ventured to commit a felony or theft. This was to deal with thieves, ravishers of women, or conspirators against the Inca; however, there were many provinces that warred on one another, and the Incas were not wholly able to prevent this.

By the river that runs through Cuzco justice was executed on those who were caught or brought in as prisoners from some other place. There they had their heads cut off, or were put to death in some other manner which they chose. Mutiny and conspiracy were severely punished, and, above all, those who were thieves and known as such; even their wives and children were despised and considered to be tarred with the same brush. . . .

We have written how it was ordered by the Incas that the statues be brought out at their feasts, and how they selected from the wisest among their men those who should tell what the life of their kings had been and how they had conducted themselves in the rule of their kingdoms, for the purpose I have stated. It should also be known that, aside from this, it was the custom among them, and a rule carefully observed, for each of them to choose during his reign three or four old men of their nation, skilled and gifted for that purpose, whom they ordered to recall all that had happened in the province during the time of their reign, whether prosperous or adverse, and to make and arrange songs so that

thereby it might be known in the future what had taken place in the past. Such songs could not be sung or proclaimed outside the presence of the Inca, and those who were to carry out this behest were ordered to say nothing referring to the Inca during his lifetime, but after he was dead, they said to his successor almost in these words: "Oh, mighty and powerful Inca, may the Sun and Moon, the Earth, the hills and trees, the stones and your forefathers guard you from misfortune and make you prosperous, happy, and blessed among all who have been born. Know that the things that happened to your predecessor were these." And saying this, with their eyes on the ground and heads hanging, with great humility they gave an account and report of all they knew, which they could do very well, for there were many among them of great memory, subtle wit, and lively intelligence, and abounding in knowledge, as those of us who are here and hear them can bear witness. After they said this, when the Inca had heard them, he sent for other of his old Indians whom he ordered to learn the songs the others bore in their memory, and to prepare new ones of what took place during the time of his reign, what was spent, what the provinces contributed, and put all this down in the quipus, so that after his death, when his successor reigned, what had been given and contributed would be known. And except on days of great celebration, or on the occasion of mourning and lament for the death of a brother or son of the Inca, for on such days it was permitted to relate their grandeur and their origin and birth, at no other time was it permitted to deal with this, for it had been forbidden by their lords, and if they did so, they were severely punished.

[The Indians] had a method of knowing how the tributes of food supplies should be levied on the provinces when the Lord-Inca came through with his army, or was visiting the kingdom; or, when nothing of this sort was taking place, what came into the storehouses and what was issued to the subjects, so nobody could be unduly burdened. . . . This involved the quipus, which are long strands of knotted strings, and those who were the accountants and understood the meaning of these knots could reckon by them expenditures or other things that had taken place many years before. By these knots they counted from one to ten and from ten to a hundred, and from a hundred to a thousand. On one of these strands there is the account of one thing, and on the other of another, in such a way that what to us is a strange, meaningless account is clear to them. In the capital of each province there were accountants whom they called *quipu-camayocs,* and by these knots they kept the account of the tribute to be paid by the natives of that district in silver, gold, clothing, flocks, down to wood and other more insignificant things, and by these same quipus at the end of a year, or ten, or twenty years, they gave a report to the one whose duty it was to check the account so exact that not even a pair of sandals was missing. . . .

The *Orejones* of Cuzco who supplied me with information are in agreement that in olden times, in the days of the Lord-Incas, all the villages and provinces of Peru were notified that a report should be given to the rulers and their representatives each year of the men and women who had died, and all who had been born, for this was necessary for the levying of the tributes as well as to know how many were available for war and those who could assume the defense of the villages. This was an easy matter, for each province at the end of the year had a list by the knots of the quipus of all the people who had died there during the year, as well as of those who had been born. At the beginning of the new year they came to Cuzco, bringing their quipus, which told how many births there had been during the year, and how many deaths. This was reported with all truth and accuracy, without any fraud or deceit. In this way the Inca and the governors knew which of the Indians were poor, the women who had been widowed, whether they were able to pay their taxes, and how many men they could count on in the event of war, and many other things they considered highly important.

As this kingdom was so vast, as I have repeatedly mentioned, in each of the many provinces there were many storehouses filled with supplies and other needful things; thus, in times of war, wherever the armies went they drew upon the contents of these storehouses, without ever touching the supplies of their confederates or laying a finger on what they had in their settlements. And when there was no war, all this stock of supplies and food was divided up among the poor and the widows. These poor were the aged, or the lame, crippled, or paralyzed, or those afflicted with some other diseases; if they were in good health, they received nothing. Then the storehouses were filled up once more with the tributes paid the Inca. If there came a lean year, the storehouses were opened and the provinces were lent what they needed in the way of supplies; then, in a year of abundance, they paid back all they had received. Even though the tributes paid to the Inca were used only for the aforesaid purposes, they were employed to advantage, for in this way their kingdom was opulent and well supplied.

No one who was lazy or tried to live by the work of others was tolerated; everyone had to work. Thus on certain days each lord went to his lands and took the plow in hand and cultivated the earth, and did other things. Even the Incas themselves did this to set an example, for everybody was to know that there should be nobody so rich that, on this account, he might disdain or affront the poor. And under their system there was none such in all the kingdom, for, if he had his health, he worked and lacked for nothing; and if he was ill, he received what he needed from the storehouses. And no rich man could deck himself out in more finery than the poor, or wear different clothing, except the rulers and headmen, who, to maintain their dignity, were allowed great freedom and privilege, as well as the *Orejones,* who held a place apart among all the peoples.

Part Four

Travel, Encounter, and Exchange:
1000–1700

Europe's late-fifteenth-century transoceanic explorations inaugurated a new age of global linkage by virtue of Columbus's sailing to the Americas. In many respects, however, the events of 1492 and following were a continuation of a process of long-range cultural exchange that had been gaining momentum throughout Eurasia and Africa since at least the opening of the Silk Road late in the second century B.C.E. The process had its periods of retreat and retrenchment, as routes closed down due to any number of factors, but the overall pattern was one of growing interchange. Between about 1000 and 1400 C.E. long-distance interchange received a boost from the travels and state-building of some newcomers — notably the Vikings, the Turks, the Franks of Western Europe, and the Mongols. To be sure, many of their travels and conquests were filled with wholesale destruction, yet these adventurers and empire builders also created new pathways for the transmission of cultures.

As important as these contacts were, none matched the historical significance of the transoceanic exchanges set in motion by Western Europe in the late fifteenth century. Earlier in that century, ships flying the flag of the small kingdom of Portugal began to probe the waters of Africa's west coast in the hope of reaching the source of North Africa's sub-Saharan gold trade and of contacting *Prester John,* the legendary Christian king believed by some to live in Africa. Although the Portuguese finally made contact with the ancient East African Christian civilization of Ethiopia, they failed to convert it to Catholicism, and their missionaries were expelled in 1633. Despite occasional setbacks, Portuguese commercial ventures along the African coastline and beyond proved to be enormously lucrative. Having reached India in 1498, the Malay coast in 1511, and China in 1513, the Portuguese were soon bringing back to Europe spices, silks, dyes, and other exotic items and reaping huge profits. Because of fierce competition among the European states, other European nations sought to rival the Portuguese by seeking new oceanic routes to East and South Asia, a region that Europeans vaguely called *the Indies.* Columbus's voyage of 1492 was only the first of dozens of Spanish enterprises that established Spain as the dominant power not in Asia, as hoped, but in a New World: the Americas. The nations of northern Europe also joined in. The French, Dutch, English, Danes, and Swedes claimed lands in the Western Hemisphere, and the French, Dutch, and English successfully challenged and broke the early Portuguese monopoly in African and Asian trade. By 1600, the European presence was beginning to be felt around the globe.

This initial burst of European expansion affected the various societies that Europeans encountered in radically different ways. It had little impact on the ancient centers of civilization in South and East Asia, whose rulers tolerated a limited amount of trade but were strong enough to prevent Europeans from undermining their political power or the cultural traditions of their subjects. In contrast, the civilizations of Mexico, Central America, and South America were all but wiped out by Spanish military conquests, economic exploitation, missionary activity, and the introduction of deadly new diseases. In the Caribbean, the initial meeting point of American Indians and Spaniards, the story was even grimmer, if that was possible. Almost all of its Neolithic peoples were eradicated by disease. The story north of the Rio Grande was more complex. Some North American cultures were obliterated soon after the first arrival of Europeans. Most of the American Indians of North America, however, faced similar threats of extinction only after 1600, when the French and English arrived in substantial numbers. Here the Native Americans' loss of territory and identity was generally not so sudden, but the process was no less painful, and the results were largely the same. In Africa, Europeans were unable to topple native rulers or impose their language and religion on most indigenous communities. Europeans largely remained on the coast, relying on Africans to bring them commodities for trade.

Tragically, in addition to gold and ivory, these commodities included human slaves. Indeed, for the first several centuries of direct European–West African contact, the slave trade dominated coastal commerce along Africa's western shores. Initially, the Portuguese shipped their African slaves to Europe and various Atlantic islands, where they primarily labored on sugar plantations. Then, in ever-greater numbers, European entrepreneurs brought these workers-in-bondage to the plantations of the New World. There Africans replaced the large numbers of American Indian forced laborers who had died off and the far fewer numbers of transported European criminals and outcasts who had also succumbed to tropical diseases and abuse. Before it ended in the nineteenth century, the trans-Atlantic slave trade robbed millions of human beings of their freedom, dignity, and lives.

Chapter 12

Adventurers, Merchants, Diplomats, Pilgrims, and Missionaries

A Half Millennium of Travel and Encounter: 1000–1500

The era from roughly 1000 to about 1500 witnessed large-scale movements of individuals and peoples across much of the Afro-Eurasian Ecumene, and it also witnessed direct contacts between Europe and the Americas. The first of the recorded contacts between Europeans and Americans proved to be a dead end; the second, however, became an epochal event that set the history of the entire human community onto a new plane. Whereas the exploits of Scandinavian seafarers who reached the shores of North America around the year 1000 left no permanent imprint on either the Americas or Europe, the arrival of Spaniards in the Americas just before the year 1500 transformed both civilizations and, ultimately, the world.

Long before Columbus and his Portuguese counterparts set sail, however, the Old Afro-Eurasian World was well on its way toward becoming the home of an increasingly interconnected human community. Turks out of the steppes of Central Asia converted to Islam and then spread their faith and culture into India, the Balkan region of southeastern Europe, and deeper into their traditional Central Asian homeland as they carved out and expanded a variety of states. In Western Europe, Scandinavian adventurers (known as *Vikings, Norse,* and *Northmen*) first pillaged and then settled in Ireland, England, western France, Iceland, and various other places. With the exception of the Scandinavians who settled in Russia and accepted Byzantine Christianity, the Vikings converted to Western Christianity, and during the eleventh century these new members of the faith of Rome became a sharp cutting edge of militant, expansionistic Western Christendom. Norse who had settled in France and had become *Norman* French expanded the boundaries of European Christendom into the Mediterranean. During the last half of the eleventh century Norman adventurers conquered southern Italy from the Byzantine Empire and Sicily from its Islamic overlords. These same Normans assaulted the Balkan possessions of the emperor at Constantinople and became an integral part of medieval Western Europe's most energetic and protracted overseas colonial adventure — the crusades in the Levant. Of all the catalysts of cultural exchange, the most explosive and impressive were the Mongols. In the course of the thirteenth century, they created a Eurasian land empire that reached from the Pacific to Ukraine. After the initial shock of their conquests, they established a *Pax Mongolica* (Mongol Peace) that opened up lines of direct communication between East Asia and Western Europe. For about a century, people, goods, ideas, and even diseases traveled faster than ever before from one end of the Eurasian landmass to the other.

A number of factors combined by 1400 to sever most of the overland routes between Europe and China that had opened up in the thirteenth century. They included the onslaught of the Eurasian-wide pandemic of the Black Death in the mid fourteenth century; massive economic depression that affected lands and peoples throughout Eurasia; the breakup of the Mongol Empire around the middle of the fourteenth century; the disruption of the ancient Silk Road routes of Inner Asia by the armies of the Turkish conqueror *Timur the Lame* (Tamerlane) between 1369 and 1405; the increasing antipathy toward foreigners and foreign adventure shown by China's *Ming* Dynasty (1368–1644); and the successes of the Ottoman Turks, who swept through Anatolia and the Balkans, finally capturing Constantinople in 1453.

To be sure, there was still a trickle of Western contact with Central, South, and East Asia in the early and mid fifteenth century. A handful of European merchants and adventurers even managed to reach the waters of the Indian Ocean by way of either the Red Sea or the Persian Gulf. Nevertheless, the heady days of regular mercantile and missionary contacts with the fabled land of *Cathay,* as China was called in the West, were now at an end — at least for the moment.

With the land routes now blocked, it fell to the kingdoms of Europe's Iberian Peninsula that had ports on the Atlantic to attempt contact by way of the ocean. The results of their attempts were extraordinary. During the last decade of the fifteenth century, Spain supported an enterprise that resulted in the European discovery of the Americas, and Portugal pushed into the Indian Ocean by way of Africa and also stumbled across Brazil in 1500.

The World Perceived

As we shall see in this chapter, the Mongol Empire established an environment conducive to long-distance travel and cultural interchange by providing an avenue across Eurasia from the Pacific Ocean to the Black Sea. We would be wrong, however, to think that long-distance travel and cultural interaction only occurred as the result of conquest and state-building. Long before the rise of the Mongol Empire, hundreds of thousands, even millions, of anonymous men and women traveling as merchants, pilgrims, missionaries, diplomats, and curiosity seekers had already made long-distance travel and its consequent cultural exchanges an important historical phenomenon. This was especially true after 1000. Indian and Chinese merchants traveled into Southeast Asia, where they influenced the evolution of a hybrid culture that has been termed *Indo-Chinese.* Arabs and Berbers in camel caravans trekked across the desert to trade salt and manufactured goods for the gold, ivory, and slaves of sub-Saharan West Africa. Italian merchants established bases in the Black Sea on the western edge of Central Asia. African, Arab, Indian, Southeast Asian, Chinese, and even a few European sailors shared the waters of the Indian Ocean. Pilgrims of many different faiths often traveled great distances to worship at their holy sites. Islamic and Christian missionaries, motivated by devotion and love, labored among foreign people who they believed would be damned to Hell without spiritual guidance. Envoys in the service of princes and spiritual leaders regularly carried important messages to faraway potentates, and some states, such as Genoa and Venice, even established resident ambassadors in distant lands. And then there were the curiosity seekers and adventurers, who simply traveled for the sheer joy and experience of it all. As the following three sources suggest, all of this travel and cross-cultural interchange had a profound impact on the ways in which people learned of and envisioned the world beyond their immediate frontiers.

A Chinese View of the World

▼▼▼

97 ▼ Zhau Rugua,
A DESCRIPTION OF FOREIGN PEOPLES

During the Age of Southern Song (1127–1279) China carried on extensive overseas trade, especially in the waters of the Indian Ocean. Indeed, China was the world leader in naval technology during that period, with ships that were larger and more seaworthy than those of any other culture. Chinese ships sailed as far west as the Arabian Peninsula and the northern regions of Africa's east coast, although most Chinese oceanic commerce was conducted nearer to home in the waters of Southeast Asia and India, where merchants from many lands traded for both local commodities and goods brought to Indian and Southeast Asian ports from points quite a bit farther away.

Toward the mid thirteenth century, a man named Zhau Rugua was appointed Inspector of Foreign Trade for the province of Fujian, which is located along China's southern coast. As inspector, he would have been responsible for levying and collecting tariffs on imported goods at Quanzhou, the province's major port. About all we know of him is his name, and the fact that he composed a descriptive catalogue of the various foreign peoples and products that China had come to know and know of through its trade networks. It is almost certain that none of his knowledge of overseas lands and cultures was firsthand. Rather, he borrowed liberally from an earlier handbook of this sort composed by Zhou Kufei in 1178. For the rest, Zhau Rugua appears to have gathered some of his information from Chinese merchants and sailors at Quanzhou, but most of it seems to have come from foreign merchants, especially Arabs. China's southern coastal cities, as well as its interior cities along the Silk Road, were home to large communities of resident alien merchants, who were attracted by the enormous profit potential offered by commerce with the Middle Kingdom. It is no exaggeration to state that China was the engine that drove Eurasia's economy during this half millennium.

The lands that Zhau Rugua described extended from Spain and Morocco in the west to Borneo in the east, and the foreign commodities that he described included such exotics as rose water from Arabia and ambergris from the waters off East Africa. Throughout his catalogue Zhau Rugua makes clear the central role played by Arab merchant sailors, like Sinbad (source 77), in carrying this high volume and variety of goods throughout the waters of the Indian Ocean and beyond. Indeed, most of the foreign lands that Zhau Rugua catalogued were part of the expanding global community of Islam. For that reason, we turn to his descriptions of Arabia — a land he knew as the country of the *Dashi* — and southern Spain, which was still in Islamic hands.

QUESTIONS FOR ANALYSIS

1. Compare the late-twelfth-century voyage from Quanzhou to overseas lands with the voyage that Faxian made from Ceylon to China in the early fifth

century (source 37). What has changed, and what has remained the same? What conclusions follow from your answers?

2. How accurately does Zhau Rugua describe the climate, landscape, and culture of the land(s) of the Dashi? What conclusions follow from your answer?
3. Assuming that Zhau Rugua reflects an informed Chinese view of the land(s) of the Arabs, how would you characterize the way in which the Arabs' land, markets, and products were seen by the Chinese? What conclusions follow from your answer?
4. What do the products traded by the Arabs suggest about late-twelfth-century commerce in the Indian Ocean?
5. How accurate is Zhau Rugua's description of southern Spain and the regions to its north?

THE LAND OF THE DASHI[1]

The Dashi are to the west and northwest of Quanzhou[2] at a very great distance from it, so that foreign ships find it difficult to make a direct voyage there. After these ships have left Quanzhou they arrive in some forty days at Lanli,[3] where they trade. The following year they go to sea again, when with the aid of the regular wind,[4] they take some sixty days to make the journey.

The products of the country[5] are for the most part brought to Sanfozi,[6] where they are sold to merchants who forward them to China.

This country of the Dashi is powerful and warlike. Its extent is very great, and its inhabitants are preeminent among all foreigners for their distinguished bearing. The climate throughout a large part of it is cold, snow falling to a depth of two or three feet; consequently rugs are much prized.

The capital of the country, called Maluoba,[7] is an important center for the trade of foreign peoples. . . . The streets are more than fifty feet broad; in the middle is a roadway twenty feet broad and four feet high for use of camels, horses, and oxen carrying goods about. On either side, for the convenience of pedestrians' business, there are sidewalks paved with green and bluish black flagstones of surpassing beauty . . .

Very rich persons use a measure instead of scales in business transactions of gold or silver. The markets are noisy and bustling, and are filled with a great store of gold and silver damasks, brocades,[8] and similar wares. The artisans have the true artistic spirit.

The king, the officials, and all the people serve Heaven. They also have a Buddha by the name of Mahiawu.[9] Every seven days they cut their hair and clip their fingernails. At the New Year for a whole month they fast and chant prayers.[10] Daily they pray to Heaven five times.

The peasants work their fields without fear of floods or droughts; a sufficiency of water for irrigation is supplied by a river whose source is not known. During the season when no cultivation is

---

[1]The Arabs.
[2]The Arabs knew this important port city as *Zayton* (as did Marco Polo).
[3]A port on the extreme northwestern coast of the island of Sumatra in Southeast Asia.
[4]The monsoon trade winds.
[5]Arabia. This sentence is confusing. The author has suddenly shifted his focus from merchants traveling by way of Sumatra to Arabia to merchants bringing their goods destined for China to Sumatra.

[6]The port of Palembang on the southeast coast of Sumatra.
[7]The coastal trading center of Merbat on the southwest corner of the Arabian Peninsula. Aden, which was located in the same region and was the Arabs' primary center for trade with Africa and India, is strangely not mentioned by name in this book.
[8]Both are richly patterned fabrics.
[9]Muhammad.
[10]The month of Ramadan.

in progress, the level of the river remains even with the banks; with the beginning of cultivation it rises day by day. Then it is that an official is appointed to watch the river and to await the highest water level, when he summons the people, who then plow and sow their fields. When they have had enough water, the river returns to its former level.[11]

There is a great harbor in this country, over two hundred feet deep, which opens to the southeast on the sea and has branches connecting with all quarters of the country.[12] On either bank of the harbor the people have their dwellings and here daily are held fairs, where boats and wagons crowd in, all laden with hemp, wheat, millet, beans, sugar, meal, oil, . . . fowl, sheep, geese, ducks, fish, shrimp, date cakes, grapes, and other fruits.

The products of the country consist of pearls, ivory, rhinoceros horns, frankincense, ambergris,[13] . . . cloves, nutmegs, benzoin,[14] aloes,[15] myrrh[16] dragon's blood,[17] . . . borax, opaque and transparent glass, . . . coral, cat's eyes,[18] gardenia flowers, rosewater, nutgalls,[19] yellow wax, soft gold brocades, camel's-hair cloth, . . . and foreign satins.

The foreign traders who deal in these wares bring them to Sanfozi and to Foluoan[20] to barter. . . .

The country of Magia[21] is reached by traveling eighty days westward by land from the country of Maluoba. This is where the Buddha Mahiawu was born. In the House of the Buddha[22] the walls are made of jade stone of every color. Every year,

when the anniversary of the death of the Buddha comes around,[23] people from all the countries of the Dashi assemble here, when they vie with each other in bringing presents of gold, silver, jewels, and precious stones. Then also is the House adorned anew with silk brocade.

Farther off there is the tomb of the Buddha.[24] Continually by day and night there is at this place such a brilliant radiance that no one can approach it; he who does is blinded. Whoever in the hour of his death rubs his breast with dirt taken from this tomb will, so they say, be restored to life again by the power of the Buddha.

MULANPI[25]

The country of Mulanpi is to the west of the Dashi country. There is a great sea, and to the west of this sea there are countless countries, but Mulanpi is the one country which is visited by the big ships of the Dashi. Putting to sea from Dobandi[26] in the country of the Dashi, after sailing due west for a full hundred days, one reaches this country. A single one of these ships of theirs carries several thousand men,[27] and on board they have stores of wine and provisions, as well as weaving looms. If one speaks of big ships, there are none so big as those of Mulanpi.

The products of this country are extraordinary. The grains of wheat are three inches long, the melons six feet round, enough for a meal for twenty or thirty men. The pomegranates weigh five catties,[28] lemons over twenty catties, salad greens weigh over ten catties and have leaves

---

[11]A reference to Egypt's Nile Valley.
[12]This seems to refer to Basra, located in southern Iraq at the head of the Persian Gulf.
[13]A waxy substance that sperm whales expel and which is added to perfumes.
[14]A tree resin used for medicine and perfume.
[15]A laxative drug processed from the juice of African aloe plants.
[16]An aromatic resin that was used for perfume and incense and also as a mild narcotic.
[17]Another aromatic tree resin.
[18]Semiprecious gems.
[19]Tree burls, or knots, formed by parasites. They are highly prized by wood carvers because of their interesting shapes.
[20]Beranang on the western coast of the Malay Peninsula.

[21]The city of Mecca.
[22]The Kaaba (see sources 55 and 57).
[23]The hajj (sources 58 and 60) is not specifically connected to the anniversary of the Prophet's death, but Islam reveres the Prophet's last sermon made while on his final pilgrimage.
[24]In Medina.
[25]Southern Spain, which was part of the Almohad Empire of western North Africa from around 1147 until the empire's disintegration after 1223 due to a bitter war of succession.
[26]Damietta in Egypt.
[27]A gross exaggeration.
[28]A *catty* was 600 grams, or about one and one-third pounds.

three or four feet long. Rice and wheat are kept in silos for ten years without spoiling. Among the native products are foreign sheep that are several feet high and have tails as big as a fan.[29] In the springtime they slit open their bellies and take out some ten catties of fat, after which they sew them up again, and the sheep live on; if the fat were not removed, the animal would swell up and die.[30]

If one travels by land [from Mulanpi] two hundred days' journey, the days are only six hours long.[31] In autumn if the west wind arises, men and beasts must at once drink to keep alive, and if they are not quick enough about it they die of thirst.

---

[29]These would be Ethiopian broad-tailed sheep, which were not to be found in Spain.

[30]This fantastic story might be based on the southern Span-

ish custom of slaughtering pigs in the springtime by cutting them lengthwise in this manner.

[31]The short winter days of northern Europe.

A European View of the World
▼▼▼

98 ▼ *THE BOOK OF JOHN MANDEVILLE*

If Zhau Rugua's catalogue illustrates a well-informed Chinese bureaucrat's vision of the world, a curious work by an otherwise unknown person who claimed to be *Sir John Mandeville,* an English knight of St. Alban's, illustrates the Western European view of the same globe. First appearing in Europe around 1360, *The Book of John Mandeville* purported to be the firsthand account of this knight's trans-Eurasian adventures between 1322 and 1356/1357, in which he claimed to have served both the sultan of Egypt and the Mongol khan of China. There is every reason to conclude that this work is a fictional tour de force by a gifted author who masked his identity behind an assumed name and a fabricated place of origin. The author's name will likely never be known, and evidence from the book's manuscripts suggests that whoever he was, he probably came from northern France, not England. As far as his purported travels are concerned, scholarly consensus is that all of his expeditions were to libraries, where he discovered quite a few travel books from which he borrowed liberally. For example, the outline of Sir John's travelogue describing his supposed journey to India and China is lifted from the genuine travel account of the Franciscan missionary Odoric of Pordenone (source 103). Mandeville amplified Friar Odoric's rather spare story by adding fables and tales from many other authors, by giving free rein to his own fertile imagination and sardonic wit, and by spicing his story with an impressive array of geographic and astronomical theories, many of them based on borrowed Arabic science.

No matter the book's questionable origins, Mandeville's book, written originally in French, was widely hand-copied (about 300 manuscripts survive) and circulated in ten European languages by 1400. Between the late 1470s and 1515, it was mass-printed in eight languages. Indeed, it became late medieval Europe's most popular travelogue in an age noted for its fascination with world travel. Even if "Sir John" did not travel to the regions he claimed to have visited, his work is historically important because it illustrates the manner in which Europeans of the fourteenth and fifteenth centuries viewed the lands and peoples beyond their frontiers. Indeed, in many ways Mandeville was instrumental in shaping that vision of the outside world on the eve of Europe's overseas explorations.

In the first selection Sir John deals with the shape and size of the Earth. Most people today are unaware that the notion that medieval European scholars believed the world was flat is a modern myth created, tongue in cheek, by the American humorist and writer Washington Irving in the nineteenth century. In the second selection Mandeville shares his putative firsthand knowledge of the wondrous land of *Prester John,* descendant of the *Magi,* or the Three Wise Kings from the East, who had visited the Christ Child. Prester John (John the priest), whose existence was firmly accepted in the West from the mid twelfth century onward, was the mythic priestly emperor of some supposedly lost Christian people. The Prester John myth was born partly out of rumors of actual distant Christian cultures — such as the Ethiopians of Africa, the Nestorians of Central and East Asia, and the Saint Thomas Christians of India's west coast — and partly out of a crusading zeal to discover Christian allies in the war against Islam. As a consequence, European adventurers as late as the sixteenth century sought Prester John in Asia and Africa.

One thing to keep in mind as you read these excerpts is that many scholars have concluded that although Mandeville certainly meant to amuse his readers, his charming stories also had a serious purpose. These commentators argue that Mandeville often used his descriptions of the exotic peoples and places whom he had supposedly encountered as a way of subtly pointing out the shortcomings of his own Christian Europe.

QUESTIONS FOR ANALYSIS

1. What was Sir John's view of the physical world? Be specific.
2. What do Mandeville's stories suggest about his attitudes toward alien customs and the world beyond Europe?
3. Many societies cherish a myth of a promised redeemer, or hero-to-come. How had the Christian West created in the mythic Prester John a person who represented the fulfillment of some of their deepest wishes?
4. In what ways, if at all, does Sir John seem to use these stories to point out his own society's flaws?
5. Reread the tale of Sinbad the Sailor (source 77) and Zhau Rugua's description of southern Spain. Leaving details aside, can you discover any common themes shared by these accounts and Mandeville's stories? What do those common motifs suggest to you?

OF THE FOUL CUSTOMS FOLLOWED IN THE ISLE OF LAMORY[1] AND HOW THE EARTH AND SEA ARE OF ROUND SHAPE, PROVED BY MEANS OF THE STAR ANTARCTIC

From India people go by the ocean sea by way of many islands and different countries, which it would be tedious for me to relate. Fifty-two days' journey from that land there is another large country called Lamory. That land is extremely hot, so that the custom there is for men and women to walk about totally naked, and they scorn foreigners who wear clothes. They say that God created Adam and Eve naked, and no person, therefore, should be ashamed to appear as God made him, because nothing that comes from nature's bounty is foul. They also say that people who wear clothes are from another world, or else they are people who do not believe in God. They say that they believe in God who created the world and made Adam and Eve and everything else. Here they do not marry wives, since all the women are common to all men, and no woman forsakes any man. They say that it is sinful to refuse any man, for God so commanded it of Adam and Eve and all who followed when he said: "Increase and multiply and fill the Earth."[2] Therefore, no man in that country may say: "This is my wife." No woman may say: "This is my husband." When they bear children, the women present them to whatever man they wish of those with whom they have had sexual relations. So also all land is held in common. What one man holds one year, another has another year, and everyone takes that portion which he desires. Also all the produce of the soil is held in common. This is true for grains and other goods as well. Nothing is held in private, nothing is locked up, and every person there takes what he wants without anyone saying "no." Each is as rich as the other.

There is, however, in that country an evil custom. They eat human flesh more happily than any other meat, this despite the fact that the land abounds in meats, fish, grains, gold, silver, and every other commodity. Merchants go there, bringing with them children to sell to the people of that country, and they purchase the children. If they are plump, they eat them immediately. If they are lean, they feed them until they fatten up, and then they eat them. They say this is the best and sweetest flesh in all the world.

In that land, and in many others beyond it, no one can see the Transmontane Star, known as the Star of the Sea, which is immoveable and stands in the north and is called the Lode Star.[3] They see, rather, another star, its opposite, which stands in the south and is called the Antarctic Star. Just as sailors here get their bearings and steer by the Lode Star, so sailors beyond those parts steer by the southern star, which we cannot see. So our northern star, which we call the Lode Star, cannot be seen there. This is proof that the Earth and sea are round in shape and form. For portions of the heavens that are seen in one country do not appear in another. . . . I can prove that point by what I have observed, for I have been in parts of Brabant[4] and seen, by means of an astrolabe, that the Transmontane Star is 53 degrees in elevation. In Germany and Bohemia it is 58 degrees; and farther north it is 62 degrees and some minutes high. I personally have measured it with an astrolabe. Understand that opposite the Transmontane Star is the other known as the Antarctic Star, as I have said. These two stars never move, and around them all the heavens revolve, just like a wheel about an axle. So those two stars divide the heavens into two equal parts, with as much above [the equator] as below. . . .

I say with certainty that people can encircle the entire world, below the equator as well as above,[5] and return to their homelands, provided they have good company, a ship, and health. And all

---

[1]Sumatra, which the Chinese called *Lanli* (source 97).
[2]The Bible, Genesis 1:22.
[3]Polaris, or the North Star, which guides mariners.
[4]A region between modern Belgium and the Netherlands.

[5]Here Mandeville refutes a notion, accepted by classical Greco-Roman geographers, that the *antipodes,* or lands south of the equator, are uninhabitable due to their extreme heat.

along the way one would find people, lands, and islands. . . . For you know well that those people who live right under the Antarctic Star are directly underneath, feet against feet, of those who dwell directly under the Transmontane Star,[6] just as we and those who dwell under us[7] are feet to feet. For every part of the sea and the land has its opposite, which balances it, and it is both habitable and traversable. . . . So people who travel to India and the foreign isles girdle the roundness of the Earth and the seas, passing under our countries in this hemisphere.

Something I heard as a youth has occurred to me often. A worthy man from our country departed some time ago to see the world. And so he passed through India and the islands beyond India, which number more than 5,000.[8] He traveled so far by sea and land and had so girdled the globe over the period of so many seasons that he found an island where he heard his own language being spoken. . . . He marveled at this, not knowing what to make of it. I conclude he had traveled so far by land and sea that he had encircled the entire globe, circumnavigating to the very frontier of his homeland. Had he traveled only a bit farther, he would have come to his own home. But he turned back, returning along the route by which he had come. And so he spent a great deal of painful labor, as he acknowledged, when he returned home much later. For afterwards he went to Norway, where a storm carried him to an island. While on that island he discovered it was the island where earlier he had heard his own language spoken.[9] . . .

That could well be true, even though it might seem to simple-minded persons of no learning that people cannot travel on the underside of the world without falling off toward the heavens. That, however, is not possible, unless it is true

that we also are liable to fall toward Heaven from where we are on the Earth. For whatever part of the Earth people inhabit, above or below [the equator], it always seems to them that they are in a more proper position than any other folk. And so it is right that just as it seems to us that they are under us, so it seems to them that we are beneath them. For if a person could fall from the Earth into the heavens, it is more reasonable to assume that the Earth and sea, which are more vast and of greater weight, should fall into the heavens. But that is impossible. . . .

Although it is possible for a person to circumnavigate the world, nonetheless, out of a 1,000 persons, one might possibly return home. For, given the magnitude of the Earth and the sea, a 1,000 people could venture forth and follow a 1,000 different routes. This being so, no person could plot a perfect route toward the place from where he left. He could only reach it by accident or the grace of God. For the Earth is very large and is some 20,425 miles in circumference, according to the opinion of wise astronomers from the past, whose words I am not going to contradict, even though it seems to me, with my limited understanding and with all due respect, that it is larger.[10]

OF THE ROYAL ESTATE OF PRESTER JOHN

This emperor, Prester John, commands a very large region and has many noble cities and fair towns in his realm, as well as many islands large and broad. For this land of India is divided into islands due to the great rivers that flow out of Paradise, dividing the land into many parts.[11] He also has many islands in the sea. . . . This Prester

---

[6]In other words, the South Pole is 180 degrees south of (or under) the North Pole.

[7]The place directly opposite on the globe.

[8]The islands of Southeast Asia.

[9]This story, especially in light of the passage that follows, seems to claim that the Englishman traveled south to India and the islands of Southeast Asia and then continued south across the South Pole and up the far side of the globe across

the North Pole to Scandinavia, and then he returned home by retracing his steps.

[10]Actually, it is closer to 25,000 miles.

[11]According to Mandeville, the *Terrestrial Paradise,* from which Adam and Eve had been expelled, lies far to the east of Prester John's country; four rivers — the Ganges, Nile, Tigris, and Euphrates — flow out of that paradise and divide the major lands of the Earth.

John has many kings and islands and many different peoples of various cultures subject to him. And this land is fertile and wealthy, but not as wealthy as the land of the Great Khan. For merchants do not as commonly travel there to purchase merchandise as they do to the land of the Great Khan, for it is too far to travel to. Moreover, people can find in that other region, the Island of Cathay, every manner of commodity that people need — gold cloth, silk, spices, and every sort of precious item. Consequently, even though commodities are less expensive in Prester John's island, nonetheless people dread the long voyage and the great sea-perils in that region. . . . Although one must travel by sea and land eleven or twelve months from Genoa or Venice before arriving in Cathay, the land of Prester John lies many more days of dreadful journey away. . . .

The Emperor Prester John always marries the daughter of the Great Khan, and the Great Khan likewise marries Prester John's daughter.[12] For they are the two greatest lords under Heaven.

In Prester John's land there are many different things and many precious gems of such magnitude that people make vessels, such as platters, dishes, and cups, out of them. There are many other marvels there, so many, in fact, that it would be tiresome and too lengthy to put them down in a book . . . but I shall tell you some part.

This Emperor Prester John is Christian, as is a great part of his country as well. Yet they do not share all the articles of our faith. They believe fully in God, in the Son, and in the Holy Spirit. They are quite devout and faithful to one another, and they do not quarrel or practice fraud and deceit.

He has subject to him 72 provinces, and in every province there is a king. And these kings have kings under them, and all are tributaries to Prester John. And he has in his lordships many marvels. In his country is a sea that people call the Gravelly Sea.[13] It is all gravel and sand, without a drop of water, and it ebbs and flows in great waves, as other seas do, and never rests at any time. No one can cross that sea by ship or any other craft and, therefore, no one knows what land lies beyond that sea. Although it has no water, people find in it and on its banks plenty of good fish of a shape and size such as are found nowhere else, but they are tasty and delicious to eat. Three days journey from that sea are great mountains, out of which flows a great river that originates in Paradise. And it is full of precious stones, without a drop of water. . . . Beyond that river, rising toward the deserts, is a great gravel plain set between the mountains. On that plain everyday at sunrise small trees begin to grow, and they grow until mid-day, bearing fruit. No one dares, however, to eat the fruit, for it is like a deceptive phantom. After mid-day the trees decrease and reenter the Earth, so that by sunset they are no longer to be seen. And they do this every day. And that is a great marvel. In that desert are many wild people who are hideous to look at, for they are horned and do not speak but only grunt like pigs. . . .

When Emperor Prester John goes into battle against any other lord, he has no banners borne before him. Rather, he has three crosses of fine gold, which are massive and very tall and encrusted with precious stones. Each cross is set in a richly adorned chariot. To guard each cross, there is a detail of 10,000 mounted men at arms and 100,000 men on foot, . . . and this number is in addition to the main body of troops. . . . When he rides out in peace time with a private entourage, he has borne before him only one wooden cross, unpainted and lacking gold, silver, or gems, as a remembrance that Jesus Christ suffered death on a wooden cross.[14] He also has

---

[12]This particular version of the Prester John myth seems to be a somewhat distorted reflection of the fact that many Mongol khans had Nestorian Christian wives.

[13]Apparently a garbled reference to the Gobi (Gravel) Desert of Central Asia.

[14]Keep in mind that *crusade* means "to bear a cross." During the 1350s the Ottoman Turks were advancing in the Balkans and putting increasing pressure on Constantinople. Western European efforts to launch crusades to counter this menace in southeastern Europe and to save Byzantium were proving ineffective.

borne before him a golden platter filled with earth, in token of the fact that his nobility, might, and flesh will all turn to earth. He also has borne before him a silver vessel full of great nuggets of gold and precious gems, as a token of his lordship, nobility, and might.

A Korean View of the World
▼▼▼

99 ▼ *THE KANGNIDO*

The most noteworthy world map from the period immediately preceding the European discovery of the Americas comes from Korea. Titled *Map of Integrated Regions and Terrains and of Historical Countries and Capitals,* but known more popularly as the *Kangnido,* the map was produced in 1402, early in the era of the Yi Dynasty (1392–1910), an age of vigorous cultural renewal. The cartographers who created this masterpiece borrowed freely from Chinese, Islamic, and Japanese maps to fashion an integrated map that included almost every known area of the world. Once one has become accustomed to the map's eccentricities, the modern viewer is astounded by its high degree of verisimilitude. To be sure, Japan is located directly south of Korea and farther away than it actually is. This might well represent a statement of supremacy over an age-old enemy by the Yi court. Also the image of Europe leaves much to be desired, but the fact remains, Europe is on the map!

The *Kangnido* was copied many times, so prominent was it to the Yi self-image and program of reform and regeneration. Although the original map is now lost, later fifteenth-century copies are extant. The map that appears here dates from around 1470.

QUESTIONS FOR ANALYSIS

1. Locate Korea. What does its relative size suggest?
2. Where does the center of the map lie? What does that suggest to you?
3. What have the mapmakers done with China, India, and mainland Southeast Asia? What do you infer from this?
4. Locate the Arabian Peninsula and Africa. What strikes you as particularly significant about these two features? In answering this question address their relative sizes and also the shape of Africa.
5. Locate Europe. Which areas are most recognizable? Which are most vague? What do your answers to these two questions suggest about the sources the Korean cartographers used for the Far West?

The Kangnido

Travel in the Age of the *Pax Mongolica*

Temujin (1167?–1227), the Mongol lord who assumed the title *Chinggis* (Ghengis) *Khan* (universal lord) in 1206, believed he had a destiny to rule the world. He and his immediate successors, particularly his grandson *Khubilai* (1214–1294), actually came close to controlling all of Eurasia. Although the Mongols were stopped in Syria, in Southeast Asia, at the borders of India and Arabia, in Eastern Europe, and in the waters off Japan, by 1279 they had still managed to create the largest land empire in history.

Beginning around the time of the rule of Khubilai Khan (r. 1260–1294) and extending for more than a half century after his death, the Mongols ruled over their enormous empire in relative peace and good order. Mongol discipline and organization made it possible to travel between Europe and China with a fair degree of safety and speed. Indeed, large numbers of merchants, ambassadors, fortune seekers, missionaries, and other travelers journeyed in all directions across the Mongol Empire. This steppe landbridge between East Asia and Western Europe was severed after 1350, however, as the Mongol Empire broke up, and the opportunity for normal direct contact between the eastern and western extremities of Eurasia was lost for a century and a half.

The following five sources trace the Mongol Era and its travelers from beginning to almost the end, from the age of Chinggis Khan to the eve of the breakup of the Mongol Empire and the renewed fragmentation of the Silk Road.

A Summons from Chinggis Khan
▼▼▼
100 ▼ Chinggis Khan, LETTER TO CHANGCHUN

In 1210 the armies of Chinggis Khan captured the city of *Zhongdu* (modern *Beijing*), the capital of the *Jin Empire,* which a Manchu steppe-people known as the *Ruzhen* had established in northern China a century earlier. Nine years later Chinggis Khan commissioned a letter to be sent to the Daoist monk *Changchun* (1148–1227), bidding him to travel north to the court of the Great Khan in order to instruct him in the Way. Evidence shows that Chinggis Khan desired instruction not in the Dao of saintly wisdom but in the way of achieving physical immortality. Changchun was the early thirteenth century's most famous master of the *Golden Lotus* sect of Daoism, whose members devoted themselves to searching in the spiritual world for the *dan,* a magical entity that contained the secret to everlasting life.

Despite his advanced age, Changchun traveled to Zhongdu in 1220, accompanied by nineteen disciples. When he arrived at his destination, Changchun discovered that the Great Khan had left, in order to campaign in the west. Changchun and his disciples set out to catch up with Chinggis Khan, finally reaching him in Afghanistan in May 1222. After instructing the Great Khan in "the ways of preserving life," Changchun received leave to return to China in April 1223, arriving back in Zhongdu in January 1224. There he settled down in a monastery provided for him by the Mongol khan and passed away on July 23, 1227, the same month and year in which Chinggis Khan died.

The letter that initiated this series of adventures for Changchun was not actually written by Chinggis Khan, since he was illiterate. In all likelihood, one of the khan's Chinese advisors composed it, using traditional Chinese modes of expression and thought to communicate the Mongol leader's general ideas.

QUESTIONS FOR ANALYSIS

1. Which traditional Chinese idioms and ways of thought do you find in this letter?
2. Notwithstanding these Chinese adornments, can you find any elements that appear to be distinctly Mongol?
3. On the basis of your answer to question 2, what would you say was the Mongol self-image?
4. What does the Great Khan's vision seem to be?
5. How does he propose to achieve it?
6. Can you find any hints in this document that Chinggis Khan saw himself as more than just a successful warlord of the steppes? Be specific.

Heaven has abandoned China owing to its arrogance and extravagant luxury. But I, living in the northern wilderness, do not have inordinate passions. I have only one coat and one food. I eat the same food and am dressed in the same rags as my humble herdsmen. I consider the people my children and take an interest in talented men as though they were my brothers. We always agree in our principles, and we are always united by mutual affection. At military exercises I am always in the forefront, and in battle I am never in the rear. In the space of seven years I have accomplished a great work, uniting the whole world in one empire. I do not myself possess extraordinary qualities. However, the regime of the Jin is inconstant, and therefore Heaven assists me in obtaining the Jin throne. The Song to the south, . . . the Xi-Xia to the east,[1] and the barbarians in the west, have all acknowledged my supremacy.[2] It seems to me that such a vast empire has not been seen since the remote time of our ancestral khans.

But insofar as my calling is high, the obligations incumbent upon me are also heavy, and I fear that in my governance there might be something lacking. To cross a river we construct boats and rudders. Likewise we invite sage men, and choose assistants, to keep an empire in good order. Ever since I came to the throne, I have constantly taken to heart the ruling of my people, but I could not find worthy individuals to occupy the offices of the three and nine.[3] With respect to these circumstances, I inquired and heard that you, Master, have penetrated the truth, and that you walk in the way of right. Deeply learned and well experienced, you have greatly explored the laws. Your holiness is evident. You have conserved the rigorous rules of the ancient sages. You are endowed with the eminent talents of celebrated men. For a long time you have lived in rocky caverns and have retired from the world. Yet people who have themselves acquired sanctity flock to you in innumerable multitudes, like clouds on the paths of the immortals. I knew that after the war[4] you had continued to live in Shandong,[5] at the same place, and I constantly thought of you. I know the stories of returning from the Wei River

---

[1]A Tangut, or proto-Tibetan, people who established a state in the Gansu region — an area of northwestern China.

[2]Although the Southern Song at first allied with the Mongols in attacking their old enemy, the Jin, they in turn were attacked by the Mongols following the total collapse of the Jin in 1234. Song resistance was so spirited that the Mongols did not complete the conquest of southern China until 1279.

[3]The emperor's three chief councilors, known as the *gong,* and the heads of the nine different imperial ministries.

[4]In which the Mongols conquered the northern regions of the Jin Empire.

[5]A peninsula and province in northeast China, it had been part of the Jin Empire.

in the same cart and of the thrice-repeated invitations in the reed hut.[6] But what shall I do? We are separated by mountains and plains of great extent, and I cannot meet you. I can only descend from the throne and stand to the side.[7] I have fasted and washed.[8] I have ordered my adjutant, Liu Zhonglu,[9] to prepare an escort and cart for you.[10] Do not be afraid of the 1,000 *li.*[11] I implore you to move your sainted steps. Do not think of the extent of the sandy desert. Show pity for the people in the present state of affairs, or have pity

on me, and communicate to me the means of preserving life. I shall personally serve you. I hope that you will at least leave me a trifle of your wisdom. Say but a single word to me and I will be happy.

In this letter I have briefly expressed my thoughts, and hope also that you, having penetrated the principles of the Great Dao, are in sympathy with all that is right and will not resist the wishes of the people. Dated: the first day of the fifth month (May 15, 1219).

---

[6]Allusions to two celebrated examples of sages who had been summoned to high office. The twelfth-century B.C.E. Zhou prince Wenwang found an old man fishing in the Wei River. His conversation proved so wise that the prince entreated him to enter his service as a minister, and took him back to court in his own cart. The other story involves Zhu Geliang, whom Liu Bei, founder of the Shu-Han Dynasty that ruled western China during the Age of the Three Kingdoms (221–265 C.E.), sought out and discovered inhabiting a reed hut. Only after repeated entreaties did Zhu Geliang consent to leave his hermitage.

[7]A hyperbolic suggestion that he, Chinggis Khan, could step aside and allow Changchun to govern.
[8]A Chinese metaphor of politeness, meaning that the host has properly prepared himself to receive an honored guest.
[9]A deserter from the Jin army who entered Chinggis Khan's service.
[10]Traditionally, Chinese kings and emperors sent carts for the sages whom they invited to serve them.
[11]A *li* is a bit more than one-third of a mile.

Traveling among the Mongols
▼▼▼

101 ▼ *William of Rubruck,*
JOURNEY TO THE LAND OF THE TARTARS

When the Mongols overran large portions of Christian Eastern Europe in a campaign that lasted from 1236 to 1242, the Latin West was forced to confront this new menace from the East. Fortunately for the West, the Mongols withdrew back to the Volga in 1242 due to the death of the Great Khan and the succession struggle that followed. This withdrawal took place, however, only after they destroyed a combined Polish and German army and, one day later, a Hungarian army.

Tales of horrendous atrocities convinced Western Europeans that these "Devil's horsemen" (see note 1) were demonic forces of the Antichrist who foreshadowed the Final Days as foretold in the Bible. In response, Pope Gregory IX called a crusade against the Mongols in 1241, and his successor, Pope Innocent IV, renewed it in 1243, but in both cases they were empty gestures. Western Europe was too caught up in internal struggles to rouse itself too much against a foe that had retreated mysteriously in 1242.

Fearing that the Mongols would return and drive even deeper into Europe (which they never did), Pope Innocent IV and King Louis IX of France tried diplomacy, dispatching a series of legations to the Khan of khans in Mongolia, which were aimed at discovering Mongol intentions, converting these so-called "enemies of God and friends of the Devil" to Christianity, and enlisting them in the West's crusade endeavors against Islam. These initial missions, which began in 1245 and lasted down to 1255, were conducted mainly by Franciscan friars, members of the religious order founded by St. Francis of Assisi in the early thirteenth century, and were met with Mongol indifference. To the Mongol mind, the West had only one option: submission.

The initial mission, which left Europe in 1245 and returned late in 1247, failed to reach any accord with the Mongols, but produced an account of Mongol culture and battle tactics by the legation's leader, Brother John of Plano Carpini. A second, even more detailed account of Mongol life and customs resulted from another embassy to the Great Khan. Between May 1253 and June 1255 two Franciscan ambassadors, William of Rubruck and Bartholomew of Cremona, traveled from Constantinople to the court of Mongke Khan (r. 1251–1259) at *Karakorum* in Mongolia and returned to the eastern Mediterranean. The mission failed to convert the Great Khan, but Brother William's report of their adventures and his observations made the trip worthwhile (at least from our perspective). An observant individual, Brother William provides us with an exceptional account of mid-thirteenth-century Mongol society.

QUESTIONS FOR ANALYSIS

1. Many people think of nomads as wanderers who aimlessly travel about with their herds. What evidence does Rubruck provide to refute this misconception?
2. At this early date, some Mongol lords flirted with Buddhism, Daoism (source 100), and Islam, and several Mongol tribes professed Nestorian Christianity. Most, however, followed none of these faiths. Describe and categorize the Mongols' religious practices as reported by Rubruck.
3. Consider the Mongols' attitude toward thunder. Why do you think these people of the steppes so feared it?
4. How would you characterize the status of women relative to men? In addressing this issue, consider the respective tasks of women and men and Mongol marriage customs.
5. On the basis of this account, how would you characterize Mongol society in the mid thirteenth century?
6. Some commentators have argued that Rubruck displays a certain sensitivity toward and even sympathy for the Mongols he encountered. Based on these selections, do you agree or disagree? Please be specific in supporting your conclusion.

THE TARTARS[1] AND THEIR DWELLINGS

The Tartars have no abiding city. . . . Each captain, according to whether he has more or fewer men under him, knows the limits of his pasturage and where to feed his flocks in winter, summer, spring, and autumn, for in winter they come down to the warmer districts in the south, in summer they go up to the cooler ones in the

---

[1]Westerners mistakenly called the Mongols *Tartars,* a corruption of *Tatars,* the name of a tribe of steppe nomads who dwelled near the Mongols. Tartar seems to have been a deliberate pun. The classical Latin name for hell was *Tartarus;* hence, the Mongols were the "Devil's horsemen."

north. They drive their cattle to graze on the pasture lands without water in winter when there is snow there, for the snow provides them with water.

The dwelling in which they sleep has as its base a circle of interlaced sticks, and it is made of the same material; these sticks converge into a little circle at the top and from this a neck juts up like a chimney; they cover it with white felt and quite often they also coat the felt with lime or white clay and powdered bone to make it a more gleaming white, and sometimes they make it black. The felt round the neck at the top they decorate with lovely and varied paintings. Before the doorway they also hang felt worked in multi-colored designs; they sew colored felt onto the other, making vines and trees, birds, and animals. They make these houses so large that sometimes they are thirty feet across. . . .

In addition they make squares to the size of a large coffer out of slender split twigs; then over it, from one end to the other, they build up a rounded roof out of similar twigs and they make a little entrance at the front end; after that they cover this box or little house with black felt soaked in tallow or ewes' milk so that it is rainproof, and this they decorate in the same way with multicolored handwork. Into these chests they put all their bedding and valuables; they bind them onto high carts which are drawn by camels so that they can cross rivers. These chests are never removed from the carts. When they take down their dwelling houses, they always put the door facing the south. . . .

The married women make for themselves really beautiful carts which I would not know how to describe for you except by a picture; in fact I would have done you paintings of everything if I only knew how to paint. A wealthy Mongol or Tartar may well have a hundred or two hundred such carts with chests. Baatu[2] has twenty-six wives and each of these has a large house, not counting the other small ones which are placed behind the large one and which are, as it were, chambers in which their attendants live; belonging to each of these houses are a good two hundred carts. When they pitch their houses the chief wife places her dwelling at the extreme west end and after her the others according to their rank, so that the last wife will be at the far east end, and there will be the space of a stone's throw between the establishment of one wife and that of another. And so the orda[3] of a rich Mongol will look like a large town and yet there will be very few men in it.

One woman will drive twenty or thirty carts, for the country is flat. They tie together the carts, which are drawn by oxen or camels, one after the other, and the woman will sit on the front one driving the ox while all the others follow in step. If they happen to come on a bad bit of track they loose them and lead them across it one by one. They go at a very slow pace, as a sheep or an ox might walk.

When they have pitched their houses with the door facing south, they arrange the master's couch at the northern end. The women's place is always on the east side, that is, on the left of the master of the house when he is sitting on his couch looking toward the south; the men's place is on the west side, that is, to his right.

On entering a house the men would by no means hang up their quiver in the women's section. Over the head of the master there is always an idol like a doll or little image of felt which they call the master's brother, and a similar one over the head of the mistress, and this they call the mistress's brother; they are fastened on to the wall. Higher up between these two is a thin little one which is, as it were, the guardian of the whole house. The mistress of the house places on her right side, at the foot of the couch, in a prominent position, a goatskin stuffed with wool or other material, and next to it a tiny image

---

turned toward her attendants and the women. By the entrance on the women's side is still another idol with a cow's udder for the women who milk the cows, for this is the women's job. On the other side of the door toward the men is another image with a mare's udder for the men who milk the mares.

When they have foregathered for a drink they first sprinkle with the drink the idol over the master's head, then all the other idols in turn; after this an attendant goes out of the house with a cup and some drinks; he sprinkles thrice toward the south, genuflecting each time; this is in honor of fire; next toward the east in honor of the air, and after that to the west in honor of water; they cast it to the north for the dead. When the master is holding his cup in his hand and is about to drink, before he does so he first pours some out on the Earth as its share. If he drinks while seated on a horse, before he drinks he pours some over the neck or mane of the horse. And so when the attendant has sprinkled toward the four quarters of the Earth he returns into the house; two servants with two cups and as many plates are ready to carry the drink to the master and the wife sitting beside him upon his couch. If he has several wives, she with whom he sleeps at night sits next to him during the day, and on that day all the others have to come to her dwelling to drink, and the court is held there, and the gifts which are presented to the master are placed in the treasury of that wife. Standing in the entrance is a bench with a skin of milk or some other drink and some cups.

In the winter they make an excellent drink from rice, millet, wheat, and honey, which is clear like wine. Wine, too, is conveyed to them from distant regions. In the summer they do not bother about anything except cosmos.[4] Cosmos is always to be found inside the house before the entrance door, and near it stands a musician with his instrument. Our lutes and viols I did not see there but many other instruments such as are not known among us. When the master begins to drink, then one of the attendants cries out in a loud voice "Ha!" and the musician strikes his instrument. And when it is a big feast they are holding, they all clap their hands and also dance to the sound of the instrument, the men before the master and the women before the mistress. After the master has drunk, then the attendant cries out as before and the instrument-player breaks off. Then they drink all round, the men and the women, and sometimes vie with each other in drinking in a really disgusting and gluttonous manner. . . .

THE FOOD OF THE TARTARS

As for their food and victuals I must tell you they eat all dead animals indiscriminately and with so many flocks and herds you can be sure a great many animals do die. However, in the summer as long as they have any cosmos, that is mare's milk, they do not care about any other food. If during that time an ox or a horse happens to die, they dry the flesh by cutting it into thin strips and hanging it in the sun and the wind, and it dries immediately without salt and without any unpleasant smell. Out of the intestines of horses they make sausages which are better than pork sausages and they eat these fresh; the rest of the meat they keep for the winter. From the hide of oxen they make large jars which they dry in a wonderful way in the smoke. From the hind part of horses' hide they make very nice shoes.

They feed fifty or a hundred men with the flesh of a single sheep, for they cut it up in little bits in a dish with salt and water, making no other sauce; then with the point of a knife or a fork especially made for this purpose — like those with which we are accustomed to eat pears and apples cooked in wine — they offer to each of those standing round one or two mouthfuls, according to the number of guests. Before the flesh of the sheep is served, the master first takes what pleas-

---

[4]More correctly *qumiz,* the Mongols' favorite alcoholic drink, which they derived from mare's milk.

es him; and also if he gives anyone a special portion then the one receiving it has to eat it himself and may give it to no one else. But if he cannot eat it all he may take it away with him or give it to his servant, if he is there, to keep for him; otherwise he may put it away in his *captargac,* that is, a square bag which they carry to put all such things in: in this they also keep bones when they have not the time to give them a good gnaw, so that later they may gnaw them and no food be wasted.

THE DUTIES OF THE WOMEN AND THEIR WORK

It is the duty of the women to drive the carts, to load the houses onto them and to unload them, to milk the cows, to make the butter and *grut,*[5] to dress the skins and to sew them, which they do with thread made out of tendons. They split the tendons into very thin threads and then twist these into one long thread. They also sew shoes and socks and other garments. They never wash their clothes, for they say that that makes God angry and that it would thunder if they hung them out to dry; they even beat those who do wash them and take them away from them. They are extraordinarily afraid of thunder. At such a time they turn all strangers out of their dwellings and wrap themselves in black felt in which they hide until it has passed over. They never wash their dishes, but when the meat is cooked, they wash out the bowl in which they are going to put it with some boiling broth from the cauldron which they afterwards pour back. The women also make the felt and cover the houses.

The men make bows and arrows, manufacture stirrups and bits and make saddles; they build the houses and carts, they look after the horses and milk the mares, churn the cosmos, that is the mares' milk, and make the skins in which it is

kept, and they also look after the camels and load them. Both sexes look after the sheep and goats, and sometimes the men, sometimes the women, milk them. They dress skins with the sour milk of ewes, thickened and salted.

When they want to wash their hands or their head, they fill their mouth with water and, pouring this little by little from their mouth into their hands, with it they wet their hair and wash their head.

As for their marriages, you must know that no one there has a wife unless he buys her, which means that sometimes girls are quite grown up before they marry, for their parents always keep them until they sell them. They observe the first and second degrees of consanguinity,[6] but observe no degrees of affinity[7]; they have two sisters at the same time or one after the other. No widow among them marries, the reason being that they believe that all those who serve them in this life will serve them in the next, and so of a widow they believe that she will always return after death to her first husband. This gives rise to a shameful custom among them whereby a son sometimes takes to wife all his father's wives, except his own mother; for the orda of a father and mother always falls to the youngest son[8] and so he himself has to provide for all his father's wives who come to him with his father's effects; and then, if he so wishes, he uses them as wives, for he does not consider an injury has been done to him if they return to his father after death.

And so when anyone has made an agreement with another to take his daughter, the father of the girl arranges a feast and she takes flight to relations where she lies hid. Then the father declares: "Now my daughter is yours; take her wherever you find her." Then he searches for her with his friends until he finds her; then he has to take her by force and bring her, as though by violence, to his house.

---

[5]A sour curd cheese.
[6]Siblings and first cousins are prohibited from marrying one another.

[7]One may wed any relative by marriage, such as a sister-in-law.
[8]The youngest son of his chief wife.

Traveling the Silk Road

▼▼▼

102 ▼ Marco Polo, DESCRIPTION OF THE WORLD

No chapter on trans-Eurasian travel in the Mongol Age would be complete without a selection from Marco Polo (ca. 1253–1324), a Venetian who spent twenty years in East Asia. A few scholars have questioned whether Marco Polo ever went to China, and some have even wondered whether he ever existed. Their conclusions, largely built on arguments from silence, in which they point to what Polo's account does not mention and to the absence of his name in all known Chinese records (despite his claim to have been in the service of Khubilai Khan), have failed to win support within the academic community. As the issue currently stands, there is no good reason to doubt the basic historicity of Marco Polo's account of his years in China, even though the story, as we have received it, contains undoubted exaggeration and human error — error that was compounded by the manner in which Polo's story was transmitted to posterity.

Around 1260 Marco's father and uncle, Niccolò and Maffeo, both merchants from Venice, set sail for the Black Sea and from there made an overland trek to the court of Khubilai. When they were preparing to return home, the Great Khan requested that they visit the pope and ask him to send 100 missionary-scholars to Cathay (northern China). The Polos arrived at the crusader port of Acre (in modern Israel) in 1269 and in 1271 received a commission from Pope Gregory X (r. 1271–1276) to return to China with two Dominican friars. The two friars quickly abandoned the expedition, afraid of the dangers that awaited them, but Niccolò's seventeen-year-old son, Marco, was made of sterner stuff. The brothers Polo, now accompanied by young Marco, began the long trek back to northern China and the court of Khubilai, arriving there in 1274 or 1275. Here apparently Marco entered the service of the Great Khan, but it is impossible to say with certainty what offices he held. Whatever the truth about Polo's position, it is clear that for close to two decades he traveled extensively over much of Khubilai's empire, and he probably functioned, at least occasionally, as one of the many foreign officials serving the Mongol, or *Yuan,* Dynasty (1264–1368).

In 1290 or 1292 the three men set sail for the West by way of the Indian Ocean and arrived home in Venice in 1295. In 1298 Marco was captured in a war with Genoa and, while in prison, related his adventures to a writer of romances known as Rustichello of Pisa. Together they produced a rambling, often disjointed account of the sites, peoples, personalities, and events Marco had encountered in Asia.

Despite its literary flaws and a self-puffery that was obvious even to fourteenth-century contemporaries, the book was widely translated and distributed throughout late medieval Europe. Its popularity was due in part to Marco's eye for detail, as the book abounds with stories and descriptions of phenomena that Westerners found fascinatingly different.

In the following selection Polo describes his journey to Cathay along the portion of the Silk Road that skirts the southern fringes of the forbidding *Taklamakan Desert.* The term *Silk Road* conjures up every sort of romantic notion in modern readers, but for the men and women who journeyed along its many routes it was anything but romantic, even though towns along the way offered pleasures and even exotic experiences. The fact that it took the Polos about three and one-half years to travel from Acre to Shangdu, the summer palace of the Great Khan, suggests how difficult and dangerous the journey was.

QUESTIONS FOR ANALYSIS

1. What were the dangers for travelers along this portion of the Silk Road?
2. Despite the dangers, what made the journey possible and even bearable?
3. Why did people inhabit towns and cities along this route?
4. What dangers did these urban people encounter?
5. What impact did the Mongols have on this part of the Silk Road?

Let us turn next to the province of Yarkand,[1] five days' journey in extent. The inhabitants follow the law of Mahomet,[2] and there are also some Nestorian Christians.[3] They are subject to the Great Khan's nephew,[4] of whom I have already spoken. It is amply stocked with the means of life, especially cotton. But, since there is nothing here worth mentioning in our book, we shall pass on to Khotan,[5] which lies towards the east-north-east.

Khotan is a province eight days' journey in extent, which is subject to the Great Khan. The inhabitants all worship Mahomet.[6] It has cities and towns in plenty, of which the most splendid, and the capital of the kingdom, bears the same name as the province, Khotan. It is amply stocked with the means of life. Cotton grows here in plenty. It has vineyards, estates, and orchards in plenty. The people live by trade and industry; they are not at all warlike.

Passing on from here we come to the province of Pem, five days' journey in extent, towards the east-north-east. Here too the inhabitants worship Mahomet and are subject to the Great Khan. It has villages and towns in plenty. The most splendid city and the capital of the province is called Pem. There are rivers here in which are found stones called jasper and chalcedony[7] in plenty. There is no lack of the means of life. Cotton is plentiful. The inhabitants live by trade and industry.

The following custom is prevalent among them. When a woman's husband leaves her to go on a journey of more than twenty days, then, as soon as he has left, she takes another husband, and this she is fully entitled to do by local usage. And the men, wherever they go, take wives in the same way.

You should know that all the provinces I have described, from Kashgar[8] to Pem and some way beyond, are provinces of Turkestan.[9]

I will tell you next of another province of Turkestan, lying east-north-east, which is called Charchan. It used to be a splendid and fruitful

---

[1]Yarkand is on the southwestern border of the *Taklamakan Desert,* which is located in the *Tarim Basin.* The Taklamakan, whose name means "those who enter never return," cannot support human life. Travelers must decide whether to take the fork that skirts the northern edge of this 600-mile-long wilderness of sand (the Northern Tarim Route) or the southern fork (the Southern Tarim Route). Yarkand is the first major city on the Southern Tarim Route for those traveling from the west.

[2]Muhammad.

[3]Various Turkish and Mongolian tribes had adopted this form of Christianity.

[4]Kaidu.

[5]The next major city along this route.

[6]Many Western Christians thought *Mahomet* was a god whom Muslims worshiped.

[7]Two highly valued quartz crystals.

[8]Kashgar, on the extreme western end of the Taklamakan, is where the northern and southern forks branch, for those traveling from the west.

[9]The region of Central Asia inhabited by Turkic peoples.

country, but it has been much devastated by the Tartars.[10] The inhabitants worship Mahomet. There are villages and towns in plenty, and the chief city of the kingdom is Charchan.[11] There are rivers producing jasper and chalcedony, which are exported for sale in Cathay and bring in a good profit; for they are plentiful and of good quality.

All this province is a tract of sand; and so is the country from Khotan to Pem and from Pem to here. There are many springs of bad and bitter water, though in some places the water is good and sweet. When it happens that an army passes through the country, if it is a hostile one, the people take flight with their wives and children and their beasts two or three days' journey into the sandy wastes to places where they know that there is water and they can live with their beasts. And I assure you that no one can tell which way they have gone, because the wind covers their tracks with sand, so that there is nothing to show where they have been, but the country looks as if it had never been traversed by man or beast. That is how they escape from their enemies. But, if it happens that a friendly army passes that way, they merely drive off their beasts, because they do not want to have them seized and eaten; for the armies never pay for what they take. And you should know that, when they harvest their grain, they store it far from any habitation, in certain caves among these wastes, for fear of the armies; and from these stores they bring home what they need month by month.

After leaving Charchan, the road runs for fully five days through sandy wastes, where the water is bad and bitter, except in a few places where it is good and sweet; and there is nothing worth noting in our book. At the end of the five days' journey towards the east-north-east, is a city which stands on the verge of the Great Desert. It is here that men take in provisions for crossing the desert. Let us move on accordingly and proceed with our narrative.

The city I have mentioned, which stands at the point where the traveler enters the Great Desert, is a big city called Lop, and the desert is called the Desert of Lop.[12] The city is subject to the Great Khan, and the inhabitants worship Mahomet. I can tell you that travelers who intend to cross the desert rest in this town for a week to refresh themselves and their beasts. At the end of the week they stock up with a month's provisions for themselves and their beasts. Then they leave the town and enter the desert.

This desert is reported to be so long that it would take a year to go from end to end; and at the narrowest point it takes a month to cross it. It consists entirely of mountains and sand and valleys. There is nothing at all to eat. But I can tell you that after traveling a day and a night you find drinking water[13] — not enough water to supply a large company, but enough for fifty or a hundred men with their beasts. And all the way through the desert you must go for a day and a night before you find water. And I can tell you that in three or four places you find the water bitter and brackish; but at all the other watering-places, that is, twenty-eight in all, the water is good. Beasts and birds there are none, because they find nothing to eat. But I assure you that one thing is found here, and that a very strange one, which I will relate to you.

The truth is this. When a man is riding by night through this desert and something happens to make him loiter and lose touch with his companions, by dropping asleep or for some other reason, and afterwards he wants to rejoin them, then he hears spirits talking in such a way that they seem to be his companions. Sometimes, indeed, they even hail him by name. Often these voices make him stray from the path, so that he

---

[10]Mongols not Tatars. See source 101, note 1.
[11]Known to the Chinese as Shanshan, it was the next significant city along the Southern Tarim Route.
[12]On the eastern edge of the Taklamakan Desert is a salt-encrusted plain of hard-baked clay known as the Lop Nor (the Salt Sea) — the dried bed of an ancient sea.
[13]Streams from distant mountains, which long ago made this a great inland salt sea, create oases.

never finds it again. And in this way many travelers have been lost and have perished. And sometimes in the night they are conscious of a noise like the clatter of a great cavalcade of riders away from the road; and, believing that these are some of their own company, they go where they hear the noise and, when day breaks, find they are victims of an illusion and in an awkward plight. And there are some who, in crossing this desert, have seen a host of men coming towards them and, suspecting that they were robbers, have taken flight; so, having left the beaten track and not knowing how to return to it, they have gone hopelessly astray. Yes, and even by daylight men hear these spirit voices, and often you fancy you are listening to the strains of many instruments, especially drums, and the clash of arms. For this reason bands of travelers make a point of keeping very close together. Before they go to sleep they set up a sign pointing in the direction in which they have to travel. And round the necks of all their beasts they fasten little bells, so that by listening to the sound they may prevent them from straying off the path.

That is how they cross the desert, with all the discomfort of which you have heard. . . .

▾ ▾ ▾

Now I will tell you of some other cities, which lie towards the north-west near the edge of this desert.[14]

The province of Kamul, which used to be a kingdom, contains towns and villages in plenty, the chief town being also called Kamul.[15] The province lies between two deserts, the Great Desert and a small one three days' journey in extent.[16] The inhabitants are all idolaters[17] and speak a language of their own. They live on the produce of the soil; for they have a superfluity of foodstuffs and beverages, which they sell to travelers who pass that way. They are a very gay folk, who give no thought to anything but making music, singing and dancing, and reading and writing according to their own usage, and taking great delight in the pleasures of the body. I give you my word that if a stranger comes to a house here to seek hospitality he receives a very warm welcome. The host bids his wife do everything that the guest wishes. Then he leaves the house and goes about his own business and stays away two or three days. Meanwhile the guest stays with his wife in the house and does what he will with her, lying with her in one bed just as if she were his own wife; and they lead a gay life together. All the men of this city and province are thus cuckolded by their wives; but they are not the least ashamed of it. And the women are beautiful and vivacious and always ready to oblige.

Now it happened during the reign of Mongu Khan,[18] lord of the Tartars, that he was informed of this custom that prevailed among the men of Kamul of giving their wives in adultery to outsiders. Mongu thereupon commanded them under heavy penalties to desist from this form of hospitality. When they received this command, they were greatly distressed; but for three years they reluctantly obeyed. Then they held a council and talked the matter over, and this is what they did. They took a rich gift and sent it to Mongu and entreated him to let them use their wives according to the traditions of their ancestors; for their ancestors had declared that by the pleasure they gave to guests with their wives and goods they won the favor of their idols and multiplied the yield of their crops and their tillage. When Mongu Khan heard this he said: 'Since you desire your own shame, you may have it.' So he let them have their way. And I can assure you that since then they have always upheld this tradition and uphold it still.

---

[14]Polo now shifts to the Northern Tarim Route. He does not claim that Kamul and the other cities that he describes in this aside were on his route eastward. Indeed, the whole tone of this section suggests he heard about these sites during his stay in China.
[15]The modern city of Hami.

[16]This smaller desert has to be the edge of the Gobi Desert, which is not a small desert and is not crossed in three days.
[17]Buddhists.
[18]Khubilai's older brother and Great Khan from 1251 to 1259.

A European Visitor to China

▼▼▼

103 ▼ Odoric of Pordenone, REPORT

The Mongols reached a stalemate with Islam in Southwest Asia, after their defeat at the Battle of Ayn Jalut in 1260 at the hands of the Mamluks of Egypt. Faced with this reality, the Mongol *il-khans* (subordinate khans) of Persia were now willing to discuss an alliance with the Christian West against the Mamluks, who controlled Egypt and Syria and were systematically dismantling the last of the crusader states. On its part, because of the crisis facing the crusader states in the Holy Land, the West was more than willing to make common cause with the Mongols.

In 1287 *Arghun,* il-khan of Persia (r. 1284–1291), a nephew of the Great Khan Khubilai, sent a Nestorian Christian monk, *Rabban* (Master) *Sauma,* to the West bearing letters for the pope, the kings of France and England, and the emperor of Constantinople, in which the Mongol prince offered to become a Christian in return for an alliance against the Mamluks.

In response to Rabban Sauma's appearance in Rome in 1289, Pope Nicholas IV dispatched a Franciscan friar, *John of Monte Corvino* (1247–ca. 1328), to the Mongols with letters for Arghun and other khans farther to the east, including the Khan of khans, *Khubilai.* In 1291 John was in Tauris (modern Tabriz), Arghun's capital, but the il-khan died in March of that year, and his successor was on the verge of embracing Islam. Moreover, between May and July of the same year the last crusader strongholds in the Holy Land fell to Islamic forces. With nothing further to be accomplished in Persia, John set out for the court of the Great Khan in China. Due to delays, John arrived at the Mongol capital of *Khanbalik* (modern Beijing) in 1294/1295, around or just after Kubilai's death. Making the best of his situation, John remained in China as a missionary, and in time was joined by other Franciscans.

One of those assistants was Friar *Odoric of Pordenone* (ca. 1265–1331), who departed for the Far East in 1322. Brother Odoric, who had already served as a missionary in southern Russia for more than a decade and in Persia for eight years, sailed from the Persian Gulf to India, and from India sailed to the port of Guangzhou (Canton), arriving there around 1323–1324. He served in China for several years, where he assisted the aged Archbishop John of Monte Corvino, but departed for home before John's death (ca. 1328). Odoric's overland journey home finally got him to Venice in 1329. Soon thereafter he fell ill, but managed to dictate his travel adventures in May 1330. He died on January 14, 1331.

Friar Odoric was neither the first nor the last medieval Catholic missionary to work in China. The mission probably survived, but barely so, the collapse of Mongol authority in China in 1368. It might well have limped along until around 1400. Although several missionaries communicated with the West through letters sent back by Italian merchants and other travelers, Odoric's *Report* is, by far, the best and most detailed account by any Western missionary in China at this time. Its excellence, in fact, attracted the plagiarizing eyes of John Mandeville (source 98). In the following excerpts Odoric describes Hangzhou, the former capital of the

Southern Song Dynasty, the Great Khan's palace complex of *Dadu,* and his imperial court.

QUESTIONS FOR ANALYSIS

1. Does Friar Odoric's account seem to reach the level of unbelievable hyperbole at any point? Be specific.
2. Which parts of this account seem to be sober reporting of fact? Be specific.
3. Based on your answers to questions 1 and 2, what is your overall evaluation of this source's worth?
4. Compare Friar Odoric's description of Hangzhou (Cansay) with that of *A Record of Musings on the Eastern Capital* (source 71). Does conquest by the Mongols appear to have affected the city in any perceptible manner? Be specific in your answer.
5. How do we infer from this source that Marco Polo and Brother Odoric were only two of many Westerners who visited China in the late thirteenth and early fourteenth centuries?
6. Based on what Odoric tells us about Dadu and about the composition and character of the Great Khan's court, how would you characterize Mongol rule in China in the early fourteenth century?
7. Compare the picture that this source gives us of the Mongol court with the image of Mongol life that emerges from sources 100 and 101. What has changed? To what do you ascribe those changes?

CONCERNING CANSAY, THE GREATEST CITY IN THE WORLD

I came to the city of Cansay,[1] which means "City of Heaven." This is the greatest city in the world and a good 100 miles in circumference. Within it there is not a square yard[2] of earth that is not heavily populated. Quite often one can find a residence that contains fully ten or twelve households. This city also has huge suburbs that contain a population larger than that of the city itself. The city has twelve principal gates, and extending out from each of these gates, for a distance of almost eight miles, are cities larger than Venice or Padua, so that one might journey six or seven days through one of these suburbs and it would seem as though he had traveled but a short distance.

This city is located on lagoons of standing and static water, like the city of Venice. It also has more than 12,000 bridges, on which are stationed guards who watch over this city for the Great Khan. Alongside the city flows a single river. Because the city is so situated, it finds itself in the same situation as Ferrara. That is, it is longer than it is wide.[3] I diligently inquired about this city and asked questions of Christians, Saracens,[4] idolaters,[5] and all others, and all said

---

[1]Hangzhou. Marco Polo also knew the city as *Kinsai,* which he also translated as "Heavenly City."
[2]The Latin is *spansa.* It is not at all clear what Friar Odoric understood a "span" to be. Perhaps this comes close. See note 19.

[3]Like Ferrara along the Po, Hangzhou is stretched out along the contours of its river.
[4]Muslims.
[5]Buddhists, Daoists, and Mongol shamans.

with one voice that it is fully 100 miles in circumference.

They also have an edict from their lord that each and every hearth[6] shall pay annually one *balis* to the Great Khan, that is five pieces of paper[7] that have an equivalent value in silk of one and a half *florins*.[8] They have a means of coping with this. Fully ten or twelve households will share a single hearth and so will pay for only a single hearth. Regardless, these hearths number eighty-five *tumans*, with an additional four *tumans* for the Saracens. Combined, they number eighty-eight.[9] One *tuman* is fully 10,000 hearths. Then there are the others: Christians, other merchants, and other transients passing through the country. This being so, I marveled at how many human bodies could manage to inhabit the same space. Yet there is a great abundance of bread there, and of pork, and rice and wine. The wine is otherwise known as *vigim*, and is reputed to be a noble beverage. Indeed, an extraordinary abundance of every other sort of food is found there. . . .

If anyone should wish to tell of or report on the vastness of this city and the great marvels contained within it, a full quire of stationery could not contain all of these matters. Truly, this is the most noble and greatest city in the world for goods that are bought and sold. . . .

CONCERNING THE GREAT CITIES OF KHANBALIK AND TAYDO AND THE PALACE OF THE KHAN

I passed through many cities and lands on my way east before arriving at the noble city of Khanbalik,[10] an exceedingly old and ancient city in the famous province of Cathay.[11] The Tartars took the city and then built another one-half mile away, which they called Taydo.[12] This second city has twelve gates,[13] spaced two miles apart from one another. A large population resides between the two cities, and together the cities have a perimeter that extends more than forty miles.[14] The Great Khan resides in this city and has a great palace, the walls of which are a good four miles in circumference.[15] Within the Great Palace's enclosure there is a man-made hill on which has been constructed another palace, the most beautiful in the world. This entire hill has been planted over with trees, and for this reason it is called *Green Mount.* A lake has been created alongside the hill and an exceedingly beautiful bridge built over it. On this lake there are so many geese, ducks, and swans that one is struck in awe. For this reason, there is no need for that lord to leave home when he wishes to go hunting. Also within this palace enclosure are thickets filled with various sorts of wild animals

---

[6]*Ignis:* literally, "fire."

[7]The Song Dynasty began printing and using paper currency in the 1120s.

[8]The *florin,* the official coin of Florence since 1252, was made from 3.53 grams of pure gold and was equal in value to a pound of silver.

[9]Someone's arithmetic is off. It should be eighty-nine.

[10]Turkish for "city of the khan." This is the usual term that Western sources use for Beijing under the Mongols. But see note 12.

[11]Northern China, which received its name from the *Khitan Mongols,* who established the *Liao* state there in 907. They were replaced by the *Ruzhen,* who set up the *Jin* state in 1125, but the name *Cathay* stuck.

[12]In 1266 Khubilai Khan ordered the construction of a new capital slightly northeast of the *Jin* capital of *Zhongdu* (Central Capital). In 1272 the newly completed capital acquired the Chinese name *Dadu* (Great Capital), and to the Mongols

was known as *Daidu.* Khubilai mandated that the entire urban complex, namely both Dadu and the former Zhongdu, was to be called Dadu, but it seems likely that even the Mongols normally used the Turkish term *Khanbalik* when referring to this complex. Dadu later became the nucleus for the Ming (1369–1644) capital of *Beijing* (Northern Capital), which took shape under the Yongle Emperor (r. 1402–1424). Regarding the Yongle Emperor, see sources 106 and 107.

[13]Apparently it had only eleven gates.

[14]Dadu alone had a perimeter of 28,600 meters, or more than seventeen and one-half miles.

[15]The palace complex had a perimeter of 3,480 meters, or a bit more than two miles.

so that he can take to the chase whenever he desires without ever leaving home.

For this palace in which he resides is vast and beautiful. Its ground floor is raised about two paces,[16] and inside there are twenty-four columns of gold. All of the walls are draped with red-leather, said to be the finest in the world. In the center of the palace there is a great cistern, more than two paces in height, totally fashioned out of a single precious stone called *merdacas*.[17] It is bound all around in gold, and in every corner there is a dragon[18] whose mouth threatens in a most menacing way. This cistern also has a hanging network of great pearls that fringe it, and these fringes of pearls are a good yard[19] wide. Drinking water for use in the royal court is dispensed through the cistern, which is fed by pipes. Nearby the cistern are many golden goblets from which those who desire to take a drink can drink. In that same palace there are also many peacocks made from gold. When one of the Tartars wishes to amuse his lord, one after another they clap their hands, upon which the peacocks flap their wings and appear to dance. Now this has to be done either through some diabolical art or by means of some underground engine.

CONCERNING THE LORD KHAN'S COURT

When that lord is seated on his imperial throne, the empress resides on his left, and one step below sit two of the other wives whom he keeps. At the bottom of the stairs are all the other women of his family. All of the women who are married have on their heads [something shaped like][20] a human foot, which is a good forearm and a half long. On the lower portion of the [so-called] foot are crane's feathers fashioned into a peak, and the entire "foot" is ornamented with great pearls. Whatever large and beautiful pearls there are in the world, they are to be found on the decorations of those ladies.

On the right-hand side of this king sits his first-born son, who is expected to reign after him. Beneath them are placed all who are of royal blood. There are also four scribes there who write down every word that the king utters. Before the khan stands an innumerable multitude of his barons. None of these dares to speak a word except if addressed by the great lord, except for the jesters, who might wish to amuse their lord. But even these jesters must not dare to do anything beyond the limits that the king has laid down for them. Before the gates of the palace stand baronial guards, on watch lest anyone tread on the threshold of the door. If they catch anyone doing that, they beat him soundly.

When this great lord desires to hold any sort of large entertainment, he has 14,000 crowned barons waiting on him at the festival, each of whom has a coat on his back whose pearls alone are worth more than 15,000 florins.

The court of this lord is well ordered, namely ranked into tens, hundreds, and thousands,[21] with all their assigned places and all answerable to one another lest any defect ever be found in the performance of their duties or in any other matter.

I, Brother Odoric, was there in this city of his for a good three years and often present at their festivals, for we Friars Minor[22] have an assigned place in his court, and it is always our duty to go and give him our blessing. So I took the opportunity to ask and inquire of Christians, Saracens, and all sorts of idolaters, as well as from those converts to our faith who are great barons in that court and who wait solely on the person of the king. They all said with one voice that of jesters

---

[16]About six feet.
[17]Jade from the region of Khotan.
[18]The Latin is *serpens,* but dragon seems a better translation than "serpent."
[19]*Spansa.* See note 2.
[20]Words in brackets are supplied by the translator.

[21]The Mongol army was organized along this decimal system, with troops organized into squadrons of tens, companies of ten tens, regiments of ten hundreds, and divisions of ten thousands.
[22]The official title of the Franciscans is the Order of Friars Minor (Lesser Brethren).

alone there are easily thirteen *tumans,* of which one alone consists of 10,000 jesters. Moreover, when it comes to other groups: Of those who care for the dogs, wild beasts, and fowl, there are fully fifteen *tumans;* of physicians who care for the king's person, there are 400 idolaters, eight Christians, and one Saracen. All of these are supplied with everything that they need from the king's court. As for the rest of his household, it is beyond counting.

Advice for Merchants Traveling to Cathay
▼▼▼

104 ▼ Francesco Pegolotti,
THE PRACTICE OF COMMERCE

Around 1340 *Francesco Balducci Pegolotti,* an agent of the Bardi banking house of Florence, composed a handbook of practical advice for merchants. Pegolotti, who served the Bardi family's mercantile interests from London to Cyprus, drew upon his years of experience to produce a work filled with lists of facts and figures on such items as local business customs, the taxes and tariffs of various localities, and the relative values of different standards of weights, measures, and coinage. In other words, the book contained just about everything a prudent merchant would want to know before entering a new market. In addition to these catalogues of useful data, Pegolotti included a short essay of advice for merchants bound for China.

QUESTIONS FOR ANALYSIS

1. What evidence is there that Pegolotti himself had not traveled to Cathay?
2. Considering that his advice is not based on firsthand experience, how knowledgeable does he appear to be on the subject, and what does this suggest?
3. Consider Pegolotti's advice regarding the types of interpreters the merchant will need. What language skills suffice to carry on this trans-Eurasian business enterprise? What does this suggest about the markets of Central Asia and northern China?
4. When and where could the trip be especially hazardous? What does this suggest about the *Pax Mongolica?*
5. Describe the type of merchant for whom this advice was written. Were these small-time traders? Big-time entrepreneurs? What inferences follow from your answer?
6. What overall impression does Pegolotti give us of this journey and its rewards?

THINGS NEEDFUL FOR MERCHANTS WHO DESIRE TO MAKE THE JOURNEY TO CATHAY

In the first place, you must let your beard grow long and not shave. And at Tana[1] you should furnish yourself with a dragoman.[2] And you must not try to save money in the matter of dragomen by taking a bad one instead of a good one. For the additional wages of the good one will not cost you so much as you will save by having him. And besides the dragoman it will be well to take at least two good menservants, who are acquainted with the Cumanian[3] tongue. And if the merchant likes to take a woman with him from Tana, he can do so; if he does not like to take one there is no obligation, only if he does take one he will be kept much more comfortably than if he does not take one. Howbeit, if he does take one, it will be well that she be acquainted with the Cumanian tongue as well as the men.

And from Tana traveling to Gittarchan[4] you should take with you twenty-five days' provisions, that is to say, flour and salt fish, for as to meat you will find enough of it at all the places along the road. And so also at all the chief stations noted in going from one country to another in the route, according to the number of days set down above, you should furnish yourself with flour and salt fish; other things you will find in sufficiency, and especially meat.

The road you travel from Tana to Cathay is perfectly safe, whether by day or by night, according to what the merchants say who have used it. Only if the merchant, in going or coming, should die upon the road, everything belonging to him will become the perquisite of the lord of the country in which he dies, and the officers of the lord will take possession of all. And in like manner if he die in Cathay. But if his brother be with him, or an intimate friend and comrade calling himself his brother, then to such a one they will surrender the property of the deceased, and so it will be rescued.

And there is another danger: this is when the lord of the country dies, and before the new lord who is to have the lordship is proclaimed; during such intervals there have sometimes been irregularities practiced on the Franks, and other foreigners. (They call "Franks" all the Christians of these parts from Romania[5] westward.) And neither will the roads be safe to travel until the other lord be proclaimed who is to reign in place of him who is deceased.

Cathay is a province which contains a multitude of cities and towns. Among others there is one in particular, that is to say the capital city, to which merchants flock, and in which there is a vast amount of trade; and this city is called Cambalec.[6] And the said city has a circuit of one hundred miles,[7] and is all full of people and houses and of dwellers in the said city. . . .

You may reckon also that from Tana to Sara[8] the road is less safe than on any other part of the journey; and yet even when this part of the road is at its worst, if you are some sixty men in the company you will go as safely as if you were in your own house.

Anyone from Genoa or from Venice, wishing to go to the places above-named, and to make the journey to Cathay, should carry linens with him, and if he visit Organci[9] he will dispose of these well. In Organci he should purchase *sommi* of silver,[10] and with these he should proceed without

---

[1]The modern city of Azov on the northeast coast of the Sea of Azov, which is an extension of the Black Sea. Tana was the farthest eastern point to which a person could sail from the Mediterranean.

[2]An interpreter fluent in Arabic, Persian, or Turkish.

[3]A Turkic people inhabiting the middle Volga.

[4]Modern Astrakhan, a city in the Volga Delta, just north of the Caspian Sea.

[5]The European term for the Byzantine Empire.

[6]Khanbalik. See source 103.

[7]Compare this with Odoric of Pordone's account (source 103).

[8]Sarai on the Volga, the capital of the il-khans of Kipchak (also known as the *Golden Horde*), who ruled Russia and Kazakhstan.

[9]Urgench on the Oxus River in Central Asia.

[10]*Sommi* were weights of silver. Each *sommo* was equivalent to five golden florins (source 103, note 8). Pegolotti calculated that the average merchant would carry merchandise worth about 25,000 florins, and the expenses for the merchant, interpreter, and two personal servants would amount to a combined sixty to eighty *sommi,* or 300–400 florins.

making any further investment, unless it be some bales of the very finest stuffs which go in small bulk, and cost no more for carriage than coarser stuffs would do.

Merchants who travel this road can ride on horseback or on asses, or mounted in any way that they choose to be mounted.

Whatever silver the merchants may carry with them as far as Cathay the lord of Cathay will take from them and put into his treasury.[11] And to merchants who thus bring silver they give that paper money of theirs in exchange. This is of yellow paper, stamped with the seal of the lord aforesaid. And this money is called balishi; and with this money you can readily buy silk and all other merchandise that you have a desire to buy. And all the people of the country are bound to receive it. And yet you shall not pay a higher price for your goods because your money is of paper. And of the said paper money there are three kinds, one being worth more than another, according to the value which has been established for each by that lord.[12]

---

[11]The Chinese (and Mongol) policy of demanding silver for paper money resulted in a significant flow of silver from the West to China before, during, and well after the fourteenth century.

[12]See source 103, note 7.

▼▼▼

Long-Distance Travel beyond the Mongol Peace

Important as the Mongol Peace was in facilitating movement and trade across Eurasia, it was not the sole factor behind the general upsurge of long-distance travel and cultural exchange after 1000. Religious motives and ties were equally important driving factors, and this was especially true for the ecumenical community that called itself *Dar al-Islam* (The House of Islam). Educated Muslims, no matter their ethnic origins or native tongues, shared a sacred language — Arabic — and could communicate with one another. They also shared the obligation of *hajj.* The pilgrimage routes that enabled African, Spanish, Turkish, Iranian, Indian, and East Asian Muslims to travel to Arabia's holy sites equally served as important avenues of cultural and material exchange. Moreover, merchants and scholars spread Islam to such faraway regions as sub-Saharan Africa and the coastal lands of Southeast Asia. Once the faith had taken root, there was even more reason to maintain contact with these societies, many of which were so distant from Islam's Southwest Asian birthplace.

In addition to religious devotion, other factors fueled long-distance travel and commerce for both Muslims and non-Muslims alike before and after the breakup of the Mongol Empire. Arabs, Persians, East Africans, Indians, Southeast Asians, Chinese, and Western Europeans had taken to the seas with increasing zeal long before the rise of Chinggis Khan and continued their interests in seafaring and naval technology throughout the thirteenth and fourteenth centuries and beyond. Chinese and Western European seafarers were in the forefront of the effort to build more seaworthy craft capable of bigger payloads and safer transportation. Borrowing extensively from the Arabs and other maritime cultures, Chinese and Western European sailors adopted and created better navigational tools, including superior coastal charts. Such efforts paid rich rewards to the merchant mariners of China and the West. By the mid thirteenth century Chinese mariners were a major force in the seaborne commerce of Southeast Asia, and Western Europeans, especially the Italians, dominated the shipping lanes of the Mediterranean.

Early in the fifteenth century Ming China sent seven massive naval expeditions into the Indian Ocean, and portions of several of those fleets reached the shores of East Africa and Arabia. Also in the fifteenth century, Western Europe, finding the overland roads to Cathay now mostly blocked, began to seek sea routes to the Indies. The consequences of those explorations were astounding. Before the century was over Europeans had sailed to East Africa, India, and the Americas.

Developments in naval engineering and navigation held the key to a new stage in human history — the joining of the Eastern and Western hemispheres — but long-distance transportation across Inner Asia also enjoyed a brief renaissance in the period following the dissolution of the Mongol Ecumene. We might think of it as the Silk Road's Indian Summer. From 1380 to 1405 the armies of *Tamerlane* swept across Eurasia, from Anatolia to the borders of China, from Russia to India. Their destructive fury became legendary and deservedly so. But they also established a new but short-lived Central Asian empire, whose capital, *Samarqand,* became the dynamic meeting place for merchants, travelers, and artisans from all over Eurasia.

The land routes of Inner Africa, particularly of West Africa, were equally vital in the thirteenth and fourteenth centuries, and remained so until new markets blossomed along Africa's west coast in the sixteenth century. Between about 1230 and 1591, the grasslands trading empires of Mali and Songhai successively flourished as a consequence of their ability to control the traffic in gold, goods, salt, and slaves that passed along the trans-Saharan caravan routes.

A Moroccan Visitor in Sub-Saharan Africa
▼▼▼

105 ▼ *Ibn Battuta,*
A DONATION TO THOSE
INTERESTED IN CURIOSITIES

The life and world travels of Abu Abdallah Muhammad ibn Battuta (1304–1369) provide eloquent testimony to the cosmopolitanism of fourteenth-century Islam. Ibn Battuta was born into the religious upper class of Tangier, Morocco, where he received an education in Islamic law and Arabic literature. In 1325 he left home to make the first of what would be several pilgrimages to Mecca. In the course of the next three decades he visited Constantinople, Mesopotamia, Persia, India (where he resided and worked as a *qadi,* or religious judge, for eight years), Burma, Sumatra, Spain, Mali, and probably southern China. In all, his travels covered about 73,000 miles, and most of his stops along the way were within the cultural confines of *Dar al-Islam,* where the sacred law of the Quran prevailed.

In 1351 Ibn Battuta returned to Morocco, but one more journey awaited him. In February 1352 he joined a camel caravan of merchants as he embarked on his last great adventure — a trip to the West African kingdom of Mali, which lay some 1,500 miles to the south of Morocco across one of the world's most inhospitable deserts. Two years later he arrived back home with marvelous tales to tell of this land of gold, whose leaders had converted to Islam in the early thirteenth century.

His days of long-distance travel now over, Ibn Battuta narrated his many travel experiences and observations to Ibn Juzayy, a professional scribe who fashioned these stories into one of the most popular forms of literature in the Islamic World: a *rihla,* or book of travels centering on the *hajj* to Mecca.

The following selection does not describe any of Ibn Battuta's several pilgrimages to Mecca; rather, it tells of his last great journey into the kingdom of Mali in West Africa's Niger River region.

QUESTIONS FOR ANALYSIS

1. What did Ibn Battuta admire most about these people? What did he find hardest to accept? Why?
2. Did Ibn Battuta understand fully all he encountered? Can you find any evidence of tension or misunderstanding?
3. In what ways were the cultures of the people whom Ibn Battuta encountered a mixture of indigenous West African and Islamic elements?
4. How organized and controlled does the state of Mali appear to be?
5. Compare fourteenth-century Mali with eleventh-century Ghana (source 91). What are their similarities and differences? Which seem more significant? What do you conclude from that answer?
6. Based on a careful study of sources 91 and 93, as well as of this document, what inferences do you draw about the social status of women in sub-Saharan West Africa?

Then we reached the town of Iwalatan . . . after a journey . . . of two whole months. It is the first district of the Sudan and the sultan's[1] deputy there is Farba Husayn. *Farba* means "deputy." When we arrived there the merchants[2] placed their belongings in an open space, where the Sudan[3] took over the guard of them while they went to the *farba.* He was sitting on a carpet under a *saqif*[4] with his assistants in front of him with lances and bows in their hands and the chief men of the Masufa[5] behind him. The merchants stood before him while he addressed them, in spite of their proximity to him, through an interpreter, out of contempt for them. At this I repented at having come to their country because of their ill manners and their contempt for white men.[6] I made for the house of Ibn Badda, a respectable man of Sala to whom I had written to

---

[1] The sultan, or king, of Mali, for whom this was an outlying province.
[2] Berbers and Arabs from North Africa.
[3] Here this Arabic word, which means "blacks," refers to the local people and not to the region.

[4] A colonnade.
[5] A Berber people of the western Sahara.
[6] Merchants from North Africa: Berbers and Arabs.

rent a house for me. He had done so. Then the *mushrif*[7] (of Iwalatan), who is called the *manshaju,* invited those who had come with the caravan to receive his reception-gift (*diyafa*). I declined to go but my companions entreated me urgently, so I went with those who went. Then the *diyafa* was brought. It was *anili*[8] meal mixed with a little honey and yogurt which they had placed in half a gourd made into a kind of bowl. Those present drank and went away. I said to them: "Was it to this that the black man invited us?" They said: "Yes, for them this is a great banquet." Then I knew for certain that no good was to be expected from them and I wished to depart with the pilgrims of Iwalatan. But then I thought it better to go to see the seat of their king.

My stay in Iwalatan lasted about fifty days. Its inhabitants did me honor and made me their guest. Among them was the qadi[9] of the place Muhammad b. Abd Allah b. Yanumur and his brother the faqih[10] and teacher Yahya. The town of Iwalatan is extremely hot. There are a few little palm trees there in the shade of which they sow watermelons. . . . Mutton is abundant there and the people's clothes are of Egyptian cloth of good quality. Most of the inhabitants there belong to the Masufa, whose women are of surpassing beauty and have a higher status than the men.

THE MASUFA LIVING IN IWALATAN

These people have remarkable and strange ways. As for their men, they feel no jealousy. None of them traces his descent through his father, but from his maternal uncle, and a man's heirs are the sons of his sister only, to the exclusion of his own sons. This is something that I have seen nowhere in the world except among the Indian infidels in the land of Mulaybar, whereas these are Muslims who observe the prayer and study fiqh[11] and memorize the Quran. As for their women, they have no modesty in the presence of men and do not veil themselves in spite of their assiduity in prayer. If anybody wishes to marry one of them he may do so, but they do not travel with the husband, and if one of them wished to do so her family would prevent her.

The women there have friends and companions among the foreign men, just as the men have companions from among the foreign women. One of them may enter his house and find his wife with her man friend without making any objection. . . .

One day I went into the presence of Abu Muhammad Yandakan al-Masufi in whose company we had come and found him sitting on a carpet. In the courtyard of his house there was a canopied couch with a woman on it conversing with a man seated. I said to him: "Who is this woman?" He said: "She is my wife." I said: "What connection has the man with her?" He replied: "He is her friend." I said to him: "Do you acquiesce in this when you have lived in our country and become acquainted with the precepts of the Shar?"[12] He replied: "The association of women with men is agreeable to us and a part of good conduct, to which no suspicion attaches. They are not like the women of your country." I was astonished at his laxity. I left him, and did not return thereafter. He invited me several times but I did not accept.

When I resolved to travel to Mali . . . I hired a guide from the Masufa, since there is no need to travel in company because of the security of that road, and set off with three of my companions. . . .

Then we . . . arrived at the River Sansara, which is about ten miles from the capital of Mali. It is their custom to prevent people from entering it except by authorization. I had written before this to the white community . . . to ask them to rent a house for me. When I reached the aforementioned river I crossed it by the ferry without

---

[7]The sultan's overseer of the town's markets.
[8]Millet.
[9]An Islamic religious judge.
[10]A teacher of religion.

[11]Religion.
[12]*Sharia,* or Islamic Sacred Law (source 58).

anybody preventing me. I arrived at the town of Mali, the seat of the king of the Sudan. . . .

THE SULTAN OF MALI

He is the sultan Mansa Sulayman.[13] *Mansa* means "sultan" and Sulayman is his name. He is a miserly king from whom no great donation is to be expected. It happened that I remained for this period without seeing him on account of my illness. Then he gave a memorial feast for our Lord Abul-Hasan[14] (may God be content with him) and invited the emirs and faqihs and the qadi and khatib,[15] and I went with them. They brought copies of the Quran and the Quran was recited in full. They prayed for our lord Abul-Hasan (may God have mercy on him) and prayed for Mansa Sulayman. When this was finished I advanced and greeted Mansa Sulayman and the qadi and the khatib and Ibn al-Faqih told him who I was. He answered them in their language and they said to me: "The sultan says to you: 'I thank God.'" I replied: "Praise and thanks be to God in every circumstance."

THEIR TRIVIAL RECEPTION GIFT AND THEIR RESPECT FOR IT

When I departed the reception gift was sent to me and dispatched to the qadi's house. The qadi sent it with his men to the house of Ibn al-Faqih. Ibn al-Faqih hastened out of his house barefooted and came in to me saying: "Come! The cloth and gift of the sultan have come to you!" I got up, thinking that it would be robes of honor and money, but behold! it was three loaves of bread and a piece of beef fried in *gharti*[16] and a gourd containing yogurt. When I saw it I laughed, and was long astonished at their feeble intellect and their respect for mean things.

MY SPEAKING TO THE SULTAN AFTER THIS AND HIS KINDNESS TOWARDS ME

After this reception gift I remained for two months during which nothing was sent to me by the sultan and the month of Ramadan[17] came in. Meanwhile I frequented the *mashwar* [council-place] and used to greet him and sit with the qadi and the khatib. I spoke with Dugha the interpreter, who said: "Speak with him, and I will express what you want to say in the proper fashion." So when he held a session at the beginning of Ramadan and I stood before him and said: "I have journeyed to the countries of the world and met their kings. I have been four months in your country without your giving me a reception gift or anything else. What shall I say of you in the presence of other sultans?" He replied: "I have not seen you nor known about you." The qadi and Ibn al-Faqih rose and replied to him saying: "He greeted you and you sent to him some food." Thereupon he ordered that a house be provided for me to stay in and an allowance to be allotted to me. Then, on the night of 27 Ramadan, he distributed among the qadi and the khatib and the faqihs a sum of money which they call *zakah*[18] and gave to me with them 33 1/3 mithqals.[19] When I departed he bestowed on me 100 mithqals of gold. . . .

THE SELF-DEBASEMENT OF THE SUDAN BEFORE THEIR KING AND THEIR SCATTERING OF DUST ON THEMSELVES BEFORE HIM AND OTHER PECULIARITIES

The Sudan are the humblest of people before their king and the most submissive towards him. They swear by his name, saying: *"Mansa Sulay-*

---

[13]The brother of Mansa Musa (source 60), Mansa Sulayman ruled Mali from 1341 to 1360.
[14]The late sultan of Morocco (r. 1331–1351).
[15]A public preacher at Friday mosque services.
[16]A vegetable oil.

[17]The month during which Muslims fast from sunrise to sunset.
[18]Alms distributed at the end of Ramadan (source 58).
[19]One *mithqal* was 4.72 grams of gold.

man ki." When he calls to one of them at his sessions in the pavilion which we have mentioned the person called takes off his clothes and puts on ragged clothes, and removes his turban and puts on a dirty *shashiyya*[20] and goes in holding up his garments and trousers half-way up his leg, and advances with submissiveness and humility. He then beats the ground vigorously with his two elbows, and stands like one performing a *raka*[21] to listen to his words.

If one of them addresses the sultan and the latter replies he uncovers the clothes from his back and sprinkles dust on his head and back, like one washing himself with water. I used to marvel how their eyes did not become blinded. . . .

WHAT I APPROVED OF AND WHAT I DISAPPROVED OF AMONG THE ACTS OF THE SUDAN

One of their good features is their lack of oppression. They are the farthest removed of people from it and their sultan does not permit anyone to practice it. Another is the security embracing the whole country, so that neither traveler there nor dweller has anything to fear from thief or usurper. Another is that they do not interfere with the wealth of any white man who dies among them, even though it be *qintar* upon *qintar*.[22] They simply leave it in the hands of a trustworthy white man until the one to whom it is due takes it. Another is their assiduity in prayer and their persistence in performing it in congregation and beating their children to make them perform it. If it is a Friday and a man does not go early to the mosque he will not find anywhere to pray because of the press of the people. It is their habit that every man sends his servant with his prayer-mat to spread it for him in a place which he thereby has a right to until he goes to the mosque. Their prayer-carpets are made from the fronds of the tree resembling the palm which has no fruit. Another of their good features is their dressing in fine white clothes on Friday. If any one of them possesses nothing but a ragged shirt he washes it and cleanses it and attends the Friday prayer in it. Another is their eagerness to memorize the great Quran. They place fetters on their children if there appears on their part a failure to memorize it and they are not undone until they memorize it.

I went into the house of the qadi on the day of the festival and his children were fettered so I said to him: "Aren't you going to let them go?" He replied: "I shan't do so until they've got the Quran by heart!" One day I passed by a youth of theirs, of good appearance and dressed in fine clothes, with a heavy fetter on his leg. I said to those who were with me: "What has this boy done? Has he killed somebody?" The lad understood what I had said and laughed, and they said to me: "He's only been fettered so that he'll learn the Quran!"

One of their disapproved acts is that their female servants and slave girls and little girls appear before men naked, with their privy parts uncovered. During Ramadan I saw many of them in this state, for it is the custom of the *farariyya*[23] to break their fast[24] in the house of the sultan, and each one brings his food carried by twenty or more of his slave girls, they all being naked. Another is that their women go into the sultan's presence naked and uncovered, and that his daughters go naked. On the night of 25 Ramadan I saw about two hundred slave girls bringing out food from his palace naked, having with them two of his daughters with rounded breasts having no covering upon them. Another is their sprinkling dust and ashes on their heads out of good manners. . . . Another is that many of them eat carrion, and dogs, and donkeys.[25]

---

[20]A skull cap.
[21]A set sequence of utterances and gestures that form the *salah*, or obligatory ritual prayer, that Muslims must engage in five times daily (sources 57 and 58).
[22]"Weight upon weight" (i.e., a large amount of wealth).

[23]Emirs, or chief men.
[24]The daily fast of the month of Ramadan ends at sunset (note 17).
[25]Unclean meat, according to quranic law.

Samarqand in the Age of Tamerlane
▼▼▼

106 ▼ Ruy González de Clavijo, *EMBASSY TO TAMERLANE*

The Byzantines retook Constantinople from its Latin overlords in 1261, but soon thereafter faced a new enemy in the *Ottoman Turks*, who appeared as a new force to be reckoned with in Anatolia around 1300. During the fourteenth century the Ottomans established a foothold in the Balkans and squeezed Byzantium from two directions — Asiatic Anatolia and Southeastern Europe. As the Byzantine Empire contracted in the face of this pressure, various popes and lords in Western Europe roused themselves to call and wage crusades in defense of the Christian Byzantines, despite the deep religious differences and historical animosities that separated Eastern and Western Christians, especially since 1204. In 1396 a combined French and Hungarian crusade army marched into the Balkans to confront the Ottomans, but Sultan Bayazid I (The Thunderbolt) crushed it at Nicopolis in Bulgaria. It seemed as though the few remnants of the Byzantine Empire would soon be overrun, and then the full fury of the Ottomans would fall upon nearby Latin Christian states, such as Hungary.

In the midst of this crisis, Byzantium and Latin Europe were given a temporary reprieve when the armies of *Timur-i leng* (Timur, or Temür, the Lame), known in the West as *Tamerlane* (1336?–1405), destroyed Sultan Bayazid's army at Ankara in July 1402. The captive sultan was transported east and died soon after. Constantinople was given another half century of life, and did not fall to the Ottomans until May 29, 1453.

Although Tamerlane was a Turkish Muslim who presented himself as the champion of Islam, he was not averse to destroying Islamic enemies in bloodbaths, as he proved in Iran, Syria, Anatolia, and elsewhere. Was it possible that the Christian West could ally with him against common Islamic enemies, such as the Ottomans and the Mamluks of Egypt and Syria?

Tamerlane, who had conquered substantial portions of the western and Central Asian lands of the former Mongol Empire, was more interested in China than the West. Indeed, he died in early 1405 just as he began moving his forces east in a campaign aimed at conquering the Ming Empire. For a few months in the period 1402–1403, however, Tamerlane conducted diplomatic exchanges with a variety of Western princes who courted an alliance with him. It was in this context that King Henry III of Castile-León dispatched several embassies to the Turkish warlord. The second of these, sent out in May 1403, consisted of three envoys, including Ruy González de Clavijo, the king's chamberlain.

After a little less than fifteen months and almost 3,000 miles of travel, Clavijo and a surviving colleague (the third envoy had died in Iran) caught up with Tamerlane at his capital, Samarqand (in modern Uzbekistan). Tamerlane, who was already preparing for his ill-fated invasion of China, received the ambassadors cordially, but refused to commit to any alliance with the Christian West. In fact, the two ambassadors and their retinue were forced to depart Samarqand in November

1404 without even a final audience with the aged and ill Tamerlane (who died two months later).

What did come out of this adventure, however, is Clavijo's detailed account of the embassy and the people and places they visited. Our selection comes from the chamberlain's description of Samarqand, an ancient city of the Silk Road.

QUESTIONS FOR ANALYSIS

1. What master plan did Tamerlane seem to have for Samarqand?
2. Tamerlane has often been described as essentially a plunderer rather than a state-builder. Based on this source, what is your considered judgment of that characterization?
3. Tamerlane's campaigns, which were often accompanied by wholesale destruction and slaughter, have been pointed to as one of many factors that helped close down the Silk Road. Based on this source, what is your considered judgment of that statement?

Now therefore that I have narrated in detail all that befell us during our stay in Samarqand, I must describe that city for you, telling of all that is there to be seen in and round and about, and of all that Timur has accomplished there to embellish his capital. Samarqand stands in a plain, and is surrounded by a rampart or wall of earth, with a very deep ditch. The city itself is rather larger than Seville, but lying outside Samarqand are great numbers of houses which form extensive suburbs. These are spread out on all sides for indeed the township is surrounded by orchards and vineyards, extending in some cases to a league and a half or even two leagues[1] beyond Samarqand which stands in their centre. In between these orchards pass streets with open squares; these all are densely populated, and here all kinds of goods are on sale with bread stuffs and meat. Thus it is that the population outside the city is more numerous than the population within the walls. Among these orchards outside Samarqand are found the most noble and beautiful houses, and here Timur has his many palaces and pleasure grounds. Round and about the great men of the government also here have their estates and country houses, each standing within its orchard:

and so numerous are these gardens and vineyards surrounding Samarqand that a traveler who approaches the city sees only a great mountainous height of trees and the houses embowered among them remain invisible. Through the streets of Samarqand, as through its gardens outside and inside, pass many water-conduits, and in these gardens are the melon-beds and cotton-growing lands. . . .

Further, this land of Samarqand is not only rich in food stuffs but also in manufactures, such as factories of silk both the kinds called zaytúmí and kincobs, also crapes, taffetas and the stuffs we call tercenals in Spain, which are all produced here in great numbers. Further, they make up special fur linings for silk garments, and manufacture stuffs in gold and blue with other colors of diverse tints dyed, and besides all these kinds of stuffs there are the spices. Thus trade has always been fostered by Timur with the view of making his capital the noblest of cities: and during all his conquests wheresoever he came he carried off the best men of the population to people Samarqand, bringing there the master-craftsmen of all nations. Thus from Damascus he carried away with him all the weavers of that city, those

---

[1]One league is about 3 miles.

who worked at the silk looms.[2] Further, the bow-makers who produce those cross-bows which are so famous: likewise armorers: also the craftsmen in glass and porcelain, who are known to be the best in all the world. From Turkey he had brought their gun-smiths who make the arque-bus,[3] and all men of other crafts wheresoever he found them, such as silver-smiths and masons. These all were in very great numbers, indeed so many had been brought together of craftsmen of all sorts that of every denomination and kind you might find many master-workmen established in the capital. Again he had gathered to settle here in Samarqand artillery men, both engineers and bombardiers, besides those who make the ropes by which these engines work. Lastly hemp and flax had been sown and grown for the purpose in the Samarqand lands, where never before this crop had been cultivated.

So great therefore was the population now of all nationalities gathered together in Samarqand that of men with their families the number they said must amount to 150,000 souls. Of the na-tions brought here together there were to be seen Turks, Arabs and Moors[4] of diverse sects, with Christians who were Greeks and Armenians, Catholics, Jacobites[5] and Nestorians,[6] besides those [Indian] folk who baptize with fire in the forehead, who are indeed Christians but of a faith that is peculiar to their nation.[7] The population of Samarqand was so vast that lodging for them all could not be found in the city limits, nor in the streets and open spaces of the suburbs and villages outside, and hence they were to be found quartered temporarily for lodgment even in the caves and in tents under the trees of the gardens,

which was a matter very wonderful to see. The markets of Samarqand further are amply stored with merchandise imported from distant and for-eign countries. From Russia and Tartary[8] come leathers and linens, from Cathay silk stuffs that are the finest in the whole world, and of these the best are those that are plain without embroi-deries. Thence too is brought musk which is found in no other land but Cathay, with balas ru-bies and diamonds which are more frequently to be met with in those parts than elsewhere, also pearls, lastly rhubarb with many other spiceries. The goods that are imported to Samarqand from Cathay indeed are of the richest and most pre-cious of all those brought thither from foreign parts, for the craftsmen of Cathay are reputed to be the most skillful by far beyond those of any other nation. . . .

From India there are brought to Samarqand the smaller spices, which indeed are the most costly of the kind, such as nutmegs and cloves and mace with cinnamon . . . all these with many other kinds that are never to be found in the mar-kets of Alexandria.[9] Throughout the city of Sam-arqand there are open squares where butchers' meat ready cooked, roasted or in stews, is sold, with fowls and game suitably prepared for eat-ing, also bread and excellent fruit both are on sale. All these viands and victuals are there set out in a decent clean manner, namely in all those squares and open spaces of the town, and their traffic goes on all day and even all through the night time. Butchers' shops are numerous, also those booths where fowls, pheasants and par-tridges are on sale: and these shops are kept open by night as by day. On the one part of Samarqand

---

[2]Tamerlane sacked the Syrian cities of Aleppo and Damascus in 1400–1401, wreaking great devastation, and leaving the economy of Syria in shambles.
[3]A heavy but portable matchlock gun fired by a single per-son. See source 109.
[4]Normally the term means a Muslim from western North Africa. Here, however, context demands that we understand it to mean a non-Arab Muslim.
[5]Syrian Christians.
[6]See source 52.
[7]Possibly the so-called Saint Thomas Christians of the west-ern coast of India, who claim origins from the missionary

work of the Apostle Thomas (source 53), but they are not Gnostics. More likely, however, he refers to *Parsis* (Persians), or Indian Zoroastrians (source 18), a small but important group in western India that traces its origins to Persian refugees who left their homeland in the eighth century fear-ing persecution from Muslim conquerors. Parsis mainly en-gage in commerce.
[8]Lands of the il-khanate of the Golden Horde north of the Caucasus Mountains.
[9]The Mediterranean's major port of entry and wholesale cen-ter for spices from the East.

stands the Castle which is not built on a height, but is protected by deep ravines on all its sides: and through these water flows which makes the position of the Castle impregnable. It is here that his Highness keeps his treasure, and none from the city without may enter save the governor of the Castle and his men. Within its walls however Timur holds in captivity upwards of a thousand workmen; these labor at making plate-armor and helmets with bows and arrows, and to this business they are kept at work throughout the whole of their time in the service of his Highness. . . .

At that time when we were his guests in Samarqand there had arrived certain ambassadors sent by the emperor of China[10] who came to Timur bearing this message, namely: that all men knew that he, Timur, was in occupation of lands formerly held in fief to China, and hence that tribute for the same yearly had been due from him to the Chinese emperor: but seeing that for seven years past no tribute had ever been paid, he, Timur, must now forthwith pay down the sum. The answer of his Highness to these ambassadors was that this was most true, and that he was about to pay what was due: but that he would not burden them, the ambassadors, to take it back to China on their return, for he himself, Timur, would bring it. This of course was all said in scorn and to spite them, for his Highness had no intention to pay that tribute. . . .

We heard presently that his Highness had issued orders that those Chinese ambassadors should forthwith all of them be hung, but whether this order was actually carried out . . . is not known to us. Now from the city of Samarqand it is six months' march to the capital of China, which is called Cambaluc,[11] and this is the largest town in that empire: and of this six months' journey two are passed going across a desert country entirely uninhabited, except by nomad herdsmen who wander over the plains feeding their flocks. During the month of June of this year, immediately before the date of our coming to Samarqand, there had arrived a caravan of eight hundred camels bringing merchandise from China. Then it was that Timur having come home from his western campaigns had received that Chinese embassy bearing the message sent him by the emperor of China: and he forthwith had ordered the whole of this caravan, men and goods, to be taken into custody and that none should return to China. . . .

Good order is maintained in Samarqand with utmost strictness and none dare fight with another or oppress his neighbor by force: indeed, as to fighting, that Timur makes them do enough but abroad. When journeying in foreign parts his Highness is everywhere accompanied by his justices who administer the law to all both in camp and palace. As to outlying provinces whither the judges are sent they give justice likewise to all and hear plaints. These judges are specially appointed, and the law has to be administered after the following system. Certain justices are maintained to give sentence in criminal matters and bloodshed arising from quarrels, while certain judges deal with money frauds such as may affect the government. Next there are justices who have it in charge to deal with the affairs of the government proctors who reside in the outlying districts and cities, and who come in to lay their cases and complaints before his Highness. Lastly they are those officials who attend to the reception of foreign embassies. Thus in three departments they give justice, and wheresoever the royal camp is set they give audience each justice in his own department; and there are three great tents erected to which are brought all litigants and criminals, where the justices hear and give sentence. But before this last is performed and done they will go and report of all matters to Timur: and then . . . the judgments are carried into effect.

---

[10]The Yongle Emperor, who was attempting to re-establish a Chinese-dominated Silk Road, such as had existed in the early Tang Dynasty (source 68). See also source 107.

[11]Khanbalik. See source 103.

Zheng He's Western Voyages
▼▼▼

107 ▼ Ma Huan, THE OVERALL SURVEY OF THE OCEAN'S SHORES

As the previous source suggests, vigorous expansionism characterized the early Ming Dynasty (1368-1644), particularly during the reign of Chengzu, known as the *Yongle Emperor* (r. 1402–1424). Between 1405 and 1421 this emperor sent out a series of six great fleets under the command of China's most famous admiral, a Muslim eunuch of Mongolian ancestry named *Zheng He* (1371–1435). If we can believe the records, several fleets carried in excess of 27,000 sailors, soldiers, and officials. The first expedition of 1405–1407 reportedly consisted of 317 vessels, including 62 massive treasure ships, some of which had 9 masts and were over 400 feet long, more than 150 feet wide (imagine a ship larger than a football field), and around 3,100 tons in weight. These armadas — as well as a seventh, which went out in 1431 and returned in 1433 — sailed through the waters of Southeast Asia and the Indian Ocean, visiting numerous ports of call in such far-away places as the Spice Islands, India, East Africa, and the Arabian Peninsula.

Following long-established Arab and Chinese sailing routes, these expeditions were certainly not voyages of exploration. Rather, their main purpose appears to have been the reassertion of Chinese prestige to the south and west. In essence, they were commissioned to accept the submission and tribute of the foreign rulers they encountered. A secondary purpose seems to have been to stimulate China's economy and strengthen its commercial position in South Asia, particularly in light of the fact that the armies of Tamerlane had disrupted certain routes along the old Silk Road.

A book that appeared in 2002, *1421: The Year China Discovered America* by Gavin Menzies, claims that the sixth expedition, which went out in 1421 and returned in 1423, divided into a number of independent squadrons. This was usual for the fleets, but what followed was not. One squadron circumnavigated the globe, sailing to both American continents, as well as to Australia and New Zealand before returning to home port. Another visited the east coast of North America and then went north to Greenland and Iceland and across the Arctic Ocean until it reached the eastern tip of Siberia. From there it sailed south to China. A third sailed to South America and then to the top of Antarctica and back across the Atlantic and Indian Oceans to Australia, and then home. Historians are skeptical of this theory and the evidence that Menzies has produced. As the issue currently stands, scholars generally agree that the squadrons of this fleet, as was true of earlier voyages, sailed no farther west than East Africa.

Wherever they sailed, all of the fleets made an impression on those whom they visited. In one area of Thailand, for example, Zheng He was remembered as a god. Despite the awe that these shows of strength engendered, China failed to gain dominance over the Indian Ocean. After the Yongle Emperor's death, the imperial court did not follow through on what had begun so well. The reasons are not too difficult to discern. The cost of mounting the expeditions was prohibitively high. Moreover, the Confucian literarcy, with its traditional contempt for commerce and foreign cultures, was on the ascendance after the Yongle Emperor's death. Although Zheng He was allowed to lead a seventh expedition westward, it proved to be China's last moment of transoceanic greatness. The court called a halt to further overseas adventures; the fleet was allowed to decay; and China deliberately and effectively forgot much of the naval technology that had made it the world's greatest maritime power in the ages of Song and early Ming.

The following account describes various sites visited in the course of three of Zheng He's expeditions in western waters. Its author, Ma Huan (ca. 1380–after 1451), a Chinese Muslim, joined the fourth voyage (1413–1415) as an Arabic translator, and upon his return transcribed his notes into book form. He later sailed on the sixth (1421–1423) and seventh (1431–1433) expeditions and amended his account accordingly, eventually publishing it in 1451.

QUESTIONS FOR ANALYSIS

1. What evidence is there that the emperor saw these expeditions as a way of extending Chinese influence abroad?
2. How did Zheng He use both diplomacy and military force to achieve this objective?
3. What evidence is there that these expeditions also served commercial purposes?
4. What evidence is there that a high level of international commerce existed in the Indian Ocean well before the coming of Zheng He's fleets?

THE COUNTRY OF MANLAJIA[1] (MALACCA)

From Zhan City[2] you go due south, and after traveling for eight days with a fair wind the ship comes to Longya strait,[3] after entering the strait you travel west; and you can reach this place in two days.

Formerly this place was not designated a "country"; and because the sea hereabouts was named "Five Islands," the place was in consequence named "Five Islands." There was no king of the country; and it was controlled only by a chief. This territory was subordinate to the jurisdiction of Xian Luo;[4] it paid an annual tribute of forty *liang*[5] of gold, and if it were not paid, then Xian Luo would send men to attack it.

In the seventh year of the Yongle period,[6] the Emperor ordered the principal envoy, the grand eunuch Zheng He, and others to assume command (of the treasure-ships), and to take the imperial edicts and to bestow upon this chief two silver seals, a hat, a belt and a robe. Zheng He set up a stone tablet and raised the place to a city; and it was subsequently called the "country of Manlajia." Thereafter Xian Luo did not dare to invade it.

---

[1]Malacca, a port on the west coast of the Malay Peninsula.
[2]In Champa (central Vietnam).
[3]The Singapore Strait.

[4]Thailand.
[5]About forty-eight ounces.
[6]1409. This would be the third expedition of 1409–1411.

The chief, having received the favor of being made king, conducted his wife and son, and went to the court at the capital[7] to return thanks and to present tribute of local products. The court also granted him a sea-going ship, so that he might return to his country and protect his land. . . .

Whenever the treasure-ships of the Central Country[8] arrived there, they at once erected a line of stockading, like a city-wall, and set up towers for the watchdrums at four gates; at night they had patrols of police carrying bells; inside, again, they erected a second stockade, like a small city-wall, within which they constructed warehouses and granaries; and all the money and provisions were stored in them. The ships which had gone to various countries[9] returned to this place and assembled; they marshaled the foreign goods and loaded them in the ships; then waited till the south wind was perfectly favorable. In the middle decade of the fifth moon they put to sea and returned home.[10]

Moreover, the king of the country made a selection of local products, conducted his wife and son, brought his chiefs, boarded a ship and followed the treasure-ships; and he attended at court and presented tribute. . . .

THE COUNTRY OF SUMENDALA[11] (SEMUDERA, LHO SEUMAWE)

The country of Sumendala is exactly the same country as that formerly named Xuwendana. This place is indeed the principal center of the Western Ocean. . . .

The king of the country of Sumendala had previously been raided by the "tattooed-face king"

of Naguer; and in the fighting he received a poisoned arrow in the body and died. He had one son, who was young and unable to avenge his father's death. The king's wife made a vow before the people, saying "If there is anyone who can avenge my husband's death and recover his land, I am willing to marry him and to share with him the management of the country's affairs." When she finished speaking, a fisherman belonging to the place was fired with determination, and said "I can avenge him."

Thereupon he took command of an army and at once put the "tattooed-face king" to flight in battle; and later he avenged the former king's death when the "tattooed-face king" was killed. The people of the latter submitted and did not dare to carry on hostilities.

Whereupon the wife of the former king, failing not to carry out her previous vow, forthwith married the fisherman. He was styled "the old king," and in such things as the affairs of the royal household and the taxation of the land, everybody accepted the old king's decisions. In the seventh year of the Yongle period[12] the old king, in fulfillment of his duty, brought tribute of local products,[13] and was enriched by the kindness of Heaven;[14] and in the tenth year of the Yongle period[15] he returned to his country.

When the son of the former king had grown up, he secretly plotted with the chiefs, murdered his adoptive father the fisherman, usurped his position, and ruled the kingdom.

The fisherman had a son by his principal wife; his name was Suganla; he took command of his people, and they fled away, taking their families; and, after erecting a stockade in the neighboring mountains, from time to time he led his men in

---

[7]Nanjing (the southern capital). The Ming court moved from the seaport capital of Nanjing to inland Beijing (the northern capital) in 1421, signaling a shift in China's focus toward the Middle Kingdom's age-old area of primary concern — the steppes and the steppe peoples who inhabited them. The Ming Dynasty also rebuilt and extended the Great Wall into the edifice we see today — massive frontier fortifications to protect China from invasions from the west and the north.

[8]China, the Middle Kingdom.

[9]Elements were detached from the main fleet and sent off on special missions.

[10]1433, the last expedition.

[11]Semudera on the north coast of the island of Sumatra and across the Strait of Malacca from Malaysia.

[12]1409.

[13]To the Ming court at Nanjing.

[14]The emperor.

[15]1412.

incursions to take revenge on his father's enemies. In the thirteenth year of the Yongle period[16] the principal envoy, the grand eunuch Zheng He, and others, commanding a large fleet of treasure-ships, arrived there; they dispatched soldiers who captured Suganla; and he went to the capital;[17] and was publicly executed. The king's son was grateful for the imperial kindness, and constantly presented tribute of local products to the court. . . .

At this place there are foreign[18] ships going and coming in large numbers, hence all kinds of foreign goods are sold in great quantities in the country.

In this country they use gold coins and tin coins. The foreign name for the gold coin is *dinaer;*[19] they use pale gold, seventy percent pure, for casting it. . . . The foreign name for the tin coin is *jiashi,*[20] and in all their trading they regularly use tin coins. . . .

THE COUNTRY OF GULI[21] (CALICUT)

This is the great country of the Western Ocean. . . .

In the fifth year of the Yongle period the court ordered the principal envoy, the grand eunuch Zheng He, and others[22] to deliver an imperial mandate to the king of this country and to bestow on him a patent conferring a title of honor, and the grant of a silver seal, also to promote all the chiefs and award them hats and belts of various grades.

So Zheng He went there in command of a large fleet of treasure-ships, and he erected a tablet with a pavilion over it and set up a stone which said, "Though the journey from this country to the Central Country is more than a hundred thousand *li,*[23] yet the people are very similar, happy and prosperous, with identical customs. We have here engraved a stone, a perpetual declaration for ten thousand ages."

The king of the country is a Nankun[24] man; he is a firm believer in the Buddhist religion[25] and he venerates the elephant and the ox.

The population of the country includes five classes, the Muslim people, the Nankun people, the Zhedi people, the Geling people, and the Mugua[26] people. . . .

The king has two great chiefs who administer the affairs of the country; both are Muslims. . . .

The people are very honest and trustworthy. Their appearance is smart, fine, and distinguished.

Their two great chiefs received promotion and awards from the court of the Central Country.

If a treasure-ship goes there, it is left entirely to the two men to superintend the buying and selling; the king sends a chief and a Zhedi Weinuoji[27] to examine the account books in the official bureau; a broker comes and joins them; and a high officer who commands the ships discusses the choice of a certain date for fixing prices. When the day arrives, they first of all take the silk embroideries and the open-work silks, and other such goods which have been brought there, and discuss the price of them one by one; and when the price has been fixed, they write out an agreement stating the amount of the price; this agreement is retained by these persons. . . .

THE COUNTRY OF HULUMOSI[28] (HORMUZ)

Setting sail from the country of Guli, you go towards the north-west; and you can reach this place after traveling with a fair wind for twenty-

---

[16]1415.

[17]Presumably Nanjing.

[18]Non-Chinese.

[19]From the Arabic *dinar.*

[20]The English would later transliterate this local word as "cash."

[21]Calicut on India's southwest coast (not to be confused with Calcutta in the northeast).

[22]1407. This was the second expedition (1407–1409). Although Zheng He was its nominal commander, he did not accompany it.

[23]A *li* is a bit more than one-third of a mile.

[24]Upper class. He probably means a member of the Kshatriya, or warrior-ruler, caste.

[25]Incorrect; he was Hindu.

[26]These would be the four castes, or varnas.

[27]Probably an accountant.

[28]Hormuz, an island off the coast of Iran and at the mouth of the Persian Gulf.

five days. The capital lies beside the sea and up against the mountains.

Foreign ships from every place and foreign merchants traveling by land all come to this country to attend the market and trade; hence the people of the country are all rich. . . .

The king of this country, too, took a ship and loaded it with lions, *qilin,*[29] horses, pearls, pre-cious stones, and other things, also a memorial to the throne written on a golden leaf; and he sent his chiefs and other men, who accompanied the treasure-ships dispatched by the Emperor, which were returning from the Western Ocean; and they went to the capital and presented tribute.[30]

---

[29]A giraffe.

[30]This probably took place at the end of the seventh expedition.

The Origins of Portugal's Overseas Empire
▼▼▼

108 ▼ Gomes Eannes de Azurara, THE CHRONICLE OF GUINEA

At the same time that Zheng He's fleets were sailing majestically through the western seas and Muslim sailors dominated the coastal traffic of virtually every inhabited land washed by the Indian Ocean (except Australia), the Portuguese were tentatively inching down the west coast of Africa. From 1419 onward, Prince Henry (1394–1460), third son of King John I (r. 1385–1433), almost annually sent out a ship or two in an attempt to push farther toward the sub-Saharan land the Portuguese called *Guinea;* only in 1434, however, did one of his caravels manage to round the feared Cape Bojador, along the western Sahara coast. Once this psychological and navigational barrier had been broken, the pace of exploration quickened. By 1460 Portuguese sailors had ventured as far south as modern Sierra Leone, an advance of about 1,500 miles in twenty-six years. Finally, Bartholomeu Dias rounded the southern tip of Africa in early 1488, and Vasco da Gama, seeking, in his words, "Christians and spices," dropped anchor off Calicut on May 20, 1498. Although da Gama lost two of his four ships and many of his crew, the profits from this small enterprise were astounding. Portugal was now in the Indian Ocean to stay.

Portugal's commercial empire was still over half a century in the future when, in 1452, Gomes Eannes de Azurara (ca. 1400–after 1472) began to compose a history of the life and work of Prince Henry "the Navigator," in so many ways the father of an empire-to-be. Azurara's history details Portuguese explorations along the coast of West Africa down to 1448. He promised a sequel because Henry was still alive and actively promoting voyages to Africa when Azurara completed *The Chronicle of Guinea* in 1453. Azurara's other duties apparently intervened, and he never returned to the topic. Still, the chronicle he managed to write is a revealing picture of the spirit behind Portugal's first generation of oceanic exploration and colonialism.

In the following excerpts Azurara explains why Prince Henry sponsored the expeditions and defends the consequent enslavement of West Africans. Trade in

Guinean slaves, which became an integral part of Portugal's commercial imperialism, began in 1441 with the capture of 10 Africans, and Azurara estimated that 927 West African slaves had come into Portugal by 1448. This humane man, who was disturbed by many of the aspects of this exploitation, could not foresee that between 1450 and 1500 roughly 150,000 more Africans would enter Portugal as slaves, and over the next four centuries untold millions of so-called heathens would be transported out of Africa by European and Euro-American slavers.

QUESTIONS FOR ANALYSIS

1. What were Henry's motives? What seems to have been foremost in his mind — commercial, political, or religious gain or simple curiosity?
2. Some modern commentators argue that Europeans initially entered the African slave trade out of a sense of racial superiority. Based on this account, do you think Azurara would agree with that assessment? In other words, how does he justify the enslavement of Africans? Please be specific in your answer.
3. It has been said that Henry was a fifteenth-century crusader. From the evidence, does this seem to be a fair judgment? Why or why not?
4. Compare this document with Christopher Columbus's letter of 1493 in the Prologue. Do they seem to share a common spirit? If so, what is it?
5. Compare the purposes behind the Portuguese and Spanish explorations with those of Zheng He's expeditions. In what ways do they differ, and to what do you ascribe those differences?

We imagine that we know a matter when we are acquainted with the doer of it and the end for which he did it. And since in former chapters we have set forth the Lord Infant[1] as the chief actor in these things, giving as clear an understanding of him as we could, it is meet that in this present chapter we should know his purpose in doing them. And you should note well that the noble spirit of this Prince, by a sort of natural constraint, was ever urging him both to begin and to carry out very great deeds. For which reason, after the taking of Ceuta[2] he always kept ships well armed against the Infidel, both for war, and because he had also a wish to know the land that lay beyond the isles of Canary and that Cape called Bojador, for that up to his time, neither by writings, nor by the memory of man, was known

with any certainty the nature of the land beyond that Cape. Some said indeed that Saint Brendan[3] had passed that way; and there was another tale of two galleys rounding the Cape, which never returned. But this does not appear at all likely to be true, for it is not to be presumed that if the said galleys went there, some other ships would not have endeavored to learn what voyage they had made. And because the said Lord Infant wished to know the truth of this — since it seemed to him that if he or some other lord did not endeavor to gain that knowledge, no mariners or merchants would ever dare to attempt it — (for it is clear that none of them ever trouble themselves to sail to a place where there is not a sure and certain hope of profit) — and seeing also that no other prince took any pains in this mat-

[1]Prince Henry. An *infante* (feminine *infanta*) was any son of a Portuguese or Spanish monarch who was not an heir to the Crown.
[2]A Muslim naval base in Morocco that Portugal captured in

1415. In 1580 possession passed to Spain, which still controls it.
[3]A wandering Irish monk of the sixth century; according to legend, he set sail into the Atlantic.

ter, he sent out his own ships against those parts, to have manifest certainty of them all. And to this he was stirred up by his zeal for the service of God and of the King Edward his Lord and brother,[4] who then reigned. And this was the first reason of his action.

The second reason was that if there chanced to be in those lands some population of Christians, or some havens, into which it would be possible to sail without peril, many kinds of merchandise might be brought to this realm, which would find a ready market, and reasonably so, because no other people of these parts traded with them, nor yet people of any other that were known; and also the products of this realm might be taken there, which traffic would bring great profit to our countrymen.

The third reason was that, as it was said that the power of the Moors in that land of Africa was very much greater than was commonly supposed, and that there were no Christians among them, nor any other race of men; and because every wise man is obliged by natural prudence to wish for a knowledge of the power of his enemy; therefore the said Lord Infant exerted himself to cause this to be fully discovered, and to make it known determinately how far the power of those infidels extended.

The fourth reason was because during the one and thirty years that he had warred against the Moors, he had never found a Christian king, nor a lord outside this land, who for the love of our Lord Jesus Christ would aid him in the said war. Therefore he sought to know if there were in those parts any Christian princes, in whom the charity and the love of Christ was so ingrained that they would aid him against those enemies of the faith.

The fifth reason was his great desire to make increase in the faith of our Lord Jesus Christ and to bring to him all the souls that should be saved, — understanding that all the mystery of the Incarnation, Death, and Passion of our Lord Jesus Christ was for this sole end — namely the salvation of lost souls — whom the said Lord Infant by his travail and spending would fain bring into the true path. For he perceived that no better offering could be made unto the Lord than this; for if God promised to return one hundred goods for one, we may justly believe that for such great benefits, that is to say for so many souls as were saved by the efforts of this Lord, he will have so many hundreds of rewards in the kingdom of God, by which his spirit may be glorified after this life in the celestial realm. For I who wrote this history saw so many men and women of those parts turned to the holy faith, that even if the Infant had been a heathen, their prayers would have been enough to have obtained his salvation. And not only did I see the first captives,[5] but their children and grandchildren as true Christians as if the Divine grace breathed in them and imparted to them a clear knowledge of itself.

---

[4]King Duarte (r. 1433–1438).

[5]West African slaves who had been captured and transported to Portugal by licensed slave hunters. As the slave trade developed, the vast majority of slaves transported out of Africa by Europeans and, later, Euro-Americans would be purchased from native African slavers (see Chapter 13, source 113).

Chapter 13

▼▼▼

Transoceanic Encounters
1500–1700

Although aggressive expansion had already been part of the dynamics of European civilization for over 700 years, its transoceanic explorations that began in the fifteenth century mark a turning point in the history not only of the West but of the entire world. Europe's push across wide expanses of ocean eventually became the single most important factor in the breakdown of regional isolation around the world and the creation of a true global community in the years after 1500.

The story is not simple. By 1700 Europeans had culturally and demographically altered forever large areas of the Americas, but they had yet to visit much of those two great continents. The major civilizations of East Asia were still successfully resisting most unwanted European influences, and European penetration of India's interior had hardly begun. At the end of the seventeenth century, Western exploration and direct exploitation of the regions of Africa beyond the coasts were even less advanced. Moreover, although it is easy from a twenty-first-century perspective to see in its early transoceanic ventures the origins of Europe's eventual dominance of the world, this would not have been apparent to most people living during these two centuries. For every area into which Europeans were expanding their influence, there was another in which they were retreating or being rebuffed. For example, sixteenth- and seventeenth-century Europeans fearfully witnessed the advancing menace of the Ottoman Turks into Europe itself.

Under Sultan *Suleiman I* (r. 1520–1566), the Ottoman Empire became a major force to be reckoned with so far as Europe was concerned. In 1522 Suleiman's armies established control over the eastern Mediterranean by seizing the island of

Rhodes. In 1526 the Turks destroyed a Hungarian army and within two decades controlled most of that Christian kingdom. By the autumn of 1529 Ottoman forces besieged Vienna but were forced to withdraw. The Ottoman Turks remained Europe's greatest challenger for the next two centuries, and many believed that the next time Ottoman soldiers advanced on Vienna they would not be stopped. Indeed, the siege of 1683 failed only by the slightest margin.

Equally impressive was the expansion of Chinese borders, especially during the reign of Emperor *Kangxi* (r. 1661–1722), when China took control of the island of Formosa (modern Taiwan), incorporated Tibet into its empire, finally turned the nomads of Mongolia into quiescent vassals, and entered into a border treaty with imperial Russia that inaugurated a long period of Sino-Russian peace. On its part, Russia carved out the largest land empire of its day through a steady process of exploration and colonization across Eurasia's eastern forests and steppes. In 1637 Russian pioneers reached the Pacific, and colonists were not far behind. Given this state of affairs, Western Europeans did not see expansion as a one-way street, nor did they see themselves as aggressors and the rest of the world as their victims.

▼▼▼

Europeans in the Americas

As Columbus's letter of 1493 indicates, Europeans almost instantly discovered that the world across the Atlantic contained exploitable sources of wealth (such as silver, gold, timber, and furs) and was capable of supporting large-scale agricultural production of such crops as sugar and tobacco, for which there was an eager European market. All these things seemed theirs for the taking, not only in the thinly populated regions of North America and eastern and southern South America, but even in the densely populated regions of Mexico, Peru, and the Caribbean.

The consequences of this attitude were catastrophic for America's indigenous peoples. By 1650 Spaniards and Portuguese ruled and exploited Mexico, the Caribbean, Central and South America, and southern portions of North America; the English, French, Dutch, and other Europeans had begun to settle the northern portions of North America's Atlantic coast and the Saint Lawrence River Basin. In the wake of these European incursions, Native American political structures disintegrated, uncounted millions of American Indians died, and traditional patterns of life and belief managed only a tenuous (but tenacious) survival.

While this sad story is true enough, it would be incorrect to say that the majority of the European colonists and the governments who supported them attempted to exterminate the Native Americans. Certainly most European colonists sought to exploit the American Indians, and even the American Indians' protectors sought to convert them to European religious beliefs, thereby offering the natives a form of cultural suicide. Moreover, there is no denying the fact that the European newcomers contained within their ranks a number of ruthless thugs who did not hesitate to brutalize and kill, sometimes on a large scale. Still, there is no credible evidence of any widespread attempts at *genocide,* or the systematic, state-sponsored annihilation of an entire people. Such a notion was inconsistent with the worldview and aims of the European colonizers who, as we saw in Columbus's letter of 1493, sought souls to save and slaves for servitude.

Europeans might have lacked the intention of killing off millions of Native Americans, but they managed unintentionally to do so, as a consequence of the viruses, bacteria, and other parasites that they carried across the Atlantic in their bodies. What is more, when West African slaves were brought to the Caribbean to replace the native populations that were rapidly dying off, additional fatal diseases came into the Americas. Smallpox, measles, diphtheria, chicken pox, whooping cough, influenza, malaria, yellow fever — all of these and more became killers when introduced into populations that lacked genetic resistance, due to their thousands of years of isolation from the Afro-Eurasian World.

The Tainos, who greeted Columbus in 1492, numbered about 1 million in 1492; by 1530 they numbered a few thousand. In 1519, the year of Cortés's arrival, the population of Mexico was about 21.5 million people; in 1532 it had fallen to about 16 million; at mid century, following the epidemic of 1545–1548, it was possibly as low as 2.5 million. That is a 90 percent decrease in the short space of thirty years! No part of the Americas was untouched; even areas not visited personally by Europeans felt the devastating effects of killer epidemics. The Mississippian Mound Culture of North America seems to have disappeared as an identifiable entity in the mid sixteenth century as a result of European diseases that traveled along native trade routes to its population centers well before Europeans ever saw the magnificent mound complexes that this culture left behind as silent witnesses of its former greatness.

The first of the following two documents hints at the critical role played by the hidden ally of disease in the Spanish *conquistadors'* conquest of Mexico. It also suggests other factors that combined to give the Spaniards their victory. The second source reveals the devastating effects of simple greed on the part of Spanish entrepreneurs in Peru.

The Battle for Tenochtitlán: An Aztec Perspective
▼▼▼

109 ▼ Bernardino de Sahagún, GENERAL HISTORY OF THE THINGS OF NEW SPAIN

Bernardino de Sahagún (ca. 1499–1590), a member of the Franciscan Order, was one of the earliest Spanish missionaries in Mexico, arriving in 1529. He soon developed a keen interest in the culture of the natives of Mexico, for whom he had deep affection and respect. He mastered the *Nahuatl* language, spoken by the Aztecs and other central Mexican peoples, and in 1545 began a systematic collection of oral and pictorial information about the culture of the native Mexicans. The result was his *General History of the Things of New Spain,* our principal source of information about Mexican culture at the time of the Spanish conquest. Many Spaniards opposed his work because they believed his efforts to preserve the memory of native culture threatened their policy of exploiting and Christianizing the American Indians. As a result, in 1578 his writings and notes were confiscated by royal decree and sent back to Spain, where they gathered dust in an archive until discovered and published in the nineteenth century.

The following selection comes from the twelfth and last book of the *General History.* Based on interviews Sahagún and his American Indian assistants had with Aztecs who had experienced the conquest some twenty-five years earlier, Book Twelve, which exists in both Nahuatl and Spanish versions, recounts the conquest of Mexico from the time Cortés arrived on the Mexican coast in April 1519 until the days following the Aztecs' capitulation in August 1521. Although scholars hotly debate the exact role of Sahagún and his assistants in composing and organizing Book Twelve, most agree that it accurately portrays Aztec views and perceptions of the events that unfolded between 1519 and 1521.

Our excerpt, translated from the Nahuatl text, picks up the story in November 1519. By then the Spaniards had gained as allies the Tlaxcalans, the Aztecs' bitter enemies, and were leaving Cholula, an ancient city that the Spaniards and their allies had sacked because of its leaders' lack of cooperation. They were on their way to Tenochtitlán, the splendid Aztec capital on Lake Texcoco, for an anticipated meeting with the Aztec emperor, Moctezuma.

QUESTIONS FOR ANALYSIS

1. What does the source reveal about the motives of the Spaniards and their allies for their attack on the Aztecs?
2. What was Moctezuma's strategy to deal with the Spaniards? Why did it fail?
3. What impression did Spanish firearms and cannons have on the Aztecs? What evidence is there that the Aztecs adjusted their strategy to counter the Spanish weapons?

4. Aside from their firearms, what other military advantages did the Spaniards have over their opponents? How decisive do these other advantages seem to have been?
5. On several occasions the Aztecs routed the Spaniards. What explains these Aztec victories?
6. How did the Aztec view of war differ from that of the Spaniards?
7. What does the source reveal about Aztec religious beliefs, values, and practices?

And after the dying in Cholula,[1] the Spaniards set off on their way to Mexico,[2] coming gathered and bunched, raising dust. . . .

Thereupon Moteucçoma[3] named and sent noblemen and a great many other agents of his . . . to go meet [Cortés] . . . at Quauhtechcac. They gave [the Spaniards] golden banners of precious feathers, and golden necklaces.

And when they had given the things to them, they seemed to smile, to rejoice and to be very happy. Like monkeys they grabbed the gold. It was as though their hearts were put to rest, brightened, freshened. For gold was what they greatly thirsted for; they were gluttonous for it, starved for it, piggishly wanting it. They came lifting up the golden banners, waving them from side to side, showing them to each other. They seemed to babble; what they said to each other was in a babbling tongue. . . .

Another group of messengers — rainmakers, witches, and priests — had also gone out for an encounter, but nowhere were they able to do anything or to get sight of [the Spaniards]; they did not hit their target, they did not find the people they were looking for, they were not sufficient. . . .

▷　Cortés and his entourage continue their march.

Then they set out in this direction, about to enter Mexico here. Then they all dressed and equipped themselves for war. They girded themselves, tying their battle gear tightly on themselves and then on their horses. Then they arranged themselves in rows, files, ranks.

Four horsemen came ahead going first, staying ahead, leading. . . .

Also the dogs, their dogs, came ahead, sniffing at things and constantly panting.[4]

By himself came marching ahead, all alone, the one who bore the standard on his shoulder. He came waving it about, making it spin, tossing it here and there. . . .

Following him came those with iron swords. Their iron swords came bare and gleaming. On their shoulders they bore their shields, of wood or leather.

The second contingent and file were horses carrying people, each with his cotton cuirass,[5] his leather shield, his iron lance, and his iron sword hanging down from the horse's neck. They came with bells on, jingling or rattling. The horses, the deer,[6] neighed, there was much neighing, and they would sweat a great deal; water seemed to fall from them. And their flecks of foam splatted on the ground, like soapsuds splatting. . . .

The third file were those with iron crossbows, the crossbowmen. Their quivers went hanging at

---

[1]For more on Cholula, see source 95.
[2]Throughout the text, the term *Mexico* refers to Tenochtitlán, the capital of the Aztec Empire. *Mexica* refers to the people of Tenochtitlán and Tlatelolco, a large suburb of Tenochtitlán.
[3]One of several acceptable modern spellings of the Aztec

emperor's name, including *Moctezuma, Motecuhzoma,* and *Montezuma.*
[4]Specially bred war dogs for use in combat.
[5]A piece of armor that covered the body from neck to waist.
[6]Having never before seen horses, some Aztecs considered them to be large deer.

their sides, passed under their armpits, well filled, packed with arrows, with iron bolts. . . .

The fourth file were likewise horsemen; their outfits were the same as has been said.

The fifth group were those with harquebuses,[7] the harquebusiers, shouldering their harquebuses; some held them [level]. And when they went into the great palace, the residence of the ruler, they repeatedly shot off their harquebuses. They exploded, sputtered, discharged, thundered, disgorged. Smoke spread, it grew dark with smoke, everyplace filled with smoke. The fetid smell made people dizzy and faint.

Then all those from the various altepetl[8] on the other side of the mountains, the Tlaxcalans, the people of Tliliuhquitepec, of Huexotzinco, came following behind. They came outfitted for war with their cotton upper armor, shields, and bows, their quivers full and packed with feathered arrows, some barbed, some blunted, some with obsidian[9] points. They went crouching, hitting their mouths with their hands yelling, singing, . . . whistling, shaking their heads. . . .

▷ Cortés and his army entered Tenochtitlán in November 1519 and were amicably received by Moctezuma, who was nonetheless taken captive by the Spaniards. Cortés's army was allowed to remain in a palace compound, but tensions grew the following spring. Pedro de Alvarado, in command while Cortés left to deal with a threat to his authority from the governor of Cuba, became increasingly concerned for the Spaniards' safety as the people of Tenochtitlán prepared to celebrate the annual festival in honor of Huitzilopochtli, the warrior god of the sun.

And when it had dawned and was already the day of his festivity, very early in the morning those who had made vows to him[10] unveiled his face. Forming a single row before him they offered him incense; each in his place laid down before him offerings of food for fasting and rolled amaranth dough.[11] And it was as though all the youthful warriors had gathered together and had hit on the idea of holding and observing the festivity in order to show the Spaniards something, to make them marvel and instruct them.[12] . . .

When things were already going on, when the festivity was being observed and there was dancing and singing, with voices raised in song, the singing was like the noise of waves breaking against the rocks.

When it was time, when the moment had come for the Spaniards to do the killing, they came out equipped for battle. They came and closed off each of the places where people went in and out. . . . And when they had closed these exits, they stationed themselves in each, and no one could come out any more. . . . Then they surrounded those who were dancing, going among the cylindrical drums. They struck a drummer's arms; both of his hands were severed. Then they struck his neck; his head landed far away. Then they stabbed everyone with iron lances and struck them with iron swords. They struck some in the belly, and then their entrails came spilling out. They split open the heads of some, they really cut their skulls to pieces, their skulls were cut up into little bits. And if someone still tried to run it was useless; he just dragged his intestines along. There was a stench as if of sulfur. Those who tried to escape could go nowhere. When anyone tried to go out, at the entryways they struck and stabbed him.

And when it became known what was happening, everyone cried out, "Mexica warriors, come running, get outfitted with devices, shields, and arrows, hurry, come running, the warriors are

---

[7]Also spelled *arquebuses*. See source 106, note 3.

[8]The Nahuatl term for any sovereign state, especially the local ethnic states of central Mexico.

[9]A volcanic glass that can be sharpened to a razor-sharp edge.

[10]Huitzilopochtli. As god of the sun, he needed daily sacrifices of human hearts and blood in order to rise from the east each morning.

[11]An image of the god was fashioned from amaranth seed flour and the blood of recently sacrificed victims.

[12]An integral part of the ceremony was the singing of hymns that extolled battle, blood, and honor on the field of conflict.

dying; they have died, perished, been annihilated, O Mexica warriors!" Thereupon there were war cries, shouting, and beating of hands against lips. The warriors quickly came outfitted, bunched together, carrying arrows and shields. Then the fighting began; they shot at them with barbed darts, spears, and tridents, and they hurled darts with broad obsidian points at them. . . .

> ▷ The fighting that ensued drove the Spaniards and their allies back to the palace enclave. Without a reliable supply of food and water, in July 1520, Cortés, who had returned with his power intact, led his followers on a desperate nocturnal escape from the city, but they were discovered and suffered heavy losses as they fled. They retreated to the other side of the lake, and the Aztecs believed the Spanish threat had passed.

Before the Spanish appeared to us, first an epidemic broke out, a sickness of pustules.[13]. . . Large bumps spread on people; some were entirely covered. They spread everywhere, on the face, the head, the chest, etc. The disease brought great desolation; a great many died of it. They could no longer walk about, but lay in their dwellings and sleeping places, no longer able to move or stir. They were unable to change position, to stretch out on their sides or face down, or raise their heads. And when they made a motion, they called out loudly. The pustules that covered people caused great desolation; very many people died of them, and many just starved to death; starvation reigned, and no one took care of others any longer.

On some people, the pustules appeared only far apart, and they did not suffer greatly, nor did many of them die of it. But many people's faces were spoiled by it, their faces and noses were made rough. Some lost an eye or were blinded.

This disease of pustules lasted a full sixty days; after sixty days it abated and ended. When people were convalescing and reviving, the pustules

disease began to move in the direction of Chalco.[14] And many were disabled or paralyzed by it, but they were not disabled forever. . . . The Mexica warriors were greatly weakened by it.

And when things were in this state, the Spaniards came, moving toward us from Tetzcoco. . . .

> ▷ Having resupplied his Spanish/Tlaxcalan army and having constructed a dozen cannon-carrying brigantines for use on the lake, Cortés resumed his offensive late in 1520. In April 1521 he reached Tenochtitlán and placed the city under a blockade.

When their twelve boats had come from Tetzcoco, at first they were all assembled at Acachinanco, and then the Marqués[15] moved to Acachinanco. He went about searching where the boats could enter, where the canals were straight, whether they were deep or not, so that they would not be grounded somewhere. But the canals were winding and bent back and forth, and they could not get them in. They did get two boats in; they forced them down the road coming straight from Xoloco. . . .

And the two boats came gradually, keeping on one side. On the other side no boats came, because there were houses there. They came ahead, fighting as they came; there were deaths on both sides, and on both sides captives were taken. When the Tenochca who lived in Çoquipan saw this, they fled, fled in fear. . . . They took nothing at all with them, they just left all their poor property in fear, they just scattered everything in their haste. And our enemies[16] went snatching things up, taking whatever they came upon. Whatever they hit on they carried away, whether cloaks, lengths of cotton cloth, warrior's devices, log drums, or cylindrical drums.

The Tlatelolca fought in Çoquipan, in war boats. And in Xoloco the Spaniards came to a place where there was a wall in the middle of the road, blocking it. They fired the big guns at it.

---

[13]Smallpox.
[14]A city on the southeast corner of Lake Texcoco.

[15]Cortés.
[16]The various American Indian allies of the Spaniards.

At the first shot it did not give way, but the second time it began to crumble. The third time, at last parts of it fell to the ground, and the fourth time finally the wall went to the ground once and for all. . . .

Once they got two of their boats into the canal at Xocotitlan. When they had beached them, then they went looking into the house sites of the people of Xocotitlan. But Tzilacatzin and some other warriors who saw the Spaniards immediately came out to face them; they came running after them, throwing stones at them, and they scattered the Spaniards into the water. . . .

When they got to Tlilhuacan, the warriors crouched far down and hid themselves, hugging the ground, waiting for the war cry, when there would be shouting and cries of encouragement. When the cry went up, "O Mexica, up and at them!" the Tlappanecatl Ecatzin, a warrior of Otomi[17] rank, faced the Spaniards and threw himself at them, saying, "O Tlatelolca warriors, up and at them, who are these barbarians? Come running!" Then he went and threw a Spaniard down, knocking him to the ground; the one he threw down was the one who came first, who came leading them. And when he had thrown him down, he dragged the Spaniard off.

And at this point they let loose with all the warriors who had been crouching there; they came out and chased the Spaniards in the passageways, and when the Spaniards saw it they, the Mexica, seemed to be intoxicated. Then captives were taken. Many Tlaxcalans, and people of Acolhuacan, Chalco, Xochimilco, etc.,[18] were captured. A great abundance were captured and killed. . . .

Then they took the captives to Yacacolco, hurrying them along, going along herding their captives together. Some went weeping, some singing, some went shouting while hitting their hands against their mouths. When they got

them to Yacacolco, they lined them all up. Each one went to the altar platform where the sacrifice was performed.[19] The Spaniards went first, going in the lead; the people of the different altepetl just followed, coming last. And when the sacrifice was over, they strung the Spaniards' heads on poles on skull racks; they also strung up the horses' heads. They placed them below, and the Spaniards' heads were above them, strung up facing east.[20] . . .

▷ Despite this victory, the Aztecs could not overcome the problems of shortages of food, water, and warriors. In mid July 1521 the Spaniards and their allies resumed their assault, and in early August the Aztecs decided to send into battle a quetzal-owl warrior, whose success or failure, it was believed, would reveal if the gods wished the Aztecs to continue the war.

And all the common people suffered greatly. There was famine; many died of hunger. They no longer drank good, pure water, but the water they drank was salty. Many people died of it, and because of it many got dysentery and died. Everything was eaten: lizards, swallows, maize straw, grass that grows on salt flats. And they chewed at . . . wood, glue flowers, plaster, leather, and deerskin, which they roasted, baked, and toasted so that they could eat them, and they ground up medicinal herbs and adobe bricks. There had never been the like of such suffering. The siege was frightening, and great numbers died of hunger. And bit by bit they came pressing us back against the wall, herding us together. . . . There was no place to go; people shoved, pressed and trampled one another; many died in the press. But one woman came to very close quarters with our enemies, throwing water at them, throwing water in their faces, making it stream down their faces.

---

[17]Elite warriors bound by oath never to retreat.
[18]American Indian allies of the Spaniards.
[19]Traditionally the sacrifice consisted of cutting the heart out of the victim.

[20]The direction of the god Huitzilopochtli. See note 9.

And when the ruler Quauhtemoctzin[21] and the warriors Coyohuehuetzin, Temilotzin, Topantemoctzin, the Mixcoatlailotlac Ahuelitoctzin, Tlacotzin, and Petlauhtzin took a great warrior named Tlapaltecatl opochtzin . . . and outfitted him, dressing him in a quetzal-owl costume.[22]. . . "Let him wear it, let him die in it. Let him dazzle people with it, let him show them something; let our enemies see and admire it." When they put it on him he looked very frightening and splendid. And they ordered four [others] to come helping him, to accompany him. They gave him the darts of the devil,[23] darts of wooden rods with flint tips. And the reason they did this was that it was as though the fate of the rulers of the Mexica were being determined.

When our enemies saw him, it was as though a mountain had fallen. Every one of the Spaniards was frightened; he intimidated them, they seemed to respect him a great deal. Then the quetzal-owl climbed up on the roof. But when some of our enemies had taken a good look at him they rose and turned him back, pursuing him. Then the quetzal-owl turned them again and pursued them. Then he snatched up the precious feathers and gold and dropped down off the roof. He did not die, and our enemies did not carry him off. Also three of our enemies were captured. At that the war stopped for good. There was silence, nothing more happened. Then our enemies went away. It was silent and nothing more happened until it got dark.

And the next day nothing more happened at all, no one made a sound. The common people just lay collapsed. The Spaniards did nothing more either, but lay still, looking at the people. Nothing was going on, they just lay still. . . .

▷ Two weeks passed before the Aztecs capitulated on August 13, 1521, after a siege of over three months' duration.

---

[21]Quauhtemoctzin was now the Aztec emperor, Moctezuma having died while in Spanish captivity.
[22]This rare bird had been sacred to the Maya and was equally sacred to the Aztecs. Its four iridescent blue-green tail feathers were highly prized.
[23]Battle darts sacred to Huitzilopochtli.

The "Mountain of Silver" and the Mita System
▼▼▼

110 ▾ *Antonio Vazquez de Espinosa,*
COMPENDIUM AND DESCRIPTION
OF THE WEST INDIES

Many of Columbus's dreams and promises for the lands he explored were never realized, but his vision that the inhabitants could be exploited proved all too correct. Queen Isabella was, by most accounts, disquieted by the idea of enslaving American Indians, but forced labor came to the new Spanish colonies nevertheless, largely because it proved economically advantageous for the colonizers, especially on their plantations and in their mines.

In 1545 an Indian herder lost his footing on a mountain in Peru while chasing his llama, and to keep from falling, he grabbed a bush, which he pulled from the ground revealing a rich vein of silver. This is the most widely told story about how the Spaniards learned of the world's richest silver mine at Potosí. Located two miles above sea level in a cold, desolate region of modern Bolivia, Potosí became the site of the Western Hemisphere's first and greatest silver rush. Within four decades Potosí had a racially mixed population of 160,000 inhabitants, making it the largest, wildest, gaudiest, and richest city in the New World. With one-fifth of all the silver extracted going directly to the Spanish crown, Potosí was a major reason why the kings of Spain were able to launch a huge naval armada against England in 1588, carry on a crusade against the Ottoman Empire in the eastern Mediterranean, and send armies off to campaigns in France, the Low Countries, and central Europe. The silver of Potosí also contributed significantly to massive inflation in Spain and, as the wealth filtered out of the Iberian Peninsula, throughout Western Europe.

The backbone of the Potosí operation was the *mita* system of labor, described in the following document by Antonio Vazquez de Espinosa (d. 1630), a Spanish Carmelite friar who abandoned an academic career to do missionary work in the Americas. He returned to Spain in 1622, where he wrote a half dozen books on the Americas and topics relating to priestly work. His best known book is his *Compendium and Description of the West Indies,* an extensive summary of observations made during his travels through Mexico and Spanish South America.

In the first part of the selection that follows Espinosa describes the mine and facilities at Huancavelica for extracting mercury, a necessary element in the refining of silver. The second portion provides a wealth of details on the mining of silver at Potosí. Throughout the document, Espinosa presents insights into the functioning of the mita system of labor, which had its roots in the Inca Empire when villages had been required to provide an annual quota of laborers for public works projects. The Spaniards continued the practice of enforced labor quotas, at first for public works, and later for work in mines, factories, and fields owned by private individuals.

QUESTIONS FOR ANALYSIS

1. What was the range of annual wages for each laborer at Huancavelica? How did this amount of money compare with the annual salary of the royal hospital chaplain? How did the annual sum of their wages compare with the cost of tallow candles at Potosí? Compare the wages of the mita workers at Potosí with the wages paid those American Indians who freely hired themselves out. What do you conclude from all these figures?

2. What were the major hazards of the work connected with the extraction and production of mercury and silver?

3. What evidence does Espinosa provide of Spanish concern for the welfare of the American Indian workers? What evidence is there of unconcern? Where does the weight of the evidence seem to lie?

4. Wherever huge profits justify the risks, there will be people who function beyond the constraints of the law. What evidence does Espinosa provide of such a phenomenon in Spanish South America?

5. How did the mita system work?

6. What appears to have been the impact of the mita system on native Peruvian society?

HUANCAVELICA

And so at the rumor of the rich deposits of mercury . . . in the years 1570 and 1571, they started the construction of the town of Huancavelica de Oropesa in a pleasant valley at the foot of the range. It contains 400 Spanish residents, as well as many temporary shops of dealers in merchandise and groceries, heads of trading houses, and transients, for the town has a lively commerce. It has a parish church with vicar and curate,[1] a Dominican convent, and a Royal Hospital under the Brethren of San Juan de Diós for the care of the sick, especially Indians on the range; it has a chaplain with a salary of 800 pesos[2] contributed by His Majesty; he is curate of the parish of San Sebastian de Indios, for the Indians who have come to work in the mines and who have settled down there. There is another parish on the other side of the town, known as Santa Ana, and administered by Dominican friars.

Every two months His Majesty sends by the regular courier from Lima[3] 60,000 pesos to pay for the mita of the Indians, for the crews are changed every two months, so that merely for the Indian mita payment [in my understanding of it] 360,000 pesos are sent from Lima every year, not to speak of much besides, which all crosses at his risk that cold and desolate mountain country which is the puna[4] and has nothing on it but llama ranches.

Up on the range there are 3,000 or 4,000 Indians working in the mine; it is colder up there than in the town, since it is higher. The mine where the mercury is located is a large layer which they keep following downward. When I was in that town (which was in the year 1616) I went up on the range and down into the mine, which at that time was considerably more than 130 stades[5] deep. The ore was very rich black

flint, and the excavation so extensive that it held more than 3,000 Indians working away hard with picks and hammers, breaking up that flint ore; and when they have filled their little sacks, the poor fellows, loaded down with ore, climb up those ladders or rigging, some like masts and others like cables, and so trying and distressing that a man empty-handed can hardly get up them. That is the way they work in this mine, with many lights and the loud noise of the pounding and great confusion. Nor is that the greatest evil and difficulty; that is due to thievish and undisciplined superintendents. As that great vein of ore keeps going down deeper and they follow its rich trail, in order to make sure that no section of that ore shall drop on top of them, they keep leaving supports or pillars of the ore itself, even if of the richest quality, and they necessarily help to sustain and insure each section with less risk. This being so, there are men so heartless that for the sake of stealing a little rich ore, they go down out of hours and deprive the innocent Indians of this protection by hollowing into these pillars to steal the rich ore in them, and then a great section is apt to fall in and kill all the Indians, and sometimes the unscrupulous and grasping superintendents themselves, as happened when I was in that locality; and much of this is kept quiet so that it shall not come to the notice of the manager and cause the punishment of the accomplices. . . .

This is how they extract the mercury. On the other side of the town there are structures where they grind up the mercury ore and then put it in jars with molds like sugar loaves on top of them, with many little holes, and others on top of them, flaring and plastered with mud, and a channel for it to drip into and pass into the jar or place where it is to fall. Then they roast the ore with a straw fire from the plant growing on the

---

[1] A parish priest and his assistant priest.
[2] A standard Spanish coin worth eight *reals* (see note 11).
[3] Lima was the capital city of the viceroyalty of Peru, one of the two major administrative units of Spanish America, covering all of Spanish South America, except for part of the Caribbean coast.

[4] A high, cold plateau.
[5] A *stade* was a measure of length, approximately one-eighth of a mile.

puna, like esparto grass, which they call ichu; that is the best sort of fire for the treatment of this ore. Under the onset of this fire it melts and the mercury goes up in vapor or exhalation until, passing through the holes in the first mold, it hits the body of the second, and there it coagulates, rests, and comes to stop where they have provided lodging for it; [but] if it does not strike any solid body while it is hot, it rises as vapor until it cools and coagulates and starts falling downward again. Those who carry out the reduction of this ore have to be very careful and test cautiously; they must wait till the jars are cold before uncovering them for otherwise they may easily get mercury poisoning and if they do, they are of no further use; their teeth fall out, and some die. After melting and extracting the mercury by fire, they put it in dressed sheepskins to keep it in His Majesty's storehouses, and from there they usually transport it on llamaback to the port of Chincha, . . . where there is a vault and an agent appointed by the Royal Council, and he has charge of it there; then they freight it on shipboard to the port of San Marcos de Arica, from which it is carried by herds of llamas and mules to Potosí. In the treatment of the silver they use up every year more than 6,000 quintals,[6] plus 2,000 more derived from the ore dust, i.e., the silver and mercury which was lost and escaped from the first washing of the ore, made in vats.

POTOSÍ

The famous Potosí range, so celebrated all over the world for the great wealth which God has created unique in its bowels and veins, lies in the Province of the Charcas, 18 leagues from the city of Chuquisaca, which was later called La Plata, on account of the great richness of this range. It is in the midst of the Cordillera, and since that is high-altitude country, that region is usually colder than Germany, so much so that it was uninhabitable for the native tribes. . . . On account of the cold, not a fly, mosquito, or [any] other unpleasant creature can live there; there was no living thing on that waste but guanacos, vicuñas, ostriches, and vizcachas, which are characteristic of that cold country. . . .

According to His Majesty's warrant, the mine owners on this massive range have a right to the mita of 13,300 Indians in the working and exploitation of the mines, both those which have been discovered, those now discovered, and those which shall be discovered. It is the duty of the Corregidor of Potosí[7] to have them rounded up and to see that they come in from all the provinces between Cuzco over the whole of El Collao and as far as the frontiers of Tarija and Tomina;[8] this Potosí Corregidor has power and authority over all the Corregidors in those provinces mentioned; for if they do not fill the Indian mita allotment assigned each of them in accordance with the capacity of their provinces as indicated to them, he can send them, and does, salaried inspectors to report upon it, and when the remissness is great or remarkable, he can suspend them, notifying the Viceroy[9] of the fact.

These Indians are sent out every year under a captain whom they choose in each village or tribe, for him to take them and oversee them for the year each has to serve; every year they have a new election, for as some go out, others come in. This works out very badly, with great losses and gaps in the quotas of Indians, the villages being depopulated; and this gives rise to great extortions and abuses on the part of the inspectors toward the poor Indians, ruining them and thus depriving the . . . chief Indians of their property and carrying them off in chains because they do not fill out the mita assignment, which they can-

---

[6]A measure of weight equaling anywhere from 100 to 130 pounds.
[7]A district military leader.
[8]This region consisted of approximately 139 Indian villages.

[9]Literally "the royal deputy," he was appointed by the Crown to serve as chief military and civil administrator over a vast region.

not do, for the reason given and for others which I do not bring forward.

These 13,300 are divided up every 4 months into 3 mitas, each consisting of 4,433 Indians, to work in the mines on the range and in the 120 smelters in the Potosí and Tarapaya areas; it is a good league[10] between the two. These mita Indians earn each day, or there is paid each one for his labor, 4 reals.[11] Besides these there are others not under obligation, who are mingados or hire themselves out voluntarily: these each get from 12 to 16 reals, and some up to 24, according to their reputation of wielding the pick and knowing how to get the ore out. These mingados will be over 4,000 in number. They and the mita Indians go up every Monday morning to the locality of Guayna Potosí which is at the foot of the range; the Corregidor arrives with all the provincial captains or chiefs who have charge of the Indians assigned them, and he there checks off and reports to each mine and smelter owner the number of Indians assigned him for his mine or smelter; that keeps him busy till 1 P.M., by which time the Indians are already turned over to these mine and smelter owners.

After each has eaten his ration, they climb up the hill, each to his mine, and go in, staying there from that hour until Saturday evening without coming out of the mine; their wives bring them food, but they stay constantly underground, excavating and carrying out the ore from which they get the silver. They all have tallow candles, lighted day and night; that is the light they work with, for as they are underground, they have need of it all the time. The mere cost of these candles used in the mines on this range will amount every year to more than 300,000 pesos, even though tallow is cheap in that country, being abundant; but this is a very great expense, and it is almost incredible, how much is spent for candles in the operation of breaking down and getting out the ore.

These Indians have different functions in the handling of the silver ore; some break it up with bar or pick, and dig down in, following the vein in the mine; others bring it up; others up above keep separating the good and the poor in piles; others are occupied in taking it down from the range to the mills on herds of llamas; every day they bring up more than 8,000 of these native beasts of burden for this task. These teamsters who carry the metal do not belong to the mita, but are mingados — hired.

So huge is the wealth which has been taken out of this range since the year 1545, when it was discovered, up to the present year of 1628, which makes 83 years that they have been working and reducing its ores, that merely from the registered mines, as appears from an examination of most of the accounts in the royal records, 326,000,000 assay pesos have been taken out. At the beginning when the ore was richer and easier to get out, for then there were no mita Indians and no mercury process, in the 40 years between 1545 and 1585, they took out 111,000,000 of assay silver. From the year 1585 up to 1628, 43 years, although the mines are harder to work, for they are deeper down, with the assistance of 13,300 Indians whom His Majesty has granted to the mine owners on that range, and of other hired Indians, who come there freely and voluntarily to work at day's wages, and with the great advantage of the mercury process, in which none of the ore or the silver is wasted, and with the better knowledge of the technique which the miners now have, they have taken out 215,000,000 assay pesos. That, plus the 111 extracted in the 40 years previous to 1585, makes 326,000,000 assay pesos, not counting the great amount of silver secretly taken from these mines . . . to Spain, paying no 20 percent or registry fee,[12] and to other countries outside Spain; and to the Philippines and China, which is beyond all reckoning; but I should venture to imagine and even assert that what has been taken from the Potosí range must be as much again as what paid the 20 percent royal impost.

Over and above that, such great treasure and riches have come from the Indies in gold and sil-

---

[10]A league is three miles.
[11]A Spanish silver coin (see note 2).

[12]The 20 percent registry fee was the royal tax on all New World silver.

ver from all the other mines in New Spain and Peru, Honduras, the New Kingdom of Granada, Chile, New Galicia, New Vizcaya,[13] and other

quarters since the discovery of the Indies, that they exceed 1,800 millions.

---

[13]New Galicia and New Vizcaya were regions and administrative jurisdictions in New Spain located in north-central and northwestern Mexico.

▼▼▼

African Reactions to the European Presence

Due mainly to the catastrophic decline of the American Indian population, Spanish and Portuguese colonists increasingly turned to African slaves for labor in the sixteenth century. Portugal, which had begun to explore the west coast of Africa in 1418, was initially in an advantageous position to supply this human chattel. During the 1480s the Portuguese established fortified posts along West Africa's Gold Coast, where it traded with such coastal kingdoms as Benin for gold, slaves, and ivory. By 1500 some 700 kilos of gold and approximately 10,000 slaves were arriving annually in Lisbon from West Africa. While engaging in this trade, the Portuguese were also pushing down the coast. Finally, in 1487–1488 Bartholomeu Dias rounded the Cape of Good Hope, opening the east coast of Africa to direct Portuguese contact. Under the leadership of Francisco de Almeida (ca. 1450–1510), the Portuguese set up fortified trading posts along Africa's east coast, thereby successfully challenging Arab hegemony over East African trade.

The Portuguese led the way, but other European maritime powers were close behind in establishing their presence in Africa. While the Spaniards concentrated on North Africa, capturing Tunis in 1535 and holding it until 1574, the English under John Hawkins instituted their own slave trade from West Africa to the New World between 1562 and 1568. After 1713, when England won the right of *asiento,* by which it was granted license to transport African slaves to the Spanish Americas, the English came to dominate the African slave trade. In 1595 the Dutch began to trade on the Guinea coast, and in 1652 they founded Cape Town on the southern tip of the continent. The first French forts in Africa appeared in 1626 on the island of Madagascar, which France annexed in 1686, and by 1637 the French were building numerous forts on West Africa's Gold Coast and exploring Senegal. Even the Prussians had a minor presence in West Africa by 1683.

Slaves and gold were the two major attractions for all these European powers on the African coasts, and many Africans were quite willing to deal in these commodities with the outside world. Arab and Berber traders had already been crossing the Sahara for centuries to purchase the goods of inner Africa, including millions of slaves. European merchants now simply opened a new door — a coastal door — to this lucrative, long-booming market.

Although Europeans were becoming a major presence along the coasts, their penetration of the interior would have to wait for a later age. The general social and political strength of most African regional kingdoms, the wide variety of debilitating and often deadly African diseases, against which Europeans had no immunities, and the absence of safe and fast inland transportation combined to block significant European thrust into the interior until the nineteenth century. The Europeans were thus forced to come largely as traders and not colonizers, and they had to negotiate with local African leaders for goods and slaves.

An African Voice of Ambivalence?

▼▼▼

111 ▾ Nzinga Mbemba (Afonso I), *LETTERS TO THE KING OF PORTUGAL*

The largest state in central West Africa by 1500 was the kingdom of Kongo, stretching along the estuary of the Congo River in territory that today lies within the nations of Angola and Zaire. In 1483 the Portuguese navigator Diogo Cão made contact with Kongo and several years later visited its inland capital. When he sailed home he brought with him Kongo emissaries, whom King Nzinga a Kuwu dispatched to Lisbon to learn European ways. They returned in 1491, accompanied by Portuguese priests, artisans, and soldiers, who brought with them a wide variety of European goods, including a printing press. In the same year, the king and his son, Nzinga Mbemba, were baptized into the Catholic faith.

Around 1506 Nzinga Mbemba, whose Christian name was *Afonso,* succeeded his father and ruled until about 1543. Afonso promoted the introduction of European culture into his kingdom by adopting Christianity as the state religion (although most of his subjects, especially those in the hinterlands, remained followers of the ancient ways), imitating the etiquette of the Portuguese royal court, and using Portuguese as the language of state business. His son Henrique was educated in Portugal and returned to serve as West Africa's first native-born Roman Catholic bishop. European firearms, horses, and cattle, as well as new foods from the Americas, became common in Kongo, and Afonso dreamed of achieving a powerful and prosperous state through cooperation with the Europeans. By the time of his death, however, his kingdom was on the verge of disintegration, in no small measure because of the Portuguese. As many later African rulers were to discover, the introduction of European products and customs caused dissension and instability. Worse yet, Portuguese involvement in the slave trade undermined Afonso's authority and made his subjects restive.

In 1526 King Afonso wrote the following three letters to King João III of Portugal. The three documents are part of a collection of twenty-four letters that Afonso and his Portuguese-educated native secretaries dispatched to two successive kings of Portugal on a variety of issues. This collection is our earliest extant source of African commentary on the European impact.

QUESTIONS FOR ANALYSIS

1. According to King Afonso, what have been the detrimental effects of the Portuguese presence in his kingdom?
2. What do the letters reveal about the mechanics of the slave trade in the kingdom? Who participated in it?
3. What do the letters reveal about King Afonso's attitude toward slavery? Was he opposed to the practice in its entirety or only certain aspects of it?
4. What steps has the king taken to deal with the problems caused by the Portuguese? What do the letters suggest about the effectiveness of these steps?
5. How would you characterize Afonso's attitude toward the power and authority of the king of Portugal? Does he consider himself inferior to the Portuguese king or his equal?
6. Based on this evidence, what do you conclude was King Afonso's conception of the ideal relationship between the Portuguese and his kingdom?

JULY 6, 1526

Sir, Your Highness should know how our Kingdom is being lost in so many ways that it is convenient to provide for the necessary remedy, since this is caused by the excessive freedom given by your agents and officials to the men and merchants who are allowed to come to this Kingdom to set up shops with goods and many things which have been prohibited by us, and which they spread throughout our Kingdoms and Domains in such an abundance that many of our vassals, whom we had in obedience, do not comply because they have the things in greater abundance than we ourselves; and it was with these things that we had them content and subjected under our vassalage and jurisdiction, so it is doing a great harm not only to the service of God, but the security and peace of our Kingdoms and State as well.

And we cannot reckon how great the damage is, since the mentioned merchants are taking every day our natives, sons of the land and the sons of our noblemen and vassals and our relatives, because the thieves and men of bad conscience grab them wishing to have the things and wares of this Kingdom which they are ambitious of; they grab them and get them to be sold; and so great, Sir, is the corruption and licentiousness that our country is being completely depopulated, and Your Highness should not agree with this nor accept it as in your service. And to avoid it we need from those (your) Kingdoms no more than some priests and a few people to teach in schools, and no other goods except wine and flour for the holy sacrament. That is why we beg of Your Highness to help and assist us in this matter, commanding your factors that they should not send here either merchants or wares, because it is *our will that in these Kingdoms there should not be any trade of slaves nor outlet for them.*[1] Concerning what is referred [to] above, again we beg of Your Highness to agree with it, since otherwise we cannot remedy such an obvious damage. Pray Our Lord in His mercy to have Your Highness under His guard and let you do forever the things of His service. I kiss your hands many times.

At our town of Kongo, written on the sixth day of July, João Teixeira did it[2] *in 1526.*
The King. Dom[3] *Affonso.*

{On the back of this letter the following can be read:
To the most powerful and excellent prince Dom João, King our Brother.}

---

[1] The emphasis appears in the original letter.
[2] That is, wrote the letter. João Teixeira was probably a Kongo-born secretary who had been baptized and educated by Portuguese missionaries.

[3] Portuguese for "lord."

UNDATED

Moreover, Sir, in our Kingdoms there is another great inconvenience which is of little service to God, and this is that many of our people, keenly desirous as they are of the wares and things of your Kingdoms, which are brought here by your people, and in order to satisfy their voracious appetite, seize many of our people, freed and exempt men, and very often it happens that they kidnap even noblemen and the sons of noblemen, and our relatives, and take them to be sold to the white men who are in our Kingdoms; and for this purpose they have concealed them; and others are brought during the night so that they might not be recognized.

And as soon as they are taken by the white men they are immediately ironed and branded with fire, and when they are carried to be embarked, if they are caught by our guards' men the whites allege that they have bought them but they cannot say from whom, so that it is our duty to do justice and to restore to the freemen their freedom, but it cannot be done if your subjects feel offended, as they claim to be.

And to avoid such a great evil we passed a law so that any white man living in our Kingdoms and wanting to purchase goods in any way should first inform three of our noblemen and officials of our court whom we rely upon in this matter, and these are Dom Pedro Manipanza and Dom Manuel Manissaba, our chief usher, and Gonçalo Pires our chief freighter, who should investigate if the mentioned goods are captives[4] or free men, and if cleared by them there will be no further doubt nor embargo for them to be taken and embarked. But if the white men do not comply with it they will lose the aforementioned goods. And if we do them this favor and concession it is for the part Your Highness has in it, since we know that it is in your service too that these goods are taken from our Kingdom, otherwise we should not consent to this. . . .

---

[4]Captives taken by King Afonso in his wars of expansion (made possible by Portuguese firearms) were sold into slavery.

OCTOBER 18, 1526

Sir, Your Highness has been kind enough to write to us saying that we should ask in our letters for anything we need, and that we shall be provided with everything, and as the peace and the health of our Kingdom depend on us, and as there are among us old folks and people who have lived for many days, it happens that we have continuously many and different diseases which put us very often in such a weakness that we reach almost the last extreme; and the same happens to our children, relatives and natives owing to the lack in this country of physicians and surgeons who might know how to cure properly such diseases. And as we have got neither dispensaries nor drugs which might help us in this forlornness, many of those who had been already confirmed and instructed in the holy faith of Our Lord Jesus Christ perish and die; and the rest of the people in their majority cure themselves with herbs and breads and other ancient methods, so that they put all their faith in the mentioned herbs and ceremonies if they live, and believe that they are saved if they die; and this is not much in the service of God.

And to avoid such a great error and inconvenience, since it is from God in the first place and then from your Kingdoms and from Your Highness that all the good and drugs and medicines have come to save us, we beg of you to be agreeable and kind enough to send us two physicians and two apothecaries and one surgeon, so that they may come with their drugstores and all the necessary things to stay in our kingdoms, because we are in extreme need of them all and each of them. We shall do them all good and shall benefit them by all means, since they are sent by Your Highness, whom we thank for your work in their coming. We beg of Your Highness as a great favor to do this for us, because besides being good in itself it is in the service of God as we have said above.

Images of the Portuguese in the Art of Benin
▼▼▼

112 ▼ *A BENIN-PORTUGUESE SALTCELLAR and A BENIN WALL PLAQUE*

For many centuries sub-Saharan Africans have crafted some of the world's most impressive artworks, especially sculptures. Since at least 500 B.C.E., West African sculptors used clay, wood, ivory, and bronze to create a variety of works that were of central importance to their various cultures. These include masks, animal figures, ceremonial weapons, religious objects, and images of rulers and other important people (see source 93). In some regions bronze casting and ivory carving were royal monopolies carried on by highly trained professionals.

Such was the case in the kingdom of Benin, located on the west coast of tropical Africa in an area that today is part of Nigeria. The kingdom, created by a people known as the *Edo,* took shape around 1300, when a number of agricultural villages accepted the authority of an *oba,* or divine king, who ruled from the capital, Benin City. By the time the Portuguese arrived in 1485 Benin was a formidable military and commercial power and also a center of state-sponsored artistic activity. Ivory carvers and bronze casters were organized into hereditary guilds and resided in neighborhoods set aside for them in Benin City. They produced bronze heads, animal and human figures, pendants, plaques, musical instruments, drinking vessels, and armlets, all of which were used by their society's elites for ceremonial and personal purposes or were exchanged in trade.

The arrival of the Portuguese affected Benin's artistic development in two important ways. First, Portuguese merchants, unable to establish Benin as a major source of slaves, turned to other commodities, including artworks, as objects of trade. Benin ivory carvers received numerous commissions from Portuguese merchants to produce condiment sets, utensils, and hunting horns for sale in Europe. Second, the Portuguese also stimulated the production of artworks for use in Benin itself by providing Benin artists through trade an increased supply of copper, which was used in the alloys that were turned into plaques and sculptures.

The two works produced in this section provide an opportunity to appreciate the high quality of Benin art and to draw some inferences about the attitudes of the people of Benin toward Europeans. The first item, an ivory carving crafted in the sixteenth or early seventeenth century, is usually identified as a *salario,* or saltcellar. It depicts two Portuguese officials, flanked by two assistants. Above them is a Portuguese ship, with a man peering out of a crow's nest.

The second work, which also dates from the sixteenth or early seventeenth century, is a copper plaque, approximately eighteen inches high and designed to be hung on a wall in the oba's palace in Benin City. (We can see the holes on the top and bottom of the plaque where it was attached.) The central figure is the oba, shown holding a spear and shield. To his right stand two attendants. The one farther away holds a C-shaped iron bar, which was used as currency in trade; the figure closer to the oba holds an *eban,* a ceremonial sword. To the oba's left stands another attendant playing a flute. The two figures in the background, on each side

A Benin-Portuguese Saltcellar

A Benin Wall Plaque

of the oba's head, represent the Portuguese. In one hand each figure holds a rectangular object, perhaps a glass mirror, and in the other hand what appears to be a goblet. They probably represent items the Portuguese offered in trade for the goods of Benin.

QUESTIONS FOR ANALYSIS

1. In the saltcellar, notice what hangs around the standing figure's neck, what he holds in his hands, and his facial expression. What is the sculptor trying to communicate?
2. Why might this image of the Portuguese official have appealed to the European purchasers for whom the work was intended?
3. Consider the plaque. What distinguishes the oba from all the other figures? Which details illustrate the oba's power and perhaps his divinity?
4. How does the representation of the Portuguese in the plaque differ from that of the saltcellar?
5. Compare the representation of the Portuguese official in the saltcellar with that of the oba in the plaque. Which strike you as more significant, the similarities or the differences? What inferences do you draw from your answer?
6. What might we infer from these works about Portuguese-Benin relations and the attitudes of the people of Benin toward the Portuguese?

The Economics of the West African Slave Trade
▼▼▼

113 ▼ James Barbot,
A VOYAGE TO NEW CALABAR RIVER IN THE YEAR 1699

Source 111 illustrates how an African king's attempt to control commerce between his subjects and the Portuguese was at least partially frustrated and how the slave trade had a number of tragic consequences for African society. This source offers another perspective. James Barbot, a French member of a late-seventeenth-century English slave-trading expedition to Ibani, describes trade negotiations with its king, William, in 1699. Ibani, or *Bonny,* as the English called it, was an island state in the Niger Delta. By the late eighteenth century it was the principal slave market of the entire Guinea coast. One English captain, who sailed to Bonny between 1786 and 1800, estimated that at least 20,000 slaves were bought and sold there annually. In this document we see how the trading system worked a century earlier.

QUESTIONS FOR ANALYSIS

1. How would you characterize trade at Ibani? Was it haphazard bartering? A well-developed system with specific currency? Something else?

2. How did the English benefit from the way in which trade was conducted?
3. What benefits did the king enjoy from this arrangement?
4. What was Barbot's attitude toward Ibani society?
5. How did the Ibani seem to regard the English?
6. What do the prices of the other commodities purchased by the English say about the relative value of one slave?
7. Who was the exploiter, and who was the exploited?
8. What does this account reveal about social structure in Ibani?

June 30, 1699, being ashore, had a new conference which produced nothing. Then Pepprell [Pepple], the king's brother, delivered a message from the king:

He was sorry we would not accept his proposals. It was not his fault, since he had a great esteem and regard for the whites, who had greatly enriched him through trade. His insistence on thirteen bars[1] for male and ten for female slaves was due to the fact that the people of the country maintained a high price for slaves at their inland markets, seeing so many large ships coming to Bonny for them. However, to moderate matters and to encourage trade with us, he would be content with thirteen bars for males and nine bars and two brass rings for females, etc.

We offered thirteen bars for men and nine for women and proportionately for boys and girls, according to their ages. Following this we parted, without concluding anything further.

On July 1, the king sent for us to come ashore. We stayed there till four in the afternoon and concluded the trade on the terms offered them the day before. The king promised to come aboard the next day to regulate it and be paid his duties. . . .

The second [of July]. . . . At two o'clock we fetched the king from shore, attended by all his *Caboceiros*[2] and officers, in three large canoes. Entering the ship, he was saluted with seven guns. The king had on an old-fashioned scarlet coat, laced with gold and silver, very rusty, and a fine hat on his head, but bare-footed. All his attendants showed great respect to him and, since our arrival, none of the natives have dared to come aboard or sell the least thing, till the king adjusted trade matters.

We had again a long talk with the king and Pepprell, his brother, concerning the rates of our goods and his customs. This Pepprell was a sharp black and a mighty talking black, perpetually making objections against something or other and teasing us for this or that *dassy*[3] or present, as well as for drinks, etc. Would that such a one as he were out of the way, to facilitate trade. . . .

Thus, with much patience, all our affairs were settled equitably, after the fashion of a people who are not very scrupulous when it comes to finding excuses or objections for not keeping to the word of any verbal contract. For they do not have the art of reading and writing, and we therefore are forced to stand to their agreement, which often is no longer than they think fit to hold it themselves. The king ordered the public crier to proclaim permission to trade with us, with the noise of his trumpets . . . , we paying sixteen brass rings to the fellow for his fee. The blacks objected against our wrought pewter and tankards, green beads, and other goods, which they would not accept. . . .

We gave the usual presents to the king. . . . To Captain Forty, the king's general, Captain Pepprell, Captain Boileau, alderman Bougsbyu, my lord Willyby, duke of Monmouth, drunken

---

[1]Bars of iron. See source 112.
[2]A Portuguese term. Here it means "chiefs and elders."

[3]A trade term meaning "gift."

Henry, and some others[4] two firelocks, eight hats, nine narrow Guinea stuffs. We adjusted with them the reduction of our merchandise into bars of iron, as the standard coin, namely: one bunch of beads, one bar; four strings of rings, ten rings each, one ditto; four copper bars, one ditto. . . . And so on *pro rata* for every sort of goods. . . .

The price of provisions and wood was also regulated. Sixty king's yams, one bar; one hundred and sixty slave's yams, one bar; for fifty thousand yams to be delivered to us. A butt[5] of water, two rings. For the length of wood, seven bars, which is dear, but they were to deliver it ready cut into our boat. For one goat, one bar. A cow, ten or eight bars, according to its size. A hog, two bars. A calf, eight bars. A jar of palm oil, one bar and a quarter.

We also paid the king's duty in goods; five hundred slaves, to be purchased at two copper rings a head.

---

[4]The king's chiefs and elders.

[5]A large cask.

Chinese and Japanese Reactions to the West

China and Japan were no exception to the rule that most societies in Asia and Africa were able to successfully resist European efforts during the sixteenth and seventeenth centuries to impose trade on Western terms and Christianity. Although ultimately rebuffed by the Chinese and Japanese, European merchants and missionaries nonetheless had good reason to believe during the sixteenth century that their labors in East Asia would be richly rewarded.

Portuguese traders reached south China in 1513, opened trade at Guangzhou (Canton) in 1514, and established a permanent trading base in Macao in 1557. In 1542 the first Portuguese merchants reached Japan and soon were reaping healthy profits by carrying goods between China and Japan. Later in the century the Dutch and English successfully entered the East Asian markets. Roman Catholic Europeans, especially the Portuguese, energetically supported missionary efforts in China and Japan, usually in cooperation with the newly founded Society of Jesus, more popularly known as the *Jesuits*. Francis Xavier and other Jesuits began preaching in Japan in 1549, and by the early 1600s they had won approximately 300,000 converts to Christianity. Catholic missionary activities in China began later, in 1579, and followed a somewhat different strategy: The Jesuits did less preaching to the common people and instead sought the support of Chinese intellectuals, government officials, and members of the imperial court. The Jesuits were moderately successful because they impressed Confucian scholars with their erudition, especially in mathematics and science, and the Chinese appreciated the missionaries' willingness to understand and respect China's culture.

For all their efforts, the economic benefits and religious gains the Westerners obtained were meager. Although the Chinese tolerated learned Jesuit missionaries, they viewed European merchants as boorish, overly aggressive, and purveyors of shoddy goods. Preferring to deal with Arabs and other foreigners, they limited trade with Europeans to Guangzhou and Macao and placed it under numerous restrictions. Missionary activity resulted in some converts, but feuding among Catholic religious orders, staunch opposition from many Chinese officials, and the unwillingness of most Chinese, even converts, to abandon such ancient rites as veneration of the ancestors caused the enterprise to wither and die.

Although European efforts to win souls and trade had a more promising start in Japan, by the mid seventeenth century the Japanese had suppressed Christianity and restricted European trade to only one Dutch ship a year. This turn of events resulted from attempts by Japanese leaders to bring stability to Japan after a century of civil war and rebellion. Convinced that European merchants and missionaries had contributed to Japan's disorder, the government outlawed Christianity and essentially closed Japan to the outside world.

The Jesuits in China
▼▼▼

114 ▼ *Matteo Ricci, JOURNALS*

The most celebrated of the Jesuit scholar-missionaries to work in China was the Italian Matteo Ricci (1552–1610). In 1582 he arrived at Macao and entered interior China the following year. A trained mathematician and scientist, Father Ricci dazzled the Chinese literarchy and court with clocks, a world map, and various pieces of scientific equipment, many of which he constructed himself. A gifted linguist, he composed more than twenty-five essays in Chinese on mathematics, literature, ethics, geography, astronomy, and, above all else, religion. He so impressed Confucian scholars that they accorded him the title *Doctor from the Great Western Ocean.* In 1601 Emperor Wanli summoned Ricci to his court at Beijing and provided him with a subsidy to carry on his study of mathematics and astronomy. When Ricci died the emperor donated a burial site outside the gates of the imperial city as a token of special honor.

During his twenty-seven years in China, Ricci kept a journal, with apparently no thought of publishing it. Shortly after Ricci's death, however, a Jesuit colleague edited and published the journal, into which he incorporated a number of other, more official sources. It became one of Europe's major sources of information about China until the late eighteenth century, when accounts by European travelers to the Middle Kingdom became more common.

When Father Ricci became the superior of the tiny Chinese mission in 1597, there were probably no more than 100 Chinese Catholics throughout the entire empire, excluding the Portuguese trading station at Macao. Thanks in large part to his and his colleagues' policy of trying to accommodate as many Chinese traditions as they could to Catholic Christianity and their genuine admiration for Confucian moral philosophy, the Jesuits were able to add to these numbers in a significant way. In 1603 Ricci instructed his Jesuits that traditional ceremonies honoring

Confucius and essential ancestral services were acceptable practices for Chinese Catholics. At Ricci's death in 1610 an estimated 2,500 converts lived in the vicinity of the Jesuits' five resident churches. By 1650 as many as 150,000 Chinese professed Catholic Christianity, out of a total population of about 150 million. Fifty years later the Christian population had risen to almost 300,000, but it was still around 1 percent of the overall population.

Many Catholic missionaries who followed Ricci, especially from other religious orders, such as the Franciscans, were not willing to accept a syncretic Chinese Catholicism that retained some vestiges of traditional Chinese worship. A heated controversy erupted regarding the so-called "rites question" and the Jesuits' missionary tactics. In the end, Catholic traditionalists won out, and the Jesuits' efforts to fuse some Chinese customs with Christianity lost out. In 1742 Pope Benedict XIV decreed that Chinese Catholics must abandon all vestiges of Confucianism. In response, the Qianlong Emperor (r. 1736–1795), a friend of the Jesuits and an admirer of Western technology and architecture, expelled the Catholic missionaries, and Chinese Catholicism was doomed. But even had the Jesuit vision prevailed, one wonders if Christianity could ever have become a major force in China. As Protestant missionaries to China later learned, too many cultural differences separated European Christianity from a culture that was already well over 3,000 years old.

In the following selection from Ricci's *Journals* we can glimpse some of the barriers and attitudes that defeated the Jesuits' efforts to transform China into a Christian civilization despite their willingness to make limited accommodations.

QUESTIONS FOR ANALYSIS

1. What most offended the Confucians who brought charges against the Jesuits and their religion?
2. The Jesuits' association with Father Ricci seems to have favored them in the course of events. Why? What was there about Ricci that gave his Jesuit colleagues an aura of legitimacy?
3. Why did Ricci view the outcome as a Christian victory?
4. How do you think the Jesuits' Confucian opponents viewed this confrontation and its resolution?
5. Imagine you are the Chief Justice and you are preparing a report to the imperial court concerning the incident, your decision, the reasoning behind it, and what you believe will be its consequences. Compose that report.
6. Compare the charges brought against the Jesuits with Han Yu's *Memorial on Buddhism* (source 73). Which are more significant, the differences or the similarities? What do you conclude from your answer?
7. Compare the failure of Christianity to permeate Chinese culture with the relative success of Buddhism 1,000 years earlier (source 72), despite opposition to it. Why did one succeed and the other fail?

During 1606 and the year following, the progress of Christianity in Nancian[1] was in no wise retarded. . . . The number of neophytes[2] increased by more than two hundred, all of whom manifested an extraordinary piety in their religious devotions. As a result, the reputation of the Christian religion became known throughout the length and breadth of this metropolitan city. . . .

Through the efforts of Father Emanuele Dias another and a larger house was purchased, in August of 1607, at a price of a thousand gold pieces. This change was necessary, because the house he had was too small for his needs and was situated in a flood area. Just as the community was about to change from one house to the other, a sudden uprising broke out against them. . . .

At the beginning of each month, the Magistrates hold a public assembly . . . in the temple of their great Philosopher.[3] When the rites of the new-moon were completed in the temple, and these are civil rather than religious rites,[4] one of those present took advantage of the occasion to speak on behalf of the others, and to address the highest Magistrate present. . . . "We wish to warn you," he said, "that there are certain foreign priests in this royal city, who are preaching a law, hitherto unheard of in this kingdom,[5] and who are holding large gatherings of people in their house." Having said this, he referred them to their local Magistrate, . . . and he in turn ordered the plaintiffs to present their case in writing, assuring them that he would support it with all his authority, in an effort to have the foreign priests expelled. The complaint was written out that same day and signed with twenty-seven signatures. . . . The content of the document was somewhat as follows.

Matthew Ricci, Giovanni Soerio, Emanuele Dias, and certain other foreigners from western kingdoms, men who are guilty of high treason against the throne, are scattered amongst us, in five different provinces. They are continually communicating with each other and are here and there practicing brigandage on the rivers, collecting money, and then distributing it to the people, in order to curry favor with the multitudes. They are frequently visited by the Magistrates, by the high nobility and by the Military Prefects, with whom they have entered into a secret pact, binding unto death.

These men teach that we should pay no respect to the images of our ancestors, a doctrine which is destined to extinguish the love of future generations for their forebears. Some of them break up the idols, leaving the temples empty and the gods to be pitied, without any patronage. In the beginning they lived in small houses, but by this time they have bought up large and magnificent residences. The doctrine they teach is something infernal. It attracts the ignorant into its fraudulent meshes, and great crowds of this class are continually assembled at their houses. Their doctrine gets beyond the city walls and spreads itself through the neighboring towns and villages and into the open country, and the people become so wrapt up in its falsity, that students are not following their course, laborers are neglecting their work, farmers are not cultivating their acres, and even the women have no interest in their housework. The whole city has become disturbed, and, whereas in the beginning there were only a hundred or so professing their faith, now there are more than twenty thousand. These priests distribute pictures of some Tartar or Saracen,[6] who they say is God, who came down from Heaven to redeem and to instruct all of humanity, and who alone, according to their doctrine, can give wealth and happiness; a doctrine by which the simple people are very easily deceived. These

---

[1]Nanchang, in the southern province of Kiangsi.
[2]New converts.
[3]Confucius.
[4]Ricci and his fellow Jesuits chose to regard all Confucian ceremonies, including those that honored the spirits of ancestors, as purely *civil rites,* rather than religious observances.
[5]Ricci (or his editor) consistently refers to China as a *kingdom,* even though it had an emperor, not a king.
[6]The reference is to Jesus Christ.

men are an abomination on the face of the Earth, and there is just ground for fear that once they have erected their own temples, they will start a rebellion. . . . Wherefore, moved by their interest in the maintenance of the public good, in the conservation of the realm, and in the preservation, whole and entire, of their ancient laws, the petitioners are presenting this complaint and demanding, in the name of the entire province, that a rescript of it be forwarded to the King, asking that these foreigners be sentenced to death, or banished from the realm, to some deserted island in the sea. . . .

Each of the Magistrates to whom the indictment was presented asserted that the spread of Christianity should be prohibited, and that the foreign priests should be expelled from the city, if the Mayor saw fit, after hearing the case, and notifying the foreigners. . . . But the Fathers,[7] themselves, were not too greatly disturbed, placing their confidence in Divine Providence, which had always been present to assist them on other such dangerous occasions.

▷ Father Emanuele is summoned before the Chief Justice.

Father Emanuele, in his own defense, . . . gave a brief outline of the Christian doctrine. Then he showed that according to the divine law, the first to be honored, after God, were a man's parents. But the judge had no mind to hear or to accept any of this and he made it known that he thought it was all false. After that repulse, with things going from bad to worse, it looked as if they were

on the verge of desperation, so much so, indeed, that they increased their prayers, their sacrifices, and their bodily penances, in petition for a favorable solution of their difficulty. Their adversaries appeared to be triumphantly victorious. They were already wrangling about the division of the furniture of the Mission residences, and to make results doubly certain, they stirred up the flames anew with added accusations and indictments. . . .

The Mayor, who was somewhat friendly with the Fathers, realizing that there was much in the accusation that was patently false, asked the Magistrate Director of the Schools,[8] if he knew whether or not this man Emanuele was a companion of Matthew Ricci, who was so highly respected at the royal court, and who was granted a subsidy from the royal treasury, because of the gifts he had presented to the King. Did he realize that the Fathers had lived in Nankin[9] for twelve years, and that no true complaint had ever been entered against them for having violated the laws. Then he asked him if he had really given full consideration as to what was to be proven in the present indictment. To this the Director of the Schools replied that he wished the Mayor to make a detailed investigation of the case and then to confer with him. The Chief Justice then ordered the same thing to be done. Fortunately, it was this same Justice who was in charge of city affairs when Father Ricci first arrived in Nancian. It was he who first gave the Fathers permission, with the authority of the Viceroy, to open a house there. . . .

After the Mayor had examined the charges of the plaintiffs and the reply of the defendants, he subjected the quasi-literati[10] to an examination in open court, and taking the Fathers under his

---

[7]The Jesuit fathers, or priests.

[8]The director of the local Confucian academy was one of the Jesuits' chief opponents.

[9]Nanjing, the southern auxiliary capital.

[10]Those who are almost learned or learned to a limited degree. This is Ricci's term for the chief tormenters of the Jesuits in Nanchang. They were Confucian scholars who had passed the first and most basic of the three Confucian civil-service examinations (offered respectively at the local, provincial, and capital levels) and thereby earned the title

Cultivated Talents. By passing the first examination level, they earned recognition simply as competent students. Hence, Ricci dismisses them as *quasi-literati.* Cultivated Talents were subject to periodic re-examination at that level and could lose their status and privileges. Only scholars who passed the provincial-level examination and became *Elevated Men* attained a permanent rank and were eligible for appointment to one of the lower civil posts. Apparently the Cultivated Talents felt threatened by the Jesuits.

patronage, he took it upon himself to refute the calumnies of their accusers. He said he was fully convinced that these strangers were honest men, and that he knew that there were only two of them in their local residence and not twenty, as had been asserted. To this they replied that the Chinese were becoming their disciples. To which the Justice in turn replied: "What of it? Why should we be afraid of our own people? Perhaps you are unaware of the fact that Matthew Ricci's company is cultivated by everyone in Pekin,[11] and that he is being subsidized by the royal treasury. How dare the Magistrates who are living outside of the royal city expel men who have permission to live at the royal court? These men here have lived peacefully in Nankin for twelve years. I command," he added, "that they buy no more large houses, and that the people are not to follow their law." . . .

A few days later, the court decision was pronounced and written out . . . and was then posted at the city gates as a public edict. The following is a summary of their declaration. Having examined the cause of Father Emanuele and his companions, it was found that these men had come here from the West because they had heard so much about the fame of the great Chinese Empire, and that they had already been living in the realm for some years, without any display of illwill. Father Emanuele should be permitted to practice his own religion, but it was not considered to be the right thing for the common people, who are attracted by novelties, to adore the God of Heaven. For them to go over to the religion of foreigners would indeed be most unbecoming. . . . It would therefore seem to be . . . [in] . . . the best interests of the Kingdom, to . . . [warn] . . . everyone in a public edict not to abandon the sacrifices of their ancient religion by accepting the cult of foreigners. Such a movement might, indeed, result in calling together certain gatherings, detrimental to the public welfare,

and harmful also to the foreigner, himself. Wherefore, the Governor of this district, by order of the high Magistrates, admonishes the said Father Emanuele to refrain from perverting the people, by inducing them to accept a foreign religion. The man who sold him the larger house is to restore his money and Emanuele is to buy a smaller place, sufficient for his needs, and to live there peaceably, as he has done, up to the present. Emanuele, himself, has agreed to these terms and the Military Prefects of the district have been ordered to make a search of the houses there and to confiscate the pictures of the God they speak of, wherever they find them. It is not permitted for any of the native people to go over to the religion of the foreigners, nor is it permitted to gather together for prayer meetings. Whoever does contrary to these prescriptions will be severely punished, and if the Military Prefects are remiss in enforcing them, they will be held to be guilty of the same crimes. To his part of the edict, the Director of the Schools added, that the common people were forbidden to accept the law of the foreigners, and that a sign should be posted above the door of the Father's residence, notifying the public that these men were forbidden to have frequent contact with the people.

The Fathers were not too disturbed by this pronouncement, because they were afraid that it was going to be much worse. In fact, everyone thought it was rather favorable, and that the injunction launched against the spread of the faith was a perfunctory order to make it appear that the literati were not wholly overlooked, since the Fathers were not banished from the city, as the literati had demanded. Moreover it was not considered a grave misdemeanor for the Chinese to change their religion, and it was not customary to inflict a serious punishment on those violating such an order. The neophytes, themselves, proved this when they continued, as formerly, to attend Mass.

---

[11]Beijing, the Ming capital.

The Seclusion of Japan

▼▼▼

115 ▼ Tokugawa Iemitsu, *CLOSED COUNTRY EDICT OF 1635 and EXCLUSION OF THE PORTUGUESE, 1639*

When the first Europeans reached Japan, they encountered a land plagued by civil war and rebellion. The authority of the *shoguns,* military commanders who had ruled Japan on behalf of the emperor since the twelfth century, was in eclipse, as the *daimyo* (great lords) fought for power. Turbulence ended toward the close of the sixteenth century, when three military heroes — Oda Nobunaga (1534–1582), Toyotomi Hideyoshi (1536–1598), and Tokugawa Ieyasu (1543–1616) — forced the daimyo to accept central authority. In 1603 the emperor recognized Tokugawa Ieyasu as shogun; the era of the Tokugawa Shogunate, which lasted to 1868, had begun.

Between 1624 and 1641 Iemitsu, grandson of Ieyasu and shogun from 1623 to 1651, issued edicts that closed Japan to virtually all foreigners. This was the culmination of policies begun under Toyotomi Hideyoshi, who had sought to limit contacts between Japanese and foreigners, especially Catholic missionaries. He and his successors viewed the missionaries' aggressive proselytizing as a potential source of social unrest and rebellion. The first document that follows, the most celebrated of Tokugawa Iemitsu's edicts, is directed to the two *bugyo,* or commissioners, of Nagasaki, a port city in southwest Japan and a center of Japanese Christianity; the second more specifically deals with the missionary activities of the Portuguese.

QUESTIONS FOR ANALYSIS

1. To what extent was the edict of 1635 directed against the activities of foreigners? To what extent was it directed against certain presumed antisocial activities by Japanese?
2. Much of the 1635 edict dealt with trade issues. What do the various trade provisions suggest about the shogun's attitude toward commerce?
3. What was the major purpose behind the 1635 edict?
4. What can you infer about the reasons for promulgating the 1639 edict?

CLOSED COUNTRY EDICT OF 1635

1. Japanese ships are strictly forbidden to leave for foreign countries.
2. No Japanese is permitted to go abroad. If there is anyone who attempts to do so secretly, he must be executed. The ship so involved must be impounded and its owner arrested, and the matter must be reported to the higher authority.
3. If any Japanese returns from overseas after residing there, he must be put to death.[1]

---

[1] Since 1597 well over 1,000 Japanese and European Christians had already been executed.

4. If there is any place where the teachings of padres[2] is practiced, the two of you must order a thorough investigation.

5. Any informer revealing the whereabouts of the followers of padres must be rewarded accordingly. If anyone reveals the whereabouts of a high ranking padre, he must be given one hundred pieces of silver. For those of lower ranks, depending on the deed, the reward must be set accordingly.

6. If a foreign ship has an objection [to the measures adopted] and it becomes necessary to report the matter to Edo,[3] you may ask the Omura domain[4] to provide ships to guard the foreign ship. . . .

7. If there are any Southern Barbarians[5] who propagate the teachings of padres, or otherwise commit crimes, they may be incarcerated in the prison. . . .

8. All incoming ships must be carefully searched for the followers of padres.

9. No single trading city shall be permitted to purchase all the merchandise brought by foreign ships.

10. Samurai are not permitted to purchase any goods originating from foreign ships directly from Chinese merchants in Nagasaki.

11. After a list of merchandise brought by foreign ships is sent to Edo, as before you may order that commercial dealings may take place without waiting for a reply from Edo.

12. After settling the price, all white yarns[6] brought by foreign ships shall be allocated to the five trading cities[7] and other quarters as stipulated.

13. After settling the price of white yarns, other merchandise [brought by foreign ships] may be traded freely between the [licensed] dealers. However, in view of the fact that Chinese ships are small and cannot bring large consignments, you may issue orders of sale at your discretion. Additionally, payment for goods purchased must be made within twenty days after the price is set.

14. The date of departure homeward of foreign ships shall not be later than the twentieth day of the ninth month. Any ships arriving in Japan later than usual shall depart within fifty days of their arrival. As to the departure of Chinese ships, you may use your discretion to order their departure after the departure of the Portuguese *galeota*.[8]

15. The goods brought by foreign ships which remained unsold may not be deposited or accepted for deposit.

16. The arrival in Nagasaki of representatives of the five trading cities shall not be later than the fifth day of the seventh month. Anyone arriving later than that date shall lose the quota assigned to his city.

17. Ships arriving in Hirado[9] must sell their raw silk at the price set in Nagasaki, and are not permitted to engage in business transactions until after the price is established in Nagasaki.

You are hereby required to act in accordance with the provisions set above. It is so ordered.

EXCLUSION OF THE PORTUGUESE, 1639

1. The matter relating to the proscription of Christianity is known [to the Portuguese]. However, heretofore they have secretly transported those who are going to propagate that religion.

2. If those who believe in that religion band together in an attempt to do evil things, they must be subjected to punishment.

3. While those who believe in the preaching of padres are in hiding, there are incidents in which that country [Portugal] has sent gifts to them for their sustenance.

---

[2]Fathers (Catholic priests).
[3]Modern Tokyo, the seat of Tokugawa government.
[4]The area around Nagasaki.
[5]Westerners.

[6]Raw silk.
[7]The cities of Kyoto, Edo, Osaka, Sakai, and Nagasaki.
[8]A *galleon*, an ocean-going Portuguese ship.
[9]A small island in the southwest, not far from Nagasaki.

In view of the above, hereafter entry by the Portuguese *galeota* is forbidden. If they insist on coming [to Japan], the ships must be destroyed and anyone aboard those ships must be beheaded. We have received the above order and are thus transmitting it to you accordingly.

The above concerns our disposition with regard to the *galeota*.

Memorandum
With regard to those who believe in Christianity, you are aware that there is a proscription, and thus knowing, you are not permitted to let padres and those who believe in their preaching to come aboard your ships. If there is any violation, all of you who are aboard will be considered culpable. If there is anyone who hides the fact that he is a Christian and boards your ship, you may report it to us. A substantial reward will be given to you for this information.

This memorandum is to be given to those who come on Chinese ships. [A similar note to the Dutch ships.]

The Great Mughals and the West

Between 1526 and his death in 1530, the Turkish lord of Afghanistan, Babur, subdued north central India with a small, well-equipped army that enjoyed the advantage of firearms received from the Ottoman Turks. This new Muslim lord of Hindustan, a direct descendant of the Mongol Chinggis Khan and the Turk Tamerlane, initiated India's *Mughal* (the Persian word for *Mongol*) Age and laid the base for the reign of his grandson Jalal ad-Din Akbar (r. 1556–1605), known to history as simply *Akbar* (the Great).

Akbar's empire encompassed only the northern half of the Indian subcontinent. His great-grandson Aurangzeb (r. 1658–1707), the last effective Mughal emperor, reigned over twice that amount of land, holding all the subcontinent except its southern tip and the island of Ceylon (modern Sri Lanka). Nevertheless, Akbar fully deserved to be known as the *Great Mughal,* a title awed European visitors to his court at Fatehpur-Sikri (the City of Victory) bestowed on him. From this court Akbar forged a centralized empire, which during his reign of more than a half century enjoyed prosperity and a fair level of peace between Hindus and Muslims. Although the Portuguese had established three major bases along the west Indian coast by 1535, Akbar was secure enough in his power to keep them and other Europeans at arm's length throughout the last half of the sixteenth century.

The European presence, however, increased in the seventeenth century. In 1603 the English East India Company — chartered on December 31, 1600, the last day of the sixteenth century — sent its first envoy to Akbar's court. After defeating a Portuguese squadron in 1639, the English established their first trading station at Madras on India's east coast and in 1661 acquired Bombay on the west coast. As Portuguese influence in India declined, other European maritime powers secured trading privileges in the Mughal Empire. The Dutch acquired several important sites on both coasts between 1640 and 1663; in 1664 France founded an East India Company, and several French trading bases followed. In time, the Dutch shifted their focus away from India to the islands of Southeast Asia, leaving the French and English to fight for control of the Indian markets.

Despite all these late-seventeenth-century incursions along India's coasts, Emperor Aurangzeb was able to hold the West and its merchants at bay for the most part, even dealing the English a military setback in the 1680s. In 1700 the directors of the English East India Company rejected as unrealistic the notion of acquiring additional territory or establishing colonies in India. The decline of Mughal authority in the eighteenth century, however, changed the situation substantially, and toward midcentury the French and British were engaged in armed struggle for control of Indian territory.

Dealing with the Faringis
▼▼▼

116 ▼ Abul Fazl, AKBARNAMA

Assisting Akbar in formulating and carrying out his largely successful policies of state was Abul Fazl (1551–1602), the emperor's chief advisor and confidant from 1579 until Abul Fazl's assassination at the instigation of Prince Salim, the future Emperor Jahangir (r. 1605–1627). Abul Fazl's death cut short his composition of the *Akbarnama,* a gigantic, laudatory history of Akbar's distinguished ancestors and the emperor's own reign. Before he was murdered, Abul Fazl carried his history to Akbar's forty-sixth year, creating a work universally regarded as one of the masterpieces of Mughal literature.

These thousands of pages of elegant Persian prose and poetry provide surprisingly few references to Akbar's or even India's relations with Europeans, or *Faringis* (Franks), as they were called at the Mughal court. This silence speaks eloquently of the level of early Mughal concern with these foreigners. The following excerpts constitute the work's major references to Europeans in India.

QUESTIONS FOR ANALYSIS

1. What aspects of European culture most fascinated Akbar?
2. What did he and Abul Fazl believe they could gain from the Faringis?
3. What did they believe they could offer the Europeans?
4. How did Akbar and Abul Fazl regard the Portuguese coastal bases?
5. What does the discussion with Padre Radif (Father Rodolfo) suggest about Akbar and Abul Fazl's attitudes toward the teachings of Europe's Christian missionaries?

6. Jesuit missionaries to Akbar's court often believed they were on the verge of converting him to Roman Catholicism. Why do you suppose they believed this? What evidence strongly indicates there was never any chance Akbar would become a Christian?

THE SIEGE OF SURAT

One of the occurrences of the siege[1] was that a large number of Christians came from the port of Goa[2] and its neighborhood to the foot of the sublime throne, and were rewarded by the bliss of an interview. Apparently they had come at the request of the besieged in order that the latter might make the fort over to them, and so convey themselves to the shore of safety. But when that crew saw the majesty of the imperial power, and had become cognizant of the largeness of the army, and of the extent of the siege-train they represented themselves as ambassadors and performed the *kornish*.[3] They produced many of the rarities of their country, and the appreciative Khedive[4] received each one of them with special favor and made inquiries about the wonders of Portugal and the manners and customs of Europe. It seemed as if he did this from a desire of knowledge, for his sacred heart is a storehouse of spiritual and physical sciences. But his . . . soul wished that these inquiries might be the means of civilizing this savage race.[5]

THE COMMODITIES OF GOA

One of the occurrences was the dispatch of Haji Habibu-llah Kashi to Goa. At the time when the country of Gujarat became included among the imperial dominions, and when many of the ports of the country came into possession, and the gov-

ernors of the European ports became submissive,[6] many of the curiosities and rarities of the skilled craftsmen of that country became known to His Majesty. Accordingly the Haji,[7] who for his skill, right thinking and powers of observation was one of the good servants of the court, was appointed to take with him a large sum of money, and the choice articles of India to Goa, and to bring for His Majesty's delectation the wonderful things of that country. There were sent with him clever craftsmen, who to ability and skill added industry, in order that just as the wonderful productions of that country [Goa and Europe] were being brought away, so also might rare crafts be imported [into Akbar's dominions].

THE MUSICIANS OF GOA

One of the occurrences was the arrival [at court] of Haji Habibu-llah. It has already been mentioned that he had been sent to the port of Goa with a large sum of money and skillful craftsmen in order that he might bring to his country the excellent arts and rarities of that place. On the 9th he came to do homage, attended by a large number of persons dressed up as Christians and playing European drums and clarions. He produced before His Majesty the choice articles of that territory. Craftsmen who had gone to acquire skill displayed the arts which they had learned and received praises in the critical place of testing. The musicians of that territory

---

[1]The siege of the west-coast port of Surat in 1573 during Akbar's campaign in Gujarat (note 6). This successful expedition gave Akbar access to the sea. Through his conquests Akbar more than tripled the empire he had inherited.
[2]The chief Portuguese stronghold in India since 1510.
[3]The act of obeisance.
[4]Akbar.

[5]The Portuguese.
[6]In 1573 Akbar conquered the northwest coastal region of Gujarat, where the Portuguese held the ports of Diu and Bassein. In theory, but not fact, these Portuguese bases were now under Akbar's control.
[7]Haji Habibu-llah. He bore the title *Haji* because he had completed the hajj, or pilgrimage, to Mecca.

breathed fascination with the instruments of their country, especially with the organ. Ear and eye were delighted and so was the mind.

THURSDAY NIGHT AT THE HOUSE OF WORSHIP

One night, the assembly in the Ibadatkhana[8] was increasing the light of truth. Padre Radif,[9] one of the Nazarene[10] sages, who was singular for his understanding and ability, was making points in that feast of intelligence. Some of the untruthful bigots[11] came forward in a blundering way to answer him. Owing to the calmness of the august assembly, and the increasing light of justice, it became clear that each of these was weaving a circle of old acquisitions, and was not following the highway of proof, and that the explanation of the riddle of truth was not present to their thoughts. The veil was nearly being stripped, once for all, from their procedure. They were ashamed, and abandoned such discourse, and applied themselves to perverting the words of the Gospels. But they could not silence their antagonist by such arguments. The Padre quietly and with an air of conviction said, "Alas, that such things should be thought to be true! In fact, if this faction have such an opinion of our Book, and regard the *Furqan* [the Quran] as the pure word of God, it is proper that a heaped fire be lighted. We shall take the Gospel in our hands, and the Ulama[12] of that faith shall take their book, and then let us enter that testing-place of truth. The escape of any one will be a sign of his truthfulness." The liverless and black-hearted fellows wavered, and in reply to the challenge had recourse to bigotry and wrangling. This cowardice and ef-

frontery displeased Akbar's equitable soul, and the banquet of enlightenment was made resplendent by acute observations. Continually, in those day-like nights, glorious subtleties and profound words dropped from his pearl-filled mouth.

Among them was this: "Most persons, from intimacy with those who adorn their outside but are inwardly bad, think that outward semblance, and the letter of Islam, profit without internal conviction. Hence we by fear and force compelled many believers in the Brahman [i.e., Hindu] religion to adopt the faith of our ancestors. Now that the light of truth has taken possession of our soul, it has become clear that in this distressful place of contrarieties [the world], where darkness of comprehension and conceit are heaped up, fold upon fold, a single step cannot be taken without the torch of proof, and that creed is profitable which is adopted with the approval of wisdom. To repeat the creed, to remove a piece of skin [i.e., to become circumcised] and to place the end of one's bones on the ground [i.e., the head in adoration] from dread of the Sultan,[13] is not seeking after God."

EUROPEAN-HELD PORTS

One of the occurrences was the appointing of an army to capture the European ports.[14] Inasmuch as conquest is the great rule of princes, and by the observance of this glory-increasing practice, the distraction of plurality[15] places its foot in the peacefulness of unity, and the harassed world composes her countenance, the officers of the provinces of Gujarat and Malwa were appointed to this service under the leadership of Qutbu-d-din Khan on 18 Bahman, Divine month (Febru-

---

[8]*The House of Worship,* where Akbar held weekly Thursday-night discussions on theological issues with Muslim, Hindu, Parsi (Zoroastrian), and Christian religious teachers.
[9]Father Rodolfo Acquaviva, a Jesuit missionary.
[10]Christian (a follower of Jesus of Nazareth).
[11]Here he refers to the *ulama,* Muslim religious teachers. Abul Fazl, who pursued a vigorous policy of religious and

cultural toleration, considered the ulama to be narrow-minded hypocrites.
[12]See note 11.
[13]Akbar.
[14]The ports of Diu and Bassein (note 6). This expedition was unsuccessful, and Abul Fazl tells us nothing more about it.
[15]The distraction of multiple rulers.

ary 1580). The rulers of the Deccan were also informed that the troops had been sent in that direction in order to remove the Faringis who were a stumbling-block in the way of the pilgrims to the Hijaz.[16]

---

[16]Pilgrims to Mecca (Mecca is located in the Hijaz, Arabia's west coast). Many Muslim pilgrims complained that, when embarking at Portuguese ports, they were forced to purchase letters of passage imprinted with images of Jesus and Mary. Orthodox Muslims consider such images blasphemous, and some Muslim ulama (note 11) went so far as to argue that it was better to forego the pilgrimage than to submit to such sacrilege.

Seventeenth-Century Commerce in India

▼▼▼

117 ▾ *Jean-Baptiste Tavernier, TRAVELS IN INDIA*

The increasing volume of French trade with seventeenth-century Mughal India attracted Jean-Baptiste Tavernier (1605–after 1689), a Parisian gem merchant, who arrived in India in 1640 on the first of five trips to the empire of the Great Mughal. Following his last voyage to India, which ended in 1668, Tavernier was able to live in wealthy semiretirement thanks to his profitable Eastern ventures. In 1670 he purchased the title of *baron of Aubonne* and settled down to write his memoirs, probably from notes he had made during his career in the East.

His *Travels in India* covers a pivotal period in Mughal-European relations. French and English merchants were becoming increasingly important in India, even as cracks were beginning to appear in the Mughal Empire under Shah Jahan (r. 1627–1658) and Aurangzeb (r. 1658–1707), whose respective building programs (Shah Jahan constructed the Taj Mahal) and military campaigns placed severe strains on the economy and general well-being of Indian society. In the following selection, Tavernier details the manner in which the Mughal government attempted to control and profit from the Western merchants and the tactics some Europeans employed to circumvent these controls and raise their profit margins.

QUESTIONS FOR ANALYSIS

1. Why do you think the English and Dutch East India companies paid a lower tariff on their imported goods and gold? What added to their costs of doing business in India, and why do you think they paid these extra expenses?
2. Did the European merchants take advantage of the Indian officials with whom they dealt? Did the Indian officials seem to resent or not want this business with the Europeans? What do your answers suggest?
3. Why do you think the officers of the Dutch and English East India companies were treated as described? Why did they refuse to engage in smuggling? What do your answers suggest about relations between the Mughal government and these trading companies?

4. What does the story of the roast pig suggest?

5. Do you perceive any significant differences in Indian-European relations between the era of Akbar and the period described by Tavernier? If so, what are they? What do these changes suggest to you?

As soon as merchandise is landed at Surat[1] it has to be taken to the custom-house, which adjoins the fort. The officers are very strict and search persons with great care. Private individuals pay as much as four and five percent duty on all their goods; but as for the English and Dutch Companies, they pay less. But, on the other hand, I believe that, taking into account what it costs them in . . . presents, which they are obliged to make every year at court, the goods cost them nearly the same as they do private persons.

Gold and silver are charged two percent,[2] and as soon as they have been counted at the custom-house the Mintmaster removes them, and coins them into money of the country, which he hands over to the owner, in proportion to the amount and standard of the bullion. You settle with him, according to the nature of the amount, a day when he is to deliver the new coins, and for as many days as he delays to do so beyond the term agreed upon, he pays interest in proportion to the sum which he has received. The Indians are cunning and exacting in reference to coin and payments; for when money has been coined for three or four years it has to lose one-half percent,[3] and it continues in the same proportion according to age, not being able, as they say, to pass through many hands without some diminution. . . .

As regards gold, the merchants who import it use so much cunning in order to conceal it, that but little of it comes to the knowledge of the customs' officers. The former do all they can to evade paying the customs, especially as they do not run so much risk as in the custom-houses of Europe. For in those of India, when anyone is detected in fraud, he is let off by paying double, ten percent instead of five, the Emperor comparing the venture of the merchant to a game of hazard, where one plays double or quits.[4] However, for some time back this has been somewhat changed, and it is today difficult to compound with the customs' officers upon that condition. The Emperor has conceded to the English Captains that they shall not be searched when they leave their vessels to go on shore; but one day an English Captain, when going to Tatta,[5] one of the largest towns of India, a little above Sindi,[6] which is at the mouth of the river Indus, as he was about to pass, was arrested by the customs' guards, from whom he could not defend himself, and they searched him in spite of anything he could say. They found gold upon him; he had in fact already conveyed some in sundry journeys which he had made between his vessel and the town; he was, however, let off on payment of the ordinary duty. The Englishman, vexed by this affront, resolved to have his revenge for it, and he took it in a funny manner. He ordered a suckling-pig to be roasted, and to be placed with the grease in a china plate, covered with a napkin, and gave it to a slave to carry with him to the town, anticipating exactly what would happen. As he passed in front of the custom-house, where the Governor of the town, the Shah-bandar,[7] and the Master of

---

[1]A city on the west coast that served as India's main port of entry for Dutch, English, and French merchants and their goods at this time.

[2]For the Dutch and English East India companies.

[3]The Indians discounted these gold coins by 0.5 percent because of the metal that had been rubbed off.

[4]Tavernier writes elsewhere that another reason the Mughals had such a lenient policy in regard to smuggling was be-

cause quranic law forbids charging interest and tariffs, and they were troubled by the practice.

[5]A city in modern Pakistan.

[6]Better known as *Sind,* this harbor at the mouth of the Indus River gave its name to the whole northwest corner of India (today Pakistan).

[7]The Mughal commissioner in charge of merchants.

the Mint were seated in a divan, they did not fail to stop him, but the slave still advancing with his covered plate, they told his master that he must needs go to the custom-house, and that they must see what he carried. The more the Englishman protested that the slave carried nothing liable to duty, the less was he believed; and after a long discussion he himself took the plate from the hands of the slave, and proceeded to carry it to the custom-house. The Governor and the Shah-bandar thereupon asked him, in a sharp tone, why he refused to obey orders, and the Englishman, on his part, replied in a rage that what he carried was not liable to duty, and rudely threw the plate in front of them, so that the suckling-pig and the grease soiled the whole place, and splashed up on their garments. As the pig is an abomination to the Muslims, and by their Law they regard as defiled whatever is touched by it, they were compelled to change their garments, to remove the carpet from the divan, and to have the structure rebuilt, without daring to say anything to the Englishman, because the Shah-bandar and the Master of the Mint have to be careful with the Company,[8] from which the country derives so much profit. As for the Chiefs of the Companies, both English and Dutch, and their deputies, they are treated with so much respect that they are never searched when they come from their vessels; but they, on their part, do not attempt to convey gold in secret as the private merchants do, considering it beneath their dignity to do so. . . .

The English, seeing that the custom of searching them had been adopted, had recourse to little stratagems in order to pass the gold, and the fashion of wearing wigs having reached them from Europe, they bethought themselves of concealing . . . [gold coins] . . . in the nets of their wigs every time they left their vessels to go on shore.

---

[8]The English East India Company.

Sources

Prologue

(1) From Cecil Jane, ed. and trans., *Selected Documents Illustrating the Four Voyages of Columbus,* 2 Vols. (London: Hakluyt Society, 1930–1933), vol. 1, pp. 2–18. Reprinted with permission of David Higham Associates. (2) Anonymous, Woodcut of 1511.

Part One ▼ The Ancient World

Chapter 1

Source 1: From *The Epic of Gilgamesh,* translated by N. K. Sandars, Penguin Classics 1960, Third Edition 1972. Copyright © N. K. Sandars, 1960, 1964, 1972. Reproduced by permission of Penguin Books Ltd. **Source 2:** Chilperic Edwards, *The Hammurabi Code* (1904), pp. 23–80, passim. Reprinted without copyright by Kennikut Press, 1971. **Source 3:** Miriam Lichtheim, *Ancient Egyptian Literature: A Book of Readings,* 3 vols. (University of California Press, 1973–1980), vol. 2 (1976), pp. 124–126. Reprinted by permission of the University of California Press. **Source 4:** From Pritchard, James B., *Ancient Near Eastern Texts Relating to the Old Testament,* 3rd edition, pp. 328, 467–468. Copyright © 1969 by Princeton University Press. Reprinted by permission of Princeton University Press. **Source 5:** James Legge, trans., *The Sacred Books of China: The Texts of Confucianism,* in F. Max Mueller, ed., *The Sacred Books of the East,* 50 vols. (Oxford: Clarendon Press, 1879–1910), vol. 3, pp. 92–95. **Source 6:** From *The Book of Songs,* edited and translated by Arthur Waley. Copyright © 1937 by Arthur Waley, pp. 23–26, 65, 78, 283–285, 318. Reprinted with permission of Grove/Atlantic. **Source 7:** Musée de l'Homme, Paris, France. Courtesy Erich Lessing/Art Resource, NY. **Source 8:** (1–6) Walter A. Fairservis, Jr., *The Roots of Ancient India: The Archaeology of Early Indian Civilization,* illustrated with drawings by Jan Fairservis (New York: Macmillan, 1971), pp. 276, 276, 279, 278, 274, 276. Copyright © 1971 by Walter A. Fairservis. Reprinted with the permission of Macmillan Publishing Company. (7–8) Courtesy of the Trustees of the British Museum. (9) Courtesy of the Ashmolean Museum, Oxford University, Oxford. **Source 9:** (1) Courtesy of Hamlyn Publishing, London. (2) Sudan Archaeological Museum, Khartoum. Courtesy of Werner Forman/Art Resource, NY.

Chapter 2

Source 10: From *The Rig Veda* translated by Wendy Doniger O'Flaherty, Penguin Classics 1981, pp. 160–162. Copyright © Wendy Doniger O'Flaherty, 1981. Reproduced by permission of Penguin Books. **Source 11:** A. J. Andrea, trans. *The Odyssey of Homer.* **Sources 12 and 13:** *Revised Standard Version of the Bible.* Copyright © 1946, 1952, 1971 by the Division of Christian Education of the National Council of Churches of Christ in the USA. Used by permission. All rights reserved.

Chapter 3

Source 14: F. Max Mueller, trans., *The Upanishads,* in Mueller, ed., *The Sacred Books of the East,* 50 vols. (Oxford: Clarendon Press, 1879–1910), vol. 1, pp. 92, 104–105; vol. 15, pp. 168–169, 173, 175–177, passim. **Source 15:** Tashinath Trmibak Telang, trans., *The Bhagavad Gita,* in F. Max Mueller, ed., *The Sacred Books of the East,* 50 vols. (Oxford: Clarendon Press, 1879–1910), vol. 8, pp. 43–46, 48–49, 51–52, 126–128, passim. **Source 16:** (1) T. W. Rhys Davids and Hermann Oldenberg, trans., *Vinaya Texts,* in F. Max Mueller, ed., *The Sacred Books of the East,* 50 vols. (Oxford: Clarendon Press, 1879–1910), vol. 13, pp. 94–97, 100–102, passim. (2) Henry C. Warrant, ed. and trans., *Buddhism in Translations* (Cambridge: Harvard University Press, 1896), pp. 117–122, passim (modernized). **Source 17:** The Buddha, "Questions That Tend Not to Edification," in Henry C. Warrant, ed. and trans., *Buddhism in Translations* (Cambridge: Harvard University Press, 1896), pp. 117–122, passim (modernized). **Source 18:** James Hope Moulton, *Yasnas* 43, 44, 45, in *Early Zoroastrianism* (London: Williams and Norgate, 1913), pp. 364–370, passim. **Source 19:** *Revised Standard Version of the Bible.* Copyright © 1946, 1952, 1971 by the Division of Christian Education of the National Council of Churches of Christ in the USA. Used by permission. All rights reserved.

Chapter 4

Source 20: F. Max Mueller, ed., *The Sacred Books of the East,* 50 vols. (Oxford: Clarendon Press, 1879–1910), vol. 39, passim. **Source 21:** From *The Analects of Confucius* by Confucius, edited by Chichung Huang, pp. 47–49, 52–53, 56, 58, 67–70, 84–85, 87, 89–90, 106. Copyright © 1997 by Chichung Huang. Used by permission of Oxford University. **Source 22:** (1) W. I. Liano, trans., *The Complete Works of Han Fei Tzu* (London: Arthur Probsthain, 1939), vol. 1, pp. 40, 45–47. Copyright © 1939. Used by permission of Arthur Probsthain. (2) Yang Hsien-yi and Gladys Yang, *Records of the Historian* (Hong Kong: Commercial Press, 1974), pp. 170–172, 177–178. Copyright © 1974. Used by permission of Commercial Press (Hong Kong), Ltd. **Source 23:** Ilza Veith, trans., *Huang Nei Ching Su Wen: The Yellow Emperor's Classic of Internal Medicine,* pp. 102–105. Copyright © 1996 by The Regents of the University of California. **Source 24:** A. J. Andrea, trans. **Source 25:** B. Jowett, trans., *Thucydides Translated into English* (Oxford: Clarendon Press, 1881), vol. 1, pp. 115–129, passim. **Source 26:** "Bacchic Maenads," an excerpt from *The Bacchae* by Euripides, W. Arrowsmith, trans. from *The Complete Greek Tragedies,* Grene & Lattimore, eds., 1959, pp. 184–187. Reprinted with permission of The University of Chicago. **Source 27:** Plato, *Apologia,* in F. J.

Church, trans., *The Trial and Death of Socrates* (London: MacMillan, 1880). With emendations by A. J. Andrea. **Source 28:** (1) Staatliche Antikensammlungen und Glyptothek Munchen. Photograph by Kuppermann. (2) Delphi Museum/Archaeological Receipts Fund, Athens. (3) The Metropolitan Museum of Art, Fletcher Fund, 1927 (27.45).

Chapter 5

Source 29: (1) German Archaeological Institute, Rome (Neg. #33.23). (2) Alinari/Art Resource, NY. (3) The Metropolitan Museum of Art, Rogers Fund, 1909 (09.39). (4) Alinari/Art Resource, NY. **Source 30:** Publius Vergilius Maro, *Aeneid,* Book 6. Selections translated by A. J. Andrea. Copyright © 2000. **Source 31:** Translated from the Latin by A. J. Andrea. **Source 32:** From Esson M. Gale, trans., *Discourses on Salt and Iron: A Debate on State Control of Commerce and Industry in Ancient China,* 1967, pp. 1–7, 3–16; modified by A. J. Andrea. Original publishers E. J. Brill, Ltd. of Leiden, 1931. Reprinted with permission of Brill Academic Publishers/The Netherlands. **Source 33:** Nancy Lee Swann, trans., *Pan Chao: Foremost Woman Scholar of China* (New York: Century Co., 1932), pp. 111–114. Reprinted with the permission of Gest Oriental Library, Princeton. **Source 34:** Excerpts from *The Edicts of Asoka,* trans. and edited by N. A. Nikam and Richard McKeon, 1958. Reprinted with permission of The University of Chicago. **Source 35:** G. Buehler, trans., *The Laws of Manu,* in F. Max Mueller, ed., *The Sacred Books of the East,* 50 vols. (Oxford: Clarendon Press, 1879–1910), vol. 25, pp. 24, 69, 84–85, 195–197, 260–326, 329–330, 343–344, 370–371, 402–404, 413–416, 420, 423, passim. **Source 36:** Translated from the Latin by A. J. Andrea. **Source 37:** From *Records of the Grand Historian of China,* 2 vols., translated by Burton Watson. Copyright © 1961 by Columbia University Press. Reprinted with the permission of the publisher. **Source 38:** (1) Museum of Fine Arts, Boston. Classical Department Exchange Fund, 1979.556. Photograph © 2003 Museum of Fine Arts, Boston. (2) Courtesy of Iraq Museum. (3) Courtesy of the University of Pennsylvania Museum, Philadelphia (neg. #S5-23340). (4) The Metropolitan Museum of Art, John Stewart Kennedy Fund, 1926 (26.123). (5) Courtesy of the National Historical Museum, Ho Chi Minh City (formerly Saigon), Vietnam.

Part Two ▾ Faith, Devotion, and Salvation: Great World Religions to 1500

Chapter 6

Source 39: From Lopez, Donald S., *Religions in China in Practice,* pp. 86–89, 90–91, and liberal borrowing from Lopez's notes. Copyright © 1996 by Princeton University Press. Reprinted by permission of Princeton University Press. **Source 40:** (1) Freer Gallery of Art, Smithsonian Institution, Washington, D.C.: Purchase, F1979.51. (2) Courtesy of the National Museum of Phnom Penh, Cambodia. (3) Bildarchiv Preussischer Kulturbesitz/Art Resource, NY. **Source 41:** From *Sources of Indian Tradition* by William Theodore de Bary et al., pp. 332–335. Copyright © 1958, Columbia University Press. Reprinted with the permission of the publisher. **Source 42:** National Museum, Madura, Tamil Nadu, India. Courtesy Giraudon/Art Resource, NY. **Source 43:** Reprinted by permission of the publishers of the Trustees of the Loeb Classical Library from *Josephus: Life Against Apion–Volume I,* Loeb Classical Library Volume L 186, translated by H. St. J. Thackeray, pp. 353, 355, 357, 359, 361, 365, 405, and 407, Cambridge, Mass.: Harvard University Press, 1926. The Loeb Classical Library® is a registered trademark of the President and Fellows of Harvard. **Source 44:** From *Crisis and Leadership: Epistles of Maimonides,* pp. 95, 96, 97, 98, 99, 102, 103, 106, 117, 121, 125, 126, 130, 131. Published 1985 by the Jewish Publication Society. Used by permission.

Chapter 7

Sources 45 and 46: *Revised Standard Version of the Bible.* Copyright © 1946, 1952, 1971 by the Division of Christian Education of the National Council of Churches of Christ in the USA. Used by permission. All rights reserved. **Source 47:** Translated from the Latin by A. J. Andrea. **Source 48:** Translated from the Latin by A. J. Andrea. **Source 49:** Arthur C. McGiffert, trans., in *A Select Library of Nicene and Post-Nicene Fathers,* 14 vols., 2nd series (Christian Literature, 1890), vol. 1, pp. 349–350, 369–370, 386–387 (modified). **Source 50:** Bridgeman-Giraudon/Art Resource, NY. **Source 51:** From *The Church History of Rufinus of Quileia,* edited by Philip R. Amidon, translated by Philip R. Amidon, Books 10 and 11, pp. 20–23. Copyright © 1997 by Philip Amidon. Used by permission of Oxford University Press. **Source 52:** Bishop Adam, "The Christian Monument," in P. Y. Saeki, *The Nestorian Documents and Relics in China* (Tokyo: Maruzen, 1951), pp. 56–61 (modified). **Source 53:** From *The Secret Teachings of Jesus* by Marvin W. Meyer, pp. 19–20, 23–24, 26–29, 32–33, 38, passim. Copyright © 1984 by Marvin W. Meyer. Used by permission of Random House, Inc. **Source 54:** Excerpt from *Gnosis on the Silk Road: Gnostic Parables, Hymns and Prayers From Central Asia* by Hans-Joachim Klimkeit. Copyright © 1993 by Hans-J. Klimkeit. Reprinted by permission of HarperCollins Publishers, Inc.

Chapter 8

Source 55: From *The Koran Interpreted,* trans. by Arthur J. Arberry, 2 Vols., 1955, George Allen and Unwin. Reprinted by permission of Harpercollins Publishers, Ltd. **Source 56:** Imam Nawawi, *Gardens of the Righteous,* trans. Muhammad Zafrulla Khan (London: Curzon Press, 1975), pp. 60–63, 65–66, 68–69, 220–224, 226–228, passim. **Source 57:** A. Guillaume, trans., *The Life of Muhammad: A Translation of Ishaq's Sirat Rasul Allah* (Oxford University Press, 1955), 181–187, passim. Reprinted by permission of Oxford University Press, Pakistan. **Source 58:** From the Al-Muwatta of

Imam Malik ibn Abnas. Kegan Paul London and New York, 1989, pp. 3, 4, 6, 8, 19, 64, 93, 94, 107, 115, 120. Reprinted with permission. **Source 59:** Hasan ibn Yusuf, "Creed Concerning the Imams," in A. A. A. Fyzec, ed. and trans., *A Sh'ite Creed* (New Delhi: Oxford, 1942). Copyright © 1942. Used by permission of Oxford University Press, New Delhi. **Source 60:** Bernard Lewis, ed. and trans., *Islam from the Prophet Muhammad to the Capture of Constantinople, Volume I, Politics and War,* Translation copyright © 1987 by Bernard Lewis. Used by permission of Oxford University Press, Inc. **Source 61:** The Shepherd's Care, "From Self to Self," and "Selections from 'Menaqibu el Arfin,'" from *Rumi: In The Arms of the Beloved* by Rumi, translated by Jonathan Star, pp. 58–59, 70–71, 193–194. Copyright © 1997 by Jonathan Star. Used by permission of Jeremy P. Tarcher, an imprint of Penguin Group (USA) Inc. **Source 62:** Al-Baladhuri, *Kitab Futah al-Buldan (The Origins of the Islamic State),* P. K. Hitti, trans. (New York, 1916), pp. 316–317. T. W. Arnold, trans., *The Preaching of Islam,* 2nd ed. (London, 1913), pp. 57–59 (modified). **Source 63:** Benjamin Ben Jonah, *The Itinerary of Benjamin of Tudela,* trans. Marcus N. Adler (London: H. Frowde, 1907), pp. 35–42, passim. **Source 64:** H. M. Elliott and John Dowson, eds. and trans., *The History of India as Told by Its Own Historians,* 8 vols. (London: Truebner, 1867–1877), vol. 3, pp. 574–588, passim.

Part Three ▾ Continuity, Change, and Interchange: 500–1500

Chapter 9

Source 65: "Chronicles of Japan," in W. G. Aston, trans., *Nihongi: Chronicles of Japan from the Earliest Times to A.D. 697,* 2 vols. (London: Kegan, Paul, Trench, Truebner, 1896), vol. 2, pp. 128–133, passim. **Source 66:** From *The Pillow Book of Sei Sh'onagon,* trans. & ed. by Ivan I. Morris, pp. 21–23, 39–40, 45–50, 117, passim. Copyright © 1991, Columbia University Press. Reprinted with the permission of the publisher. **Source 67:** From *The Taiheiki: A Chronicle of Medieval Japan,* trans. by Helen Craig McCullough. Copyright © 1959, Columbia University Press. Reprinted with the permission of the publisher. **Source 68:** From *The Selected Poems of Du Fu,* trans. Burton Watson, pp. 2, 5–6, 8–9, 26–27, 52. Copyright © 2002, Columbia University Press. Reprinted with the permission of the publisher. **Source 69:** From Colin Mackerras, ed and trans., *The Uighur Empire According to the T'ang Dynasty Histories: A Study in Sino-Uighur Relations, 744–840,* 1972, pp. 62–68. Reprinted with permission of University of South Carolina Press. **Source 70:** Reprinted with the permission of The Free Press, a Division of Simon & Schuster Adult Publishing Group, from *Chinese Civilization: A Sourcebook* by Patricia Buckley Ebrey. Copyright © 1981 by The Free Press. All rights reserved. **Source 71:** "The Attractions of the Capital," trans. Clara Yu, in *Chinese Civilization and Society: A Sourcebook,* by Patricia Buckley Ebrey. (New York: Free Press, 1981), pp. 100–102, 104–105, passim. **Source 72:** From *Lives of the Nuns: Biographies of Chinese Nuns from the Fourth to Sixth Centuries,* pp. 20–21. A translation of *Pi-ch'iu-ni chuan,* compiled by Shih Pao-ch'ang. Translated by Kathryn Ann Tai, 1994. Romanization from Wade-Giles to Pinyin by A. J. Andrea. **Source 73:** From Edwin O. Reischauer, *Ennin's Travels in T'ang China,* pp. 221–224. Copyright 1995 by John Wiley & Sons, Inc. This material is used by permission of John Wiley & Sons, Inc. **Source 74:** From *A Collection of Tales From Uji: A Study of Translation of Uji Shui Monogatari,* D. E. Mills, trans., 1970, pp. 390, 392–393. Reprinted with the permission of Cambridge University Press. **Source 75:** Charles Pellat, *The Life and Works of Jahiz,* trans. D. M. Hawkes (Berkeley, CA: University of California Press, 1969), pp. 251, 257–258, 265–267, passim. **Source 76:** Extract from *The Travels of Ibn Jubayr* by R. J. C. Broadhurst published by Jonathan Cape, 1952, pp. 313–325, passim. Used by permission of The Random House Group Limited. **Source 77:** *The Arabian Nights' Entertainments* (London: George Routledge, 1890), pp. 113–116. **Source 78:** Taken from *A Biography of the Tripitaka Master of the Great Ci'en Monastery of the Great Tang Dynasty* published by the Numata Center for Buddhist Translation and Research, 1995, pp. 93–95. Reprinted with permission. **Source 79:** Edward C. Sachau, trans., *Alberuni's India* (Delhi, 1910), pp. 17–25, passim. **Source 80:** Franklin Edgerton, ed. and trans., *Vikrama's Adventures,* 2 vols. (Cambridge, Mass.: Harvard University Press, 1926), vol. 1. pp. 228–230. Copyright © 1926 by Harvard University Press. Reprinted by permission.

Chapter 10

Source 81: (1 and 2) Alinari/Art Resource, NY. **Source 82:** *Procopius,* The Great History Series, H. R. Trevor-Roper, General Editor, edited by Mrs. Averil Cameron. Reprinted with the permission of Washington Square Press, a division of Simon & Schuster. Copyright © 1967 by Washington Square Press. From *Secret History,* trans. Richard Atwater (Ann Arbor: University of Michigan Press, copyright 1961), pp. 67–68, 70–71, 89–94, passim. Reprinted by permission of the University of Michigan Press. **Source 83:** Alinari/Art Resource, NY. **Source 84:** Oliver J. Thatcher and Edgar H. McNeal, trans., *A Source Book for Medieval History* (New York: Charles Scribner's Sons, 1905), p. 107; D. C. Munro, trans., University of Pennsylvania Translations and Reprints (Philadelphia: University of Pennsylvania, 1900), vol. 6, no. 5, pp. 16–27, passim. **Source 85:** From *The Works of Liudprand of Cremona,* translated by F. A. Wright, pp. 243–245. Copyright © 1930, Routledge. Reprinted with permission of Taylor & Francis Books Ltd. **Source 86:** (1) Courtesy Bayerische Staatsbibliothek, Munchen. (2) Herzog August Bibliothek Wolfenbüttel. **Source 87:** Baldric of Dol, "The Jerusalem History," in A. C. Krey, trans., *The First Crusade: The Accounts of Eye-Witnesses and Participants* (Princeton, N.J.: Princeton University Press, 1921), pp. 33–36. **Source 88:** From *The Alexiad of the Princess Anna Comnena,* translated by

E. A. S. Dawes, pp. 33–34, 248–250. Copyright © 1967, Routledge. Reprinted with permission of Taylor & Francis Books Ltd. **Source 89:** Reprinted material from Harry J. Magoulias, trans., *O City of Byzantium: Annals of Niketas Choniates,* 1984, pp. 314–317, with the permission of Wayne State University.

Chapter 11

Source 90: G. S. P. Freeman-Greenville, ed. and trans., *The East African Coast: Select Documents* (Oxford: Clarendon Press, 1962), pp. 14–17, passim. Reprinted by permission of Mr. Freeman-Greenville. **Source 91:** J. F. P. Hopkins, trans., and N. Levtzion and J. F. P. Hopkins, eds., *Corpus of Early Arabic Sources for West African History* (Cambridge: Cambridge University Press, 1981), pp. 79–83, passim. Copyright © University of Ghana, International Academic Union, Cambridge University Press, 1981. Reprinted with permission of Cambridge University Press. **Source 92:** From G. W. B. Huntingford, *The Glorious Victories of 'Amda Seyon, King of Ethiopia,* 1965, pp. 53–65, passim. Reprinted by permission of Oxford University Press/UK. **Source 93:** *Yoruba Woman of Authority* from 1978 Ibadan University Press and the Nigerian Federal Department of Antiquities. Photograph courtesy of the Library of Congress. **Source 94:** (1) Maya People, "Ball Player as a War Captive," terra-cotta with traces of pigment, Late Classic period, circa 600–900, New Orleans Museum of Art: Museum purchase, Women's Volunteer Committee Fund, 74.211. (2) Denver Art Museum Collection: Gift of William I. Lee, 1986.617. Photo by Denver Art Museum © 2003. All rights reserved. (3) The Detroit Institute of Arts, acc #77.49. Founders Society Purchase, Katherine Margaret Kay Bequest Fund and New Endowment Fund. Photograph © 1993 The Detroit Institute of Arts. **Source 95:** (1) From *Book of the Gods and Rites and the Ancient Calendar,* by Fray Diego Duran, translated by Fernando Horcasitas and Doris Heyden, © 1971. Reprinted with permission of the University of Oklahoma Press. (2) Biblioteca Nacional Madrid/Institut Amatller d'Art Hispanic. **Source 96:** From *The Incas of Pedro de Cieza de Leon,* translated by Harriet de Onis, pp. 165–167, 169–174, 177–178, passim. Edited, with an inroduction, by Victor Wolfang von Hagen, © 1959. Reprinted with permission of the University of Oklahoma.

Part Four ▾ Travel, Encounter, and Exchange: 1000–1700

Chapter 12

Source 97: Friederich Hirth and W. W. Rockhill, *Chau Ju-Kau: His Work on the Chinese and Arab Trade in the Twelfth and Thirteenth Centuries,* entitled *Chu-fan-chï* (Saint Petersburg: Imperial Academy of Sciences, 1911), pp. 111–116, 124–125, 142–143, revised by A. J. Andrea. **Source 98:** The "Cotton Manuscript" of the British Museum, printed

1625, ch. 20, 30; adapted into modern English by A. J. Andrea. **Source 99:** Courtesy Omiya Library at Ryukoku University. **Source 100:** Chinggis Khan, *Letter to Changchun,* adapted by A. J. Andrea from E. Bretschneider, *Mediaeval Researches from Eastern Asiatic Sources* (London, 1875), pp. 37–39. **Source 101:** Christopher Dawson, ed., *The Mongol Mission* (New York: Sheed and Ward, 1955), pp. 93–98, 103–104, passim. **Source 102:** From *The Travels of Marco Polo,* translated by Ronald Latham, Penguin Classics 1958, pp. 82–85, 87–88. Copyright © Ronald Latham, 1958. Reproduced by permission of Penguin Books Ltd. **Source 103:** Translated from the Latin by A. J. Andrea. **Source 104:** Henry Yule, ed. and trans., *Cathay and the Way Thither,* 2nd ed. (rev. by H. Cordier), 4 vols. (London: Hakluyt Society, 1913–1916), vol. 3, pp. 151–155. **Source 105:** J. F. P. Hopkins, trans., and N. Levtzion and J. F. P. Hopkins, eds., *Corpus of Early Arabic Sources for West African History* (Cambridge: Cambridge University Press, 1981), pp. 284–286, 288–291, 296–297, passim. Copyright © University of Ghana, International Academic Union, Cambridge University Press, 1981. Reprinted with permission of Cambridge University Press. **Source 106:** From *Ruy González de Clavijo, Embassy to Tamerlane, 1403–1406,* trans. by Guy Le Strange, Harper & Bros., 1928, pp. 285–292, 294–295, passim. **Source 107:** Ma Huan, *The Overall Survey of the Ocean's Shores* (London: Hakluyt Society, 1970), pp. 108–109, 113–117, 120, 137–140, 165, 172. Copyright © 1970. Used by permission of the publisher. **Source 108:** Gomes Eannes de Azurara, *The Chronicle of the Discovery and Conquest of Guinea,* trans. Charles Raymond Beazely and Edgar Prestage, 2 vols. (London: Hakluyt Society, 1896), vol. 1, pp. 27–29, 83–85.

Chapter 13

Source 109: James Lockhart, ed. and trans., *We People Here: Nahuatl Accounts of the Conquest of Mexico* (Berkeley: University of California Press, 1993), pp. 96, 98, 100, 106, 108, 110, 112, 132, 134, 136, 180, 182, 186, 188, 210, 216, 218, 238, 240, 242. **Source 110:** Antonio Vazquez de Espinosa, *Compendium and Description of the West Indies* (Washington, DC: Smithsonian Institution, 1942), pp. 621–625, 629, 631–634. **Source 111:** Copyright © 1964 by Basil Davidson. Reprinted by permission of Curtis Brown, Ltd. **Source 112:** (1) A Benin-Portuguese Saltcellar, courtesy of the Trustees of The British Museum. (2) A Benin Wall Plaque, Multiple Figures, Edo Peoples, Benin Kingdom, Nigeria, Photograph by Franko Khoury, mid 16th–17th century, copper alloy, H x W x D: 45.6 x 35 x 8.9 cm. Purchased with funds provided by the Smithsonian Collection Acquisition Program, National Museum of African Art, 82-5-3, Smithsonian Institution. **Source 113:** Awnsham Churchill and John Churchill, eds., *Collections of Voyages and Travels,* 3rd ed., 8 vols. (London: H. Lintor, 1744–1747), vol. 5, p. 459; modernized by A. J. Andrea. **Source 114:** Louis J. Gallagher, S. J., trans., *China in the Sixteenth Century: The Journals of Matthew Ricci: 1583–1610* (New York: Random House,

1953). **Source 115:** David John Lu, ed. and trans., *Sources of Japanese History* (New York: McGraw-Hill, 1974), vol. 1, pp. 207–209. **Source 116:** Henry Beveridge, trans., *The Akbar Nama of Abu-l-Fazl,* 3 vols. (New Delhi: Ess Ess Publications, 1902–1939), vol. 1, pp. 37, 207, 322–323, 368–370, 410–411. **Source 117:** Jean-Baptiste Tavernier, *Travels in India,* 2nd ed., ed. William Ball, trans. V. Ball (Oxford: Oxford University Press, 1925), pp. 7–11. Used by permission of the publisher.